Butterflies of New Jersey

Butterflies of New Jersey

A GUIDE TO THEIR STATUS, DISTRIBUTION, CONSERVATION, AND APPRECIATION

Michael Gochfeld and
Joanna Burger

RUTGERS UNIVERSITY PRESS
New Brunswick, New Jersey

Library of Congress Cataloging-in-Publication Data

Gochfeld, Michael.
    Butterflies of New Jersey : a guide to their status, distribution, conservation, and
appreciation / Michael Gochfeld and Joanna Burger.
        p.   cm.
    Includes bibliographical references and index.
    ISBN 0-8135-2354-0 (cloth : alk. paper).—ISBN 0-8135-2355-9 (pbk. : alk. paper)
    1. Butterflies—New Jersey. I. Burger, Joanna. II. Title.
    QL551.N3G635   1997
    595.78′9′0942—dc20   96-18111
                                                                                 CIP

British Cataloging-in-Publication information available

Manufactured in the United States of America

Photographic Editor: Guy Tudor

Publication of this book was made possible by a generous grant from
the Geraldine R. Dodge Foundation.

To the butterflies and all who watch or care about them, this book is dedicated,

and to our friends and field companions,

to our children, Deborah and David,

and nieces and nephews,
Jennifer and Douglas; Kathy and Eddie; Michael, David, and Daniel; Jacob and Andrew; Benjamin, Eric, Elizabeth, and Emily, and to their parents, our brothers and sisters,

and above all to our parents
Alex and Anne Gochfeld, and Melvin and Janette Burger

Contents

List of Illustrations and Tables

Photo Editor's Note

Several fine books provide excellent illustration of virtually all of New Jersey's butterflies, so the challenge here was to select color photographs that particularly represent both the geographic and taxonomic diversity of New Jersey's butterflies. I have tried also to highlight some of the state's well-known butterfly locations.

Plates 1, 2, 3, illustrate a selection of several families typical of northern and central New Jersey, including both widespread and marginal species. The Pipevine Swallowtail is a Palisades specialty and the Arctic Skipper a High Point State Park specialty. Lakehurst is an important butterfly locality in central New Jersey and two of its specialty species are shown in Plate 4. The Pine Barrens are the largest natural area in the state and cover much of southern New Jersey. Two of its highly local specialties, one of wet and the other of dry habitats, are shown in Plate 5. Plate 6 illustrates two rare and local species of southern New Jersey. The Rare Skipper was only recently discovered in the state while the Bronze Copper, formerly more widespread, is declining, with a few localities known in northern as well as southern New Jersey. Cape May is a mecca for butterfly watchers in late summer and two of its specialties are shown in Plate 7. Plate 8 shows the Red-banded Hairstreak, a relatively recent invader of New Jersey as well as a roost of migrating Monarchs to round out the selection.

Guy Tudor
Forest Hills, New York

Figures

Photographs

Color Plates (gallery)

Tables

List of Illustrations and Tables

xi

Foreword

Now is an exciting time to take up butterflying, an outdoor activity at roughly the same stage of development as birding was in the 1930s. For the first time, field guides have begun to appear that allow butterfliers to identify live butterflies in the field with binoculars. Because our knowledge of butterfly distribution, behavior, life histories—everything!—is still so scanty, the information learned from the field efforts of each individual is important.

But before you contribute to our future knowledge of butterflies in New Jersey, you should know the past. Mike Gochfeld and Joanna Burger have created an important book that is like the butterflies themselves—a memory of the past and a guide to the future.

First the past. As a child, on the south shore of Long Island, I would read guide books by day and dream of butterflies at night. One of my favorite books was by Alexander Klots, who, in addition to providing much information in readable form, would occasionally lace his accounts with sly humor. Here my friends and I learned about some of the local and habitat-restricted butterflies found at Lakehurst, New Jersey, and the adjoining pine barrens—Hoary Elfin, Bog Copper, Georgia Satyr. Klots talked especially about Georgia Satyrs—saying that he always found them in the long grass to the south of the railroad station but rarely to the north. When we got a little older we saved our money for a bus ride to this mythical locality. We found Klots's railroad tracks without too much trouble but the railroad station itself was gone! Without exact instructions, we never did locate the nearby bog. Later in life I returned to this area and found Klots's Bog, where hundreds of Bog Coppers flew tremulously at my feet, and bobbing Georgia Satyrs weaved through the tall grasses. Still, almost fifty years after Klots wrote about it, this wonderful little bog is waiting for you.

Moving into the present, it seems as if the Garden State should be a natural for butterflies—and it is! Although noticeably smaller than the neighboring Empire and Keystone states, New Jersey actually boasts a larger number of butterfly species. Although not far in absolute distance, there is a huge faunistic distance between the Kittatinny Ridge of northwestern New Jersey and the Cape May peninsula in the south. Many of the butterflies found in New Jersey have a distributional break within the state—the dividing line between areas where the species occurs and does not normally occur, cuts through the state. Aphrodite Fritillaries, Meadow Fritillaries, Harris' Checkerspots, Baltimore Checkerspots, and Acadian Hairstreaks are found in northern New Jersey but not in the south. Red-banded Hairstreaks, and Aaron's Skippers are found toward the southeast, but not in the northwest. Other special species are found in the New Jersey Pine

Barrens. It is probably easier to find Hessel's Hairstreaks in New Jersey than anywhere else. Rare Skippers and Arogos Skippers, some of the rarest butterflies east of the Mississippi, have recently been respectively discovered and rediscovered in the state. There are a multitude of butterflying experiences packed into the outlines of this small state.

Mike Gochfeld and Joanna Burger have assembled a wealth of information, extracted from historical sources, more recent publications, communications from currently active field workers, and their own field impressions. Their species accounts will give you an excellent picture of the known historical and current status of each species in New Jersey, when they fly, and where to search for them. Use this book to plan your outings in the state. Look up the historical status of a species of interest and the current status listed in the book. Then, go out and search likely habitats at appropriate times of the year. What is the status of this species in your area?

The real value of this book lies in the future. As you and other readers use it to explore New Jersey's butterflies, a larger constituency will develop that has a stake in conserving this valuable resource—the Earth's way of remembering its past. And so we can hope that New Jersey's fields of color and flowers, filled with dashing skippers and dreamlike fritillaries, will not become only a dim memory—a fairy-tale world recalled to our grandchildren.

Jeffrey Glassberg,
President
North American Butterfly Association

Preface

With the first sunny days of late winter, when our leafless landscape is still chilled by icy breezes, the first of our butterflies, the Mourning Cloak, flutters across our path through woodland clearings. From that day, usually in early March, until the killing frosts of November, is the season of butterflies. As spring advances and warm sun daily bathes the meadow, the early spring flowers are visited by Cabbage Whites, and Spring Azures appear in our forests. Our walks in summer are enlivened by brilliant butterflies moving erratically across our field of view. Striking orange and black Monarchs drift majestically over the field heading for a patch of milkweeds. Dramatic Fritillaries, spangled with silver, move deliberately from flower to flower, spending hour after hour exploring our Butterfly Bushes (*Buddleia*). Our gaze is directed high and low, from brilliantly patterned swallowtails sailing overhead to tiny blues at our feet.

With careful attention we become accustomed to picking out the smaller butterflies and skippers that hang from the flowers in our garden. With close-focusing binoculars and macro lenses we watch and photograph the different species that visit our yard, and on weekends we seek out butterflies in other habitats—the hills of northwestern New Jersey, the holly forests at Sandy Hook, the Pine Barrens, the salt marshes, and of course Cape May Point.

With careful record keeping, we find that some species, such as Peck's Skipper and Pearl Crescent, are abundant for a few weeks and then disappear only to reappear at intervals throughout the season, while others such as the Cabbage Whites and Orange Sulphurs are present almost any time. Thus there is a succession of different species flying through our gardens, meadows, and woodlots as the summer months unfold. This discovery leads to a fascination with the seasonality of butterflies, the pattern of habitat use, and the life cycles of each new species identified.

A butterfly's day begins slowly. Butterflies hide in their roosting spots on a tree or low in the grass until they warm up sufficiently to fly about. In midsummer, some are flying and feeding by 8 A.M., but often it is 10 A.M. before there is much activity. We usually find a lull on really hot afternoons, with some resurgence of activity well before dusk. As nightfall approaches, the butterflies disappear. "Disappear" is the right word, because only occasionally have we actually seen them fly to their nighttime roost.

The daily cycle is repeated each morning. First none, then slowly one, then two, appear and begin to visit flowers or seek their mates. This rhythm of butterfly activity is different from that of birds, frogs, and mammals, some of the other animals that also claim our attention as naturalists.

Butterflies can live in small city parks, suburban gardens, farmland, and extensive natural areas such as our National Parks and Wildlife Refuges (NWRs). Naturally, the diversity of butterflies increases with the size and diversity of habitats. But, with careful and judicious plantings, even the smallest garden can attract a variety of butterfly species that changes with the season.

The wonderful thing about studying butterflies on a local or regional scale is the dynamic nature of their populations. A species may suddenly colonize an area where it has not been seen before, thrive for a number of years, and then, just as suddenly, disappear, perhaps to reappear somewhere else. A species such as the Regal Fritillary may decrease dramatically over a wide area of its range, just when another such as the Common Ringlet is expanding. The availability of new hosts introduced by the human hand enables some species such as the Wild Indigo Duskywing to greatly expand their range, but in other cases, such as the West Virginia White, the introduced exotic may be a toxic trap, seducing females to lay their eggs while killing the larvae.

Butterfly populations have not always fared well. In the past century, New Jersey's human population has increased nearly tenfold, resulting in a great reduction in suitable habitat for butterflies. Indeed, around the world the loss of habitat in the face of expanding human populations is the number-one factor adversely affecting wildlife and biodiversity. Also, after World War II, when chemical insecticides became readily available, there was a massive assault on insects in New Jersey, as elsewhere in the United States. Agricultural crops were sprayed, as were forests attacked by Gypsy Moths, salt marshes populated by mosquitoes, and even residential communities where mosquitoes were a nuisance.

In those early days of chemical euphoria, pesticides were used with great abandon. In the 1940s and 1950s, most of the pesticides were the persistent organochlorines that caused chronic effects in wildlife, nearly eliminating such dramatic bird species as the Brown Pelican, Peregrine Falcon, and Bald Eagle. The disappearance of butterflies killed outright by pesticides failed to capture public notice. Now, a half-century later, it is impossible to completely evaluate how much insecticides contributed to the decline of our insect fauna.

Although the overall long-term effects of such spraying remain a controversial subject, we personally witnessed the declines of a number of "common" species, such as the Tiger Swallowtail, during the period of suburban spraying in the early 1950s. The effects of the Gypsy Moth control program beginning in the 1970s were much worse, for a number of woodland butterfly species, unintended victims, may have been eliminated from New Jersey during this time.

Indirectly, this war on insects, which involved massive spraying of large areas of the countryside without regard for nontarget species, has been the motivating force for the environmental movement of the past 30 years. However, it was not butterflies but the loss of dramatic birds that really alerted the public to the massive species declines and die-offs caused by this indiscriminate spraying.

In 1962, marine biologist Rachel Carson published her book *Silent Spring*, and awakened the nation to the extensive ecological damage caused by the unbridled use of pesticides. Although she focused her book on bird mortality and did not mention butterflies at all, butterfly populations were probably even more susceptible. Unlike most species of birds, a number of butterflies are restricted to small areas or a specialized habitat, making such local populations very vulnerable.

Fortunately, many populations that had almost been eliminated by the overuse of pesticides have apparently recovered, although others have not. Unfortunately, systematic censusing of butterflies did not begin until 1975, after the main damage was already done. Many local populations may have declined or disappeared from our meadows and fields without our even knowing they were there.

With a reawakening of interest in our environment, scientists, government agencies, and the public have become more interested not only in the population stability of large birds and mammals, but in the biodiversity of all organisms. Butterflies are particularly appealing because they are beautiful, conspicuous, abundant, and active at midday. The past five years have witnessed a tremendous increase in interest in watching, studying, and protecting butterflies.

For both of us, an interest in butterflies began while we were young children growing up in rural New York State: MG in northern Westchester County and JB in Schenectady County. Like so many country children, we developed an avid interest in natural history. We captured frogs, salamanders, turtles, and snakes and watched them for weeks in terraria or outdoor pens before we reluctantly released them. Our collections of leaves, rocks, and insects were stuffed into various containers in whatever nooks and crannies we could commandeer. Both of us had butterfly collections, with Joanna having had the advantage of finding many dead butterflies trapped in the greenhouses on her parents' farm. With our adolescence, some of the collecting activities dissipated, but not our fascination.

In the 1950s, many suburban communities had contracted for weekly "fogging" to rid their environs of mosquitoes. This resulted in a rapid diminution in the diversity of butterflies and many other insects—perhaps even mosquitoes. Documenting this decline of several species and the very gradual recovery of some species over a period of years became a long-term interest in our high school years.

When we moved into our house in Somerset, New Jersey, in 1981, we immediately began identifying and cataloging the various plant and animal species on our one acre of land. Our yard had previously been a horse paddock, and we had the dubious good fortune of being able to watch plant succession firsthand, as the completely barren landscape gradually accumulated a surprising variety of wildflowers. To the natural immigrants we added several beds of "butterfly flowers" as well.

Partly because of the initial paucity of flowers and also because we were surrounded by woods, our early butterfly lists were fairly paltry. By the mid-1980s, we had begun to get seriously into butterfly watching on our various birdwatching trips around the state. As bird watchers, we were accustomed to rising before dawn and then relaxing during the hotter parts of the day, so butterflies posed a serious health threat for us: butterfly activity increased just as the morning's avian activity waned, and they continued to keep our attention until late afternoon, when it was time to focus on birds again. There was no rest for the weary.

For reawakening our interest in butterflies, we have to thank our friends: Guy Tudor, president of the New York City Butterfly Club, Charlie Leck and Bert Murray, our colleagues at Rutgers, and Patti Murray, a professional nature photographer. Charlie, Bert, and Patti introduced us to some local butterfly spots, and Guy convinced us that skippers required our attention as well. However, it was not until Guy led us into the New Jersey Pine Barrens on an April morning a decade ago specifically to look for duskywings and elfins that we began studying butterflies on a statewide basis.

We asked Guy what information was available about New Jersey butterflies, and he produced for us an annotated copy of Comstock's (1940) paper, "Butterflies of New Jersey." It made for very interesting reading because it provided some information on habitats and egg laying, but it gave only the most cursory distribution and status accounts. Furthermore, the localities told us only where collectors had looked for butterflies, not where they were likely to occur. It was shortly thereafter that we decided to assemble a book on New Jersey's butterflies.

Because we had grown up studying birds in New York, we had as our models the books by Ludlow Griscom (*Birds of the New York City Region*, 1923), Allan D. Cruickshank (*Birds Around New York City*, 1942), and John Bull (*Birds of the New York Area*, 1964). These books, appearing with startling regularity, kept current our understanding of an important avifauna. In our view, butterflies deserved equal time.

Our preliminary list, based both on observations and on the literature, was circulated in 1989. We were pleased to receive serious criticisms from several people who pointed out its shortcomings, particularly of the published information. Of particular concern was the historical tendency to attribute a butterfly to all of New Jersey if it had been collected at least once in the North and once in the South. Moreover, early collectors weren't trying to survey the distribution and status of butterflies over a large area.

In the ensuing years we have gathered enough information to present a general picture of the status and distribution of New Jersey's butterflies, and to identify many shortcomings in our information base. We believe that the function of a regional book is to stimulate observers to focus on gaps in the literature or what is now routinely called a database. Although any regional list of butterflies is inevitably a snapshot that soon becomes out of date, it is essential to have it as a point of reference. With the increasing interest in biodiversity, such milestones are important.

We think it is important to develop a thorough knowledge of one's local fauna, and a state or regional book can provide an observer with the "top line," that is, the number of species that can reasonably be expected to occur in any local area in a given year or season. We have done this on our own acre as well as in the 50-acre mosaic of fields and second-growth woodland behind our house. In 1985 this habitat was threatened with development, and indeed a wide swath of trees behind our house was bulldozed. Its trees were eaten by a voracious machine which spat them out as woodchips and sawdust.

Imagine our surprise when, the following spring, we began to find many new species of butterflies in our yard. This open corridor served as a veritable highway, and through the years we have censused it at least weekly. We encountered a few species that seemed highly unusual, but we had no clear reference base to determine just how unusual it was when, for example, a Baltimore Checkerspot visited our yard one day. Now nearly a decade later we can say with conviction that it was indeed very unusual.

There was no way to tell whether, for example, the Hobomok Skipper should be looked for in our area. Although we saw many Zabulon Skippers, several years passed before we saw our first Hobomok. We had always seen American Coppers when we were growing up, and we expected this species because our lawn was riddled with Sheep Sorrel, their host plant. Yet only once has an American Copper ventured into our yard.

One morning in early September we spotted a large orangish brown skipper with a conspicuous white V of spots on its underwing. We immediately recognized this as a Leonard's Skipper, with which we had already become familiar at Ward Pound Ridge in Westchester County, New York. There was no book to tell us that it was quite rare in Central New Jersey and that local colonies were vulnerable to mowing or habitat succession. Indeed, our tiny colony of these skippers seems to be hanging on by a thread, for we see only a few individuals each year.

Much of the early information on New Jersey's butterfly fauna came from a relatively small number of collectors. Comstock listed sixty-one people who had collected in New Jersey over an 80-year period; that's about half the number who participated in the first annual field trip of the North American Butterfly Association (NABA) in New Jersey in May 1994. Although we always envisioned collectors as combing the countryside in search of new species, our review of published information and collections suggests that, in fact, they returned over and over again to relatively few fruitful areas. Indeed, one collector published a list of his favorite collecting areas so that future collectors could avoid "fruitless searches." Thus, New Jersey's northern Coastal Plain fauna is represented in large part by collections from only three localities: Lakehurst, Lakewood, and Jamesburg. Remarkably, virtually no collections were made in Hunterdon or Monmouth Counties, while Hudson, Essex, and Camden Counties were well represented.

We were surprised to learn that early collectors were apparently much more interested in seasonality than in long-term trends, for a surprising number of specimens in the museums we checked have labels that list the month and date, but not the year. This is true in Comstock's work as well. Although early writers knew that butterfly populations vary from year to year (they wrote of "good years" and "bad years"), they obviously did not consider such variability important, nor did they anticipate any long-term trends.

We, on the other hand, consider such trends of major importance, and a large part of our text is devoted to documenting the historical and current status of butterflies in different parts of the state. For a state the size of New Jersey, we have decided to focus on the main geographical divisions or ecological zones rather than on the artificial basis of counties. We think this is a crucial feature of understanding biodiversity and documenting both the declines and increases in our fauna. With the recent national interest in biodiversity, it is all the more important to have a good data base on butterflies as a current reference and for future use in determining trends associated with changes in human activities or natural events within the state. This book is intended to accompany such popular and readily available identification guides as Jeffrey Glassberg's *Butterflies Through Binoculars* and Paul Opler's *Field Guide to Butterflies*.

In assembling this book we have faced many challenges and data gaps, but the quest for better information has given us much pleasure and satisfaction. We have had the good fortune to make field trips to many parts of the state with some very knowledgeable people, and expect to continue such ventures in the future. We trust that this book will be a stimulus to many people to learn about butterflies, and to help them enjoy their fascination and understand these insects' complex lives.

Acknowledgments

Over the years many friends and colleagues have accompanied us into the field in search of butterflies or have otherwise contributed to our appreciation and knowledge of their behavior, ecology, and distribution. We thank Rich Cech, Harry Darrow, Jim Dowdell, Jeff Glassberg, Michel Kleinbaum, Michelle Le-Marchant, John Lawrenson, Charlie and Mary Leck, Fred Lesser, Patti and Bert Murray, Paul Opler, Harry Pavulaan, Bob and Peg Ridgeley, Carl Safina, Dale Schweitzer, Art Shapiro, Jim Springer, Ted Stiles, Pat and Clay Sutton, Guy Tudor, Richard Walton, Wade and Sharon Wander, Chris and Paula Williams, David Wright, John and Mary Yrizarry, Bob Zappalorti, and Harry Zirlin.

We especially appreciate the stimulation and advice provided by Guy Tudor, president of the New York City Butterfly Club. He critically reviewed all the species accounts and served as the photo editor. Dale Schweitzer and Harry Pavulaan graciously provided a detailed critique of many of the species accounts, and Pavulaan provided extensive advice regarding the treatment of the Azures. Jeff Glassberg, president of NABA, whose book on butterfly identification, *Butterflies Through Binoculars*, will profoundly influence how people look at butterflies, provided valued advice. Charles and Mary Leck and Patti and Bert Murray were enthusiastic contributors at many stages. Jim Dowdell and Pat Sutton provided information about butterfly populations of the Cape May area. Wade and Sharon Wander provided detailed information about northwestern New Jersey, while Rick Cech, Harry Darrow, and John Yrizarry provided valuable information about northern New Jersey and adjacent New York. Charles Leck shared his experience regarding central New Jersey, and Dale Schweitzer provided information particularly about the Pine Barrens and the Delaware Valley. We have benefited greatly from Arthur Shapiro's writings and the additional information he provided when MG visited him in California.

We thank Scott McVey for his interest and the attention he gave to our project, and the Geraldine P. Dodge Foundation for its generous support of publication under its Welfare of Animals program.

We greatly appreciate the efforts of Rick Cech, Dale Schweitzer, Jeff Glassberg, Harry Pavulaan, Pat Sutton, Guy Tudor, David Wright, and Larry Niles, who read all or part of the manuscript and made valuable comments and corrected a number of errors. Undoubtedly many errors remain, and readers will enjoy the opportunity to correct them through future fieldwork.

Rick Cech, Jeffrey Glassberg, and Patti Murray provided color illustrations. Tim Casey, Chair of Entomology, Michael May, Curator of Entomology, and their staff graciously provided assistance at the Pepper Library and at the Entomology

Museum of Rutgers University. Fred Rindges of the American Museum of Natural History in New York provided valuable historical information on New Jersey lepidopterists, and Robert Robbins of the U.S. National Museum in Washington, D.C., provided additional information.

Last but not least we thank our editor, Karen Reeds. Our copy editor, Alice Calaprice, labored diligently to bring order to a complicated text.

We look forward to sharing field experiences with these and many new acquaintances in years to come. Our children, Deborah and David, and our nieces and nephews, Jacob, Douglas, Eric, Elizabeth, Benjamin, Emily, and Andrew, have joined us in the field and added sharp eyes to our ventures.

MG thanks his high school mentors, Martin Brech and Ralph O'dell, who shaped his field peregrinations, and his college and graduate advisors, George T. Jones, Edward J. Kormondy, Max Hecht, and Wesley Lanyon, who gave academic form to his inquiries. JB thanks Meg Stewart and A. Benton, who stimulated her interests in college, and H. B. Tordoff and Dwain Warner, who gave her the strength and confidence to pursue every academic interest.

Our Amazon Parrot, Tico, shared with us many hours of manuscript preparation on the computer, cheerfully chewing up discarded pages and walking across the keyboard keys when he felt it was time for us to eat or go to bed.

Finally, our parents stimulated our interest in nature when we were small children, pointing out small warblers in the treetops, killdeer nesting amid the squash plants, and butterflies sipping from flowers. Their love of nature flowed as strongly to us as did their other teachings, and we are forever grateful for their encouragement.

SECTION I

About Butterflies

CHAPTER 1

Introduction: Butterflies around Us

Butterflies, with their vivid hues and flashing patterns, capture the attention of all people who observe their natural surroundings. They are second only to birds in their popularity, and much has been learned about their distribution, life histories, and behavior. But only about a third of the butterfly species in a region are bright and conspicuous. Many species, particularly the Skippers, are what bird watchers would call "little brown jobs," inconspicuous in appearance and so similarly marked that care and experience are needed to tell them apart. Fortunately, many books have been written about butterflies, and there are excellent guides that help both novice and expert in identifying them.

Butterflies figure prominently in ancient and medieval art and poetry. Miriam Rothschild (1991), for example, has assembled a fascinating historical account, oddly called *Butterfly Cooing Like a Dove*, which reproduces many artistic and literary renditions of butterfly form and meaning. Butterflies are frequently pictured in commercial advertising, and a new business involves raising butterflies (mainly Monarchs and Painted Ladies) for release en masse at weddings and other festive occasions.

A small and faithful group of naturalists has always been interested in collecting butterflies, and some have raised them to study their biology, physiology, genetics, and mimicry. But in recent years the number of people that identify, watch, attract, list, and photograph butterflies has increased dramatically (Glassberg 1993a). Like birds, butterflies command more than their fair share of scientific scrutiny. The number of scientists studying a group is inversely related to the number of species in the group. Thus, more people study the 700 or so species of North American butterflies than study the 10,000+ species of moths. Butterflies and the professional and amateur scientists who study them have contributed greatly to our understanding of evolution, plant-animal coevolution, genetics, mimicry, behavior, ecological chemistry, population ecology and conservation biology (Ford 1964, Brower 1969, Sheppard 1975, Gilbert and Singer 1975, Vane-Wright and Avery 1984, Pullin 1995).

As butterflies have become more popular, interest has extended to butterfly conservation, photography, and gardening (Xerces Society 1990). Many parts of the country now offer "butterfly houses" where people may walk among free-flying butterflies. Butterfly counts and censuses and butterfly trips analogous to birding trips (except for the hours) are now popular. And gardeners are planting species chosen to attract butterflies and encourage them to breed.

Butterflies and moths comprise the order Lepidoptera, one of about twenty-six subgroupings (orders) of the insects. A number of professional societies are devoted to the study of insects in general (entomology) and butterflies and moths (lepidopterology) in particular. The resurgence of interest in butterflies has resulted in the appearance of groups catering more to the amateur and beginner, on both the international (Xerces Society), national (North American Butterfly Association [NABA]), and local levels (e.g., New York City Butterfly Club, Northern New Jersey Butterfly Club), all devoted to studying, conserving, and enjoying butterflies.

Many butterfly watchers are also bird watchers, and many of the features and principles of bird study are now being applied to butterflies, with newsletters and club meetings fostering wider interest. For some, butterflies provide the added advantages not available to bird watchers: you can enjoy them without having to be up at 5 A.M., having a trained ear, or spending the morning straining one's neck gazing into the treetops. For others, butterflies are something to look at during the midday lull in bird activity.

Although technically the study of Lepidoptera is referred to as lepidopterology, most students of butterflies refer to themselves as "lepidopterists." But most people who have recently begun to watch butterflies are more likely to consider themselves "butterfly watchers" or "butterflyers." To both—the serious lepidopterist and the serious butterfly watcher—this book is dedicated.

The key to watching, studying, and conserving butterflies is to be able to identify them and to have an up-to-date species list with detailed information on their status, distribution, habitats, seasonality (or phenology), and relevant behavioral information. For New Jersey, these requirements are well filled by the appearance of several recent volumes.

The remarkable volume *Butterflies through Binoculars* by Jeffrey Glassberg, president of the North American Butterfly Association (Glassberg 1993b) focuses attention on the butterflies known to occur between Boston and Washington, D.C. Glassberg's emphasis on identifying butterflies by their appearance in the field revolutionizes butterfly identification. Virtually all species likely to occur in New Jersey are illustrated with photographs depicting butterflies as the observer is likely to see them in life. Descriptions, though brief, are accompanied by information on how to distinguish them from similar species. Glassberg's book joins the ranks of other identification books for North America. Robert Pyle's *The Audubon Society Field Guide to North American Butterflies* (1981) provides photographs of almost all species in North America, including those that occur in New Jersey. Paul Opler's *Field Guide to Eastern Butterflies* (1992), in the Peterson Field Guide series, provides range maps, drawings, and field marks. For the traveling butterfly watcher, some excellent state and regional butterfly books are being published.

With these and other excellent books mentioned in appendices C and D, the observer should be able to identify most individuals of most butterfly species, though some, particularly certain skippers, are very difficult, and worn or aberrant individuals of many other species may not be identifiable in the field. This problem is not unique to butterflies: bird watchers, too, are sometimes faced with a worn individual in unusual plumage that defies identification. However, unlike birds, butterflies offer no vocal cues to their identities, and only with experience will subtle behavioral cues become apparent. Given the excellent identification guides already available, this book will focus on the status and distribution of butterflies rather than on how to identify them.

Rationale and Outline for This Book

We have planned this book, which is the first account of New Jersey's butterflies in more than 50 years, to provide information on the current and historical status and distribution of all species known to have occurred in the state. It should greatly enhance readers' appreciation of the butterflies around them, and also challenge them to provide updated information, since butterfly populations are highly dynamic.

In view of the increasing concern about biodiversity and conservation, this book identifies gaps in knowledge and changes in status which we hope will lead to further study and improved management of butterfly habitats and protection of populations. To accomplish this goal, we have presented detailed historical accounts of the status of butterflies so that long-term trends can be identified. We also expect this book to encourage and stimulate beginning butterfly watchers in and around New Jersey. Those concerned with conservation are likely to think of the mature forest as the desirable ecological habitat, but most butterfly species thrive in open country and edge habitats, making forest management often inimical with their interests.

The book is divided into three sections. Section I, "About Butterflies," contains chapters on the characteristics of butterflies; taxonomy and nomenclature; the study of status and distribution; and life cycles, phenology, and behavior. Section II, "About New Jersey," contains chapters on the geography of New Jersey; the history of butterfly studies; ecology, habitats, and butterfly gardening. Section III contains the annotated list of the approximately 145 species of butterflies recorded from New Jersey as well as several species that have been recorded in neighboring states but have not yet been seen in New Jersey. For each of these species we summarize its range, its current and historical status in New Jersey, information from relevant checklists and publications, and information on its habitats, phenology, larval foods, and overwintering. For species that are neither widespread nor threatened, suggestions are given on where and when to find them. For those butterflies that are declining or in trouble, we provide information on the conservation status.

It is hard to believe that more than 50 years have passed since the last comprehensive review of New Jersey's butterfly fauna. During that interval, major faunal publications have appeared for many states, including Shapiro's (1974a) paper on New York, the New York City Butterfly Club's booklet on New York City (including northern New Jersey; Cech 1993), and Woodbury's (1994) book on butterflies of the Delmarva peninsula (Delaware, Maryland, and Virginia).

In this book we have included information intended for both the beginning butterfly watcher and the experienced lepidopterist, for both amateurs and professionals. It has been observed that "a professional is someone who gets paid to study Lepidoptera; an amateur is someone who has to pay money to study Lepidoptera" (Powell 1989). However, when it comes to butterflies, this distinction is blurred, for much of the information on life history and distribution has been presented by people for whom butterflies were an avocation rather than a paying job.

Although it is important to study a fauna on a local habitat or landscape scale, since that is the unit that will ultimately have to be managed, it also is important to consider the fauna of the state as a whole. It is essential to determine the current status and distribution of butterflies in New Jersey, particularly which ones are threatened or endangered and require vigorous protection. Understanding and documenting biodiversity and the conservation of wildlife are responsibilities of state agencies, in this case New Jersey's Department of Environmental Protection, through its Endangered and Nongame Species Program and its Natural Heritage Program. These programs are concerned with the conservation status of New Jersey's butterflies (see chapter 10 and tables 15 and 16).

Sources of Distributional Information

Opler and Krizek (1984) provide distributional maps for butterflies in the eastern United States, and these indicate the range of many species in New Jersey. However, often the entire state is shaded in, even for species that we know are highly localized. Less widely available is Opler's (1983) *County Atlas* (reprinted as Opler 1995), which shows each county in which each butterfly has been documented. Because of New Jersey's small size, the distribution of its butterfly fauna cannot be separated from the status in adjacent states.

At the end of the last century, John B. Smith of Rutgers University published a list of insects of New Jersey (Smith 1890); shortly thereafter, Beutenmüller (1893) published a list of butterflies recorded within 50 miles of the American Museum of Natural History in Manhattan. In the present century, the knowledge of New Jersey's butterfly fauna has been summarized by Smith (1900, 1910) and Comstock (1940). There have been dramatic changes in New Jersey's landscape in the past 50 years, but there have also been great differences in the way information is presented and the kind of information that is deemed important. Many early collectors, for example, were not at all interested in populations or trends; they were more interested in varieties or aberrant specimens, in extreme date records (the earliest emergence or latest persistence of a butterfly), or in new host plant records. Many of these early lepidopterists reared butterflies, both to document their life history and to obtain fresh specimens for their collection. They little dreamed of the long-term population trends that might take place.

Even as recently as 1940, Comstock's summary lacked detail on status and distribution. He lamented "there are a number of localities . . . which no longer exist as good collecting areas" and "Many of the less common species recorded from them thirty or more years ago are now scarce or absent." He specifically mentioned the degradation of the Orange Mountains, of Paterson, Greenwood Lake, Lake Hopatcong, and Five Mile Beach (now Wildwood), among others. However, his concern was perhaps more for the inconvenience to collectors than for the threats to butterfly populations. Comstock provided relatively little information on habitat or status for most species, although he reported on egg laying, larval behavior, hosts, phenology, and, for some species, which life stage overwintered. In the published accounts, ironically, more attention is given to rare and vagrant species than to widespread and common ones.

These Smith and Comstock publications were based primarily on reports by collectors or examinations of private and museum collections, and this approach is not necessarily an adequate representation of a fauna. Collectors have traditionally focused on certain species, particularly on rare or extralimital (out of range) records, or those unusually early or late in the season; these are likely to be disproportionately represented in collections. Also, collectors pursue fresh specimens; therefore most of the time periods based on specimens in collections are useful for determining the early dates, but they underestimate the actual flight periods, since the butterflies may persist in worn condition (unattractive to collectors) for days and weeks.

A substantial improvement was Shapiro's (1966) work on the Delaware Valley fauna covering a 35-mile radius around Philadelphia's City Hall, including extreme northern Cumberland and Atlantic Counties, extreme southern Hunterdon

County, and most or all of Mercer, Burlington, Camden, Gloucester, and Salem Counties. It represents the first modern treatment of part of the New Jersey butterfly fauna. Although he cited historical records, he based his report largely on field and laboratory work conducted by him and his students. His Staten Island report (Shapiro and Shapiro 1973) provides detailed coverage of an area immediately adjacent to New Jersey and provides a glimpse of what the butterfly fauna of northeastern New Jersey would have been prior to its extensive urbanization. Leck (1973) provided a preliminary list of butterflies of the Hutcheson Memorial Forest, a complex of old fields and mature forest in Somerset County.

More recently, the New York City Butterfly Club published a checklist of all butterflies recorded within 50 miles of lower Manhattan (Cech 1993), and the Cape May Bird Observatory published a checklist for Cape May County (Wright and Sutton 1993). But New Jersey is, in a way, remarkable for the paucity of such local lists and papers.

Changes in landscape inevitably result in long-term changes in butterfly populations. Although most of New England and the Mid-Atlantic states were covered with Canadian and Hudsonian Life Zone forests, including Oak-Hickory, Beech-Maple, and such soil-determined (edaphic) variants as Pine Barrens, there is controversial evidence that Native Americans cleared areas of forest by burning them to facilitate hunting (Russell 1981a,b). At the time of European "discovery," there was already a patchwork of field and forest, perhaps with corridors allowing penetration of open-country butterflies from the central prairies to the Atlantic coast.

During the colonial period, the clearing of forests was a primary activity, valued in itself for the production of timber, release of land for agriculture, and elimination of fearsome wild beasts. Forest land dwindled rapidly with only a few relict stands surviving the ax, and populations of most butterflies (except Anglewings and Satyrs) must have increased. Following the industrial revolution in the mid-nineteenth century and the increasing urbanization at the turn of the century, the economy of the region changed, and much agricultural land was allowed to undergo natural succession which proceeded at varying rates. Thus the amount of New Jersey's landscape that is forested is about the same today as it was a century ago (42%; see table 11), but the character of these tracts has been altered.

Fires ignited by lightning or by accident periodically opened up new areas, particularly in the Pine Barrens. With the advent of railroads, fires ignited by sparks and hot cinders occurred commonly (Russell 1981a,b). Another change wrought during the colonial period was the introduction of innumerable alien flowering plants from the Old World, which dramatically altered the composition and diversity of many plant communities. The net impact of this change on butterfly faunas is not clear, but it probably benefited some generalist species at the expense of some specialists.

Overall, the late nineteenth century may have been a time of unusual abundance and diversity of butterflies. In the early twentieth century, much land was being reclaimed by forests, with the resulting decline of some open-country species whose tenure in the northeastern United States may have been relatively recent and temporary (A. E. Brower 1960). These declines were probably hastened by habitat loss due to suburban sprawl, which has occurred mainly in northern and central New Jersey.

The mid-twentieth century began an era of widespread use of chemical insecticides, many of which were designed to be highly toxic particularly to Lepidoptera. The heavy spraying of forests to control Gypsy Moths (*Lymantria dispar*) had a serious negative impact on a number of forest-adapted butterflies and may have contributed significantly to the disappearance of some species from our fauna.

Inevitably, a book of this sort is static and challenges observers to gather the kind of information which quickly renders it out of date. That is the tradition of state books on flora and fauna. It is always tempting to wait for additional information to accumulate before publishing a work such as this, but a half-century is long enough, and there have been great changes that deserve to be chronicled.

Much remains to be studied regarding New Jersey's butterfly fauna. For most parts of the state, there is no published documentation of species occurrence and status, and for virtually all parts there is inadequate published information on the *phenology*[1] (seasonal cycle of occurrence) of even the most common species. The feeding and host plants of most species are known but may vary from place to place, or even from decade to decade. Shapiro's (1979) study of the reliance of the Wild Indigo Duskywing (*Erynnis baptisiae*) on Crown Vetch (*Coronilla varia*) is a good example of new information arising from careful observation. Particularly for local and declining species it is important to know what hosts they actually use in New Jersey so that appropriate habitat management measures can be taken.

The annotated list of butterflies in this book has been assembled from extensive fieldwork, published accounts, examination of specimens, and personal communications with many people, yet inevitably the work of some will have been overlooked. Hence, any such list is always preliminary. We provide it in the hope and expectation that the increasing number of active field naturalists and butterfly watchers will add to our understanding of all species, but particularly of those species whose status is indicated as poorly known or unknown.

There are also many New Jersey species for which the status is changing. Just since we began writing a decade ago, at least one species, Mitchell's Satyr (*Neonympha mitchellii*), has been lost from our fauna, while the Common Ringlet (*Coenympha tullia*) has invaded the state, and the Arogos Skipper (*Atrytone arogos*) has been rediscovered after 20 years of absence. No list can be more than a snapshot of butterfly status, and any list is intended to encourage new and additional records and revisions.

1. Technical terms defined in the glossary (appendix B) are printed in italics the first time they appear.

CHAPTER 2

What Are Butterflies?

The millions of organisms that make up our living world are divided into about twenty-eight major categories called Phyla, and by far the largest of these is the Arthropod phylum (Arthropoda means jointed legs), which includes the insects, spiders, shrimps, crabs, and their allies. Phyla are further subdivided into classes, one of which, the Insecta, contains most living things on Earth. To date, about 750,000 species of insects have been described and named by scientists, and this makes up about 76% of the approximately 990,000 known animal species (fig. 1) and about 54% of all species, including plants as well as animals. However, Harvard biologist E. O. Wilson, author of *Biodiversity*, estimates that this is less than one-third of all existing species. Based on studies in the canopy of the Amazonian rain forest, Erwin (1983) estimated that there might be as many as 30 million species, of which the vast majority are insects.

The insects (Insecta) include about twenty-six orders, one of which is the Lepidoptera—the butterflies and moths. In general, the insect body has three portions: the head (which guides the insect and contains the mouthparts for feeding), the thorax (which bears the locomotory apparatus, wings and legs), and the abdomen (which bears the reproductive and food-processing organs).

The term "butterflies," as distinct from moths, is usually applied to the subclass Rhopalocera, which includes the true butterflies and the skippers. However, many early books on "butterflies" excluded the skippers, which early authors considered intermediate between butterflies and moths. Many recent authors still emphasize the distinction by writing of "butterflies" and "skippers," for example, Shapiro's (1974a) monograph on the *Butterflies and Skippers of New York State* and Iftner et al.'s (1992) *Butterflies and Skippers of Ohio*; others do not, for example, Opler and Krizek's (1984) *Butterflies East of the Great Plains* and Glassberg's (1993b) *Butterflies through Binoculars*. All four of these books cover the true butterflies and skippers. Conversely, *The Butterflies of Delmarva* (Woodbury 1994) does not cover the skippers at all.

Even the separation of moths from butterflies is somewhat artificial, according to Murphy and Ehrlich (1984), who suggest joining butterflies and most moths in a suborder, Glossata. In the past, some authors referred in their writings to butterflies as "diurnal Lepidoptera" or simply "diurnals," although many moths are diurnal as well. Other artificial subdivisions sometimes used to refer to the butterflies and larger moths are "Macrolepidoptera" and "Ditrysia." The innumerable, hard-to-identify, tiny moths a few millimeters in length are considered Microlepidoptera, often dismissed as "Micros." There are more than ten times as many moths as butterflies, and many of these are "micros."

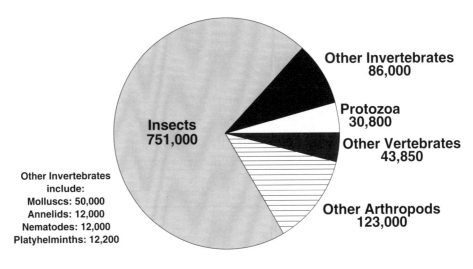

Figure 1. Estimated number of known animal species (based on Wilson 1988). Insects comprise 76% of known species and a much higher percentage of those yet to be discovered and described.

Other Invertebrates
86,000

Protozoa
30,800

Insects
751,000

Other Vertebrates
43,850

Other Invertebrates
include:
Molluscs: 50,000
Annelids: 12,000
Nematodes: 12,000
Platyhelminths: 12,200

Other Arthropods
123,000

The Lepidoptera are a fairly large order as the known insects go, and even in North America there are undoubtedly numerous species of microlepidoptera that have not yet been identified or described by scientists. In the tropics, the number of new species of these moths waiting to be discovered and *described* is certainly great, and judging by the progress in discovering hitherto unrecognized *sibling species* among well-known North American butterflies, there are many new butterfly species to be described there as well. Many of these species are probably already endangered due to habitat loss. With the mounting interest in biodiversity (Wilson 1988), there is a recognition and fear that many species of animals, including insects, are becoming extinct before they are even known to science.

It is difficult to reconstruct the evolutionary history of butterflies because the fossil record is exceedingly poor. The earliest Arthropods were present in the ocean more than 500 million years ago, and terrestrial scorpionlike creatures are found in the fossil record from 435 million years ago (Scott 1986). There is still controversy about the age of the Lepidoptera, which Scott places at more than 200 million years old; but Emmel et al. (1992) say that the earliest Lepidoptera appeared with the flowering plants in the Cretaceous, about 140 million years ago. They are believed to have evolved from a common ancestor with the Caddisflies, and the butterflies later evolved from an ancestral moth, probably by the beginning of the Cretaceous period, about 144 million years ago (Shields 1976). Probably all modern butterfly families had appeared by the end of the Cretaceous, 66 million years ago, about the time that the earliest mammals first appear in the fossil record.

There are remarkably few definite fossil butterflies. Only forty-four have been documented, nearly half of these from the Florissant shales northwest of Colorado Springs (Emmel et al. 1992). These date from the Oligocene (about 35 million years ago), and most of these were already known to Scudder (1875), indicating the dearth of recent discoveries.

There is general agreement that butterflies evolved with the flowering plants, since most butterfly species use one or more species of flowering plants as their host plant (the plant on which they lay their eggs and on which their caterpillars develop). A few species use conifers as their hosts, and, uniquely, the larvae of Harvesters feed on other insects (Woolly Aphids). Both the plants and butterflies underwent a major spurt of evolutionary radiation during the Cretaceous period. As new kinds of plants arose offering new niches, certain butterflies evolved the ability to exploit those plants. As their herbivory became a threat, plants evolved adaptations to "escape" being eaten, often resulting in newly differentiated species, which in turn offered an evolutionary challenge to new kinds of butterflies. This accounts in part for the fact that certain families of Angiosperms contain many species that are hosts to many species of butterflies, whereas other families are used by only a few species of butterflies or none at all. This phenomenon of coevolution has been extensively studied in the tropics, particularly by Keith Brown and his colleagues in Brazil. They showed that the Heliconiine butterflies coevolved in complex ways with the Passion Flower family (Passiflora; Benson et al. 1976).

Although the butterflies (as a subgroup of Lepidoptera) are a relatively small component of the insects, they have attracted a very large scientific following, no doubt because of their conspicuousness and intrinsic beauty. Despite, or perhaps because, so many people have studied butterflies, their classification is still controversial (Ackery 1984). Even Samuel Scudder, writing in 1889, summarized more than a dozen classification schemes put forward by earlier scientists.

The following classification is adapted from the chart developed by Philip Ackery (1984), based in large part on the work of Paul Ehrlich (1958, Ehrlich and Ehrlich 1967) and others. It is based on more characters than many earlier classifications, but it too is probably not the last word. Only the families and subfamilies [1] represented in New Jersey are included in table 1.

A number of writers have tried to estimate the number of butterfly species in the world, beginning with Kirby's (1872) estimate of 7,700. Ehrlich and Raven (1964) put the number between 15,600 and 18,600, and Robbins (1982) estimated between 15,900 and 18,225 butterfly species. Using newer references, Shields (1989) arrived at an estimate of 17,280 species. By contrast, there are probably about ten times as many moths (Shields 1989).

Any such estimate must take into account the fact that the diversity of some families, particularly the Lycaenidae (Coppers, Hairstreaks, and Blues) and the Hesperiidae (Skippers) in the Oriental (Asia) and Neotropical (Central and South America) regions is poorly known. Species estimates are approximate and depend on how well the group is known both worldwide and in North America, and what one considers to be distinct species. Table 2 summarizes the approximate numbers of species of the major butterfly groups in the world, North America, and New Jersey.

Skippers versus Butterflies

Taxonomists distinguish the true butterflies (Papilionoidea) from the skippers (Hesperioidea) on the basis of wing venation and by the presence of a spur on a portion of the front leg (tibia) of the true butterflies. Skippers generally have thicker, more mothlike, bodies. The skippers themselves are divided into two major groups or subfamilies. There is no difficulty in recognizing that the fold-winged or grass skippers (Hesperiinae) are distinct, but many of the spread-winged skippers (Pyrginae) look and behave more like true butterflies.

Like typical insects, most butterflies have six legs (three pairs) attached to their thorax. In many groups, however, the front pair of legs is reduced, and this distinction is widely used as a *taxonomic* character to distinguish among families of

---

1. The scientific names applied to families end in "idae" while the scientific names applied to subfamilies end in "inae."

Table 1. Classification of Higher Categories of Butterflies of New Jersey (Modified from Ackery 1984)

Kingdom: *Animalia*	The animal kingdom
Phylum: *Arthropoda*	Joint-legged creatures
Subphylum: *Hexapoda*	Six-legged creatures
Class: *Insecta*	Insects
Order: *Lepidoptera*	Butterflies and moths
Suborder: *Rhopalocera*	Butterflies (including skippers)
Superfamily: *Papilionoidea*	True Butterflies
Family: *Papilionidae*	Swallowtails
Subfamily: *Papilioninae*	Swallowtails
Family: *Pieridae*	Whites and yellows
Subfamily: *Pierinae*	Whites
Subfamily: *Coliadinae*	Yellows and sulphurs
Family: *Lycaenidae*	Lycaenids or Gossamer Wings
Subfamily: *Miletinae*[a]	Harvester
Subfamily: *Theclinae*[a]	Hairstreaks
Subfamily: *Lycaeninae*[a]	Coppers and Blues
Family: *Riodinidae*[a]	Metalmarks[b]
Family: *Nymphalidae*[c]	Nymphalids or Brushfoots
Subfamily: *Heliconiinae*[d]	Fritillaries
Subfamily: *Nymphalinae*[d]	Anglewings, Brushfoots, etc.[e]
Subfamily: *Apaturinae*[f]	Emperors and Goatweeds
Subfamily: *Satyrinae*[c]	Nymphs, Satyrs, Ringlets
Subfamily: *Danainae*[c]	Monarch and Milkweed butterflies
Subfamily: *Libytheinae*[c,g]	Snouts
Superfamily: *Hesperioidea*	Skippers
Family: *Hesperiidae*	Skippers
Subfamily: *Pyrginae*	Spread-winged Skippers
Subfamily: *Hesperiinae*	Grass, folded-wing

a. Opler and Krizek (1984) divide the Lycaenidae differently. They recognize the subfamily Lycaeninae (Harvesters, Coppers, Hairstreaks, and Blues) as distinct from the Riodininae (Metalmarks), and then use the following subgroups as tribes: Gerydini (Harvester), Lycaenini (Coppers), Theclini (Hairstreaks), and Plebejini (Blues).
b. The Metalmarks have sometimes been included as a subfamily, the Riodininae of the Lycaenidae.
c. The subfamilies now included in the Nyphalidae have often been treated as full families in the past.
d. These two subfamilies are more closely related than are the other families of Nymphalids.
e. Scott (1986) refers to these as Spiny Brushfoots.
f. The Emperors are sometimes placed with the Goatweed butterflies in Charaxinae.
g. Ehrlich (1957a) retained the family Libytheidae while including Satyrinae, Nymphalinae, Heliconiinae, and Danainae in the Nymphalidae.

butterflies. There are three types of forelegs among male butterflies, described by Robbins (1987) as follows:

> Type I found in the Swallowtails, the Whites and Sulphurs and the Skippers. The forelegs are fully developed and are used for walking as well as cleaning the antennae. The "tarsus" of the foreleg has five segments.

> Type II found in the Blues, Coppers and Hairstreaks, but not in the Metalmarks. The forelegs are used for walking, but not for cleaning the antennae. The "tarsus" of the foreleg is fused into one segment and retains spines.

> Type III found in all subfamilies of Nymphalidae including the Snouts and also in the Metalmarks. The foretarsus is fused, but has no spines or claws and is greatly reduced so it is not used for walking or cleaning the antennae.

The following are some of the characteristics of the butterfly families and some of the subfamilies found in New Jersey.

Swallowtails (*Papilionidae*). This is a worldwide family of large, brightly col-

Table 2. The Butterfly Fauna of the World, North America, and New Jersey

	World-wide	North America	New Jersey
Swallowtails	600	30	7
Whites and Sulphurs	1100	55–60	12
Blues, Coppers, Hairstreaks	7000[a]	100	28[g]
Metalmarks	1300[b]	24	1
Nymphalids	6400	215	39
snouts	< 12	1[c]	1
nymphalids	3000	150–160	29[d]
satyrids	3000	50	8
milkweeds	300	4	1
Skippers	3000[f]		57[e]
spread-wing	1150[f]	110	20
grass	2150[f]	135	37
	ca 18,000	680	143

NOTE: The numbers of species listed are approximate and are adapted from Pyle (1981), Robbins (1982), and Shields (1989).
a. An estimated 7000 species, but only 5000 have been described.
b. About 90% of these are found in the American tropics (Neotropics).
c. The Eastern and Western Snouts are now considered conspecific by several authors.
d. Includes 14 fritillaries, crescents, and checkerspots, 7 anglewings, and 8 other nymphalids.
e. Includes 21 Spread-winged skippers (Pyrginae) and 36 Grass skippers (Hesperiinae).
f. Scott (1986) estimates 3650 skippers with 2150 grass skippers.
g. Includes Appalachian and Summer as well as Spring Azures.

What Are Butterflies?

13

ored butterflies, many of which have a conspicuous tail on the hind wing. All legs are fully developed and function for walking and cleaning antennae. Some species are host specific (their larvae can develop on only one type of host plant), while others feed on many species, but for the most part their hosts are confined to a few families, Rutaceae (citrus), Apiaceae (formerly called Umbelliferae; carrot family), Lauraceae (Spicebush, Sassafras), and Aristolochiaceae (Pipevines).

Whites and Sulphurs (*Pieridae*). This worldwide family comprises butterflies that are mainly white, yellow or orange. The species in New Jersey range from the rather small Little Yellow to the Cloudless Sulphur. All legs are fully developed and function for walking and cleaning antennae. Several species do not have distinct flight peaks, but breed more or less continuously from spring to fall. They have a basic larval design, usually green color with whitish or yellow longitudinal stripes. Their host plants are mainly in the Brassicaceae (also called Cruciferae; mustards and cresses) and the Fabaceae (also called Leguminosae; clovers and peas).

Gossamer Wings or Lycaenids (*Lycaenidae*). This is by far the largest of the butterfly families. In any one location there are several species that are highly similar in appearance (Malaysia has ninety-six species in a single genus of hairstreaks, *Arophala*). Although females have six functional legs, the forelegs of the males are reduced in size. Caterpillars of many species feed on flowers as well as or instead of leaves. The larvae of many hairstreaks and blues are attended by ants that feed on a honeydue secretion emitted by the caterpillar and in turn guard it from predators. The Harvester (*Feniseca tarquinius*) in the subfamily Miletinae[2] is unique in that its larvae are carnivorous on woolly aphids.

Metalmarks (*Riodinidae*). The metalmarks are a very diverse, primarily Neotropical, family of medium-sized butterflies, many of which are characterized

2. Not to be confused with "Melitaeinae" which has been applied by some authors to the crescents.

by fine, reflective markings on their wings. The forelegs are greatly reduced, more like Nymphalids, while the larvae are closer to the Satyrids. Only one species, the very localized Northern Metalmark (*Calephilus borealis*), is found in New Jersey.

The highly diverse family Nymphalidae, as currently understood, includes not only the Brushfoot butterflies, but also the Satyrids, the Milkweed Butterflies, the Snouts, and the mainly tropical subfamilies, Heliconiinae and Charaxinae. The forelegs are reduced in size and are not used for either walking or cleaning antennae.

Snouts (*Nymphalidae, Libytheinae*). There are reasonable arguments that this small group of butterflies should be designated as a separate family, Libytheidae. All North American snouts have recently been united as a single species, American Snout (*Libythea carinenta*). The larvae of this species feed only on Hackberry trees (*Celtis* spp), and males set up patrolling beats around their host trees. Occasionally in the western United States, Snouts engage in massive migratory flights.

Nymphalids (*Nymphalidae, Nymphalinae*). Also called Brushfoots (fritillaries, checkerspots, crescents, anglewings). It is difficult to characterize this highly diverse group. The forelegs are reduced in size and are not used for either walking or cleaning antennae. Most of these butterflies are brightly colored above, but some have very *cryptic* patterns below and are well camouflaged when their wings are closed. For some species the larvae occur together in large groups.

Admirals (*Nymphalidae, Limenitidinae*). The Red-spotted Purple, Viceroy, and their allies, the Admirals (excluding the Red Admiral), are sometimes separated as a subfamily (Ehrlich and Ehrlich 1961). The larvae form a tube by rolling a leaf and securing it with silk threads, forming the *hibernaculum* in which they overwinter. Our species use tree hosts: cherries, willows, and poplars.

Emperors (*Nymphalidae, Apaturinae*). Not substantially distinct from Nymphalinae (Scott 1986). Forelegs as in Nymphalinae. New Jersey's two emperors are *obligate* Hackberry feeders. The pupae are flattened sideways and rest flat on leaves.

Satyrids (*Nymphalidae, Satyrinae*). These are mostly brown butterflies, with varying patterns of eyespots. Most use grasses or sedges as their hosts. The forelegs are reduced in size and are not used for walking, but serve to sense the substrate on which the butterfly is perched. They usually perch with the wings closed, so the dorsal surface is seldom visible.

Milkweed Butterflies (*Nymphalidae, Danainae*). The forelegs are greatly reduced. The Monarch (*Danaus plexippus*) is the only representative in New Jersey of this widespread family in which larvae are known to sequester cardiotoxic substances derived from their host plants.

Skippers. The skippers apparently derive their name from their supposedly rapid "skipping" flight. Many of these are "the little brown jobs" of the butterfly world. They have broad heads and are mothlike with proportionately shorter wings and fatter bodies than the true butterflies. Only one family (Hesperiidae) and two subfamilies (Pyrginae, Hesperiinae) occur in New Jersey. The names applied to the genera of skippers have varied greatly, but since the publication of the Evans (1955) catalog there has been a tendency for stabilizing the number of genera in use and their names (Burns 1992).

Spread-wing Skippers (*Hesperiidae, Pyrginae*). These include duskywings (*Erynnis*) and cloudywings (*Thorybes*) which usually perch with their wings spread open or flat. Most species are dark grayish, brownish, or blackish, with fine white spotting, and they pose serious identification problems. The widespread, common and conspicuous Silver-spotted Skipper (*Epargyreus clarus*) belongs to this subfamily but usually perches with its wings closed. Most Spread-wing Skippers (pyrgines) do not use grasses as their host plants; many use legumes.

The Grass Skippers, also called Branded or Folded-wing Skippers (*Hesperiidae, Hesperiinae*). These often perch with their wings closed together above their backs, but they have a unique basking posture in which they open their hind wings flat but raise their forewings at more than a 60° angle. Males of many species show a black mark called a *stigma* on the dorsal forewing, which in many cases has a distinctive size or shape that facilitates identification. This mark gives rise to the name "Branded Skippers." In our region all are some shade of orange or brown with markings of white, buff, orange, brown, or black. The group name "Grass Skippers" is appropriate since virtually all species use only grasses or sedges as their hosts (the Brazilian Skipper, which uses Cannas, is an exception).

The Skippers are generally inconspicuous, although they are sometimes the most numerous butterflies encountered. Many older books ignored the Skippers, considering them nonbutterflies, and indeed many field observers find them frustrating to identify and would just as soon overlook them. They do provide identification challenges, particularly when worn, but most of our local skippers are readily identifiable with experience and practice.

Systematics, Taxonomy, and Nomenclature

To better appreciate the distinctions among groups of butterflies and to understand why so many different classifications and names exist both in popular books and in the scientific literature, it is important to understand some of the basic features of systematics and taxonomy and of classification and nomenclature.

The science of *systematics* is a study of the evolutionary relationships among organisms, or how they got to be the way they are. *Taxonomy* is the way that organisms are classified and named according to some method or plan, usually a reflection of their presumed evolutionary relationships. *Classification* is the product of taxonomic study resulting in ordering organisms in some convenient way. *Nomenclature* is the technical process of applying unique names to the organisms. The processes blend into one another, but there are important conceptual distinctions. Ernst Mayr (1954, 1969) distinguished taxonomy as the "theory and practice of classifying organisms" while nomenclature is the "system of names" applied to them.

Ehrlich and Murphy (1981) cautioned that nomenclature often could not achieve its goals of being unique and stable, while at the same time reflecting the evolutionary relationships among species. They warned that nomenclature is a separate practice, though many other writers believe that nomenclature must attempt to reflect evolution. Murphy and Ehrlich (1984) reviewed the challenges of butterfly taxonomy at all levels from family to subspecies. They estimated that there are about 15,000 species of butterflies, with the species level taxon the hardest to define.

Although each butterfly is an individual, we are usually interested in the *population* of butterflies, the number of individuals of any species in an area. A population might refer to the Appalachian Browns (*Satyrodes appalachia*) in a forest, the Pearl Crescents (*Phyciodes tharos*) in a park, the Eastern Tiger Swallowtails (*Papilio glaucus*) in a county, or the Monarchs in a state. For some species such as the Bog Copper (*Lycaena epixanthe*), which show high habitat specificity and a low tendency to disperse from one bog to another, each bog may have its own population, often referred to as a *colony*. In that case the populations at different bogs may be relatively isolated from one another simply by distance.

Many butterflies habitually move long distances, and such individuals have the possibility of encountering other individuals of their own species in another population. This results in *gene flow* among populations, and as long as there is gene flow the populations will not evolve into different entities. Such populations are referred to as *open*, and the breeding within such populations is referred to as *panmixis*. When there are several populations with only a small amount of interchange between them, the term *metapopulation* is applied to the larger group, and this is becoming an increasingly important concept in conservation biology.

The individuals within any given population are not all exactly alike (their *phenotypes* may vary). Their differences may be apparent visually (pattern variability, size variability) or may involve some behavioral or physiological attributes. This variation may have a genetic basis (their *genotypes* may differ) or may be environmentally induced. In the past, some of the pattern variants or aberrations were given taxonomic names as if they were subspecies or varieties.[3]

Variation is important because in different places or under different environmental conditions, different variants may be favored. Thus, over time, a population may develop a certain appearance in one part of its range that differs consistently from the appearance of populations in another part of the species' range. In that case they may be named as different subspecies. The evolution of these differences is the concern of evolutionary biologists and of systematists.

Systematics involves many areas of biology, from anatomy to biochemistry to behavioral ecology. Various lines of evidence are adduced to understand how organisms are related and how they may have evolved. Systematics can focus on "higher categories" such as the relationships among families and orders, or on "lower categories" such as relationships among species or the process of *speciation* itself. The early systematists were morphologists, who relied mainly on the structure and appearance of organisms to determine their classification. Increasingly, systematists are turning to biochemical characters and molecular biology to help sort out complicated relationships among highly similar organisms.

Speciation

Most people, both scientists and butterfly watchers, are primarily interested in species. A butterfly lister probably does not care whether the American Snout he or she is seeking is in the Nymphalidae or in its own unique family. Nor does it matter, for the sake of a list or a photograph, who its nearest evolutionary neighbors are. Scientists study morphology, biochemistry, anatomy, ecology and behavior of individuals, populations, and species, but unless they are specifically interested in systematics and evolution, they tend not to make interspecific comparisons, even when they should. Indeed, the comparative study of species within genera and of genera within families has been viewed as descriptive and archaic, and only with the resurgence of interest in biodiversity have these pursuits become respectable again.

Ernst Mayr (1963) is credited with championing the *biological species* concept as opposed to describing species solely on the basis of morphological distinctiveness, which he called the "typological species" approach that ignores variation within a species. However, much earlier, Henry Skinner (1896) made the same point, in a paper showing that many dramatic variations (for example, the presence or absence of silver spots on the ventral surfaces of fritillaries or the presence or absence or differences in eye spots in satyrids) occur within the same popula-

3. In this book, varieties, aberrations, or forms that are not taxonomic categories are put within single quotation marks.

tion in some cases or are signs of physiological responsiveness to the environment in others.

Central to Mayr's understanding of speciation was his emphasis on the importance of *geographic isolation* in allowing different populations of a species to evolve in different ways by adapting to different habitats, and therefore eventually becoming different species. Mayr (1963) argued that the differences that precluded two forms from interbreeding freely had a genetic basis that must have evolved when the two species were separated or isolated (for example, during periods of glaciation).

When two populations have been isolated (usually because of geological or ecological conditions) for many generations (usually thousands of years), they accumulate genetic differences (sometimes subtle, sometimes enough to be recognizable) that may influence how they behave or reproduce. Should the geological or ecological barriers change, they may come into *secondary contact*, at which time they may find themselves so different that they are reproductively isolated and do not even attempt to interbreed. Or depending on the degree of genetic differentiation, their interbreeding may or may not produce viable offspring, and these offspring may or may not be fertile. Even if fertile, the subsequent generations produced by these interbreeding offspring may be at some physiological or behavioral disadvantage. In any of these cases, there will be a powerful selective force against those parents in the two contacting populations that attempt to interbreed. Thus the members of the two "species" that are able to avoid interbreeding would leave behind more young than those that do interbreed. In some cases, however, the offspring of those that interbreed might be better adapted to the environment in their contact zone than either of the parents, and this might promote the rapid evolution of a new population of intermediate organisms, in which case they would be determined to be a single species.

The application of this understanding of speciation led to the conclusion that two populations represent separate species if

- They do not successfully interbreed in areas where their populations are in contact (*sympatric*), or
- If they do interbreed they do not produce fertile hybrids, or
- If their hybrids are fertile, the subsequent generations are less successful at survival or reproduction (are selected against by natural selection).

This understanding, which has become known as the *biological species concept* of speciation, is now recognized as an oversimplification. However, it remains a useful way of understanding how speciation may occur or how subspecies within a species may develop.

Paul Ehrlich (1961) challenged this approach, pointing out that for many so-called species, even among the well-studied birds and butterflies, the criteria cannot be adequately tested. Either the "species" do not come in contact (i.e., they are *allopatric* rather than *sympatric*) and the hypothesis of speciation is never tested, or they do different things in different areas of sympatry (i.e., they behave as two separate species in one area but as the same species in another). Ehrlich argued that, wishful thinking to the contrary, species are not defined biologically, and he suggested that the "biological species concept" has "outlived its usefulness" as far as taxonomy was concerned.

Ehrlich went on to argue that physical or phenetic similarity should be the basis of classification, and that classification is a means of organizing information, not an end in itself. He believed that it was often fruitless to try to apply the biological species concept rigorously, while Shapiro (1982) argued that the biological species concept was still useful even if it was often difficult to apply with confidence.

Several different approaches to evolution can be discerned among systematists, often resulting in acrimonious controversy. *Phylogenetic* or *cladistic systematists* attempt to reconstruct the branching patterns in evolution by comparing the similarities and differences among organisms in a formal fashion. Cladistics operates on two overriding principles. All members of each branch must share a common ancestor (i.e., must be *monophyletic*), and each branching point must be defined on the basis of shared derived characters. In a cladistic analysis, each identifiable or measurable character has the same weight as any other character, on bifurcations in the evolutionary tree. *Evolutionary systematists* also try to reconstruct the evolutionary history of their organisms, but they rely more on inference by weighting some characters more heavily than others. Reduced forelegs, for example, count for more than a miniscule change in wing venation. Much of the modern classification of butterflies and birds has been based on this approach, championed by Mayr and others.

Pheneticists argue that it is hopeless to reconstruct evolution, and that organisms should simply be classified on their attributes—their similarities and differences (Ehrlich 1964)—ignoring how they got that way. Pheneticists emphasize the artificiality of the species (Sokal and Crovello 1970), an idea championed for some groups of insects through the process of *numerical taxonomy* (Sokal and Sneath 1963). Any of these approaches can produce a usable classification of organisms—a system that can be used to store and retrieve information about organisms or which can provide the order for listing species in a book or checklist.

All of the above approaches of *taxonomy* involve sorting out organisms based on similarities and differences. Because these similarities and differences result from evolutionary processes, many taxonomists argue that the resulting taxonomy should reflect, as accurately as possible, the evolutionary history of a taxon. This is contrary to a strictly phenetic classification, in which two organisms that look the same may be put in the same category, even if they represent convergent evolution. At present, the classification of butterflies is mainly an evolutionary/phylogenetic one, but several authors, for example Scott (1984) and Robbins (1987), have attempted to reconstruct it within a cladistic framework.

As scientists investigate various groups of butterflies, they periodically reach new conclusions regarding the degree of differentiation, hence the shuffling of species. Thus, for example, recent systematic work has resulted in lumping the Olive Hairstreak with several other Hairstreaks and splitting the Spring Azure into several species.

Taxonomy

Taxonomy delineates groups of organisms, or *taxa*, which deserve a name. Thus *glaucus* is a species-level *taxon* within the genus-level *taxon Papilio* within the subfamily-level taxon *Papilioninae* within the family-level taxon *Papilionidae*. The taxonomic hierarchy (table 3) for any species indicates how it fits into the rest of the living world. The product of taxonomy is a classification, usually in the form of a list or data base. Classifications are inherently limited by the fact that we process information linearly, for example, from left to right or from top to bottom, while the process of evolution does not lend itself to such linearity. Thus it is easy to see that *Papilio glaucus* is in the family Papilionidae, but not how it should be listed in relation to other species of *Papilio*, or how these are related to other butterflies. Problems arise when two authorities hold different opinions about the relationships among taxa. Furthermore, some faunal books list higher categories (classes, orders, and families) in some accepted or presumed

Table 3. Simplified Taxonomic Hierarchy of Humans and Eastern Tiger Swallowtail

	Humans	Tiger Swallowtail
Kingdom	*Animalia*	*Animalia*
Phylum	*Chordata*	*Arthropoda*
Class	*Mammalia*	*Insecta*
Order	*Primate*	*Lepidoptera*
Superfamily	*Hominoidea*	*Papilionoidea*
Family	*Hominidae*	*Papilionidae*
Subfamily	*Homininae*	*Papilioninae*
Genus	*Homo*	*Papilio*
Species	*sapiens*	*glaucus*

Table 4. Finer Taxonomic Subdivisions in the Taxonomic Hierarchy of the Eastern Tiger Swallowtail

Kingdom	Animal	Animal kingdom
Phylum	*Arthropoda*	Arthropods
Class	*Insecta*	Insects
Order	*Lepidoptera*	Butterflies and moths
Suborder	*Ditrysia**	
Section	*Macrolepidoptera***	
Subsection	*Rhopalocera*	Butterflies and skippers
Superfamily	*Papilionoidea*	True butterflies
Family	*Papilionidae*	Swallowtails and allies
Subfamily	*Papilioninae*	Swallowtails
Tribe	*Papilionini**	
Genus	*Papilio**	Swallowtails
Species	*glaucus*	Eastern Tiger Swallowtail

SOURCES: Derived from Scott 1986; Miller and Brown 1981.
* Some taxa do not have a convenient common name.
** A confusing term which includes the larger moths.

"evolutionary" order, but then they list the species and sometimes even the genera in alphabetical order.

It is readily apparent that in addition to the seven major steps of this hierarchy, other levels are frequently used to show more subtle relationships. Table 4 shows how groups can be divided even more finely to reflect relationships. Thus, orders can be divided into suborders or even infraorders, families into subfamilies and tribes, genera into subgenera, and species into subspecies.

Descriptions of New Species

When a new species is recognized, the scientist naming it provides a formal technical *description*. Most of our species were described more than a century ago (some more than two centuries ago). Modern descriptions must include the designation of a *type specimen*, the original specimen on which the original author based the description. Future generations of scientists should be able to find this type specimen in a museum. This is particularly important for little-known species from tropical areas that may be described under different names by different scientists, in which case it becomes difficult to piece together exactly what the correct name (usually the first one used) should be. However, if one can examine the original type specimen associated with a name, it is possible to determine what kind of butterfly the name originally referred to.

Remarkably, many of the butterfly species of North America do not have identifiable type specimens (Miller and Brown 1981), and many presumed types have been designated in subsequent taxonomic revisions. This means that no one knows for sure what kind of butterfly the originally named butterfly was. These types represent the best guess of taxonomists one hundred or more years after the fact, and this guesstimate has posed an obstacle to understanding butterfly taxonomy and nomenclature. Many of the descriptions of species in the eighteenth and early nineteenth century were based on illustrations, particularly those of Abbot, rather than specimens, and these illustrations have become important documents in butterfly taxonomy. Unfortunately, book dealers have learned that it is lucrative to tear the color plates out of antique books and sell them individually, with the result that many important natural history works have become rare.

Lumping versus Splitting

Taxonomists differ in their basic attitude toward their craft, and some reflect either a *lumper* or a *splitter* tendency. Lumpers like to emphasize the similarities among organisms, and therefore put two or more similar groups together under the same name. For example, two similar "species" are likely to be considered a single species (*conspecific*) or related genera may be placed together (for example, the elfin genus *Incisalia* and hairstreak genus *Mitoura* have been merged into, or lumped with, *Callophrys*).

Splitters like to emphasize the uniqueness of each kind of creature, and are likely to keep two species separate unless the evidence for lumping them is overwhelming. To splitters, slight differences have taxonomic significance. Thus Miller and Brown (1981), for example, recognized far more genera in their book than most other authors (they are generic splitters). Many scientists fall in between, varying in the type of evidence they require to split or lump.

Lumping and splitting reflect individual understandings and preferences, and also seem to run in waves. The late nineteenth and early twentieth centuries were the heyday for description of new species, particularly those from the tropics. Every morphologically distinct form was likely to be designated a species. Sometimes even the male and female of a species originally received different names. Mayr (1963) refers to this as the "typological species" practice.

Beginning mainly in the 1940s, biologists interested in different groups of animals began to examine more closely the relationships among numerous "species" that had been described. Many of these were found to be different forms of a single species, classified mainly on their ability to interbreed where their ranges overlapped, and their ability to produce fertile hybrids that were not at any evolutionary disadvantage. Challenges arose where two species did not overlap (had *allopatric* ranges), but biologists guessed that they might interbreed if they did overlap. There followed a flurry of lumping, so that in birds the number of species-level groups or taxa was cut in half, from more than 16,000 to just about 8600. When, in their quest for understanding relationships, lumpers group several different forms together under a single name, the other species names are no longer used and are said to be *synonyms* of the name that is applied.

With the burgeoning interest in biodiversity in the mid-1980s, scientists began to reexamine many species and discovered that splitting them would better represent their relationships. New techniques of molecular biology, similar to those used in the courtroom for identifying parents or perpetrators,[4] can show that in some cases even highly similar appearing forms may represent two genetically distinct groups that deserve to be called separate species. The applications of molecular approaches to systematics is rapidly growing, and many new techniques

---

4. Readers may be interested to know that Jeffery Glassberg, president of the North American Butterfly Association, was one of the developers of these molecular techniques.

and markers are being sought to improve the taxonomic utility. Molecular techniques, however, are far from being the last word.

By carefully documenting the life history of butterflies, scientists often discover two or more species lurking under a single name. These are called *sibling species* or *cryptic species*. This phenomenon is well illustrated by the Azures (*Celastrina*). The various Azures look extremely similar but have different hosts, life cycles, and flight periods. Until recently, the Appalachian Azure was treated as a variety of the Spring Azure (for example, Pyle 1981, Scott 1986), though Opler and Krizek (1984) already considered it a separate species. Moreover, scientists now believe that there are other species, for example the "Summer Azure" still lurking in the Spring Azure "complex" (Pavulaan, pers. comm.). David Wright (1995) indicated several other forms which differ ecologically and may require separate taxonomic designations in the future (see Spring Azure species account).[5]

Nomenclature

The process of describing a new species must follow rules (International Code of Zoological Nomenclature) set down by the International Commission on Zoological Nomenclature. Both the Code and the Commission are abbreviated ICZN. This is an official international body that governs scientific names of animals. There are rules applicable to both the lower-level (genus, species, subspecies) and the higher-level categories (class, order, family), as well as the in-between ranks. The ICZN actually adjudicates situations where a species is referred to by two names or where a name has been applied to two species. For example, for many years the scientific name *ajax* was applied to the Zebra Swallowtail, but it has been suppressed by the ICZN because Linnaeus originally illustrated the Black Swallowtail and Tiger Swallowtail as well as the Zebra Swallowtail, under the name *ajax* (Zirlin 1994a).

Some of the rules concern *priority*; the earliest name unequivocally assigned to a species takes precedence over subsequent names assigned to that species. This is particularly relevant to scientific publications of the 1700s and 1800s, when scientists had much more difficulty communicating, and a taxonomist in one country might describe and name a species already named by another taxonomist somewhere else. When someone realizes that the two names actually apply to the same species, the earliest name is designated as having *priority*, and the latter name(s) are reduced to *synonymy*. The rules of nomenclature are quite complicated, but they do serve to put some order into the process. These rules, such as the rule of priority, do not apply to English names; therefore, the NABA Standing Committee on English names developed rules for these names as well (NABA 1993,1995).

When a butterfly is first described, it must be given a scientific name. The original describer must decide to what genus the butterfly belongs, based on its anatomical and other attributes, and then designate a type specimen and, thereby, a type locality. The describer does have great discretion, however, over the name given to the species. The only limitation is that a name already used for another species in the genus cannot be used, even if the name has subsequently been reduced to synonymy (in other words, even if no species in the genus currently bears that name).

Thus, when Carolus Linnaeus (also known as Linné), the father of modern

---

5. Although these additional "species" of Azures have not been widely recognized, they are mentioned in this book, to encourage observers to be aware of their possible occurrence in different parts of the state.

taxonomy, was assigning names to the various species of swallowtails, he named them after characters from Homer's *The Odyssey* (Zirlin 1994a), while dusky-wings were named after Roman poets (Zirlin 1993). Opler and Krizek (1984) provide a brief etymological account of the meaning of the names of each butterfly. Once a species has been named, future systematists may decide to shift a species to a different genus, based on new knowledge or understanding of relationships. The species may retain its original species name but will have a new genus name, and this is sometimes referred to as a "new combination." Thus Linnaeus (1758) assigned almost all butterflies to the genus *Papilio*, but most of the species he named are now placed in other genera.

Use of Authorities

In many taxonomic books and checklists dealing with butterflies, the scientific names (genus and species) are followed by the name of the person who first described the butterfly and sometimes the year of the description (table 5). This is referred to as the *authority*. Where the current genus name is the same as in the original description, the name and year are given without parentheses. This is the case, for example, for the swallowtails which Linnaeus originally assigned to the genus *Papilio* and which are still there. Linnaeus's name follows without parentheses. However, for the other species Linnaeus assigned to this genus, his name follows in parentheses since they are now listed in other genera. In some works (e.g., Iftner et al. 1992), the name given is the authority who described the subspecies that occurs in an area rather than the species to which it is now assigned.[6]

The role of authority used to be very important in defining a scientific name. If the same name was applied to two different species, the person's name following it would indicate which species was meant. Most popular natural history books such as field guides dispense with the authority. In this book we include the authority, partly because it shows when a species was first described. It also shows the diversity of people who had a hand in naming our butterfly fauna (see table 5).

Scientific versus Common Names of Butterflies

Organisms can be referred to by two kinds of names. The *scientific names* are those applied when the organism is described and are supposed to be used universally. Rules of nomenclature require that they be Latin or Latinized. But organisms, particularly common and conspicuous ones, are also given a *vernacular name* (also called a *common name*) in local languages. Thus each of our butterflies has both a scientific name and a vernacular or "English" name.

Scientific names are used by scientists and technical people when communicating with one another, particularly in international meetings or publications, since an insect species is likely to have different common names in Germany, England, France, Spain, and North America, or even different names in different parts of North America. Theoretically at least the same scientific name should apply throughout the world, though this is not always the case. Murphy and Ehrlich (1983) argue emphatically that people should not use common names in referring to butterflies; they worry about the lack of universality or uniqueness and the language barriers that inevitably arise. Pyle (1984) counters that common names are essential tools for helping the uninitiated learn about butterflies.

6. In this book, the authority listed is the one who first described the species. Where a different subspecies is present in New Jersey, it is mentioned in the "Range" section and the authority is given there.

Table 5. Years of Original Descriptions and the Authorities Who Named Species and Subspecies of New Jersey Butterflies

Year/Authority	Species
1758 Linnaeus	Pipevine Swallowtail
1758 Linnaeus	Tiger Swallowtail
1758 Linnaeus	Spicebush Swallowtail
1758 Linnaeus	Mustard White (E)
1758 Linnaeus	Cabbage White (E)
1758 Linnaeus	Cloudless Sulphur
1758 Linnaeus	Gulf Fritillary
1758 Linnaeus	Red Admiral (E)
1758 Linnaeus	Mourning Cloak (E)
1758 Linnaeus	Painted Lady (E)
1758 Linnaeus	Monarch
1758 Linnaeus	Long-tailed Skipper
1761 Linnaeus	Small Copper/American Copper (E)
1763 Johansson	Orange-barred Sulphur
1763 Johansson	White Peacock
1763 Johansson	Eyed Brown
1764 Mueller	Common Ringlet (E)
[1767 Linnaeus	Cloudless Sulphur (ssp. *ebule*)]
1771 Pallas	Arctic Skipper (E)
1773 Drury	Palamedes Swallowtail
1773 Drury	Baltimore Checkerspot
1773 Drury	Pearl Crescent
1773 Drury	Regal Fritillary
1773 Drury	American Lady
1773 Drury	Red-spotted Purple (White Admiral)
1775 Cramer	Meadow Fritillary
1775 Denis & Schiffermuller	Silver-bordered Fritillary
1775 Fabricius	Black Swallowtail
1775 Fabricius	Great-spangled Fritillary
[1775 Fabricius	Red-spotted Purple (ssp. *astyanax*)]
1775 Fabricius	Common Wood Nymph
1775 Cramer	Bronze Copper
1775 Cramer	Silver-spotted Skipper
1775 Cramer	Peck's Skipper
1775 Cramer	Variegated Fritillary
1776 Cramer	Gray Comma
1776 Cramer	Viceroy
1777 Cramer	Zebra Swallowtail
1777 Cramer	Giant Swallowtail
1777 Cramer	Great Purple Hairstreak
1777 Cramer	American Snout
1777 Cramer	Little Wood Satyr
1778 Denis & Schiffermuller	Compton Tortoiseshell
1779 Cramer	Sleepy Orange
1780 Cramer	Spring Azure
1781 Fabricius	Pearly Eye
[1782 Stoll	Black Swallowtail (ssp. *asterias*)]
1782 Stoll	Brazilian Skipper
1787 Fabricius	Aphrodite
1790 Stoll	Southern Dogface
1793 Fabricius	Carolina Satyr
1793 Fabricius	Crossline Skipper
1793 Fabricius	Juvenal's Duskywing
1793 Fabricius	Coral Hairstreak
1793 Fabricius	Least Skipper
1793 Fabricius	Red-banded Hairstreak
1793 Fabricius	Harvester
1793 Fabricius	Common Sootywing

(*continued*)

Table 5. (*continued*)

Year/Authority	Species
1793 Drury	Fiery Skipper
1797 J. E. Smith	Clouded Skipper
1797 J. E. Smith	Georgia Satyr
1797 J. E. Smith	Southern/Northern Hairstreak
1797 J. E. Smith	Southern Cloudywing
1798 Fabricius	Questionmark
1808 Ochsenheimer	European Skipper (E)
1809 Hubner	Falcate Orange Tip
1809 Hubner	Banded Hairstreak
1818 Hubner	Gray Hairstreak
1819 Hubner	Olive Hairstreak
1819 Godart	Clouded Sulphur
1819 Godart	Milbert's Tortoiseshell
1822 Hubner	Common Buckeye
1823 Hubner	Pine Elfin
[1824 Godart	Banded Hairstreak (ssp. *falacer*)]
1824 Godart	Frosted Elfin
1824 Godart	Eastern Tailed Blue
1824 Latreille	Swarthy Skipper
1824 Latreille	Tawny-edged Skipper
1829 Boisduval & LeConte	Checkered White
1829 Boisduval & LeConte	Little Yellow
1829 Harris	Mustard White
1832 Geyer	Hoary Edge
1832 Geyer	Whirlabout
1833 LeConte	Striped Hairstreak
1833 Boisduval & LeConte	Bog Copper
1833 Boisduval & LeConte	White M Hairstreak
1833 Boisduval & LeConte	Tawny Emperor
1834 Boisduval & LeConte	Hackberry Emperor
1834 Boisduval & LeConte	Sleepy Duskywing
1834 Boisduval & LeConte	Arogos Skipper
1834 Boisduval & LeConte	Zabulon Skipper
1834 Boisduval & LeConte	Rare Skipper
1836 Boisduval	Large Orange Sulphur
1837 Kirby	Brown Elfin
1837 Kirby	Northern Crescent
1837 Boisduval & LeConte	Gold-banded Skipper
[1841 Harris	Gray Hairstreak (ssp. *humuli*)]
1841 Doubleday	Silvery Blue
1842 Harris	Eastern Comma
1847 Doubleday & Hewitson	Silvery Checkerspot
1852 Boisduval	Orange Sulphur
1852 Boisduval	Sachem
[1852 Kirtland	[Eastern] Snout (ssp. *bachmanii*)]
1857 Lucas	Zarucco Duskywing
[1861 Edwards	Common Ringlet (ssp. *inornata*)]
[1862 Harris	American Copper (ssp. *americana*)]
1862 Harris	Indian Skipper
1862 Harris	Leonard's Skipper
1862 Harris	Hobomok Skipper
1862 Harris	Dun Skipper
1862 Edwards	Early Hairstreak
1862 Edwards	Acadian Hairstreak
1862 Edwards	Summer Azure
1862 Edwards	Atlantas Fritillary
1862 Edwards	Common Roadside Skipper
1862 Edwards	Little Glassy Wing
1862 Edwards	Green Comma
1863 Edwards	Appalachian Grizzled Skipper
[1863 Edwards	Arctic Skipper (ssp. *mandan*)]
[1863 Edwards	Sachem (ssp. *huron*)]

Table 5. (*continued*)

Year/Authority	Species
1863 Edwards	Black Dash
1863 Edwards	Long Dash
1863 Edwards	Delaware Skipper
1863 Edwards	Ocola Skipper
1863 Scudder	Persius Duskywing
1864 Scudder	Harris' Checkerspot
1864 Scudder	Cobweb Skipper
1864 Scudder	Northern Broken Dash
1864 Scudder	Pepper and Salt Skipper
1864 Scudder	Mulberry Wing
1864 Scudder	Salt Marsh Skipper
1865 Reakirt	Tawny Crescent
1865 Edwards	Broad-winged Skipper
1865 Edwards	Twin-spot Skipper
1866 Edwards	"Edwards Azure" (*violacea*)
1866 Grote & Robinson	Northern Metalmark
1867 Grote & Robinson	Edwards Hairstreak
1867 Grote & Robinson	Henry's Elfin
1867 Grote & Robinson	Two-spotted Skipper
[1868 Edwards	Southern [Northern] Hairstreak (*ontario*)]
1868 Scudder	Dusted Skipper
1869 Scuder	Mottled Duskywing
1869 Edwards	Eufala Skipper
1870 Scudder & Burgess	Dreamy Duskywing
1870 Scudder & Burgess	Horace's Duskywing
1870 Scudder & Burgess	Columbine Duskywing
1870 Scudder	Northern Cloudywing
1870 Edwards	West Virginia White
1870 Edwards	Hayhurst's Scallopwing
1871 Edwards	Dotted Skipper
1872 Grote	Checkered Skipper
[1876 Scudder	Brown Elfin (ssp. *croesides*)]
1879 Edwards	Dion Skipper
1889 French	Mitchell's Satyr
[1889 Harris	Striped Hairstreak (ssp. *strigosum*)]
[1890 Skinner	Dotted Skipper (ssp. *slossonae*)]
1890 Skinner	Aaron's Skipper
[1891 Neumogen	Large Orange Sulphur (ssp. *maxima*)]
1907 Cook & Watson	Hoary Elfin
1908 Tutt	Appalachian Azure
[1909 Fruhstorfer	Red Admiral (ssp. *rubria*)]
1922 Bell	Confused Cloudywing
[1924 Davis	Georgia Satyr (ssp. *septentrionalis*)]
[1929 Harris	Mustard White (ssp. *oleracea*)]
1936 Clark	Northern Pearly Eye
1936 Forbes	Wild Indigo Duskywing
1942 McDunnough	Hickory Hairstreak
[1942 Munroe	White Peacock (ssp. *guantanamo*)]
[1942 Michener	Gulf Fritillary (ssp. *nigrior*)]
1947 Chermock	Appalachian Brown
1950 Rawson & Ziegler	Hessel's Hairstreak
[1971 Shapiro	Broad-winged Skipper (ssp. *zizaniae*)]
[1977 Kohler	Silver-bordered Fritillary (ssp. *myrina*)]

Summary of Numbers of New Jersey Butterfly Species Named in 20-year Periods

1750–1769	16	1830–1849	17	1910–1929	1
1770–1789	29	1850–1869	36	1930–1949	4
1790–1809	18	1870–1889	10	1950+	1
1810–1829	13	1890–1909	4		

NOTE: (E) designates a species first described from its European representative. [Brackets and indentation] indicate that the New Jersey subspecies is not the nominate race.

Different scientists have also used different scientific names for the same butterfly. The choice of name may reflect their understanding of the nomenclatorial history—or which name was properly attached to the butterfly in question. Or the choice may reflect their belief regarding the relationships among butterflies and their relative degree of similarity or difference to closely related species. Thus the Eastern Tiger Swallowtail is called *Papilio glaucus* by most authors, but *Pterourus glaucus* by others (e.g., Pyle 1981). The insect is the same, but the choice of genus names reflects different degrees of subtlety in defining relationships at the genus level.

Serious lepidopterists have always prided themselves on using scientific names, and there has been a long-standing controversy over whether the vernacular names should even be mentioned in scientific publications. It has long been assumed that scientific names are preferable for communicating among experts because they are more stable, better known, and more scientific. This is an illusion. They are, however, more international. Scientific names are more likely to be the same from place to place but certainly not from time to time. Unlike with birds, however, most publications on insects and most technical—and even some popular—publications on butterflies (for example, Howe 1975), use only the scientific names, considering it almost a badge of honor to ignore the vernacular names (Gochfeld 1993; Glassberg 1994c). In fact, in the United States, the English names of most butterflies have become fairly well standardized, while there have been dramatic reappraisals of butterfly taxonomy, resulting in many changes in scientific names.

Remarkably, the very first issue of the journal *Psyche* (journal of the Cambridge Entomological Club) in 1874 begins with the praise of common names, and the promise to publish common names for many New England species (Anon 1874). Ironically of fifty-two butterfly names published in that issue more than a century ago, twenty-nine of the vernacular names are those currently used, compared with only sixteen of the scientific names (to be fair, many of the species names are still used, even though the generic names have been changed).

Ehrlich and Murphy (1981) performed a similar analysis of publications from Holland (1898) to Miller and Brown (1981) and found that name changes, particularly on the generic level, were frequent. They found that generic splitting was rampant from 1930 to 1980, as seen in the works of McDunnough (1938) and Miller and Brown (1981). They emphasized that the scientific names of organisms should be stable over time, universally recognized from country to country, and sufficiently unique to avoid confusion regarding what organism is meant (Ehrlich and Murphy 1981).

In March 1893, the first article in the first issue of the Journal of the New York Entomological Society (Slosson 1893) began: "Entomologists differ now, as they have always differed, as to the advisability and practicability of having a popular and simple as well as a scientific and technical nomenclature in their own branch of natural history." Slosson used vernacular names to communicate with her collectors, but she also recognized their importance in "popularizing entomology." As recently as 1983, Murphy and Ehrlich (1983) have argued strongly against the use of common names for butterflies, even suggesting that the Lepidopterists' Society abandon its attempt to standardize English names in North America. They claimed that many of the vernacular names do not connote relationships. Pyle (1984), on the other hand, pointed out that names such as Swallowtail are much more stable in indicating the family to which these butterflies belong than the changing scientific names that have been applied. The debate continues in the pages of *News of the Lepidopterists' Society* (e.g., Gochfeld 1993), while the NABA has clearly decided to use English names in lieu of scientific names.

There is an active effort to standardize the vernacular names of butterflies. Miller (1992) has published a list of *Common Names of North American Butterflies*, including a recommended English name as well as those used in other publications. This synonymy is valuable because the common names of many species were not standardized, particularly in the last century, and have changed over time or differed in different parts of the country. Many of the names used by Pyle (1981) and Scott (1986) are not standard, but the work of Opler and Krizek (1984), and more recently Glassberg (1993b) and Opler (1992), contributed to standardization.

NABA (1995) has recently published its *Checklist & English Names of North American Butterflies*, which will very likely become the most widely used standard. The NABA committee recognized that some of its choices, particularly the relatively few newly coined names, would not be popular, but it chose to bite a very important bullet. We have adopted the NABA names in this book with very few exceptions, listing some commonly used alternative names in square brackets.

Taxonomic Sequence of Butterflies

Different books list the families and species of butterflies in different sequences. Although most begin with the swallowtails and end with the skippers, others begin with the skippers, then get to the true butterflies, and begin these with the swallowtails. Each sequence has its proponents and its evolutionary rationale. Many systematists, students of biological relatedness, argue that the taxonomic sequence should reflect the evolutionary history of organisms, with the earliest or most primitive at the front of the list. Beginning in the 1950s the futility of this requirement was realized, for organisms evolved at different rates and the fact that an organism was here now did not tell us its degree of specialization or primitiveness (Ehrlich 1958, Ehrlich and Murphy 1982). Moreover, even primitive or old lineages show a high degree of specialization to modern environments. The sequences offered in various books reflect then current understandings of evolutionary relatedness, and it was certainly desirable to keep apparently related species together in a book or plate, since these were often the most similar in appearance.

There is no magic order that truthfully reflects the evolution of butterflies. The order used in this book is basically that used by other popular books such as Opler and Krizek (1984), Opler (1992), and Glassberg (1993b), and is the order used in the NABA (1995) checklist.

Variation among Butterflies

Even within a single species of butterfly there may be substantial variation in appearance from time to time (temporal variation), place to place (spatial or geographic variation), or from host to host (ecological variation). The appearance or *phenotype* of a butterfly is determined in part by its genetic makeup (*genotype*) and in part by environmental conditions or by accident. Variation may be discrete (also called categorical, distinctive, or discontinuous) or may show all gradations (continuous variation). Examples of discrete variations called *polymorphisms* include the yellow and black morphs of the female Eastern Tiger Swallowtail. Examples of continuous variations include the color gradations of the Great Spangled Fritillary from bright orange to dark brown. Temperature, humidity, and photoperiod during larval development are known to contribute to this variation. Thus, for Pearl Crescents the short daylengths in spring and fall result in the more heavily marked individuals (known as the variety 'marcia'), while those emerging in summer are less well marked (variety 'morpheus'). This kind of variation is called *seasonal polyphenism*.

A century ago, Skinner (1896) discussed these environmental causes of variation, noting that "nearly, if not all, butterflies produced from wintering chrysalids are different in appearance from the subsequent summer brood or broods." For example, he found that the early emerging Mustard and Cabbage Whites are whiter with more restricted black markings, while early emerging Tiger Swallowtails are paler than the summer brood. He remarked on both color and morphological variation in Lycaenids, although some of those variants are now recognized as different species. Conversely, in California, early and late Orange Sulphurs have darker markings on the dorsal hind wing than their midsummer counterparts, which Hoffmann (1978) attributed to thermal adaptations. Darker pigment helps the insect warm up on cool spring and autumn mornings, while paler pigmentation reduces overheating in midsummer (Watt 1995).

Skinner (1896) also commented, in passing, on *industrial melanism*: "Woody coverts and proximity to the sea, as also the smoke of towns and manufacturing districts, are associated with variety and melanism," although it wasn't until a half-century later that genetic mechanism and the role of avian predation in selecting for melanism was clarified (Kettlewell 1955). Skinner apparently believed that the pollution itself influenced coloration directly, as do nutrition, temperature, and humidity.

Geographic Variation and Subspecies

Where the variation has a geographical basis, for example the Common Wood Nymph (*Cercyonis pegala*), subspecies or races are described and given a Latin or Latinized subspecific name. Thus in the northern United States and perhaps extreme northern New Jersey, most or all common Wood Nymphs lack the conspicuous and familiar yellow patch on the forewing and belong to the subspecies *nephele*. In the southern United States and most of New Jersey, most or all Common Wood Nymphs have a yellow patch and belong to other subspecies. Where two subspecies are in contact, intergrades are frequently found, a result of interbreeding. Conversely, where two forms overlap in range but do not interbreed, or produce either infertile or selectively disadvantaged hybrids, that is taken as evidence that they are separate species.

In other species there may be continuous or *clinal variation* in size and/or color from north to south or east to west, such that very large individuals predominate in one part of their range and very small individuals in another part. In some cases, for example, in the *pawnee* and *leonardus* subspecies of Leonard's Skipper (*Hesperia leonardus*) in the Missouri Valley (Spomer et al. 1993), the extremes of the *cline* may be given subspecific names and are called "clinal subspecies" to designate that the variation is continuous rather than discrete.

Applications of the subspecies concept are not at all straightforward and have been extensively debated (see, for example, Murphy and Ehrlich 1984). A subspecies is usually considered to be a geographically distinct entity, but problems arrive when the same characteristics appear in widely separated parts of the range. Thus Harvesters in western Maryland appear very similar to those from the Maritime Provinces that are called a separate subspecies *tarquinius novascotiae*, but in between are Harvesters which appear different and belong to a different subspecies. Thus it would not be appropriate to call the west Maryland insects *novascotiae* (Simmons and Andersen 1970), even if they were indistinguishable. However, the unique appearance may result from similar ecological conditions in western Maryland and Nova Scotia, and such ecologically determined forms have sometimes been considered ecotypes or even ecological races.

Where two or more discrete forms occur together over a large part of their range, they are not usually treated as subspecies, but are called *morphs*, and the situation is referred to as *polymorphism*. Ernst Mayr (1963) first used the term "polyphenism" to describe phenetic variability of a nongenetic nature (for example, the seasonal variation in markings in the Cabbage White), as opposed to polymorphism, which connotes a genetic basis for variation (e.g., the black morph of the female Eastern Tiger Swallowtail). Whereas polymorphism usually applies to discrete types rather than continuous variation, Oliver (1970) maintained that polyphenism can be either continuous or discrete. Such variants have been called "varieties" or "forms" as well as morphs, and in the past were given a scientific name. In current practice, however, the names of varieties are not part of a scientific name, and in this book we designate them by single quotation marks rather than by italics.

Some entomologists, for example, Wilson and Brown (1953), argue that the subspecies concept is not applicable to many insects, and that units named as subspecies are difficult to define. Ehrlich (1957b), however, recognized that the concept worked much better in some groups of insects than in others. Even within the butterflies there may be some species where it makes sense to recognize stable geographic variation as a subspecies, and other cases where one has continuous variation (clinal variation) such that it is difficult to determine the boundaries between two subspecies.

When the variation does not have a genetic basis, it is not reasonable to accord it a subspecific name. For example, ecological or physiological variability is well known and deserves to be studied. The resulting morphs may even be given varietal names, but they are not subspecies. Examples of ecological variation include the Atlantis Fritillary (*Speyeria atlantis*), which in Colorado has a silvered variety, sometimes designated a subspecies *S. a. atlantis*, and an unsilvered form sometimes called *S.a.hesperis*. The two varieties occur in the same geographic areas with a preference for different habitats, but display similar courtship and apparently interbreed freely such that Scott (1988a) concluded that they were indeed conspecific.

In addition there are many butterflies that simply have an abnormal appearance due to a chance mutation or unusual environmental conditions during their development. Many of these aberrations have also been given names and have been valued by collectors. Some are recurrent aberrations, whereas others have been found only once.

CHAPTER 3

The Status and Distribution of Butterflies

This book is primarily about the status and distribution of the butterflies of New Jersey. Whereas "distribution" refers to the places that a butterfly is found, the meaning of "status" is not as obvious. Status refers to the numbers or populations of butterflies and how those numbers change over time, either in the short run (hours, days, or weeks) or in the long run (over a period of years and decades).

Many species of butterflies are conspicuous, and compared with most other insects their status and distribution are relatively well known. The status of some New Jersey butterflies has changed dramatically over the past century, whereas for others we find no evidence of change. Indeed, fifty years ago Comstock (1940) remarked that "the present list adds few [species] to those known to occur thirty years ago as butterflies are mostly obvious creatures and future additions to the State list will probably occur more as strays than as permanent residents."

Today, there are few additions to Comstock's list, mostly species that have been recently recognized or separated taxonomically (for example Hessel's Hairstreak, Hickory Hairstreak, Appalachian Brown, and several "species" of Azures). These were here in Comstock's time but were not considered distinct species. Two species not listed by Comstock are the Rare Skipper, which has been found as a resident in southern New Jersey, and the Common Ringlet, which has recently (1994) invaded northern New Jersey. The former may simply have been overlooked. Only three vagrant species (Mustard White, Atlantis Fritillary, and Zarucco Duskywing) have been added to Comstock's (1940) list. Only one of the species Comstock indicated in his supplemental list has become a "resident," the Red-banded Hairstreak. Indeed, in the past half-century we have probably lost more resident species (e.g., Regal Fritillary, West Virginia White, Persius Duskywing, Appalachian Grizzled Skipper) than we have added. This is particularly surprising because the list of birds recorded from New Jersey has grown dramatically in the 1900s, from 340 species recorded by Stone in 1909 to 414+ species listed for 1983 by Leck (1984).

Although there are approximately 700 species of butterflies and 700 species of birds that occur regularly in North America, the patterns of distribution are very different. Compared to birds, many more of the butterfly species have ranges confined to the tropical regions of the country, or they have small ranges in the montane western states. Although more than half of North American bird species have been recorded in New Jersey (Leck 1984), only about 20% of North American butterflies have ever been found in the state.

Status

The status of any species can be viewed as two-dimensional: abundance and regularity, which in turn are influenced by season and distribution.

Abundance or numerosity reflects the number of individuals encountered at a particular place and time. Some species tend to be solitary, while others are present by the dozens or hundreds during their peak flight periods. Numbers may vary from year to year; a normally rare species may show unusual abundance in some years, or vice versa. For example, the Fourth of July Butterfly Counts (4JC) clearly demonstrated the peak abundance of Monarchs in 1991 and a 75% decline in 1992, with a modest recovery subsequently (Swengel 1994b).

Regularity or frequency refers to how often a species is encountered in a given location. Some butterflies may be encountered daily (albeit in small numbers), others only a few times in a season. Some species are resident in New Jersey, completing their entire life cycle here, while others are seasonal immigrants, usually eliminated entirely during the winter, then reinvading from the south. Vagrants are species that do not occur regularly and cannot be expected to occur every year. Some apparently wandered to New Jersey more frequently in the past, whereas others (e.g., Long-tailed Skipper, Ocola Skipper) are more common today and may deserve elevation from "vagrant" to "irregular immigrant." Arbitrarily, vagrant species for which there are five or fewer New Jersey records are designated "accidental."

Seasonality refers to the time of year the butterflies are present. The season can range from March to November, but few species can be found throughout this period; many are apparent for several months, and others, the so-called *univoltine* species, are present as adults for only a few weeks out of the entire season. Many of the species that seem to be present for most of the season actually appear as two or more relatively synchronized broods, each with some representatives on the wing for 2–4 weeks. Peak abundance is reached when most of the adults of a brood have emerged and before they have begun to die off.

The seasonal pattern of emergence for a species is called its *phenology*. In the species list, the designations given under phenology are for central and northeastern New Jersey, unless otherwise specified. In southern New Jersey, butterflies are likely to emerge up to two weeks earlier, and in extreme northwestern New Jersey emergence is likely to occur up to two weeks later. The phenology schedule can also vary from year to year, leading butterfly watchers to describe a season as "early" or "late." For example, after a warm 1990–91 winter and a very warm spring, butterflies emerged three weeks earlier than usual; and after a warm 1994–95 winter and a very cool spring, emergence was about a week later than usual.

Distribution refers to the localities where the butterflies are found. Quite a few of New Jersey's butterflies can be found throughout the state, that is, in every county and in most open habitats. Some southern species reach their northern limit in southern New Jersey and some northern species occur only in our northwestern counties. Among the latter are woodland species that are not found south or east of the *Fall Line*—the demarcation between the *piedmont* and the Coastal Plain (see chapter 5). Many other New Jersey butterfly species are localized in their distribution, limited, for example, to the South, the Northwest, or the Coastal Plain. Others are simply localized to a specific habitat.

The larvae of some species are *monophagous*, and feed on only a single food plant, for example the Northern Metalmark is restricted to areas where its host plant, the Round-leaved Ragwort (*Senecio obovatus*), occurs. Other species have become restricted (or even eliminated) by the loss or fragmentation of their habitat. Some localized species may be occasionally or locally abundant, for example, the Bog Copper (*Lycaena epixanthe*), but most of the localized species are uncommon or rare, and several are THREATENED or ENDANGERED.

Expansions and Declines

Comparing the current status of a species with its historical status is often frustrated by lack of quantitative information in the past. The words "common" or "often encountered" or "not rare" mean different things to different people at different times. Moreover, an observer would consider ten Pipevine Swallowtails "unusually common" while ten Cabbage Whites might be "unusually rare." As a species increases or decreases in number, our attitudes about its commonness or rarity may change as well. For example, American Coppers used to be very numerous when and where we grew up, and we would regularly see hundreds in a day; today we would consider that many an unusual abundance in most localities. Similarly, we used to think of Monarchs as abundant along the shore in September, and we would often see 100 or more in a day. After 1991, however, when they were truly abundant, 100 individuals in a day seem somehow less spectacular. We can hardly imagine the abundance reported by Hamilton (1885), who wrote that "miles of them is no exaggeration" and estimated that millions passed by Brigantine.

Since much of the early information about butterflies was based on collections made by individuals with different interests who covered different areas, this information is difficult to compare with modern sight-record census techniques. An individual who tracks populations in a locality over many years can provide the best indication of which species are declining or which might be expanding. The Fourth of July Butterfly Counts provide excellent data when they are conducted over the same area by the same people in the same manner, year after year.

In the Historical Status section of the species accounts, we have tried to assess whether species are stable, whether they have increased or decreased, expanded or contracted their range, or whether data are insufficient to make a comparison. Table 6 lists species which we believe have increased (22 species) or decreased (30 species) over the past 50 years. Some other species have shown increases followed by decreases and vice versa, and a long-term trend is not evident. Accidental and vagrant species are not included.

Seasonal Immigrants

Some southern species reach the northern limit of their range in New Jersey, and others extend north along the Coastal Plain to western Long Island. Several southern immigrant species do not arrive in most years until it is too late in the season to reproduce; others may arrive, produce one or more local broods, but then be eliminated by cold winter weather. Shapiro (1974a) noted this latter pattern for the Fiery Skipper in upstate New York and the Ocola Skipper on Long Island. He also identified several species (Cloudless Sulphurs, Gulf Fritillary, and Little Yellow) that do not have their usual host species in New York, although the last does find potential hosts on New Jersey's Coastal Plain and it also breeds on western Long Island.

Human-Assisted Occurrence

Humans transport butterflies to unusual locations both deliberately and accidentally. For some species such as the Brazilian Skipper, the occurrence in New Jersey

Table 6. Butterflies That Have Increased or Decreased in New Jersey in the Past 50–100 Years

Increases[d]	Decreases	
Cabbage White[a]	Pipevine Swallowtail	
Orange Sulphur	Giant Swallowtail	(P)
Banded Hairstreak	Checkered White[b]	
Olive Hairstreak	West Virginia White[b]	(?P)
White M Hairstreak	Clouded Sulphur[c]	
American Snout	Bronze Copper[b]	
Variegated Fritillary	Acadian Hairstreak	(?P)
Meadow Fritillary	Frosted Elfin[b]	
Compton Tortoiseshell	Appalachian Azure	(?P)
Hackberry Emperor	Northern Metalmark	
Tawny Emperor	Aphrodite[b]	(?P)
Common Ringlet	Regal Fritillary[b]	(X)
Horace Duskywing	Silver-bordered Fritillary	
Wild Indigo Duskywing	Silvery Checkerspot	(P)
European Skipper	Tawny Crescent[b]	(X)
Indian Skipper	Baltimore Checkerspot	
Little Glassywing	Green Comma	(?P)
Delaware Skipper	Gray Comma	(?P)
Broad-winged Skipper	Northern Pearly Eye	(P)
Black Dash	Eyed Brown	
Dusted Skipper	Mitchell's Satyr[b]	(X)
	Carolina Satyr	
	Dreamy Duskywing	
	Mottled Duskywing[b]	(P)
	Columbine Duskywing	
	Persius Duskywing	(?P)(X)
	Appalachian Grizzled Skipper[b]	(P)
	Two-spotted Skipper[b]	
	Common Roadside Skipper	
	Arogos Skipper[b]	

a. Much of its increase occurred in the early part of the century.
b. Its decline is part of a regional decline in the northeastern United States.
c. May have declined due to competition or hybridization with the increasing Orange Sulphur.
d. Some increases are only apparent because the species was not adequately recognized or collected in the past.
(P) Pesticide spraying for mosquito and Gypsy Moth control was a factor in decline.
(?P) Pesticide spraying for mosquito/Gypsy Moth control probably contributed to decline.
(X) No longer known to occur in New Jersey.

has been suspected of being related to imported fruit shipments. The origin of the Small Tortoiseshell, which has shown up at Jamaica Bay and in Manhattan, may be related to plant shipments arriving at John F. Kennedy Airport, and indeed the arrival of this species in Nova Scotia via a packing crate from England has been documented (Scott and Wright 1972). There is an increasing commercial trade in live butterflies both for recreational and educational purposes. People contract to have hordes of butterflies (usually Monarchs or American Ladies) released en masse to celebrate weddings or other events. Schoolchildren can purchase larvae and pupae of a variety of species and raise them to adulthood. Perversely, the new environmental ethic encourages children to release their prizes into the wild. Since Zebra and Giant Swallowtails are two of the most popular species sold for rearing in New Jersey, any record of these species in the state may be considered suspect. Various other species that are common in New Jersey (for example Monarchs, American Lady, Viceroy, and various swallowtails) are also sold for raising and release, but the relatively few released are not likely to be noticed. Such releases, however, may disrupt local gene pools and should be discouraged. Exotics such as the Zebra Longwing (*Heliconius charitonus*) seen by Michel Kleinbaum at Ward Pound Ridge, Westchester County, New York (in 1995), and the European Peacock (*Inachis io*) seen by N. Wagerik on Staten Island (September 1995) may have been exotic releases or human-assisted escapes rather than self-propelled accidentals.

Some people have deliberately transplanted eggs, larvae, or pupae with the intention of introducing a species to a new area. Except in the management of THREATENED or ENDANGERED species, this practice should be discouraged since the consequences of such introductions are not predictable. Any transplantations that are done should be carefully documented and monitored in case the species does become established.

Describing Status and Abundance

It is difficult to convey the status of a butterfly in New Jersey in a few words. The important features of a status statement are to convey the likelihood or probability that an observer will encounter that species at a particular place and date, or to indicate the need for special concern or protection. If we had adequate data and space, we could make statements about the number of days per year when a species could be encountered as well as the number of individuals seen on a typical or "good" day. For most species, however, we do not have adequate data and must resort to generalizations. In this book we have tried to make the generalizations as meaningful as possible, and to offer different status statements for different parts of the state. Table 7 lists the maximum counts for each of the species recorded on the sixty-four New Jersey Fourth of July Counts.

In the future, observers making systematic surveys and censuses (e.g., as part of the state Atlas Project) at a particular locality will provide us with much firmer quantitative data. Many butterfly watchers keep a daily list of the species they see and the locations. It is also good to record actual numbers of butterflies seen on a given date at a particular place, even if the estimate is only approximate. Such records are preferable to simply writing "common."

For status, we indicate whether a species is resident (i.e., completing its life cycle in the state each year), probably or possibly resident, or whether it is a seasonal immigrant, vagrant, or accidental:

Vagrant—a species that does not normally breed or occur in New Jersey and visits on a rare and irregular basis, not occurring in most years; also called "strays."

Accidental—a species with five or fewer self-propelled records in the state. Human-assisted visits should not be counted as accidentals.

Absent—a species that does not occur in a particular place, except as a vagrant or accidental.

Human-Assisted—species that are believed to have reached New Jersey artificially, either by ship or plane, often in shipments of plant matter, or which have been released at a new location.

In the absence of numbers, we have employed the following semiquantitative terms to give a general indication of the abundance of each species. If one goes to the appropriate habitat at a time of year when the adult butterflies are active and the weather is suitable, by consulting the terms one can get an idea of the likelihood of encountering each species. These terms are similar to those used by Glassberg (1993b), except we add the designations "fairly common" and

Table 7. Summary of Sixty-four Fourth of July Butterfly Counts from New Jersey, 1975–1995 (includes all New Jersey species whether or not recorded on a Count)
Extracted from the Annual Reports published by the Xerces Society and NABA

English Name	Scientific Name	Percent of counts	Number of counts	Maximum number
Pipevine Swallowtail	*Battus philenor*	22	14	22
Zebra Swallowtail	*Eurytides marcellus*			
Black Swallowtail	*Papilio polyxenes*	58	37	116
Giant Swallowtail	*Papilio cresphontes*			
Eastern Tiger Swallowtail	*Papilio glaucus*	83	53	41
Spicebush Swallowtail	*Papilio troilus*	84	54	78
Palamedes Swallowtail	*Papilio palamedes*			
Checkered White	*Pontia protodice*			
Mustard White	*Pieris napi*			
West Virginia White	*Pieris virginiensis*			
Cabbage White	*Pieris rapae*	100	64	1403
Falcate Orangetip	*Anthocharis midea*			
Clouded Sulfur	*Colias philodice*	73	47	337
Orange Sulfur	*Colias eurytheme*	81	52	3216
Dog Face	*Colias cesonia*			
Cloudless Sulfur	*Phoebis sennae*	5	3	1
Orange-barred Sulfur	*Phoebis philea*			
Large Orange Sulfur	*Phoebis agarithe*			
Little Yellow	*Eurema lisa*			
Sleepy Orange	*Eurema nicippe*			
Harvester	*Feniseca tarquinius*	2	1	3
American Copper	*Lycaena phlaeas*	69	44	310
Bronze Copper	*Lycaena hyllus*	6	4	5
Bog Copper	*Lycaena epixanthe*	8	5	152
Great Purple Hairstreak	*Atlides halesus*			
Coral Hairstreak	*Satyrium titus*	64	41	49
Acadian Hairstreak	*Satyrium acadica*			
Edwards Hairstreak	*Satyrium edwardsii*	13	8	14
Banded Hairstreak	*Satyrium calanus*	59	38	177
Hickory Hairstreak	*Satyrium caryaevorum*	11	7	4
Striped Hairstreak	*Satyrium liparops*	41	26	31
Southern Hairstreak	*Satyrium favonius*	8	5	13
Brown Elfin	*Callophrys augustinus*			
Hoary Elfin	*Callophrys polios*			
Frosted Elfin	*Callophrys irus*			
Henry's Elfin	*Callophrys henrici*			
Eastern Pine Elfin	*Callophrys niphon*			
Olive Hairstreak	*Callophrys gryneus*	27	17	29
Hessel's Hairstreak	*Callophrys hesseli*	2	1	1
White M Hairstreak	*Parrhasius m-album*	8	5	1
Gray Hairstreak	*Strymon melinus*	58	37	56
Red-banded Hairstreak	*Calycopis cecrops*	11	7	5
Early Hairstreak	*Erora laeta*			
Eastern Tailed Blue	*Everes comyntas*	84	54	310
Spring Azure	*Celastrina ladon*			
Summer Azure	*Celastrina neglecta*	64	41	151
Appalachian Azure	*Celastrina neglectamajor*			
Silvery Blue	*Glaucopsyche lygdamus*			
Acmon Blue	*Plebejus acmon*			
Northern Metalmark	*Calephilus borealis*	3	2	5
American Snout	*Libytheana carinenta*	19	12	49
Gulf Fritillary	*Agraulis vanillae*			
Variegated Fritillary	*Euptoieta claudia*	23	15	20
Great Spangled Fritillary	*Speyeria cybele*	55	35	236
Aphrodite	*Speyeria aphrodite*	5	3	3

(*continued*)

Table 7. (*continued*)

English Name	Scientific Name	Percent of counts	Number of counts	Maximum number
Regal Fritillary	*Speyeria idalia*			
Atlantis Fritillary	*Speyeria atalantis*			
Silver-bordered Fritillary	*Boloria selene*	6	4	9
Meadow Fritillary	*Boloria bellona*	11	7	7
Silvery Checkerspot	*Chlosyne nycteis*			
Harris' Checkerspot	*Chlosyne harrisii*			
Pearl Crescent	*Phyciodes tharos*	81	52	1884
Northern Crescent	*Phyciodes selenis*			
Tawny Crescent	*Phyciodes batesii*			
Baltimore Checkerspot	*Euphydryas phaeton*	9	6	51
Questionmark	*Polygonia interrogationis*	70	45	26
Eastern Comma	*Polygonia comma*	17	11	16
Green Comma	*Polygonia faunus*			
Gray Comma	*Polygonia progne*			
Compton Tortoiseshell	*Nymphalis vau-album*	5	3	12
Mourning Cloak	*Nymphalis antiopa*	39	25	32
Milbert's Tortoiseshell	*Nymphalis milberti*			
American Lady	*Vanessa virginiensis*	77	49	79
Painted Lady	*Vanessa cardui*	41	26	35
Red Admiral	*Vanessa atalanta*	80	51	32
Common Buckeye	*Junonia coenia*	42	27	111
White Admiral	*Limenitis a. arthemis*	3	2	1
Red-spotted Purple	*Limenitis a. astyanax*	58	37	47
Viceroy	*Limenitis archippus*	25	16	17
Hackberry Emperor	*Asterocampa celtis*	41	26	13
Tawny Emperor	*Asterocampa clyton*	28	18	12
Northern Pearly Eye	*Enodia anthedon*	11	7	17
Eyed Brown	*Satyrodes eurydice*	5	3	6
Appalachian Brown	*Satyrodes appalachia*	33	21	36
Carolina Satyr	*Hermeuptychia sosybius*			
Georgia Satyr	*Neonympha areolata*	3	2	8
Mitchell's Satyr	*Neonympha mitchelli*			
Little Wood Satyr	*Megisto cymela*	86	55	91
Common Ringlet	*Coenonympha tullia*			
Common Wood Nymph	*Cercyonis pegala*	86	55	285
Monarch	*Danaus plexippus*	84	54	126
Silver-spotted Skipper	*Epargyreus clarus*	91	58	97
Long-tailed Skipper	*Urbanus proteus*			
Golden-banded Skipper	*Autochton cellus*			
Hoary Edge	*Achalarus lyciades*	31	20	8
Southern Cloudywing	*Thorybes bathyllus*	25	16	10
Northern Cloudywing	*Thorybes pylades*	13	8	15
Confused Cloudywing	*Thorybes confusis*			
Hayhurst's Scallopwing	*Staphylus hayhursti*	3	2	1
Dreamy Duskywing	*Erynnis icelus*			
Sleepy Duskywing	*Erynnis brizo*			
Juvenal's Duskywing	*Erynnis juvenalis*			
Horace's Duskywing	*Erynnis horatius*	31	20	68
Mottled Duskywing	*Erynnis martialis*			
Zarucco Duskywing	*Erynnis zarucco*			
Columbine Duskywing	*Erynnis lucilius*			
Wild Indigo Duskywing	*Erynnis baptisiae*	30	19	249
Persius Duskywing	*Erynnis persius*			
Appalach. Grizzled Skipper	*Pyrgus wyandot*			
Common Checkered Skipper	*Pyrgus communis*	16	10	7
Common Sootywing	*Pholisora catullus*	36	23	79
Arctic Skipper	*Carterocephalus palaemon*			

Table 7. (*continued*)

English Name	Scientific Name	Percent of counts	Number of counts	Maximum number
Swarthy Skipper	*Nastra lherminier*	36	23	43
Clouded Skipper	*Lerema accius*			
Least Skipper	*Ancyloxphya numitor*	53	34	86
European Skipper	*Thymelicus lineola*	17	11	221
Fiery Skipper	*Hylephila phyleus*	2	1	0
Leonard's Skipper	*Hesperia leonardus*			
Cobweb Skipper	*Hesperia metea*			
Dotted Skipper	*Hesperia attalus*	5	3	4
Indian Skipper	*Hesperia sassacus*	2	1	1
Peck's Skipper	*Polites peckius*	23	15	36
Tawny-edged Skipper	*Polites themistocles*	16	10	7
Crossline Skipper	*Polites origenes*	28	18	19
Long Dash	*Polites mystic*			
Whirlabout	*Polites vibex*			
Northern Broken Dash	*Wallengrenia egeremet*	38	24	43
Little Glassy Wing	*Pompeius verna*	34	22	57
Sachem	*Atalopedes campestris*	17	11	66
Arogos Skipper	*Atrytone arogos*			
Delaware Skipper	*Anatrytone logan*	36	23	27
Rare Skipper	*Problema bulenta*	16	10	66
Mulberry Wing	*Poanes massasoit*	30	19	44
Hobomok Skipper	*Poanes hobomok*	6	4	5
Zabulon Skipper	*Poanes zabulon*	13	8	20
Aaron's Skipper	*Poanes aaroni*	20	13	269
Broad-winged Skipper	*Poanes viator*	39	25	455
Dion Skipper	*Euphyes dion*	9	6	27
Black Dash	*Euphyes conspicua*	11	7	63
Two-spotted Skipper	*Euphyes bimacula*	3	2	2
Dun Skipper	*Euphyes vestris*	58	37	118
Dusted Skipper	*Atrytonopsis hianna*			
Pepper and Salt Skipper	*Amblyscirtes hegon*			
Common Roadside Skipper	*Amblyscirtes vialis*	2	1	3
Eufala Skipper	*Lerodea eufala*			
Twin-spot Skipper	*Oligoria maculata*			
Brazilian Skipper	*Calpodes ethlius*			
Salt Marsh Skipper	*Panoquina panoquin*	36	23	691
Ocola Skipper	*Panoquin ocola*			

"occasionally common," and we use "uncommon" to refer to individuals not seen on a daily basis. The categories refer to the observations of a single individual rather than several parties that might be deployed on a Fourth of July Count. The following relative designations are for general guidance only and the suggested numbers apply to species such as whites, sulphurs, and crescents, whereas anglewings and swallowtails would be considered abundant at much lower numbers.

Superabundant—one may find more than 500 individuals in a given place, or a 4JC total greater than 2,000.

Abundant—one is likely to find more than 20 at the right time and place. A species may be locally or temporally abundant for a brief time, and rare or absent the rest of the year. For a 4JC, a count exceeding 500 would be considered abundant.

Common—one is likely to find 5–20 in a day on all days during its appropriate flight period, and more than 100 on a 4JC.

Table 8. Comparison of Factors Affecting the Activity and Status of Butterflies and Birds

Variability due to	How Important for	
	Butterflies	Birds
Time of day	quite	somewhat
Immediate weather conditions	very	somewhat
Daily fluctuations	quite	slight
Week-to-week or seasonal changes	very	quite
Habitat scale	very	quite
Year-to-year scale	very	somewhat

Fairly common—one is likely to see 1–4 individuals daily on most days during the appropriate flight period, and more than 10 on a 4JC.

Uncommon—one is likely to see 1–4 individuals several times in a season, but not daily.

Occasionally common—one is likely to find 5–20 individuals a few times in a season.

Locally common—a species that is uncommon, rare, or absent in most habitats or localities, but common in its preferred habitats.

Rare—rarely seen at any time or place; one is likely to find it only a few times (< 5 days) a year, and usually only single individuals.

Irruptive—a species that is usually rare or absent, but may occasionally become common or abundant.

Finding a vagrant or stray can be a very exciting experience. Although such events are usually considered to have low biological significance, Shapiro (1993) argues that these irregular visitations occurring at long intervals may be important sources of future colonization during periods of rapid environmental change, and therefore deserve systematic data collection and documentation.

Butterfly status is more difficult to understand and convey than bird status, because their numbers fluctuate more rapidly (from week to week and year to year) under the influence of several environmental factors, as shown in table 8. Nonetheless, some generalizations can be made. The Cabbage White, for example, can be seen in almost any open habitat on almost any day during its long flight season. It may be present by the hundreds over some meadows, or as stray individuals along a forest roadside. Other species, such as Eastern Tiger Swallowtail, are likely to be seen in small numbers in most places and in many weeks during most years.

Other species have more restricted flight periods and habitats and will be found in only a few choice localities. At the right time or place, such species might be represented by dozens of individuals (e.g., the locally common Bog Copper), or they might be altogether difficult or impossible to find (e.g., Silver-bordered Fritillary). Thus the likelihood of finding a particular species on a given day is dependent on its seasonal cycle or phenology, which may vary from year to year. Prior to first emergence or between broods, even common species such as Peck's Skipper will not be seen.

The status in a given year also depends on status in previous years, even for a relatively common species. If a species has had several years of low productivity there will be few survivors to contribute to next year's population, and it may take several years for it to become common again. However, species may have a year of unusual abundance followed by several years of much lower numbers. This was true for the Monarch, which reached a high population level in 1991, and the Red-banded Hairstreak and American Lady, which reached high levels in 1992.

Status Unknown

A number of species have been reported in New Jersey in the past, but we have few recent records. They may simply be rare vagrants or species that have declined and disappeared from the state (become *extirpated*). It is possible that they were never really residents in New Jersey, for it is often difficult to interpret the brief remarks in the writings of J. B. Smith (1890–1910) and Comstock (1940). Moreover, those that have declined or disappeared in neighboring states are now less likely to wander into New Jersey than in former times.

As with birds, some butterfly species can occur as long-distance vagrants and may appear in the state only at long intervals. With our increasing cadre of knowledgeable observers, we should get an increasing number of records of these vagrants. At the same time, identification and documentation of rare resident species becomes a significant concern. Responsibility for the designation of status within New Jersey and for the protection of threatened and endangered species is under the aegis of the Endangered and Nongame Species program of the New Jersey Department of Environmental Protection.

CHAPTER 4

Life Cycles, Phenology, and Butterfly Behavior

Several books offer extensive chapters on butterfly biology, life cycles, and behavior. These range from the more technical accounts in *The Biology of Butterflies* (Vane-Wright and Ackery 1984) to the more popular accounts in *The Lives of Butterflies* (Douglas 1986). The adult butterfly has one primary responsibility: finding a mate and reproducing. Females have the added burden of producing high-quality eggs and laying them on suitable hosts, often in an inconspicuous manner. To accomplish this overriding "purpose," butterflies must recognize appropriate habitat, feed to obtain sufficient energy, and avoid predators and inclement weather.

The four-stage life cycle of the butterfly from egg to adult offers the classical example of complete metamorphosis among insects: egg, larva (caterpillar), pupa (chrysalis), and adult (imago). But within this basic scheme is great variety, and the stages can be quite variable in duration. Although butterflies are relatively well studied among all animal species, White (1986) emphasizes how little we know about the biology of many species, including some of the longest life stages. In a well-studied checkerspot, for example, more than 60% of the lifespan occurs in *diapause*, but virtually no biochemical or physiological studies of this important life stage exist.

A single cycle may take about a month, but it may be interrupted by winter so that eggs laid in late summer may not result in an emerging (or *eclosing*) adult until the following spring. Many butterflies are univoltine, and there is a delay in development, called the diapause, such that eggs laid in spring may not hatch, or pupae formed in spring may not *eclose*, until the following year. Even in the tropics, many species actually halt their development for weeks or months to avoid unfavorable dry seasons. Diapause allows the larvae to mature and the adults to emerge when conditions are most favorable.

Some species have only a single adult brood in a year. The adult emerges in spring or summer, lays eggs, and then disappears, with no new adults emerging until the following year. These are single-brooded or *univoltine* species. In other species, a second brood of adults emerges during the summer, and they in turn reproduce; they are double-brooded or *bivoltine*. Many species have three broods or, as in the case of the Cabbage White or several other species, even more. In some species, the broods are highly synchronous and the period of adult flight are discrete, with several weeks intervening when no flying adults can be found. In other species, the broods overlap, the cycles are not synchronous, and adults can be found on most days from spring to fall; their phenology is described as "continuous." At the opposite extreme are certain species of sub-Arctic latitudes that require two years to complete their life cycle (*biennialism*). In some cases, all adults are synchronous and none fly in the intervening year; in other cases there are *allochronic* subpopulations, so some adults fly each year (Masters 1979).

Some butterflies exhibit territorial behavior, defending a favorable location, not usually a food source, from intruders, particularly conspecific males (Rutkowski 1994). Such stations are usually defended only during favorable parts of the day, but may be defended several days in a row.

In some species, males take up mating stations to "meet" females moving through the area. In others, males patrol or cruise for potentially receptive females. Once a male identifies a potential mate, he lands near or even on her, exposing her to a variety of visual, tactile, and chemical stimuli. Often, the male buffets the female with his wings. The female may respond with a rejection posture, often turning her abdomen down, and rapidly fluttering her wings. Or she may allow the male to make sexual contact (Rutowski 1984).

Males transfer sperm to the female in a *spermatophore* which contains protein, lipids, and hydrocarbons, at least some of which are used by the female for nutrition and maturation of eggs. These packets, amounting to 6% of body weight, represent a significant contribution of the male (Marshall 1985). Some female butterflies mate only once, while others may mate several times and lay several batches of eggs. Flight duration for the adult butterfly varies, and longevity is particularly important for the latter group. In many species, most adults may survive for only about 7–12 days after emergence (Scott 1973)—a busy week during which they must obtain fuel, find mates and host plants, breed, and lay eggs. Adults of other species may survive weeks or months, and indeed even very worn and tattered individuals may remain reproductively active. The phenology of a population at a location is often difficult to describe precisely. Usually there are 1–3 obvious peaks of abundance with few or no adults flying between the peaks. But sometimes there is a low peak, which may be called a "partial brood." Shapiro (1967) suggested that some of these are merely delayed emergence of some members of an earlier brood and called these "false broods."

Phenology is often shown graphically with black bars of varying thickness. Both the New York City Area checklist (Cech 1993) and *Butterflies through Binoculars* (Glassberg 1993b) provide these graphs for many New Jersey species. Indeed, Glassberg shows graphs for five years, indicating how much variability there can be from year to year. At present, however, our knowledge of butterfly cycles throughout the state is inadequate to provide such charts on a statewide basis, hence their absence from this book.

Clench (1967) diagrammed the phenology of several species of skippers in western Pennsylvania and suggested that the peaks were offset to minimize competition for nectar resources; that is, the peak of one species' abundance corresponded to the troughs in another. Shuey (1986), however, has questioned whether the data were good enough to substantiate the temporal displacement in phenology, and he indicated that there were other explanations that would account for the observed timing at any locality. There was little direct evidence that two different species of skippers actually were competitors.

The best way of minimizing competition would be to avoid flying and feeding where and when conspecifics are feeding. Yet remarkably the emergence of many species is often highly synchronized. One day there are none, the next day many. This is presumably to maximize the likelihood of finding mates. One of the purposes of this book is to stimulate local observers to keep detailed phenological information from their own localities, thus allowing future temporal and spatial refinements. Such details should be recorded for each species.

Table 9 shows the flight periods of Pearl Crescents in our yard in Somerset for

Table 9. Flight Periods of Pearl Crescents at Somerset, New Jersey (1988–1990)

	May			June			July			Aug			Sept			Oct		
	E	M	L	E	M	L	E	M	L	E	M	L	E	M	L	E	M	L
1988	0	6	9	4	0	0	3	10	10	4	0	0	No observations					
1989	0	6	10	10	4	3	10	10	10	10	2	8	10	9	9		2	
1990	5	10	2	0	0	0	4	8	7	0	0	5	5	No observations				

NOTES: Each number indicates the number of days out of each 10-day period, that the butterflies were present. E = early, M = mid, L = late.

3 years, based on the number of days they were recorded in each 10 day period. The patterns are consistent from year to year, but the timing differs.

Host Specificity

Except for the Harvester and some blues, butterfly larvae feed on plant material. Some species use or tolerate many different hosts, while others are more host specific. Hovanitz and Chang (1962ab) showed that development rate and survival of Cabbage White and related species varied depending on the host plant, and showed that these variables could be altered by raising succeeding generations on formerly unfavorable hosts.

Host specificity refers to the use of a narrow range of caterpillar foodplants. The highest level of host specificity (*monophagy*) occurs in those butterflies that use a single plant species, for example, the Northern Metalmark uses only the Round-leafed Ragwort and the Harris' Checkerspot only the Flat-topped Aster (*Aster umbellatus*). Monarchs are somewhat less host specific; they can raise their young on several different species of milkweeds, but all are in the genus *Asclepias*. A lower degree of specificity is shown by the Cabbage White, an abundant species which uses many different host plants but virtually all of them are in the Mustard family (Brassicaceae); indeed, all species of *Pieris* use either plants in the Mustard or Caper (Capparidaceae) families (Chew 1979).

Understanding the host specificity of butterflies is important in learning where to find them and how to protect their populations. The study of host specificity is complicated by the fact that some butterflies may lay eggs on plant species on which they cannot survive or on which they grow but fail to mature (Chew 1995), or they may ignore species that are perfectly suitable and available but somehow not attractive. Much information has been gained by raising larvae on a variety of hosts in the laboratory, but one cannot be sure that a plant species used in the lab will be used under natural conditions. The tendency for a butterfly species to use hosts in two closely related families may be real, or it may reflect the fact that biologists are likely to experiment by offering leaves from families closely related to known hosts. Shields et al. (1969) cautioned that merely seeing a female butterfly laying eggs on a plant does not constitute a "host record," since the viability of larvae must be ascertained. They point out that the literature is replete with erroneous host plants for various butterflies, and in our species accounts we will question some of the published plant hosts.

Table 10 groups the butterflies of New Jersey according to their degree of host specificity. Those butterflies known to use only one host species (monophagy) are listed first. The second group are those that use mainly one host, but have been found occasionally or locally on other hosts. A third group uses two species or more regularly, but the species are mainly in a single genus or family, hence are closely related. A fourth group has a relatively narrow host range (known from only two host species, for example), but the hosts are in different families. In

Table 10. Degrees of Host Specificity of New Jersey Butterflies

A. Species believed to be narrowly host specific or monophagous (using a single host species), at least in New Jersey

Zebra Swallowtail	Pawpaw	*Asimina triloba*
Palamedes Swallowtail	Red Bay	*Persea borbonica*
Bog Copper	Cranberry	*Vaccinium macrocarpum*
Red-banded Hairstreak	Winged Sumac	*Rhus coppalina*
Juniper [Olive] Hairstreak	Red Cedar	*Juniperus virginianum*
Hessel's Hairstreak	Atlantic White Cedar	*Chamaecyparis thyoides*
Hoary Elfin	Bearberry	*Arctostaphylus uva-ursi*
Henry's Elfin	American Holly	*Ilex opaca*
Northern Metalmark	Round-leaved Ragwort	*Senecio obovatus*
Harris Checkerspot	Flat-topped White Aster	*Aster umbellatus*
Tawny Crescent	Wavy-leafed Aster	*Aster undulatus*
Golden-banded Skipper	Hog Peanut	*Amphicarpa bracteata*
Hayhurst's Scallopwing	Lambquarters	*Chenopodium album*
Mottled Duskywing	New Jersey Tea	*Ceanothus americanus*
Columbine Duskywing	Wild Columbine	*Aquilegia canadensis*[a]
Appalachian Grizzled Skipper	Dwarf Cinquefoil	*Potentilla canadensis*

NOTE: Several skippers are currently known to use only a single species of grass or sedge, but they are listed separately in section D of this table.

B. Species that feed almost exclusively on one host but may occasionally use or lay on closely related species

Pipevine Swallowtail	Pipevines	*Aristolochia*	Also Wild Ginger[b]
Clouded Sulphur	White Clover	*Trifolium repens*	Occasionally other legumes
American Copper	Sheep Sorrel	*Rumex acetosella*	Occasionally other *Rumex*
Edwards' Hairstreak	Scrub oak	*Quercus ilicifolia*	Can feed on Black Oak
Sleepy Duskywing	Scruboak	*Quercus ilicifolia*	Also occasionally on black oak
European Skipper	Timothy	*Phleum pratense*	Also other grasses

C. Species that feed on two or more members of the same or closely related genera

Giant Swallowtail	Hercules Club and Prickly Ash	*Zanthoxylum*	Rutaceae
Checkered White	Peppergrass	*Lepidium*	Occasionally other Brassicaceae
West Virginia White[c]	Toothworts	*Dentaria diphylla* & *D. laciniata*	Brassicaceae
Orange Sulphur	Legumes, particularly Alfalfa	*Medicago sativa*	Fabaceae
Sleepy Orange	Sennas	*Cassia*	Fabaceae
Bronze Copper	mainly Curly Dock, also Water Dock	*Rumex crispus* & *R. orbiculatus*	Polygonaceae
Great Purple Hairstreak	Mistletoe	*Phoradendron flavescens*	Loranthaceae
Coral Hairstreak	Black Cherry, occasionally others	*Prunus*	Rosaceae
Acadian Hairstreak	Black and Silky Willows	*Salix nigra* & *S. sericea*	Salicaceae
White M Hairstreak	Various oaks	*Quercus*	Fagaceae
Pine Elfin	Pines	*Pinus*	Pinaceae
American Snout	Hackberries and other *Celtis*	*Celtis*	Ulmaceae
Milbert's Tortoiseshell	Stinging Nettles	*Urticaria*	Urticaceae
Hackberry Emperor	Hackberries and other *Celtis*	*Celtis*	Ulmaceae
Tawny Emperor	Hackberries and other *Celtis*	*Celtis*	Ulmaceae
Gulf Fritillary	Passion Flower vines	*Passiflora*	Passifloraceae
Variegated Fritillary	Violets	*Viola*	Violaceae
Great Spangled Fritillary	Violets	*Viola*	Violaceae
Aphrodite	Violets	*Viola*	Violaceae
Regal Fritillary	Violets	*Viola*	Violaceae
Atlantis Fritillary	Violets	*Viola*	Violaceae
Silver-bordered Fritillary	Violets	*Viola*	Violaceae
Meadow Fritillary	Violets	*Viola*	Violaceae

(*continued*)

Table 10. (*continued*)

C. Species that feed on two or more members of the same or closely related genera

Pearl Crescent	Asters	*Aster*	Asteraceae
Monarch	Milkweeds	*Asclepias*	Asclepiadaceae
Wild Indigo Duskywing	Crown Vetch and Wild Indigo	*Coronilla varia, Baptisia tinctoria*	Fabaceae
Southern Cloudywing	Beggars Ticks and Bush Clover	*Desmodium, Lespedeza*	Fabaceae
Juvenal's Duskywing	Oaks	*Quercus*	Fagaceae
Horace's Duskywing	Oaks	*Quercus*	Fagaceae
Brazilian Skipper	Wild and horticultural	*Canna*	Cannaceae

NOTE: Many subtropical species that are not regular in the United States are genera-specific, using *Aristolochia* or *Passiflora* or *Cassia*.

D. Species utilizing only grasses and or sedges (Poaceae) [d] (including virtually all Satyridae and virtually all Hesperinae with the exception of the Brazilian Skipper)

Northern Pearly Eye	Grasses	
Eyed Brown	Sedges	*Carex*
Appalachian Brown	Sedges	*Carex*
Carolina Satyr	Grasses	
Little Wood Satyr	Grasses	
Common Wood Nymph	Grasses	
Arctic Skipper	Grasses	
Swarthy Skipper	Little Bluestem	*Andropogon scoparius*
Clouded Skipper	Various grasses	
Least Skipper	Grasses 3 species	
European Skipper	Timothy	*Phleum pratense*
Fiery Skipper	Crabgrass and others	*Digitaria*
Leonard's Skipper	Grasses	
Cobweb Skipper	Blue-stem grasses	*Andropogon*
Indian Skipper	Grasses	
Peck's Skipper	Grasses	
Tawny-edged Skipper	Grasses	*Panicum*
Crossline Skipper	Grasses, 2 spp.	
Long Dash	Grasses, including *Poa*	*Poa*
Whirlabout	Grasses, 3 spp.	
Northern Broken Dash	Grasses	*Panicum*
Little Glassy Wing	Purpletop	*Tridens flavus*
Sachem	Grasses, 3 spp.	
Arogos Skipper	Blue-stem grasses	*Andropogon*
Delaware Skipper	Grasses	
Rare Skipper	Tall Cordgrass	*Spartina cynosuroides*
Mulberry Wing	Tussock Sedge	*Carex stricta*
Hobomok Skipper	Grasses	*Panicum* and *Poa*
Zabulon Skipper	Grasses	
Broad-winged Skipper	Mainly reeds	*Phragmites*, also *Zizania* and *Carex*
Dion Skipper	Sedges and rushes	*Carex* and *Scirpus*
Black Dash	Sedges	*Carex*
Dun Skipper	Mainly sedges; Comstock says Purpletop	*Carex* and ? *Tridens flavus*
Dusted Skipper	Blue-stem grasses	*Andropogon*
Pepper and Salt Skipper	Grasses, 3 sp.	
Roadside Skipper	Grasses	
Eufala skipper	Sorghum and Sugar Cane	
Twin-spotted Skipper	Grasses	

E. Species using various members of several genera of a single family

Cabbage White	Mustards	Brassicaceae
Eastern Tailed Blue	Legumes	Fabaceae [e]
Red Admiral	Mainly nettles	Urticaceae

Table 10. (*continued*)

E. Species using various members of several genera of a single family

Viceroy	Willows (*Salix*) and Poplars (*Populus*)	Salicaceae
Long-tailed Skipper	Leguminous vines: *Desmodium, Wisteria*	Fabaceae
Common Checkered Skipper	Mallows: Malva, Hollyhock, Hibiscus	Malvaceae
Hoary Edge	Legumes	Fabaceae
Northern Cloudywing	Legumes	Fabaceae

F. Species with narrow host range but in more than one family

Hickory Hairstreak	Oaks and hickories	Fagaceae and Juglandaceae
Baltimore Checkerspot	Turtlehead and English Plantain (*Chelone glabra, Plantago lanceolata*)	Scrophulariceae
Questionmark	Nettles and elm family	Urticaceae and Ulmaceae
Eastern Comma	Nettles and elm family	Urticaceae and Ulmaceae

G. Species for which the host is not definitely known

Northern Crescent	Presumably asters		Compositae
Georgia Satyr	Presumably grasses or sedges		Poaceae
Mitchell's Satyr	Presumably grasses or sedges		Poaceae
Confused Cloudywing	Presumably *Lespedeza*		Fabaceae
Persius Duskywing	Controversial: willows and poplars, or Lupines	*Salix* or *Populus* *Lupinus*	Salicaceae Fabaceae
Dotted Skipper	Maybe Switch Grass	*Panicum virgatum*	Poaceae
Aaron's Skipper	Uncertain, possibly Spike Grass	*Distichlis spicata*	Poaceae
Two-spotted Skipper	Probably sedges or grasses		Poaceae
Salt Marsh Skipper	Probably Spike Grass	*Distichlis spicata*	Poaceae

a. Columbine Duskywing may also use horticultural varieties of Columbine.
b. Studies in Pennsylvania suggest that Wild Ginger is not an alternative host there.
c. West Virginia White also lays on Garlic Mustard (*Alliaria petiolata*), an unsuitable host.
d. The Poaceae has traditionally been called the Graminae.
e. The Fabaceae has traditionally been called the Leguminosae.
f. The Brassicaceae has traditionally been called the Cruciferae.

some cases the families are closely related themselves, for example, the Ulmaceae and Urticaceae used by some of the Anglewings. A special case not included in any of the lists is the Harvester, North America's only carnivorous butterfly, whose larvae feed on several species of woolly aphids.

Remarkably little documentation exists on host plant use in New Jersey. Inevitably, new field observations will turn up exceptions to the existing host list, and in some localities species may develop preferences or tolerances for other new hosts. These changes may be driven by the increasing availability of a host, for example, the use of Crown Vetch (*Coronilla varia*) by the Wild Indigo Duskywing or Wild Indigo (*Baptisia tinctoria)* by the Frosted Elfin. In New England, some populations of Mustard Whites (but not West Virginia Whites) are tolerating and using the invading Garlic Mustard (*Alliaria petiolata*; Courant et al. 1994). Certainly any species that could exploit Asiatic Bittersweet (*Celastrus orbiculatus*), Japanese Honeysuckle (*Lonicera japonica*), or Japanese Knotweed (*Polygonum cuspidatum*), for example, will have abundant hosts available in the future as these plants spread rapidly at the expense of native flora. On the other hand the spread of weeds may be facilitated if they are not eaten significantly by any insects.

In Somerset we are witnessing the sudden invasion of lawns by Mouse-ear (*Hieracium pilosella*), a short, yellow hawkweed that forms a dense mat, crowding out other plants. As this alien spreads in central New Jersey, it will be interesting to see whether it becomes an important nectar source.

Exotic species can be a trap, as in the case of West Virginia Whites laying on Garlic Mustard, which is highly available but is not suitable for their larvae. Will this intense natural selection favor those few West Virginia Whites which can discriminate and lay their eggs only on their traditional and suitable hosts, Rock Cresses (*Dentaria* spp)? Will some larvae show tolerance for Garlic Mustard, a trait which would spread quickly? Or will populations disappear before they learn to avoid Garlic Mustard (Courant et al. 1994)?

Predation and Other Adversity

Sooner or later, most animals are eaten by other animals, and such predation has played an important role in the evolution of behavior and morphology of prey. Predation on butterflies has been extensively studied, mainly experimentally, because of its role in selecting for the complex mimicry patterns by which apparently palatable species are protected by their resemblance to inedible or toxic species. In this way, butterfly biology has made some of its most important contributions to understanding behavior, ecology, and evolution. The classic cases of the Viceroy mimicking the Monarch and various swallowtails mimicking the Pipevine Swallowtail are the main examples in our region, although each of these cases turns out to be anything but simple. However, predation is also interesting in its own right as a phenomenon influencing a butterfly's population dynamics.

Predators come in very many shapes and sizes, ranging from primates (especially humans) down to mites. Birds, monkeys, and lizards capture adult butterflies. Rodents are very important predators of the more sedentary larval and pupal stages of the butterfly. Mice (Brower et al. 1984) and even cattle have been reported feeding on wintering Monarchs that lay on the ground under the roosts in the mountains of Mexico (Urquhart and Urquhart 1976).

Birds are generally considered to be the major predators who exert a selective influence on butterfly mimicry. However, actual observations of birds capturing butterflies are infrequent, and whether birds are important enough predators to be a selective factor in mimicry has engendered a lively debate for more than a century. One occasionally sees birds in erratic flight attempting to capture a flying butterfly in midair, but more often birds simply ignore flying butterflies, even when they flutter continuously around the same flowering bush for minutes at a time. If birds ignore butterflies most of the time, how can they be an important predator?

Many conflicting reports have appeared in scientific publications and newsletters (e.g., Collenette 1935, Carpenter 1937; Shapiro 1974b), and through the years scattered observations of bird predation on butterflies have been reported. To some this seems sufficient argument that birds eat butterflies, while others point to each anecdote as further evidence of the rarity of such events. Over the past decade we have seen Yellow-rumped [Myrtle] Warbler (*Dendroica coronata*) and House Sparrows (*Passer domesticus*) attempt to catch Cabbage Whites on nine occasions, with five successes. Olson (1962) mentioned Song Sparrows (*Melospiza melodia*) catching four species of butterflies (all Lycaenids). But these are clearly rare events.

Several studies show that birds take resting or roosting butterflies more often than flying or feeding ones, and this may be the secret of their success. With carefully controlled studies in the laboratory and in the field in New Jersey and Texas, Codella (1986) showed that predators, including birds, do take large numbers of roosting swallowtails, mainly at night but also on cold rainy days, when the butterflies are immobile for hours at a time.

The importance of bird predation is apparent at the huge Monarch roosts in California and Mexico, even though this species is generally considered distasteful and even toxic. There have been several studies of bird predation on Monarchs, since a variety of species including orioles and grosbeaks prey on Monarchs at their roosts (Calvert et al. 1979; Urquhart 1987). In Mexico at least seven species of birds were found preying on Monarchs at least occasionally. Flocks of orioles and grosbeaks visited the roost daily and killed an estimated 15,000 butterflies per day, destroying over two million during the 135 days that the butterflies occupied the roost. This accounted for 9% of the estimated total population (Brower and Calvert 1985). One pair of Rufous-sided Towhees (*Pipilo erythrophthalamus*) ate an average of 22.7 Monarchs per day at a California winter roost, thereby accounting for a 7% overall mortality (Sakai 1994). Careful studies showed that 29% of the Monarchs at the Mexican site labeled "Site Alpha" had such low cardenolide concentrations that they would be considered palatable by bird standards (Fink and Brower 1981), and direct observations showed that in 37% of the captures, birds released the butterfly without eating it, apparently sensing that they had captured a more toxic individual (Calvert et al. 1979). Thus Monarchs have what researchers have called a *palatability spectrum*, and birds are able to taste and distinguish the more palatable from the more toxic (Brower et al. 1969).

Since actual predation events are seldom witnessed, one can infer predation by the disappearance of butterflies, or by certain other telltale signs. Birds will generally de-wing larger species such as swallowtails, and the four wings may be found under a perch (Urquhart 1987). Smaller species such as Wood Nymphs, however, may be eaten, wings and all (Bowers and Wiernasz 1978). Much of the evidence concerning the importance of bird predation involved the finding of "beak marks" on butterfly wings (Shapiro 1974b). These are usually triangular cuts from which researchers infer that the butterfly was captured and released.

By counting the percentage of butterflies that show such marks, people have estimated the frequency of unsuccessful predatory attempts on butterflies. Beak marks can be studied in newly collected butterflies, or they can be found in museum specimens taken many years earlier. Carpenter (1933) showed that different kinds of marks on butterfly wings probably corresponded to the different beak shapes of the predators. Small narrow marks were probably made by warblers, and broad, triangular marks by large-billed finches. Carpenter (1941) also showed that distasteful species have more beak marks than palatable ones, presumably because the latter have been eaten and the former released. He cautioned, however, that specimens with beak marks are considered imperfect and are often discarded rather than placed in a museum collection.

These ragged marks have been open to alternative explanations; perhaps they are not beak marks at all. This controversy dates back at least to 1862, when the differential frequency of beak marks on various butterfly species was first reported (Brower 1984). Also, they provide little information on how many butterflies are actually killed and eaten since the eaten ones don't get counted. Do the marks indicate that the bird found the butterfly distasteful and released it, or do they indicate that the butterfly struggled and escaped before the predator could kill it? Does a lack of marks indicate that birds have learned to avoid an unpalatable species, or that they have a perfect kill record when they capture a

Photo 1. Viceroy revealing at least three distinct "beak marks" and other tears, despite its mimetic status. If these are real beak marks, then more than one bird tried and rejected this individual. Viceroys are known to have some degree of unpalatability. (Photographed at Higbee Beach, Cape May, by Joanna Burger)

butterfly? Photo 1 illustrates a Viceroy with at least three notches that could be interpreted as "beak marks" as well as a tear. This ragged individual understandably had difficulty flying. Photo 2 shows a Red-spotted Purple with a torn hind wing, suggesting it had escaped from a predator. It had no evident flight impairment. Both of these are considered palatable species, although the Viceroy illustration is consistent with reports that this species is sometimes distasteful in its own right. Malcolm Edmunds (1974) examined the various possibilities that might account for different frequencies of beak marks on two species:

- One is easier to catch than the other.
- One is palatable and the other distasteful and is therefore released more often
- One struggles and escapes from the bird more often
- One lives longer than the other and is more likely to be caught for that reason
- One may have eyespots that cause birds to attack the wings rather than the body

The controversy over the importance of bird predation will continue until further ecological and behavioral studies provide better data. Since our entire understanding of natural selection for mimicry in adult butterflies hinges on an active and voracious, visually guided predator, such studies are of great importance and even anecdotes of bird predation on butterflies (successful or unsuccessful) should be reported in newsletters. This is one area where a butterfly watcher can make an important contribution by keeping careful notes of attempted and actual predation, reporting both predator and prey identification and the circumstances of the attack.

The palatability spectrum applies within a species (some individuals are more unpalatable than others) and between species. Sargent (1995) presented a large variety of moths and butterflies to Blue Jays (*Cyanocitta cristata*) and other birds, and ranked them in terms of their palatability. Moths were generally more palatable than butterflies. Some butterflies, such as the Great Spangled Fritillary,

Photo 2. Red-spotted Purple, a palatable species, revealing tear marks suggestive of struggle and escape, rather than "beak marks." (Photographed at Schooleys Mountain Park, Morris County, by Joanna Burger)

were consumed 100% of the time, while others, such as Buckeye and Viceroy, were consumed only 50% of the time and the Monarch was eaten only 35% of the time. Strangely, none of the seven Silver-bordered Fritillaries was eaten.

Dramatic as the North American examples of mimicry are, they pale by comparison with the great variety of mimetic complexes of South American and African butterflies, where dozens of species may be involved. Both of these continents have monkeys that may have been important in selecting for mimicry. Monkeys are known to be selective feeders, tasting and testing fruits before consuming them in quantity, and there is no reason why they wouldn't quickly learn about the edibility of butterflies. Much less has been published regarding primates as predators, but within 30 minutes of observation at Monkey Jungle in Florida, we saw different Squirrel Monkeys (*Saimiri sciureus*) nimbly and unhesitantly capture and eat a Malachite Butterfly (*Siproeta stelenes*) and a Dorantes Skipper (*Urbanus dorantes*). We then noted that the number of butterflies in the monkey enclosure was far less than the number outside.

Lizards, too, are visual predators and are believed to exert a significant impact on butterfly populations, particularly in the tropics (e.g., *Ameiva* lizards in Panama) (Boyden 1976). At Iguazu Falls on the Brazil-Argentina border, the small iguanid lizard *Tropidurus torquatus* may specialize on butterflies that land nearby, and it even leaps into the air to take passing butterflies (Ehrlich and Ehrlich 1982). However, Odendaal et al. (1987) noted that lizards are quite content to eat Pipevine Swallowtails, and if they tolerate the inedible species, they would be less effective at selecting for mimicry. Although frogs have not been reported as important predators on butterflies, we observed a green frog leap two feet into the air to capture a Hummingbird Moth (*Hemaris thysbe*), Cabbage White, and even a Tiger Swallowtail foraging on the lower part of a *Buddleia* bush next to our pond. Other visually guided predators include dragonflies and mantids.

Mantids are aggressive predators and will wait on flowering plants to ambush any insects, including butterflies. Certain dragonflies will actually dart out to seize butterflies in flight. In New Jersey we have seen the Eastern Pondhawk or Green Clearwing (*Erythemis simplicicollis*) take Cabbage Whites.

The most obvious predators in most parts of New Jersey are Crab Spiders (*Misuma*) and Ambush Bugs (*Phymatidae*), although other spiders such as Green Lynx Spider (*Peucetia viridans*) have been found preying on butterflies (J. W. Brown 1990). In New Jersey, immature Red-spotted Crab or Goldenrod Spiders (*Misuma vatia*) and Jagged Ambush Bugs (*Phymata erosa*) commonly capture butterflies. Elsewhere, other species, including *Phymata fasciata*, are important (Fales 1976). These creatures hide themselves in flower heads, where they are remarkably camouflaged and wait patiently (we have found them on the same head for at least six days) until a butterfly or other insect lands to nectar. The predator then seizes the butterfly, usually by the probing tongue, and hangs on while the insect struggles vigorously to escape. They may inject a venom to speed their quarry's death. Once the prey is lifeless, the predator sucks liquid contents from the thorax and then releases the dead butterfly. We usually find the entire body, including wings, below the flower, unless ants carry it away. A butterfly struggling vigorously or "perched" motionlessly upside down or under a flower head is a tell-tale sign of such predation. Photo 3 shows a Crab Spider consuming a female Cabbage White.

In Somerset, we have found that the main victims are Cabbage Whites. Is this simply because of their abundance, and the predators take butterflies randomly? Or as we suspect, is the local predator population selected to prefer those flowers that are attractive to the most abundant prey species. The Cabbage White is almost the only butterfly to nectar at Purple Loosestrife (*Lythrum salicaria*), yet the Crab Spiders and Ambush Bugs are often found on these flowers, even where the plants are not numerous. By contrast, of twenty-five observations of crab spider predation in Maryland, 80% were on skippers (mainly Silver-spotted and the Sachem), and no whites were represented (Fales and Jennings 1977).

Spiders are important predators, although butterflies can often extricate themselves when they first touch a web. Some spiders, such as an orb-weaving spider (*Nephila clavipes*) of Brazil, have a specific behavioral sequence they use for releasing unpalatable butterflies from their webs (Vasconcellos-Neto and Lewisohn 1984). Photo 4 shows an Orb-weaving Spider that has wrapped up an Orange Sulphur.

Any garden or field offers the opportunity to document such predation events, and in appendix G we provide an example of record keeping for predation events. Unfortunately, the camouflaged predators themselves are hard to find until they have actually snared a butterfly. But after the initial capture, we have been able to chart their progress over a period of days as the predator lingers first in a flower head where it has been successful, and then moves to an adjacent head to try again. We mark each predation site with a strip of plastic ribbon numbered with a permanent marker, and we can often track the activity of an individual predator for several days. The crab spiders also take honeybees, small spiders, and other prey, so that butterflies may not even be a major part of their diet. A careful observer can record where and when predation occurs, noting both the predator and the victim, and one can even estimate the frequency of predation, although butterflies are usually dropped after 4–8 hours, or are sometimes spirited away by birds.

Mite parasites occur on butterflies and feed on hemolymph in the wing veins (Treat 1975), and minute flies of the midge family Heleidae have been reported feeding in a similar manner (Bauer 1961).

For the overall population biology of a butterfly, predation and parasitism of

Photo 3. Peck's Skipper captured by a Red-spotted Crab spider on Daisy Fleabane. The capture occurred under the flower, and the spider was teased into view for the picture. (Photographed at Somerset by Michael Gochfeld)

Photo 4. Black and Yellow Orb Spider wrapping an Orange Sulphur in its web. (Photographed at Somerset by Joanna Burger)

the early life stages has a much greater impact than predation on the adult. Vertebrates such as rodents and birds can be important predators on Lepidopteran eggs, larvae, and pupae, and no doubt select for *crypsis* (camouflage) at those vulnerable life stages. However, this would not influence the evolution of mimicry in the adult butterflies unless mimicry and crypsis were genetically linked. It is likely that predation by invertebrates on butterflies is of far greater importance to butterfly populations than vertebrate predation, and involves all stages. Scorpions and spiders, true bugs and beetles, dragonflies, mantids, and ants, flies and wasps—all take one or more stages. Even cannibalism occurs among butterfly broods; for example, when preparing to pupate, mature larvae of Gray Hairstreaks may be eaten by their younger and more active siblings (Guppy 1959). Overall, the butterfly watcher is more likely to encounter examples of invertebrates eating butterflies; some of these examples are mentioned below.

Butterfly watchers are not likely to witness predation on eggs, larvae, and pupae unless they keep track of these life stages day after day or raise them in captivity. Viruses, fungi, and other insects take their toll. No doubt the most important predators are the minute parasitoid wasps. Female wasps search for eggs or caterpillars on which to lay one or more eggs of their own. Eventually these hatch into a wasp larva that eats away its host and then completes its own life cycle on or near its dead victim. Thus one may watch a butterfly egg for days only to see a wasp larva emerge. In some cases, an entire brood of caterpillars may be parasitized. This no doubt selects in part for solitary egg laying by butterflies. The endangered Homerus Swallowtail (*Papilio homerus*) of Jamaica, for example, is regularly victimized by three species of wasps, and in one case eighteen adult wasps emerged from a single parasitized egg. The wasps killed 76% of the Swallowtail eggs, accounting for 87% of the entire egg mortality (Garraway and Bailey 1992).

Laying eggs solitarily (one to a leaf or plant) reduces future food competition for the caterpillars, but also makes it more difficult for wasps to parasitize all the eggs. Yet some butterflies lay large numbers of eggs together. Baltimore caterpillars have elaborate behaviors to discourage wasps from laying eggs on them (Stamp 1981, 1982). Tawny Emperors lay eggs in large pyramid-shaped clusters, such that the internal eggs are protected, even when most of the eggs in the outside layer turn out to be parasitized (Friedlander 1985).

Mimicry, discussed below, presupposes that some butterflies are unpalatable or toxic to predators, which in most cases is based on alkaloid chemicals which the caterpillars consume by feeding on certain plants. The chemicals stored in the caterpillar's body, end up in the adult's body, and lead to rejection by predators. However, this is not the only chemical defense, for certain Neotropical butterflies sequester alkaloids as adults from flowers (mainly in *Eupatorium*-type flowers) and by sucking liquid from decomposing vegetation (K. S. Brown 1984).

Antipredator Behavior

Although many hazards await all stages of butterfly life, the butterflies are by no means passive, helpless victims. They too have evolved effective antipredator strategies. Anyone who has tried to net a flying butterfly is aware of their ability to take evasive actions. When captured, butterflies are capable of struggling vigorously, which may help them gain escape from both vertebrate and invertebrate predators. Indeed, the literature is impressive for the relatively small number of accounts of predation on flying adult butterflies. In addition, butterflies take advantage of both cryptic and distractive coloration, the former often apparent on the ventral surface and the latter on a boldly colored dorsal surface. Eyespots or patches of bright color are believed to startle or frighten some attackers when a butterfly suddenly opens and closes its wings. Hairstreaks have eyespots and tails on their hind wings, as far from the head as possible. A predator may mistakenly think that this is the head, seize the tail, and be left with worthless fragments, while the butterfly escapes (Robbins 1993). We often see butterflies with the corners of the hind wing, the so-called anal angle, missing.

Crypsis, or camouflage, is very important to many adult butterflies. Although we tend to think of butterflies as having bright and striking patterns, many of the brightest species (for example Questionmarks and Red Admirals) actually have an indistinct, camouflaged pattern on the ventral sides of the wing, making them difficult to see while resting or feeding. A common camouflage pattern, often called a "dead-leaf" pattern, involves patches of gray and black with darker wavy lines that resemble dead leaves or bark. We never thought of the bright yellow sulphurs as being cryptic until a Cloudless Sulphur landed on a leaf in a sun-dappled forest and disappeared before our eyes. Some species, such as the Red Admiral, have the best of both; they can be cryptic at rest, but if disturbed they suddenly flash open their wings, revealing an unsuspected bold pattern that may momentarily startle the predators, allowing the butterfly to escape.

Some of the bold patterns, such as the white bands on the wings of White Admirals, are considered *disruptive* patterns, which confuse a predator about the actual outline of the butterfly or may contribute to its camouflage. Whether these patterns actually work as suggested requires careful observation.

Other life stages have their protective attributes as well. Eggs, larvae, and pupae may be cryptically colored or placed in inconspicuous locations. Crypsis is extremely important, and larvae come in a variety of subdued shades of green or brown, which may resemble twigs, leaves, or some combination of the two. Some swallowtail larvae are gray and whitish at certain stages and resemble bird droppings. Other larvae are boldly marked and may resemble snakeheads. Douglas (1986) provides a good summary of these defenses.

There are behavioral protections as well. Larvae may wriggle vigorously when touched (Stamp 1982), or they may drop suddenly on a silken thread which they can climb up once danger has passed. Other defenses include rigid or sharp physical structures such as *scoli*, or the ability to vomit or secrete noxious chemicals. Some larvae have rigid hairs that can be both physically and chemically irritating.

Ecological Chemistry

One of the most famous defense strategies available to some butterflies is to render themselves unpleasant or toxic by storing certain chemicals in their tissues. In most cases this is accomplished when the larvae eat the leaves of certain plants (for example, pipevines *Aristolochia* or milkweeds *Asclepias*) and sequester the cardenolide (heart poisons) synthesized by the plants in their bodies (Brower and Glazier 1975). These chemicals are retained during metamorphosis so that the emerging adults have certain quantities of these chemicals. Predators (presumably mainly birds) that capture and taste such butterflies are likely to drop them, and the butterflies may therefore escape if they have not been lethally wounded. Major contributions from the laboratory of Miriam Rothschild (1961, 1972) and Lincoln P. Brower (Brower and Brower 1964, Brower 1969) and their colleagues in many subsequent publications have created the exciting field of "ecological chemistry."

Although certain butterflies are protected by their unpalatability, not all individuals in a population have the same concentrations of cardenolides, hence there is a *palatability spectrum*, where some individuals are hardly protected at all. Other species whose larvae are unable to tolerate the plants that contain the cardenolides can take advantage of the unpalatable species, by mimicking them (see the next section). Finally, some butterflies are able to extract pyrrolizidine chemicals from the nectar of certain flowers, and use those distasteful chemicals to render themselves unpalatable (Brown 1984).

Mimicry

Mimicry, is divided into two classes, which are named after the nineteenth-century biologists who recognized them. However, they actually blend into one another. *Batesian mimicry*, named after the Amazon explorer Henry W. Bates, occurs when a palatable species such as the Black Swallowtail or Red-spotted Purple very closely resembles an unpalatable species such as the Pipevine Swallowtail so that predators avoid it. A New Jersey graduate student, Sylvio Codella (1986), performed extensive experiments on this "system," showing that both male and female Black Swallowtails are protected when they are roosting with their wings closed, because their ventral surface closely resembles that of the Pipevine. Once trained to taste and reject Pipevines, birds will avoid both species, while naive birds consume both sexes of Black Swallowtail avidly.

Müllerian mimicry, named after Fritz Müller, occurs when one inedible species closely resembles another inedible species, and both thereby gain protection since a bird that has tasted a member of either species will remember to avoid both in the future. This is often linked with a conspicuous "warning coloration" also known as *aposematic coloration*. These bright colors make it easier for a predator who has made the mistake of capturing one of these butterflies to learn not to eat such butterflies again. Brightly colored tropical species in the subfamily Heliconiinae offer many examples of both kinds of mimicry (Brower et al. 1963). A detailed technical discussion of the evolution of butterfly patterns is provided in the book by Nijhout (1991), and there are numerous excellent reviews of mimicry, including those of Turner (1977), Douglas (1986), and Waldbauer (1988). Beautifully illustrated accounts are given by van Sommern and Jackson (1959), Brower (1969), and Owen (1971). Therefore only a brief discussion of mimicry is offered here.

There have been few actual field demonstrations of the effectiveness of mimicry, and much of the discussion has been theoretical and is "largely unproven" (Douglas 1986). The major body of experimental studies in this country has been provided by Jane van Zandt Brower (1958a,b) and Lincoln Brower (1969) and their students.

One of the major contributions of population geneticists to the discussion of mimicry has been the mathematical demonstration that the mimic must be less numerous than the model. Otherwise the selective predator is likely to learn about the palatability of the mimic before discovering the unpalatability of the model. This appears to be true for the Monarch and Viceroy, the latter usually being less common throughout its range. In parts of the range where the Pipevine Swallowtail is particularly common, such as in the Great Smokies, several species occur that appear to mimic it. The mimetic black morph of the female Eastern Tiger Swallowtail is particularly common there, and it is less common or even absent where there are few or no Pipevine Swallowtails (Brower and Brower 1962). However, in other parts of its range the reverse is true. In New Jersey, the Pipevine is generally rarer than any of its mimics, and is usually rarer than all of its mimics together. The mimetic Eastern Tiger Swallowtail black morph is generally uncommon in New Jersey, yet it does occur.

What is the explanation for mimicry in a situation that violates the rule about the model being more numerous than the mimic? One possibility is that visual predators have been genetically programmed through the experience of prior generations to avoid certain patterns. Another possibility is that even if the model is tasted first by only a small percentage of predators, that is sufficient to confer some measure of protection—thus mimicry does not have to work all the time to benefit the mimic species. Another possibility is that the mimicry has little to do with bird predation.

The case of the Viceroy mimicking the Monarch is considered the classic North American example of Batesian mimicry (J. Brower 1958a), but recent studies show that Viceroys may be unpalatable as well, in which case the mimicry is

Müllerian (Ritland and Brower 1991). Although people quickly learn to distinguish the Viceroy because of its slightly smaller size and the black line across its hind wing, most predators apparently do not make this distinction, although no doubt they could learn to do so if offered the opportunity. Remarkably, in some places, some Viceroys have only an indistinct black line, suggesting that they are being selected for increasing similarity to the Monarch.

On their Mexican mountain wintering grounds, Monarchs are eaten by several species of birds. Either these butterflies have lost some of their toxicity with time, or the birds have come to tolerate the noxious cardenolide defenses. Indeed, nearly a third of the Monarchs tested at their Mexican wintering sites had such low concentrations of noxious chemicals that birds did not reject them (Fink and Brower 1981). Elsewhere, reports of birds capturing Monarchs are scarce, though McIsaac (1991) reported a Barn Swallow (*Hirundo rustica*) that captured a Monarch and then released it in a "fraction of a second." The extent to which birds can be a driving force for the evolution of mimicry will no doubt continue to be debated.

If mimicry really confers protection against predators, it is essential to understand who the predators are. It has always been assumed that birds are the primary predators, and indeed many butterfly specimens have grooves and cuts that appear to be made by bird beaks. Yet there are remarkably few direct observations of birds capturing flying butterflies. Codella (1986) found that most predation occurred at night or during cold weather when the swallowtails were roosting with their wings closed.

Since the Viceroy mimics the Monarch and the Red-spotted Purple mimics the Pipevine Swallowtail, Platt et al. (1971) hit on the idea of training some Blue Jays to avoid Monarchs (without ever seeing or tasting a Pipevine Swallowtail), while others were exposed to Pipevines but not Monarchs. Once trained to avoid either of these unpalatable species, the Blue Jays were offered a choice between the two mimetic species, a Viceroy and a Purple, both of which are relatively palatable (the Purple more so than the Viceroy). As expected, Jays trained to avoid Monarchs almost always ate Red-spotted Purples and ignored Viceroys, while those trained to avoid Pipevine Swallowtails almost always chose Viceroys.

Birds are not the only predators to consider. In Panama, the large ground-dwelling *Ameiva* lizards capture butterflies and have learned to reject unpalatable species while continuing to eat palatable ones (Boyden 1976). There are, of course, many invertebrate predators, but since most are not visually guided, it is not clear how mimicry would affect their predation rates.

Hilltopping

Hilltopping is a common behavioral phenomenon in many species of butterflies. Hilltoppers show a propensity for flying around or along hilltops or ridge tops, and are found there in greater numbers than on slopes or valleys. Yet in any one area only a small proportion of the species are hilltoppers.

Hilltopping males fly to the summit of hills or ridges and perch there or patrol for females. This behavior is unrelated to the availability of food (Scott 1968). Hilltopping males tend to be present at lower density than non-hilltopping species, and Scott pointed out that a high density among hilltoppers would lead to interference in finding mates. Hilltopping provides the opportunity for a species that has a low population density to achieve a critical level of abundance at certain points to facilitate mating (Scott 1968), and observations indicate that hilltopping behavior is involved in mate location (Shields 1967; Scott 1968; Lederhouse 1982). Hills need not be very high to focus this behavior, and an observer situated on a hill or ridge may find butterflies concentrated there. Most hilltopping butterflies fly low over the ground, below 10 feet (3 meters), but Tiger Swallowtails fly higher. In one study, 94% of Tiger Swallowtails flew above 20 feet (6 meters), while only 2% of four other swallowtail species occurred above 20 feet (Turner 1990).

Not surprisingly, hilltopping has been studied mainly in the western United States (Shields 1967) where montane topography is more varied. Males of some species, such as the Great Purple Hairstreak, select prominent perches on ridge-tops and defend these against other males, and dominant males are able to defend perches or territories that are most likely to be attractive to females (Alcock 1983). The relative low relief of New Jersey ridges and hills offers an opportunity to determine the relative importance of hilltopping to New Jersey butterflies.

Puddling

Puddling is the tendency of butterflies, mainly males, to gather at moist spots on bare soil. In very hot or arid regions this is one way to obtain moisture, but it is also a way of obtaining essential trace elements such as sodium (Arms et al. 1974). Butterflies will sometimes land on a bare arm to sip sweat rich in sodium. They are also attracted to fresh urine or even feces (plate 3a). Photo 5 shows 500 whites and sulphurs of five species puddling near a village well in Zaire. Around this community well at Tonga, Zaire, we found 125 Swallowtails of five species jammed together in an area of one square foot, while nearby, on fresh mud, were the whites and sulphurs, sipping water and perhaps other nutrients while people tramped nearby to fill their pails.

Migration

Migration is a conspicuous aspect of the life of certain species (Williams 1958). Although several species engage in mass movements, these are usually one-way events, whereas true migration is considered a two-way event. The Monarch engages in the most dramatic annual migrations and is one of the few species that actually migrates both ways—south in autumn to its wintering roosts, and then northward in spring to breed. Much has been written about its migration and its colossal winter roosts (Urquhart 1976, 1987; Brower 1995). Other species such as Snouts and Painted Ladies exhibit dramatic mass emigrations of millions in some years, but these are one-way trips, carrying them far northward, where they breed and then die.

Life Histories

The life history of a butterfly species includes details regarding its ecology, behavior, and the timing and duration of its four life stages. These in turn are influenced by geography and climate, and thus vary from place to place and year to year. The life cycles of most of our common butterflies were investigated more than a hundred years ago, and Samuel Scudder summarized much of this information in his three-volume work published in 1889. Although the general features of life history are known for most New Jersey species, there are many gaps in knowledge regarding what the species actually do in different parts of the state. The larval hosts, for example, have been reported for almost all species, but it is not known whether these hosts are the ones used or preferred in New Jersey.

Although most skippers are known to feed on grasses, the actual species of grass used by many skippers are not known. For some species there are discrep-

Photo 5. Five hundred whites and sulphurs of five species puddling at a village well at Tonga, Zaire. (Photographed by Joanna Burger)

ancies between hosts reported by early authors (e.g., J. B. Smith 1910) and more recent authors (Shapiro 1974a; Opler and Krizek 1984). As the vegetation of New Jersey changes, butterflies encounter new potential hosts, and some species may be able to exploit them. The classic example is the use of Crown Vetch by Wild Indigo Duskywings (Shapiro 1979), which has allowed this insect to expand its range and increase in number.

It is apparent that female butterflies sometimes, or perhaps often, lay their eggs on plants unsuitable for larval development. Such fatal mistakes are an important selective factor, encouraging females to accurately identify suitable hosts, but females may not always have the physiological capability of making correct identifications. There are, undoubtedly, suitable hosts which are not attractive to females, but on which larvae can survive and mature; this offers another subject for study.

The pages of scientific journals carry numerous studies of the life history and breeding biology, behavior and physiology of butterflies, and butterflies have contributed greatly to our understanding of behavior, ecology, evolution, development, and conservation. Like ornithology, this is a field where the amateur can make important contributions to understanding behavior, biology, distribution, and changes in population status.

Topics for Future Study

Serious observers have the opportunity to add substantially to our understanding of butterfly status, behavior, ecology, and population biology in their locality through long-term monitoring. This kind of monitoring is now being taken seriously in the interests of understanding and preserving biodiversity. Binoculars, notebook, and patience are the main tools.

In all cases, the first requirement is the accurate identification of the butterflies one is observing. Some kinds of information require long-term, laborious study (e.g., the determination of host specificity or the relationships among sibling species such as the Azures). Other kinds of information can be obtained by careful documentation of casual observations (e.g., novel predators).

The conservation status is of particular importance, as Dale Schweitzer (1987, 1989) has emphasized. Understanding why certain species are restricted to certain habitats within their range can be aided by determining with what plants or other habitat characteristics the butterflies associate, or by watching their behavior at particular flowers. In some cases, the butterfly's occurrence may be influenced by the presence or absence of competing butterflies or of predators or parasites. The presence of certain blues may be influenced by the presence or absence of the ant species that tend their larvae. Interactions among species, social dominance at favored feeding areas, and predation by both vertebrates and invertebrates are inadequately known.

The Fourth of July Counts provide a standardized national census scheme for butterflies. Their value is enhanced if they are conducted in the same way by the same number of parties year after year (Swengel 1990). Other approaches to sampling butterfly populations include conducting a repeated transect sample through a particular area throughout the year. This allows one to detect all species regardless of their phenology, and provides better information on abundance.

We recommend that each observer adopt one or more particular habitats, such as a field or park, and census it in the same way on a regular basis (every one or two weeks throughout the season). Newsletters such as the NABA *Anglewing* or local club newsletters such as *Mulberry Wing* are suitable places for publishing such results.

An additional project initiated in 1996 is a statewide atlas to document butterfly distribution. Many observers will be needed to survey various habitats throughout the state to provide a comprehensive picture of the occurrence and status of New Jersey's butterflies. This is being coordinated by the NABA chapters in cooperation with New Jersey Audubon Society and the Department of Environmental Protection.

SECTION II

About New Jersey and Its Butterflies

CHAPTER 5

New Jersey's Geography

New Jersey has an area of 7509 square miles (19,223 square kilometers), ranking forty-sixth among the states in area, yet its population of about 7.7 million (1990) places it ninth, and its 1029 people per square mile ranks it number one in density. From High Point to Cape May it is a distance of 166 miles (266 km), and from Sandy Hook to Cape May it is 125 miles (200 km). New Jersey's greatest width is 57 miles (91 km). The geographic center of the state is 5 miles east of Trenton.

New Jersey is also the most densely industrialized state. No state has a higher proportion of its workforce employed in manufacturing. The pharmaceutical and chemical industries lead New Jersey's manufacturing sector, giving the state an industrial appearance along the northern New Jersey Turnpike. In addition, these industries have left a legacy of hazardous waste pollution, which has put New Jersey at the forefront of states eager to clean up their environment.

Visitors who arrive in New Jersey via the Northeast are often surprised to learn of the extensively rural character of the southern half of the state. Nearly a fifth of its land area is still in agriculture, and 42% is forested, including large segments incorporated in the Pine Barrens Reserve; in State Parks, State Forests, Wildlife Management Areas (WMA), and National Wildlife Refuges (NWR); and the National Seashore. There are a variety of detailed (e.g., Heston 1924) and popular (e.g., Dorwart 1992) historical accounts of the settlement of New Jersey.

Climate

New Jersey lies between 39° and 41° latitude. Despite its extensive coastline and proximity to major bodies of water, New Jersey experiences a fluctuating continental climate, carried to it by prevailing westerly winds. The winter air mass movement from the Northwest brings cold Arctic weather, while the summer movement from the Southwest brings hot, humid weather and rainfall from the Gulf of Mexico. New Jersey experiences dramatic seasonal swings from summer highs averaging 70°F to winter lows below 30°F (fig. 2). The growing season ranges from 255 days at Cape May to 220 days in the extreme Northwest (fig. 3).

The precipitation in New Jersey is relatively steady across the year, with an average of at least 3 inches every month and no more than 5 inches in any one month, resulting in an overall precipitation of about 40 inches in the South and 48 inches in the extreme northwest. The wettest months are July and August, with a second, winter peak in March (fig. 4). Most of this precipitation falls as rain, particularly in the South, where snowfall averages less than 15 inches, compared with about 50 inches in the North (Collins and Anderson 1994). There

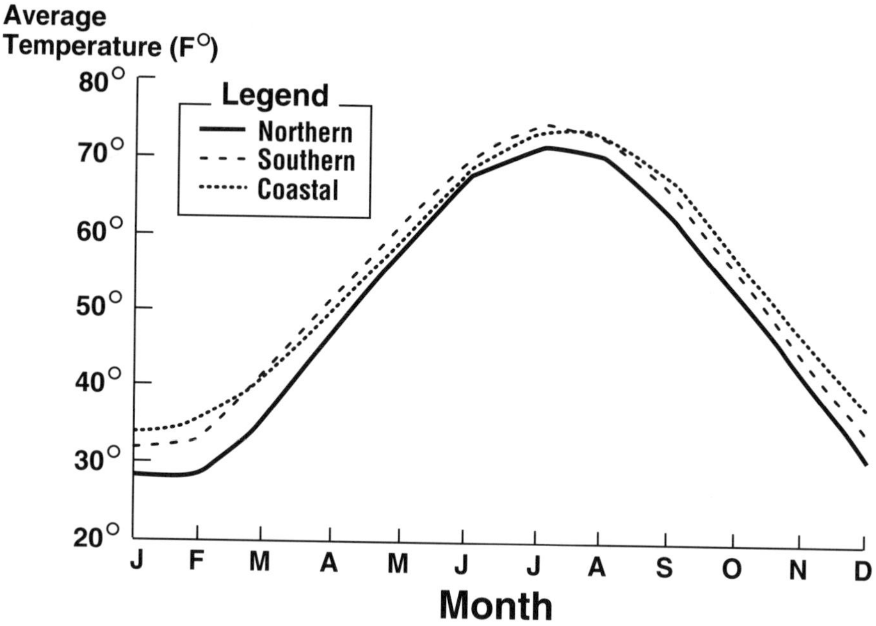

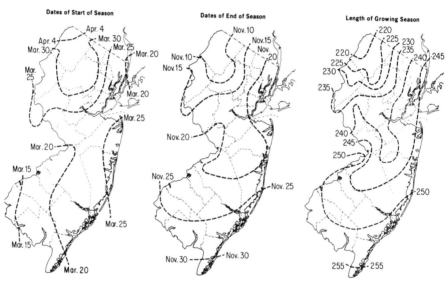

Figure 2. Monthly average temperatures for northern, southern, and coastal New Jersey (from U.S. Department of Commerce 1993).

Figure 3. Growing seasons in New Jersey (after Collins and Anderson 1994: 46), based on data in Biel 1958.

is substantial year-to-year variation in both the amount of snowfall and the duration of snow cover, with the winters of 1993–94 and 1995–96 setting records for frequency, amount, and duration of snowcover throughout the state, while the 1994–95 winter was nearly snowless.

The severity of winter has a direct impact on overwintering butterfly stages as well as indirect effects on the phenology of the flowering plants on which newly emerging butterflies will depend. The effect is complicated. Extreme cold may kill many hibernating insects, particularly those at the northern extreme of their range. But prolonged snow cover may be beneficial by providing an insulating layer that protects eggs and larvae.

Geologic History

During the Pleistocene, ice sheets covered northern New Jersey (fig. 5) and played a major role in shaping our landscape. Three of the four ice sheets of the last

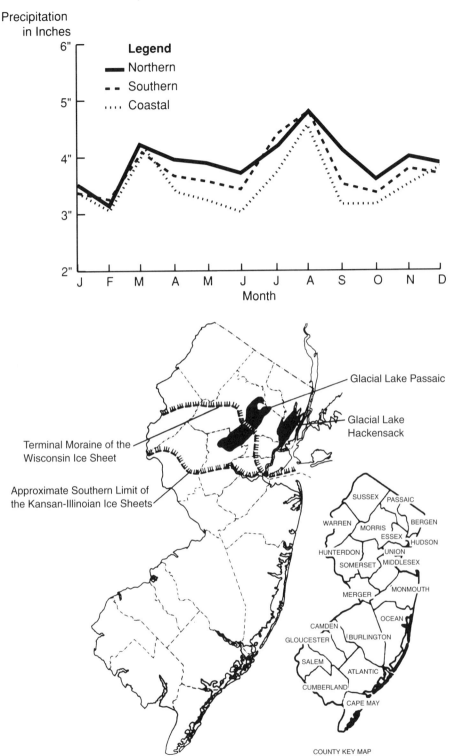

Precipitation in Inches

Legend
— Northern
-- Southern
.... Coastal

Month

Figure 5. The Pleistocene glacial margins and glacial lakes of northern New Jersey (after Collins and Anderson 1994:27), based on original data from Widmer 1964.

Glacial Lake Passaic

Glacial Lake Hackensack

Terminal Moraine of the Wisconsin Ice Sheet

Approximate Southern Limit of the Kansan-Illinoian Ice Sheets

SUSSEX
PASSAIC
BERGEN
WARREN
MORRIS
ESSEX
HUDSON
HUNTERDON
UNION
SOMERSET
MIDDLESEX
MERGER
MONMOUTH
CAMDEN
OCEAN
GLOUCESTER
BURLINGTON
SALEM
ATLANTIC
CUMBERLAND
CAPE MAY

COUNTY KEY MAP

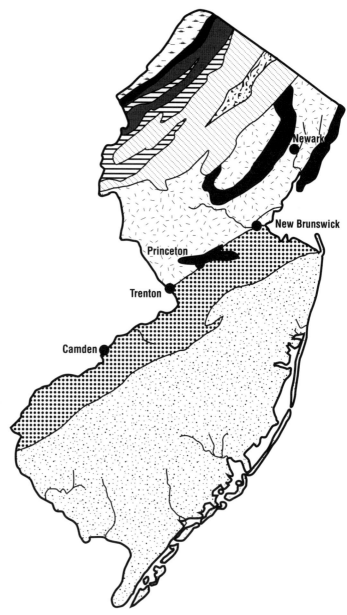

Figure 6. Geologic bedrock of New Jersey (modified from Collins and Anderson 1994:34—35). Shows nearly half of the state underlain with sand. The northern quarter has a more complex bedrock than shown here.

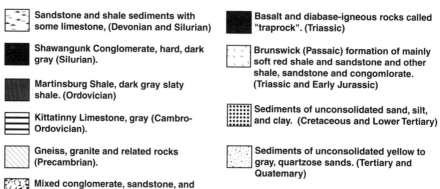

Sandstone and shale sediments with some limestone, (Devonian and Silurian)

Shawangunk Conglomerate, hard, dark gray (Silurian).

Martinsburg Shale, dark gray slaty shale. (Ordovician)

Kittatinny Limestone, gray (Cambro-Ordovician).

Gneiss, granite and related rocks (Precambrian).

Mixed conglomerate, sandstone, and shale.

Basalt and diabase-igneous rocks called "traprock". (Triassic)

Brunswick (Passaic) formation of mainly soft red shale and sandstone and other shale, sandstone and congomlorate. (Triassic and Early Jurassic)

Sediments of unconsolidated sand, silt, and clay. (Cretaceous and Lower Tertiary)

Sediments of unconsolidated yellow to gray, quartzose sands. (Tertiary and Quatemary) glaciation reached central New Jersey, and remarkably their margins nearly co-incided. The last retreated between 12,000 and 15,000 years ago (Wolfe 1977). Humans, presumably hunter-gatherers, are believed to have appeared in New Jersey about 10,000 years ago, and artifacts dated at 7000 years have been found in the Delaware Valley.

The geologic bedrock map (fig. 6) based on J. C. F. Tedrow (1963) shows that nearly half the state, corresponding to the Inner and Outer Coastal Plain, lies mainly on sand. The area from the mouth of the Raritan River to Trenton is the edge of a zone of red Brunswick shale, and this is the line that J. B. Smith repeatedly referred to as the Red Shale Line, demarcating two distinct faunal areas of the state. It lies close to the Fall Line, which separates the Coastal Plain from the Piedmont, a feature discussed by geologists but sometimes ignored by ecologists. Reference to the Fall Line will facilitate our discussion of butterfly distribution. For additional information, see Kemble Widmer's *The Geology and Geography of New Jersey* (1964).

Precolonial Times and European Settlements

Relatively little is known of the Native American occupants of New Jersey up until the time the first colonists arrived around the 1620s and found the land occupied by the Lenapé and Iroquois tribes (Russell 1981a,b). The Iroquois Indians discouraged seventeenth-century colonists from settling the Kittatiny Valley, but the Lenapé (Delaware) Indians were more tolerant. The Piedmont and Inner Coastal Plain were settled, and much of their forest cover was cleared for farming by the Europeans.

The Indians themselves had a significant impact on their environment, but the details are controversial. Collins and Anderson (1994:55) vividly describe eye-witness accounts of the Indians setting fires to burn forests and facilitate hunting. Russell (1981b), however, determined that the Indians generally did not use fire deliberately to clear the land. Nonetheless, at least some clearings and early successional stages were there even before European colonization.

Whatever effect the Native Americans may have had was soon overshadowed by the European settlers, since their population grew rapidly (fig. 7). By 1700 more Europeans were living in New Jersey than Native Americans. As the number of colonists grew, so did the demand for farmland and timber. Land that was unsuitable for agriculture was still logged for timber and firewood, and even though forests tended to regrow, the species composition was inevitably altered. The period from 1850 to 1860 was a period of maximal deforestation, and very little native forest remained standing. Thereafter, the demand for wood decreased, and forest gradually reclaimed much of the land that had proved undesirable for farming.

Railroads played a dual role in the landscape of the mid-1800s. They opened up areas of New Jersey, providing ready access from both New York and Philadelphia to many more communities than are served by the rail lines today. In addition, sparks from passing locomotives were an important source of ignition for forest fires, thereby opening up land for butterflies.

People and Landscape

The growth of New Jersey's population was rapid and continued well into the twentieth century (fig. 7). The state has experienced several growth spurts, one in colonial times, another in the 1860s and 1870s (growth exceeded 3.5% per year), and prior to World War II; but generally population growth has remained

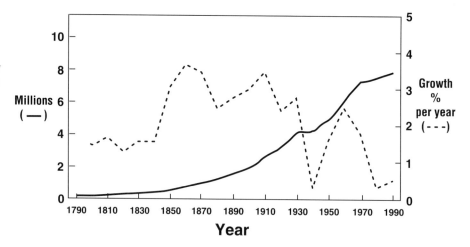

Figure 7. Growth in New Jersey's population (in thousands on left axis) from 1790 to 1990 (*World Almanac 1993*), and population growth rate (in percent per year on right axis).

between 1.6% and 2.8% except during the depression years. Growth has been negligible since 1970, but this figure can be deceiving. Although the state's overall population has remained stable recently, there has been a dramatic shift of population, particularly in central New Jersey. Many people have been relocating from urban to suburban developments, thereby greatly increasing the residential land area. By contrast, many of the nineteenth-century settlements in the Pine Barrens have since been abandoned (McPhee 1967).

Table 11 shows the change from 900,000 people in 1870 to about 7.7 million in 1990. This corresponds to a growth of about 750%. The counties with the slowest growth were Salem (157%), Warren (168%), and Hunterdon (192%); those with the fastest growth were Ocean (3300%), Bergen (2500%), and Atlantic (1400%).

Two columns in table 11 show the percentage of the state's population and area in each county. Thus Hudson has 7.2% of New Jersey's population on only 0.6% of its land (12,291 people per square mile), and Salem has 0.8% of the population on 4.6% of the land (191 per square mile). Seven of the counties have a higher population density than Barbados (1530 per square mile), usually considered the most densely populated nation in the Western Hemisphere (World Almanac 1993).[1]

By the end of the 1800s, most of the forest clearing in the northern part of the state had taken place. Table 11 shows that Hunterdon, Sussex, and Warren Counties have all had a significant increase in forested area in the present century. Conversely, several southern counties—Cumberland, Ocean, Atlantic, and Cape May—showed a decrease. The amount of forested area is largely a reflection of land set aside for public use.

Geographic Features

There are several ways of subdividing New Jersey geographically. One can refer to northern, central, and southern areas (fig. 8), or to the North and the South divided by the Fall Line (fig. 8), or to certain arbitrary geographic areas (fig. 9), or to its physiographic regions (fig. 10) with their corresponding vegetation zones (see next section). Northern New Jersey is generally the area from the New York

---

1. The average density for the entire United States is 68 people per square mile.

Table 11. Human Population Growth and Forest Cover in New Jersey's Twenty-one Counties

	Human population		Percent growth	% of state total in 1990		1990 population density[c] /sq mile	Thousands of acres of forest		Percent of land in forest	
	1870[b]	1990[c]		People[a]	Area		1899[d]	1987[e]	1899[d]	1987[e]
Atlantic	14,163	223,300	1,477	2.9	7.5	403	315.5	na	88%	na
Bergen	31,042	823,900	2,554	10.7	3.1	3,589	59.3	na	40%	na
Burlington	53,774	392,700	630	5.1	10.9	489	305.1	296.5	59%	57%
Camden	42,977	500,500	1,065	6.5	3.0	2,255	68.8	na	48%	na
Cape May	8,529	92,400	983	1.2	3.5	366	122.1	na	73%	na
Cumberland	34,688	138,600	300	1.8	6.7	278	197.6	139.1	62%	41%
Essex	143,907	777,700	440	10.1	1.7	6,176	26.0	na	32%	na
Gloucester	24,758	231,000	833	3.0	4.4	706	77.3	na	37%	na
Hudson	129,288	554,400	329	7.2	0.6	12,291	1.4	na	5%	na
Hunterdon	36,961	107,800	192	1.4	5.8	251	38.2	99.6	14%	36%
Mercer	46,470	323,400	596	4.2	3.0	1,461	15.3	na	11%	na
Middlesex	45,057	669,900	1,387	8.7	4.1	2,210	60.2	na	31%	na
Monmouth	46,316	554,400	1,097	7.2	6.4	1,164	90.3	90.3	30%	30%
Morris	43,161	423,500	881	5.5	6.4	887	138.5	141.2	46%	47%
Ocean	12,658	431,200	3,307	5.6	8.5	688	357.0	204.0	87%	50%
Passaic	46,468	454,300	878	5.9	2.5	2,449	74.1	na	60%	na
Salem	23,951	61,600	157	0.8	4.6	191	58.4	58.4	27%	23%
Somerset	23,514	238,700	915	3.1	4.1	790	29.9	na	15%	na
Sussex	23,168	130,900	465	1.7	7.0	252	134.5	210.0	40%	62%
Union	41,891	492,800	1,076	6.4	1.4	4,748	15.4	na	23%	na
Warren	34,419	92,400	168	1.2	4.8	257	59.7	108.9	26%	47%
State total	907,160	7,700,000	749	100.2	100		33,434.1	1,348.0	41%	42%

Groups of counties for which only aggregate forest area data are available:[a]

							1899[d]	1987[e]	1899[d]	1987[e]
Bergen, Essex, Hudson, Passaic, Union							176.2	111.2	39%	25%
Camden, Gloucester							146.1	143.7	42%	41%
Mercer, Middlesex, Somerset							105.4	147.2	19%	27%
Atlantic, Cape May							437.6	274.4	82%	52%

SOURCES:
a. Data mainly from Collins and Anderson (1994).
b. Beers (1874).
c. Census of Population and Housing, March 1991, New Jersey Department of Labor, Trenton.
d. Vermeule (1899).
e. DiGiovanni and Scott (1990).
na = Data not available.

State line south to Warren, Morris, and Essex Counties. Central New Jersey includes Hunterdon, Somerset, and Union to Mercer, Middlesex, and Monmouth Counties. Southern New Jersey is generally the area from Burlington and Ocean Counties south to Cape May (fig. 8).

Geographically, there are two major subdivisions—the hilly uplands of the Northwest and the Coastal Plain; but within these regions there is an array of habitats that accounts for the diversity of New Jersey's flora and fauna. Notably there is an intermingling of southern species extending northward along the coastal plain, while species of the Canadian and even Hudsonian Life Zones enter in the Northwest and may extend south along the Delaware Valley.

An important geographic feature is the invisible "Fall Line" (fig. 8), a diagonal line separating the upland Piedmont from the relatively flat Coastal Plain, and several elements of the butterfly fauna are influenced by this break. So named because of the waterfalls on the Schuylkill River (Philadelphia) and the Delaware

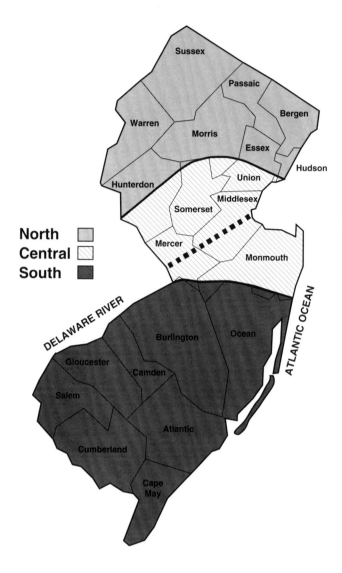

Figure 8. Division of New Jersey into northern, central, and southern regions, as used in this book. The Fall Line is indicated.

North ▢
Central ▢
South ■

River (Trenton) which occur in the zone of sudden altitudinal change (Shapiro 1966), the Fall Line parallels the lower reaches of the Delaware from New Hope to Salem, and crosses into New Jersey through Trenton and Princeton, extending to Raritan Bay.

New Jersey can also be divided into subregions (fig. 9) designated by a mixture of geographic and vegetational characteristics. Although it is partly artificial, this system is useful for describing the distribution of many butterfly species. There is some overlap between adjacent regions, which are as follows.

Northwestern NJ (NW)—Sussex, most of Warren, and parts of Morris and Passaic Counties, including the hilly country of the Kittatiny ridges and valleys, covered by hardwood forests, with several parks and forests, notably High Point and Stokes. This region is important because a number of butterfly species have historically reached their southern limit here. It is referred to in this book as "the Northwest."

Northeastern NJ (NE)—the Palisades, and Bergen, Hudson, and part of Passaic Counties, much of which are now heavily urbanized. This included the Crystalline Highland region mentioned by Comstock (1940).

Central NJ (C)—from Union County to Burlington, including the Watchung

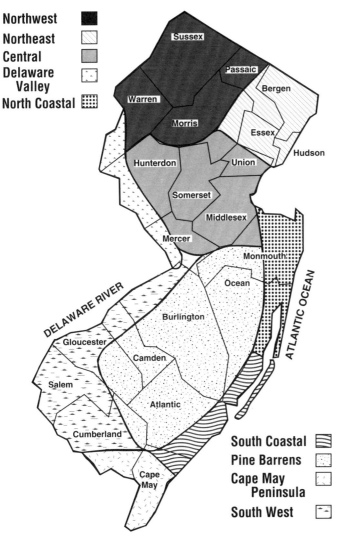

Northwest ⬛
Northeast ▨
Central ▨
Delaware Valley ⬚
North Coastal ▦

Figure 9. The geographic areas of New Jersey referred to in this book.

Sussex
Passaic
Bergen
Warren
Morris
Essex
Hudson
Hunterdon
Union
Somerset
Middlesex
Mercer
Monmouth
Ocean
DELAWARE RIVER
Burlington
Gloucester
Camden
ATLANTIC OCEAN
Salem
Atlantic
Cumberland
Cape May

South Coastal ▤
Pine Barrens ⬚
Cape May Peninsula ◱
South West ⬓

Mountains. This is low-lying suburban and agricultural land, including major urban areas (Newark, New Brunswick, Trenton, Camden).

Delaware Valley (DV)—cuts through upland areas of New Jersey, from the Delaware Water Gap to Camden. The Delaware River greatly influences habitats in the western part of the State. A number of plant species reach their limits in the Delaware Valley.

Southwest NJ (SW)—includes Camden, Salem County, and Gloucester County, bordering the wider reaches of Delaware River and Delaware Bay.

Coastal NJ (Coast)—includes the barrier beaches and salt marshes of the Atlantic Coast from Sandy Hook to Cape May. The salt marshes have been greatly modified by mosquito control measures. All were ditched prior to World War II to drain water and control mosquitos. There has also been intensive spraying for mosquito control, which still continues in some counties.

Pine Barrens (PB)—includes a large, partially preserved area of pinelands, bogs, and cedar swamps from Monmouth to Cape May Counties. It has a fairly rich specialized fauna. The core of the Pine Barrens is encompassed by the Pinelands Reserve.

Cape May Peninsula (CM)—includes Cape May and part of Cumberland

Counties. The fauna here shows strong southern affinities. Five Mile Beach, now completely occupied by the Wildwoods, was once "one of the most prolific collecting grounds" (Smith 1910).

Vegetation Zones

Dividing New Jersey into major vegetation zones is also useful for understanding the distribution of butterflies. Beryl Robichaud Collins of Rutgers University and Karl Anderson of the New Jersey Audubon Society have written a very useful book called *Plant Communities of New Jersey*, which emphasizes the substantial diversity of New Jersey's native vegetation. This diversity and the state's geographic location account for the relative richness of the fauna of this relatively small, densely populated state. Much of the following information has been adapted from this source and other volumes in the Jerseyana series published by Rutgers University Press.

New Jersey lies in the vegetation zone characterized as the Eastern Deciduous Forest (Braun 1950). It is in the Upper Austral Life Zone, except for the northwestern corner, which is in the Transition Zone. Before its vegetation was influenced by European colonists, the land was mostly forested, except for the clearings made by Native Americans and natural fires. The pinelands are fire adapted and require periodic fires to eliminate competitors. However, in the past 350 years the landscape has been substantially altered. More than half of the land area is urban or suburban, but, as Collins and Anderson (1994) point out, fortunately the greatest human population density occupies the biologically least interesting part of the state. Relatively few of the butterflies were ever confined to or even most numerous in the northeastern corner, for example. Perhaps the main exception is the Pipevine Swallowtail, which has its largest population along the Palisades.

There are five physiographic zones in New Jersey (fig. 10). Their boundaries extend as nearly parallel lines from northeast to southwest. Only a superficial account of each zone and its dominant vegetation will be mentioned, and the reader should consult the Collins and Anderson book for greater detail on the species composition and successional and dominant vegetation which give each of these zones their character. The zones are Ridge and Valley, Highlands, Piedmont, Inner Coastal Plain, and Outer Coastal Plain.

Ridge and Valley Zone—the Kittatinny Ridge and Valley Zone of northwestern New Jersey, occupying 635 square miles or 8.5% of New Jersey's area. High Point (1803 feet), the highest point in New Jersey, lies on the Ridge, which separates the Delaware River Valley from the Kittatinny Valley. Together these formations occupy a major portion of Sussex and Warren Counties. Its geologic history has left the ridge area covered in most places by thin, relatively acid soil of lower fertility. In many places, erosion has exposed the underlying bedrock. The valleys have deeper, more fertile soil. The area is characterized by many small glacial lakes. Relatively natural forest occurs along the ridge in High Point State Park, Stokes State Forest, and at the Delaware Water Gap. Fewer and smaller public park areas are preserved in the valleys.

Highlands—encompasses 900 square miles (12% of the state), including most of Passaic and Morris Counties and parts of Warren and Hunterdon Counties. They are about 20 miles wide in the North, and include parallel ridges and valleys and large glacial lakes such as Hopatcong, as well as the Great Swamp and Troy Meadows, which are remnants of the much larger Passaic Lake of glacial times (Widmer 1964). The average elevation of the Highlands is nearly 1000 feet, with a range from about 350 feet to 1500 feet.

Schooley's Mountain in extreme northwestern Morris County is an important

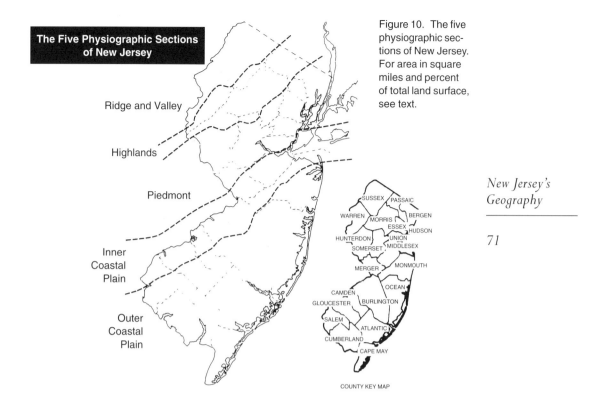

The Five Physiographic Sections of New Jersey

Ridge and Valley

Highlands

Piedmont

Inner Coastal Plain

Outer Coastal Plain

SUSSEX / PASSAIC
WARREN / MORRIS / BERGEN
ESSEX / HUDSON
HUNTERDON / UNION
SOMERSET / MIDDLESEX
MERGER / MONMOUTH
CAMDEN / OCEAN
GLOUCESTER / BURLINGTON
SALEM
ATLANTIC
CUMBERLAND
CAPE MAY

COUNTY KEY MAP

Figure 10. The five physiographic sections of New Jersey. For area in square miles and percent of total land surface, see text.

landmark in the Highlands and is important as a historical collecting site for butterflies. Many northern species, hardly known in New Jersey today, were collected there by Aaron in the late nineteenth century (Smith 1910).

The Piedmont—occupies 1500 square miles, or about 20% of the state. Whereas the human population in the Ridge and Valley and in the Highlands is relatively sparse and rural, in the Piedmont we begin to see more dense suburbs. Like the former two zones, it is part of a much larger geologic formation extending from New England into the South Atlantic states. Since glacial times its bedrock has eroded more than that of the Highlands, so it has a lower average elevation, sloping downward from 400 feet in the north to 100 feet in the south along the Delaware and to sea level at Newark Bay. All of the northeastern counties (Bergen, Hudson, Essex, and Union) as well as most of Somerset and part of Middlesex and Hunterdon lie in this section.

Inner Coastal Plain—the narrowest zone, but not the smallest, since it extends all the way from Raritan Bay to Salem County on Delaware Bay, covering 1075 square miles or 14.3% of the state. It includes the transportation corridor between New York and Philadelphia and was heavily settled at an early date. Its habitats are generally moister (more mesic) than the outer coastal plain, and it originally supported a variety of forests, most of which have long since disappeared or been severely altered by human activities and exotic species.

The original flora of the Inner Coastal plain was very diverse, containing elements of both the Piedmont and Outer Coastal Plain. About one-seventh of the plant species that occurred naturally on both the Piedmont and Inner Coastal Plain also grew on the Outer Coastal Plain, while a similar proportion of those found on the Inner and Outer Coastal Plains also grew on the Piedmont (Collins and Anderson 1994, based on a 1910 report by Witmer Stone, *The Plants of Southern New Jersey*).

Outer Coastal Plain—cover 3,400 square miles (45.2%) and occupies almost all of the state south of Trenton, extending northward to Sandy Hook. It includes the Pine Barrens as well as specialized coastal forests and almost all of the salt marsh vegetation. Many southern plants and quite a few southern butterflies reach the northern limit of their range in this section.

The Outer Coastal Plain is separated from the Inner Plain by a mini-divide of hills ranging from the Atlantic Highlands near Sandy Hook to Mount Laurel in the Delaware Valley. Although the highest of these is only 373 feet, they divide the drainage of the east-flowing rivers and creeks of the outer coastal plain from those flowing into the Delaware River or Bay.

The Wetlands

Like the terrestrial landscape, New Jersey's wetlands have been drastically altered by human activities. Draining and filling of marshes were considered great accomplishments until the 1960s, when the Wetlands Preservation Act became law. Far from assuring the permanency of wetlands, the act only restricts the kinds of development that can impact on wetlands but does not assure the management or maintenance that may be necessary to preserve their character.

Wetlands include lakes, ponds, streams, rivers, bogs, fens, and a variety of marshes and swamp forests. The distinctions between these are not always sharp. Most of the large lakes are in the glaciated northern part of the state. In the south, many of the ponds are either temporary (drying up in the summer) or boggy. There are a large number of rather sterile artificial lakes on the coastal plain in residential developments and old sand quarries.

New Jersey is famous for its salt and brackish coastal and estuarine marshes (Burger 1996), which occupy about 4% of its surface and occur in three regions: the northern marshes from the lower Hudson Valley to Newark Bay and the Arthur Kill (17 square miles), the Atlantic Coast from Sandy Hook to Cape May (170 square miles), and the Delaware Bay from Cape May to Salem (138 square miles). There are subtle gradations between true salt marsh and the brackish marsh found a few miles upriver, where fresh water dilutes the salt water.

Although only a few butterflies are found on the salt marshes, three of these, the Salt Marsh Skipper, Aaron's Skipper, and Rare Skipper, are essentially restricted to that habitat. Zonation of salt marsh vegetation is influenced mainly by the height above water and by tides. Many of the islands in Barnegat Bay, for example, are covered by a single grass species, the Salt Marsh Cordgrass (*Spartina alterniflora*). On slightly higher areas of marsh, or at the interface between the marsh and uplands, are other zones of vegetation, including the finer and more delicate Salt Hay (*S. patens*), Spike-grass (*Distichlis spicata*), and bushes such as Marsh Elder (*Iva frutescens*) and Groundsel Bush (*Baccharis halmifolia*). Many of the islands were created artificially by dredging of boat channels and deposition of sand and muck in piles that soon became vegetated, so the plant succession can hardly be called "natural succession." Many are being overgrown by the familiar Phragmites (*Phragmites communis*). Ditching of islands created rows of elevated muck that were also invaded by bushes (Burger and Shisler 1978). Nonetheless, there clearly is a succession, with a tendency for Phragmites and bushes to invade the higher salt marsh areas. On the other hand, during winter, sheets of ice may grind away some of this vegetation, thereby resetting the cycle of succession.

Swamp forests have the appearance of woodlands, but for most or all of the year, the ground is covered by water. The most dramatic example is the Great Swamp National Wildlife Refuge. Swamp forests with different tree compositions are found in South Jersey at the Tuckahoe Wildlife Management Area, among other places.

Bogs and fens differ from marshes in their general appearance. They are fringed by trees and bushes, and mosses often grow in dense mats out over the water. They are defined by their organic soil base. Bogs are characterized by low oxygen content, low fertility, high acidity, and they are often covered by a mat of *Sphagnum* mosses. Their substrate is peat, which can be many feet thick and in some cases has been mined for garden peatmoss or fuel. Fens develop on limestone soils and are not acid; they are characterized by sedge (*Carex* spp.) vegetation.

Plant Succession

Many ecology books, including Collins and Anderson (1994), describe in detail the process of plant succession, which consists of a more or less orderly progression from a low, simple, pioneering flora which colonizes newly cleared or burned land, to grassland, brushland, low forest, and ultimately mature forest. It has been customary and remains useful to speak of climax habitats—the forest type that will be more or less stable in an area under the influence of soil quality and climate, and in the absence of human destruction, fire, or natural catastrophes.

At one time the forest of northwestern New Jersey was dominated by oaks (*Quercus* spp.) and American Chestnut trees (*Castanea dentata*), which Braun (1950) designated oak-chestnut forest.[2] The American Chestnut trees are gone from the northeastern United States, killed in the early twentieth century by an introduced fungus, the Chestnut Blight. In their place is a mixed deciduous forest dominated by oaks. Braun depicted the Coastal Plain vegetation as pine-oak. Within each of these zones are subtypes of forests with specialized flora and fauna, for example the White Cedar swamps of the Pine Barrens and the Holly forests of the Coastal Plain.

On the relatively dry, infertile ridge tops, this oak forest has a large number of Chestnut Oaks or it may culminate in a Scrub Oak-Pitch Pine (*Quercus ilicifolia, Pinus rigida*) plant community. On the cooler, moister slopes and ravines, Hemlocks (*Tsuga canadensis*) and various hardwood species survive, providing a very different habitat extending as far south as the Watchung Preserve in Somerset County. However, like the Chestnut before it, the Hemlock is now threatened by an introduced pest, the aphidlike Woolly Adelgid, and many hemlock groves are already devastated.

We are likely to feel that deforestation and urbanization are destructive to habitat and biodiversity, but most of New Jersey's butterflies are open-country species, and succession to forested lands can be catastrophic for them. They thrive in openings and on the edges of forest rather than within the mature forest itself. Historically, fire has played an important role in reopening forests for such species, and the control of fire thus can have a negative impact on some butterfly populations. This is clear from the occurrence of fire-adapted vegetation in the Pine Barrens. Some pine cones, for example, require fire to open the cones and release the seeds, allowing them to generate.

Exotic Plant Species

About one quarter of the plant species recorded from New Jersey are aliens or exotics (Collins and Anderson 1994) that were not here before European

---

2. Not to be confused with Chestnut Oak (*Quercus prinus*), which is a tree species that forms extensive stands on exposed ridge tops in northwestern New Jersey.

colonization. But that figure underestimates the impact of alien species. For example, on the road shoulders of highways, more than half of the species and much more than half of the biomass belongs to alien species. Furthermore, where agricultural land has reverted to forest, much of the understory consists of exotics that have replaced the native vegetation. In the absence of natural insect herbivores or diseases, many of these alien plant species flourish, outcompete the native flora, and become severe pests.

In some cases, butterflies have adapted to using some alien species as larval hosts, for example, Crown Vetch and Queen Anne's Lace (*Daucus carota*). In other cases, adaptation does not occur and the butterfly disappears. The loss of suitable hosts may be an important contributor to the decline of certain butterfly species.

Several noteworthy plant pests exist in New Jersey. None have become as serious a pest as the highly invasive Kudzu vine (*Pueraria lobata*), which covers fields, hillsides, and the edges of forests over much of the southeastern United States. The Common Phragmite, which is native to North America, has greatly increased its range inland in the present century, due to changes in hydrology wrought by urbanization and agriculture. It is exceedingly aggressive, crowding out and replacing native cattails (*Typha*). As a redeeming feature, it is the main host of the Broad-winged Skipper. The alien Purple Loosestrife now fills many wet fields, marshes, and lake edges. No American butterfly larvae are known to feed on it, and in central New Jersey only the Cabbage White regularly nectars at its flowers.

These invasions are taking place today and may dramatically alter the landscape, as was done earlier by another alien, the Gypsy Moth. Although first recorded in New Jersey in 1919, the Gypsy Moth (*Lymantria dispar*) did not cause serious defoliation until 1971, with a peak in 1981, when it affected 800,000 acres or about one-sixth of the state's area (Collins and Anderson 1994). The widespread and recurrent use of pesticides to control the moth had a more damaging effect on butterfly populations than the Gypsy Moth's own impact on the forests.

CHAPTER 6

History of New Jersey
Butterfly Studies

Approaches to the study of butterflies have been inextricably interwoven with the history of scientific thought in general and biology in particular over the past 250 years. This chapter provides a chronology of studies and publications relevant to the butterfly fauna of New Jersey. The early publications on butterflies were generally on a global or continental scale. Only in the late nineteenth century do we find publications dealing with butterflies of specific localities such as New Jersey.

Although New Jersey was one of the earliest colonies to be settled and is situated between the population centers of New York and Philadelphia, it is apparent that the early eighteenth-century naturalists, in their quest for discovering species, concentrated their efforts on the southern regions of the United States, and even on the tropics. Thus, several common New Jersey butterflies were originally named from specimens captured in the southern United States or the West Indies (e.g., Black Swallowtail) and sent to Europe for identification.

The Eighteenth-Century—Linnaean Period

Although European naturalists before Linnaeus collected, illustrated, and/or named butterflies, the origin of a universally accepted naming system for organisms, including butterflies, dates back to the tenth edition of the *Systema Naturae* of Carolus Linnaeus[1], published in 1758. This marks the official beginning of the binomial system of scientific nomenclature, whereupon each described entity or species was given a generic and specific name in Latin or Latinized Greek. For the few North American species that also occurred in Europe, the name Linnaeus used for the European populations automatically extended to conspecific populations in North America. But early explorers also sent specimens to Linnaeus from around the world, so he had them available when he set about the huge task of naming living things.

Appendix C has a chronology of some of the early writings in which New Jersey butterflies were described, and table 5 lists each New Jersey species and subspecies and the year and authority for its original description. Linnaeus placed most butterflies into a single genus, *Papilio*. The tenth edition of his *Systema Naturae* already provided recognizable descriptions and genus and species

---

1. Late in life Linnaeus (1707–1778) adopted the spelling Karl von Linné. His first edition of *Systema Naturae* actually dates from 1735, but was not strictly binomial. Only in the 10th edition (1758) did he assign a genus and species name to each plant and animal.

names for several species that occur in New Jersey, mainly the most conspicuous ones.

The late 1700s was a time of global exploration and heightened interest in natural history. Captain Cook completed his first circumnavigation of the globe in 1771, and other explorers ranged from Newfoundland to the West Indies and returned to Europe with exciting biological novelties, many of which ended up in the private "natural history cabinets" of the nobility. Linnaeus, his students, and others examined such specimens and gave them their original scientific names. Many of the cabinets were poorly curated, however, allowing the specimens to disintegrate. Furthermore, the collections were often broken up on the death of their owner, so that the original or *type* specimens of many species described in this period cannot be traced.

The 1760s and 1770s saw the publication of several other works that illustrated and/or named North American butterflies: those of Johansson in 1763; of Charles Clerck, a student of Linnaeus who published his *Icones* in 1764; Drury in 1773; and of Denis and Schiffermüller in 1775 and 1778. During the same period, the Dutch artist Peter Cramer published four large volumes of *Papillons Exotiques* illustrating and describing butterflies, including many from North America.

Johann Christian Fabricius (1745–1808), also a Linnaeus student, served in the court of the king of Denmark and published a series of works on entomology between 1775 and 1798. Although many of his descriptions are brief, some (for example, the Question Mark, Aphrodite, Pearly Eye, and Harvester) are sufficiently detailed to be recognizable, thereby gaining acceptance from the International Commission on Zoological Nomenclature and having priority as names for these species.

At the end of the eighteenth century, Jacob Hubner, an Austrian, published *Sammlung exotischer Schmetterlinge*, which included illustrations of a number of North American species (Falcate Orange Tip, Banded and Olive Hairstreaks, and Common Buckeye) but essentially no text. In the same period, James Edward Smith published a two-volume work, *Natural History of the Rarer Lepidopterous Insects of Georgia*, including plates by the English artist John Abbot. Abbot had lived in Georgia, and their work (Smith 1797) contains the original description of several North American species, including the Georgia Satyr.

The Nineteenth Century and American Contributions

Abbot's drawings also figured prominently in the work of Boisduval and LeConte (1833), who named ninety-three American species, including the Checkered White, Bog Copper, White M Hairstreak, and Hackberry Emperor. Dr. Thaddeus Harris described several species in the period 1829 to 1842, including the Eastern Comma, and in 1841 he published *A Report on the Insects of Massachusetts which are Injurious to Vegetation*. The first comprehensive treatise on North American butterflies was the catalog published by John Morris in 1860. This work, however, was a compilation of many previously published descriptions.

The Civil War was a landmark for the intellectual awakening of science, and the modern era for various disciplines can be traced to this period. Many scientific journals first appeared between 1865 and 1900. The first modern compendium on our butterflies was William Edwards's *The Butterflies of North America*, published in three well-illustrated volumes appearing between 1868 and 1897. This did not cover all of the North American species but included several original descriptions of species that are only marginally part of our fauna, for example, the West Virginia White, Acadian Hairstreak, and Green Comma. Edwards is among the first to publish on the biology of butterflies, including a pioneering life history of the Monarch (Edwards 1878), and he made a major effort to understand the polymorphism of the Spring Azure (Edwards 1883). Herman Strecker attempted to publish a more complete catalog giving nomenclatorial synonyms, but apparently he abandoned this effort in 1878 after publishing one volume of *A Complete Synonymical Catalogue*.

During this same period, Samuel Hubbard Scudder published a number of papers on butterflies as well as a comprehensive three-volume work, *The Butterflies of the United States and Canada with special reference to New England* (1889). This rare work, with its many fine colored plates, makes for very interesting reading. In his detailed review of prior classifications of butterflies are no fewer than fifteen different ideas about the relationships among butterflies and how they should be classified.

In the late 1880s we begin to see the publication of books popularizing natural history. C. J. Maynard published a small book called *The Butterflies of New England* in 1886, and G. H. French published a volume entitled *The Butterflies of the Eastern United States*. Maynard followed this in 1891 with a poorly illustrated volume that purported to be *A Manual of North American Butterflies*. Scudder (1893a,b) published two popular volumes on butterflies. The close of the nineteenth century also saw the initial publication of W. J. Holland's (1898) *The Butterfly Book*, which sold 65,000 copies. It was the only comprehensive listing of butterflies of the United States and Canada, and provided seventy color plates. Holland revised it in 1921 and again in 1931. Most butterfly students and collectors living in the first half of the century used this book.

In addition to the books and catalogs mentioned above, many of these authors (e.g., Boisduval and LeConte, Edwards, Scudder) and others published smaller reports throughout the nineteenth century in which species were described for the first time. By 1900 virtually all species regularly occurring in North America had been described (see table 5), although taxonomic revisions have resulted in some forms being elevated to species rank.

The Twentieth Century and North American Studies

In the early twentieth century, the number of publications devoted largely or entirely to butterflies increased rapidly, with greater attention given to popularizing the study of natural history in general, and butterflies in particular, including their life cycles. These books focused on common and usually showy species of True Butterflies and ignored the Skippers. Mary Dickerson (1901) published a popular but detailed account of the life histories of common butterflies in *Moths and Butterflies*, illustrated with 200 photographs of all life stages. The Comstocks' *How to Know the Butterflies* (Comstock and Comstock 1904) illustrated 123 common eastern butterflies, based mainly on those occurring in New York. Ellen Robertson-Miller (1912) produced the *Butterfly and Moth Book*, which illustrated life histories with drawings and photographs. In 1931 Comstock's long awaited revision of *The Butterfly Book* appeared. James Halliday McDunnough (1877–1962) was one of the most prominent systematic entomologists. A professional musician who received his Ph.D. in Berlin, he switched to entomology as a profession. He served most of his professional life at the Canadian National Museum in Ottawa and published many papers on the systematics of Lepidoptera, primarily moths. His major contribution to butterflies is embodied in the *Check Lists of the Lepidoptera of Canada and the United States of America* (1938–39), and he is credited with recognizing the Hickory Hairstreak as a separate species.

How to Know the Butterflies (Ehrlich and Ehrlich 1961) and *The Butterflies of North America* (Howe 1975) provided enhanced approaches to identifying butterflies, although the former was illustrated only in black and white while the latter included paintings of butterfly specimens.

Studies of Butterflies in New Jersey and Its Surroundings

Progress in understanding the diversity, ecology, and behavior of New Jersey's butterfly fauna is closely linked with naturalists and scientists from New York and Philadelphia. Many scientists, both professional and amateur, from those cities repeatedly visited New Jersey locations to collect butterflies. Nonetheless, one of the premier entomologists of the late nineteenth and early twentieth centuries was a New Jerseyan, John Bernard Smith (1858–1912), the state entomologist and professor of entomology at Rutgers University (1889–1912).

J. B. Smith was internationally recognized for his research work on mosquito biology and control, and he was the pioneer in eliminating breeding habitat by ditching (now viewed as a mixed blessing). In 1897 Smith was among the first to recognize that insects showed "an outstanding difference in the amount of resistance to poisons, either external or internal" (Porter 1952). He edited various scientific journals and was elected president of several societies. He was at the forefront of economic entomology, writing extensively on a variety of agricultural pests, but he was primarily a lepidopterist who devoted much of his professional career to moths. He (Smith 1884b) suggested a division of butterflies into five families—Papilionidae, Nymphalidae, Erycnidae, Lycaenidae, and Hesperiidae—but he altered the order of these families in several subsequent publications.

His most monumental contributions were the three editions of a catalog of New Jersey's known insect fauna which include lists of New Jersey's butterflies. The first edition was published in 1890. This was followed by revisions dated 1899 (published 1900) and dated 1909 (published 1910). The John B. Smith Entomology Building on the Rutgers University campus in New Brunswick is named for him. Several useful short biographies of Smith have been written (Howard et al. 1912; Osborn 1912; Mallis 1971).

Smith was a prominent figure in entomology circles. Mallis (1971:320) provides an amusing account of acrimonious debates between Smith and another prominent entomologist, the moth and mosquito expert Harrison Gray Dyar, noting that "the feud reached the stage where Dyar named an insect *corpulentis* in honor of the rotund Smith, and Smith reciprocated the honor by naming one *dyaria*."

William Beutenmüller, a member of the New York Entomological Society and a staff member of the American Museum of Natural History, contributed many butterfly records to Smith. He also published the *Descriptive Catalogue of the Butterflies Found within Fifty Miles of New York City* (Beutenmüller 1893), and updated these brief accounts of their life histories in *The Butterflies of the Vicinity of New York City* (Beutenmüller 1902).

Henry Skinner (1861–1926), a lepidopterist at the Philadelphia Academy of Sciences, was a founder of *Entomological News*, which he edited from 1890 to 1910. He received an M.D. degree in 1884 and practiced gynecology until 1900, when he devoted himself to Lepidoptera studies full-time and became curator of the insect collection at the academy. He collected widely in the Philadelphia area and specialized on the skippers, publishing many papers on their systematics. These are some of the first rigorous discussions of the importance of variation in butterfly morphology and appearance. In 1890 he described Aaron's Skipper from Cape May.

William Thompson Davis (1862–1945), who lived most of his life on Staten Island, specialized on cicadas and named many North American species. He published major faunal papers on the butterflies of Staten Island in 1893 and 1910 (the latter dated 1909). Although each species receives only brief mention, his works contain important records of species that have since vanished from our area or are much rarer visitors today than formerly; conversely he did not record some species that are common today.

Samuel Francis Aaron (1862–1947) served as curator of insects at the Philadelphia Academy of Natural Sciences. He collected butterflies mainly in southern New Jersey, but also at Schooleys Mountain, and his records contributed significantly to Smith's catalogs. Aaron's Skipper is named after him.

William Phillips Comstock (1880–1956), scion of the Comstock publishing family, was educated at Columbia University and held a variety of jobs until turning "professional" in 1932. He moved to Newark in 1907, and in 1934 he became a research associate at the Newark Museum, then moved to the American Museum of Natural History (AMNH) in 1944. He was a member of the Newark Entomological Society and other professional associations. He published thirty-two scientific papers, eight of them before 1920 and the rest after 1940, with an emphasis on butterflies from the West Indies and on the Lycaenidae. In 1940 he published *Butterflies of New Jersey*, the only statewide compendium since Smith (1910). Minibiographies of Comstock can be found in dos Passos (1956a) and Mallis (1971).

Cyril Franklin dos Passos (1887–1986), cousin of the renowned writer John Dos Passos, began his professional life as a lawyer, retiring at age 40 to take up the career of entomology (Wilkinson 1988a). His interest was triggered by his wife, Viola Harriet Van Hise, who specialized in North American moths, while Cyril began to specialize in butterflies. In 1931 they moved to a 90-acre estate at Mendham (Morris County), New Jersey, where he spent the remainder of his life. He became a research associate at the American Museum of Natural History in 1936, having worked there unofficially for many years. His special interest was in types of North American species and subspecies of butterflies. Wilkinson (1988b) provided an annotated bibliography of 120 entomological papers, the first appearing in 1934, when dos Passos was 47. The papers by dos Passos and Grey in 1947 on the fritillary genus *Speyeria* are considered a turning point, reversing the "splitting history" of butterflies, whereby every distinctive form had been accorded species status. The dos Passos collection of more than 65,000 butterflies is in the American Museum of Natural History in New York.

Dos Passos had a strong interest in the literature of butterfly systematics, and he published bibliographies of faunal papers and catalogs that had been published on North American butterflies (dos Passos 1956b, Field et al. 1974). Many of his papers concern the type specimens of butterflies with the designation of type localities and the selection of the appropriate scientific name, and he authored several applications to the International Commission on Zoological Nomenclature to suppress some names and validate others. Among these was a proposal that the ban on intemperate language or deliberately offensive nomenclature be transferred from the formal rules of nomenclature to a code of ethics. Among his major works was *A Synonymic List of the Nearctic Rhopalocera* (dos Passos 1965).

Dos Passos's major faunal interest, as reflected in his papers, was the north country from Maine and New Brunswick, Canada, to Alaska. He did make contributions specific to New Jersey; for example, he described the life histories of the Northern Metalmark (dos Passos 1936) and Falcate Orange Tip (dos Passos and Klots, 1969), and reported variation in eye color of Sulphurs collected at Mendham (dos Passos 1948). He also reported the occurrence of the West Virginia White in New Jersey, based on a specimen collected near Springdale, Sussex County, in 1966.

Otto Buckholz, an amateur collector who lived in New Jersey, amassed a collection of about 125,000 specimens of butterflies and moths from all over North America. His collection is now housed in the AMNH. Joseph Muller collected about 25,000 butterflies in New Jersey, many taken after 1955, and his collection is also in the AMNH. He first raised the question as to whether air pollution might be affecting insect populations in New Jersey (Muller 1976).

C. Brooke Worth, a physician researcher who worked on insect-transmitted diseases with the Rockefeller Foundation in India, South Africa, and Trinidad, "retired" to a 63-acre farm in Eldora, Cape May County. There, in addition to studies of birds, he made important studies on moths and mosquitoes and wrote a number of popular books (including *Of Mosquitoes, Moths, and Mice*; Worth 1972) on his natural history studies and experiments. Although his work was mainly with moths rather than butterflies, his writings provide an excellent account of the natural history of southern New Jersey. His farm has now become a Nature Conservancy reserve.

A number of modern-day New Jersey lepidopterists have published contributions to our knowledge of butterflies. J. Benjamin Ziegler suggested a generic revision of the North American hairstreaks based mainly on their genitalia (Ziegler 1960), and with Rawson (Rawson and Ziegler 1950) he described Hessel's Hairstreak.

Arthur M. Shapiro, now a professor at the University of California, Davis, contributed greatly to the knowledge of butterfly ecology and behavior in and around New Jersey in the 1960s and 1970s, and his three major faunal papers on butterflies of the Delaware Valley (1966), Staten Island (Shapiro and Shapiro 1973), and New York State (1974a), greatly advanced knowledge of New Jersey's butterflies.

Robert C. Lederhouse began his studies of swallowtails at Cornell University. He spent six years at Rutgers University in Newark before joining the faculty of Michigan State University in 1987. He and his students (Berger 1986, Codella 1986) conducted a variety of studies on ecology, breeding biology, mimicry, and predation of swallowtails, particularly the Black and the Tiger Swallowtails.

Dale Schweitzer, a New Jersey lepidopterist employed by the Nature Conservancy, studies butterflies and particularly moths. He serves on the Endangered and Nongame Species Council and has contributed substantially to the conservation of New Jersey invertebrates in general. His studies of distribution and ecology have focused mainly on the lower Delaware Valley and the Pine Barrens, and he has been the chief technical resource for invertebrates for the Natural Heritage Program.

David Wright has been studying the biology and systematics of lycaenids, particularly the perplexing complex of Azures, in addition to his extensive study of the life history of the Bog Copper. His studies of reproductive biology, host preferences, and biochemistry have revealed several sibling species (see p. 168) among the Azures. His Cape May County checklist (Wright 1989; Wright and Sutton 1993) is the first comprehensive county checklist for New Jersey, and he has recently coauthored a county atlas of New Jersey Butterflies (Iftner and Wright 1996). David Iftner of Sparta, New Jersey, recently authored the comprehensive and well-illustrated *Butterflies and Skippers of Ohio* (Iftner et al. 1992) and issued a preliminary edition of a *County Atlas of New Jersey Butterflies* (Iftner and Wright 1996). He is documenting distribution of New Jersey butterflies including the examination of New Jersey butterflies in many public and private collections, to validate historical records of occurrence. Jeffrey Glassberg of Morristown, New Jersey, wrote the innovative book *Butterflies Through Binoculars,* the first in a series of regional field guides. He is also the founder and president of the North American Butterfly Association. He contributes many feature articles to *American Butterflies,* as well as to other publications on lepidoptera.

Many other professional and amateur naturalists and lepidopterists are actively contributing to our understanding of butterfly biology and habitats in New Jersey. A partial alphabetical list includes: Don Adelberg (deceased), Peter Bacinski, Bob Barber, Jeanette Bowers-Altman, Tom Bredin, Rick Cech, William J. Cromartie, Harry Darrow, Jim Dowdell, Rick Dutko, Vince Elia, Jeffrey Glassberg, Tom Halliwell, Robert Holt, Linas Kudzma, Charles and Mary Leck, Molly Monica, Bertram and Patti Murray, Harry Pavulaan, Dale Schweitzer, Jim Springer, Gayle Steffy, Eric Stiles, Ted Stiles, Clay Sutton, Patricia Sutton, Guy Tudor, Nick Wagerik, Richard Walton, Wade and Sharon Wander, David Wright, John Yrizarry, Louise Zemiatus, and Harry Zirlin.

The Nongame and Endangered Species program under Larry Niles, the Cape May Bird Observatory under Peter Dunne, and Herpetological Associates under Robert Zappalorti have encouraged such studies.

The many members of the New York City Butterfly Club have compiled what is probably the largest local data base of butterfly field records, which have been a major asset in compiling this volume. The recently formed Northern New Jersey Butterfly Club (and in the future other chapters of NABA) will enhance this effort by encouraging many more amateur butterfly watchers to participate in field activities.

The City of Cape May's Environmental Commission sponsored the Cape May Water Conservation Garden, including butterfly plantings. The Cape May Bird Observatory planted two butterfly gardens in the State Park. The Cape May Taxpayers' Association planted the Pavilion Circle Gardens for butterflies.

Iftner and Wright have compiled a county by county Atlas of New Jersey Butterflies, which was published in 1996. The next stage in understanding butterfly status and distribution will be the compilation of a locational atlas. This approach to documenting biodiversity is still in its infancy.

CHAPTER 7

Ecology and Butterfly Habitats

Although New Jersey is a small state with relatively flat relief, it does offer substantial habitat diversity, from the Palisades and the hilly hardwood forest of the north, to the salt marshes and brushy vegetation of the coast. Each of the regions and vegetation zones supports several different types of terrestrial and wetland habitats. Pine woods, bogs, and cedar swamps are found in the Pine Barrens, and hardwood forests and even coniferous forests occupy the Kittatinny Mountains in the northwest. Butterflies frequent mainly the edges of this array of woodland habitats as well as brushy fields, dry and wet meadows, swampy grasslands, roadsides, and other habitats that share sunlight and low vegetation but differ in floral composition, the availability of host plants, and the proximity of certain forest types.

Each species of butterfly can be characterized ecologically by the habitats it prefers, tolerates, or shuns, and by the foods it consumes (usually at the larval stage). The more foods a species can use, the greater are its habitat options; and the broader its habitats, the wider its potential range.

Thus, plant-species composition may be more important than the general appearance or physiognomy of the landscape in determining the presence or absence of a butterfly species. From the list of host preferences (table 10) it is apparent that for many of New Jersey's butterflies only a single genus or family of host can be identified. In some cases, closely related butterfly species have very different hosts (indeed, some seemingly identical or sibling species are distinguished mainly by their host), while in other cases (e.g., fritillaries on violets) similar species have similar hosts. It is not surprising that some of the most widespread and diverse plant families, such as the Fabaceae (formerly known as Leguminosae: legume and bean family), the Brassicaceae (formerly the Cruciferae: mustard and cabbage family), Violaceae (violets), and the Poaceae (formerly known as Graminae: grasses and sedges), are important hosts for many butterflies.

However, a few relatively small plant families also act as hosts. The uses of Pipevine and Dutchman's Pipe (Aristolochiaceae) by the Pipevine Swallowtail is unique in New Jersey, but in the tropics throughout the world, many other species use vines of this genus as a source of *alkaloids*, which the larva sequesters in its tissues and which ultimately renders the adult unpalatable and noxious as well. The same is true of Passionflower Vines (Passifloriaceae) used by a wide variety of tropical butterflies.

Whether a butterfly is "habitat specific" may depend mainly on whether its host plant is habitat specific. For example, the Northern Metalmark is found mainly on exposed limestone ridges, presumably because this is where its host plant, the Round-leaved Ragwort, thrives in New Jersey, and it may not have such a narrow habitat distribution elsewhere in its range.

Other butterflies are confined to highly specific habitats occurring on certain kinds of soil. Specific habitat types are important for several species. Thus, the cranberry bogs of the Pine Barrens are home to Bog Copper and Georgia Satyr, while the extirpated Mitchell's Satyr was confined to limestone fens. These habitats are limited in number, and the species that occupy them become vulnerable if any of their habitat is lost.

Conversely, many of New Jersey's butterflies are widespread and can be found in a variety of open habitats (fields, parks, and gardens), in most or all counties. Their habitat preferences are usually described in the most general terms.

Habitat Preferences

Forests of Northwestern New Jersey

The forests of northern New Jersey are quite diverse and provide a selection of butterfly hosts. Yet it is the gaps in these forests—the glades, abandoned clearings, old burns—and the edges, roadways, and powerline cuts with their rich flora of flowering herbs and shrubs that provide the most diverse habitats for butterflies, offering sun and a choice of nectar sources and larval host species. To the extent that these are maintained, either by fire, clear-cutting, or by periodic mowing, these cuts provide stable habitat for butterflies.

New Jersey's butterfly fauna includes a northern element that becomes more common in the Catskills or the Adirondacks. Prominent among these are the Arctic Skipper, Pepper and Salt Skipper, and Compton Tortoiseshell. They are found in clearings and particularly along dirt roads winding through forests. The Tortoiseshell and the Gray Comma, like their more common relatives, the Question Mark and Eastern Comma, should be looked for resting on the surface of dirt roads, while the two skippers have been found on flowers (particularly geraniums) along road shoulders.

The limestone ridges of northwestern New Jersey are home to the Northern Metalmark, a species with a tenuous foothold in New Jersey. It has often been found under the high voltage powerline at Springdale, but that habitat is being overgrown, and without habitat management this butterfly may be eliminated from our fauna.

Freshwater Wetlands

There is a variety of freshwater wetlands, with subtle differences and characteristic species. Shuey (1985) made a detailed survey of thirty-seven Ohio/Michigan wetlands of six major types, all of which also occur in New Jersey. Marshes are flooded throughout the year, while sedge meadows, dominated by species of *Carex*, typically dry out in the summer.

Several New Jersey butterflies (e.g., Broad-winged Skipper, the Black Dash, Dion's Skipper, and Mulberry Wing) range both southward along the coastal plain and westward along the southern Great Lakes. These wetland-associated species occupy habitats, particularly fens and bogs, that were formed at the edge of the Pleistocene glacier. Fens and bogs occur in depressions with no drainage; fens occur mainly on glaciated terrain over limestone, while bogs occur in the Pine Barrens as well and are covered by sphagnum. Unfortunately, many fens are wrongly called "bogs." They are a boggy habitat dominated by sedges, and are scattered over northern New Jersey. This habitat was once the home of Mitchell's Satyr, a species that has apparently been eliminated from the state, although some of its habitat remains intact. Several other species, including Acadian Hairstreaks, use this habitat now. Shuey (1985) found that fens are the richest type of wetlands.

Bogs and Swamps

Mostly within the southern region and the outer coastal plain of New Jersey are a number of species found mainly in bogs. New Jersey is one of the leading producers of cranberries, and many wetlands have been created or modified specifically for this crop. Butterflies shun the actively worked bogs because of heavy pesticide use; but once abandoned, such bogs may become suitable for species such as the Bog Copper, Georgia Satyr, and Two-spotted Skipper.

Swamps are forested areas with standing water and occur both in northern and southern New Jersey. The Great Swamp National Wildlife Refuge, for example, offers a high diversity of habitats, including wet meadows and swamp forests. The boardwalk and trails through the swamp forest offer one the opportunity to find Northern Pearly Eye and as well as Appalachian Brown, the former of which is much less common in central than in northern New Jersey. Tuckahoe Wildlife Management Area and many other WMAs offer a more southern type of swamp forest.

The interface between White Cedar swamps and bogs is a good location for the highly local Hessel's Hairstreak. This species, one of the last North American butterfly species to be recognized and described, was named by New Jersey lepidopterists (Rawson and Ziegler 1950). It is a bright-greenish insect, quite similar to the much more widespread Juniper [Olive] Hairstreak with which it was formerly confused. It has been found on the edge of blueberry fields along Route 72 and in the cedar swamps at Warren Grove, and it occurs in small numbers in many of the relict cedar swamps in southern New Jersey.

Dry Forests

The Elfins, a group of very similar butterflies with complex cryptic patterns, occur in drier habitats, mainly in southern New Jersey. The Brown and Pine Elfins are widespread in the pine and pine-oak barrens. The other three species are more restricted. The holly thickets (*Ilex opaca*) on the Outer Coastal Plain, including Sandy Hook in the North and the Tuckahoe WMA in the South, are places to find Henry's Elfins. Bearberry flats (*Arctostaphylos uva-ursi*), on edges of pine woodlands, are the habitat of the Hoary Elfin. The Frosted Elfin occurs in dry forest areas such as the Assunpink WMA, where its main host, the Wild Indigo (*Baptisia tinctoria*), occurs. The Assunpink WMA is one of the most important butterfly areas on the Inner Coastal Plain.

In early spring, the Juvenal's Duskywing is often very abundant along Pine Barrens roads, and a few Sleepy Duskywings can be found among them. As one drives along dirt roads, groups of these butterflies are disturbed from their basking and they fly up, only to resettle quickly as one passes. Cobweb Skippers occupy the same habitat, but are usually found only singly.

Two species, the Falcate Orange Tip and Dion Skipper, have two populations that occur in different parts of the state. The Orange Tip occupies the Pine Barrens edge and hilly woodlands in the north, and the Dion Skipper is in marshy areas in the north and in or near Pine Barren bogs. The relationship of these populations in the different habitats remains to be studied.

Coastal Marshes

Several species of skippers are characteristic of coastal marshes and adjacent areas. The Broad-winged Skipper is relatively widespread since it uses the highly invasive Phragmites grass. The Salt Marsh Skipper and Aaron's Skipper occupy many of the salt marshes on both coasts, while the Rare Skipper is more local in New Jersey. Probably because of their very low diversity and their historical inaccessibility to early collectors, salt marsh butterfly faunas have had very few formal studies. Our fieldwork on islands in Barnegat Bay indicates that population density of the Salt Marsh skipper is low, and we have yet to find either an Aaron's or a Rare Skipper there; however, all three species can be common in marshes farther south in New Jersey.

Serpentine Barrens

"Serpentine" is a loose characterization applied to rock that gives rise to "serpentine soils" that support "serpentine vegetation." They tend to have high nickel, chromium, and magnesium content, and quite low silica (Brooks 1987). Although serpentine is a common bedrock underlying Staten Island and parts of northern New Jersey, it is only where this stratum is exposed at the surface that one gets a "serpentine barrens" vegetation with sparse, low tree cover and a relatively low diversity of understory plants. New Jersey has no serpentine barrens. The only exposure of serpentine in the state is at Castle Point, Hoboken, an area that is now almost entirely developed. However, serpentine barrens occur both on Staten Island and west of Philadelphia at Nottingham County Park. Several species, such as the Common Roadside Skipper, Dusted Skipper, and Mottled Duskywing, are characteristic of such habitats.

Effects of Pesticides

No account of New Jersey's butterfly fauna would be complete without mentioning pesticides. Pesticides, particularly insecticides, are designed to kill living things, and many have been developed specifically to kill Lepidoptera. In the post-World War II period, organochlorine, organophosphate, pyrethroid, and other chemical families of pesticides have been widely used in agriculture and forestry as well as for domestic use on residential lawns and gardens. Their effect on insect ecology has been profound. In the 1950s, for example, there was widespread spraying to control mosquitoes, both in marshes and in residential communities, with the result that some species disappeared and others were greatly reduced. At Mohegan Lake, Westchester County, New York, where a residential community was fogged weekly during the early 1950s, Eastern Tiger Swallowtails virtually disappeared between 1951 and 1958, and other less conspicuous species must have declined as well.

The first wave of heavy pesticide use came between 1948 and 1960, mainly for mosquito control. A second wave came in the 1970s and 1980s to control Gypsy Moth infestations in northern New Jersey. Although not everyone agrees (e.g., A. E. Brower 1960), several species have apparently suffered long-term declines or may have been eliminated entirely by spraying. The disappearance of the Appalachian Grizzled Skipper is probably due in large part to spraying of its restricted forest habitat (Schweitzer 1989). Other species that were either reduced or perhaps eliminated from New Jersey include the Giant Swallowtail, Appalachian Azure, Silvery Checkerspot, and Mottled Duskywing. Other possible victims include the West Virginia White, Harvester, Acadian Hairstreak, Green Comma, Gray Comma, Northern Pearly Eye, and Persius and Columbine Duskywings.

The role of pesticides in reducing or eliminating a species is hard to assess, and it is often unclear why many species thrive and survive today in sprayed areas while their neighbors disappeared. Perhaps phenology played a role, since many of the victims are univoltine.

Habitat Change

In the long run, the butterfly fauna has been and will continue to be most influenced by changes in the available habitat. It is an oversimplification to speak of habitat loss, although draining, plowing, paving and mowing all have devastating impacts on many butterfly species. The clearing of forests, however, has historically opened up formerly unavailable habitats and greatly increased the species diversity of butterflies. Regrettably, there is no documentation of the status of most butterfly species prior to 1890, and we cannot be certain which species invaded New Jersey and the eastern United States after European colonization.

Often overlooked, though no less important, is the fact that much of the land that was cleared one or two centuries ago is now reverting to woodland. During early successional stages, abandoned land may attract a high diversity of butterflies, but as mature forest grows, relatively fewer species will use these habitats. The effect of succession can be seen on the powerline cut near Springdale, where tall brush and trees are shading out the Round-leaved Ragwort host of the Northern Metalmark. Similarly, Klot's Bog at Lakehurst is being invaded by Red Maples (*Acer rubrum*). Because new wetlands are not being created and because fire is being controlled, it becomes important to manage the early successional stages that still exist, otherwise more species will inevitably disappear from the state.

CHAPTER 8

Butterfly Distribution and Censuses

There are numerous published records of New Jersey butterflies, and a wealth of information in the field notes of collectors and observers whose records remain unpublished. Some New Jersey localities have been intensively studied (see the Gazetteer in Appendix A) and the fauna is well known, yet for most areas of even a small state like New Jersey, the status of butterflies is poorly known and inadequately documented.

Before World War II, much butterfly collecting was done in the vicinity of railroad stations, as visitors from the major cities traveled throughout the state by rail. Collectors repeatedly visited these productive or accessible locations, such as Lakehurst, while many of the intervening areas were ignored. The pattern continues today as butterfly watchers flock to the most productive areas to observe unusual or rare species, while for the rest of New Jersey there is little information.

The Fourth of July (4JC) counts (see below) rectify this situation somewhat, for counters are encouraged to cover their 15-mile diameter circle as thoroughly as possible. But unless many parties are afield, most circles are covered only superficially along roads or in parks, again based on accessibility and habitat quality. These counts provide an improved picture of the state's fauna overall, at least for the period of late June and early July.

There has been a compelling need for an atlas project, repeated at intervals, to document distribution, status, and trends. This project began in 1996, with the goal of publishing the first atlas in the year 2000.

Local Lists of Butterflies

Concentrated studies of butterfly diversity in a localized area will prove very valuable, particularly with information documenting how the populations of different species change over a season or from year to year. Harry Clench (1979) described the benefits of and approaches to documenting the butterflies in a region. At Powdermill Nature Reserve in western Pennsylvania, for example, he found that the number of new species he encountered did not begin to level off until the fifth year, and he was still finding new species at the reserve in the tenth year. Systematic lists with estimates of abundance would complement the one obtained from the Fourth of July Counts. With the modern emphasis on butterfly listing, the concept of a yard list or a park list seems very natural, and comparisons among lists can provide valuable information on the status of species and trends over time.

Some professional and amateur lepidopterists have published their yard lists for all to compare. For example, a 5.5-acre hilltop farm in New Britain, Connecticut, yielded forty-four species in one year, and an additional twenty-four species were collected within one mile (Austin and Austin 1956). W. H. Howe (1958) reported that his 9-acre farm in Kansas yielded sixty-four species in one year, with an additional eighteen collected within a mile. At Goshen, Cape May County, Pat and Clay Sutton have recorded sixty-eight species in their garden, while Wade and Sharon Wander have identified sixty-one species in a three-year period in their yard in Newton, Sussex County.

Over a period of ten years, we have observed fifty-seven species on our half-acre suburban yard in Somerset (Somerset County), with another five species within 300 meters; but in any one year, we have found only about forty species. Moreover, the number of species has steadily declined over the past five years as natural succession is resulting in denser, more closed vegetation, and as surrounding areas are being developed.

Yard listing, if done systematically, allows each participant to concentrate intensely on repeated monitoring of a small, well-known area. Careful record keeping, including dates and estimates of numbers, will contribute greatly to documenting the butterfly fauna.

Censusing Butterflies

Counting butterflies has become a popular recreational activity, but it is also a potential source of serious and important information for documenting the status and population trends of butterflies. Listing can take on a serious role when an observer begins to record data on butterflies in a systematic and repeatable fashion. To obtain the most useful data, one should adopt a method that is simple to use, quick, accurate, and precise, and can be used from year to year. No single sampling technique offers all of the necessary features:

Simplicity—it must be easy to conduct, require a minimum of equipment, and easy to teach to others.

Speed—one must be able to sample the target area in a limited period of time, preferably within a 1–2 hour period under optimal weather conditions; an all-day census may run into unfavorable weather in the afternoon, for example, which influences future interpretation of the results.

Accuracy—the ability to get the right answer; the number of butterflies counted should be close to the number actually present and an accurate identification of species must be made.

Precision—since no method can be completely accurate (some butterflies will be missed while others are counted twice), the method should be consistent with regard to its biases; a method that overcounts on one day and undercounts on another is weaker than one that consistently underestimates by a fixed percentage.

Mark-Recapture

This technique is often considered the "gold standard" for censusing butterflies, but few butterfly watchers will undertake it. Gall (1985) provides a detailed comparison of different approaches and statistical techniques using mark-recapture data. He discusses the various assumptions and the strengths and limitations of the different techniques. The observer nets as many butterflies as possible on day 1 and marks them, usually with an indelible marker. At a future time (usually hours or 1–2 days later), the observer counts the number of butterflies that are marked compared to the total seen (or netted). Thus, if twenty Clouded Sulphurs were marked on day 1, and on day 2 there were fifteen marked individuals out of thirty seen (50%), one would calculate that the original population on day 1 was about forty (twice the number actually marked). This technique (often referred to as a Lincoln Index) assumes that no butterflies immigrate into or emigrate from the study area between the two censuses, and it also assumes that no adults emerge or die in between.

These studies require considerable experience, time, and effort and are subject to their own biases. If the initial capture and marking affects a butterfly's behavior, causing it to emigrate or die or otherwise changing the probability that it will be resighted, the mark-recapture method will give inaccurate estimates. People who have studied the behavior of marked butterflies (e.g., Singer and Wedlake 1981) note that they are more likely to migrate out of the area, and furthermore the marks may also render them conspicuous to predators.

Fourth of July Counts

In 1975 the Xerces Society began coordinating a nationwide series of counts called the Fourth of July Counts, patterned after the Audubon Christmas Bird Counts. Since 1993 the counts have been sponsored by the North American Butterfly Association (NABA). Although these counts began too late to capture status changes occasioned by the post-World War II boom in the U.S. population, suburban development, and pesticide use, they are nonetheless an important source of information on the status of North America's butterfly fauna. Nationwide, only four of these counts have been held annually since 1975 (Swengel 1990, 1993b). The counts held in New Jersey in the 1990s are shown in figure 11.

As of 1995, New Jersey has had ten count circles. Instructions for beginning a count in a new location can be obtained from the NABA coordinator: Ann Swengel, 909 Birch Street, Baraboo, WI 53913.

Most of the counts are held between mid-June and mid-July, although a few in the southwestern United States are held at times that are more favorable for these regions. Both amateurs and professionals participate. Counts are conducted in one day and can cover a full 15-mile diameter (177 square mile) circle, or they may concentrate on a single park or sanctuary. In New Jersey most counts are of the former type, though the Greenwood Sanctuary count covers only that sanctuary in Bergen County.

Where there are many participants and many parties, it is possible to cover most of the count circle quite thoroughly. However, an individual or even a few people usually cannot adequately census such a large area and must focus their attention on specific parts of the circle. The value of censuses lies in sampling the area the same way year after year.

Nationwide the counts have grown from 1975 (29 counts with 108 participants) to 1995 (296 counts with 2946 participants) (see all 4JC count reports; see also Swengel 1993a, 1994a). It is encouraging to note that the number of new counts each year has increased, but there is a disturbing countertrend: despite the sixty new counts in 1992, twenty-five former counts were not repeated. There are various reasons for this: lack of time, lack of interest, loss of habitat.

Many articles have been written identifying the strengths and weaknesses of the Christmas Bird Counts, and some of these points apply to the butterfly counts as well (Swengel 1995). A count with few observers cannot readily be compared

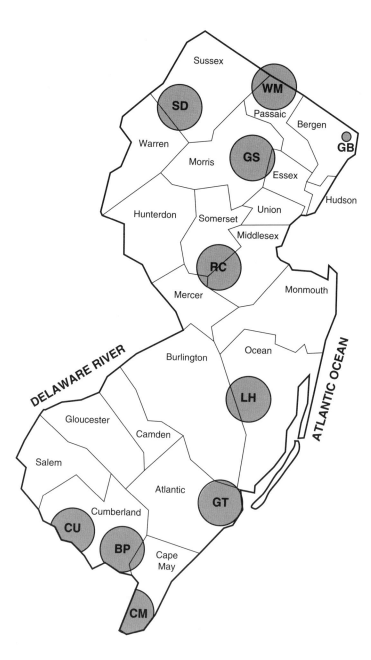

Figure 11. The ten current Fourth of July Butterfly Counts in New Jersey. Each circle represents a 15-mile diameter count area. The year in parentheses is the first year each count was conducted. BP=Belleplain Count (1991); CM=Cape May (1991); CU=Cumberland (1991); GA=Galloway Township (1981); GB=Greenbrook Sanctuary (sanctuary only) (1976); GR=Great Swamp (1994); LA=Lakehurst (1995); RC=Raritan Canal (1988); SD=Springdale (1992); WM=West Milford (New Jersey portion only) (1991)

to counts with many observers; therefore, it is customary to describe the number of butterflies encountered by "party-hour." The number of parties tends to be relatively similar from year to year; but as counts become more popular, and as there are more experienced observers, the number of parties may grow. This increase has to be considered when analyzing for long-term trends, and inevitably it produces better coverage and higher counts. Comparisons of trends from year to year are usually based on party-hours (Swengel 1994b). Nonetheless, some bias occurs, because as parties grow larger, observers can spread out and encounter more butterflies, particularly in fields and meadows where observers are not confined to well-worn paths.

Counts are conducted by one or more parties over a one-day period. If the weather is unfavorable on count day, an alternative day may be chosen. But because many counters are constrained by other counts and other schedules, many counts must go forward despite unfavorable weather, introducing a potential bias that can be overcome only by having a lot of counts in an area and by recognizing that a single count alone does not provide definitive information about butterfly status or trends in a particular place and year.

Several interesting phenomena have already been documented via these counts. Although many butterfly species are known to undergo dramatic shifts in abundance from year to year, independent of long-term trends in their populations, the 4JC can identify these cycles and distinguish those that occur on a local level from those that occur nationwide. For example, Swengel (1994b) pointed out that in 1991 the Monarch showed a nationwide boom in population, while in 1992 their numbers in the eastern United States were 90% lower than in 1991, but approximately at their long-term average. However, only through a network of systematic counts could we detect that in the Midwest the Monarch, though 60% below its 1991 level, was still more numerous than its long-term average. In 1993, the eastern population rebounded somewhat, the midwestern population continued to decline, and the Pacific population declined to the lowest levels ever recorded (Swengel 1994b).

See table 7 for a list of all butterfly species recorded from New Jersey, those sighted to date on the sixty-four published 4JC, the number of counts for each species, and the maximum number of individuals on any single count.

Distribution and Censuses

Other Types of Counts

Although the Fourth of July Counts correspond to the period of greatest butterfly diversity, they do not adequately sample all species. Spring counts would provide information on a number of mainly univoltine species that are completely missed by the 4JC, while late summer counts would record southern immigrants that do not reach our area until after mid-August (for example, the Little Yellow).

In our region regular late summer butterfly counts are held at the Gateway National Recreation Area, covering areas such as Jamaica Bay and Floyd Bennett Field, New York. All told, forty-four species were recorded in eleven years. Six of these, including the vagrant Long-tailed Skipper, have been recorded only once, while twelve were recorded on all eleven counts (table 12). None of the species showed a clear tendency to increase or decrease over these eleven years. Of the twenty species recorded on five or more counts, ten had their highest numbers among the first five counts and ten among the last six counts. Three species, the Broad-winged, Peck's, and Zabulon Skippers, which were barely recorded on the first five counts, have become regular on the last four counts, but this may reflect peculiarities of phenology rather than a population trend.

Area and Transect Censuses

It is valuable to census some areas repeatedly throughout the season. Such censuses, usually conducted by one or two individuals, have the advantage of providing data on all species regardless of their phenology and also tend to use more repeatable methods. Depending on where they live, butterfly watchers should consider adopting a census area, whether it be their yard or a park, and consistently sample the butterfly populations there.

An area census involves a direct count of the number of individuals present, usually in a plot of a particular size (say an acre), and then extrapolating from the small area to a much larger area of relatively homogeneous habitat to obtain

Table 12. Species Recorded on All Eleven Late Summer Counts at Gateway National Recreation Area

Black Swallowtail	[10]	Eastern Tailed Blue	[72]
Cabbage White	[227]	Pearl Crescent	[45]
Clouded Sulphur	[66]	Red Admiral	[31]
Orange Sulphur	[148]	American Lady	[33]
American Copper	[68]	Monarch	[1950]
Gray Hairstreak	[28]	Swarthy Skipper	[140]

NOTE: The maximum count in any year is shown in [brackets]; courtesy New York City Butterfly Club.

an estimate of density (individual per acre, hectare, or square mile) at a particular time and place. This requires careful sampling to assure that the area censused is representative of the larger area.

Transect sampling is particularly suited to linear habitats such as streams, dirt roads, railroads, or powerlines. In order to provide comparable data from year to year, the sampling should be conducted in the same manner. Several methods have been developed and tested by butterfly ecologists, and Nielson and Monge-Najera (1991) compared the usefulness of four of these methods, named after their original authors, while walking steadily along a 90-meter trail in Costa Rica:

> *King method*—all butterflies seen are counted and the distance at which each individual is first spotted is recorded (they did not record butterflies more than 5 meters away).

> *Sides*—all individuals seen within 5 meters on either side of the observer are counted (both sides of the trail); this is not much different from the King Method.

> *Pollard*—all individuals seen in front of the observer at a range of 5 meters or less in a band 5 meters wide are counted.

> *Douwes*—all individuals seen to the right of the observer within a range of 5 meters are counted.

As one might imagine, the King method (which counts all butterflies) yields higher counts but is not necessarily more precise, since individuals can be sampled multiple times. Moreover, a single observer would have to be vigilant on both sides of the trail, thereby increasing the likelihood of overlooking some individuals. The last two methods are variants of the others. Nielson and Monge-Najera (1991) concluded that the Douwes method (counting on one side of the trail only) was the simplest and most productive.

The Douwes method is the approach that we have been using in sampling a 300-meter road cut behind our home. It is about 4–12 meters wide, and we walk slowly along one edge, counting each butterfly we see. We also record the activity of the butterfly at the time we first notice it (flying, feeding, fighting, attempting to mate, mating, resting), the species of flower on which it is feeding or the substrate on which it is resting, and its interactions with other butterflies (chasing, etc). We also record the general abundance of flowers along this route so we can chart their change through the season. We record all butterflies to the right of the trail on the outbound walk, and return along the same path counting all butterflies on the other side (thereby approximating the King method, but with greater precision).

The transect approach can be applied to areas that are not linear, by simply turning the transect at various angles to fit into the available area. Douwes (1976) found that this provided a very consistent population estimate, with good agreement among three different observers. For two species of fritillaries censused in Sweden, it was estimated that about 30% of the population was counted compared with the mark-recapture estimate. The main stipulation is that the path remain the same from day to day and year to year. Where the transect covers a mosaic of habitats (open fields, forest, lawns, marshes), separate records should be kept for each segment.

When the recording technique is consistent, one can simply compare the total number of butterflies seen on the different censuses. However, for making comparisons among locations or habitats, it is usually preferable to take an average frequency per linear distance. This is probably more reliable than attempting to compute the density from transects, since the transects are often not in homogeneous habitat. Readers wishing to undertake serious study of butterfly populations will certainly want to read Pollard and Yates's book, *Monitoring Butterflies for Ecology and Conservation* (1993).

CHAPTER 9

Butterfly Gardening

In New Jersey, the most densely populated state in the nation, development continues to replace natural landscapes. Urbanization, industrialization, and suburbanization are converting woodlands, meadows, and farm fields into manicured lawns and pavement. Small vacant lots overgrown with native vegetation are disappearing from many areas of metropolitan New Jersey. Wild areas are shrinking in size, and remaining habitats are being fragmented. Creating butterfly gardens[1] as oases in private yards and public parks can play a role in conserving butterfly populations, maintaining diversity, and providing an aesthetic and educational resource. Each preserved area can serve as a reservoir for repopulating other nearby habitats should they become available.

In addition to its benefits for conservation, creating a butterfly garden provides hours of enjoyment and entertainment as well as opportunities to observe and photograph the behavior and ecology of butterflies. One can now have one's own "yard list" of butterflies, and can study their seasonal use of the yard and different flowers. One can observe courtship and mating behavior, host plants and nectaring preferences, and one can watch interactions among butterflies and between butterflies and predators.

Creating a butterfly garden involves providing the butterflies with the habitat, food, water and shelter they require for all four life stages. "Host plants" are the plants that caterpillars feed on as they grow, and "nectar plants" are the plants that adult butterflies feed on to obtain energy necessary for reproduction. Both are essential for a successful butterfly garden.

Obviously the number and diversity of butterflies that one can attract will depend on the location and size of the yard. Small gardens in urban areas will have a limited pool of species to draw on and will mainly attract large mobile or migratory species such as swallowtails and Monarchs. Larger lots in suburban and rural areas will have greater diversity. In our butterfly garden in suburban Somerset, we regularly record forty species in a year and occasionally fifteen species in a day.

To attract the greatest number of butterflies, flowers and shrubs should be planted in full sun. Other ingredients for a butterfly garden include flat rocks for basking in the sun, shrubs and trees that provide a varying amount of protection (for sleeping and resting), wet mud, and shallow water for drinking.

Flower colors range from white to yellow, blue to pink, red, and purple, and

---

1. The term "butterfly garden" has also been used to refer to the keeping of free-flying butterflies (usually indoors) as described by Rothschild and Farrell (1983), but today these are usually referred to as "butterfly houses."

some butterflies seem to show a preference for certain colors (Pearl Crescents prefer yellow flowers, for example). In general, masses of flowers are more attractive than solitary flowers scattered about the garden. Where space is very limited, opt for larger beds of a few favorite species, rather than single plants of many species. The fragrance or odor of a flower is obviously important, and plants have evolved their fragrances to attract insects for pollination.

Nectar must be available throughout the season, so careful thought must be given to the mix of species you plant so that some are in flower at all times. This is particularly challenging for those butterflies that emerge in early April, when few New Jersey wildflowers or horticultural perennials are in bloom, as well as for those that persist after mid-September, when floral diversity is low. The flowering season of individual plants can be prolonged by picking off the dead flowers before they go to seed (dead-heading); once they are setting seed, further flowering is inhibited.

Quite a variety of colorful books and manuals on butterfly gardening is now available, from which the reader can gain many ideas on how to landscape a garden for both human and butterfly visitors. These books provide lists of species suitable for gardening. The North American Butterfly Association includes gardening articles in its *American Butterflies* magazine and distributes newsletters devoted to butterfly gardening. Both provide lists of nurseries for purchasing suitable plants.

Even with the benefit of books, the butterfly gardener will have to experiment to identify the best plantings. A surprising feature is that different plant species seem to "perform" differently in different gardens. In some New Jersey gardens, Lilac flowers (*Syringa* spp.) are a major attraction for swallowtails, but we have never seen butterflies at our own Lilacs. This may reflect the color of the blooms, their density (we have three scattered bushes rather than a hedge), their position with respect to other trees, as well as other flowers that may be available to compete for butterfly attention.

In our garden, Everlasting Pea (*Lathyrus*) is a major drawing card for various skippers, and Silver-spotted Skippers will hang out in our pea patch all day. Yet others tell us that they never see anything on this plant. We wonder whether certain populations of butterflies become "imprinted" chemically or visually on certain local flowers, or whether the flowers themselves vary in nectar production depending on soil conditions. We can certainly detect variation in the attractiveness of flower species from day to day. Many flowers don't seem very attractive when they first open, but butterflies will flock to them a week later. Then, as nectar production declines, butterflies ignore them, long before the flowers go to seed.

Wherever you go, however, the story about Butterfly Bush (*Buddleia*) is the same. It is a major drawing card. We can sometimes see eight species at once on our bush, plus the two species of Clearwing Moths. When it is in bloom, nothing else can compare with its attracting power. Many nearby flowers never entertain a butterfly when the *Buddleia* is in full flower (July–September). However, our bush never blooms before July 15, so we need many other flower species to attract butterflies before that. Many flowers have only limited appeal to people and butterflies, but may be desirable, because they offer nectar at a time when other sources are unavailable.

Butterfly Life Cycles: Planning Your Garden

Understanding the life cycle of butterflies will help in designing a garden that fulfills all of their needs throughout the year. Many popular books provide detailed accounts of the anatomical, physiological, and biochemical transformations accompanying the metamorphic stages of the life cycle. Eggs generally are the size of a pinhead and may go unnoticed. Females seek out the appropriate food plant for egg laying. The eggs normally hatch in four to seven days, but some species overwinter as eggs.

The caterpillars' main task is to eat and grow larger. They have voracious appetites and will eat their way through the leaves of many garden plants. The successful butterfly gardener must therefore learn to love the ragged scrawls and patterns that caterpillars create on the leaves of prized plants. Caterpillars grow quickly, going through five distinct stages, or *instars*, after each of which they shed their skin and eat some more.

Some caterpillars are host specific (see table 10), feeding on the leaves of only one or a few different plants. Many species seem to be *family specific*; for example, Monarchs feed only on milkweeds, and some skippers and satyrids feed only on grasses. Other species are *generalists*, feeding on plants from many different families. When the fifth instar has finished feeding, it forms a *chrysalis*, or pupa.

Inside the newly formed chrysalis, sometimes in little more than a week, the caterpillar is transformed into a butterfly. The caterpillar sheds its head, and it forms a new head with compound eyes, a hollow and flexible tongue, jointed legs, sex organs, and delicate wings. Butterflies usually emerge from their chrysalis early in the morning, and then rest for hours as their wings straighten and harden; by midmorning the adult is searching for a mate and food. This sequence can be interrupted by *diapause*, a long period of suspended animation.

For many butterflies, the adult stage is short-lived (1–2 weeks), although some, like the Monarch and Mourning Cloak, may live for months. Adult butterflies have good vision and excellent smell and taste, which they use to detect mates from great distances, to discriminate nectar, and to locate larval food plants for egg laying.

Understanding all of the life stages will help in designing a butterfly garden. A successful butterfly garden will meet the needs of all four stages.

Creating the Garden

Creating a butterfly garden involves several steps: (1) choosing a location; (2) selecting the plantings; (3) considering the garden within the context of your neighborhood; (4) recording butterfly use and reconsidering the selection.

Location

Geography will have a strong influence on your garden, both in terms of the local butterfly fauna and the growing season. For example, in southern New Jersey several species of elfins might be induced to visit a garden that contained American Holly (Henry's Elfin), Bearberry (Hoary Elfin), or Wild Indigo (Frosted Elfin), but these wouldn't work in the Northwest.

Presumably one has little choice in their overall location for relatively few people will include "butterfly garden compatibility" in their criteria for purchasing a home. But once settled, you can create an entirely new garden, or gradually switch your present, traditional garden to one that includes both native and non-native species, as well as showy and less showy nectar-bearing species. We had the mixed blessing of creating our garden out of a completely barren yard that had formerly served as a horse paddock. Alternatively, one may have the opportunity to create a butterfly garden on someone else's land, for example in a local park or botanical garden.

A main determinant should be sunshine—lots of it. You should consider several designs, keeping in mind the needs of the butterflies (for food plants, nec-

Table 13. Nectar Plants for New Jersey Butterfly Gardens

Plant	Bloom Period	Species Attracted
Butterfly Bush	**July–Oct**	**Swallowtails, Nymphalids, Monarchs, Skippers**
Butterfly Weed	**June–July**	**Fritillaries, Crescents, Coral and Olive Hairstreak**
Common Milkweed	**June–July**	**Hairstreaks, Skippers**
Swamp Milkweed	**July–Aug**	**Hairstreaks, Skippers**
Purple Cone Flower	**July–Sept**	**Miscellaneous**
Dogbane	June–July	Hairstreaks, Nymphalids
Black Knapweed	July–Oct	Swallowtails, Pierids, Nymphalids, Skippers
Queen Anne's Lace	June–Sept	Snout, Hairstreaks
Orpine	Aug–Sept	Buckeyes, Skippers
Goldenrods	July–Oct	Nymphalids, Monarchs
Globe Amaranth	Aug–Sept	Skippers
New England Aster	Sept–Oct	Monarchs, Pierids, Skippers*
Heath Aster	Sept–Oct	Pierids, Skippers**
Black-eyed Susan	July–Sept	Crescents, Hairstreaks
Alfalfa	July–Aug	Blues, Sulfurs, Skippers
Bee-balm	July	Nymphalids
Red Clover	June–Oct	Swallowtails, Pierids, Nymphalids
Jo Pye Weed	July–Sept	Nymphalids, Skippers
Everlasting Pea	June–Sept	Skippers, Sulfurs
Mimosa	June–Aug	Swallowtails
Zinnias	July–Sept	Swallowtails
Wild Geranium	May–June	Early spring species

NOTE: **Boldface indicates first choice, high priority flowers.**
*Other purple asters such as New York Aster are also suitable.
**Other white asters and fleabanes are also suitable.

tar sources, shelter, water, perches) and your tolerances (for native flowers and "weeds," partially eaten leaves, and large homogeneous masses of color).

Plant Selection

Your design should include the placement of herbs, shrubs, vines, and perhaps trees, as well as a water and mud source. Be sure to include pathways so that you can actually see all parts of the garden close up. Tables 13 and 14 provide a general list of nectar sources and caterpillar hosts that will be suitable for many parts of New Jersey. But you need to consider your plantings as an experiment. Consult various butterfly gardening books for other suggestions. The size of the available garden space obviously puts a constraint on the variety and number of butterfly plants one can have. In the smallest garden a single Butterfly Bush may be the only option. A single Milkweed plant may be adequate to induce a passing female Monarch to lay, but a group of Milkweeds would be needed to gain the full benefit of their floral attraction for Hairstreaks, Brushfoots, and Skippers.

Local Context

Your surroundings will influence the butterflies you can attract, but you should also become familiar with the types of plants that are nearby. They will give a clue as to what will thrive in your garden, and they provide a reservoir of butterflies that will invade your garden if you plant the same species. On the other hand, since most gardens can have only a few trees, and trees provide shade, learn which trees are nearby. If your neighborhood has oaks and hackberries, for example, that will support duskywings and emperors. If not, you might consider planting a hackberry. Tiger Swallowtails use a variety of trees as hosts, and if

Table 14. Larval Hosts for New Jersey Butterfly Gardens

Eastern Tiger Swallowtail	**Lilac**, also Wild Black Cherry
Black Swallowtail	**Parsley, dill, fennel**, also Queen Ann's Lace
Spicebrush Swallowtail	Sassafras & Spicebush
Sulphurs	**Alfalfa and other Legumes**
Eastern Tailed Blue	**White Clover**
Spring Azure	Wild Black Cherry
"Edwards' Azure"	**Flowering Dogwood**
Summer Azure	**New Jersey Tea**
Gray Hairstreak	various **Clovers**
Other Hairstreaks & Elfins	Oaks, **Lupines**
Snout, Hackberry & Tawny Emperors	**Hackberries (*Celtis*)**
Fritillaries	**Violets**
Pearl Crescent	**Asters**
Baltimore Checkerspot	**Turtlehead** (near water)
Anglewings	Nettles
Mourning Cloak	Willows and Aspen
American Lady	**Sweet Everlasting (*Gnaphalium obtusifolium*)**
Red Admiral	Nettles
Common Buckeye	English Plantain
Red-spotted Purple	Wild Black Cherry, also poplars & oaks
Viceroy	Aspens and willows
Wood Nymphs and Satyrs	Various grasses (try Purple Top, *Tridens*)
Monarch	**Milkweeds (*Asclepias*), Butterflyweed**
Grass Skippers	Various grasses, particularly Bluestems (*Andropogon*)—leave unmowed lawn area

NOTES: **Boldface: These are plants worth trying in your garden.**
Regular Font: Plants probably found in your neighborhood.

none of these are nearby, consider planting a Lilac or Wild Black Cherry (usually considered a weed tree).

Record and Reconsider

Record what species you see using certain flowers, and reconsider future plantings. Don't be bound by what you read in the various books (or in this chapter, for that matter), since not every flower will thrive in your garden, nor will it necessarily attract the butterflies that the books list. We have tried growing Lantana and Spanish Needle, flowers which are very attractive to butterflies in the southeastern United States, but which seem unappealing in our area. Although many people will, at a minimum, keep a list of the butterflies attracted to their yard, it will also be valuable to note what flowers they visit and when. This will influence the flowers and plants you should use in future years. Make sure that there also are caterpillar host plants for species that regularly visit the garden, and certain hosts may someday attract wandering individuals of species you've never seen before. Our Dutchman's Pipe (*Aristolochia*) has been climbing a fence for several years, waiting in vain for the attentions of a passing Pipevine Swallowtail.

Tips for Creating a Butterfly Garden

1. Locate the garden in a sunny area.
2. Landscape your garden with the nectar-producing flowers which adult butterflies prefer.
3. Provide food plants (host plants) for caterpillars of species that you see regularly. There are simply too many host species to include in a single garden, so concentrate on attracting those butterfly species that one can reasonably expect to see. This involves learning what butterfly species are

present in the neighborhood. Also, find out what plants and trees are located next door so you don't have to duplicate them.

4. Plan for continuous color and flowering throughout the season (at least from April through October). Cresses and Mustards, Flowering Chive, Wild Geranium, and Wood Sorrel are suitable in the early spring before Milkweeds and Butterfly Bush bloom. Gill-over-the-Ground attracts a few butterflies, but is too invasive to deliberately introduce into a garden. Various asters are suitable for late September and October, when Butterfly Bush ceases to bloom.

5. Use group plantings for large splashes of color rather than isolated plants.

6. Create shallow puddles or damp areas for a water source (a dripping hose will do).

7. Provide flat rocks for basking places for butterflies to use in the early morning and late afternoon. These may be close to a wet, muddy area for drinking.

8. If your garden area is large enough, provide a sizable, unkempt area where native plant species grow wild. This should be mowed only once a year in November, to prevent the encroachment of small trees, shrubs, blackberries, and wild rose. And use the highest possible blade setting, to leave as much base to the grasses as possible. Let the clippings lie in place for mulch. The wild grasses are particularly important as host plants for various skippers and satyrids, and Bluestem meadows[2] are becoming popular.

9. Rotting fruit can attract certain species of butterflies. Mount overripe fruit on nails or platforms off the ground so that mammals don't consume them at night.

10. Dog and cat lovers should remember that feces and urine attract some of the prettier butterflies (Red-spotted Purple, Red Admiral, Question mark, Mourning Cloak, Tiger Swallowtail).

11. Try commercially available butterfly feeders and nectar. This works in some places but not everywhere.

Tips for Plant Sources

1. Friends and other butterfly enthusiasts can often provide plants or seeds for some wildflowers.

2. Most nurseries carry standard plants such as Butterfly Bush, asters, composites, and others.

3. Collect your own wildflower seeds. In most cases it is not practical or necessary to dig up wildflowers themselves, although this can be done in areas that are scheduled for development. New Jersey has a list of rare, endangered, and threatened plant species (do *not* dig up or disturb these plants).

4. Contact and join the New Jersey Native Plant Society. They rescue plants from places being developed and also conduct wildflower plant sales.

5. There are a number of wildflower nurseries, and they can be contacted for purchase of many native species. Plants often take better initially than seeds.

6. Local butterfly clubs can become involved in fostering butterfly gardens by raising and sharing plants and seeds of appropriate species.

7. Check the butterfly gardening articles in *American Butterflies* for the names of suppliers.

---

2. Little Bluestem grass (*Schizachryium* [= *Andropogon*] *scoparius*) is host for several species of skippers.

Tips for Maintaining the Garden

1. Butterflies are insects, so use biological control or insecticidal soaps for pest management; do not use insecticides.
2. Cut off dead flowers, which will encourage further flowering and flowering for a longer period of time. This is called "dead-heading."
3. Consider not using herbicides on the lawn and letting species such as Sheep Sorrel (*Rumex acetosella*) intrude. This is a host for the American Copper. Better yet, let areas of lawn grow up with wildflowers and grasses (Little Bluestem is a good choice). If your lawn is invaded by the Mouse Ear Hawkweed, dig up the pioneers. It is not particularly attractive to butterflies, and will rapidly exclude *all* other plants.
4. Mulch flowers so they remain in good condition.

Butterflies beyond Your Garden

1. Consider your garden as a small part of your total neighborhood, and plan accordingly. Butterflies will use the whole neighborhood.
2. Educate and encourage your neighbors to plant butterfly plants, or to maintain plants, trees, and shrubs that are host and nectar-producing plants. Start them with a really successful plant such as a pink or purple Butterfly Bush. The more nectar sources there are in more yards, the larger the number of butterflies that will be attracted to your area in general.
3. Encourage your town to leave meadows and roadsides unmowed so wildflowers can attract butterflies to your neighborhood.
4. Encourage your local and state department of transportation to leave roadsides unmowed and to plant native flowers. Meadow wildflower mixes can be used that include horticultural wildflowers. Some of these mixtures contain *Coreopsis*, *Cosmos*, Purple Coneflower, and other species native to the central United States that are attractive to butterflies.

Some Suitable Plants for Some New Jersey Gardens

This subtitle is a deliberate "hedge," since as mentioned above, each gardener will have to experiment to find the plants that work best in his or her garden. It is not possible to provide a detailed account of all the species that one should or could have in a butterfly garden, but we provide details on a few plant species that ought to be a high priority because of the variety of butterflies they attract. The success of any planting in attracting butterflies depends on what butterflies are available nearby that can be attracted and on how well the plant grows.

Table 13 provides a list of flowers suitable as adult nectar sources, and Table 14 provides a list of appropriate larval host plants. The following species are well suited for butterfly gardening in New Jersey.

Butterfly Bush, *Buddleia davidii* (and its varieties)—A must for the garden. One large bush is sufficient, although a row of two or three is desirable. The pink and light purple varieties seem to be preferable to the white or orange flowers. These bushes should be cut back severely in the spring or late fall, since they flower on the new branches. We also prune our Butterfly Bush after new growth has started to encourage branching and to keep it lower so we can readily see the butterflies closer to eye level. If allowed to become too woody, these bushes may die, particularly after a harsh winter; but even a seemingly dead bush may send up fresh shoots from underground buds. Cut off the flower heads after they turn brown to encourage new flower buds to develop. *Buddleia davidii* is the

main species, but other species are given horticultural names. The bush will grow 8–15 feet tall, depending on how it is pruned. Dwarf varieties are also available, but in our garden these are not as attractive as the larger kind.

Butterfly Weed or Orange Milkweed (*Asclepias tuberosa*)—A popular garden plant, particularly attractive to Pearl Crescents, Coral Hairstreaks and Great Spangled Fritillaries (photo 6). It grows well on sandy soil or on well-drained slopes. Its seeds can be harvested and planted, or it can be allowed to self-seed, though it seems to have a poor germination rate. Young plants can be purchased from nurseries, but they often do not flower in the first year. In our area this is the least attractive of the milkweeds we discuss, both as a nectar source and as a host for the Monarch. However, elsewhere in New Jersey its orange flowers are like a beacon, attracting large numbers of fritillaries and other species. It partly depends on what butterflies are numerous in the vicinity and what other flowers are available.

Common Milkweed (*Asclepias syriaca*)—Widespread in the countryside, with its familiar white cotton seeds. It is easy to establish in a yard and it proliferates well, but it may die out after a few years. It can send up shoots in places where it is not wanted, and it is very obviously a weed. However, it is also one of the best nectar sources for a great variety of butterflies, and it flowers before the Butterfly Bush. So it is a must for gardeners who can tolerate it. It has a relatively short flowering period, mainly in June. This can be prolonged a bit by mowing down about half the stems in early June. A variety of other very colorful insects use this plant as a host. It is a favored host for the Monarch. Flowers late summer.

Swamp Milkweed (*Asclepias incarnata*)—One of our favorite butterfly plants. It is not easily obtained commercially, but can be readily grown from seeds. It likes poorly drained soil, but does not need a swamp, and if well watered it will thrive in lawns. It is an excellent nectar source for many butterflies, particularly hairstreaks, and is also a suitable host for the Monarch. Flowers late summer.

Scarlet Milkweed (*Asclepias curassavica*)—A tropical plant that must be treated as an annual in New Jersey. It is a very attractive nectar source and can be propagated from seeds each year.

Indian Hemp or **Dogbane** (*Apocynum cannabinum*)—In large stands in some areas, a wonderful nectar source attracting many species, particularly hairstreaks. Small stands, however, seem to be less attractive and may not be worth planting. We recommend trying to cultivate it for a year or two. It is not generally commercially available, but seeds can be collected from wild plants. We refrigerate them for six weeks before planting.

Black Knapweed (*Centaurea nigra*)—An alien that is widespread in New Jersey. It is clearly a weed, and looks like a weed in the early summer, but once it is covered with pink flowers it is very attractive to many species from swallowtails to skippers.

Purple Cone Flower (*Echinacea purpurea*)—Native to the prairies and a hardy and attractive addition to a butterfly garden, this plant works well in some places. One can usually purchase single plants from nurseries that handle perennials and then propagate them from seeds, which are produced in abundance. Unfortunately, deer like them as well.

Canada Thistle (*Cirsium arvense*). This species is very attractive to a large variety of butterflies in late June. It is not an excellent garden plant, but if one's yard has sufficient room, a stand of these thistles will amply repay the planting effort. Other thistles such as Bull Thistle (*C. vulgare*) also attract butterflies, including swallowtails and Great Spangled Fritillaries. But gardeners should think twice (at least) before introducing thistles into their yard.

Tickseed Sunflowers (*Bidens* spp.)—A familiar weed that produces bright yellow flowers in September which are available for nectaring by late-season visitors.

Black-eyed Susans (*Rudbeckia* spp.)—Both wild and horticultural varieties are often attractive, but they are not a high priority in New Jersey.

Queen Anne's Lace (*Daucus carota*)—A "weed" that easily persists in a yard, or can be planted if it doesn't colonize naturally. It is a larval host for the Black Swallowtail and also a nectar source for various species, including American Snout and hairstreaks. In our area it is not nearly as attractive as the species mentioned above.

The **Eupatoriums**—Joe Pye Weed and Boneset (there are several local species of each in New Jersey), these do quite well, and can be attractive nectar sources, particularly for hairstreaks. Edinger (1995) wrote a brief account telling how to propagate these species from seed. Red-banded Hairstreaks seem to prefer Boneset to Milkweed (at least in our garden). Find a stand of these plants in summer and return in autumn to collect seeds, which can be planted at that time.

Asters—Most flower in the fall and are often the mainstay of butterflies in late September and October. Several species will naturally invade most suburban yards. Others can be started from seeds gathered in late fall. A mixture of purple flowering species (particularly New England Aster) and white species (Heath Aster is a good choice) will increase the likelihood of attracting autumn visitors.

Clovers—Red Clover is an excellent nectar flower for many butterflies. White Clover is less attractive but is an important larval host for blues and sulphurs. Alfalfa is especially attractive to the Orange Sulphur.

Sedum or **Orpine** (*Sedum* spp.)—In southern New Jersey the white-flowered *Sedum* blooms in September. It is an excellent place to find Buckeyes and many other species, including some rare wanderers from the south such as the Ocola Skipper. Even one or two plants seem to be attractive, but large stands are better. In our garden in Somerset they have not proven attractive, perhaps because of better competing sources such as *Buddleia*. At any rate, the pink-flowered varieties, which are the ones usually sold in nurseries, seem less attractive than the white forms.

Globe Amaranth (*Gomphrena*)—Forms beds of round white, pink, or purple flowers especially attractive to skippers in late summer. A large bed (at least 4 by 4 feet) is desirable. We did not get good germination of seeds we collected from our flowers.

Goldenrods (*Solidago* spp.)—Various species are found all over the state; they readily invade yards. Pearl Crescents are attracted to several goldenrod species. Painted Ladies frequently nectar on Seaside Goldenrod (*S. sempervirens*) while moving along the coast. Slender Fragrant Goldenrod (*S. tenuifolia*) seems to be a major draw in southern New Jersey.

Zinnias—Large beds of brightly colored zinnias are attractive to swallowtails. However, the vast majority of zinnias available from nurseries are "double" varieties with little or no nectar, so look for those that have the small, yellow central heads where nectar is produced.

Wild Geranium (*Geranium maculatum*)—Blooms in May before most other butterfly flowers, but this normally shade-dwelling flower attracts butterflies mainly when it is in sunshine. In northwestern New Jersey it is the nectar source used by Arctic and Pepper and Salt Skippers.

Flowering Chive—A large bed of these purple, May-blooming flowers is attractive to skippers at a time when few other flowers are available.

Beebalms and Bergamots (*Monarda* spp.)—These plants provide a variety of colorful flowers that are reported to be attractive to butterflies in some localities, but we have had little success with them.

Verbena (*Verbena bonariense*)—Hardy in southern New Jersey and rivals *Buddleia*.

Many horticultural flowers have been bred as double flowers for their showy blooms, and the stamens and ovaries have been modified as petals. These plants are sterile and produce little or no nectar. So avoid double flowers of any species.

There are many other popular garden flowers that will occasionally attract butterflies. Swallowtails will nectar at both native and ornamental lilies. Marigolds are often attractive, particularly to Nymphalids. Pansies and Johnny-Jump-Ups are horticultural violets and are suitable larval hosts for some Fritillaries. Various herbs such as oregano and thyme are sometimes attractive.

Larval Hosts

Most species of milkweeds (*Asclepias*) are used by Monarchs, but Butterfly Weed is less attractive than either Swamp or Common Milkweed. Parsley (*Petroselinum hortense*) beds attract Black Swallowtails (we recommend a dozen or more plants at least).

Various legumes such as clover and alfalfa are attractive to sulphurs and to some of the spread-winged skippers. Asters are useful for Pearl Crescents, nettles for Red Admirals and anglewings, and Everlastings for American Ladies.

Grasses are important hosts for skippers and satyrs. The benefits of planting a Little Bluestem (*Andropogon scoparius*) meadow have been described by Sara Stein (1995). A second choice would be Purple Top (*Tridens flavus*). These can be mixed with tall wildflowers to create a prairielike habitat. Other grasses used include species of *Poa*, *Eragrostis*, and even Bermuda Grass (*Cynodon dactylon*). We allow a large part of our lawn to go wild, and mow it once in the autumn to keep it from undergoing succession.

Many species of butterflies use trees as their larval hosts. These include such common species as oaks, dogwoods, spicebush, cherry, and lilac. However, planting trees is a challenge since, unlike with flowers, it is more difficult to change your mind once they have taken root and grown. Most large trees are not useful as nectar sources but serve mainly as host plants. The drawback to trees is that sooner or later they provide shade, which is definitely undesirable for a butterfly garden. It is probably better to rely on trees that are available in the neighborhood. For example, for those species such as hairstreaks or duskywings that use oaks, it is not likely that one can create a population by planting a few trees. Thus if there are no oaks nearby, a few young oaks will not attract hairstreaks, while if there are a lot of oaks nearby there may already be a thriving population, and one can attract them simply by providing nectar sources such as Common Milkweed and Dogbane. Sassafras (*Sassafras albidum*) bushes are the host of Spicebush Swallowtail; Black Locust (*Robinia pseudoacacia*) hosts Silver-spotted Skippers; Wild Black Cherry (*Prunus serotina*) attracts Eastern Tiger Swallowtail and Striped Hairstreak; and last but not least, Hackberries (*Celtis occidentalis*) host emperors and the American Snout. Some of these trees will invade naturally in many rural areas.

There are a few exceptions to the no-tree rule. A hackberry tree (*Celtis*) in the corner of the yard may attract the three specialist species (Hackberry Emperor, Tawny Emperor, and Snout). Some trees are also excellent nectar sources. Our Rose-of-Sharon flowers often attract Tiger Swallowtails. The fluffy pink flowers of Mimosa trees are very attractive for swallowtails, particularly the Tiger Swallowtail. However, in central New Jersey these are subject to disease and may die after a few years. If you can get one to flourish it will be worthwhile. If the disease is present in your neighborhood, you will find out about it quickly enough.

Transplantation of Butterflies

After one has gone to the trouble of planting suitable host species, one may be tempted to import the appropriate butterflies by finding their eggs, caterpillars, or pupae and bringing them to one's garden. In general, this is a not a good idea. Most such transplantations usually will not take, but if they do they may result in changes in the local balance among species. So wait for the butterflies to visit and establish themselves naturally. This is also more engaging and challenging, and makes one's yard list more useful and important.

Wildflower and Prairie Mixes

In principle, this would be a good way to establish a butterfly meadow. We have reviewed the species composition of several mixes, and found that although they may contain many pretty flower species, they are *not* usually the right species for attracting butterflies. Before buying a mix, check the species composition to make sure that it contains Coneflowers, Black-eyed Susans, Red Clover, and/or Asters.

Sources of Information on Butterfly Gardening

North American Butterfly Association
909 Birch St.
Baraboo, WI 53913
(Its quarterly magazine *American Butterflies* and newsletters provide articles on butterfly gardening and on sources of plants.)

New Jersey Native Plant Society (for sources of native plants)
Cook College Office of Continuing Education
P.O. Box 231
New Brunswick, NJ 08903-0231

Cape May Bird Observatory (particularly for southern New Jersey)
New Jersey Audubon Society
707 E. Lake Drive, P.O. Box 3
Cape May Point, NJ 08212
Phone: 609-884-2736

Friends of the Rutgers Gardens
Cook College Office of Continuing Education
P.O. Box 231
New Brunswick, NJ 08903
Phone: 908-932-9271

Books and Leaflets

Many volumes on butterfly gardening have been published in the past decade, some of which are mainly photographic albums of butterflies in gardens, and others of which are mainly of regional interest. For additional information, see Jane Ruffin's review of butterfly gardening books (Ruffin 1993a). The following publications are particularly relevant to butterfly gardening in New Jersey.

Pat Sutton. 1990. How to create a butterfly and hummingbird garden. *New Jersey Audubon* 16(2): 1–4 (Summer 1990). Reprint available from Cape May Bird Observatory. This is a remarkably concise and useful introduction that includes lists of flowers and host plants suitable for New Jersey.

Xerces Society. 1990. *Butterfly Gardening.* Sierra Club Books, San Francisco. $20.00. This book is as much about butterflies and watching butterflies as it is about gardening and attracting butterflies. The photographs are spectacular, including unbelievable photos of butterflies in flight by Kazuo Unno. There are chapters on overall garden design and on choice of flowers. An appendix lists fifty-three New Jersey butterfly species and their host plants. The book also has a detailed listing of addresses for supply houses, nurseries, and societies. This is a must for the butterfly gardener anywhere.

Mathew Tekulsky. 1985. *The Butterfly Garden.* Harvard Common Press, Boston. $8.95. This volume provides details on the steps involved in developing a butterfly garden. It also has chapters on butterflies, life cycles, and rearing butterflies. Most valuable are suggestions on the kinds of observations one should make in a butterfly garden.

John V. Dennis and Mathew Tekulsky. 1991. *How to Attract Hummingbirds and Butterflies.* Ortho Books, Chevron Co., San Ramon, CA. $8.95. It is perhaps ironic that one of the largest manufacturers of agricultural chemicals should publish an attractive volume on butterfly gardens. It has much the same information as Tekulsky's book, but in a very different format. It provides illustrations and range maps for twenty-six butterfly species, which are not a good selection since many of the species commonly encountered in gardens are omitted.

Jane Ruffin. 1993. *Where Are the Butterfly Gardens?* Lepidopterists' Society, Manhattan Beach, CA. This slender volume provides information on the locations of public butterfly gardens that one can visit for ideas about garden design.

North American Butterfly Association. Leaflet on "Top Butterfly Nectar Flowers for New Jersey." A list available from NABA includes species *not* to plant in our area.

Recent Articles of Interest in *American Butterflies*

Swengel, A. Butterfly gardening with prairie plants. *Amer. Butterflies* 3(1): 12–19 (Spring 1995).

Pillar, R. 1995. The Gaea gardener: Black Cohosh. *Amer. Butterflies* 3(1): 29–30 (Spring 1995).

Stein, S. 1995. The Little Bluestem meadow: Plant your field of dreams and the butterflies will come. *Amer. Butterflies* 3(2): 24–28 (Summer 1995).

Stein, S. 1995. The Little Bluestem meadow: How to restore, plant and manage a backyard meadow. *Amer. Butterflies* 3(3): 24–38 (Fall 1995).

Meyers, E. 1995. The Gaea gardener: Wild Cherries. *Amer. Butterflies* 3(2): 29–30 (Summer 1995).

Edinger, G. 1995. Native *Eupatoriums* for the butterfly garden. *Amer. Butterflies* 3(4): 24–29 (Winter 1995).

Condon, M. A. 1995. The Gaea gardener: False Nettle. *Amer. Butterflies* 3(4): 30 (Winter 1995).

CHAPTER 10

Butterfly Conservation in New Jersey

The butterfly fauna of any region is dynamic, undergoing increases and decreases depending on climatic conditions, habitat quality, and human interventions. Some of the changes are merely fluctuations or cycles that occur over periods of a few years, but others are long-term trends. The documentation of such trends is a major emphasis of this book, and is discussed for each species. In general, more species are declining than are increasing, and this is hardly surprising in view of the loss of natural habitat around urban population centers and the historic use of pesticides. Nonetheless, the situation is generally quite hopeful. Many butterfly species are not fussy and will thrive in habitats that humans manage for their mutual enjoyment and benefit, and species that were not completely eliminated by pesticides are capable of recovering.

In Britain and the United States, the disappearance of certain Blue butterflies was noted (Pyle 1995). The Royal Entomological Society formed a Committee for Protection of British Lepidoptera as early as 1925, although Pyle notes this focused attention more on discouraging the overexploitation of certain showy species, rather than on the overall loss of habitat. Yet even in the mid-1960s, during a climate of environmental concern, papers on butterfly conservation were not considered acceptable for publication, and only after 1965 (Pyle 1967) came a spate of publications on the conservation of butterflies and their habitats.

Of greatest concern in conservation are the species that are endemic to a region, that is, they occur only in that region and nowhere else and are host specific and/or habitat specific. Endemism reaches its highest levels on islands and mountains. Although no species of butterflies are endemic to New Jersey, Schweitzer (1987) found six endemic moths. No other northeastern state had more than one endemic species. Morever, he found that several other rare moths occur mainly in New Jersey.

The next element of concern are those species that are habitat specific. Due to landscape changes, many butterfly populations become fragmented, thriving only in parks or reserves where habitat can be protected and managed. Pollard and Yates (1993) distinguish between species that can survive in the mosaic (they used the term "matrix") of fields, hedges, and roadside vegetation, and therefore range widely, and "island" species that are restricted to a local biotope such as a fen or limestone outcropping. Mitchell's Satyr is a prime example of such a species. It has disappeared from New Jersey and Ohio, and is endangered elsewhere (North Carolina, Michigan, Indiana).

Species that are of limited conservation concern are those whose occurrence in New Jersey has always been marginal or uncertain. The Green Comma, for example, is a northern forest species which may historically never have been a regular New Jersey resident. Although it would be a welcome addition to our fauna if it colonized or recolonized the forests of northwestern New Jersey, a management program to protect it alone would not be warranted.

The key to protecting any organism is to secure and protect its habitat, and to manage it in a way that is favorable to the species' needs. Even fifty years ago, Comstock (1940) noted that a significant loss of important butterfly collecting sites and habitats had occurred in the period from 1910 to 1940, and he could hardly have imagined the changes the next 50 years have brought to New Jersey's landscape. But it is only recently that people have begun to think of butterflies (or indeed any invertebrates) as something to conserve. Butterfly conservation has fared better than most invertebrate protection efforts because of their intrinsic and wide-ranging aesthetic appeal. Moreover, recent interest in preserving bio-diversity (Wilson 1988) has increased interest in understanding butterfly faunas as well.

Agriculture has greatly altered the landscape of southern New Jersey, while urbanization would render the northeastern part of the state largely unrecogniz-able to a nineteenth-century butterfly. Different agricultural practices—cropping or grazing—and different rotations of fallow land may favor one butterfly species at the expense of another (Pollard and Yates 1993). As agricultural land is aban-doned, some of it is developed for housing, and some undergoes succession and eventually becomes forest. Some butterflies can make use of a habitat over a long period of succession from grassland to forest, whereas others are typical of only one successional stage and will disappear when forest reclaims an open landscape.

The history of the landscape of the northeastern United States has involved a changing patchwork of forests, of clearing and reforestation (Russell 1981a,b). If it weren't for urbanization and paving, this cycle might continue unabated for centuries; but with a burgeoning population, and a population shifting from cit-ies to countryside, there is an inevitable loss of area that can provide suitable habitats for butterflies.

Protection of habitat is critical, but so is insect diversity. The loss of insects during periods of heavy pesticide use in the past 50 years must not be underesti-mated. Insecticide spraying against mosquitoes and Gypsy Moths has probably eliminated a number of butterfly species, and greatly reduced the populations of others.

Both federal and state governments have mechanisms for listing butterflies as "threatened" or "endangered" as well as "vulnerable" or "of special concern." Some species may soon become threatened or endangered if steps are not taken to stop their decline.

Conservation Status Terminology (used by both federal and state agencies)

Threatened—a species that has declined and become so localized that it is likely to become endangered if there is no protection or other change in status.

Endangered—a rare and local species or population that is likely to disappear in the foreseeable future without some intervention.

Extirpated (synonymous with locally extinct or historic)—a species that for-merly occurred in New Jersey but no longer occurs here, though it survives elsewhere.

Extinct—a species that no longer survives anywhere. In North America, only one species, the Xerces Blue, is known to merit this dubious distinction, although others, such as the Uncomphagre Fritillary and perhaps Mitchell's Satyr, may be approaching that status.

Readers should be aware that other definitions (particularly for the "threatened" status) have been proposed by the International Union for the Conservation of Nature.

"Island" species, those confined to restricted habitats, are likely to become *vulnerable* as their special habitat islands are swallowed in a sea of suburban development, agriculture, or even mature forest. Among the species that have disappeared from New Jersey are several of these species, for example, the Mitchell's Satyr and the Appalachian Grizzled Skipper. The Regal Fritillary, with its dependence on prairie grasslands, probably became an island species in the northeastern United States as remnant grassland patches shrank and then disappeared.

The two New Jersey butterflies considered endangered by federal agencies are Mitchell's Satyr (*Neonympha m. mitchelli*) and the Arogos Skipper (*Atrytone a. arogos*). The Satyr was last recorded in 1988; the Skipper was not recorded between 1974 and 1994, and was presumed to be extirpated but was "rediscovered" in 1995. In New Jersey, the determination of the status and conservation of butterflies is the responsibility of the Endangered and Nongame Species Program of the New Jersey Department of Environmental Protection. The program is currently developing a protocol specifically designed to deal with butterflies in our changing state, and it operates with the Endangered and Nongame Species Advisory Committee to consider the plight of dwindling populations of all wildlife. As of February 1995 the extirpated Mitchell's Satyr was the only butterfly officially listed as endangered by the state of New Jersey.

A national network called the Natural Heritage Program has been established to identify plant or animal species of special concern and locate their habitats. In New Jersey this is also based in the NJDEP. Species are listed on a Global (G), State (S), and Regional (R) basis, and their status is designated by numbers from 1, meaning in critical difficulty, to 5, meaning secure (see table 15). This system is primarily an inventory data base and does not have regulatory impact. The Natural Heritage Program can rank a species as "critical" more easily than the species can be formally listed as "endangered."

Even if a species occurs on a protected area or nature reserve its survival cannot be guaranteed. Appropriate long-term management of habitat may be required to prevent the incursion of undesirable species or succession, from changing a habitat beyond the butterfly's range of tolerance. In the future, new management of parks may dictate other uses for a currently protected habitat. Old fields may be mowed for picnic grounds or ball fields, for example. Such "multiple use" philosophy sometimes results in no use at all for butterflies and natural ecosystems. Moreover, in New Jersey, the State House Commission has the authority to exchange some public land for other land, without much public comment or oversight. Pesticide use can jeopardize butterflies even in protected areas. If the park management chooses to spray to control some insect pest, it may inadvertently eliminate nontarget species as well. Finally, a *relict* population thriving on a reserve may be eliminated by chance events such as a hurricane or an unusually cold winter.

Considering what can happen to a localized butterfly population, we identify several additional species that should be considered for threatened or endangered status in New Jersey (table 16). Loss of habitat is the main factor contributing to

Table 15. Natural Heritage Program Rankings of Conservation Status

1: ENDANGERED; known from one or two stations with very few individuals. Habitat limited.

2: THREATENED; known from 2–5 locations, few remaining individuals. Habitat limited. At risk of becoming endangered.

3: INSECURE; known from 6–20 locations, limited habitat, or other risk factor. At risk of becoming threatened.

4: APPARENTLY SECURE; little likelihood of becoming threatened in the foreseeable future.

5: SECURE.

H: Historically recorded but not encountered in past decade. However, possibility of persistence exists if habitat not fully surveyed. If rediscovered, it would most likely become status 1.

X: EXTIRPATED; surveys of suitable remaining habitat support absence.

U: UNKNOWN; status unknown, needs more information. May also be designated by question mark.

Table 16. Conservation Status of Selected New Jersey Butterfly Species[a]

Species	Current understanding	Our status recommendation	Natural Heritage Rankings		NYC, region[f]
			Global	State	
Giant Swallowtail	Probably extirpated as a breeder	survey	G5	S1-2	R1
Checkered White	Few known colonies, erratic	vulnerable	G5	SH[b]	R1/R2
West Virginia White	Probably extirpated	survey	G4	S1-3[h]	R1
Falcate Orange Tip	Locally abundant				R3
Little Yellow	Erractic, nonresident				R2
Bronze Copper	Declining, very few known colonies	THREATENED	G5	S1?	RH
Bog Copper	Locally abundant, limited habitat	survey			R2
Acadian Hairstreak	Few known colonies	survey	G5	S3[c]	
Edward's Hairstreak	Local, inadequate information	survey/monitor	G4	S2-4	
Hickory Hairstreak	Local, inadequate information	survey/monitor	G4?	SU	
Southern/Northern Hairstreak	Universally scarce, inadequately known	survey			
Frosted Elfin	Very few known colonies	THREATENED	G4	SU	R2/R3
Hoary Elfin	Few known colonies	survey			RH
Henry's Elfin	Locally common	monitor	G5	S3-4	R1
Hessel's Hairstreak	Locally uncommon	survey	G3-4	S3-4	R1
Appalachian Azure	Declining, poorly known	survey	G4	SU	R3
Northern Metalmark	Dwindling due to habitat succession	ENDANGERED	G3-4	S2-3	R1/R2
Regal Fritillary	EXTIRPATED	vigilance	G3[i]	SX	R1[i]
Silver-bordered Fritillary	Highly local, declining	survey/monitor	G5	S2-3	R1
Silvery Checkerspot	Possibly extirpated	survey	G5	SH	R2/R3
Harris' Checkerspot	Highly local, few populations	survey/monitor	G4	S3?	R2/R3
Tawny Crescent	EXTIRPATED if ever resident	vigilance	G3-4[i]	SX	
Gray Comma	No recent records	survey	G5	SU[h]	
Hackberry Emperor	Local, usually uncommon				R3/R4
Tawny Emperor	Local, usually uncommon				R3-4
Northern Pearly Eye	Locally uncommon	monitor	G5	S3-4	
Eyed Brown	Inadequate information	monitor	G5	S1-3[d]	
Mitchell's Satyr	Listed as ENDANGERED, but EXTIRPATED	survey	G2	SH	RX
Georgia [Lakehurst] Satyr	Highly local in bogs	monitor	G5	S3	
Gold-banded Skipper	Probably never resident	vigilance	G4	SH	
Confused Cloudywing	Questionable resident	vigilance	G4	SU	
Mottled Duskywing	Possibly extirpated or very local		G4	SH	RH
Columbine Duskywing	No recent records	vigilance	G4	SU	R1
Persius Duskywing	Possibly extirpated	vigilance	G4	SH	RH
Appalachian Grizzled Skipper	Probably extirpated	vigilance	G2[i]	SH	RH
Hayhurst's Scallopwing	Highly local and uncommon	monitor	G5	S3-4	
Arctic Skipper	Marginal, known from one locality	monitor	G5	S1	
Leonard's Skipper	Few known populations, declining	vulnerable/survey	G4	S2-3	R2

110

Table 16. (*continued*)

Species	Current understanding	Our status recommendation	Natural Heritage Rankings Global	State	NYC, region[f]
Dotted Skipper	Small numbers at scattered sites	survey	G4	S1-2	RH
Arogos Skipper	ENDANGERED, recently rediscovered	survey/monitor	G4	SH[g]	RH
Long Dash	Highly local	survey/monitor	G5	S3?	
Rare Skipper	Locally common, few localities	monitor	G2-3[i]	S2	
Aaron's Skipper	Locally common	monitor	G4	S3-4[e]	
Two-spotted Skipper	Few known populations, declining	survey	G4	S3-4	RH
Pepper and Salt Skipper	Few known colonies	monitor	G5	S2-3	
Common Roadside Skipper	Very few recent sightings	vigilance	G5	S3-4	RH
Dion Skipper	Widespread, uncommon				R1/R2
Dusted Skipper	Inadequate information, uncommon, local				R3/R4

a. These are species for which there is a section on *Conservation Status* in the species accounts.
b. The Checkered White periodically appears at various localities and is not extirpated.
c. There are no known secure populations of Acadian Hairstreak.
d. Due to its similarity to the more numerous Appalachian Brown, the status of the Eyed Brown should be considered uncertain. It may be widespread in northern New Jersey.
e. Aaron's Skipper is highly local, but sometimes abundant.
f. New York City Regional data from New York Butterfly Club (1992).
g. Would be listed as S1 if it is found to be resident rather than vagrant.
h. More likely should be SH.
i. Under consideration for federal listing as THREATENED if more information becomes available.
j. If lumped with Grizzled Skipper, status would be G3.

the decline of these species, but as species become more rare, they become more attractive to collectors, particularly those who engage in the sale or trade of rare species. Such nonscientific collecting poses a threat of eliminating local populations of threatened or endangered species. These species require special attention, and butterfly watchers can make a unique contribution to their conservation by documenting their occurrence, phenology, and habitat use. Some other species, such as the Checkered White, have declined but are not readily protected or managed, and are therefore not on our list; others such as the Baltimore Checkerspot are species of special concern, but are not yet threatened. For some species, like the Acadian Hairstreak and Appalachian Azure, the status is currently too poorly known. For such species we recommend a formal survey of likely habitats in different parts of the state to ascertain whether the species is indeed resident. For many other species we recommend a formal monitoring program, conducted at the appropriate time(s) and place(s) each year, to ascertain if a population is declining to a point where it should be listed as threatened.

There are a number of species whose status in New Jersey is a mystery, such as the Columbine and Persius Duskywings. Others have New Jersey at the extreme margin of their range, such as the Gray Comma, or outside their range, such as the Green Comma and Gold-banded Skipper. The New York City Area checklist (Cech 1993) lists twelve extirpated species out of ninety-nine surviving, regularly occurring species (11%). The figure for Staten Island is about 13% extirpated, although Shapiro and Shapiro (1973) made dire predictions of 80% extirpation by the twenty-first century. For New Jersey, we estimate at least eight extirpated species and 109 regular species (7% extirpation). The species that have probably disappeared from New Jersey but were probably resident in the past include the Giant Swallowtail, West Virginia White, Great Purple Hairstreak, Regal Fritillary, Mitchell's Satyr, Mottled and Persius Duskywings, and Appalachian Grizzled Skipper. Species such as the Zebra Swallowtail, Mustard White, Tawny Crescent, and Green Comma probably never were residents in modern times (i.e., in the past two hundred years).

Most butterflies have a more or less continuous distribution, but some have a disjunct distribution, that is, parts of their range are isolated from other parts. Such distributions suggest that the species is already subject to habitat fragmentation, which may be a characteristic of species that are in trouble, such as Mitchell's Satyr and Arogos Skipper.

The Natural Heritage Program has identified additional species that need attention in New Jersey (table 16). These species should be searched for in appropriate habitats, and their occurrence should be documented. Once they are found, it is important to determine whether their occurrence is sporadic or consistent and what nectar sources and host species are being used in New Jersey so that they can be protected. Surprisingly, the actual host species used by a number of New Jersey butterflies are not known (see table 10). It is also important to know how many populations or colonies of local species there are in New Jersey. A species with a large population in only one locality may be more vulnerable than a species with multiple small populations.

Once the status and distribution of a species have been determined, it is possible to develop a management strategy aimed at protecting the species' habitat. Determination of land ownership may be followed by acquisition as public land, but protection of private lands is also desirable. Incentives may be provided to landowners to keep appropriate habitats secure from farming or development, and to maintain habitat at a suitable successional stage.

Despite the dramatic changes in New Jersey's landscape and the distressing number of declining species, there are still grounds for optimism. Conservation methods have been effective in setting aside and protecting habitats. Coupled with scientifically based management, even a fragmented landscape can contribute to biodiversity and perpetuate the enjoyment of butterflies. Recent books on butterfly conservation include Pollard and Yates (1993) on the methods and applications of monitoring, and Pullin (1995) on the role of biology and ecology in protecting rare butterflies.

Butterfly conservation is catching on in other parts of the world as well. Largely through the efforts of groups such as the Xerces Society, efforts are underway to conserve butterflies in tropical regions threatened by human population growth and habitat exploitation. These include butterfly farming ventures and the purchase of critical habitat. Purchase may offer the only hope for preserving the fir forests of the Monarch's Mexican wintering areas (Aridjis and Brower 1996), which are threatened by logging.

SECTION III

New Jersey's Butterfly Fauna

Introduction: Explanation of the Species Accounts

The species list that follows is based on many publications, from Smith (1890) to the present, as well as many reports of specimens, photographs, and sight records provided by many people we have contacted. New information has been extracted from other sources, including *Mulberry Wing* (publication of the New York Butterfly Club), *News of the Lepidopterists' Society*, and a variety of scientific journals as well as personal records provided by a number of regional contributors.

A species list should include species to look for or species to validate, so we have included hypothetical species as well as species never recorded in New Jersey but recorded in adjacent states in square brackets. Some of these are likely to be found in New Jersey in the future, and some may never be found here.

Our list places a heavy emphasis on understanding the historical changes in status by contrasting the reports of current observers with the lists published twenty, fifty, and one hundred years ago. We think this historical documentation is unique and is a valuable asset in making decisions about butterfly conservation. It is also an important part of understanding the changes in New Jersey's natural world, which is particularly critical today as the nation recognizes the importance of preserving biodiversity across all groups of organisms.

State butterfly books traditionally emphasize county records, and we have tried to indicate county occurrences, particularly for rare species. However, county borders are often artificial (some do follow river valleys), so it is not crucial to attribute a record to a particular county. Furthermore it is often difficult to assign a record to a county. Many of the old specimen labels contain only a town, without indication of whether the specimen was collected in the town itself or a few miles away. Smith (1910) refers to the "Newark" collectors, for example, without knowing how far afield they ranged.

For towns located on a county line, it is unsafe (and probably unimportant) to assign the specimen to one county or the other. For example, specimens labeled "Westville" could have been obtained on the Camden or Gloucester side of the border. Fortunately, the Lecks, for example, can tell us that their observations and specimens from Kendall Park were all in Middlesex County, even though the village lies on the Somerset County line. But Mr. Wormsbacher, long deceased, can no longer tell us whether his Palamedes Swallowtail was taken in Bergen or in Hudson County (it has been published both ways).

Even today, many Fourth of July Count circles (including most of those in New

Table 17. The Composition of New Jersey's Butterfly Fauna

	Total	Definitely resident	Possibly resident	Regular immigrant	Uncertain	Vagrant accidental	Former resident
Swallowtails	7	4				1	2
Whites and sulphurs	12	5		3		3	1
Harvester	1	1					
Coppers, Blues, Hairstreaks	28	24	1		1	1	1
Metalmarks	1	1					
Snout	1	1					
Nymphalids, Angelwings, Emperors	29	18	1	3		3	4
Satyrids	9	6	1			1	1
Monarch	1	1					
Spread-winged Skippers	19	11	2	1		3	3
Grass Skippers	37	27	3	3		4	
Total	145	99	8	10	1	16	11

Jersey) cover more than one county, so the summary count list does not provide county occurrence data.

In this book we trace history back only about 150 years, so the term "never resident" can be assumed to refer only to the past 150 years. Ranges and status may have been much different two centuries ago, and they certainly were different before European settlement.

As we currently understand it, New Jersey's butterfly fauna, including extirpated species and accidentals but not hypotheticals, totals about 145 species broken down as shown in table 17. The information covers the period through 1995. Of these, about 50–60 occur in any part of the state during the summer, and with diligent searching throughout the state, it should be possible to find about 80 species in a season afield, with 100 as a probable maximum. About 100 species are recorded annually by the New York City Butterfly Club within 50 miles of the New York City area.

The information provided for each species varies with its status. For wide-spread common species, less attention is paid to distributional details, while rare, local, or vagrant species receive a disproportionate amount of attention. Conversely, there is usually more biological information regarding common species, while many of the rare species have not been extensively studied anywhere.

The species accounts provide a brief introduction to interesting aspects of the species, indicate where and when they are likely to be found, and identify gaps in our knowledge that the observer of butterflies, whether professional or amateur, may be able to fill. Even species that are listed as widespread and common may be absent from the extreme habitats of New Jersey such as salt marshes, sandy beaches, deep forests, or urban areas. Species listed as *immigrants* are those that do not or cannot overwinter in New Jersey but appear, either annually or at irregular intervals, as invaders from the south. *Irruptive* species are those immigrants which are not annual visitors, but which occasionally become quite common in the state.

Within its known range, a butterfly may be confined to highly localized habitats where its preferred host species are found. In addition, habitat fragmentation has proceeded rapidly, and changes in land use have allowed formerly productive butterfly habitats to succeed into forest or to vanish into developments. Thus a butterfly may occur in only a small portion of what is listed as its range.

This book should both enhance one's understanding of the species one sees often and focus attention on those seen rarely. It is not an identification book per se, but will help with identifications by indicating which species are likely to occur and which are not. It is intended to be used in conjunction with Glassberg's *Butterflies through Binoculars*, Opler's *Field Guide to Eastern Butterflies*, and Pyle's *The Audubon Society Field Guide to North American Butterflies*.

Organization of the Species Accounts

The *header line* of each species account includes the following:

English or Common Name [Alternative names], *Scientific name* (Authority, year) (by whom and when the species was described).

[Square brackets] around the header line indicate that there are no documented New Jersey records for the species, but it is included because of its occurrence nearby in adjacent states or its hypothetical status.

The English name (also called Common Name or Colloquial Name) is bold-faced; the names we use conform, in almost all cases, to those recently selected by the Standing Committee on English Names of the North American Butterfly Association (NABA 1995). For the most part, these names are the same as those used by Opler (1992). Where an alternative English name has been widely used, it is given in square brackets.

The scientific names likewise reflect the NABA (1995) checklist and are generally those used by Opler and Krizek (1984), Opler (1992), and Glassberg (1993b), but some adjustments have been made to reflect new understandings of relationships, particularly generic lumping.

In cases where the scientific name has recently changed, the usual or former name is given beneath the header line.

Range. The overall range given is based on Opler and Krizek (1984) and Scott (1986), and Opler's *County Atlas* (1983, 1995). The published maps in Opler and Krizek (1984) tend to overstate the distribution in New Jersey, since complete shading is provided for some species that are highly local.

We have based the distribution in New Jersey on a great many published and unpublished sources as well as recent field work. Depending on the species, the distribution is mentioned by region (figs. 8, 9) or Ecological Zone (fig. 10). Specific localities are not provided for most widespread species or for very rare resident species. Shapiro (1966) cautioned that providing specific location information might jeopardize a population's survival by attracting collectors, but it might also discourage observers from finding new populations or colonies of a species.

For both distributional and current status we have relied on our own observations and on the people listed below. Personal records are listed by (name) or by (date, name). When someone reports the records of others that could not be verified with the original person, they are reported as (name, pers. comm.).

(Cech): Rick Cech
(Darrow): Harry Darrow
(Dowdell): Jim Dowdell
(Glassberg): Jeff Glassberg
(Kudzma): Linas Kudzma
(Lawrenson): John Lawrenson
(Lecks): Mary and Charles Leck
(LeMarchant): Michelle LeMarchant
(Murrays): Patti and Bert Murray
(Pavulaan): Harry Pavulaan

(Schweitzer): Dale Schweitzer
(Springer): James Springer
(Sutton): Pat and Clay Sutton
(Tudor): Guy Tudor
(Walter): Steve Walter
(Wagerik): Nick Wagerik
(Wanders): Sharon and Wade Wander
(Williams): Paula and Chris Williams
(Wright): David Wright
(Yrizarry): John and Mary Yrizarry

Other Sources

(Mulberry Wing): Newsletter of the New York City Butterfly Club.

(Opler's Atlas): Paul Opler's *County Atlas*, initially dated 1983 and republished in 1995 with records valid through 1987 (Opler, pers. comm).

(Rutgers Collection): Entomology Museum of Cook College, Rutgers University, contains mainly specimens from Comstock's collection.

(4JC): Annual reports of the Fourth of July Butterfly Counts published by the Xerces Society and, since 1993, by the NABA.

Current Status—summarizes the distribution and status in New Jersey based on information from a wide variety of sources. The indications of frequency of occurrence and relative abundance are influenced by seasonality which is described under *Phenology*. A species can occur throughout New Jersey yet be highly localized (i.e. a few colonies in the northern, central and southern parts of the State). In some cases the highest number recorded on a New Jersey 4JC is given (see table 18).

Historical Status—compares the current status with information from published sources that are detailed in table 19. We make comparisons between Current Status (post-1985) and previous decades. Under this section are direct quotes or comments from the eight historical sources that have been abstracted for each New Jersey species. Additional information from other sources is included where relevant.

Wherever possible, direct quotations are given from the references used, since for the most part these are no longer readily available. In some cases these are followed by our explanation or comment in {curly brackets}. No orthographic or spelling changes have been made in direct quotes. Some spellings such as Mt. Holly and Ft. Lee as used by Smith are changed to Mount Holly and Fort Lee to conform with current usage.

Smith (1890–1910) emphasized the relative paucity of information regarding New Jersey's insect fauna, particularly for the northwestern part of the state, which was not readily accessible to collectors living in New York or Philadelphia. He relied heavily on information provided by M. S. Crane of Caldwell and E. M. Aaron of Philadelphia, as well as published accounts by Strecker, Edwards, and Scudder. Smith also cited a list, provided by the Newark Entomological Society, of insects collected in the vicinity of Newark. Since the actual localities were not given and their proximity to Newark is therefore uncertain, these records are mentioned as "Newark." Smith often uses the term "throughout" to refer to butterflies that had been collected both in northern or southern New Jersey, without providing a picture of status in intervening areas or indicating the regularity of occurrence.

Comstock (1940) updated Smith's lists. He also used the term "throughout" to refer to a species recorded from both northern and southern New Jersey, even if it was highly local and rare. He used the term "Northern District" to refer to the entire area northwest of the Fall Line. This district includes the Piedmont, the Highlands (which he called the Crystalline Highlands), the Appalachian Valley, and the Kittatiny Range. He also divided the Coastal Plain into a Middle District (Delaware Valley), Pine Barrens, Coastal District, and Cape May Peninsula, but he referred to these subdivisions very little.

Delaware Valley (1966) status is based on the paper by Shapiro (1966) covering a circle with a 35-mile radius centered at Philadelphia's City Hall, including all of Camden and Gloucester, nearly all of Salem, half of Burlington, and extreme western Atlantic and northern Cumberland Counties. Shapiro used the term "general," which can be considered a synonym for "widespread."

Table 18. Bibliographic Sources for Historical Status Information for the Species Accounts

Smith (1890, 1900, 1910). The Lepidoptera sections of three major reports on the insects of New Jersey.

  Smith (1890). *Catalogue of Insects Found in New Jersey.* Geological Survey of New Jersey, Trenton. Pages 271–283.

  Smith (1900). *Insects of New Jersey.* Twenty-seventh Annual Report of the State Board of Agriculture for 1899. MacCrellish and Quigley, Trenton. Pages 369–383.

  Smith (1910). *A Report of the Insects of New Jersey.* Annual Report of the New Jersey State Museum, 1909. Pages 407–424. MacCrellish and Quigley, Trenton.

Comstock (1940). Comstock, W. P. Butterflies of New Jersey. *Journal New York Entomol. Soc.* 48: 47–84.

Shapiro (1966). Shapiro, A. M. *Butterflies of the Delaware Valley.* Special Publ. of American Entomolgical Society.

Shapiro and Shapiro (1973). Shapiro, A. M., and A. R. Shapiro. The ecological associations of the butterflies of Staten Island (Richmond County, New York). *J. Research Lepid.* 12:65–126.

New York City Area (1993). Cech, R., ed. *A Distributional Checklist of the Butterflies and Skippers of the New York City Area (50-mile Radius) and Long Island.* New York City Butterfly Club, New York. 28 pages.

Cape May (1993). Wright, D., and P. Sutton, *Checklist of Butterflies of Cape May County, NJ.* Cape May Bird Observatory, Cape May Pt., New Jersey. 4 pages.

New Jersey's Butterfly Fauna

117

Staten Island (1973) status is based on the paper by Shapiro and Shapiro (1973). Staten Island is geologically and ecologically close to New Jersey and we follow Smith (1890, 1900, 1910) in considering Staten Island as part of New Jersey's faunal region. It shares features with the Pine Barrens of New Jersey and Long Island and is at the interface of the northern and southern faunas. Much of north-central Staten Island is underlain by serpentine bedrock that outcrops on hills and ridges. This important habitat is virtually nonexistent in New Jersey. We also examined two papers by Davis (1893, 1910) that list the butterflies of Staten Island, and these are quoted when not specifically referenced by Shapiro and Shapiro (1973). Although the Davis (1910) paper appears in an issue dated 1909, it includes a number of records from 1910, which must reflect its true publication date.

New York City Area (1993) status is based on the pamphlet edited by Rich Cech (1993); it covers the status of butterflies within 50 miles of lower Manhattan based on records compiled by the New York City Butterfly Club as well as historical information.

Cape May (1993) status is based on the revised county checklist published by the Cape May Bird Observatory (Wright and Sutton 1993). In simple checklist form, it lists the species that have been recorded or should be looked for in Cape May County, with a brief indication of their status, seasonality, and whether they still occur in the county.

Conservation Status—used only for those species that we consider vulnerable, threatened or endangered, or which have been ranked by the Natural Heritage Program (see chapter 10). It provides a brief discussion plus recommendations for obtaining better information. If this section is absent, one should not assume that the species is secure in the state.

Habitat. Since butterflies in general are species of open country, it is not always easy to ascribe a specific habitat to a species. Some New Jersey butterflies are restricted to specific habitats (e.g., salt marshes, bogs, or fens, and these are indicated in more detail). We have coined the term "cuts" to refer to linear openings: powerlines, railroad lines, and dirt roads through woodlands.

Phenology. We list the number of broods and the general flight period(s), usually for Central New Jersey, unless otherwise specified. Butterflies generally emerge about two weeks earlier in the South, about two weeks later in the North-west, with some variation from year to year.

We found the data for most of New Jersey too sparse and variable to provide phenology graphs. For northern New Jersey, refer to Cech (1993) and Glassberg (1993b). Thus we give only a general indication of phenology, embracing the main temporal range of occurrence, and break down some accounts to give data for both the northern area (based on Cech 1993) and southern area (based on Shapiro 1966). In some cases, extreme dates are reported; however, extreme dates reported in the literature often underestimate late records since, as Comstock (1940) noted, collectors usually discarded worn specimens. In recent years many of the late record dates have been substantially surpassed. In this section the term "North" refers to northern New Jersey and "South" to southern New Jersey (fig. 8b).

Caterpillar Foodplants. This section is much more complicated than one might infer from its simple designation in most popular texts. A true larval host is one on which the female lays eggs and the larvae can develop and mature. Discrepancies are likely to arise at the edges of a range or during range expansion of either the insect or the plant. Some females are observed to lay on plants on which caterpillars can't mature (Dethier 1941). Sometimes these are in the same family as suitable hosts (Straatman 1962; Courant et al. 1994). In many cases butterflies can be raised in the laboratory on plants they do not normally use in nature. Many published host plant records fail to meet these criteria and some simply represent misidentifications. We have tried to indicate these. Many plants that are used only in the southern or western United States and do not occur in New Jersey are reported by Opler and Krizek (1984) and/or Scott (1986), but are not mentioned here.

The English names of plants follow Anderson's (1983) New Jersey checklist. Not all of the English names are in widespread use, and some of the scientific names used there are no longer current. Most notably, the Little Bluegrass widely referred to as *Andropogon scoparius* has been shifted more recently to the genus *Schizachryium*. With some trepidation we continue to refer to it as *Andropogon* in this volume.

Some of the largest plant families, including those extensively used by butterflies, have both a traditional and a "new" scientific name now adopted by most botanists. These names are as follows:

	New Name	Traditional Name
Grass family	Poaceae	Graminae
Composite family	Asteraceae	Compositae
Mustard family	Brassicaceae	Cruciferae
Mint family	Lamiaceae	Labiatae
Carrot family	Apiaceae	Umbelliferae

Overwintering Stage. The life stage in which the species overwinters is based mainly on information provided by Comstock (1940) and Opler and Krizek (1984). Note that there are many species for which this information is lacking in New Jersey, indicating either that the stage is unknown or that it is not likely to overwinter in New Jersey.

Comments. In this section we provide a variety of additional information on taxonomy, identification, temporal population trends, behavior, reproductive biology, and conservation. Many species have been extensively studied and only a few interesting studies are mentioned, while other species have received virtually no attention at all. In some cases, noteworthy records are provided for local or rare species. Several books (Opler and Krizek 1984, Iftner et al. 1992) list the nectar sources used by adult butterflies. We have mentioned some favored nectar sources under *Habitat* or *Comments* for a few species, but did not attempt a comprehensive list. Often it is not possible on casual observation to tell when a butterfly has actually consumed nectar or is merely testing a flower.

Where to Find It. This section is used only for regular but local residents. It is not included for vagrant species, for widespread common species, or for rare species. This includes localities in adjacent states for species that are not regular in New Jersey.

Papilionidae, Swallowtails

This worldwide family of about 600 species contains the largest and some of the most dramatic and common butterflies as well as some of the world's most endangered species. Swallowtails reach their maximum diversity in northern South America, where over seventy species occur. By contrast, only thirty species occur in North America, with only sixteen species in the northern parts (Slansky 1972). Of the thirty species known in North America, seven have been recorded in New Jersey, of which three (Eastern Tiger, Black, and Spicebush) are common and widespread throughout the state and are familiar visitors to gardens and parks. The evolutionary relationships among the different subgroups of Swallowtails remains an area of active study, with new approaches resulting in some modifications of the taxonomy (Miller 1987; Tyler et al. 1994). Tyler et al. (1994) have published an extensive monograph on American Swallowtails, covering taxonomy, evolution, ecology, behavior, and physiology as well as cultural and conservation issues.

All New Jersey Swallowtails are in the subfamily Papilioninae. The subfamily has further been divided into tribes, with the Pipevine Swallowtail (*Battus*) in the Troidini, which includes the birdwings; the Zebra Swallowtail (*Eurytides*) in the Kite Swallowtail tribe Graphiini; and all other New Jersey swallowtails in the tribe Papilionini.

Various generic names have been used in the past, and we follow Opler and Krizek (1984) in including species sometimes assigned to *Pterourus* within *Papilio*. Since all Swallowtails described by Linnaeus and his contemporaries were originally placed in the genus *Papilio*, those remaining in the genus include the authority name without parentheses.

Swallowtails lay smooth spherical eggs, and some of its caterpillars resemble bird droppings. Our species spend the winter in the chrysalid stage.

Pipevine Swallowtail, *Battus philenor* (Linnaeus, 1771) Plate 1a

Range: Massachusetts to Florida and Texas including parts of New Jersey. Opler's Atlas shows no records from Coastal Plain counties other than Cape May. The subspecies *philenor* occurs in New Jersey.

Current Status: Highly localized breeder. Can be common in appropriate localities (e.g., Bergen County). Sporadic elsewhere. Common on the Palisades where its host plant *Aristolochia* covers steep hillsides. Recent sightings in Stokes Forest (1994). Essentially absent from the Coastal Plain. Rare in central and most of southern New Jersey, with several 1995-96 sightings in Cape May and Cumberland counties (C. & P. Sutton, Dowdell). Codella (1986) did not record it during his studies in the Great Swamp, nor have we found it in Somerset. Recorded from Iselin (1986) and Sandy Hook (1989). Uncommon in Delmarva (Woodbury 1994). Today it is only common along the Palisades and at Greenbrook Sanctuary.

Historical Status: For the past century this species has been described as local or locally common. However, it has apparently declined since it is known from fewer localities, despite the increased number of observers. Considered occasionally common near Philadelphia (Skinner and Aaron 1889; Shapiro 1966).

Smith (1890–1910): "Throughout," uncommon to occasionally common.

Comstock (1940): "Throughout. . . . Sometimes common locally." Eight localities from Newton to Fort Lee, plus Five Mile Beach.

Delaware Valley (1966): "Common . . . in the coastal plain," recorded generally from Camden and Burlington Counties southward, including Pine Barrens.

Staten Island (1973): "Rare immigrant. Perhaps colonizing the Island at times though rarely, if ever overwintering." "There are no native host plants."

New York City Area (1993): "Irregular southern immigrant; also extremely local breeder along the New Jersey palisades and in botanical gardens." Usually rare to uncommon.

Cape May (1993): "Rare," probably not breeding in county.

Habitat: Edges of, glades in, and cuts through woodlands. Visits gardens. Occurs consistently along the Palisades, where its Pipevine host is abundant.

Phenology: Probably three broods late April to September, commoner late in season. Peaks in May and July with small numbers in September.

Caterpillar Foodplants: Larvae feed on Dutchman's Pipe (*Aristolochia durior*) and other pipevines in the genus *Aristolochia*. This limits their breeding distribution. Also reported on Wild Ginger (*Asarum canadense*), but Saunders (1932) remarked that larvae did not eat Wild Ginger, and Fee (1979) tried unsuccessfully to get a female to oviposit on this plant and to get larvae to eat it. He suggested that Wild Ginger is probably not a larval food plant for this species. Skinner and Aaron (1889) reported larvae on Morning Glory (*Ipomoea*) near Philadelphia.

Overwintering Stage: Pupa.

Comments: This distasteful species is the model in a complex system of Batesian mimicry. It is mimicked by Black, Spicebush, and female Tiger Swallowtails, Red-spotted Purple, and some moths. Codella, a Master's degree student at Rutgers University, showed that captive Blue Jays (*Cyanocitta cristata*) quickly learn to reject this species and subsequently reject the mimics as well (Codella 1986). However, Anoles (*Anolis carolinensis*) in Texas regularly ate this species (Odendaal et al. 1987). Mimics are more common and mimicry is more perfect in areas where the Pipevine Swallowtail is more abundant (Brower and Brower 1962).

Females avoid laying eggs on leaves that already have an egg and continue their search for vacant leaves (Rausher 1979). Pupae are mainly brown (small proportion of green pupae) and the texture of the substrate, rather than its size or color, influences where the larvae will pupate (Hazel and West 1979). Pupae are mainly on coarse-grained bark or rock substrate (West and Hazel 1979).

Iftner et al. (1992) note that the Pipevine Swallowtail was formerly more common in northern Ohio but has declined, apparently because Dutchman's Pipe is no longer frequently planted as an ornamental. This may be true in New Jersey as well, since few nurseries now supply the hardy *Aristolochia*.

Where to Find It: Regular in late summer at Greenwood Sanctuary (Bergen County) nectaring on thistles along road. Also on slopes of Palisades Park at end of Engelwood Avenue, where rocky hillsides are covered by Pipevine. Look for it in late morning while the sun still strikes the steep east-facing slopes. On warm afternoons the swallowtails ride updrafts along the face of the Palisades and cross to the west along a broad front (Darrow).

Zebra Swallowtail, *Eurytides marcellus* (Cramer, 1777)

Referred to as the Ajax Swallowtail in many old writings. The scientific name *ajax* is no longer used, since Linnaeus applied it to at least three species.

Range: Western New York to southern Florida and Texas. Rare visitor as far east as Rhode Island (Pavulaan 1990). Opler and Krizek (1984) show it occurring throughout New Jersey except extreme northwest; however, early records are mainly from northern New Jersey and the Delaware Valley, with coastal records from Ocean and Cape May Counties and no records from most central counties (Opler's Atlas). The subspecies reaching New Jersey is *marcellus*.

Current Status: Vagrant. Very few recent records including sightings along the Delaware Valley. A September 1995 record from Sailor's Snug Harbor, Staten Island (Peggy Smith, reported by Wagerik, pers. comm.). There are no breeding records, but its host, Pawpaw, occurs sparsely in central and western New Jersey, for example at Trenton Marsh. The Zebra occurs commonly as close as Elks Neck State Park, Cecil County, Maryland, but does not wander northward. Unfortunately, larvae and pupae of this butterfly are commercially available and the resulting adults are usually released, making suspect any record of this species outside its normal range and especially away from its preferred habitat.

Historical Status: There are scattered old records suggesting that it formerly occurred more commonly in New Jersey. Its host is rare and there are no documented breeding records. It was rare near Philadelphia in the late nineteenth century (Skinner and Aaron 1889, who believed it was possibly declining). Beutenmüller (1892) considered it "probably accidental" around New York City, but Wormsbacher collected five specimens at Jersey City after 1910 (Comstock 1940). If it was ever resident, it occurs now only as a rare vagrant with many years between sightings. Reported as a rare vagrant on Long Island in 1912, with the statement that it was "not uncommon formerly in . . . Brooklyn" (Engelhardt 1913).

Smith (1890): On "Newark list," local, but not rare {not shown for Essex County in Opler's Atlas}.

Smith (1900): "Not rare locally . . . single specimens . . . in almost all parts of the state" {but no southern localities listed}.

Smith (1910): "Local throughout . . . usually only single examples at long intervals." Records mostly in North, but also from Anglesea.

Comstock (1940): "Occasionally throughout." Localities include Woodridge, Jersey City, Lakehurst, and Anglesea.

Delaware Valley (1966): Rare and sporadic. Local breeder "relatively common wherever . . . papaw occurs." Recorded from Gloucester (Williamstown) and Salem Counties (Salem, Quinton, Palatine).

Staten Island (1973): "There are no modern records of this species or its food plant . . . anywhere near New York City." Davis (1910) gives four records from 1886 to 1902 (June to August).

New York City Area (1993): "Historic records from New Jersey and one from Rockland County."

Cape May (1993): A "stray."

Habitat: A species of forest edges, river flood plains, and glades where Pawpaw occurs. Males engage in hilltopping behavior.

Phenology: In mid-Atlantic states two or three broods early April–autumn. Most historical records in June–July (Smith 1900).

Caterpillar Foodplant: Papaw *Asimina triloba*.

Overwintering Stage: Pupa.

Comment: This interesting representative of the Neotropical Kite Swallowtails rarely occurs in New Jersey. In the mid-Atlantic states there are three broods, each of which has a different appearance. Early spring forms are paler with fewer black markings, more red spots, and shorter tails. Adults emerging in late spring have more black and smaller red markings, whereas the summer brood is the largest and darkest of all. Early naturalists gave different names to each of these "forms": 'marcellus,' 'telamonides,' and 'lecontei,' respectively.

Black Swallowtail, *Papilio polyxenes* (Fabricius, 1775)

Range: Central Maine to southern Florida and Texas to northern South America, including all of New Jersey. The subspecies in New Jersey is the eastern North American race *asterias* described by Stoll in 1782.

Current Status: Widespread and occasionally abundant, occurring in most parts of the state. Particularly common at Brigantine [Forsyth] National Wildlife Refuge. Peak 4JC count 116 (1994 Raritan Canal).

Historical Status: Numbers may be declining throughout the region, even though host plants are abundant. Its status should be monitored. It is likely that this species became abundant in the eighteenth century with widespread planting of host plants and the spread of the alien Queen Anne's Lace.

Smith (1890–1910): Common throughout.

Comstock (1940): "Throughout sometimes so abundant" as to injure crops {a situation not likely to be encountered today, perhaps because carrots and parsley are not major cash crops in New Jersey}.

Delaware Valley (1966): "Very common . . . throughout . . . rare in some years."

Staten Island (1973): "Common and widespread," "fluctuates greatly in numbers."

New York City Area (1993): "Locally fairly common along the coastal plain, less so inland."

Cape May (1993): "Common."

Habitat: Very broad from old fields and forest edges to gardens, but mainly in extensive fields, particularly of Red Clover. Engages in hilltopping along the Palisades. Well adapted to suburban and even urban habitats. May be declining as large open field habitat becomes fragmented.

Phenology: Up to three broods mid-April–October.

Caterpillar Foodplant: Includes various wild and domestic members of the carrot family (Apiaceae, formerly Umbelliferae), including Queen Anne's Lace (*Daucus carota*) and Parsley, Carrots, and less often Dill and Fennel.

Overwintering Stage: Pupa.

Comment: The male, with its broad yellow band across both wings, is readily identified, but females may be difficult to separate from Spicebush Swallowtails (see Glassberg 1993b:24). Occasionally reported as a pest on carrots and parsley.

This species has been extensively studied by Robert Lederhouse and his students at Rutgers University. Codella (1986) showed that both male and female Black Swallowtails are effective Batesian mimics of the Pipevine Swallowtail, particularly when their ventral surface is exposed, as it is when roosting at night. He also showed that predation is the major cause of mortality in New Jersey (though not in Texas), that most predation takes place at night or on wet chilly days, and that most predation is by birds. Mimicry is closer in areas of the southeastern United States where the Pipevine Swallowtail is more numerous (Brower and Brower 1962).

The pupae occur in both green and brown color morphs. Short photoperiod results in the brown morph, but during midsummer the pupae may be brown or green, depending on the background color of the larvae and the light reaching their undersurface (West et al. 1972). The average adult survival is 10.2 days (Lederhouse 1983). The territoriality of this species has been well studied. In one study, early-arriving males claimed better territories, of higher relative elevation, but the territories (which averaged 75 square meters) were clumped (sev-

Photo 7. Male Black Swallowtail nectaring at a Bull Thistle. The entire field was converted to a housing development the following year. (Photographed in Franklin Township by Michael Gochfeld)

eral male territories close together), and therefore the group acted like a lek (Lederhouse 1982). Some populations have a substantial preponderance of males (Lederhouse 1983).

A noteworthy recent inland record was >50, seen in Franklin Twp (Somerset County) in a field of Red Clover, July 11, 1994 (Raritan Canal 4JC). By 1995 this field had been developed for housing (see Photo 7).

Giant Swallowtail, *Papilio cresphontes* (Cramer, 1777)

Listed in the genus *Heraclides* by some authors.

Range: Western New York and formerly southern New England to southern Florida and Texas, west to the Great Plains and south to the West Indies and northern South America. Opler and Krizek (1984) show it occurring over all of New Jersey, and Opler's Atlas shows records for the northern tier of counties and for Salem, Camden, and Atlantic Counties.

Current Status: A vagrant; not recorded in New Jersey in most years. One 1994 Sussex County record (Hampton, 6/17/94; Glassberg), a 1990 New York record (*Mulberry Wing*), and a 1984 sighting at Brighton, Sussex County (Schweitzer). Its host, Prickly Ash, is not uncommon in northwestern New Jersey. This species is not common in adjacent states (Schweitzer), and is considered a nonbreeding stray to Delmarva (Woodbury 1994). The larvae and pupae of this species are sold commercially and the resulting adults are often released, rendering suspect any sighting of this species in New Jersey.

Historical Status: Formerly resident in northern New Jersey but apparently declined after spraying for mosquitoes and Gypsy Moths (Schweitzer). It is uncertain that spraying was directly responsible for the decline (Tudor). Never resident in southern New Jersey where its hosts do not occur, and only sporadic records from Atlantic, Camden, and Salem Counties. Occasionally found near Philadelphia in 1880s (Skinner and Aaron 1889).

Conservation Status: Extirpated as a breeder. Although globally secure, it is rated S1–2 by the Natural Heritage Program. There should be periodic surveys in areas where Prickly Ash is common to determine if it recolonizes the state.

Smith (1890–1910): Occasional, "isolated specimens . . . throughout," including Fort Lee, Caldwell, Newark, Staten Island, New Brunswick, Trenton.

Comstock (1940): "Throughout . . . occasional . . . but where Prickly Ash is common, several may be seen in a day." Specimens listed are from Sussex to Essex Counties. {The designation "throughout" is not supported by the collecting sites.}

Delaware Valley (1966): "Rare and sporadic . . . strays from Maryland," but reported as regular near Philadelphia (Shapiro and Shapiro 1973). Recorded from Camden, Salem, and Atlantic Counties.

Staten Island (1973): "No modern records." Records from 1882, 1893, and once subsequently.

New York City Area (1993): "Formerly an erratic breeder on coastal plain; no verified breeding sites now exist in our region." "Extremely rare southern stray" (Nassau County, NY, 9/3/90).

Cape May (1993): Never recorded but, listed as a "species to look for."

Habitat: Woodland edges, cuts, and open habitats and gardens.

Phenology: Two broods May–June and August–September, the latter being more numerous.

Caterpillar Foodplants: In New Jersey uses Prickly Ash (*Zanthoxylum americanum*); elsewhere recorded using Hercules Club (*Z. clavaherculis*) and Hop Tree (*Ptelea trifoliata*). In southeastern United States uses citrus trees.

Overwintering Stage: Pupa.

Comment: A striking and conspicuous species, the Giant Swallowtail is not likely to be overlooked, hence its apparent rarity today reflects a real and significant decline from its past status. In southeastern United States sometimes a minor pest on citrus.

Eastern Tiger Swallowtail, *Papilio glaucus* (Linnaeus, 1758)

Listed in the genus *Pterourus* by some authors.

Range: Southern Canada to southern Florida and Texas, including all of New Jersey. The subspecies *glaucus* occurs in New Jersey.

Current Status: Widespread and relatively numerous with late spring and summer broods. Numbers vary from year to year. The species was unusually numerous in 1994 and was much scarcer in 1995. Maximum 4JC total 41 (1993 Raritan Canal).

Historical Status: No long-term change apparent. Always reported as common.

Smith (1890–1910): Common throughout.

Comstock (1940): "Throughout."

Delaware Valley (1966): "Commonest swallowtail . . . everywhere."

Staten Island (1973): "Frequent to common."

New York City Area (1993): Generally the commonest swallowtail.

Cape May (1993): "Common."

Habitat: Very diverse and widespread. This is more of a canopy species than most of our butterflies, and it is commonly seen flying high across roads. It is a frequent garden visitor.

Phenology: Three broods April (rarely March)–September, with peaks in early May, June, and August.

Caterpillar Foodplants: Over its entire range it utilizes a variety of species in seven families (Rosaceae, Oleaceae, Salicaceae, Corylaceae, Magnoliaceae, Betulaceae, Aceraceae; L. P. Brower 1958) and is thus the most polyphagous of our swallowtails. In the Northeast it uses a variety of trees, mainly Wild Black Cherry (*Prunus serotina*), but also ash (*Fraxinus* sp.), Lilac (*Syringa vulgaris*), Tulip Tree

(*Liriodendron tulipifera*), and rarely Spicebush (*Lindera benzoin*; Scriber et al. 1975).

Overwintering Stage: Pupa.

Comment: The light-phase females are distinguished from males by the more extensive blue on the dorsal hind wing. The dark female morph, a mimic of the distasteful Pipevine Swallowtail, is usually uncommon, amounting to fewer than 2% of all individuals in most parts of New Jersey, but they tend to be commoner in areas where the Pipevine Swallowtail is more common, exceeding 90% of all females in northern Georgia and the Great Smokies (Brower and Brower 1962). Clarke and Sheppard (1959, 1962) did extensive research on the genetic control of the female mimicry. Melanism is controlled by a gene on the W chromosome and the gene occurs only in females. Females produce daughters of their own morph (Clarke et al. 1976). Skinner and Aaron (1889) reported that both morphs were equally common near Philadelphia, a situation that is certainly not true today.

Since experiments show that the dark females suffer less predation, particularly in areas where the Pipevine model is numerous, and dark females may outnumber yellow ones (Brower and Brower 1962), it is challenging to explain why there are any yellow female Tiger Swallowtails at all. After a while, one would expect that selection would eliminate yellow females entirely. Perhaps there is a benefit to females from being yellow which counterbalances the benefit that dark females gain from not being eaten. In a classic study, Burns (1966) showed that dark females are less vulnerable to predators, but pale females attract more mates, resulting in a balanced polymorphism; Levin (1973) found no difference in the number of eggs laid or larvae produced between yellow and dark females. Jeffords et al. (1979) suggested that the light phase persisted because it was less conspicuous to predators, but it is certainly quite conspicuous to the human observer. The geneticists Clarke and Sheppard (1962) believed that migration of yellow females into areas where yellow females were being eaten would explain the persistence. It is not clear that any of these explanations is sufficient to explain why the polymorphism exists. We suspect that the predation pressure may never be high enough to eliminate the yellow females entirely.

Females of this species regularly have more than one mating based on counts of sperm packets (spermatophores) when the females are dissected (Lederhouse and Scriber 1987). Females tend to select host plants that are concentrated near clumps of nectar sources (Grossmueller and Lederhouse 1987). Females spend most of their time in the vicinity of nectar sources or host plants while males are more often found near flyways where transient females may be encountered. In most years (unless the season is unusually late), males exhibit protrandry (emerging days before the first female; Berger 1986).

The Canadian Tiger Swallowtail (*P. canadensis*, formerly *P. glaucus canadensis*) has recently been separated as a distinct species (Hagen et al. 1991), based on morphology and physiology. Its females are always yellow due to the existence of an autosomal gene that suppresses black coloration (Scriber et al. 1990), and its range does not coincide with the Pipevine Swallowtail. This smaller, univoltine species reaches central New York and has not been recorded in New Jersey. Experimental crossing of a female Canadian Tiger Swallowtail with a melanistic male Eastern Tiger Swallowtail did produce fully black female hybrids (Scriber and Evans 1986), but when male Canadian Tigers are crossed with dark morph female Eastern Tigers, no dark offspring are produced (Clarke and Sheppard 1959).

Larvae that experience long photoperiod, warm temperature, and good nutrition pupate and metamorphose into adults without diapause, while those experiencing short days, cool nights, and limited food undergo diapause, thereby overwintering as pupae (Hagen et al. 1991). Experiments with Eastern Tiger Swallowtail larvae raised at high temperatures produced females that were intermediate between light and dark phase (Ritland 1986).

Spicebush Swallowtail, *Papilio troilus* (Linnaeus, 1758)

Listed in the genus *Pterourus* by some authors.

Range: Central New York and southern New England to southern Florida and Texas, including all of New Jersey. The subspecies *troilus* occurs in New Jersey.

Current Status: Widespread and relatively numerous throughout the state, but rarely abundant.

Historical Status: No apparent change, always listed as common to abundant.

Smith (1890–1910): Common throughout.

Comstock (1940): "Throughout."

Delaware Valley (1966): "Very common . . . general, common in pine barrens."

Staten Island (1973): "Abundant and general."

New York City Area (1993): "Widespread" in woods and gardens.

Cape May (1993): "Common."

Habitat: Open areas in and around deciduous and oak-pine forests, often seen well inside forests. A species of woodland glades and cuts. Commonly visits gardens.

Phenology: Three broods late April–mid-September.

Caterpillar Foodplants: Spicebush (*Lindera benzoin*) and Sassafras (*Sassafras albidum*). Elsewhere reported on Tulip Tree (*Liriodendron tulipifera*) and other trees in southern and western parts of its range.

Overwintering Stage: Pupa.

Comment: Away from the Coastal Plain this is the commonest dark swallowtail. It is considered a mimic of the Pipevine Swallowtail with which its range largely coincides. The first instar caterpillar is a bird-dropping mimic.

Palamedes Swallowtail, *Papilio palamedes* (Drury, 1773)

Range: Resident from Dismal Swamp and southern Delmarva (Virginia coastal plain) to southern Florida, Texas, Caribbean, and southern Mexico; vagrant to New Jersey and western Long Island (Shapiro 1974a). Opler's Atlas shows records for Cape May and Staten Island.

Current Status: Accidental. No recent records. Common north as far as southeastern Virginia (Dismal Swamp), where it is abundant. Rare in Delaware.

Historical Status: One or two old records, including Cape May. Reported to have bred on Staten Island in 1896, also on Long Island. No modern records. Always as a stray.

Smith (1890–1900): Not recorded.

Smith (1910): One specimen from "Fairview *fide* Wrms." {There are at least four Fairviews in New Jersey, but this one must refer to Bergen County.}

Comstock (1940): On supplemental list as a "Rare visitor from the South" based on a specimen (7/8/1908) from West Hoboken by Henry Wormsbacher. This is undoubtedly the same as Smith's Fairview specimen. {Opler's Atlas map has the dot misplaced in Union County}.

Delaware Valley (1966): One vagrant Delaware specimen (8/19/59, Wilmington). "Reaches . . . coastal plain of Maryland, Cape May, N.J."

Staten Island (1973): "A very rare stray, recorded by Comstock (1940) citing as his source Davis, Fort Wadsorth" in June. The specimen is unknown and this would be only the second record for the species north of Cape May.

New York City Area (1993): Not mentioned.

Cape May (1993): A "stray."

Habitat: In southeastern United States a species of riverine forests and broad-leaf swamps.

Phenology: Not resident in New Jersey.

Larval Host: Its known host Red Bay (*Persea borbonica*) occurs north to southern Delaware. In the laboratory, larvae will eat Sassafras, and other members of the Laurel family, but not Sweet Bay (*Magnolia virginiana*; Scott 1986), on which larvae have been reported.

Comment: The historical information on this species is confusing to say the least. There are, however, no recent records. Although larger than the Black Swallowtail with more yellow markings, this species could easily be overlooked by those unfamiliar with its appearance. The type locality of this tropical species is designated "New York" (Miller and Brown 1981).

Both Comstock (1940) and Smith (1910) refer to a Wormsbacher specimen of this species taken in 1908; the former attributes it to West Hoboken (Hudson County) and the latter to Fairview (Bergen County), close to the Hudson County line.

Pieridae, Whites and Sulphurs

The Whites and Sulphurs comprise a Cosmopolitan family that reaches its greatest diversity in the tropics. The Whites feed mainly on members of the Mustard and Cabbage family (Brassicaceae, formerly called Cruciferae) or the Caper family (Capparidaceae), and the Sulphurs feed on clovers and beans (Fabaceae, formerly called Leguminosae). The eggs are laid singly and the caterpillars are not social, nor do they build tent shelters. Worldwide there are about 700 species of whites and 300 species of sulphurs, three of which (Cabbage White, Orange Sulphur, Clouded Sulphur) are among the most conspicuous and widespread butterflies in the state. The Little Yellow and Cloudless Sulphur are fairly regular annual immigrants from the South.

Subfamily *Pierinae*, Whites

Our species are medium to smallish, all-white butterflies with varying patterns of black spots or dark wing veins, except for the prominent orange apex on the forewing of the male Orange Tip. They utilize the Brassicaceae family as hosts.

[Florida White, *Appias drusilla* (Cramer, 1777)]

Range: Southern Florida and Texas to Brazil. Opler's Atlas shows a Long Island, NY, record and one in western New York, with no other records north of Florida. The Florida subspecies is *neumoegeni* (described by Skinner in 1894).

Status: No definite New Jersey records or recent New York records.

Historical Status: This south Florida species is a very rare vagrant collected in a few northern locations, with one specimen from Riverhead, Suffolk County, NY (7/3/24); reported also from Queens and Erie Counties, NY (Shapiro 1974a).

Comstock (1940) listed it on the supplemental list based on two specimens taken at Canarsie, Brooklyn (6/10/1906).

Comment: This is such a characteristically southern Florida insect that one would hardly expect it to reach New Jersey. Perhaps it is one of the species that was a more common vagrant in the early part of the century than it is today.

Checkered White, *Pontia protodice* (Boisduval and LeConte, 1829)

Range: Southern New York to southern Florida, and west to California, including all of New Jersey except northwestern counties.

Current Status: Highly localized with very few recent records. However, where it occurs it is likely to be common. We discovered a colony at Newark Airport in 1993 (Gochfeld 1994) which was still active in 1996. One seen at Higbee Beach in 1990 (P. Sutton), but no regular colonies known in southern New Jersey. Last documented colony in Ocean County in 1964 at Lakehurst (Schweitzer). A colony at Trenton Marsh (1993, Lecks). Recorded on eight of eleven late summer butterfly counts at Jamaica Bay, NY.

Historical Status: This species appears to have undergone a dramatic decline in the past century, particularly the past 50 years, over a large part of its range in the northeastern United States (as far as North Carolina). Beutenmüller (1893) reported that this once common species had virtually disappeared around New York City but was still abundant in southern New Jersey. Although listed as common on Cape May County checklist (Wright 1989) the status was corrected to "rare" (Wright and Sutton 1993). Reported at Collier's Mills and Kendall Park as late as 1980 (Leck).

Glassberg (1993b) notes that authors have been stating for the past century that it has declined, leading him to conclude that it may never have been common except during sporadic outbreaks. Dickerson (1901) wrote that the Checkered White was commonly known over nearly all of the United States. Skinner and Aaron (1889) reported that it had already become rare near Philadelphia; we infer that they had found it commoner in earlier years. Like Beutenmüller (1893), they attributed the decline to the population increase of Cabbage Whites. However, for reasons explained under Comments, we doubt that the Cabbage White had much to do with the decline of the present species. Beutenmüller (1893) caught 200 in two hours near Camden in 1886, and Shapiro (1966) records it as common to locally abundant in the Delaware Valley. Pavulaan (pers. comm.) reports it quite common even as early as March at Brentwood, Long Island, NY, in the early 1960s, but absent after about 1965. Cech (1995) cites Alan Worthington's caution that historical accounts over the past decade indicate the species is very cyclical and may have alternated being common and rare, and this is consistent with Comstock's (1940) account.

Conservation Status: Protection of an erratic resident like this species is not practical. It is certainly vulnerable in New Jersey, but both its nectar source and larval host plants are abundant, and colonies can thrive in extremely marginal habitat, including along the edges of industrial sites, barren fields, and beaches.

Smith (1890): "Occasional throughout . . . southern part of the state." Specimens from Mount Holly and Westville.

Smith (1900): "South of the red shale line it is sometimes locally abundant." Burlington, Gloucester, Salem, and Camden Counties; also Lake Hopatcong.

Smith (1910): Variable numbers, more common in South; only Hopatcong and Paterson in North.

Comstock (1940): "Generally south of and sparingly north of the Fall Line." "Large broods frequently occur followed by years of scarcity." {Strangely, most localities listed are north of Fall Line.}

Delaware Valley (1966): "Common to locally abundant in the coastal plain . . . reinforced by immigrants." Rare north of Philadelphia. Recorded as "general from Camden, Medford, and Batsto south, locally in the pine barrens; very common in Gloucester Co." {This suggests a serious decline in the past 25 years.}

Staten Island (1973): "Locally common to abundant . . . on the coastal plain." "Perhaps not always wintering successfully."

New York City Area (1993): "Irregular coastal plain migrant; beaches, weedy fields . . . not recorded every year . . . very rare breeder at Jamaica Bay." {Also recorded at Marine Park and Arverne; no 1995 records.}

Cape May (1993): "Rare." {One recent record (9/20/89, Suttons); no established colonies.}   *Habitat*: The open barren areas behind sandy beaches and the wastelands of former landfills and industrial sites are suitable habitat for this species. The bright yellow-flowered Camphorweed (*Heterotheca subaxillaris*) is an indicator of its habitat.

Phenology: Two to four broods April–late November, but mainly late July–September.

Larval Host: Mainly Wild Peppergrass (*Lepidium virginicum* spp.), but also other cruciferous plants such as Shepherd's Purse (*Capsella bursa-pastoris*).

Overwintering Stage: Pupa.

Comment: In flight this species is very similar to the Cabbage White, although it may have a more fluttery demeanor. Although its decline is sometimes attributed to the increasing abundance of Cabbage Whites, this is likely to be an oversimplification. In New Jersey and Long Island, the two occur together, and often the Checkered White is locally more numerous. At Jamaica Bay this species was most common wherever Cabbage Whites were also most common (1984, Pavulaan). Although adults use a variety of nectar sources, they are most consistently associated with Camphorweed, and white butterflies flying near this flower should be checked carefully.

The occurrence of this species is unpredictable. It has long been known that colonies flourish for a few years, then may disappear for a few years (Rawson 1945; Shapiro 1978). Smith (1910) wrote: "Some seasons it is very common throughout its range and then for several years in succession only isolated examples are seen, or it may be entirely absent." In California, also, the Checkered White undergoes frequent local extinctions and colonizations, with extinctions related to winter stress (Shapiro 1978). It shows much genetic homogeneity over a wide area, reflecting its extensive migration and colonization, resulting in gene flow between distant populations (Shapiro and Geiger 1986).

Where to Find It: Colonies are not predictable. There is presently (1993–96) a colony at Newark Airport, where this species can be viewed through the chain link fence in Long-Term Parking Lot D, near bus stops 2 and 9, at least in August. Should be looked for in vacant coastal fields when the abundant yellow composite, Camphorweed, is blooming.

Mustard White, *Pieris napi* (Linnaeus, 1758)

Sometimes listed in the genus *Artogeia*; sometimes listed under the specific name *oleracea* before it was lumped with Old World *napi*.

Range: Northern Eurasia and across North America from Maritime Provinces to Canadian Rockies, extending from the edge of tundra through the Canadian Zone forests. Formerly reached coastal plain in Connecticut and Rhode Island. Southern limit in Appalachians uncertain (Hovanitz 1962). Map in Opler and Krizek (1984) shows it reaching central New York and northern Massachusetts; not shown from New Jersey or adjacent New York or Pennsylvania. New York records mainly from Adirondacks northward (Shapiro 1974a). No records in Opler's Atlas. The subspecies *oleracea*, described by Harris in 1929, would be the form likely to reach New Jersey.

Current Status: Accidental or hypothetical. Reported from Springdale in 1966 (dos Passos 1966), but no recent records. The record in Cech (1993) probably refers to this specimen.

Historical Status: Beutenmüller (1893) knew of no specimens other than the one mentioned by Smith (1890). Smith (1910) wrote: "It is our native cabbage butterfly, which has been almost exterminated . . . by the imported species . . . in some years none at all." Dos Passos mentioned specimens from Paterson and

"Carney" which Comstock (1940) had assumed should be referred to the West Virginia White. Dos Passos (1966) reported collecting an individual at Springdale (7/8/66), and he in turn assumed that this reflected a long-established population rather than a vagrant. This is the only modern New Jersey record known to us. Formerly common in eastern Massachusetts but already rare by the 1860s (Scudder 1889, Hovanitz 1962). Chew (1981) attributed its disappearance from areas where it was formerly common to land use changes that eliminate its favored host plants. Klots (1951) reported that it had become entirely restricted to Canadian Zone forest and was not recorded south of the Catskills in New York.

Smith (1890): "Orange Mountains; rare."

Smith (1900): Rare in North.

Smith (1910): Occasional, both North and South, but decreasing. {As Comstock (1940) pointed out, Smith was probably in error when he reported that this was New Jersey's native white butterfly.}

Comstock (1940): Not listed. "Records of *oleracea* (Smith's 'List') probably refer" to the next species {*virginiensis*}.

Delaware Valley (1966): No records. Erroneously reported by Williams (1941).

Staten Island (1973): Either this or *P. virginiensis* may have been collected in 1858–59. But Shapiro and Shapiro (1973) note that even that occurrence was reported on hearsay. Davis (1893) quotes a letter from A. R. Grote: "I believe that I remember clearly that I took *P. oleracea* on Staten Island between 1856 and 1859." Davis notes that this rare insect would be overlooked among the very common Cabbage Butterflies.

New York City Area (1993): On the list of "Extirpated/Extralimital Species." The southern limit of range just north of the 50-mile diameter circle. "Found in the New York region during the last quarter of the nineteenth century; also in far northwestern New Jersey in the early 1970s." {This probably refers to the dos Passos specimen dated 1966.}

Cape May (1993): Not listed.

Habitat: Fens and wet deciduous forests, and farm edges. Prefers partially shaded habitats.

Phenology: Not applicable in New Jersey. In New England it is triple brooded, appearing first in mid-April, again in late June, and finally in late July.

Caterpillar Foodplants: Toothwort (*Dentaria diphylla*), rock cresses (*Arabis* spp.), *Nasturium officinale*, mustards (*Brassica* spp.), and winter cresses (*Barbarea* spp.). Thrives on crops such as turnip, cabbage, radish, and mustard as well as on Watercress and various wild cresses.

Comment: This species has probably not been a regular part of the New Jersey fauna in recent history. It is probable that early records refer to the next species below, which can be highly similar to the Mustard White, even to the extent of showing prominent wing venation. If the dos Passos specimen was indeed this species, it was far out of the current range. The nearly all-white summer form of Mustard White would be very difficult to distinguish from West Virginia White. However, the West Virginia White is considered univoltine, so a July specimen of that species would be highly unusual.

Hovanitz (1963) points out that in the northeastern United States, *napi* and *virginiensis* are almost entirely allopatric, but where their ranges come together (Connecticut and probably New York and the northern Great Lakes), one finds individuals that are intermediate and that the relationship of the two forms is unclear and perhaps not constant from place to place. However, he did not find evidence of free interbreeding, as would be predicted between two subspecies of the same species. This suggests that the two forms were partially isolated, and that time will tell whether they increase or decrease the amount of interbreeding.

P. napi is shown as occurring no closer than southwestern Connecticut (Hovanitz 1963), but Opler's Atlas does not show documented records from Connecticut.

Although some authors have attributed the decline of the Mustard White to the ascendancy of the Cabbage White, their hosts and habitats are sufficiently different that competition is unlikely to play any role. Hovanitz (1963) argued that loss of forest habitat was the main contributor to the decline of Mustard White, but even this is oversimplified, since the species has disappeared from areas that are still well forested.

West Virginia White, *Pieris virginiensis* (Edwards, 1870)
Sometimes listed in the genus *Artogeia*, and formerly considered a subspecies of *P. napi*.

Range: Appalachian distribution from central Vermont to northeastern Ohio and to northern Georgia, including northern and central New Jersey (Opler and Krizek 1984). Not on Delmarva (Woodbury 1994). In New York, occurs or occurred across southern tier from Erie to Westchester Counties (Shapiro 1974a).

Current Status: Apparently formerly resident, but now very rare or probably extirpated in New Jersey. Status unknown, but no recent records, despite efforts to find colonies in northwestern New Jersey where its food plants, Toothworts, are common (Wander).

Historical Status: It was already noted as declining rapidly by Shapiro (1974a); Shapiro (1966) comments: "There are two old and *very* dubious records from Camden Co. N.J. . . . perhaps based on spring forms of *rapae*." Also reported from Warren to Union Counties. It has declined over a large part of its northeastern range, and is no longer found in areas where it occurred regularly even 20 years ago. Glassberg (1993b) notes that it is absent from many areas where its host plant occurs. Some of the northeastern United States populations should be considered THREATENED. Still occurs and may be locally common in Massachusetts (*Massachusetts Butterflies*, Feb. 1994). It is apparently stable in Ohio (Iftner et al. 1992) and in West Virginia, where it is still common (Tudor). The decline was coincidental with the massive spraying to control mosquitoes and Gypsy Moths, but this is not likely to be the sole cause. The superabundant Garlic Mustard (*Alliaria petiolata*), which has invaded its range, is toxic to its larvae, but apparently seduces females to lay on it, even where their normal hosts are present (Bowden 1971, Porter 1994). The larvae do not survive on this exotic plant, and this may contribute to its decline. This would also be a powerful selective force favoring females that learn to discern that this host is unsuitable (Chew 1995) or larvae that can survive. Indeed, Western Whites (*Pieris occidentalis*) lay fewer eggs on a host that is toxic than on preferred hosts, but some females do lay on the toxic plant (Chew 1977).

Conservation Status: Probably extirpated. There should be periodic surveys of suitable habitat where stands of Toothwort occur. One should not assume that white butterflies laying on Toothwort are necessarily this species, since Cabbage Whites can be found in woodland areas and will lay on these plants. Conversely, a population in Ontario was discovered in a woodland where Toothworts were scarce (Tasker 1975).

Smith (1890–1910): Not listed. {Comstock concluded that the records Smith listed under *oleracea* pertain to the present species which was often considered only a subspecies.}

Comstock (1940): "Occasionally throughout." Records given from Blairstown and Paterson to Camden, but Comstock expresses uncertainty about old records.

Delaware Valley (1966): No definite records; occurs in higher woodlands to north and west.

Staten Island (1973): Either this or *P. napi* may have been collected in 1858–59 {see previous species}.

New York City Area (1993): Reported in southeastern New York {northern Westchester County} but not since 1985.

Cape May (1993): Not listed.

Habitat: A species of forest openings in rich deciduous woodlands. This species prefers bottomlands along south-facing cliffs, where its host plants occur.

Phenology: One brood mid-April–early May. However, it may occasionally have a partial second brood due to inhibition of its normal diapause (Shapiro 1971, Courant and Chew 1995).

Caterpillar Foodplants: Toothworts (*Dentaria diphylla* and *D. laciniata*), but will develop on other cresses in the laboratory, including Watercress.

Overwintering Stage: Pupa.

Comment: Although this butterfly was first described in 1870, it was for a long time considered a subspecies of the Mustard White. Indeed, its range, extending from the southern Appalachians into the St. Lawrence region, is inserted between the New England and Great Lakes ranges of *P. napi oleracea* and could well qualify it as as a geographic subspecies of Transition Zone forest (Hovanitz 1963). Partly for that reason, early biologists did not necessarily distinguish between the two species, and when Smith (1890) refers to *P. napi* as the common white butterfly of New Jersey in the last century, Comstock (1940) corrected him by saying that this was almost certainly *P. virginiensis*. Klots (1951) recognized this as a distinct species, but Hovanitz (1963) indicated the uncertain species status of the West Virginia White.

The main distinction in spring is that the ventral veining on the West Virginia White appears smudged, whereas in the Mustard White the veins are sharply demarcated. The summer form of Mustard White is normally unmarked white below, but it can be smudged and appear virtually indistinguishable from the West Virginia White, which generally does not have a summer brood in most areas. However, a Massachusetts population included a partial summer brood in which the adults resembled the summer brood of Mustard White, lacking the black venation. These individuals presumably used Watercress (*Nasturtium officinale*) as their host since Toothworts were no longer available (Courant and Chew 1995).

It is reported that the two may have formerly overlapped in the Catskills, with the West Virginia White feeding on Toothworts (*Dentaria*) and the Mustard White on Wintercress (*Barbarea*). Their flight peaks are said not to coincide. The Mustard White is common in April and late June, and the West Virginia White is common only in May (Hovanitz 1963). Where the two species are or have been sympatric, interspecific pairings are very rare. Most laboratory hybrids have reduced viability.

Where to Find It: No known colonies in New Jersey, but occurs in the Catskills. One should look for this species in forest glades in northwestern New Jersey, but should not assume that white butterflies found there belong to this species. It must be distinguished both from Cabbage White and Mustard White. Records should be documented by recognizable photographs or a specimen.

Cabbage White, *Pieris rapae* (Linnaeus, 1758)

Sometimes listed in the genus *Artogeia*. In Europe called Small White. Also known as European Cabbage Butterfly or simply Cabbage Butterfly. Farmers refer to it as Cabbage Worm.

Range: Central Maine to central Florida, including all of New Jersey and west across the continent into northern Mexico, but scarce along Gulf Coast.

Current Status: Our most abundant and probably most widespread butterfly. Shuns forested areas but common in residential and agricultural areas and on edges of woodlands. Found also along the outer beaches and on salt marsh islands. Often seen by the hundreds over meadows and cruciferous (cabbage, cauliflower, broccoli) crops. Among New Jersey butterflies, this is currently the only potential agricultural pest, particularly in retail nurseries. There are peak years, with 1291 on the 1989 Raritan Canal 4JC and 1403 on the 1993 Cape May 4JC.

Historical Status: No recent change. This Eurasian species was accidentally introduced near Quebec around 1860, near New York in 1871, and at various other localities (Charleston, Chicago). It spread rapidly (Scudder 1877). By 1889 it was described as "painfully common" near Philadelphia (Skinner and Aaron 1889), and "exceedingly common" around New York City (Beutenmüller 1893), and by the turn of the century it occupied virtually all of the United States (Dickerson 1901; Weed 1917). It was already widespread and common in New Jersey by 1890. It probably reached its present abundance early in the twentieth century.

Smith (1890–1910): "The common cabbage butterfly; found everywhere." Often injurious to crops.

Comstock (1940): "Throughout."

Delaware Valley (1966): "Most generally abundant butterfly . . . everywhere."

Staten Island (1973): "Abundant and general." Already common in early 1890s (Davis 1893).

New York City Area (1993): "Ubiquitous."

Cape May (1993): "Abundant."

Habitat: Ubiquitous except in forests.

Phenology: Except for species that overwinter as adults, this is usually the earliest butterfly to emerge. Continuous broods overlapping March–November; persists into December until killing frost occurs. There is hardly a day between mid-April and late September when the species cannot be seen. There are usually clear second- and third-brood peaks in early June and mid-July, but peaks become less obvious later in the season.

Caterpillar Foodplants: Various crucifers including wild cresses and mustards and Wild Peppergrass (*Lepidium*), often on Nasturtium (Pavulaan), but also crops such as cabbage, broccoli, cauliflower, radish, collards, kale, and Water Cress. Shapiro (1966) reports "at least sixteen species of Cruciferae" used in the Delaware Valley, and Scott (1986) lists over forty species, some of which result in slow larval development. On outer beaches uses Sea Rocket (*Cakile edentula*). Populations in some places use Garlic Mustard (*Alliaria petiolata*). In Somerset females are frequently associated with this plant.

Larvae grow much faster on kale than on nasturtium or Watercress, and had 10% mortality on the first and 90% on the last (Hovanitz and Chang 1962a). Within ten generations of being grown on either kale or mustard, a strain can be selected to manifest a hereditary preference for the species on which it is raised (Hovanitz and Chang 1963).

Overwintering Stage: Pupa.

Comment: This species is well known to farmers and horticulturists, who call it the Cabbage Worm or Cabbage Moth and many voice surprise when told it is a butterfly. Some authors attribute the decline of several other whites to the ascendancy of this abundant species. It is not clear, however, that there is a causal relationship, particularly since the three declining species of Whites use different hosts, and hence are not likely to be in direct competition. It is possible that there is confusion in mate selection, and this should be studied where Cabbage Whites occur with other white species.

Dickerson (1901) noted that the Cabbage White populations exploded in

North America in the 1860s and 1870s in the absence of natural controls, but by 1900 ichneumon flies and other parasites on the larvae had increased such that "the balance of nature is now rapidly being restored." Of one hundred larvae she collected, 85% were killed by parasites. The initial population explosion of this species in the last century was largely sustained by cruciferous crops, but also by many introduced roadside weeds as well as garden flowers (*Nasturtium*).

This butterfly is characterized as having an "open" population structure, in that individual males and females disperse relatively long distances (several hundred meters), which enhances the interbreeding or panmixis over a relatively large distance (Emmel 1972).

The eastern North American populations of this butterfly are genetically homogeneous, reflecting a high degree of gene flow. However, some peripheral populations (New Brunswick, Canada, and northern California) appear to be genetically quite distinct, despite less than a century of isolation (Vawter and Brussard 1983).

In the mid-Atlantic states this species is invading woodlands where Garlic Mustard has become abundant (Pavulaan).

[Great Southern White, *Ascia monuste* (Fabricius, 1775)]

Range: A Neotropical species resident from coastal Florida, the Gulf Coast, and western Mexico to Argentina. Irruptive northward to Missouri and Delmarva. The Florida race *phileta* might occasionally reach New Jersey, where many of its cruciferous hosts occur.

Comment: It is surprising that this species, recorded several times in Delmarva, has never been found in the Philadelphia area or New Jersey.

Falcate Orangetip, *Anthocharis midea* (Hubner, 1809) Plate 3b

Range: Southwestern New England to southern Georgia and Texas. Opler and Krizek (1984) show it throughout New Jersey, and Opler's Atlas documents records in all counties but Salem, but it is rare or absent over most of central and northwestern New Jersey. The northern populations (e.g., Massachusetts and Ohio south through Appalachians) are assigned to the subspecies *annickae* (described by dos Passos and Klots 1969).

Current Status: An early spring species that is locally common, with two apparently separate populations, one in the Pine Barrens and southern New Jersey and one in the Lower Hudson Valley and northern New Jersey. Quite local in distribution but may be abundant, as at Assunpink; smaller numbers at Sandy Hook. At least six colonies known in Sussex County, including top of Sunrise Mountain (Wander).

Historical Status: Has apparently declined in the northern parts of the state, but may be more common on Coastal Plain than in the last century.

Smith (1890–1910): "Locally throughout" {but locations given are clearly concentrated in North (Delaware Water Gap to Ramapo Mountains) and in South (Camden to Seven Mile Beach)}.

Comstock (1940): "Locally, throughout. . . . Sometimes very common in Northern District."

Delaware Valley (1966): "Locally common . . . sporadically into coastal plain New Jersey."

Staten Island (1973): "Never . . . recorded from Staten Island."

New York City Area (1993): Rare to uncommon, but occasionally numerous. Sandy coastal plain.

Cape May (1993): "Common."

Habitat: This species of open deciduous woodland and edge occurs in two disjunct locations—the fringes of the Pine Barrens (particularly at Assunpink WMA) to Cape May, and in the hills of northern New Jersey and the lower Hudson Valley. At Assunpink it occurs in a mosaic of old fields and deciduous woodlands.

Phenology: One brood early April to early May (to mid-May in North). Peak numbers are late April and early May.

Caterpillar Foodplants: Cruciferous plants, mainly the rock cresses *Arabis* spp., but also toothworts (*Dentaria*) and pepper grass (*Lepidium*). Preferred hosts vary geographically. Seen nectaring on Small-flowered Bittercress (*Cardamine parviflora*) at Assunpink (Tudor); this plant is a known host (Scott 1986).

Overwintering Stage: Pupa.

Comment: This characteristic early spring butterfly with a brief flight period frequently flies in cool cloudy weather (Pavulaan). It occurs in more wooded areas than Cabbage White, and the males with their orange wingtips are readily recognizable. The flight is weak and fluttery, and they usually fly about 1 m above the ground or lower.

Where to Find It: Deciduous forest edges and old fields of Assunpink Wildlife Management Area in early to mid-May. Also at Sandy Hook and Lakehurst.

Subfamily *Coliadinae*, Sulphurs

The Common Sulphurs

The Common Sulphurs include the Clouded Sulphur *Colias philodice* and the Orange Sulphur *C. eurytheme*. These are widespread, familiar butterflies which occur together over most of North America and hybridize in many localities. Some authors have treated them as conspecific, but they do not hybridize randomly even though they are genetically extremely closely related (Watt 1995). Moreover, cross-matings are more likely to occur when the female is an 'alba' morph than with normally colored females (Pavulaan).

If the hybrids were at a selective disadvantage because females didn't recognize them as appropriate mates, then the relative frequency of hybridization would change over time, becoming less frequent. Since the two species actively expanded their ranges in recent times, their species-isolating behaviors may not yet have evolved completely.

Taylor (1972) studied these sulphurs in various parts of the United States, including western Arizona, which had been colonized by Common Sulphur only four years earlier. He found evidence of hybridization throughout the range, but in all cases, each species mated preferentially with its own species, not at random. This was true even in western Arizona, where the newly arrived Clouded Sulphurs could distinguish their own species from Orange Sulphurs. Even sulphurs captured in areas where only one species occurred were able to mate preferentially with their own species. Thus they are behaving like separate species, with incomplete isolating mechanisms.

In both species some females are very pale (form 'alba'). These white females cannot be reliably distinguished in the field; and they make up about one-fourth of the females in some areas. It is significant that white females also occur in some European *Colias* species, but white males are not found. Among all Sulphurs, thirty-five out of the forty-eight species in the genus *Colias* have a white ('alba') female morph. The gene for 'alba' results in transforming the yellow or red pigment to white. Surprisingly, the highest frequency of 'alba' occurs in the colder climates (Watt 1973), which is contrary to what one would expect if temperature regulation were the selective factor, and it is contrary to the occurrence of darker yellow individuals at colder times of the year, when the darker pigment absorbs heat and facilitates thermoregulation.

The genetics of this sex-limited dimorphism is complicated (Remington 1954). Lorkovic and Herman (1961) showed that ratios of yellow to white female offspring could be explained by one pair of autosomal genes, in which the white allele is dominant to yellow or orange, but the expression of which is modified by a second gene locus that allows white to be expressed only in females.

Whereas typical Clouded Sulphurs are very pale yellow, Orange Sulphurs may be bright orange or may have the orange confined to the base of the wings. Hybrids and backcrosses span the range of variation between the two species. Thus not all individuals can be assigned to a "species," although some fieldworkers call any butterfly with any orange area an "Orange Sulphur."

The late Robert Silberglied (Silberglied and Taylor 1978) found that the female Sulphurs do not recognize conspecific males by their visible coloration (yellow vs. orange), but by the ultraviolet reflectance (present in Orange Sulphurs but absent in Clouded Sulphurs). Only the female Orange Sulphur relies on this cue (since only the male Orange Sulphur has it). Interestingly, although hybrids show some orange and are often called "Orange Sulphurs," this default practice may be wrong, as these butterflies do not have the ultraviolet reflectance, and female Orange Sulphurs therefore do not recognize them as Orange Sulphurs.

This requires further study. If the female Orange Sulphurs do not recognize the partially orange males as conspecific, then butterfly watchers probably shouldn't either. We therefore recommend listing four types of these Sulphurs: (1) obvious Clouded Sulphurs, (2) obvious Orange Sulphurs, (3) intermediate or indeterminate individuals with a hint of orange, and (4) white females. Counting the proportion of intermediate individuals may provide clues as to whether the number of individuals is increasing (hybridization is becoming more frequent) or decreasing (isolation is becoming more perfect).

Clouded Sulphur, *Colias philodice* (Godart, 1819)

Range: Canada to central Georgia and west to the Pacific Coast and south to Guatemala, including all of New Jersey. The subspecies *philodice* occurs in New Jersey.

Current Status: Widespread, often common and occasionally abundant, but numbers fluctuate from year to year (populations very low in 1991). Occurs throughout New Jersey in appropriate habitat.

Historical Status: With the increasing abundance of Orange Sulphurs, this species has apparently declined in the past 50 years, but it is still common in most areas of New Jersey. Beutenmüller (1893) graphically describes "dense masses" and "swarms," phenomena that are seldom seen in New Jersey today.

Smith (1890–1910): Common throughout, "quite abundant."

Comstock (1940): "Throughout."

Delaware Valley (1966): Abundant and widespread.

Staten Island (1973): "Common and widespread."

New York City Area (1993): Common. May have declined as next species below has increased.

Cape May (1993): "Common."

Habitat: Very diverse. Found in any open area including cuts through forest. Greatest abundance over fields of alfalfa and clover.

Phenology: Up to four broods March–December.

Caterpillar Foodplants: Mostly White Clover (*Trifolium repens*), but other "clovers" such as Red Clover (*Trifolium pratense*), Alfalfa (*Medicago sativa*), and White Sweet Clover (*Melilotus alba*) are sometimes used.

Overwintering stage: Larva and pupa.

Comment: Some hybridization with the Orange Sulphur; see below. This was formerly the widespread common Sulphur over the eastern U.S., but in many places the Orange Sulphur now outnumbers it, particularly in southern New Jersey.

Both species of *Colias* have dimorphic females, with some proportion occurring in an "alba" or white form. These are often confused with Cabbage Whites until they settle to nectar. Despite extensive hybridization, the two species do show assortative mating, apparently based on differences in their ultraviolet reflectance patterns (Silberglied and Taylor 1973). Interbreeding occurs more often with white than with orange females.

The identification of Clouded Sulphur has become a problem, and by convention any Sulphur showing orange (regardless of extent) is not called Clouded Sulphur (see above). Pure lemon-yellow individuals are usually identified as this species, but Pavulaan (in litt.) cautions that some all-yellow individuals have the broader black margins and more angular forewing apex of the Orange Sulphur. These may be hybrids or a yellow morph of Orange Sulphur. The fairly common "white" females pose a serious identification problem. The white females of this species have a narrower black margin on the dorsal wing surface than the next. But there is much variation and hybrids make it difficult to identify these females, even in the hand. In general, it is best to simply note "white female sulphur."

We have seen Clouded Sulphurs as much as 10 miles out to sea in early October, possibly migrating.

Orange Sulphur [Alfalfa Butterfly], *Colias eurytheme* (Boisduval, 1852)

This southwestern species has invaded the northeastern United States since the 1930s and is now one of the commonest butterflies.

Range: Canada to southern Florida and Texas to California, and southern Mexico.

Current Status: Widespread and usually common. In most parts of New Jersey usually outnumbers the Clouded Sulphur. May be superabundant (hundreds) over alfalfa fields; ca. 1000 estimated in old fields at Rio Grande (Cape May County, 6/18/89), and 3216 in a day (Cumberland County 4JC, 1993). Populations were relatively low in 1991.

Historical Status: Its dramatic status change in New Jersey is apparent by comparing Smith's (1890–1910) statements with Comstock's observation that "in the last fifteen years this species has become almost as numerous as *philodice*." Skinner and Aaron (1889) considered it very rare near Philadelphia. Beutenmüller (1893) knew of only two records in the New York City area (Astoria in Queens, N.Y.C., and Newark). As alfalfa cultivation became common after 1870, this western species rapidly spread eastward (Shapiro 1966) until it is now one of the most numerous butterflies in the east. It colonized Maine beginning in the 1940s (A. E. Brower 1960).

Smith (1890): "Occasionally . . . Newark," also Mount Holly.

Smith (1900): Mount Holly, scarce at Camden; Long Island: "very occasional."

Smith (1910): "Hardly a regular inhabitant of the state."

Comstock (1940): "Throughout."

Delaware Valley (1966): "Abundant and general."

Staten Island (1973): "The most abundant butterfly."

New York City Area (1993): "Ubiquitous . . . less common in spring."

Cape May (1993): "Abundant."

Habitat: All open habitats with main abundance over fields of alfalfa.

Phenology: Multiple broods—March–December in South; April and August–October or occasionally November in North. However, it is most common after

Photo 8. Orange Sulphur on Red Clover. (Photographed near Higbee Beach, Cape May, by Joanna Burger)

July. Next to the Cabbage White, this is usually the latest butterfly seen in autumn. Recorded up to Dec. 16 near Philadelphia as fresh individuals which emerge from the otherwise overwintering pupae during warm winter spells when temperature exceeds 60°F (Shapiro 1962b). In the mild winter of 1994, recorded through end of December.

Caterpillar Foodplants: A variety of clovers including Alfalfa (*Medicago sativa*), White Sweet Clover (*Melilotus alba*), and White Clover (*Trifolium repens*), and also vetches (*Vicia*).

Overwintering Stage: Larva and pupa.

Comment: The females occur as either an all orange, a yellow-orange, or white form. It hybridizes with the Clouded Sulphur, and 8% of specimens taken on Staten Island (1970–71) and 15–25% of those from the Delaware Valley showed hybridization with *C. philodice* (Shapiro 1966; Shapiro and Shapiro 1973). To complicate matters, this species very rarely has an all-yellow form which still has the characteristic ultraviolet reflectance (Silberglied and Taylor 1973), but looks more like a Clouded Sulphur. The average developmental cycle is egg 5 days, larva 18 days, pupa 7 days (see Photos 3 and 8).

[**Southern Dogface,** *Colias cesonia* (Stoll, 1790)]

Often listed simply as Dog Face; usually listed in the genus *Zerene* or *Cesonia*.

Range: Resident range is southern third of United States from South Carolina to Arizona, and thence south to the West Indies and Argentina. Opler and Krizek (1984) show irruptive distribution northward over most of New Jersey (except extreme Northwest) and Long Island. However, there are no New Jersey records. Opler (1983) shows records from Philadelphia area and Staten Island. The subspecies *cesonia* occurs in North America.

Current Status: No New Jersey records known to us, although there are specimens from Staten Island and Queens, NY. This mainly western species is not usually common even in the southeastern states.

Historical Status: No records. Simmons and Andersen (1962) report large

Plate 1a. Pipevine Swallowtail, a highly local species resident mainly in northeastern New Jersey. (Photographed by Rick Cech)

Plate 1b. Mourning Cloak, a widespread, early spring and summer species. (Photographed in Somerset by Joanna Burger)

Plate 2a. Arctic Skipper, a northern species recently discovered at High Point State Park, Sussex County. Typically seen nectaring on Wild Geranium. (Photographed by Jeffrey Glassberg)

Plate 2b. Northern Metalmark, a highly localized and declining monophagous species (Photographed along the Springdale powerline, Sussex County, by Rick Cech)

Plate 3a. Hackberry Emperor, a pugnacious species that often flies out to investigate an approaching person. Often rests on tree trunks. (Photographed on wooden fence at Somerset by Joanna Burger)

Plate 3b. Mating pair of Falcate Orangetips (male on right). (Photographed at Hook Mountain, Rockland County, New York by Jeffrey Glassberg)

Plate 4a. Dotted Skipper is usually considered rare and local, but may be widespread in the Pine Barrens. (Photographed on Common Milkweed at Lakehurst by Jeffrey Glassberg)

Plate 4b. The northern "race" of Georgia Satyr. (Photographed at Klots' Bog, Lakehurst, by Rick Cech)

Plate 5a. Hessel's Hairstreak, a recently described, monophagous insect typical of the White Cedar Swamps of the Pine Barrens. (Photographed nectaring at Sand Myrtle, near Chatsworth, by Jeffrey Glassberg)

Plate 5b. The Hoary Elfin is found on Bearberry Flats in the Pine Barrens in early May. (Photographed at Warren Grove by Rick Cech)

Plate 6a. The Rare Skipper is a southern, coastal specialty, emerging in mid-July. (Photographed on Swamp Milkweed in Atlantic County, by Jeffrey Glassberg)

Plate 6b. Bronze Copper is a declining species with few known locations, mainly in southern New Jersey. (Photographed on Swamp Milkweed by Rick Cech)

Plate 7a. Cloudless Sulphur, the large yellow butterfly frequently seen flying in southern New Jersey in late summer and fall. At rest its undersurface is pale greenish, allowing it to disappear among the foliage. (Photographed at Cape May by Rick Cech)

Plate 7b. American Snout, a hackberry specialist, is frequently found in the hackberry grove near the Higbee Beach parking lot. Note the "snout" formed by the elongated labial palps. The underwing pattern is cryptic, but it shows a bright orange and black pattern when it opens its wings. (Photographed by Rick Cech)

Plate 8a. The Red-banded Hairstreak has invaded New Jersey from the South in the past 50 years, with a population explosion occurring in 1991. (Photographed in our yard at Somerset by Patti Murray)

Plate 8b. In autumn, migrating Monarchs form roosts of hundreds or thousands of individuals, mainly along the coast. This small roost was photographed in a salt marsh near Stone Harbor by Joanna Burger.

numbers in Charles County, Maryland (9/8/60), and 1961 was also an invasion year (Shapiro 1966), but none were recorded in New Jersey.

Smith (1900): "Staten Island in June–July 1896.

Comstock (1940): On supplemental list based on specimens from Staten Island (July 1896), and Flushing, NY (July 12).

Delaware Valley (1966): "Infrequent immigrant . . . sometimes in numbers." 1961 was an invasion year, but no records from New Jersey.

Staten Island (1973): "The only records near New York City are given by Davis . . . summer 1896, apparently frequent and perhaps breeding."

New York City Area (1993): Rarely strays up the coastal plain. "Reported to have bred on Staten Island in 1896, also on Long Island. No modern records."

Cape May (1993): Never recorded but listed as a "species to look for."

Habitat: In the southern United States occurs in dry open woodland and prairies of the Lower Austral and Lower Sonoran Zones.

Phenology: Not applicable. In the southern United States flies virtually throughout the year.

Larval Host: Various members of the pea family, including False Indigo (*Amorpha fruticosa*), Alfalfa (*Medicago sativa*), and various clovers.

Comment: The outer margin of the "dogface" pattern on the dorsal forewings reflects ultraviolet.

Cloudless Sulphur [Giant Cloudless Sulphur], *Phoebis sennae* (Linnaeus, 1758) Plate 7a

Range: A permanent breeding resident in southeastern U.S. north to South Carolina. It is often the most common and conspicuous Sulphur in the Neotropics. It immigrates almost annually to southern New England and Long Island and is shown throughout New Jersey except the Northwest (Opler and Krizek 1984). The North American subspecies *ebule* was described by Linnaeus in 1767.

Current Status: Quite common in some years, rare or absent in others, but mainly occurs in southern New Jersey and along Coastal Plain. Usually more common in late summer and early fall. Earliest central New Jersey record 7/8/92 (Raritan Canal 4JC). Northward movements probably follow the Coastal Plain. Regularly irruptive to western Long Island. Increased sightings in northern New Jersey since 1990. There were more 1995 records at Cape May and on Long Island than in many years.

Historical Status: No clear long-term change, but has increased since the mid-1980s. Was reported as very rare near Philadelphia but common in southern New Jersey in 1880s (Skinner and Aaron 1889).

Smith (1890–1910): Local mainly in south and occasionally common in fall. Scattered records in north to Fort Lee and Staten Island.

Comstock (1940): "Coastal area and occasionally inland." Migration rates exceeding fifty per hour, and "swarms" mentioned along outer beaches in September from Cape May to Manasquan.

Delaware Valley (1966): "Immigrant . . . nearly every year, often in numbers, in the coastal plain."

Staten Island (1973): "No modern records." {This is remarkable since the species is now fairly regular on Staten Island and western Long Island in late summer.}

New York City Area (1993): "Irregular late summer migrant along the coast . . . not known to breed."

Cape May (1993): "Common" as a migrant. Migrating swarms reported by Shapiro (1966). Nearly absent in some years (P. Sutton).

Habitat: Any open areas. In migration may be seen over water, in outer beaches, or in suburban corridors. Sometimes quite common in the city of Cape May.

Phenology: June–November. Reported as mid-September–October by Shapiro (1966), hence its earlier occurrences in recent years may represent a real trend. However, it is scarce in July, and only three have been seen on the 64 4JC, all in 1992. This followed unusually mild winters in the southern states (Garrahan 1994). Has bred in Cape May area in years when they arrive early.

Caterpillar Foodplants: Various Wild Sennas (*Cassia* spp.), several of which occur in New Jersey, including Senna (*C. marilandica*), and Sensitive Plant (*C. nictitans*). Found on Partridge Pea (*C. fasciculata*), 9/25/93, Jane Ruffin.

Overwintering: Does not usually overwinter in New Jersey.

Comment: Tends to move long distances along outer dunes, forest edges, roads, and rivers. Due to its rapid, uninterrupted, high flight, its former occurrence was likely underestimated by collectors in New Jersey. Usually seen in flight, alighting infrequently. Seldom seen at flowers, but prefers those with long tubular corolla (for example Trumpet Vine, *Campsis radicans*, Pavulaan).

Orange-barred Sulphur, *Phoebis philea* (Johansson, 1763)

Range: A Neotropical species (northern Mexico and West Indies to southern Brazil) that occurs in southern Florida. Irruptions to northeastern Florida with scattered records in about half of the northeastern states including Monmouth County, NJ, New York, Connecticut (Opler's Atlas), and Rhode Island (Garrahan 1994). The subspecies *philea* would occur in New Jersey.

Current Status: An accidental visitor. No recent records are known to us.

Historical Status: One old Asbury Park record (Sept. 1930s). Sporadic northern records were mainly in the 1930s. This accidental species may have been a more common invader 60 years ago, considering the large number of observers looking for rare species today.

Smith (1890–1910): Not listed.

Comstock (1940): On supplemental list based on a specimen from Asbury Park (Sept. 9) and from New York City.

Delaware Valley (1966): Not listed.

Staten Island (1973): Not listed.

New York City Area (1993): Not listed.

Cape May (1993): Never recorded but listed as a "species to look for."

Habitat: In the southeastern United States, variable, including hardwood hammocks, forest edges, cuts, and gardens.

Phenology: Not applicable in New Jersey.

Larval Host: Sennas genus *Cassia*.

Comments: This species is often uncommon even in Florida, although it is adapting to urban parks and gardens. Its more frequent occurrence during the 1930s may have corresponded to its arrival in the United States. It is highly unlikely that this species would be seen in New Jersey. In the field it must be distinguished with care from the preceding and following species.

Large Orange Sulphur, *Phoebis agarithe* (Boisduval, 1836)

Range: A Neotropical species occurring south to Peru. It is fairly common in southern and central Florida and southern Texas. Opler and Krizek (1984) show breeding in southern and central Florida, with irruptions only to southern Georgia and up the Mississippi Valley (probably from Mexico); single records in Ocean County, NJ, Maine, and Wisconsin (Opler's Atlas). The northern subspecies is *maxima*, described by Neumoegen in 1891.

Current Status: Accidental. No recent records.

Historical Status: An accidental visitor.

Smith (1890–1910): Not listed.

Comstock (1940): On supplemental list based on a specimen from Beach Haven, Sept. 3.

Delaware Valley (1966): Not listed.

Staten Island (1973): Not listed.

New York City Area (1993): Not listed.

Cape May (1993): Not listed.

Habitat: In the southeastern United States, a species of glades and edges in subtropical hammocks and scrub and gardens.

Phenology: Not applicable in New Jersey. Flies all year in southern United States.

Caterpillar Foodplants: Trees of the Mimosoidea subfamily, mainly the genus *Pithecellobium*. Also on *Inga vera* in Jamaica.

Comments: Females of this species are either orange or white. A 1995 record in Rochester, NY.

Little Yellow [Little Sulphur], *Eurema lisa* (Boisduval and LeConte, 1829)

Range: Opler and Krizek (1984) show breeding range from Chesapeake Bay southward along Gulf Coast to Mexico, with irruptions throughout New Jersey and to Maine. However, in New Jersey it is common only in the Cape May area, and it is usually rare away from the Coastal Plain. Opler's Atlas documents records from about half the counties. The subspecies *lisa* occurs in New Jersey.

Current Status: Rare over most of the state, and generally uncommon along the Coastal Plain. Probably occurs annually in Cape May and at Sandy Hook. Its host is the genus *Cassia*, at least three species of which occur in New Jersey, but this butterfly is apparently not a resident in New Jersey. Opler (1983) shows scattered records on the Coastal Plain and lower Delaware Valley, with none from northwestern and northern counties. It was unusually common in 1993 but inexplicably rare in 1995 with no records at Cape May (Dowdell). A 1994 Parsippany record is unusual.

Historical Status: This species is less common today than at the turn of the century, for Smith (1900, 1910) clearly describes this species as very common in the southern coastal part of the state: "There is no time during the summer when it is not likely to be met with along the shore" (Smith 1910). He described it as "local and rarely common north of the red shale line," when today it would be considered very rare there. Skinner and Aaron (1889) likewise considered it "locally moderately common" near Philadelphia, and Shapiro (1966) considered it resident in southern New Jersey. Beutenmüller (1893) considered it "rather common in sandy places." It occurred occasionally in the 1970s in Princeton, where mating was observed in 1973 (Leck).

Smith (1890): "Not rare throughout the state."

Smith (1900): "Throughout the state," June to October. "Local and not common north of red shale," "but the most common species at Anglesea and along the shore in Cape May County in September."

Smith (1910): Local throughout, not common in North; very common in South along shore.

Comstock (1940): "Throughout . . . common in coastal district, less numerous above Fall Line."

Delaware Valley (1966): "Resident . . . general from . . . Camden and the central pine barrens south."

Staten Island (1973): "Common and widespread," "regular immigrant, breeding but not usually overwintering."

New York City Area (1993): "Local and uncommon in open, sandy areas." "Mostly an immigrant but also breeds on beach areas of western Long Island."

Cape May (1993): An "uncommon" migrant.

Habitat: Various open habitats including barren fields near the coast, forest edges, cuts, and roadsides.

Phenology: Enters region from late June/July onward until November. Shapiro (1966) reports three broods mid-May–June, mid-July, and August–September, the latter being most numerous. "Occurrence is sparse until August and September when it is often common" (Comstock 1940). Unusually late records at Lincoln Park, Morris County, 10/23/1993 (Tudor and Cech), and at Manasquan Inlet, Monmouth County, 10/29/92 (*Mulberry Wing*).

Caterpillar Foodplants: In South uses the genus *Cassia*, particularly Wild Sensitive Plant (*C. nictitans*), locally on Partridge Pea (*C. fasciculata*). Also on Wild Senna (*C. marilandica*). These host plants are common in the state.

Overwintering Stage: Not known to overwinter in New Jersey.

Comment: In most years this species appears in midsummer as an immigrant from the South and produces one or more broods until eliminated by cold weather. This species rarely has white females.

Sleepy Orange, *Eurema nicippe* (Cramer, 1779)

Range: Across the southern United States from the Carolinas to southern California through the West Indies and Central America to Brazil. Irrupts northward to southern New England across to central California. Opler and Krizek (1984) show breeding from southeastern Virginia (regularly only from North Carolina) southward. In New Jersey, documented from Gloucester to Cape May and from Essex to Middlesex Counties, as well as Ocean County (Opler's Atlas).

Current Status: Now an uncommon and irregular immigrant from the South, perhaps occurred more regularly in past, but seen about every other year in southwestern New Jersey (Schweitzer). Particularly common in 1988.

Historical Status: Unclear; may have been more common formerly. Beutenmüller (1893) reports an influx into New York City in 1880, with the species rare thereafter. Davis (1910) found this species much commoner on Staten Island at the turn of the century than it is now. Skinner and Aaron (1889) considered it plentiful south of Camden. Most old records are from southern counties, but it was collected in Essex, Union, and Middlesex Counties as well.

Smith (1890): "I have seen it quite generally throughout the State, but nowhere common." Rare at Caldwell.

Smith (1900): "Throughout . . . but somewhat local and never very abundant." Localities include Essex County to Staten Island and Camden to Atlantic City. {Not shown from Atlantic County in Opler's Atlas.}

Smith (1910): "Local throughout . . . rarely common." Records are concentrated in Northeast (e.g., Elizabeth, Staten Island) and in South (Camden to Atlantic City).

Comstock (1940): "Locally, Coastal Plain."

Delaware Valley (1966): "A regular immigrant, often overwintering in the coastal plain and sometimes common." "General in coastal plain but rare in pine barrens."

Staten Island (1973): "Irregular immigrant, breeding often." At least two broods in 1971. Davis (1910) recorded flights in 1880, 1891, 1896, 1906, 1907, 1910.

New York City Area (1993): On accidental list. "Historically rare late fall stray"; several Staten Island records from 1880–1910, seen as late as 1971. No recent records.

Cape May (1993): A "rare" migrant.

Habitat: Open fields, pinelands, woodland cuts, and roadsides.

Phenology: Comstock (1940) reports records from August to November. Smith (1910) records peaks in May–June and September–October. Shapiro (1966) reports broods in May–June, July–August, and sometimes September–October. Peak numbers in August. One in November at Cape May (Dowdell).

Caterpillar Foodplants: Genus *Cassia*. At the turn of the century it bred on *Cassia marilandica* on Staten Island, but that species has been extirpated (Shapiro and Shapiro 1973). Probably uses Partridge Pea (*C. fasciculata*). Raised on Wild Senna (*C. hebecarpa*) (Iftner et al. 1992), a species not listed for New Jersey (Anderson 1983).

Overwintering Stage: Does not overwinter in New Jersey.

Comment: Shapiro (1966) twice saw swarms of hundreds in southern New Jersey in midsummer. In most years breeds as far north as Washington, D.C. (Pavulaan). The pupae of this species may be either green or black or various speckled intermediates, and this pattern appears to have a genetic basis (Evans 1958).

[**Dainty Sulphur,** *Nathalis iole* (Boisduval, 1836)]

Range: From southern Georgia through Florida to the West Indies and from Louisiana to southern California, south to Colombia. It is a regular immigrant in the West to the Great Lakes and northern Plains, but in the East it is rare north of South Carolina. Opler's Atlas shows records from Maryland and southeastern Pennsylvania and several from northwestern Pennsylvania.

Status: No New Jersey records.

Lycaenidae, Harvesters, Coppers, Blues, and Hairstreaks

This is the largest family of butterflies. Males have the forelegs somewhat reduced, but they are fully developed in the female. Many species in this family are called *myrmecophilus* because their larvae associate with ants. Some species are *obligate myrmecophiles*, requiring ants to tend their larvae in order for the larvae to survive, while others can apparently take it or leave it. Some of these interactions are truly mutualistic, where both the ants and the butterfly benefit, while others are more parasitic, benefiting the butterfly at the expense of the ants. In most cases, the ants tend and protect the larvae in order to harvest their energy-rich secretions (Fiedler 1994). In more extreme cases, the ants actually carry the late instar larvae back to their nest, and the larvae then switch to preying on ant pupae; in some cases, they actually elicit feeding by the ants (Cottrell 1984). Caterpillars of many nonmyrmecophile species utilize flowers and buds rather than leaves.

Most species are quite sedentary, and migration is an infrequent event.

An alternative classification (Opler and Krizek 1984; Scott 1986) is to include the Metalmarks (Riodininae) as a subfamily, with all others in the Lycaeninae, and treat the Harvester, Hairstreaks, Coppers, and Blues as tribes of the Lycaeninae.

Subfamily *Miletinae*, Harvesters

There are about fifty species in this group, occurring mainly in the Asian and African tropics. Only one species occurs in North America.

Harvester, *Feniseca tarquinius* (Fabricius, 1793)

Range: The entire eastern United States, from extreme eastern and southern Canada west to Minnesota and south to northern Florida and Texas, including much of New Jersey; but the species is highly local. Opler's Atlas shows records in the extreme northwest and from Bergen County to Sandy Hook, with additional records from Trenton to Gloucester County, but essentially no records from the Atlantic and Delaware Bay coastal plains. The subspecies *tarquinius* occurs in New Jersey.

Current Status: Poorly known and not recorded every year. This unique carnivorous butterfly is generally rare, except where Woolly Aphids occur on alder (*Alnus* spp.), Beech (*Fagus grandifolia*), and other trees; even there it is uncommon and is usually seen solitarily. Occurs periodically at Scherman-Hoffman Audubon Sanctuary in Bernardsville (Wander), Hutcheson Forest (8/29/92, Leck), and Frelinghuysen Arboretum (Wander). Recorded also at Springdale (Wanders), near Annandale, Hunterdon County (Kudzma), Higbee Beach (1990, *fide* Dowdell), Lakehurst (July 1995, Dowdell), and at Cheesequake State Park (1994).

Historical Status: Apparently always rare and local, but also erratic, appearing in an area for a few years and then disappearing. Specimens in Rutgers Collection from Springdale, Caldwell, and Andover.

Smith (1890–1910): "Generally distributed, but local and nowhere common," but specimens only from Newark and Mount Holly.

Comstock (1940): "Locally, throughout . . . sometimes numerous."
{All localities are in North.}

Delaware Valley (1966): "Sporadic and uncommon to rare . . . erratic." Recorded from Mercer, Gloucester, and Camden Counties.

Staten Island (1973): "Frequent but sporadic."

New York City Area (1993): "Rare and irregular in lowland alder thickets, bogs, and stream edges."

Cape May (1993): "Rare."

Habitat: Deciduous forest edge or clearings, often along streams or swamps.

Phenology: Two or three broods May (occasionally late March)–September with peaks in mid-May and late August in North.

Caterpillar Food: This species is unique in North America in that its larvae feed on Woolly Aphids (Homoptera: Eriosomatidae), mainly the genera *Schizoneura* and *Pemphigus*. Shapiro and Shapiro (1973) noted that the Harvester persisted on Staten Island despite the disappearance of alder and first suggested they might use Woolly Aphids of beech or ash. Iftner et al. (1992) report use of Woolly Aphids on Winterberry (*Ilex verticillata*) and Balsam-Apple (*Echinosystis lobata*). Associated with *Prosophila* aphids on American Beech trees at Scherman-Hoffman Sanctuary and Frelinghuysen Arboretum (Wander) and Hutcheson Forest (Leck). Possibly associated with Tulip Tree (*Liriodendron*) at Annandale (Kudzma).

Overwintering Stage: Pupa.

Comments: This species is apparently erratic, occurring for a few years in one locality, then disappearing, hence its alternative name, the Wanderer (Weed 1917). Adults feed on aphid honeydew and bird droppings. Caterpillars are covered with long white hairs and often with faint flecks of whitish wax secreted by the aphids.

Where to Find It: In July, search beech groves at Scherman-Hoffman Sanctuary or Frelinghuysen Arboretum for evidence of woolly aphid infestation.

Subfamily *Lycaeninae*, Coppers

There are about fifty species in this primarily Holarctic group. A few representatives occur in the tropics and New Zealand. Many species use members of the

Polygonaceae as larval hosts, but in New Jersey, the Bog Copper uses Cranberry (Ericaceae). Many species, including the three in New Jersey, have large dull orange (coppery) wing patches.

American Copper, *Lycaena phlaeas* (Linnaeus, 1761)

The systematics of this species require further study. Some authorities believe the American Copper is only recently derived from a Eurasian species, the Small Copper (*L. phlaeas*), which was perhaps introduced to North America as recently as colonial times (Opler and Krizek 1984). There is, however, no direct evidence to support this, and *americana* differs from all European populations.

Range: Central Maine and North Dakota to northern Georgia and Arkansas, including all of New Jersey. The American form described by Harris in 1862 as *Lycaena americana* is now treated as a subspecies, *L. phlaeas americana*.

Current Status: Widespread and often locally abundant, but absent from many likely looking areas even where its host plant is abundant. Common in highlands and also in Cape May and Cumberland Counties. Uncommon in most of Pine Barrens. Can be abundant at Lakehurst (125 in one field, 6/29/88, MG), but surprisingly rare in Somerset and on the Raritan Canal 4JC.

Historical Status: No apparent change in some parts of the state, but has substantially decreased in central New Jersey, for example, at Princeton Junction (Leck).

Smith (1890–1910): "Common throughout."

Comstock (1940): "Throughout . . . usually common."

Delaware Valley (1966): "Locally common."

Staten Island (1973): "Frequent but local."

New York City Area (1993): "Fairly common to locally abundant."

Cape May (1993): "Common."

Habitat: Various disturbed open habitats, including pastures, old fields, forest glades, and cuts; also coastal flats.

Phenology: up to four broods late March–early December with peaks in May, July, and late August–September.

Caterpillar Foodplants: Sheep sorrel (*Rumex acetosella*) and other members of the *Rumex* genus.

Overwintering Stage: Pupa.

Comment: Although this is a widespread and often abundant species that uses a ubiquitous host, its distribution in New Jersey is puzzling. It appears to be associated with oak barrens and is virtually absent from many likely looking areas in central New Jersey where its host abounds. In Ohio, too, its populations are localized (Iftner et al. 1992).

Its scientific name *L. phlaeas*, used in most modern books, reflects its status as a subspecies of Small Copper (*L. phlaeas phlaeas*) of Europe. Although some authors question whether it is indeed conspecific with the Small Copper, treating it as *L. americana* has not gained general acceptance. Indeed, some have suggested that we use the name Small Copper to apply to the American forms, arguing that this is not the only American copper. However, neither is it the only small one, so American Copper seems to have remained the name of choice.

Bronze Copper, *Lycaena hyllus* (Cramer, 1775) Plate 6b

Often listed as *L. thoe* in older books.

Range: Newfoundland and Alberta south to Maryland and Colorado, including all of New Jersey. Opler's Atlas shows records for Sussex, Mercer, Burlington, and Cape May Counties as well as most northeastern counties.

Current Status: Poorly known. Now a rare species in the New York metropolitan area (Glassberg 1989). It has probably declined throughout its New Jersey range and is now highly local, rarely found, and is usually not numerous. Formerly in Troy Meadows. Four colonies known in Sussex County (Wander), and three in Cumberland and Salem counties (C. Sutton).

Historical Status: This species has always been local and not common, but it appears to have declined over much of the northeastern United States (Glassberg 1989). Still fairly common on Delmarva (Pavulaan). There are specimens in the Rutgers Collection from Chatham (6/26/48) and Rutherford/Carlstadt (9/23/10). Absent from most coastal plain counties (Opler's Atlas).

Conservation Status: Because this species is now so local, we recommend that it be listed as a state THREATENED species; it is possibly ENDANGERED. The Natural Heritage ranking is S1?, indicating the need for additional distributional data. It tolerates disturbed habitat, and its wetland habitat is amenable to management and protection from further development. Weakening of wetland protection laws and regulations will further jeopardize this species.

Smith (1890): Rare and local in North (Schooley Mountain, Newark, Caldwell).

Smith (1900): Local, not common in North. (Additional site: Secaucus salt marshes.)

Smith (1910): "Local, not common in North." (Additional sites: Paterson, Elizabeth, Staten Island.)

Comstock (1940): "Locally" north of Fall Line.

Delaware Valley (1966): "Very rare and erratic." Was apparently regular at Tinicum on the outskirts of Philadelphia, but in New Jersey recorded only from Burlington County (Willingboro).

Staten Island (1973): "Locally frequent. . . . Davis found this species rare." {Now extirpated; Cech 1993.}

New York City Area (1993): "Known colonies in the New York City area have been lost to development." Formerly occurred at Idlewild, Queens, NY, now covered by J. F. Kennedy Airport (Tudor).

Cape May (1993): "Rare."

Habitat: A species of wet meadows and disturbed habitat on flood plains, also marshes and fens, and fallow farmland. Glassberg (1993b) suggests that this may be a species of early wetland succession.

Phenology: On Staten Island, two broods June–July and August–September (Shapiro and Shapiro 1973).

Caterpillar Foodplants: Curly dock (*Rumex crispus*); also reported to use Water Dock (*Rumex orbiculatus*; Iftner et al. 1992) and Knotweeds (*Polygonum*) in New Jersey (Smith 1910).

Overwintering Stage: Egg.

Comment: In the past it has been found over most of New York and Long Island, including Rockland County (Shapiro 1974a) and Staten Island (Shapiro and Shapiro 1973). The host plant of this species is abundant. The butterfly has declined possibly due to habitat loss, but it typifies disturbed, early successional habitats.

Bog Copper, *Lycaena epixanthe* (Boisduval and LeConte, 1833)

Range: Maine to northern Minnesota, south to New Jersey and northern Pennsylvania; Opler and Krizek (1984) map includes all of New Jersey except extreme South. However, Opler's Atlas records it from all southern counties except Salem. Not in Delmarva (Woodbury 1994).

Current Status: This is a local species found mainly in the unworked cranberry bogs of the Pine Barrens, where it is often common, and sometimes abundant in late June and early July. It is rare in northern New Jersey but has recently been recorded at a historic site (Mashipacong Bog) in northwestern New Jersey. Occurs in many bogs in the Pine Barrens with up to 300 seen in a day near Manahawkin (Dowdell). It is sparsely distributed south of the Mullica River (Schweitzer).

Historical Status: Smith's lists reflect the increased reconaissance of bog habitats near the turn of the century. No numbers are mentioned. This species is vulnerable to the disappearance of unworked cranberry bogs, and its current habitat at Lakehurst is threatened by forest succession.

Smith (1890): One locality.

Smith (1900): Three localities between Newark and Jamesburg. {The habitat for the "Newark" specimen is unknown.}

Smith (1910): Five locations, including Browns Mills and Lakehurst.

Comstock (1940): "Pine Barrens in cranberry bogs." Localities: Mashipacong, Lakewood, Jamesburg, Lakehurst.

Delaware Valley (1966): "Common to abundant . . . very local." Widespread in bogs.

Staten Island (1973): "Not recorded by Davis but probably formerly occurred on the bogs." {If so, it was extirpated very early.}

New York City Area (1993): "Extremely local in pine barren acid bogs with cranberry"; on eastern Long Island and southern New Jersey.

Cape May (1993): "Local" and "uncommon."

Habitat: Confined to cranberry bogs. Has one of the narrowest habitat ranges of any New Jersey species.

Phenology: Single brooded early June to late July. Peak abundance June 10–15 in Cumberland and Burlington Counties; late June at Lakehurst. In most years, few are flying after July 10. Total flight period in Atlantic County 6/12 to 7/10. Flight period averages four weeks, with males appearing first.

Caterpillar Foodplants: Cranberry (*Vaccinium macrocarpon*); also on *V. oxycoccos* (Opler and Krizek 1984).

Overwintering Stage: Egg.

Comments: The range of this obligate bog species reflects the limit of Pleistocene glaciation. Wright's (1983) life history of this species is considered the most thorough documentation of life stages for any North American species (White 1986). During its brief flight period this species may be quite abundant. They nectar almost exclusively on Cranberry blossoms (Wright 1983). This species is known from a number of New Jersey bogs and may occur in many others that have not been explored. Nonetheless, its habitat is jeopardized by plant succession, and management may be necessary to maintain favorable conditions for this and other bog-loving species. In Ohio it disappeared due to drainage of bogs (Iftner et al. 1992).

This species is very variable in appearance, and Comstock (1940) noted that seven named aberrations have been captured in New Jersey.

Where to Find It: Klots' Bog along the railroad tracks in Lakehurst is an accessible locality. Look during last week of June. Walk southeast along tracks, across a stream, and look for trail leading left (east) into bog.

Subfamily, *Theclinae*, Hairstreaks and Elfins

There are about 2000 species in this group, about half occurring in the Neotropics. The hairstreaks and elfins in New Jersey are finely marked gray and brown butterflies (some have a bright blue upper surface). They have a quick, erratic flight, then land with their wings closed. Except for the Gray Hairstreak, the upper surface is seldom seen. Most rely on trees as larval hosts.

Great Purple Hairstreak, *Atlides halesus* (Cramer, 1777)

Range: Southern United States from Virginia (formerly New Jersey) to central Florida and west to Arizona and California, extending north along Pacific Coast to Oregon and south to southern Mexico. Opler and Krizek (1984) show range from central New Jersey to central Florida, but Opler's Atlas documents records only from Cape May, Gloucester, Mercer, and Somerset Counties. The only New York records (not shown in Opler's Atlas) are from Brooklyn (no date) and Suffolk County (7/18/29) (Shapiro 1974a).

Current Status: No records in the present century, and today very rare north of Virginia.

Historical Status: Probably resident in the last century in New Jersey, but extirpated due to decline of its host (Schweitzer).

Smith (1890): No status indicated, but records from Cape May, Gloucester, Westville (Gloucester County) and "Newark."

Smith (1900–1910): "Very occasional occurrence" and no additional records.

Comstock (1940): On supplemental list as an "occasional visitor."

Delaware Valley (1966): "Included on the basis of a record . . . near Westville, NJ."

Staten Island (1973): Not listed.

New York City Area (1993): "No evidence of recent vagrancy." One old record from Brooklyn and one specimen from eastern Long Island (not shown in Opler's Atlas).

Cape May (1993): Historically present; no recent record.

Habitat: Openings and cuts in deciduous forest.

Phenology: In Virginia, three broods March–November.

Caterpillar Foodplants: Mistletoe (*Phoradendron flavescens*). This arboreal parasite once occurred in southern New Jersey and along the Delaware Valley, but collectors essentially eliminated it by the early twentieth century.

Comment: This spectacular butterfly does not normally range north of the range of Live Oak (*Quercus virginiana*). Mistletoe does occur in Cape May and Cumberland Counties, though it is rare. This species regularly engages in hilltopping (Alcock 1983).

Where to Find It: It is usually uncommon and local on Delmarva (Woodbury 1994).The nearest reliable location is the Dismal Swamp in southeastern Virginia.

Coral Hairstreak, *Satyrium titus* (Fabricius, 1793)

Listed in most publications as *Harkenclinus titus*.

Range: Across southern Canada and northern U.S. to northern California; south to Georgia and northwestern Florida, northern Texas, and Mexico, including all of New Jersey. The subspecies *titus* occurs in New Jersey.

Current Status: Widespread and fairly common in early summer and must occur throughout the state, although documented records are lacking for many counties in northern New Jersey (Opler's Atlas). High 4JC count 49 (1993, Belleplain).

Historical Status: No apparent change in past 50 years, but has certainly increased since a century ago. Smith's accounts are puzzling for he mentions localities with no status information, suggesting that he was not very familiar with it. Beutenmüller (1893) also lists it as rare with only one New York City record in addition to those of Smith.

Smith (1890): Mount Holly and "Newark."

Smith (1900): Several sites from Hopatcong to Staten Island and also Jamesburg.

Smith (1910): Only one additional site listed.

Comstock (1940): "Locally, throughout . . . sometimes common."

Delaware Valley (1966): "Resident," "scarce on coastal plain."

Staten Island (1973): "Frequent, locally common."

New York City Area (1993): "Fairly common to common."

Cape May (1993): "Common."

Habitat: Various open habitats and forest cuts and edges.

Phenology: Single brood late May–mid-August. In North, rare before mid-June and rare after July.

Caterpillar Foodplants: Wild Black Cherry (*Prunus serotina*), also Wild "Plum" (Smith 1910); occasionally on other cherries; (*P. virginiana*) (Shapiro 1966).

Overwintering Stage: Egg.

Comment: Of all our local butterflies, this species shows the strongest preference for Butterfly Weed (*Asclepias tuberosa*) as a nectar source, but also uses other milkweeds. Seldom seen on *Buddleia*. Its pale green eggs are deposited on twigs.

Acadian Hairstreak, *Satyrium acadica* (Edwards, 1862)

Range: Nova Scotia to British Columbia and south to New Jersey and Idaho. In mountains barely reaches northwestern Maryland (Simmons and Andersen 1978a). Opler and Krizek (1984) show it in northern and central New Jersey. The subspecies *acadica* occurs in New Jersey.

Current Status: Status poorly known. Probably rare in the state, and highly local; few recent records in northern New Jersey; two locations in Sussex County (July 1994–95; Wander). Not in southern New Jersey (Schweitzer). Very local but not rare on Long Island (Shapiro 1979), and locally common in northern Westchester County, NY (Glassberg).

Historical Status: Never common and always local, but lack of recent records indicates a decline, probably due to habitat loss. Specimens in Rutgers Collection are from Newton (8/16/12) and Greenwood Lakes. A colony was at Colesville, northern Sussex County, in July 1965 and 1966 (Muller 1976). In the 1960s, fairly common in milkweed/dogbane fields south of Stokes Forest (Darrow). Opler's Atlas shows records for Warren, Sussex, Passaic, Bergen, and Essex Counties and Staten Island; also a questionable record for Ocean County.

Conservation Status: The Natural Heritage Program lists this with an S3 status. There are, however, few known colonies in the state, although there are many small fens that could support this species. Surveys should be conducted specifically to look for this species between mid-June and early July.

Smith (1890): No documented records.

Smith (1900): Greenwood Lake.

Smith (1910): Hewitt and Greenwood Lake.

Comstock (1940): "Crystalline Highlands, Appalachian Valley." Localities: Hewitt, Dover, Newton, Ogdensburg, Newfoundland. {Records are from Sussex to Bergen Counties.}

Delaware Valley (1966): "Uncommon and very local." Shapiro (1962a) found a colony at Cheltenham Twp just north of Philadelphia, but it occurs more regularly in the Poconos.

Staten Island (1973): "Very local," three localities, including Tottenville. {This colony is apparently gone; Tudor.}

New York City Area (1993): "Locally fairly common at marsh edges" {but mainly north of New York City}.

Cape May (1993): Not listed.

Habitat: Fens, wet fields, streamsides, and other wet habitats, and sometimes sandy plains where willows occur.

Phenology: Single brood June–August, but scarce after mid-July.

Caterpillar Foodplants: Black (*Salix nigra*) and Silky Willows (*S. sericea*). Colony at Edgewood, NY, used Beaked Willow (*S. bebbiana*) (Pavulaan).

Overwintering Stage: Possibly egg (Comstock 1940).

Comments: It is surprising that this species is not better known from New Jersey. Black Willow is certainly widespread, and the butterfly should occur in many parts of northern New Jersey. There are recent records from Orange County, NY, and a large population in western Suffolk County, Long Island (Walter). The colony at Colesville, Sussex County (1965–66) yielded several aberrant specimens with creamy rather than orange spots on the ventral hind wing (Muller 1976). Courtship and mating mainly in late afternoon near sunset (Pavulaan).

Edwards' Hairstreak, *Satyrium edwardsii* (Grote and Robinson, 1867)

Range: Disjunct; an eastern population from Maritime Provinces and southern Maine to northern Georgia, including New Jersey. Also a race from Michigan and western Kentucky westward. Opler's Atlas shows scattered records in most northern counties and from Mercer and Ocean to Gloucester and Burlington Counties, but not in most of central New Jersey or the Cape May Peninsula. Not listed for Delmarva (Woodbury 1994).

Current Status: Unknown in most of the state, but locally common in North, where Scrub Oak occurs, including Stokes Forest, Springdale, and Sunrise Mt. (Sussex County), Hibernia (Morris County). Sparsely distributed in southern New Jersey; collected in Cumberland County in 1994 (Schweitzer). Fairly common in oak-pine scrub on Long Island, where often very abundant in early July with counts exceeding 200 in a day.

Historical Status: Inadequate data. Apparently always a very local species. Rutgers Collection has specimens from Hewitt and Newton.

Conservation Status: Natural Heritage ranking is S2–4, indicating inadequate information. Requires surveys to establish its distribution and monitoring of known colonies. Probably secure as long as Scrub Oak habitat is protected.

Smith (1890): "Newark" with no specific locality.

Smith (1900): Newark and Jamesburg.

Smith (1910): Reported as abundant at Newark; additional sites in Passaic County.

Comstock (1940): "Northern District." Localities: Greenwood Lake, Newfoundland, Newton, Hewitt, Newark.

Delaware Valley (1966): "Locally common." Recorded from Gloucester, Burlington, Mercer, and Atlantic Counties. Reported as fairly widespread in Pine Barrens {but this is questionable and needs verification}.

Staten Island (1973): "Apparently rare." First and only specimen 1971.

New York City Area (1993): "Locally common to abundant" near Scrub Oak.

Cape May (1993): Never recorded, but listed as a "species to look for."

Habitat: This species is quite habitat restricted, occurring in oak savannahs, Pine Barrens, and powerline cuts where Scrub Oak occurs. Shows a strong preference for nectaring on New Jersey Tea (*Ceanothus americanus*) and Common Milkweed (*Asclepias syriaca*).

Phenology: Single brood mid-June–early August.

Caterpillar Foodplants: Scrub Oak (*Quercus ilicifolia*, but can also feed on Black Oak (*Q. velutina*).

Overwintering Stage: Egg.

Comment: It is abundant in the Albany, NY, pine-oak barrens and in parts of Long Island pine barrens, but not in the New Jersey Pine Barrens. Since Scrub Oak occurs in several areas of New Jersey, it is possible that it is limited by the distribution of its ant attendant (Schweitzer). This myrmecophilic species is attended by the ant *Formica integra*, which may be necessary for its survival (Webster and Nielson 1984). Banded Hairstreaks, particularly females, may be mistaken for this species.

Banded Hairstreak, *Satyrium calanus* (Hubner, 1809)

Range: Nova Scotia to Manitoba and south to central Florida, Texas, and Colorado, including all of New Jersey. The subspecies *falacer* (described by Godart in 1824) occurs in New Jersey.

Current Status: Occurs throughout New Jersey and is the commonest *Satyrium* hairstreak in central and northern New Jersey. Numbers extremely variable from year to year (Schweitzer) and from place to place (Tudor). In 1995 the species was superabundant near Lakehurst, while numbers were low elsewhere in the region.

Historical Status: Both Smith and Beutenmüller (1893) considered this uncommon. This species may have increased between 1900 and the 1950s since it is now often common, particularly in central New Jersey.

Smith (1890–1910): Throughout, but not common, with localities from Paterson and Staten Island to Camden and Five Mile Beach.

Comstock (1940): "Throughout." Localities from Newton to Five Mile Beach.

Delaware Valley (1966): "Common and widespread" from Camden northward. Common in oak-pine woodlands.

Staten Island (1973): "Abundant . . . extremely abundant on dry acid sand."

New York City Area (1993): "Commonest and most widespread woodland hairstreak."

Cape May (1993): "Common."

Habitat: A forest species occurring in glades, edges, and cuts; may visit nearby gardens.

Phenology: Single brood June–August, usually disappearing entirely by mid-July.

Caterpillar Foodplants: Several white oak species, including White Oak (*Quercus alba*), Chestnut Oak *(Q. prinus)*, and sometimes hickories (*Carya*) and Butternut (*Juglans cinerea*). Reported on "oak, chestnut, hickory, and walnut" (Smith 1910).

Overwintering Stage: Egg.

Comment: Common Milkweed (*Asclepias syriaca*), New Jersey Tea (*Ceanothus americanus*), and Dogbane (*Apocynum*) are its favorite sources of nectar. It spends much time in the canopy, with feeding peaks in midmorning and late afternoon. May also occur with Edwards' Hairstreak near Scrub Oak. On Staten Island occasionally seen in "thousands" (Shapiro and Shapiro 1973). The type locality of the subspecies *falacer* is "near Philadelphia" (Miller and Brown 1981).

Hickory Hairstreak, *Satyrium caryaevorum* (McDunnough, 1942)

This species was first recognized as distinct in 1942.

Range: Disjunct distribution probably due to inadequate data. Eastern population from southern Vermont to New Jersey and Pennsylvania, including all of New Jersey; Opler's Atlas documented records from most northern and central counties, but not Atlantic, Cape May, or Cumberland. Not listed on Delmarva (Woodbury 1994). Other populations from Great Lakes to southern Appalachians and in central United States.

Current Status: Not often reported, probably due to confusion with very similar Banded Hairstreak. May be locally common, but is generally uncommon in the Northwest (Wander) and absent in most of the South (Dowdell) and Delaware Valley (Schweitzer).

Historical Status: Impossible to assess from published accounts since the species was not described until 1942, and even then many literature records are suspect. Some specimens of Banded Hairstreak were presumably this species.

Conservation Status: Inadequate information. Requires surveys and monitoring, with careful documentation of identification.

Smith (1890–1910): Not listed.

Comstock (1940): Not listed.

Delaware Valley (1966): "Rather common" reported from Mercer, Gloucester, and Burlington Counties. {Its commonness in the area remains to be verified.}

Staten Island (1973): "Abundant," the commonest hairstreak at Tottenville (Shapiro). {Its presence today needs verification.}

New York City Area (1993): "Local and usually uncommon." Irruptive in some years.

Cape May (1993): Not listed.

Habitat: Forest clearings, edges, and cuts.

Phenology: Single brood late June–July (rarely to August).

Caterpillar Foodplants: Hickories (*Carya* spp.). Shapiro (1966) reported females laying eggs on shoots of American Chestnut (*Castanea dentata*).

Overwintering Stage: Not reported, presumably egg.

Comment: Often associates with Banded Hairstreak, but generally much less common and very difficult to distinguish, particularly when the anal corner of the hindwing is damaged. Opler and Krizek (1984) note that it is usually separable by the appearance and alignment of the postmedian band of spots. Glassberg (1993b) points out several subtle distinctions, particularly useful when both species are present for comparison; the longer inward projection of the blue anal spot appears to be the most consistent character. Shapiro (1966) noted that males are more visibly distinct than females. However, many individuals are difficult to determine and genitalic examination is desirable. Females can be distinguished under a magnifying glass. In any case, sight records should include a description of how the identification was made, and should be interpreted with caution. This species is certainly both misidentified *and* overlooked.

Striped Hairstreak, *Satyrium liparops* (LeConte, 1833)

Range: Maritime Provinces to Manitoba, south to central Florida and Texas, including all of New Jersey. Fairly common in North but generally rare in South (Opler and Krizek 1984). The subspecies *strigosum* (described by Harris in 1889) occurs in New Jesey.

Current Status: Probably throughout state. May be locally common, although not usually as common as Banded Hairstreak. Highest 4JC total 31 (1993 Cumberland).

Historical Status: It is difficult to identify any trends in this species. Smith (1890–1910) mentioned a few specific localities, and Beutenmüller (1893) could account for only three specimens within 50 miles of New York. Thus it was very rare a century ago. It is puzzling that Shapiro found it rare in the Delaware Valley (Shapiro 1966) but abundant on Staten Island (Shapiro and Shapiro 1973). Did this reflect a change from the 1960s to the 1970s or a real geographic difference?

Smith (1890): "Newark" without specific location.

Smith (1900): Newark, Elizabeth, Jamesburg, without status.

Smith (1910): Additional sites Lakehurst and Five Mile Beach.

Comstock: "Locally, throughout."

Delaware Valley (1966): "Rare and sporadic."

Staten Island (1973): "Abundant locally."

New York City Area (1993): Widespread. Often solitary.

Cape May (1993): "Uncommon."

Habitat: Forest clearings, edges, and cuts.

Phenology: Single brood June–July, and occasionally August.

Caterpillar Foodplants: Quite varied, including several species in the Ericaceae and Rosaceae families (Opler and Krizek 1984). These include Black Chokeberry (*Aronia melanocarpa*), Swamp Blueberry (*Vaccinium corymbosum*; Comstock 1940), Blueberry (*Vaccinium arboretum*), and cherry (*Prunus* sp.). Larvae also reported to feed on various other trees, including "oak, holly, plum, thorn and apple" (Smith 1910). Reported to use "Hop-Hornbeam (*Carpinus carolinensis*) [*sic*, or *Ostrya*?]" and Hawthorn (*Crataegus* spp.; Shapiro 1974a).

Overwintering Stage: Egg. Laid on host twigs.

Comment: The orange cap on the blue anal spot immediately distinguishes this species from the Banded and Hickory Hairstreaks with which it is sometimes found.

Southern or Northern Hairstreak, *Satyrium favonius* (J. E. Smith, 1797)

Often listed in the genus *Fixsenia*. The NABA Checklist (1995) uses the name Southern Hairstreak, which here is doubly misleading since the subspecies occurring in New Jersey has long been called Northern Hairstreak (*S. ontario*), and the species does not have a particularly southern (nor for that matter a northern) distribution. An alternative name would be very desirable. Retaining the name Northern would be preferable to Southern.

Range: The northern race *ontario* (described by Edwards in 1868) has a disjunct range that includes New Jersey. On the Coastal Plain it is found from eastern Massachusetts to South Carolina and from southwestern Georgia and the Florida Panhandle to Louisiana. It is also scattered through the Appalachians and Ozarks from Ohio and Michigan to Mississippi and Texas. The southern race *favonius* occurs along the coast of South Carolina through most of Florida. The map in Opler and Krizek (1984) shows occurrence over all of New Jersey, but there are few records from few localities, and it is unrecorded in most of central New Jersey. It occurs regularly, probably annually, around Lakehurst and Cape May in early July.

Current Status: Poorly known. A local and usually rare species, but locally and briefly common (Lakehurst, late June to early July). Apparently numbers very variable from year to year and much sought after by collectors. Recorded on Cape May and Belleplain Counts in 1993. Occasionally at Cape May (Dowdell); Highest 4JC total 7/3/95, Lakehurst, was a national high.

Historical Status: Always a rare species, Holland (1931) considered it so rare that he suggested it might be an aberrant form of a better-known species. Comstock's account is confusing, implying that both the southern and northern subspecies have occurred in New Jersey; the southern form does not occur regularly north of coastal Georgia. Northern Hairstreak occurs regularly in southern Orange County, New York (Yrizzary), and also has occurred on Long Island (Shapiro 1974a). Darrow (pers. comm.) reports that a collector took 100 specimens near Lakehurst in one week ca. 1960.

Conservation Status: Considered "one of the rarest northeastern butterflies" (Shapiro 1974a). Not ranked by Natural Heritage Program. This species is an erratic resident, locally fairly common in some years and nearly absent in others. There are few known colonies, and collection pressure can be a serious threat. It does not appear consistently at the same place, so "colony" may be a misnomer. In Maryland the Northern Hairstreak is uncommon, but several localities produced individuals in ten straight years (Simmons and Andersen 1970). There are so few known localities that it should be considered vulnerable, and it requires survey and monitoring.

Smith (1890): "Newark" without specific locality.

Smith (1900): One specimen from Anglesea.

Smith (1910): No additional records.

Comstock (1940): On supplemental list *favonius* is mentioned as an occasional visitor from the South based on two specimens from Anglesea {undoubtedly an error}. The form *ontario* was once bred from larvae found at Newark (1892). Comstock mentioned it as very rare with only about twenty records anywhere in a half-century.

Delaware Valley (1966): "Very rare . . . probably resident" recorded from Burlington County (Medford Lakes, Browns Mills, Chatsworth), Salem County (Palatine), Gloucester County (Folsom). The occurrence of the Southern form was reported erroneously by Williams (1941).

Staten Island (1973): Not listed.

New York City Area (1993): "Scattered records, mostly single individuals. Has occurred on Long Island.

Cape May (1993): "Uncommon."

Phenology: Single brood mid-June–mid-July. Apparently emerges a few days earlier than Banded and Hickory Hairstreaks, though this requires careful study.

Caterpillar Foodplants: Oaks. In New Jersey probably mainly on White Oak (*Q. alba*); also uses Post Oak (*Q. stellata*); in the southern U.S. on Live Oak (*Quercus virginiana*).

Comment: Confusion may arise over the name of this species since the Northern Hairstreak (usually listed as *Fixsenia ontario*) has recently been lumped with the Southern Hairstreak and they have been transferred to the genus *Satyrium*. Robbins (1994) explains that there are many intermediate individuals where the two forms overlap in the Carolinas and northern Georgia, hence their treatment as a single species. When the two former "species" (Southern Hairstreak *S. favonius*, and Northern Hairstreak *S. ontario*) were lumped, the scientific name *favonius* had priority, since it had been described earlier (1797 versus 1868). However, such rules of priority do not apply to vernacular names. Indeed, the species as a whole is neither particularly northern nor southern. When two species are lumped, it is appropriate to coin a new common name for the combined species, as for example the following bird species: Northern Oriole, Northern Flicker, and Yellow-rumped Warbler. Note below that when the Olive and Juniper Hairstreaks are lumped, the scientific name of the former was applied, while the English name of the latter was deemed more appropriate (NABA 1995).

Opler and Krizek (1984) state that *favonius* is named after the "western spring wind [Latin]," certainly a neutral name for this species. An alternative name would be the Scarce Hairstreak since it is generally rare throughout its range.

The Genus *Callophrys*

In this volume we follow the treatment suggested by Harry K. Clench and published by J. Benjamin Ziegler (1960) in uniting the green hairstreaks (subgenus *Mitoura*) and elfins (subgenus *Incisalia*) under the generic name *Callophrys*, based on common features of both male and female genital structures. This generic lumping has also been adopted by NABA (1995).

Brown Elfin, *Callophrys augustinus* (Kirby, 1837)

Usually listed in the genus *Incisalia*. The species name is sometimes incorrectly listed as *augustus*; *augustinus* is correct for technical reasons of the ICZN (Ferris 1989).

Range: Newfoundland to Alaska; in East, south through Appalachians to northern Georgia. Opler and Krizek (1984) show it occurring throughout New Jersey except along the Delaware Bay shore. But Opler's Atlas shows it absent from the North except for Passaic County. The subspecies in New Jersey is *croesoides* (described by Scudder in 1876).

Current Status: Very common in early spring in the Pine Barrens. Very local elsewhere where its hosts, particularly blueberry, occur. Absent from most of northern New Jersey.

Historical Status: Difficult to assess. No change since 1940. Smith (1910) reports it as formerly abundant but decreasing on Staten Island. There is no evidence that this species has changed status in the present century.

Smith (1890–1910): Local from Staten Island to Gloucester County, with a record from Paterson.

Comstock (1940): "Throughout . . . frequently abundant, Pine Barrens."

Delaware Valley (1966): "Abundant in pine barrens."

Staten Island (1973): "Status uncertain." Had declined already by 1910. Not definitely found in 1970–71, but listed as common at Watchogue (Davis 1893).

New York City Area (1993): "Widespread."

Cape May (1993): "Common."

Habitat: Clearings and cuts in pine and pine-oak barrens. In New Jersey it is associated mainly with blueberries and sheep laurel, occurring mainly on dry habitats, while in southern Ohio it is associated mainly with Mountain Laurel (Iftner et al. 1992) and elsewhere with acid bogs (Opler and Krizek 1984) and with serpentine formations.

Phenology: One brood early April–May and occasionally early June.

Caterpillar Foodplants: Plants of the Heath family (Ericaceae). In New Jersey, on Blueberries (*Vaccinium* spp.), Bearberry (*Arctostaphylos uva-ursi*), Black Huckleberry (*Gaylussacia baccata*), Leatherleaf (*Chamaedaphne calyculata*), and Labrador Tea (*Ledum groenlandicum*). Among Blueberries, the Low Bush Blueberry (*V. vacillans*) is a particularly good host. Eggs reported on Sheep Laurel (*Kalmia angustifolia*; Pavulaan 1940) and on Mountain Laurel (*K. latifolia*; Iftner et al. 1992). Elsewhere reported on plants in a few other families (Scott 1986).

Overwintering Stage: Pupa in sand or leaf litter.

Comment: This is the commonest elfin in the Pine Barrens in spring. It is found, often abundantly, in open pine woods and pine-oak scrub, along the edges of clearings and roadways. Ziegler (1953) published notes on its life history.

Hoary Elfin, *Callophrys polios* (Cook and Watson, 1907) Plate 5b
Usually listed in the genus *Incisalia*.

Range: Disjunct distribution from Nova Scotia to Alaska; in East from central Maine to southern New Jersey and Delaware Valley with disjunct populations in Appalachians and northern Great Lakes. Not listed for Delmarva (Woodbury 1994). Opler's Atlas records it from Middlesex, Ocean, Burlington, Atlantic, and Cumberland Counties. The subspecies *polios* occurs in New Jersey.

Current Status: Its preferred habitat is barren flats covered with its host, Bearberry *Arctostaphylus uva-ursi*. This local species may be fairly common and occasionally abundant in May in Ocean County. Although few colonies are known it is probably widespread. Recorded near Collier's Mills (common 4/27/74; Leck) and near Warren Grove (many observers), where up to 100 recorded in late May. It should be widespread in the dwarf barrens, since its host is very widespread. Not in Cape May County (Dowdell)

Historical Status: A highly local species with no apparent change in status. It was first described as distinct in 1907 with Lakehurst as the type locality. It has apparently disappeared from eastern Long Island, NY, where its host remains abundant (Cech 1993).

Smith (1890–1900): Not listed.

Smith (1910): Listed from Lakehurst and Lakewood, the latter reported as its type locality. {Miller and Brown (1981) report Lakehurst as the type locality.}

Comstock (1940): "Pine Barrens . . . Occasionally numerous."

Delaware Valley (1966): "Resident," uncommon and local. Occurs in Pine Barrens.

Staten Island (1973): Not listed.

New York City Area (1993): "Extremely local or extirpated, still exists in the New Jersey pine barrens."

Cape May (1993): Not recorded, but listed as a "species to look for."

Habitat: Open flats in the Pine Barrens where Bearberry occurs.

Phenology: One brood late April–mid-June (peak in late May).

Caterpillar Foodplants: Bearberry (*Arctostaphylos uva-ursi*); also Trailing Arbutus (*Epigaea repens*; Shapiro 1966).

Overwintering Stage: Pupa.

Comment: This species should be widespread in clearings in the Pine Barrens wherever its host occurs.

Where to Find It: Open flats of Bearberry about one mile northwest of Warren Grove in mid-May. Take Simm's Road to Beaver Dam Road to open field by communication tower.

Frosted Elfin, *Callophrys irus* (Godart, 1824)

Usually listed in the genus *Incisalia*.

Range: Disjunct from southern Maine to Wisconsin south to northern Florida and eastern Texas. Opler and Krizek (1984) report that "it always occurs in extremely local colonies," but their map is misleading in showing it throughout New Jersey. The subspecies *irus* occurs in New Jersey.

Current Status: A highly localized and generally uncommon species. Very few colonies are known (Schweitzer 1987). There is a large colony near Vineland (Cech) and one at Assunpink WMA, where up to forty have been found in early May. It was seen at Brigantine NWR in 1977 (Leck).

Historical Status: This species may have declined in some neighboring states and in New Jersey, where it is now known from few localities. Recorded historically from a few northern (Sussex, Hunterdon, Essex) and from most southern counties. Still occurs at several colonies in Suffolk County, NY, but highly local.

Conservation Status: Surveys in suitable habitat should be undertaken to detect additional colonies. It is listed as SU, pending additional information. Based on the very few known colonies it should be considered as THREATENED in New Jersey.

Smith (1890): Gloucester and Westville "also taken by Newark collectors."

Smith (1900–1910): Many localities from highlands to Anglesea.

Comstock (1940): "Locally, throughout. . . . Not uncommon; Pine Barrens."

Delaware Valley (1966): "Fairly common" but local.

Staten Island (1973): "Frequent . . . near host plant."

New York City Area (1993): "Very local colonies . . . eastern Long Island . . . Assunpink, NJ." {No mention of the Staten Island population.}

Cape May (1993): "Local" and "uncommon."

Habitat: Cuts and glades in oak woodlands where its hosts occur. In New Jersey it is found with Wild Indigo.

Phenology: One brood early May–early June.

Caterpillar Foodplants: Some populations feed on Lupine (*Lupinus perennis*), but in New Jersey only known on Wild Indigo (*Baptisia tinctoria*). Schweitzer (pers. comm.) questions whether this species was ever a Lupine specialist in New Jersey. Elsewhere also reported on Rattlebox (*Crotalaria sagittalis*; Shapiro 1966) and False Blue Indigo (*Baptisia australis*). Smith (1910) erroneously reported the larvae on wild plum and huckleberry.

Overwintering Stage: Pupa.

Comment: Its temporal status is uncertain. Glassberg (1993b) reports that its numbers fluctuate markedly from year to year, and new colonies have been discovered recently. It is rarely seen nectaring. In different parts of its range it feeds on either Wild Indigo or Lupine, and there may be subtle differences between these populations. Larvae tend to be different as well: pale green and unmarked on Lupine and prominently striped on Wild Indigo. These ecotypes may represent sibling species (Schweitzer, pers. comm.).

Where to Find it: Assunpink WMA (see Appendix) has the best-known colony of this species. Also found along powerline cuts in Belleplain State Forest. Learn to recognize its host, Wild Indigo.

Henry's Elfin, *Callophrys henrici* (Grote and Robinson, 1867)

Usually listed in the genus *Incisalia*.

Range: Nova Scotia to Wisconsin and central Maine to central Florida and Texas. Opler and Krizek (1984) show it occurring throughout New Jersey, but it is a local species on the Coastal Plain. The subspecies *henrici* occurs in New Jersey.

Current Status: Occasionally common in May, but local, occurring mainly on Coastal Plain where Holly grows (e.g., Cape May, Tuckahoe, Brigantine NWR, Sandy Hook). As Holly forests are widespread on the Coastal Plain of New Jersey, this species may actually be very widespread. Sometimes abundant in Cumberland County (up to 30 in a day) and at Sandy Hook (up to 60 in a day), and also found at Higbee Beach (Dowdell) and Brigantine NWR (Leck).

Historical Status: It is difficult to determine if there has been a change. Although Smith (1890–1910) had a few records, the species was not mentioned at all by Beutenmüller (1893). Now that observers know where to look, the species is found regularly and is often common in May. However, it may be another species such as the Red-banded Hairstreak, which has increased in recent decades. In North has occurred in Sussex and Essex Counties.

Conservation Status: The Natural Heritage Ranking is S3–4, and the known colonies of this species should be monitored.

Smith (1890–1910): Localities from Staten Island to Gloucester County.

Comstock (1940): "Locally, Northern District." "Rare." {This may be in error since it occurs mainly south of the Fall Line today.} "The several records given in Smith's 'List' for this species are omitted as doubtful through misidentification." {Comstock apparently erred and Smith was probably right.}

Delaware Valley (1966): "Very rare and sporadic."

Staten Island (1973): Not definitely recorded and not listed.

New York City Area (1993): Known only from Sandy Hook; locally common in southern New Jersey.

Cape May (1993): "Common."

Habitat: Open woods and edges, glades or cuts through hardwood or mixed pine-oak forests where holly occurs; often on sandy soils but also on edges of wooded swamps.

Phenology: One brood late April–late May.

Caterpillar Foodplants: Very variable. In New Jersey mainly on American

Photo 9. Henry's Elfin resting on dead stalk. (Photographed at Sandy Hook by Joanna Burger)

Holly (*Ilex opaca*). Most reports from northeastern United States mention holly, huckleberry (*Gaylussacia*), or blueberry (*Vaccinium*), but in the Appalachians it uses Redbud (*Cercis canadensis*) and in Michigan Maple-leafed Viburnum (*Viburnum acerifolium*). Wild Plum (*Prunus pensylvanica*; Shapiro 1966) and Persimmon (*Diospyros texana*) and "cherry" (Smith 1910), are also reported, but these hosts have not been verified by recent studies.

Comment: The type locality of the species is Philadelphia. Comstock (1940) did not find records of this species south of the Fall Line, although it occurs today mainly on the Coastal Plain, and he dismissed records in Smith (1910) as misidentifications. However, ironically, Comstock's northern records are now viewed as questionable. In view of its use elsewhere of *Vaccinium*, this species should be sought in the Pine Barrens as well. The very different host preferences east and west of the Appalachians make this a candidate for careful systematic study. Greenish highlights on the ventral surface are apparent in a small proportion (less than 10%) of Henry's Elfins from Cape May and become more common southward, until it is predominant in North Carolina (Pavulaan). Photo 9 shows a Henry's perched on a grasshead.

Where to Find It: Sandy Hook and Tuckahoe WMA are regular places to find this species from mid-April to early May. Look for it both on bare ground and in the holly canopy before noon. Also found along Pine Swamp Road in Belleplain State Forest (Dowdell, pers. comm.).

Eastern Pine Elfin, *Callophrys niphon* (Hubner, 1823)
Usually listed in the genus *Incisalia*.
Range: Nova Scotia to Alberta and central Maine to northern Florida and Texas. Opler and Krizek (1984) show it throughout New Jersey, but it is highly

local. The subspecies *niphon* occurs in southern New Jersey, but most Pine Barrens specimens are assignable to the northern *clarkii* (Pavulaan).

Current Status: Fairly common and regular in Pine Barrens in spring. Occurs south to northern Cape May County with up to twenty seen in a day (Dowdell). Also present but rare at Stokes State Forest and Delaware Water Gap, where White Pine is the host. Collected in garden in Kendall Park (4/20/1976; Leck). Occasionally near Lakehurst (Tudor).

Historical status: No evidence of change.

Smith (1890–1910): Localities from Staten Island to Camden and Five Mile Beach.

Comstock (1940): "Pine Barrens . . . Not common."

Delaware Valley (1966): "Common in New Jersey pine barrens," widespread.

Staten Island (1973): "Extirpated." Apparently common in 1881, but no subsequent records. Its host pines have been greatly reduced.

New York City Area (1993): "Widespread in pine-oak woodland on Coastal Plain."

Cape May (1993): "Common."

Habitat: Openings and cuts through pine and pine-oak woodland.

Phenology: One brood mid-April–late May and occasionally mid-June.

Caterpillar Foodplants: Various species of pines, including mainly the hard pines—Scrub, Pitch, and Jack Pines (*Pinus virginiana, P. rigida, P bansksiana*). Less common with White Pine (*P. strobus*), but this is the host in northern New Jersey. Shapiro (1966) reports "probably also red cedar" (*Juniperus*), but it is not often associated with that species. Eggs are laid on the new growth.

Overwintering Stage: Pupa.

Comment: This is a fairly common species in the Pine Barrens in April and early May, but is greatly outnumbered by the Brown Elfin. Sometimes seen in the canopy.

Where to Find It: Widespread but not numerous throughout the Pine Barrens. Usually seen singly. Regular as far south as Belleplain State Forest.

Juniper Hairstreak [Olive Hairstreak], *Callophrys gryneus* (Hubner, 1819)

Usually listed in genus *Mitoura*. The Olive Hairstreak of eastern North America has recently been lumped with several western forms. The NABA Checklist calls the new species the Juniper Hairstreak, since all members use Juniper as their host.

Range: The newly lumped species ranges over the entire United States to Mexico. The 'Olive' Hairstreak (subspecies *gryneus*) ranges from southern Maine and central Vermont to southern Minnesota, south to northern Florida, Georgia, and Texas, including all of New Jersey.

Current Status: Can occur wherever its host, Red Cedar (*Juniperus virginiana*) occurs. Sometimes common in early summer. Local but fairly common in Northwest, although it has decreased since 1990 (Wander). Near Cape May may be common nectaring on beach plum on the dunes. Unusually scarce in Somerset in 1995.

Historical Status: No apparent change this century. The species is probably more common today than in colonial times due to the increase of its host after clearing of hardwood forests.

Smith (1890): Locally not rare in Passaic Valley, also "Newark".

Smith (1900): Widespread north of red shale line, also at Anglesea.

Smith (1910): "Throughout the state, locally common."

Comstock (1940): "Locally, throughout . . . occasionally common."

Delaware Valley (1966): "Locally common," fairly widespread.

Staten Island (1973): "Extinct," its food plant also nearly extinct. No extant specimens for Staten Island.

New York City Area (1993): Coastal Plain; can be fairly common near its host.

Cape May (1993): "Common."

Habitat: Old fields, juniper savannahs, and forest edges where its host occurs. However, there are many juniper stands where this hairstreak is not found. It prefers stands with some young trees 2–4 m in height. Occurs in Pine Barrens and on red shale area, and elsewhere also on serpentine soils.

Phenology: Spring brood late April–late May; summer brood, mainly in July, rarely before July 8 and rarely after mid-August. In the New York City area and the Pine Barrens, the May brood is more numerous, while in Sussex and Somerset Counties, the spring brood is very scarce.

Caterpillar Foodplant: Red cedar (Juniperus virginiana). A Catbriar (Smilax rotundifolia) is mentioned in earlier papers (e.g., Smith 1900, 1910), but this has not been verified and seems unlikely. It is considered host specific on Red Cedar.

Overwintering Stage: Pupa.

Comment: Robbins (1994) explained that where the "Olive" and "Siva or Juniper" Hairstreaks come in contact in western Texas one finds a whole spectrum of wing patterns indicating interbreeding. Scott (1986) reports similar findings for the other members of the complex, thus supporting their treatment as a single species. The Juniper Hairstreak appears to be host specific, ovipositing only on Red Cedar, although Remington and Pease (1955) showed that the caterpillars can mature when raised on White Cedar (Chamaecyparis thyoides), which is the host of the next species.

Adults perch mainly on junipers and orient their bodies according to polarized light. They roost in taller trees, but tend to perch at a height of about 2 m (Johnson and Borgos 1976) or higher (Pavulaan).

The phenology requires further study. The spring brood has not been observed at all in some colonies in Sussex County (Wander) and Somerset County (Gochfeld), where the summer brood is common.

Hessel's Hairstreak, Callophrys hesseli (Rawson and Ziegler, 1950) Plate 5a

Usually listed in the genus Mitoura.

This highly localized and usually uncommon species was not recognized as a distinct species until 1950, hence its prior status is unknown.

Range: Highly disjunct distribution from extreme southern Maine to Florida, including localities in southern half of New Jersey and Long Island (formerly). Not recorded from most of New York (Shapiro 1974a) or from most of New Jersey (Opler 1983).

Current Status: Confined to vicinity of white cedar swamps, but may be occasionally common. Recorded from Ocean, Burlington, Atlantic, and Cape May Counties (Opler's Atlas). Widespread in south (Schweitzer); found from Lebanon State Forest to northern Cape May County (Great Cedar Swamp). It has not yet been found in the North, although there are White Cedar stands that should be checked.

Historical Status: Difficult to determine since the species was not recognized until 1950. Some specimens identified as 'Olive' Hairstreaks are actually this species.

Smith (1890–1910): Not listed.

Comstock (1940): Not listed.

Delaware Valley (1966): "Very local and always uncommon."

Staten Island (1973): Not listed.

New York City Area (1993): "Still reasonably common in New Jersey 'throughout' pine barrens."

Cape May (1993): "Local" and "uncommon."

Habitat: In and around White Cedar swamps.

Phenology: First brood late April–mid-May, with a small and irregular second brood in July.

Caterpillar Foodplant: White Cedar (*Chamaecyparis thyoides*) (Rawson et al. 1951).

Comment: This species is not conspicuous, spending most of its time in the canopy and nectaring in the understory mainly in morning and late afternoon, so that it is difficult to inventory even in suitable habitat. Most New Jersey colonies are in regenerated White Cedar stands (Schweitzer 1989). It is very similar to the more widespread Juniper [Olive] Hairstreak but tends to be brighter green (see Glassberg 1993b).

Where to Find It: Blueberry fields and open sandy areas adjacent to White Cedar swamps, for example, along Route 72 at mile post 9, about 4 miles west of Route 539. Look for patches of Sand Myrtle (*Leiophyllum buxifolium*) and Button Bush (*Cephalanthus occidentalis*) along dirt roads at the edge of the wetlands. It also nectars at various blueberries, and the July brood also nectars on Swamp Milkweed (*Asclepias incarnata*). Also occurs near Warren Grove and in Belleplain State Forest.

White M Hairstreak, *Parrhasius m-album* (Boisduval and LeConte, 1833)

Sometimes listed in the genus *Panthiades.*

Range: Massachusetts and Rhode Island west to Kansas and south to southern Florida and Texas and to northern South America; can occur anywhere in New Jersey.

Current Status: Generally a southern species that is rare and local in most of the state, particularly in the Northwest. Seen with some regularity near Lakehurst and in late summer near Cape May, where it may be fairly common with up to six seen in a day. One Somerset record in 10 years (MG). The spring brood is apparently rare or usually unrecorded.

Historical Status: This southern species has been expanding its range northward in the past two decades, as is apparent from its former rarity. Beutenmüller (1893) had no records for the northern part of New Jersey. In New York State, Shapiro (1974a) recorded only two records, from Staten Island (10/5/71) and Rockland County (9/13/67), but there are now many records. In the past 50 years it has become regular and occasionally fairly common at Cape May.

Smith (1890–1900): Not listed.

Smith (1910): Atlantic City, Orange Mountains (April 28), and Lake Hopatcong.

Comstock (1940): "Occasional visitor, southern species." Records from Orange Mountain and Hopatcong to Atlantic City. {Apparently very few new records since 1910.}

Delaware Valley (1966): "Very rare and sporadic, but possibly breeding."

Staten Island (1973): "A single record" 10/5/71.

New York City Area (1993): Widespread but sparse; near oakwoods. May be increasing.

Cape May (1993): "Uncommon."

Habitat: Edges of and cuts through deciduous forest. Seems particularly attracted to Slender Fragrant Goldenrod (*Solidago tenuifolia*) as a nectar source in southern New Jersey (Tudor).

Phenology: Three broods late April–September.

Caterpillar Foodplants: Several species of oaks, including Live Oak (*Q. virgiana*) in South. Hosts in New Jersey are not known. The pupa may actually emit a high-pitched chirp when disturbed (Clench 1961).

Overwintering Stage: Not reported by Comstock (1940) or Opler and Krizek (1984).

Comment: The early spring brood apparently uses little nectar and is likely to be overlooked, but reported on Sassafras flowers in spring (Pavulaan).

Where to Find It: Easiest in September in Delaware Bay coastal plain, where Slender Fragant Goldenrod occurs (near Higbee Beach and Delmont).

Gray Hairstreak, *Strymon melinus* (Hubner, 1818)

Range: Nova Scotia to British Columbia and south to Florida, California, and South America; throughout New Jersey, although map in Opler and Krizek (1984) show it as not resident in northern New Jersey. The subspecies *humuli* (described by Harris in 1841) occurs in New Jersey.

Current Status: Widespread and sometimes common in North and often abundant in South. However, usually few individuals seen in any one day. Maximum of four individuals on the eight Raritan Canal 4JC (1988–1995). Maximum of six at Lakehurst in August. Maximum 4JC total fifty-six (1993 Cumberland County).

Historical Status: No apparent change. Has always been considered common.

Smith (1890–1910): Local throughout.

Comstock (1940): "Throughout."

Delaware Valley (1966): "Commonest hairstreak," widespread.

Staten Island (1973): "Common and general."

New York City Area (1993): "Widespread but seldom abundant." Coastal plain; commonest in late summer.

Cape May (1993): "Common."

Habitat: Very diverse. Found in any open habitat, including gardens, and along woodland edges.

Phenology: Up to four broods mid-April–early November.

Caterpillar Foodplants: Very diverse, with apparent preference for legumes and Malvaceae. Clovers including *Trifolium, Melilotus, Lespedeza*, Tick Trefoil (*Desmodium*), Knotweeds (*Polygonum*), and various other species (Shapiro 1966). Apparently favors flowers and perhaps even pollen (Guppy 1959). Scott (1986) lists more than eighty plants in twenty-nine families.

Overwintering Stage: Pupa.

Comment: Although not usually numerous, this Hairstreak is very widespread and can be found almost any time during its long flight period.

Red-banded Hairstreak, *Calycopis cecrops* (Fabricius, 1793) Plate 8a

Range: Southeastern New York and Rhode Island to southern Florida and west to Mississippi Valley, including central and southern New Jersey. Not documented in most northern counties.

Current Status: This species has been extending its range northward (reaching Rhode Island in 1995; Pavulaan). It became relatively common over much of the state in 1990–91, particularly the Coastal Plain, but was less common in 1992–94. Often common in Cape May and Cumberland Counties and near Toms River. Less numerous in central New Jersey; most counts fewer than ten per day. Up to twelve recorded at Assunpink in August (Tudor). Rare in the Northwest, but has been reported near Sterling Forest, NY (Yrizarry).

Historical Status: Has increased greatly. Formerly very rare and irregular and

Photo 10. The rare White M Hairstreak nectaring at Common Milkweed. Note the white spot on the costal margin of the hind wing (photographed at Somerset by Joanna Burger).

listed by Comstock (1940) among species that were not regular inhabitants of New Jersey. Apparently only one record before 1940. Opler's Atlas did not list records for the five northwestern counties. For New York, Shapiro (1974a) recorded it only from New York City and Long Island.

Smith (1890–1900): Not listed.

Smith (1910): One specimen from Manasquan.

Comstock (1940): On supplemental list as an "occasional visitor" from the South with specimens only from Manasquan and Long Island, NY. {Only one record between 1890 and 1940.}

Delaware Valley (1966): "Rare but apparently breeding locally."

Staten Island (1973): "Frequent to locally common."

New York City Area (1993): "Currently undergoing an explosive range expansion."

Cape May (1993): "Common."

Habitat: Forested edges and clearings and cuts and nearby old fields.

Phenology: Two broods late May–June and August–October.

Caterpillar Food: In some areas this species associates with Winged or Dwarf Sumac (*Rhus copallina*), which is common on the Coastal Plain of New Jersey. Elsewhere associated with other species of sumac (Anacardiaceae) or the euphorb *Croton linearis*. The caterpillars probably feed mainly on sumac leaf litter rather than on live plant material (Scott 1986, Pavulaan).

Comment: This is among the species showing the most dramatic range extension and population increase in New Jersey in the past half-century.

[Early Hairstreak, *Erora laeta* (Edwards, 1862)]

Range: Disjunct; an Appalachian species extending from Nova Scotia and Maine to northern Georgia, scattered records in north-central states. New York records mainly from central counties but also from Sullivan and Ulster Counties (Shapiro 1974a). Occurs in southwestern Pennsylvania (Simmons and Andersen 1978b). Map in Opler and Krizek (1984) includes extreme northwestern New Jersey; a record from Sussex County (Opler 1983).

Current Status: Accidental. No definite records. Northwestern New Jersey is at the margin of its primarily Appalachian distribution. It could be a vagrant or extirpated or exceedingly rare. The species occurs to the west in Pennsylvania and could occur in New Jersey.

Historical Status: One specimen attributed to F. G. Stiles in Sussex County (Opler, pers. comm.). Comstock (1940) reported that the only specimen is one from Atlantic City (July 1), but that was based on a mislabeled specimen. Reported in the 1880s by Aaron and Skinner which Shapiro (1966) remarks is "almost certainly an introduced specimen." Rare in New York with records as near as Ulster and Sullivan Counties (Shapiro 1974a).

Smith (1890–1910): Not listed.

Comstock (1940): On supplemental list based on the Atlantic City specimen. {This accounts for one of the localities on the map in Opler's Atlas; but the location is certainly not accurate.}

Delaware Valley (1966): "Not recorded," "always rare." Found in Alleghenian area northwest of Philadelphia and in Poconos.

Staten Island (1973): Not listed.

New York City Area (1993): Not listed.

Cape May (1993): Not listed.

Habitat: It is a species of beech woods and maple-beech-hemlock (Shapiro 1974a).

Phenology: Not known in New Jersey; in New York probably has two broods May–early June and a smaller brood in summer. Flies mid-April in western Maryland and early May in southwestern Pennsylvania (Simmons and Andersen 1978b).

Caterpillar Foodplants: American Beech (*Fagus grandifolia*) and Beaked Hazel (*Corylus cornuta*), possibly also White Oak (*Quereus alba*; Pavulaan).

Comment: Generally considered one of the rarest butterflies in eastern North America. "It occurs in the most unlikely place when least expected" (Simmons and Anderson 1978b). In addition to the possible Sussex County record, the only New Jersey records are the single mislabeled specimen from Atlantic City and a questionable record from Cape May, both of which are inappropriate habitat.

Where to Find It: No known New Jersey localities but should be sought in Sussex County at higher elevations (Stokes, High Point) in late May. The only reliable site in the northeastern states is Mount Greylock in western Massachusetts.

Subfamily *Polyommatinae*, Blues

The Blues (subfamily Polyommatinae) comprise a North Temperate assemblage of small, sexually dimorphic butterflies that reach much greater diversity in Eurasia than in North America. Many of the species have strict host preferences, usually for legumes, and many are myrmecophiles, their larvae must be attended by ants.

Some of the most endangered butterflies in North America are Blues, and the extinct Xerces Blue of San Francisco Bay has lent its name to the Xerces Society, thereby becoming a metaphor for invertebrate conservation. Worldwide, many of the Lycaenids are endangered and the International Union for the Conservation of Nature (IUCN) has published a monograph on the conservation biology of this group (New 1993).

[Marine Blue, *Leptotes marina* (Reakirt, 1868)]

Range: Southern California to south Texas (rarely Florida) to northern Central America, irrupting sporadically north and eastward to northern California,

Colorado, Illinois, Ohio, and recently New York. Has not been found in New Jersey.

The first East Coast record documented by photographs was at Fort Tilden, Queens, N.Y., Aug. 29, 1993 (Walter 1993), apparently part of an invasion that brought the species to Ohio and western New York (Glassberg 1993e).

Habitat: Very variable, tropical lowland including deserts and agricultural fields (e.g., Alfalfa).

Phenology: Its population outbreaks would occur in August–September.

Caterpillar Foodplants: Various members of the Fabaceae family.

Comments: This species has become urbanized in southern California (Brown 1990) and is now widespread and common in gardens and coastal habitats (Tudor). It could occur in New Jersey during an outbreak year. The individual observed in Queens possibly crossed New Jersey en route.

Eastern Tailed Blue, *Everes comyntas* (Godart, 1824)

Range: Central Maine and southern Canada to Colorado and south to northern Florida and Central America. Throughout New Jersey. The subspecies *comyntas* occurs in New Jersey.

Current Status: Widespread and usually common, sometimes abundant. Highest 4JC total 310 (1992, Cape May).

Historical Status: No apparent change.

Smith (1890–1910): "Common throughout."

Comstock (1940): "Throughout. . . . Usually common."

Delaware Valley (1966): "Abundantly . . . throughout."

Staten Island (1973): "Abundant."

New York City Area (1993): "Common to abundant."

Cape May (1993): "Abundant."

Habitat: Ubiquitous, including any open country and edges of, and cuts through, woodland where clover occurs. Frequently found over lawns or other short vegetation.

Phenology: Four broods April–November.

Caterpillar Foodplants: Many species of legumes. Mainly White Clover (*Trifolium repens*) but also Alsike Clover (*T. hybridum*), Tick-Trefoil (*Desmodium canadense*), Alfalfa (*Medicago sativa*), Sweet Clovers (*Melilotus* spp.), and Bush Clovers (*Lespedeza* spp.).

Overwintering Stage: Full-grown larva.

Comment: This is one of the most common and most widespread, though somewhat inconspicuous, butterflies in New Jersey (photo 11). However, it was quite uncommon in Somerset during the August 1995 drought. Beginners may confuse this with the Azures, which are larger and more likely to fly high, while Tailed Blues spend most of their time within one meter of the ground. Spring females are partly blue while summer females are wholly black above.

The Azures

The taxonomy and systematics of the American azures has long been controversial. Early authors considered our Spring Azure conspecific with the Holly Blue (*Celastrina argiolus*) of Eurasia, since John Abbot's illustration in 1797 was labeled as *argiolus*, the treatment returned to by Ferris (1989). However, the great morphologic variability of this species has been recognized for more than a century, and several varieties or morphs are often distinguished:

'violacea': Smaller, darker, more distinctly marked with larger spots; but without the black margin of 'marginata' or the discal patch of 'lucia'

Photo 11. Eastern-tailed Blue male resting on a dried Self-heal flower cluster. This is one of the smallest and most numerous and widespread butterflies in New Jersey. (Photographed in our yard in Somerset by Michael Gochfeld)

'marginata': gray below with broad black margin, but lacking the black patch
'lucia': Brownish or blackish discal patch below,
'lucimargina': Discal patch plus heavy black border
'neglecta': pale white below with smaller spots

W. H. Edwards was probably the first to provide extensive systematic study of this group, and he originally described the forms 'neglecta' (1862) and 'violacea' (1866) as distinct species, and 'marginata' as an intermediate form. The form 'lucia' had been described by Kirby (1837). Based on a flawed experiment, Edwards (1883) concluded that they all represented one species. He recognized that some forms ('marginata,' 'lucia') did not occur in Virginia but were predominant in southern Canada and New England. He believed that the early spring population gave rise to the May population, which is now recognized as Appalachian Azure (*C. neglectamajor*) and to the June brood, now treated as the Summer Azure (*C. neglecta*) because 1% of the larvae from his Spring Azure females emerged at those times, although the remainder pupated and remained in diapause until the following spring.

Edwards recognized that most of the spring adults were univoltine for he says (1883:89): "Eggs laid by *Violacea*, in April or early May . . . produce *Neglecta*, in June so far as known, but most of the chrysalids hibernate." Edwards had a lot of trouble keeping his chrysalids alive, and with better technique he might have recognized the distinct phenologies a century ago. Beutenmüller (1893) knew about the differing host preferences, pointing out that the spring females laid eggs in flower buds of Flowering Dogwood, while the late spring brood laid on Black Cohosh, and the summer brood on Wingstem (*Actinomeris alternifolia*).

Today, the Azures are undergoing intensive systematic reinvestigation because of the evidence that the designation "Spring Azure" hides several so-called sibling species (species that eventually prove to be genetically or biologically distinct, but have masqueraded under the guise of another species for a long time). Two species with primarily Appalachian distributions, the Dusky Azure (*Celastrina ebenina*) and Appalachian Azure (*C. neglectamajor*), have already been separated from the Spring Azure, and David Wright and Harry Pavulaan are sorting out several additional entities that are currently included in the Spring Azure complex, but which differ in their phenology and host preferences. There is strong evidence supporting recognition of the Summer Azure (*C. neglecta*).

The Azures of New Jersey may best be represented as follows:

Spring Azure, *Celastrina ladon*
  *Northern Azure, *Celastrina lucia*
  *Edwards' Azure, *Celastrina violacea*
  *Cherry Gall Azure, *Celastrina* sp.
  *Pine Barrens Azure, *Celastrina* sp.
Summer Azure, *Celastrina neglecta*
Appalachian Azure, *Celastrina neglectamajor*

One or more of the four entities marked by an asterisk may prove to be good species, or they may represent ecological races, host specific races, or phenological races (Pavulaan). Until they are better understood, they tax our traditional approaches to taxonomy. (Pavulaan, and Wright 1994). Moreover, it is not clear which of the entities was represented by the original species name *Celastrina ladon* (Cramer), since his description could apply to any of these (Pavulaan).

For clarification of the current status of Azures we are indebted to the work and extensive comments of Wright and Pavulaan. We hope we have reflected the current understanding fairly, if not clearly. In the treatment that follows we provide both the traditional treatment of the Spring Azure, and also summarize the status of the other entities recognizing that they are still preliminary. The NABA Checklist (1995) treats several of these as subspecies of *C. ladon*, but they are not subspecies since they regularly occur together, albeit in different proportions at different times and places.

Spring Azure, *Celastrina ladon* (Cramer, 1780)
Traditional Spring Azure Complex (excluding Summer Azure).
Also listed in the genus *Lycaena* with various species names including *pseudargiolus* in older publications.
Range: Labrador and Maine to northern Florida and across North America to Panama; throughout New Jersey.
Current Status: Widespread and sometimes abundant.
Historical Status: Edwards (1883) uses terms such as "swarms" and "myriads," suggesting that these were at one time superabundant, occurring in much greater numbers than is typical today or even 40 years ago.
Smith (1890–1910): Locally common throughout.
Comstock (1940): "Throughout. . . . often very common."
Delaware Valley (1966): Resident throughout. Shapiro (1966) studied this species extensively and recognized *neglectamajor* as possibly distinct.
Staten Island (1973): "Summer form common and widespread." Spring form *violacea* was rare in 1971.
New York City Area (1993): "Common and widespread, often in woodlands."
Cape May (1993): "Abundant."
Habitat: Deciduous forest edges, glades, and cuts, as well as old fields and gardens.
Phenology: Univoltine. Mid-March to mid-April for some entities and April to mid-May for others ("Cherry Gall Azure" and "Pine Barrens Azure"). Populations emerging after early June are herein designated Summer Azures.
Caterpillar Foodplants: Early broods use mainly Flowering Dogwood (*Cornus*

florida), viburnums (*Viburnum* spp.), blueberries (*Vaccinium* spp.) and cherries (*Prunus* spp.). It includes entities using leaf galls of Wild Black Cherry (*Prunus serotina*) and hollies (*Ilex* spp.).

Overwintering Stage: Pupa.

Comment: The butterflies are highly variable from the pale 'violacea' with large spots, pale wing margins, and no patch, to 'marginata' with its dark wing margin and to 'lucia' which has brown patches on the wings. All three forms may be found together in the spring, although the proportions vary from place to place. The darker forms predominate at higher latitudes, whereas 'violacea' is the only representative in some southern populations. This is a very complex taxon. The species *neglectamajor* has already been separated as a distinct species, and the summer *neglecta* is treated separately here, as well. The form *violacea* may also be distinct (Glassberg 1993b, Wright 1995). Since the frequency of the color forms or morphs varies geographically, several have been considered to be subspecies, but this is inconsistent with the usual use of the term subspecies.

Some or all of the following entities may prove to be distinct species. Since all are "Spring Azures" it may be most convenient to drop that name entirely. One of the following is the true *Celastrina ladon* as originally described, but it is not clear which. The first two entities fly in early spring; the latter two in later spring.

Northern Azure, *Celastrina sp.*

Treated as *c. l. lucia* by Pratt et al. (1994).

If the entities listed below prove to be distinct species, the Northern Azure, which ranges across Canada and south through New Jersey, will remain as a wide-ranging generalist. It occurs in northern New Jersey with, and at the same time as, "Edwards' Azure" and also in the Pine Barrens, but earlier than the "Pine Barrens Azure."

Current Status: Probably the common "Spring Azure."

Habitat: Widespread in various woodlands and scrubby areas with blueberries.

Phenology: The archetypical Spring Azure, emerging in late March and April, and mostly gone by early May.

Caterpillar Foodplants: Blueberries (*Vaccinium* spp.) in Pine Barrens. In northern New Jersey also on cherries (*Prunus* spp.) and Viburnums (*Viburnum* spp.). Reported on cherries in New England.

Overwintering Stage: Pupa.

Comment: The 'lucia' and 'marginata' forms are most common, while other forms similar to 'violacea' occur. The darker forms predominate at higher latitudes, and also in the Pine Barrens. All three forms fly together in varying proportions. A "lucimargina" form also occurs (Scott 1986).

Edwards' Azure, *Celastrina violacea* (Edwards, 1866)

Treated as "Edwards" Spring Azure *C. l. violacea* by NABA (1995).

Range: Southern Maine through Appalachians to central Ohio and eastern Kentucky, to central Georgia. Disjunct populations in southern Michigan, southeastern Missouri, and central Arkansas. This is mainly an Appalachian and Ozark entity. Absent from much of the Coastal Plain. Occurs in New Jersey west of the Fall Line.

Current Status: Uncertain. The 'violacea' morph is widespread and common, but could refer either to other "Spring Azures" or to "Edward's Azure."

Habitat: Cuts and stream edges in rich deciduous woodlands, and in scrubby woods where blueberries occur. Not in the Pine Barrens.

Phenology: One brood, early April–early May, peaking in mid-late April.

Caterpillar Foodplants: Larvae feed on unopened flower buds of Flowering Dogwood (*Cornus florida*), its main host. At the northern edge of its range where this tree is less common, it uses *Viburnum*, *Prunus*, and *Vaccinium* (Wright 1995), which are probably the hosts in northwestern New Jersey (Pavulaan).

Overwintering stage: Pupa.

Comment: Originally described by Edwards as a separate species. Wing scales differ structurally from other azures and are most similar to Dusky Azure. Males are more violet than the "Northern Azure", with which they may fly. Most individuals are 'violacea,' but in Michigan and New England, some 'marginata' and 'lucia' individuals occur. There is also a 'lucimargina' form with dark margin and dark patch (Pavulaan, in litt.). The wing margin tends to be checkered pale and dark in specimens from northern New Jersey (Pavulaan). It should be sought in northern and western New Jersey outside the Pine Barrens.

Cherry Gall Azure, *Celastrina* sp.

Treated as "Cherry Gall" Spring Azure, *C. ladon* subsp. by NABA (1995). All information from Wright (1995) and Pavulaan and Wright (1994).

Range: Poorly known. Main range is from eastern Massachusetts to extreme eastern Ohio and northern West Virginia. Many disjunct populations in Nova Scotia, central Maine, southern Quebec, eastern Ontario, western New York, and southeastern Michigan. In New Jersey occurs northwest of the Fall Line. The map in Wright (1995) shows it in the Pine Barrens as well, but that refers to the next entity, the "Pine Barrens Azure."

Current Status: Unknown. May be locally common west of Fall Line (Wright 1995).

Habitat: Open woodlands and old fields with Black or Chokecherry trees.

Phenology: Mid-May–early June. Usually after, but can overlap latter part of flight period of Spring Azure (or "Edward's" and "Northern" Azures).

Caterpillar Foodplants: Leaf galls of Wild Black Cherry (*Prunus serotina*). In Poconos, uses leaf galls on Chokecherry (*P. virginiana*). Also reported on Naked Withe-Rod (*Viburnum nudum*) on Long Island. In Canada, feed on Sarsparilla (*Aralia hispida*) and Nannyberry (*Vibrunum lentago*) flowers. The cherry flower buds used by larvae of the Spring Azure are gone by the time the larvae of this species emerge (Wright 1995).

Overwintering Stage: Pupa.

Comment: Most individuals are pale 'violacea' forms, brighter and paler blue than the few Spring Azures that remain to fly with it. Wing margin usually white (Pavulaan). This entity is slightly smaller than the very similar Appalachian Azures which would be flying at the same time. Wright (1995) cautions that "field separation from Spring Azures and Appalachian Azures remains problematical." As with other azures, more northern populations have higher percentages of the darker 'lucia' and 'marginata' forms. These can be found in the Poconos.

Pine Barren Azure, *Celastrina* sp.
Treated as part of the Cherry Gall Azure by Wright (1995), but this distinct entity might be either a smaller race of the Cherry Gall Azure or a distinct species. It is very similar in appearance to the larger Appalachian Azure but would not occur with that species.
Range: Pine Barrens of southern New Jersey.
Current Status: Poorly known.
Habitat: Forested Coastal Plain including the Pine Barrens and woodlands along Delaware Bay.
Phenology: Early to late May, usually after the "Northern Azure" flights.
Caterpillar Foodplant: Feeds on flowers of Inkberry (*Ilex glabra*) in the Pine Barrens and on American Holly (*I. opaca*) in Cape May County.
Comment: Typically very pale beneath. Like the Cherry Gall Azure the wing margin is usually white, but 'marginata' and 'lucia' forms occur infrequently. This form or population obviously requires detailed study. If this proves to be a full species it may be New Jersey's only endemic species.
Where to Find It: It is reported common near cedar swamps of the Pine Barrens in late May. It nectars at Inkberry (*Ilex glabra*) and Sand Myrtle (*Leiophyllum buxifolium*). The pale May "brood" mentioned by Dowdell (1993) for the Cape May area is probably this "species."

Summer Azure, *Celastrina neglecta* (Edwards, 1862)
Treated as "Summer" Spring Azure *C. l. neglecta* by NABA (1995). It is treated here as a discrete species (photo 12).
Range: Eastern North America from Nova Scotia and southern New Brunswick, south to central Florida and across the southern tier of Canada to southeastern Alberta and south through Great Plains to central Texas and Gulf Coast. Occurs throughout New Jersey, but in southern New Jersey some places have Summer Azures and others do not (Schweitzer).
Current Status: Although not traditionally treated as a separate species, the status of the Summer Azure has been regularly documented. It is known to be widespread and common in many parts of New Jersey, even in places where there are no spring broods. The Azures recorded on the Fourth of July Counts belong to this species. It rarely becomes as numerous as the Spring azure often does.
Historic Status: No evidence of change. Most authors did not specifically mention the summer form. Shapiro and Shapiro (1973) report the "summer form common and widespread."
Habitat: Very variable. Open country including parks and gardens and woodland glades and cuts.
Phenology: Three broods between June and September, rarely in late-May. Later broods may be partial.
Caterpillar Foodplant: The early brood uses flowers of many species including summerblooming Dogwoods (*Cornus* spp.) other than Flowering Dogwood. Also reported on New Jersey Tea (*Ceanothus americana*), Meadowsweet (*Spiraea*), and Sumac (*Rhus*). Also use composites, mints, and legumes (Wright 1995). May even use Black Cohosh (*Cimicifuga racemosa*]. In Maryland, Wingstem (*Actinomeris alternifolia*) is main host of the second and third broods.
Overwintering Stage: Pupa.

Photo 12. Summer Azure on a honey-suckle leaf. Note absence of dark margin or dark hindwing patch, and indistinct spotting. (Photographed June 20 at Somerset by Michael Gochfeld)

Lycaenidae

171

Comment: Lepidopterists have long suspected that the Summer Azure was a separate species from the Spring Azure. It flies in many disturbed areas (e.g., urban parks) where the spring brood is not known to occur (Tudor). Characterized by pale whitish undersides with very small spots. In flight they tend to be pale blue or whitish due to white scales on the upper surface.

Appalachian Azure, [Appalachian Blue], *Celastrina neglectamajor* (Tutt, 1908)

Range: Appalachians from western Connecticut to western Virginia and Tennessee and northern Georgia with disjunct occurrrence in Ozarks. In New York occurs mainly in Hudson Valley (including Orange and Rockland Counties) (Shapiro 1974a); occurs in northern and central New Jersey. Not listed for Delmarva (Woodbury 1994).

Current Status: Local and probably uncommon. Status is poorly known since it is usually not distinguished from Spring Azure. There are few definite records.

Historical Status: Difficult to determine since the species was only recently separated from Spring Azure and since it may be overlooked. It may also have declined due to Gypsy Moth spraying (Schweitzer). Opler's Atlas records it from Middlesex, Mercer, Burlington and Gloucester Counties, which does not conform to our understanding of its habitat. Some historical records may represent the similar Cherry Gall Azure or Pine Barren Azure (Pavulaan).

Conservation Status: The species is probably declining in New Jersey; the Natural Heritage ranking is SU, indicating the need for additional information. Appropriate habitat containing the host plant should be surveyed for this species in late May and early June, when the Spring and Summer Azures should be uncommon or absent.

Smith (1910): Not specifically mentioned.

Comstock (1940): Although not recognized as a distinct species, it was identified as a form that flies between the broods of Spring Azure with at least one record as far south as Middlesex County.

Delaware Valley (1966): Recognized as a possibly distinct species recorded in Gloucester and Mercer Counties. {It would be expected mainly in northern New Jersey.}

Staten Island (1973): Not listed.

New York City Area (1993): "Rare to uncommon in rich deciduous woods."

Cape May (1993): Not listed.

Habitat: Deep deciduous forests near streams or ridges, where its host abounds, often venturing to forest edges.

Phenology: Single brood mid-May–early June. The larvae enter diapause and do not emerge until the following spring.

Caterpillar Foodplants: Unopened buds of Black Cohosh (*Cimicifuga racemosa*). Reports that it uses Maple-leafed (*Viburnum acerifolium*; Shapiro 1966) and other viburnums are incorrect (Pavulaan), and may refer to Edwards' Azure.

Overwintering Stage: Pupa.

Comment: Formerly considered a race of *C. ladon*, Opler and Krizek (1984) treated it as a separate species. Adults fly between the Spring Azure and Summer Azure peaks with slight overlap. It is apparently absent from the Coastal Plain. Pavulaan and Wright (1994) note the difficulty in identifying adults and that larvae are often easier to find than adults.

Glassberg (1993b) notes that this large grayish white species is similar to the 'violacea' form of Spring Azure but is "best identified by an intimate knowledge of the local brood sequence of azures." The largest American azure is very similar to the Summer Azure and is virtually identical to the smaller Cherry Gall Azure (Pavulaan and Wright 1994). The largest Azures, it appears, "washed out with tiny spots." (Wright pers. comm.).

How to Find It: Pavulaan suggests seeking out the hostplant in mid-May when it has flower buds that resemble tiny green corn cobs. The tiny white eggs may be found between the flower buds. Later the adults emerge and nectar at Blackberry blossoms seldom found far from its food plant (Pavulaan and Wright 1994). In June–July the Summer Azure lays on the elongated flowering spikes of the same plant.

[**Silvery Blue**, *Glaucopsyche lygdamus* (Doubleday, 1841)]

Range: Disjunct distribution from Nova Scotia to British Columbia, with populations in south-central New York (Shapiro 1974a), southeastern Pennsylvania (formerly), the Appalachians, and the northern Great Plains.

Current Status: No records in New Jersey.

Historical Status: Scudder (1889) included New Jersey in the range of this species, but Smith (1890) knew of "no specimens from this state." It has occurred in the Delaware Valley along the western border of the state (Dirig and Cryan 1991). Formerly occurred near Philadelphia. Its former colony sites have been developed. Still locally common in Allegheny Mountains (*G. l. lygdamus*) and in New England (*G. l. couperi*). The subspecies *lygdamus* occurred in central New York until 1969 but has since disappeared.

Smith (1890): No New Jersey specimens.

Smith (1900–1910): Not listed.

Comstock (1940): Not listed.

Delaware Valley (1966): "Rare," no records in New Jersey portion of the area.

Staten Island (1973): Not listed.

New York City Area (1993): Not listed.

Cape May (1993): Not listed.

Habitat: A species of shale barrens on rocky and sandy soils in open woodlands. The subspecies *lygdamus* is more restricted to true "barrens" than *couperi*.

Phenology: One brood in New York late May–mid-June. In Ohio it flies mainly in early April–mid-May.

Caterpillar Foodplants: Vetch (*Vicia* spp.) and Everlasting Pea (*Lathyrus*).

Comment: We can find neither definite nor hypothetical records for New Jersey. In view of its decline in nearby Pennsylvania and New York, it is not likely to occur in the state in the near future. Both of those populations were disjunct, separated from the main Appalachian range. However, Glassberg (1993b) notes that it has a propensity for "suddenly appearing in an area and establishing a colony." The northern subspecies *couperi*, which feeds on vetch and is apparently more habitat tolerant, is extending its range southward into northern New England and New York (Dirig and Cryan 1991) and may eventually reach New Jersey.

[**Melissa Blue,** *Lycaeides melissa* (Edwards, 1873)]
Also known as Karner or Orange-bordered Blue.

Range: Very disjunct distribution. No records in New Jersey but formerly reported from nearby northeastern Pennsylvania and Brooklyn (Opler and Krizek 1984), although the latter site is not shown in Shapiro (1974) and there is no suitable habitat. The subspecies *samuelis* occurs in the northeastern United States.

Current Status: No definite New Jersey records; historic records for the New York City area are hypothetical.

Historical Status: Under the name, *L. scudderii*, Beutenmüller (1893) mentions "a number from this neighborhood are in the collection of the late S. L. Elliot." Many of Elliot's specimens, including apparently these, are unlabeled, so it is not even certain they came from the New York City area. Moreover, *scudderii* is now a subspecies of the very similar Northern Blue (*Lycaeides ida*), which has not occurred in the northeastern United States. Specimen attributed to "NJ" shown for Sussex (Iftner and Wright).

Habitat: The nearest population (Albany, NY) is mainly a pine barrens species.

Phenology: In New York, two broods peak in late June and mid-August.

Larval Hosts: Wild Lupine, *Lupinus perennis*.

Comment: A highly local species with a very disjunct range in the Northeast. It is a habitat-restricted, lupine-specialist confined to sandy soils where its host persists; it is generally declining rapidly and requires habitat management by fire (Schweitzer 1989). The New York Pine Bush population is threatened by habitat loss to development and succession and by collecting. The Ohio populations are endangered by habitat succession (Iftner et al. 1992). The subspecies *samuelis* was named by the novelist Nabokov in 1944.

[**Acmon Blue,** *Icaricia acmon* (Westwood and Hewitson, 1852)]
Range: Western United States east to the Great Plains, where it is sometimes the commonest blue.

Current Status: Extirpated, but never a regular resident.

Historical Status: Undetermined, either accidental or human assisted. Opler and Krizek (1984:122) state: "A colony, probably the result of an accidental introduction, was once found near Camden, New Jersey." None of the other authors (Smith, Comstock, or Shapiro) mention this event.

Riodinidae, Metalmarks

The Metalmark family (Riodinidae) has its main diversity in tropical America. Many metalmarks have patterns of metallic spots or flecks on their wings. Only one species occurs in New Jersey. Wilbur McAlpine (1971) published a systematic "revision" of the genus *Calephilus* in which he recognized thirty-seven species, of which twenty-five species and seven subspecies were described as "new."

Northern Metalmark, *Calephelis borealis* (Grote and Robinson, 1866) Plate 2b

Range: Disjunct distribution from western Connecticut to southeastern Pennsylvania and in the Appalachians from western Maryland to eastern Kentucky and west through Ohio and Indiana. Recorded from Sussex, Warren, Essex, and Mercer Counties and from Philadelphia vicinity; formerly from Orange County NY (Opler's Atlas).

Current Status: Highly localized to a few hillsides in Sussex County, and generally rare, but may be fairly common where it occurs. One thriving colony at Swartswood State Park (1995; Wander).

Historical Status: Although never common, this species appears to have declined since the early 1980s at its few known sites. Close monitoring is required to determine whether this is a serious trend or a fluctuation. No evidence that it persists in Mercer or Essex Counties, and no recent records from Warren County.

Conservation Status: Declining. Its well-known Springdale site is becoming overgrown and requires management. The Swartswood colony should be monitored. Given the small number of known sites and their vulnerability to succession, this species should be considered at least THREATENED and probably ENDANGERED in New Jersey, even though at least one of the sites is secure from development. It is absent from most seemingly suitable places (Schweitzer 1987), although its food plant is quite widespread (Wander). The Natural Heritage ranking is S2–3. This species requires surveys for new sites, monitoring of existing colonies, and habitat management to retard succession and protect its host plant.

Smith (1890–1900): Only location at Delaware Water Gap.

Smith (1910): Additional specimens from Newton and Springdale; was more numerous in 1907.

Comstock (1940): "On limestone outcrops, Appalachian Valley and Kittatinny Range," including Newton and Delaware Water Gap.

Delaware Valley (1966): "Generally rare, and quite local." Often overlooked. Listed for New Hope, PA, and for Mercer County (Ewingville).

Staten Island (1973): Not listed.

New York City Area (1993): "Threatened." Extremely local colonies on dry open hillsides {only in Fairfield, CT, and Sussex County, NJ; Tudor}.

Cape May (1993): Not listed.

Habitat: Open woodlands on barren hillsides, shale, or limestone outcroppings and ridges (dos Passos 1936). Elsewhere also on serpentine.

Phenology: One brood late June–mid-July.

Caterpillar Foodplants: Round-leaved Ragwort (*Senecio obovatus*). Shapiro (1966) mentions *S. aureus* and *Erigeron philadelphicus* as possible alternative hosts, but these require verification. The Ragwort is much more widespread than the butterfly (Wander).

Comment: The type locality is Orange County, NY. Now known in New Jersey from about a half-dozen localities in Sussex County, and variously reported as rare and temporarily common. It is certainly THREATENED in New Jersey. Probably extirpated from southeastern Pennsylvania due to development. The New Jersey populations are highly localized on exposed hillsides, and Iftner et al. (1992) note that Ohio colonies are often confined to a few square meters corresponding to localized stands of its host.

Where to Find It: The powerline cut in the Springdale area near Newton, in Sussex County, NJ, has several accessible points where this species has been found in late June and early July.

Nymphalidae, Snout, Brush-footed butterflies and their allies, including Fritillaries, Crescents, Anglewings, Emperors, Satyrids, and Milkweed Butterflies

This is a very diverse family with confusing and controversial systematics. In the broadest sense, the Nymphalidae as conceived by Ehrlich and Ehrlich (1961) and Opler and Krizek (1984) embraces not only the Nymphalids (crescents, fritillary, and anglewings), but the long-winged heliconids (Heliconiinae), nymphs and satyrs (Satyridae), Monarch (Danaidae), and sometimes the Snouts (Libytheidae) as well. All of these butterflies have the forelegs severely reduced and appear to be four-legged. The larvae of many nymphalids feed colonially.

Even among those who recognized the various subfamilies, there are different treatments. For example, the Fritillary genera (*Euptoieta, Speyeria, Boloria*) are treated as a tribe, Argynnini, of the Nymphalinae (Scott 1986) or as part of the subfamily Heliconiinae (NABA 1995), or both the heliconiines and the fritillaries are included in the subfamily Nymphalinae, without tribal distinction (Opler and Krizek 1984).

Subfamily *Libytheinae*, Snouts

The Snouts are often treated as a separate family of about eight species, and Ehrlich (1957a) favored family status noting that as a subfamily this would be by far the most distinctive in the Nymphalidae. Snouts occur in the tropical and subtropical regions of the Old and New Worlds. The forelegs are greatly reduced in the male, but only slightly reduced in the female. The labial palps are elongated and extend in front of the face. This is less pronounced in some Old World species.

American Snout, *Libytheana carinenta* (Cramer, 1777) Plate 7b

Usually listed as the Eastern Snout, *L. bachmanii*; all of the American Snouts are now considered a single species.

Range: Primarily tropical. Permanent resident from southeastern Virginia and North Carolina to Florida and across North America to Arizona and south to Argentina. Regularly migrates northward to southwestern New England, northern Great Plains, and central California. Occurs over most of New Jersey except extreme northwest. Occurs sporadically north to Maine and Ontario. The subspecies in New Jersey is *bachmanii* described by Kirtland in 1852.

Current Status: Populations fluctuate from year to year. Usually rare to uncommon and local as an immigrant; to be sought wherever Hackberries occur. Most records are of single individuals, but occasionally abundant as in 1994. Up to forty per day in hackberry grove near Rutgers University stadium (Piscatway; C. Leck). Maximum 4JC total 49 (1994, Cape May). More common on the Coastal Plain than inland, particularly at Cape May (Higbee Beach), Sandy Hook, and Tottenville (Staten Island). Quite rare in northwestern New Jersey, even though Hackberry is common. Recent records from southern Orange County, NY, where *Celtis* is not common. We have had three records in ten years in Somerset.

Historical Status: It has possibly increased somewhat in the past quarter century. Old records are all from Mercer and Ocean Counties southward. In New York State, formerly recorded only from Long Island and New York City (Shapiro 1974a), but now more widespread.

Smith (1890): Localities: Gloucester, "Newark," and Sandy Hook were common in 1886.

Smith (1900): "Local, but sometimes not uncommon." Additional sites include Hopatcong and Fort Lee in North and Avalon and Camden in South.

Smith (1910): "Local and sometimes common." Additional site is Lakehurst.

Comstock (1940): "Locally, throughout."

Delaware Valley (1966): "Usually quite uncommon to rare," local. Records from Gloucester, Burlington, and Mercer Counties.

Staten Island (1973): "Rare and sporadic." {It has apparently increased since 1971.}

New York City Area (1993): "Irregular coastal immigrant and uncommon local breeders."

Cape May (1993): "Common."

Habitat: Woodland edges, clearings, and cuts near Hackberries. Mainly on Coastal Plain.

Phenology: Two broods early June–July (occasionally in May) and August continuing into September. Recorded May–mid-November at Cape May (Dowdell).

Caterpillar Foodplants: Various species of Hackberry (*Celtis*); in New Jersey mainly on *C. occidentalis*.

Overwintering Stage: Adult.

Comment: The Eastern race *bachmanii* has often been treated as a separate species. Scott (1986) explains that the characters separating the various American subspecies grade into one another. This is one of three Hackberry specialists. Although renowned for mass migrations in the southwestern United States, it is usually uncommon in the Northeast. This species is cryptic with its wings folded, but has a conspicuous distractive pink pattern when it opens its wings.

Where to Find It: Usually close to Hackberry trees. Late summer at Higbee Beach around the parking lot is fairly reliable.

Subfamily *Heliconiinae*, Heliconians and Fritillaries

This mainly tropical family includes some of the most brilliantly colored species, as well as some of the most complex examples of mimicry. In addition to the Gulf Fritillary, two species, the Zebra (*Heliconius charitonius*) and Julia (*Dryas iulia*), are common in Florida. The NABA Checklist (1995) includes the Fritillary genera *Euptoieta*, *Speyeria*, and *Boloria* in this subfamily. These are medium to large orange insects with complex patterns of black dots and scrawls.

Gulf Fritillary, *Agraulis vanillae* (Linnaeus, 1758)

This is the northernmost-ranging Heliconian butterfly.

Range: South Carolina to Florida and the southwestern United States through the Caribbean and Neotropics to Argentina. Opler and Krizek (1984) show it for most of New Jersey (except Northwest) and Long Island, and Opler's Atlas shows records from Cape May, lower Delaware Valley around Philadelphia and near Glassboro. Long Island records from Brooklyn to Suffolk County (Shapiro 1974a). A stray to Delmarva (Woodbury 1994) with several records since the 1960s (Simmons and Andersen 1978c). The subspecies *nigrior*, described by Michener in 1942, occurs in eastern United States.

Current Status: Vagrant (possibly human assisted). A subtropical species that rarely reaches New Jersey. Recent records from Port Norris in 1992 (Schweitzer) and at Cape May Point (Sept. 1994; C. Sutton) and (10/1/95; Walton).

Historical Status: Apparently more common as a vagrant in the late nineteenth century, but considered "exceedingly rare" by Skinner and Aaron (1889). They suspected that it was being introduced with horticultural Passionflower vines. Very few twentieth-century records.

Smith (1890): Recorded from Cape May, Seven Mile Beach, Camden.

Smith (1900–1910): "Occasional." No new sites are reported.

Comstock (1940): "Occasional visitor." Mentions the same three sites as in Smith (1890).

Delaware Valley (1966): "Very rare immigrant . . . more frequent . . . at Cape May." Salem County record, 10/9/61.

Staten Island (1973): A rare migrant from South, recorded once (11/1/70).

New York City Area (1993): "Historically a very rare vagrant along the coastal plain as late as 1970 (Staten Island). . . . Not seen here in recent times."

Cape May (1993): A "stray" migrant not seen most years.

Habitat: Open areas from coastal dunes to gardens, pastures, and forest edges.

Phenology: Would probably occur after late summer; has been recorded August–October.

Caterpillar Foodplants: Passionflower (*Passiflora* spp.).

Comment: This conspicuous butterfly is abundant in the southeastern United States and it is certainly puzzling that it was recorded on a number of occasions up to 1970, but only rarely in the past 25 years despite the great increase in butterfly observers who would have no trouble identifying this distinctive species.

[Zebra, *Heliconius charitonius* (Linnaeus, 1767)]

Range: Florida Peninisula and extreme southern Texas through the West Indies and Mexico to Venezuela and Peru. Irruptive northward to coastal South Carolina and Georgia and in the West to Missouri. A recent local record at Ward Pound Ridge, Westchester County, NY (July 1995; Kleinbaum). The Florida race is *tuckeri* described by Comstock and Brown in 1950.

This species is commonly sold for raising and releasing, and as there are no records north of South Carolina (Opler's Atlas), any records in New Jersey should be suspected of being human-assisted.

Variegated Fritillary, *Euptoieta claudia* (Cramer, 1775)

Range: Across the southern United States, the Caribbean, and through the Neotropics to Argentina. Opler and Krizek (1984) show it as a permanent resident from North Carolina to Florida and Texas and an immigrant as far north as southern Canada and Maine, and throughout New Jersey. New York records clustered on western Long Island and scattered across the southern tier (Shapiro 1974a).

Current Status: Usually uncommon, but occasionally locally common, mainly in South and on Coastal Plain. Present most years but numbers vary greatly (Schweitzer); sometimes common and some years absent (Dowdell 1993). Uncommon to rare in central New Jersey and absent in northern New Jersey. Regular in small numbers on the Inner Coastal Plain (Leck). Up to forty seen in a day in Cumberland County (Dowdell). Very uncommon in Northwest with only three sightings in three years (Wanders), but more common near Sterling Forest, NY, with up to twenty-three in a day (Yrizarry). These summer immigrants do breed locally, but do not overwinter.

Historical Status: No dramatic change, but possibly more common today than a century ago; Skinner and Aaron (1889) considered it rare near Philadelphia, but surprisingly Beutenmüller (1893) reported it only as "not common." Typically it is a rare to uncommon visitor on the Coastal Plain. Rare in western Somerset County with records from Hutcheson Memorial Forest. In some it has been common, and in other years (e.g., 1989) nearly absent.

Smith (1890): Localities from Mount Holly and Atlantic City to Cape May, but also recorded northward and to "Newark."

Smith (1900): Probably occurs everywhere south of red shale, from Cape May to Elizabeth and to Camden.

Smith (1910): Delaware to Cape May and north to Jersey City. Rare to seasonally common on Staten Island.

Comstock (1940): "Occasionally locally common."

Delaware Valley (1966): "Rather common . . . a southern and western species."

Staten Island (1973): Scarce . . . less than a dozen specimens . . . earliest July 11. . . . Not known to breed."

New York City Area (1993): "Uncommon immigrant and possible sparse colonist . . . does not overwinter. Absent some years."

Cape May (1993): "Common" as a migrant.

Habitat: Mainly found in sparsely vegetated fields and vacant lots, early successional stages. It may be sensitive to field succession.

Phenology: There is no evidence that it overwinters in New Jersey. Rarely seen in May, but there are two peaks of northward movement along the Coastal Plain in June and August–September. Extreme dates late May–November. It does not winter in Delmarva but is found there occasionally in April (Woodbury 1994).

Caterpillar Foodplants: Violets (*Viola* spp.). Also reported on Passionflower (*Passiflora*) and rarely on Orpine (*Sedum*) (Comstock 1940). In New York, used Common Blue Violet (*V. papilionacea*) and Northern Downy Violet (*V. fimbriatula*; Shapiro 1974a). Its larvae have been reported elsewhere on several other families, including Asclepiadaceae, Passifloraceae, Plantaginaceae, and Portulacaceae (Scott 1986). Reported on May Apple (*Podophyllum peltata*), an unlikely host rich in alkaloids, and on Tick Trefoils (*Desmodium*; Smith 1900).

Comment: Characteristically this species is found close to the ground. It has probably increased in the past decade. It undergoes remarkable emigrations from the southwestern United States into central Canada, but although it occurs throughout the United States except the Pacific Coast, it has not been extensively studied.

Where to Find It: Short grass and barren fields at Higbee Beach and Cape May Point in late summer.

Great Spangled Fritillary, *Speyeria cybele* (Fabricius, 1775)

Range: Southern Canada to the Pacific Coast and south to northern Georgia. The nominate subspecies *cybele* occurs throughout New Jersey.

Current Status: Widespread, often common and sometimes abundant. A conspicuous summer species, particularly away from Coastal Plain. Remarkably rare in southern New Jersey with perhaps "3–4 records in past 5 years" from Cape May County (Dowdell). Generally uncommon in Cumberland County as well (Schweitzer).

Historical Status: There has probably been a considerable change since this species, formerly reported as more common in the South, is now common in central and fairly common in northern New Jersey, but is rare in the extreme South.

Smith (1890): "Common throughout."

Smith (1900): "Common throughout" {but all localities are in north}.

Smith (1910): "Throughout . . . less numerous in the northern areas than in the south." {This statement is paradoxical given today's status.}

Comstock (1940): "Throughout." Abundant east of Fall Line.

Delaware Valley (1966): "Abundant."

Staten Island (1973): "Formerly common . . . but now unaccountably rare, perhaps at an abnormal . . . low level in 1971."

New York City Area (1993): "Common in uplands, much less so on coastal plain."

Cape May (1993): "Uncommon."

Habitat: Very widespread ranging from openings and cuts through woods to any open habitat and gardens.

Phenology: Up to three peaks in South mid-June–September, rarely May–early October. Two peaks in North mid-June–mid-July and late August–September, but individuals continually present June–September. These peaks result from a single brood with a complex seasonal pattern. Typically males emerge in June (rarely late May), with females emerging at the end of June about three weeks later (Shapiro 1966). Males persist until late July. Females may estivate in July–August, reemerging in late August and persisting through September (Pavulaan).

Caterpillar Foodplants: Violets (*Viola*) spp. Recorded on Round-leaved Yellow Violet (*V. rotundifolia*) on Staten Island (Shapiro 1974a) and on Common Blue Violet (*V. papilonacea*; Opler and Krizek 1984).

Overwintering Stage: First-stage larva.

Comment: Uses a great variety of nectar sources, and particularly fond of Butterfly Weed (*Asclepias tuberosa*), but will forsake that for *Buddleia*. They tend to have long nectaring bouts on a single plant. If undisturbed an individual will remain on a milkweed head for an hour, leaving for a few seconds to circle around. We have observed individuals visiting a *Buddleia* almost continuously for 8 hours. They are tolerant of conspecifics and sometimes three or more will feed from the same flower head.

Aphrodite, [Aphrodite Fritillary] *Speyeria aphrodite* (Fabricius, 1787)

Range: Maritime Provinces to Rocky Mountains, south to mountains in northern Georgia, including northern and central New Jersey. Although subspecies have been named, they are not well marked (but New Jersey populations would belong to the subspecies *aphrodite*).

Current Status: Uncertain, probably rare and local. This northerly species is very similar to Great Spangled. It is much less common, more local, and occurs mainly at scattered sites in northwestern New Jersey where Wander estimated about one for every 200 Great Spangled Fritillaries. It is absent from the coastal plain south of Massachusetts.

Historical Status: Since early authors considered this rare and since it is rare today, there has apparently been no long-term change. However, it is probably rarer in the 1980s and 1990s than in the 1950–1960 period, perhaps due to insecticide spraying, and is apparently declining in surrounding areas such as Westchester County, NY (Tudor). Old records from the Coastal Plain (Mercer to Gloucester Counties) are either misidentifications or represent vagrants at a time when the species was more numerous in the North. It was fairly common in central Long Island in 1960s (Pavulaan).

Smith (1890): Schooley and Orange Mountains, also "Newark."

Smith (1900–1910): Local, occurring "north of red shale line" with records from extreme Northwest to Newark and Staten Island. Records also from Camden and Moorestown "but these may need verification."

Comstock (1940): West of Fall Line with records from extreme North to Jamesburg (Middlesex County).

Delaware Valley (1966): "Generally rare." More common 1958–61 than 1961–64. Recorded from Mercer, Camden, Gloucester, and Atlantic Counties.

Staten Island (1973): "Local but frequent, on acid-soil areas on the west shore and at Tottenville." {Not recorded recently.}

New York City Area (1993): "Rare resident of upland fields" north of New York. Getting less common.

Cape May (1993): Not listed.

Habitat: Open woodlands and adjacent wet meadows and dry fields associated with Milkweeds. It appears more restricted in habitat than the previous species, but that may simply reflect its rarity.

Phenology: One brood June–September, mainly mid-July–late August.

Caterpillar Foodplants: Violets, including Northern Downy (*V. fimbriatula*), Lance-leaved (*V. lanceolata*), and Primrose-leaved (*V. primulifolia*) on Staten Island (Shapiro 1974a).

Overwintering Stage: First-stage larva.

Comment: Shapiro and Shapiro (1973) note that Staten Island may represent its southern limit on the Coastal Plain and that it is not known to extend into the Pine Barrens.

Regal Fritillary, *Speyeria idalia* (Drury, 1773)

Range: Formerly Maritime Provinces and central Maine to Rocky Mountains, south to northwestern North Carolina. Formerly widespread but local in New Jersey. New York records clustered in Southeast and on Long Island (Shapiro 1974a). Now occurs mainly in prairie regions in central United States, where still locally common in suitable habitat.

Current Status: EXTIRPATED; no recent New Jersey records.

Historical Status: Records documented from Sussex, Bergen, Essex, Morris, Middlesex, Somerset, Mercer, Burlington, Camden, Atlantic, Cumberland, and Cape May Counties (Opler's Atlas). Even in the past its populations fluctuated. Considered locally common around New York City (Beutenmüller 1893). Apparently showed some increase between 1890 and 1910, and described as plentiful in some years and rare in others, near Philadelphia (Skinner and Aaron 1889). A Staten Island record in 1971.

Conservation Status: EXTIRPATED. It has declined drastically throughout the Northeast, disappearing from most of New England by 1960, and from most of New Jersey before 1970, at which time it was even becoming rare in western Pennsylvania (Wagner 1995). Since it is absent from most surrounding areas, it is not likely to recolonize New Jersey spontaneously. In addition to its state SX ranking, this species is accorded a G3/C2 rank, indicating that it is in trouble over much of its range. Hammond and McCorkle (1983) emphasize that many populations of *Speyeria* butterflies are declining, and that this group seems unusually vulnerable to human disturbance of their habitats. Controlled burning designed to maintain prairie habitat is often carried out during the larval stage with unintended lethal results (Swengel 1993b).

Smith (1890): "Found throughout . . . ; usually not common." Reported as common at Caldwell.

Smith (1900): "Throughout . . . sometimes locally common"; however, all records are from northern and central New Jersey: Newark, Staten Island, Jamesburg.

Smith (1910): "Throughout the State and locally common."

Comstock (1940): "Throughout" with records from Mashipacong (Sussex County) to Fairton (Cumberland County).

Delaware Valley (1966): "Scarce and local . . . erratic." Recorded from Camden, Burlington, and Mercer Counties. {It is remarkable that a decline was not noted at this time.}

Staten Island (1973): "Apparently rare today." One recent specimen, Tottenville, 7/5/71.

New York City Area (1993): "Regionally endangered, very possibly extirpated." At Montauk, Long Island, several in 1984 (Pavulaan) and last recorded 7/10/88 (Cech 1993).

Cape May (1993): Listed as "historically present." {No recent records.}

Habitat: Apparently relatively specialized to prairie or undisturbed tall grassland habitat. Agriculture is inimical to this species' survival.

Phenology: Mid-July–mid-August (and September on Staten Island; Smith 1900).

Caterpillar Foodplants: Violets including Bird's Foot Violet (*V. pedata*). Not adequately documented in New Jersey.

Overwintering Stage: As first-stage larva which hatches in fall but does not feed until spring.

Comment: Populations on Martha's Vineyard, Nantucket, Block Island, and eastern Long Island have disappeared since mid-1980s. Last Long Island record in 1988. A colony persists in southeastern Pennsylvania. This species was probably never common in New Jersey.

Captive rearing efforts are underway to reintroduce Regal Fritillaries. The species is extremely prolific, one captive female laying more than 2,450 eggs over her 12-week flight period (Wagner 1995). However, egg and larval mortality are extremely high. Wild females lay on or near violets at the time that leaves are withering, and when caterpillars hatch two weeks later their food plant is no longer available. They enter diapause until the following spring, when new violet leaves unroll. Unless the causes of its decline can be reversed or mitigated, reintroductions are not likely to lead to stable populations.

Atlantis Fritillary, *Speyeria atlantis* (Edwards, 1862)

Also called Mountain Silver-spot.

Range: Maritime Provinces and northern Maine to northern Great Plains, and south in Appalachians to Virginia. Opler and Krizek (1984) include northwestern New Jersey, but Opler's Atlas shows only one New Jersey location, in Morris County. Recorded throughout eastern New York, as close as northern Orange County (Shapiro 1974a) and in southeastern Pennsylvania, including Bucks County. The subspecies *atlantis* would occur in New Jersey.

Current Status: Accidental. Recorded by Joseph Muller in Morris County (Chester; 7/8/78; Glassberg 1993b), and by Molly Monica at the same location (7/30/78; specimen identified by C. dos Passos). These are the only known New Jersey records.

Historical Status: No records before or after 1978.

Smith (1890–1910): Not listed.

Comstock (1940): Not listed.

Delaware Valley (1966): "A species of northerly distribution and higher elevations" occurs in upland and lowland Bucks County. No New Jersey records.

Staten Island (1973): Not listed.

New York City Area (1993): "Never common around New York City . . . should be sought in northwestern New Jersey."

Cape May (1993): Not listed.

Habitat: A common species of wet meadows and bogs of the Canadian and Hudsonian Life Zones.

Phenology: One brood June–August.

Caterpillar Foodplants: Violets. Northern Blue Violet (*Viola septentrionalis*) in New York (Shapiro 1974a).

Comment: This species should be looked for in northwestern New Jersey. It does not occur in the Poconos, but does occur in the eastern Appalachians as close as Wayne County, PA. The occurrence of two specimens at one locality suggests that this may have been a transient colony in an irruption year.

Silver-bordered Fritillary, *Boloria selene* (Denis and Schiffermuller, 1775)

Range: Labrador across northern tier of states to Alaska and Eurasia. In East, from Maritime Provinces to northern Virginia. In New Jersey formerly occurred throughout (Opler's Atlas). Recorded virtually throughout New York State, including nearby Orange County (Shapiro 1974a). The New Jersey subspecies is *myrina* (described by Kohler in 1977).

Current Status: An uncommon and highly local species. A 1991 record from Burlington County (Gochfeld and Tudor). Two highly local populations in Cumberland County are in jeopardy. Two localities known in Sussex County (Wanders). One colony recently found in Middlesex County (near Pigeon Swamp; Williams) and one in Ocean County (Butterfly Bogs; MG and JB).

Historical Status: Has apparently declined dramatically in the past 50–75 years. Beutenmüller (1893) considered it abundant in swampy places. Its wetland habitat is disappearing. Former records from Kendall Park (1977; Leck) and Griggstown along the Delaware-Raritan Canal (1982; Leck).

Conservation Status: A declining species that is vulnerable, but not yet threatened. Surveys should be conducted to discover new colonies, and existing colonies should be monitored. State status is S2–3.

Smith (1890–1910): "Common throughout." Abundant on cranberry bogs. Localities: "Newark," Staten Island, Jamesburg, Westville.

Comstock (1940): "Throughout." Most records in northern and central New Jersey, but recorded from Dennisville, Cape May County.

Delaware Valley (1966): "Uncommon." Was common around Philadelphia until 1920. Records from Salem, Gloucester, Camden, Burlington, and Mercer Counties.

Staten Island (1973): "Two colonies known, but . . . suitable habitats . . . have decreased."

New York City Area (1993): "Formerly more common." Now only one known colony in Orange County, NY.

Cape May (1993): "Rare."

Habitat: A species of sedgy meadows, marshes, and bogs and cuts mainly west of the Fall Line.

Phenology: Two broods June–September or even early October, with peaks in late June–early July and August. Three broods in Rhode Island (May, July, September; Pavulaan).

Caterpillar Foodplants: Various violets (*Viola*). The host requirements and preferences are not well known.

Overwintering Stage: Partially grown larva.

Comment: This species has declined greatly, perhaps concurrent with the increase in the Meadow Fritillary; however, the two use different habitats and are not likely to be in competition. It is found in the same habitat as Bronze Copper, and like that species has suffered from habitat loss.

Meadow Fritillary [Eastern Meadow Fritillary], *Boloria bellona* (Fabricius, 1775)

Range: Southeastern Canada to Northwest Territories and British Columbia, south to northwestern North Carolina. Northern and central New Jersey. The subspecies *bellona* occurs in New Jersey.

Current Status: A local species apparently requiring broad expanses of low grasslands. May be quite numerous when found. Very rare or absent on Coastal Plain; in fact, rare east of Fall Line.

Historical Status: This species was apparently common at the turn of the century, then less common in much of the early twentieth century. It has increased greatly and expanded its range in the past 30 years in some areas (Glassberg 1993b). The clearing of forests in colonial times apparently created new habitat, allowing the spread of this species; but where development of agricultural into industrial/residential "habitat" has occurred, this species is receding. It is decreasing in much of southern New England (Pavulaan).

Smith (1890–1910): Common throughout, but more common in North. Includes records from Camden and Cape May.

Comstock (1940): "Throughout" {but sites mentioned are all from northern and central New Jersey}.

Delaware Valley (1966): "Common to abundant northwest of the Fall Line . . . sporadic southward." Around north rim of Pine Barrens from Gloucester County northward.

Staten Island (1973): "Apparently greatly decreased in numbers since" 1910.

New York City Area (1993): "Generally common but local, absent from coastal plain."

Cape May (1993): Listed as "historically present."

Habitat: Open flat grasslands, including meadows and pastures.

Phenology: Three broods late–April to September (rarely later). Peaks in mid-May, early July, and late August.

Caterpillar Foodplants: Violets (*Viola* spp.), including Woolly Blue (*V. sororaia*) and Northern White (*V. pallens*) in New York (Opler and Krizek 1984).

Overwintering Stage: Partially-grown larva.

Comment: A species "well known for its irruptive tendencies." (Shapiro and Shapiro 1973). Weed (1917) remarked that where their habitats came together the Meadow and Silver-bordered Fritillaries were "commonly associated."

Subfamily *Nymphalinae*, Brushfoots (Checkerspots, Crescents, Anglewings, Ladies)

Depending on one's definition, there are about 1100 species in the Nymphalinae (Scott 1986). Opler and Krizek (1984) included the Heliconian butterflies in this subfamily. One indicator that this subfamily is too diverse is that there is no clear way of characterizing it. Most authors include the Fritillaries in Nymphalinae.

[Gorgone Checkerspot, *Chlosyne gorgone* (Hubner, 1810)]

Range: Disjunct distribution from Great Plains and Mississippi Valley west to Rocky Mountains and south to Mexico with populations in Kentucky and northwestern Georgia. Collected in northern New York (Lewis County, July 1970; Shapiro 1974) and northeastern Pennsylvania (Opler and Krizek 1984).

Status: No records from New Jersey but has occurred, as in two adjacent states. The status of the New York colony discovered by Shapiro is unknown (Pavulaan).

Caterpillar Foodplants: Sunflowers *Helianthus*, Loosestrifes *Lysismachia*.

Silvery Checkerspot, *Chlosyne nycteis* (Doubleday and Hewitson, 1847)

Range: Maritime Provinces to Manitoba and south to northern Georgia and Arizona including northern and central New Jersey {west of Fall Line}. The subspecies *nycteis* occurs in New Jersey.

Current Status: Unknown, possibly EXTIRPATED; there are no definite localities. It is surprisingly rare in New Jersey in recent years, considering that it occurs at least uncommonly in southeastern New York and southeastern Pennsylvania.

Historical Status: It was formerly known from a few localities and mainly west of the Fall Line and was uncommon. Beutenmüller (1893) considered it "quite rare" near New York City. It may have declined even more in New Jersey, possibly a victim of insecticide spraying (Schweitzer).

Conservation Status: Possibly extirpated, but if still resident it is THREATENED or ENDANGERED. Surveys should be conducted to find colonies. The state ranking is S1.

Smith (1890): Local and "not common." Specimens from Gloucester and Mount Holly, reported from "Newark."

Smith (1900): Recorded from Hopatcong and Greenwood Lake to Mount Holly, but common only at Greenwood Lake in extreme northern New Jersey. Not usually common.

Comstock (1940): "Locally" in North.

Delaware Valley (1966): A local resident, mainly in the Piedmont, recorded from Salem, Camden, Gloucester, Mercer Counties.

Staten Island (1973): "Rare in acid scrub"; not reported by Davis (1910).

New York City Area (1993): "Rare to locally common in woodland clearings. Occurs on Hook Mountain, Rockland County, NY.

Cape May (1993): Not listed.

Habitat: Open areas in and adjacent to deciduous forests, including second growth. Often along streams or rivers, but also on dry ridges and in serpentine areas.

Phenology: One brood mid-May–mid-July (may be two broods in South). All records from Smith (1900) are June–July. Reported as partially double brooded in Westchester, NY (Shapiro and Shapiro 1973) and as double brooded (mid-May–early June and late July–early September) in Delaware Valley (Shapiro 1966), but recent observations in Bronx and southern Westchester find only a single brood in June into early July.

Caterpillar Foodplants: Uses a "wide variety of composites" (Opler and Krizek 1984), including Woodland Sunflower (*Helianthus divaricatus*), Wingstem (*Actinomeris alternifolia*), and Asters. Elsewhere reported on Crown-beard (*Verbesina helianthoides*; Iftner et al. 1992); in Delmarva associates with Thin-leaved Sunflower (*H. decapetalus*; Woodbury 1994).

Overwintering Stage: Partially grown larva.

Comment: This species should be looked for; at present, there are no known colonies in New Jersey. It resembles a Pearl Crescent but appears to be larger and longer winged. A field mark, reliable when present, is that some of the six black submarginal dots on the dorsal hind wing have orange centers, whereas they are solid black on the crescent. Often rests on the ground close to water.

Harris' Checkerspot, *Chlosyne harrisii* (Scudder, 1864)

Range: Maritime Provinces and northern Great Plains south to northern Pennsylvania and northern New Jersey. The subspecies *harrisii* occurs in New Jersey. Does not reach Delmarva (Woodbury 1994).

Current Status: Sparsely distributed and uncommon to rare where it occurs. Colonies known in Morris, Passaic, and Sussex Counties. May be locally common in lower Hudson Valley. Probably host restricted. It is near the southern extreme of its range. Known localities are at Troy Meadows (Glassberg); near Hibernia, Morris County (up to twelve seen in a day; Dowdell); near Oak Ridge; and near Ogdensburg (Sussex County; Wander).

Historical Status: Poorly documented. A few northern New Jersey locations are listed. Records for Sussex, Morris, Essex, and Union Counties shown in Opler's Atlas and also in Passaic (Pavulaan, pers. comm.). Beutenmüller (1893) considered it "very rare." The Comstock collection (Rutgers Collection) has specimens from Great Swamp (6/9/70), from Chatham (no date), and from Hemlock Falls (Essex) in 1902, and nineteen specimens taken 6/22/12 at Greenwood Lakes. Either the species was common at that time, or the collector took so many specimens because it was rare.

Conservation Status: The state ranking is S3?. It is known from very few populations, and is certainly vulnerable and probably THREATENED.

Smith (1890): Schooley Mountain and "Newark."

Smith (1900): Also Orange Mountain.

Smith (1910): Also Hewitt.

Comstock (1940): "Locally" north of Fall Line {records mainly in extreme Northwest}.

Delaware Valley (1966): "Does not enter our area . . . in New Jersey in the northern highlands."

Staten Island (1973): Not listed.

New York City Area (1993): "Rare to fairly common," highly local, north of New York City.

Cape May (1993): Not listed.

Habitat: Wet brushy meadows and edges of bogs where its host occurs. Klots (1951) pointed out that the presence of Blue Flag (*Iris*) is a good indicator of habitat where this species may be found.

Phenology: Single brood late May–late June. (June–July; Shapiro 1966).

Caterpillar Foodplants: A monophagous host specialist requiring Flat-topped White Aster (*Aster umbellatus*).

Overwintering Stage: Partially grown larva.

Comment: This highly local species should be looked for in moist wooded areas of northwestern New Jersey, where there are probably more colonies. Bowers (1983) provided experimental evidence that this species is a Batesian mimic of the unpalatable Baltimore. It is occasionally highly irruptive, becoming briefly superabundant (e.g., northern Pennsylvania in 1995; Pavulaan).

The Crescents, *Phyciodes*

The species status of the 'Pearl Crescent' is much researched by several investigators. Like the Azures, this complex undoubtedly includes several sibling species. The Northern Crescent has been separated, but it is not clear that it is the same from place to place. In the southwestern United States the complex also appears to contain more than one species (Scott 1994).

Pearl Crescent, *Phyciodes tharos* (Drury, 1773)

Range: Southern Maine and central New York to Rocky Mountains and south to southern Florida, Texas, and Mexico. The subspecies *tharos* occurs throughout New Jersey.

Current Status: Widespread and often abundant; sometimes superabundant with more than 500 seen in a day. One of our most regular and numerous butterflies. Peak 4JC numbers 1884 (1993 Cumberland).

Historical Status: No apparent change. Always reported as common to abundant for all parts of the state.

Smith (1890–1910): "Common throughout."

Comstock (1940): "Throughout."

Delaware Valley (1966): "Common to very abundant everywhere."

Staten Island (1973): "Abundant everywhere."

New York City Area (1993): "Widespread and abundant."

Cape May (1993): "Abundant."

Habitat: Ubiquitous, occurring in any open grassy habitat from woodland glades to agricultural areas.

Phenology: Up to four broods April–November.

Caterpillar Foodplants: Asters (*Aster* spp.)

Overwintering Stage: Partially grown larva.

Comment: The Pearl Crescent is often abundant, making it particularly challenging to distinguish the next two much rarer species. It uses a wide variety of nectar sources with the autumn broods showing a preference for yellow flowers such as goldenrods (*Solidago* spp.), Tickseed Sunflowers (*Bidens* spp.), Black-eyed Susans (*Rudbeckia* spp.) and Butterfly Weed (*Asclepias tuberosa*).

The Pearl Crescent is one of the prime examples of discontinuous seasonal polyphenism among eastern butterflies. On the one hand, there may be substantial color variation in a population encountered at any one time or place. However, in addition, the ventral wing surface of the spring and fall broods (form 'marcia') is more strongly patterned than in the summer brood (form 'morpheus'). Oliver (1976) showed that the two forms were determined by photoperiod, apparently independent of temperature.

Using electrophoretic techniques to study gene frequencies, Vawter and Brussard (1975) found very little genetic differentiation between Pearl Crescent populations from Alabama, Texas, and Ithaca, NY.

Experiments crossing male and female crescents from different parts of the range (Oliver 1972) revealed that in some cases the hybrids had higher survival and faster growth than one or both parent forms, while in other cases there was slower growth and poorer survival. When hybrids have significantly lower survival or fecundity than parents, natural selection will favor those parents who avoid hybridizing. In this case, Oliver (1972) found that the farther apart the source populations, the more likely they were to be genetically incompatible.

Northern Crescent, [*Northern Pearl Crescent*]*Phyciodes selenis* (Wright, 1905)

Also listed as *Pyciodes pascoensis* and as *P. tharos* type B. Scott (1994) revised the Crescents and provides compelling arguments that the name with priority is *P. cocyta* (Cramer, 1777). Listed as a subspecies of Pearl Crescent by Miller and Brown (1981). The nomenclature is still not settled.

Range: Newfoundland to British Columbia, South in Rocky Mountains to New Mexico and Arizona. Possibly disjunct populations in Appalachians, reaching southeastern New York and northwestern New Jersey. In New Jersey known only from Sussex County.

Current Status: Unknown. Collected in Sussex County by Adelberg (specimen in USNM). There are a few recent sight records, including Newton (July 1993; Cech) suggesting there is possibly a population in northwestern New Jersey. However, it cannot reliably be identified by sight.

Historical Status: Originally described as a race of Pearl Crescent and only recognized as a distinct species in 1980, hence its historical status cannot be determined.

Smith (1890–1910): Not listed.

Comstock (1940): Species not distinguished in 1940.

Delaware Valley (1966): Species not distinguished in 1965.

Staten Island (1973): Not listed.

New York City Area (1993): Not listed.

Cape May (1993): Not listed.

Habitat: "Moist open areas near streams" (Opler and Krizek 1984).

Phenology: One brood June–July, possibly a second brood in some places.

Caterpillar Foodplants: Asters; has been raised on Panicled Aster (*Aster simplex*) in the laboratory (Opler and Krizek 1984) on which it lays (Scott 1994). Also uses Smooth Aster (*A. laevis*).

Comment: This species is very similar to the Pearl Crescent, and if it occurs regularly is apparently very rare and local in New Jersey. It was considered a subspecies of Pearl Crescent until Oliver (1979a, 1980) showed that although the two interbreed, the hybrids are at a selective disadvantage, because male emergence is delayed. There are no barriers to courtship between the two (Scott 1994).

There are relatively few locations given in New York and Pennsylvania (Opler's Atlas), suggesting that the species is either truly rare or often overlooked among the abundant Pearl Crescents.

Tawny Crescent, *Pyciodes batesii* (Reakirt, 1865)

Range: Disjunct distribution from Nova Scotia, southern Quebec and southern Maine, west to Alberta and south to Pennsylvania and Montana, with scattered populations through the Appalachians. New York records scattered through central counties (Shapiro 1974a). The map in Opler and Krizek (1984) shows historical occurrence in central western New Jersey, with records in Mercer, Camden, Burlington, and Gloucester Counties (Opler 1983).

Current Status: The species has declined over a wide area of the United States, and if it ever occurred regularly in New Jersey it is now EXTIRPATED. It has declined greatly in New York and has probably disappeared from Ohio, if it was ever resident there, since recent specimens attributed to this species are Pearl Crescents (Shuey et al. 1987).

Historical Status: The type locality was designated as Gloucester (Klots 1951). However, Scott (1994) redesignated the type locality as Winchester, VA, since the specimens originally described are similar to those that most recently occurred in Virginia. Shapiro (1966) lists records from several counties, but no other records known to us. Beutenmüller (1893) mentions it recorded from eastern Long Island, presumably in error. It has "declined drastically throughout the northeast" (Glassberg 1993b), persisting near Philadelphia to early 1980s and in central New York to early 1990s." The only stable population known to Shapiro (1974a) was in Onondaga County, NY, and that population too has apparently disappeared. Both its present and historical status are difficult to evaluate because of its similarity to Pearl Crescent.

Conservation Status: Natural Heritage Rankings are SX, G3–4. There is little likelihood that this species will become reestablished in New Jersey, but observers can be vigilant for this possibility. In eastern North America, the Tawny Crescent survives only in eastern Ontario and Quebec and in the Great Smokies of North Carolina; otherwise, it no longer occurs between New York and Georgia. Scott (1994) attributes this loss largely to fire suppression and reforestation, which eliminated the open habitat the species requires. Overcollecting may have contributed to the disappearance of the highly publicized, last remaining New York colony (Scott 1994).

Smith (1890–1910): Only the type specimen from Gloucester.

Comstock (1940): "The only record is from Gloucester in the original description in 1865."

Delaware Valley (1966): "Apparently rare and local, but perhaps overlooked." Lists New Jersey records from Burlington (Mount Holly), Camden (Clementon), Gloucester (type locality), and Mercer (Bakersville).

Staten Island (1973): Not listed.

New York City Area (1993): Not listed.

Cape May (1993): Not listed.

Habitat: Pastures, and fields on dry limestone or rocky hillsides, and the tops of bluffs along rivers, in association with beard grasses (*Andropogon*; Opler and Krizek 1984). Often attributed to wet meadows, where it may sometimes be found, but its habitats were usually dry (Scott 1994).

Phenology: One brood mid June–early July.

Caterpillar Foodplants: Wavy-leafed Aster (*Aster undulatus*; Comstock 1940, Scott 1994).

Comment: This species may have been a rare resident in southwestern New Jersey but has disappeared concurrent with its general decline in the eastern United States. As a host specialist it must have been vulnerable to habitat changes. There were no twentieth-century records until Shapiro's (1966) reports (see above). Male Tawny Crescents confined with female Pearl Crescents did not mate with them, but hybridization studies using forced matings with Pearl Crescent produce hybrids with developmental and growth abnormalities and with reduced survival, confirming that these are distinct species (Oliver 1979).

Baltimore Checkerspot, [Baltimore] *Euphydryas phaeton* (Drury, 1773)

Range: Eastern United States from Nova Scotia, southern Ontario, and Minnesota south to northern Georgia and Arkansas. In New Jersey, the subspecies *phaeton* occurs in central and northern counties; rarely on Coastal Plain. Opler's Atlas shows no records from Ocean, Atlantic, and Gloucester Counties (nor from Hunterdon).

Current Status: This species is declining, probably due mainly to loss of shallow freshwater marshes and wet meadows. It is very local, but may be occasionally common, and even locally abundant in Sussex County with a maximum of fifty per day (Wander). It has always been rare in the South and in the Pine Barrens (Schweitzer) and is apparently absent from Cape May and Cumberland County (Dowdell; Schweitzer). A colony at Trenton Marsh (Lecks).

Historical Status: Declining. Always rare in southern New Jersey.

Smith (1890): "All over the state."

Smith (1900–1910): "Throughout . . . sometimes locally abundant." Localities from Hopatcong to Camden.

Comstock (1940): "Throughout." {Records from Newton to Cape May Court House; almost all records are in North.}

Delaware Valley (1966): "Local, but often common." Recorded from Gloucester, Burlington, Salem, Mercer, and Camden Counties.

Staten Island (1973): "Rare and local today."

New York City Area (1993): "Mostly . . . marshy upland meadows, bog edges," "scarce on coastal plain." {No recent Long Island records; Tudor.}

Cape May (1993): "Local" and "rare."

Habitat: There are two ecological races of Baltimore, the marsh form *phaethon* and the upland *ozarkae*, the status of which remain to be clarified in New Jersey.

Phenology: Single brood June–July.

Caterpillar Foodplants: Its historical host is Turtlehead (*Chelone glabra*), although upland populations in some areas switching to English Plaintain (*Plantago lanceolata*; Cech 1993), a trend first noted in Connecticut, which may occur in New Jersey. Larvae found on Smooth False Foxglove (*Gerardia flava*) at Greenbrook Sanctuary (1983 4JC). Smith (1910) reported a variety of hosts from the early literature including honeysuckles and viburnums. Recorded using Bearded Penstemon (*Penstemon digitalis*) in Northwest (Wanders) and larvae found on Arrowwood (*Viburnum recognitum*) at Trenton Marsh (Lecks). The life cycle of this species is complex. Females lay masses of yellow eggs, and the larvae live in communal webs on Turtlehead. Late larvae undergo diapause, hibernating in leaf litter, and emerge in spring, whereupon they disperse to various other plants including plaintains (*Plantago* spp.) to complete their development.

Overwintering Stage: Partially grown larva.

Comment: This butterfly is distasteful to birds and its bright colors apparently serve as warning coloration (Bowers 1980). The caterpillars are likewise conspicuous with orange and brown stripes. The two subspecies, the marsh-dwelling *phaeton* (mainly in the Northeast) and the upland dwelling *ozarkae* (mainly in the Southwest), are geographically separated. The former traditionally uses Turtlehead as its host plant, while the latter uses *Gerardia* (Vawter and Wright 1986). However, within the range of *phaeton* one finds both marsh and upland populations which require study (Shapiro 1974a); the latter is reported to use *Gerardia*. A biochemical study indicates that the two forms are closely related and do not represent distinct species (Vawter and Wright 1986).

In Virginia, the average clutch size was 274 (Stamp 1982). The larvae are colonial and live in a web which they repair if damaged. Wasp parasitism is common. Caterpillars defend themselves by thrashing their body back and forth (Stamp 1984).

This species occasionally reaches superabundance, as for example the 10,000+ adults in Bristol County, MA (1989 4JC).

Anglewing Butterflies

The next seven species in the genera *Polygonia* and *Nymphalis* comprise the "Anglewing" butterflies. They winter as adults, which may emerge very early in the spring. The Mourning Cloak, typically on the wing in March, is the only one that regularly nectars, showing a fondness for milkweed flowers. These species prefer rotting fruit, sap, or dung. Most species have a complex brown and gray "dead leaf" underwing pattern that is cryptic when the wings are folded.

Question Mark, *Polygonia interrogationis* (Fabricius, 1798)

Range: Maritime Provinces to the Rocky Mountains and south to central Florida and Gulf Coast; throughout New Jersey.

Current Status: Widespread and sometimes fairly common. We would hardly consider this species "abundant" anywhere today. Up to sixteen recorded on a Raritan Canal 4JC and highest total 26 (1994, Springdale).

Historical Status: No apparent long-term change. Smith (1890) referred to it as abundant, but it was apparently less common 20 years later (Smith 1910).

Smith (1890–1910): "Throughout," sometimes common.

Comstock (1940): "Throughout . . . abundant."

Delaware Valley (1966): "Usually numerous and . . . general."

Staten Island (1973): "Common."

New York City Area (1993): "Fairly common most years."

Cape May (1993): "Common."

Habitat: Openings in and edges of deciduous woods.

Phenology: Two broods March–December. Hibernating adults can emerge as early as late March.

Caterpillar Foodplants: Main hosts are Stinging Nettles (*Urtica* spp.) and False Nettle (*Boehmeria cylindrica*; Shapiro 1966) but also on elms (*Ulmus* spp.), Hackberry (*Celtis occidentalis*; Comstock 1940), on Hops (*Humulus lupulus*) and Japanese Hops (*H. japonicus*). Basswood (*Tilia americana*) mentioned by Smith (1910).

Overwintering Stage: Adult.

Comment: Frequently found sunning on dirt roads and tree trunks. There is a strong polyphenism. The summer brood adults tend to be darker, while the over-wintering fall brood is bright orange; those surviving to spring are also bright orange. Many migrate south in fall. Very similar to the next species but tends to be larger. Adults sometimes feed on animal dung, fermented fruit, and even aphid honeydew, but seldom on flowers.

Eastern Comma [Comma or Hop Merchant], *Polygonia comma* (Harris, 1842)

Range: Maritime Provinces and southern Maine to central plains and south to central Georgia and Louisiana, with scattered disjunct populations on Gulf coastal plain to Florida; throughout New Jersey, but less common in South.

Current Status: Widespread but usually uncommon. Becomes more common away from the Coastal Plain.

Historical Status: No apparent change.

Smith (1890–1910): "Throughout," more local and less common than the Question Mark.

Comstock (1940): "Throughout . . . sometimes locally abundant."

Delaware Valley (1966): Resident, nearly as common as preceding species. Widespread.

Staten Island (1973): "Infrequent . . . widespread."

New York City Area (1993): "Uncommon to fairly common."

Cape May (1993): "Uncommon."

Habitat: Openings and edges of deciduous forest, often seen on dirt roads.

Phenology: Two or three broods March–November. In central New Jersey usually seen earlier in spring and later in fall than Question Mark.

Caterpillar Foodplants: A wide variety of species in the nettle family (Urticaceae) and elm family (Ulmaceae). Shows a preference for Hops (*Humulus*; Smith 1910).

Overwintering Stage: Adult.

Comment: Like the Question Mark, it has a dark summer and an orange fall brood. It is usually less common than the Question Mark in midsummer, particularly on Coastal Plain. It was unusually common in 1994. Seldom nectars but often seen on dung (photo 13).

Green Comma, *Polygonia faunus* (Edwards, 1862)

Range: Newfoundland to central Alaska, south in Appalachians to northern Georgia (shown as disjunct population from West Virginia southward; Opler and Krizek 1984), southern Rocky Mountains and central California mountains, absent from central and southern Great Plains. New York records mainly in Adirondacks and Catskills. Historic records from Sussex and Morris Counties (Opler's Atlas). The subspecies *faunus* would occur in New Jersey.

Current Status: Unknown. No recent records. If it was ever resident it should probably be considered EXTIRPATED. However, it could still occur as a vagrant. Still occurs in Poconos (Tudor).

Historical Status: Always highly local and rare, this species has declined, possibly due to pesticide spraying. It was collected at enough localities to indicate that it probably was resident in the North, at least intermittently, although Beutenmüller (1893) considered it "very rare." Like several other primarily northern species, it has retreated from the southern edge of its range in New Jersey. No records in past 50 years.

Smith (1890): Only from Schooley Mountain.

Smith (1900): Schooley Mountain and other localities in north.

Smith (1910): "Local, northern hills," including Westwood (Bergen County).

Comstock (1940): "Kittatiny Range . . . March–November. One brood. . . .

Photo 13. Comma on dung. The Angle-wings rarely visit flowers, but are occasionally seen feeding at dung or rotting animals. (Photographed at Springdale, Sussex County, by Joanna Burger)

Very scarce in state." Specimens from Mashipagcong Pond, 7/6; Lake Lackawanna, 9/6; and Schooley Mountain.

Delaware Valley (1966): Sometimes common in Poconos and Catskills, rare in covered area. In New Jersey not recorded south of Orange Mountains.

Staten Island (1973): Not listed.

New York City Area (1993): "Locally common in boreal habitats in upstate New York. May occur sparingly in northwestern New Jersey."

Cape May (1993): Not listed.

Habitat: Openings in boreal woodlands such as spruce forests.

Phenology: Hibernaters emerge in July (rarely in May) and persist until September or October.

Caterpillar Foodplants: "Birch, willow, currant, gooseberry" (Comstock 1940). Possibly birch (Shapiro 1966). In the western United States, usually on willow (Scott 1988b).

Overwintering Stage: Adult.

Comments: This northern species was probably always marginal in New Jersey, and should be sought in the extreme northwestern part of the state.

Where to See It: No known New Jersey locality. Can be found in the Adirondacks in spruce-fir forests, for instance at Moose River Plains.

Gray Comma, *Polygonia progne* (Cramer, 1776)

Range: Maritime Provinces to the Great Plains; from northern Maine to western North Carolina; occurs over most of New York (Shapiro 1974a) and is shown for northern and central New Jersey (Opler and Krizek 1984) with records from Sussex, Essex, Somerset, Hunterdon, Mercer, Burlington, and Camden Counties (Opler's Atlas). Recorded as a stray in Delmarva (Woodbury 1994).

Current Status: Rare in Northwest; no currently documented populations. Has occurred in Stokes Forest. Recent records in May 1983 (Cech 1993) and along Delaware River in Warren County.

Historical Status: There are relatively few historical records, and fewer recent records. Beutenmüller (1893) considered it "less common than" Question Mark and Comma, implying that it was not vary rare in the New York City area. It is clearly rarer today than 50 years ago. With former records on Staten Island and in southern New Jersey, we must assume that this species has greatly declined; another retreating northern species. The Rutgers Collection has specimens from Springdale and the Delaware Valley.

Conservation Status: Natural Heritage Listing is SH, indicating no recent records. This northern species, still fairly common in the Adirondacks, may have been severely affected by pesticide spraying. Surveys should be conducted to see if it persists in suitable habitat.

Smith (1890): "Caldwell, common."

Smith (1900): "New Brunswick northward, throughout the state; somewhat local and occasionally common." One Camden specimen.

Smith (1910): "Local throughout the northern half of the State."

Comstock (1940): North of Fall Line. "Not common." Specimens from Hemlock Falls, Hamburg, Irvington, Greenwood Lakes, Stanhope, Lake Lackawanna, Andover, with only one southern locality, Camden.

Delaware Valley (1966): "Scarce and local" recorded from Mercer (Washington Crossing, Princeton Junction), Hunterdon (Raven Rock), Burlington (Mount Holly), and Camden (Clementon) Counties.

Staten Island (1973): Two specimens, 2/24/1906 and 10/6/71 (Tottenville).

New York City Area (1993): "Common to our north." {Fairly common is a more typical status.}

Cape May (1993): Not listed.

Habitat: Clearings in and cuts through deciduous woods of the Transition Life Zone and mixed deciduous-coniferous woodlands.

Phenology: Two broods—hibernators emerge in May, broods emerge in early July and mid-August–October.

Caterpillar Foodplants: Wild Gooseberry (*Ribes rotundifolium*), some other species of Currants (*Ribes* spp.), Pinxter Flower (*Rhododendron nudiflorum*; Shapiro 1966), and rarely on elms (*Ulmus* spp.).

Overwintering Stage: Adult.

Comment: The fall brood emerges in October when it is likely to be overlooked since relatively few observers are in the field. Larvae have a variety of predator avoidance tactics (Scott 1988b) including the ability to descend rapidly on a silken threat when disturbed. They induce vomiting when eaten by birds, and they have sharp, physical scoli around the neck (these can even produce micropunctures in human skin).

Compton Tortoiseshell, *Nymphalis vau-album* (Denis and Schiffermüller, 1778)

Range: Holarctic. Maritime Provinces and northern Maine across northern New York to Minnesota, expanding southward to central New Jersey and southern Pennsylvania. Occurs over most of New York (Shapiro 1974a) and Cape May. A stray to Delmarva (Woodbury 1994) and Cape May. The North American race *j-album* (described by Boisduval and LeConte in 1833) occurs in New Jersey.

Current Status: This is one of the few species which invades from the North. It has not been detected every year, but has apparently been increasing since 1980. Widespread and fairly common in northwestern New Jersey, where it is resident. Occurs in Somerset County, but not recorded at Somerset town until 1996 (MG). Only a vagrant in southern New Jersey. More common north and west of New Jersey, with a substantial resident population in southern Orange County, NY (Yrizarry).

Historical Status: Very rare and local in northern New Jersey and New York City at the turn of the century (Beutenmüller 1893). Although still local, this species has apparently showed an increase since 1980 for reasons that are obscure; perhaps partly due to increased observers.

Smith (1890): Schooley Mountain and "Newark."

Smith (1900): "Locally north of the red shale." Additional sites: Staten Island, Caldwell, Orange Mountain, and Camden.

Smith (1910): "Local throughout . . . much more frequent northwardly." Additional records: Lakehurst and Barnegat.

Comstock (1940): "Throughout state locally." Specimens from extreme Northwest and from Barnegat and Lakehurst. {These latter localities would be unusual today.}

Delaware Valley (1966): "Sporadically." Outside of invasion years when it is abundant, only a few individuals are seen. No New Jersey records in this area. {This is apparently still true.}

Staten Island (1973): "No modern records. . . . Perhaps extinct in the entire New York City region." A number of specimens were reported by Davis (1910).

New York City Area (1993): Varies from year to year but usually scarce. "Most common inland . . . some coastal movement."

Cape May (1993): First recorded 8/20/95 near Rio Grand by Dale Russelet (P. Sutton)

Habitat: Open areas in and around deciduous and coniferous forests of the Canadian to Transition Life Zones.

Phenology: Two broods—hibernators emerge late March or April, then a brood July–September. An adult may live 11 months. In October, seek hibernation sites. Proctor (1976) describes fourteen adults entering a narrow crevice at the corner of a radio relay tower 10 m above the ground.

Caterpillar Foodplants: Preference for birch, particularly Gray and Paper Birches (*Betula populifolia, B. papyrifera*) and Quaking Aspen (*Populus tremuloides*), but also on other poplars (*Populus*) and willows (*Salix*) (Shapiro 1966).

Overwintering Stage: Adult. Often winters in groups in crevices in buildings (Smith 1910). This is a species that might benefit from "butterfly houses."

Comment: The North American form was described, originally as a separate species, by Boisduval and LeConte (1833), giving the locality as "env. New York, Philadelphia, and New Harmony, Indiana"; as with many of their descriptions, it was apparently based on a drawing by Abbot rather than on a specimen.

Mourning Cloak, *Nymphalis antiopa* (Linnaeus, 1758) Plate 1b

Range: Holarctic; eastern Canada across North America to central Mexico; northern Maine to northern Florida. The subspecies *antiopa* is said to occur in northeastern North America (Miller and Brown 1981), but our populations more closely resemble other European races (Klots 1951; Pavulaan), in which case they require a separate name.

Current Status: Widespread and sometimes fairly common but usually seen singly. Usually the earliest spring butterfly; often flying on warm days in March.

Historical Status: Probably no real change, but it is not usually "common" at present, with most counts showing fewer than ten individuals.

Smith (1890–1910): "Common throughout."

Comstock (1940): "Throughout."

Delaware Valley (1966): "Common". Numbers vary from year to year.

Staten Island (1973): {Common.}

New York City Area (1993): "Usually common." "Most fall . . . records are coastal migrants."

Cape May (1993): "Common."

Habitat: Open areas in and around deciduous forest.

Phenology: Two "broods"—March (rarely February)–end of December (as in 1994). Adults emerge mainly in March and early April and produce the brood that will emerge in July–August. These adults are seen flying until early October, when they seek shelter for winter hibernation, but they may reemerge on warm, sunny days.

Caterpillar Foodplants: Black Willow (*Salix nigra*) and other willows, Cottonwood (*Populus deltoides*) and aspen (*P. tremuloides*), American Elm (*Ulmus americana*). Occasionally on Hackberry (*Celtis*) and blackberry (*Rubus* spp.).

Overwintering Stage: Adult.

Comment: Estivates in late summer. Adults may live 11 months. They nectar more than most anglewings, particularly on milkweeds, but also use fermented fruit and tree sap. In Britain, the same species is called the "Camberwell Beauty."

Milbert's Tortoiseshell, *Nymphalis milberti* (Godart, 1819)

Also called "Small Tortoiseshell" in Comstock (1940) and Shapiro (1966), but that is the name of the next species. Often listed in *Aglais*.

Range: Newfoundland to California; northern Maine to Pennsylvania. Occurred over most of New York but not around New York City since 1910 (Shapiro 1974a). Infrequently irruptive to northern and central New Jersey. The subspecies *milberti* occurs in New Jersey.

Current Status: Poorly known. It is scarce in the Catskills and is occasionally seen in New Jersey. A sight record from Culver's Lake, Sussex County (August 1995; Tetlow), suggests it may still be a rare, local resident or an erratic immigrant. It is rare in Massachusetts, occurring in forested areas such as Mount Greylock (*Mass. Butterflies*, February 1994) and is absent most years around Philadelphia (Glassberg 1993b).

Historical Status: Very rare a century ago (Beutenmüller 1893). Never very common, but formerly apparently more widespread in northern New Jersey (Smith 1910), including several records in October 1910 at Newark and Keyport, corresponding to records in Manhattan and Brooklyn (Davis 1911). Was recorded rarely in the 1950s and 1960s. A specimen was taken at Green Pond (8/56; Forster) and a sight record of two near Culver's Pond in 1970 (Darrow); then virtually no records for 25 years. This is another species retreating northward.

Smith (1890): Schooley Mountain.

Smith (1900): Schooley and Orange Mountains northward, rare near Camden.

Smith (1910): Additional records from Staten Island, Swartswood Lake, and Paterson.

Comstock (1940): North of Fall Line "usually scarce but some seasons locally very numerous." Specimens from Northwest and Camden.

Delaware Valley (1966): "More widespread and familiar" than Compton Tortoiseshell. {This is certainly not true today.} Recorded from Mercer, Burlington, and Camden Counties.

Staten Island (1973): "Presumably extinct on Staten Island." Records for 1886, 1902, and 1910 (all September or October).

New York City Area (1993): "Not seen in New York City area since 1910" (Shapiro 1974a).

Cape May (1993): Not listed.

Habitat: Moist fields adjacent to deciduous woods. Often found basking on dirt roads.

Phenology: Two broods—hibernators emerge in May–June and produce a brood emerging July–September, occasionally early October. Most records in June–July. A November record from Camden (Comstock 1940).

Caterpillar Foodplants: Stinging nettles (*Urticaria*), including *U. gracilis* and *U. dioica*.

Overwintering Stage: Either as pupa or adult.

Comment: It visits flowers more than other anglewings except for the Mourning Cloak. It is closely related to the next species.

[**Small Tortoise Shell** *Nymphalis urticae*] (Linnaeus 1758)

Listed in the genus *Aglais* in most European books.

A European species with several recent New York City Records (1989–95). Two of the records are from Jamaica Bay; the most recent is from Manhattan. Either previously overlooked as a human-assisted vagrant, or perhaps there is a small unknown colony in the New York City area. Should be looked for in northeastern New Jersey (Glassberg 1992).

New York City Area (1993): "No known North American populations." Records include Jamaica Bay (Aug. 31–Sept. 2, 1988, and Aug. 25–26, 1991) and two Manhattan records at Riverside Park (10/15/90), and Central Park West (10/11/95).

Habitat: In Europe very widespread in open habitats adjacent to forests and one of the commonest visitors to suburban gardens and urban parks, where it is attracted to *Buddleia*.

Caterpillar Foodplant: Stinging Nettle (*Urtica dioica*), the host plant in Europe, is widely naturalized in eastern North America.

Comment: This species has also been recorded from Albany, NY, and Nova Scotia (Glassberg 1992). The Nova Scotia specimen was known to have arrived in a packing crate from England (Scott and Wright 1972). Should be sought in northeastern New Jersey.

[**California Tortoiseshell** *Nymphalis californica* (Boisduval) 1852]

Range: Southern British Columbia south through mountains to southern California, Arizona and New Mexico. Rare enormous outbreaks result in eastward movement across Great Plains. Opler's Atlas shows about eight sites in eastern United States, including southern Vermont, western Pennsylvania, and western New York. "Somehow introduced near Buffalo in the late 19th century and survived about 20 years" (Shapiro 1974a).

Current Status: Never recorded in New Jersey, but recorded in two adjacent states, hence could show up during one of its unusual emigration years.

Habitat: Edges of montane woodland from Transition to Hudsonian Zone of western mountains.

Phenology: Adults overwinter, emerging in spring to produce one or more summer broods, which emigrate to higher altitudes. Adults of latest brood migrate to lower altitude to hibernate (Scott 1986).

Caterpillar Foodplants: Several species of *Ceanothus* (Rhamnaceae). Only one species, New Jersey Tea (*C. americanus*), occurs in New Jersey.

American Lady, [American Painted Lady] (*Vanessa virginiensis* (Drury), 1773)

The name was shortened to avoid confusion with Painted Lady (NABA 1995). Has also been called Painted Beauty and Hunter's Butterfly.

Range: Southern Canada across North America to northern South America. Maritime Provinces to southern Florida and Caribbean; throughout New Jersey.

Current Status: Widespread and often fairly common, particularly in 1991 and

1992. High count of seventy-five at Sandy Hook (5/3/92) and 79 (1995, Cumberland 4JC).

Historical Status: No apparent long-term change, but numbers fluctuate greatly from year to year.

Smith (1890–1910): "Common throughout."

Comstock (1940): "Throughout."

Delaware Valley (1966): "Very common to abundant . . . throughout." "Not subject to the fluctuations . . . which characterize its relatives." {Such fluctuations have occurred in New Jersey in recent years.}

Staten Island (1973): "Frequent," widespread.

New York City Area (1993): "Widespread breeder and migrant."

Cape May (1993): "Common to abundant," migratory.

Habitat: Ubiquitous from coastal dunes to forest openings. Frequently visits gardens where individuals will spend hours on a single *Buddleia* bush; also favors fields of Common Milkweed.

Phenology: Three broods early May–early November.

Caterpillar Foodplants: Mainly Sweet Everlasting (*Gnaphalium obtusifolium*), as well as related composite species in the genera *Anaphalis*, *Antennaria*, *Artemesia*, and *Arctium* and possibly other families (Opler and Krizek 1984).

Overwintering Stage: Usually as adult in southern states; sometimes as pupa.

Comment: Sometimes migrates with the next two species.

Painted Lady, [Cosmopolitan Painted Lady] (*Vanessa cardui* (Linnaeus), 1758)
Sometimes referred to as the Cosmopolite.

Range: Nearly worldwide, including North and South America, Eurasia and Africa as well as isolated islands. It is not truly resident in most of the United States, but regularly emigrates northward from Mexico and the southwestern deserts, eventually ranging from Canada to southern Florida. Throughout New Jersey.

Current Status: Erratic immigration patterns. Rare in some years and widespread and common in other years. Outnumbered previous species in central New Jersey in 1991 with up to thirty-five in a day (1991, Raritan Canal 4JC).

Historical Status: No apparent change, but, like the last species, its numbers vary dramatically from year to year, and in some years very few are seen.

Smith (1890–1910): "Common throughout."

Comstock (1940): "Throughout. Numerous some years, absent others."

Delaware Valley (1966): Interyear variation from rare to abundant.

Staten Island (1973): A variable migrant, abundant in 1970, rare in 1971.

New York City Area (1993): "Rare in early 1980s; common since."

Cape May (1993): "Uncommon" as a migrant.

Habitat: Ubiquitous from coastal dunes to forest openings. Often associates with American Ladies in milkweed fields; on coastal dunes frequently nectars on Seaside Goldenrod.

Phenology: Three or four broods April–December. It is continuously brooded and does not diapause.

Caterpillar Foodplants: More than 100 host plants have been recorded (Opler and Krizek 1984). In our area uses the alien Bull Thistle (*Cirsium vulgare*) and other thistles, *Carduus* spp. Also on various other composites (Shapiro 1966) including on Burdock (*Arctium*) and on Hollyhock (*Althaea*; Comstock 1940).

Overwintering Stage: Does not overwinter in New Jersey.

Comment: This is the world's most widespread butterfly. The Painted Lady has a very wide range in North America from coast to coast and from sea level to 3960 meters elevation (Pike's Peak, CO). It occurs throughout most of the Old

World, but has a very limited range in Australia, where it is replaced by a closely related species, and except where introduced, it is absent from the Pacific Islands.

It is a highly migratory species (Abbott 1951) that does not overwinter in New Jersey, but recolonizes its northeastern range nearly every year. It often engages in spectacular migrations in the western United States. In emigration years a large population builds up when favorable temperature and rainfall produce flourishing vegetation in the southwestern deserts of northern Mexico and Arizona (Tilden 1962). It then engages in extensive migrations involving four generations (Abbott 1962).

Red Admiral, *Vanessa atalanta* (Linnaeus, 1758)

Range: North America to central America, Europe to Middle East, Asia, and North Africa, Hawaii, and New Zealand. Canada to Key West; throughout New Jersey. The subspecies *rubria*, described by Fruhstorfer in 1909, occurs in the eastern United States.

Current Status: Widespread and often fairly common, though seldom abundant except in irruption years when migrants from South invade. A dramatic northward migration occurred throughout the spring and summer of 1990. Thousands were migrating north in early May 1990 at Cape May (Suttons). A very large migration westward on the south shore of Long Island was observed on Sept. 9, 1912 (Davis 1912).

Historical Status: No apparent long term change; considered abundant by most writers, and occasionally abundant today.

Smith (1890–1910): "Common throughout," more abundant in September.

Comstock (1940): "Throughout . . . often abundant in fall."

Delaware Valley (1966): "Usually abundant," widespread.

Staten Island (1973): "Frequent and widespread."

New York City Area (1993): "Fairly common to abundant breeder and coastal migrant; numbers vary greatly from year to year."

Cape May (1993): "Common to abundant."

Habitat: Ubiquitous, especially when migrating. Otherwise usually associated with open areas in and around deciduous woodlands. Also fairly common in the Pine Barrens.

Phenology: Two broods April–December. Hibernators emerge in April, fresh adults from overwintering pupae in May, and new broods mid-June–mid-July and late August–September.

Caterpillar Foodplants: Mainly Nettles (*Urtica*) and False Nettle (*Boehmeria cylindrica*).

Overwintering Stage: Adult. The fall brood overwinters and may emerge in the spring. Some overwinter as pupae.

Comment: Adults rarely nectar but sometimes feed on fermented fruit, sap, or bird droppings. The males wait on sunny branches or tree trunks and sally out at passing females or other intruders, including humans. Bitzer and Shaw (1979) studied the territoriality of Red Admirals on a university campus (Iowa State) and found that territories were oriented along lines such as walls and sidewalks. The males held territories for about 2 hours in late afternoon and usually did not return the next afternoon. Males engage in towering spiral flights when chasing conspecific males, but not when chasing other species of butterflies. Territorial males attacked intruding males, with some having as many as twenty intruders per hour.

This butterfly clearly illustrates the contrast between a cryptic ventral surface and a conspicuously marked upper surface. Bitzer and Shaw (1979) did not reach a conclusion whether the males opened their brightly colored upper-wing surfaces as a threat display or to attract mates.

Common Buckeye, *Junonia coenia* (Hubner, 1822)

Range: Permanent range is from North Carolina across Gulf States to west Mexico and coastal California (Opler and Krizek 1984; Scott 1986) but regularly immigrates to central Maine and southern Canada (absent from northern Rockies). Does not overwinter, but an immigrant to most of New Jersey. Recorded regularly from Long Island and lower Hudson Valley but absent from most of New York (Shapiro 1974a).

Current Status: Often abundant on the southern Coastal Plain, becoming uncommon northward and quite rare in the Northwest (Wander). Counts of over 100 per day are not unusual at Cape May.

Historical Status: No apparent change. The reports below are applicable today.

Smith (1890–1910): Widespread south of red shale and often common; occasional in North and West.

Comstock (1940): "Abundant south of Fall Line, more sparingly in Northern District."

Delaware Valley (1966): "Usually present in the coastal plain and often quite common." May occasionally breed north of Fall Line.

Staten Island (1973): "Common," widespread, "especially on beaches." "Probably does not overwinter."

New York City Area (1993): "Coastal migrant and colonist, rare inland."

Cape May (1993): "Common to abundant."

Habitat: Open areas with bare ground, particularly numerous along the coast.

Phenology: Three broods May–November, rarely March or December. Usually does not reach Delmarva until late April and New Jersey until early May, but recorded March 1992 (New Brunswick, Murrays).

Caterpillar Foodplants: English Plantain (*Plantago lanceolata*), also Red-stemmed Plantain (*P. rugelii*), Toadflax (*Linaria* spp.), False Foxglove (*Aureola*). Gerardias (*Gerardia*) and Snapdragons (Comstock 1940). In Delmarva, Purple Gerardia (*Gerardia purpurea*) is the favored host (Woodbury 1994), and it is used on Long Island and Cape May (Dowdell) as well (Tudor).

Overwintering Stage: Adult.

Comments: This is one of the most conspicuous butterflies in southern New Jersey in late summer and fall. The March record suggests that it may overwinter at least occasionally in or close to New Jersey. The development of the complex wing pattern of bars and eyespots has been reported by Nijhout (1980). The two black bars on the front edge of the dorsal forewing is a pattern that occurs in many genera of nymphalids. Two very similar Buckeyes occur in Florida and the Neotropics, and very similar species are found in Africa and Australasia.

Migrants arriving in spring and early summer are usually smaller and paler than the brood produced locally in summer which often has a reddish brown postmedian band below. The autumn brood is the largest and most brightly colored above. The underside of the hind wing is very variable; many are quite bronze, and some individuals are quite reddish below (form 'rosa'). Some late females have metallic green on the upper forewing (Pavulaan).

Males perch mainly on bare ground in flat areas and wait for females. Scott (1975) considered that this species had the most variable courtship behavior. Males investigate any passing objects motorcycles to conspecific females.

Where to find it. This widespread species is often abundant around Cape May Point in September and can be found in parks and gardens, particularly nectaring around *Sedum*. Also regularly seen on the dikes at the Brigantine (Forsyth) National Wildlife Refuge. Caterpillars on *Gerardia* at Cape May.

White Peacock, *Anartia jatrophae* (Johansson, 1763)

Range: This is a widespread and common Neotropical species that regularly reaches South Carolina and "occasionally" North Carolina (Opler and Krizek 1984). Accidental in New Jersey and Massachusetts (Glassberg 1993b). The race in eastern North America is *guantanamo*, (described by Munroe in 1942).

Current Status: Accidental. One New Jersey sight record at Port Norris (Cumberland County) (August 1988; Schweitzer).

Historical Status: Not applicable.

Smith (1890–1910): Not listed.

Comstock (1940): Not listed.

Delaware Valley (1966): Not listed.

New York City Area (1993): Not listed.

Cape May (1993): Not listed.

Habitat: A conspicuous and distinctive species at lawns, gardens, and roadsides in the South that would be readily identified by any observer.

Caterpillar Foodplants: Members of the Vervain (Verbenaceae), Ruellia (Acanthaceae), Figwort (Scrophulariaceae), and Mint (Lamiaceae) families (Opler and Krizek 1984; Scott 1986). Of its documented host species, only Peppermint (*Mentha piperita*) and Balm (*Melissa officinalis*) occur in New Jersey.

Overwintering Stage: Does not overwinter.

Comment: It is exceedingly rare north of South Carolina, where it is confined to the coast. It is one of the few butterflies that uses mints as a host.

Subfamily *Limenitidinae*, Admirals and Viceroy

This subfamily is not recognized in most books, and they are usually treated as part of the Nymphalinae group.

Red Spotted Purple and **White Admiral,** *Limenitis arthemis* (Drury, 1773)

Range: Maritime Provinces to Alaska and the Rocky Mountains, south-central Florida and central Texas. The Red-spotted Purple (race *astyanax*, described by Fabricius in 1775) occurs from southeastern Maine, southern New England, and central New York to Florida and from Minnesota to Texas. It occurs throughout New Jersey. The White Admiral race, including *arthemis*, occurs from New England and southern New York westward and northward to Alaska, and may be a vagrant to northern New Jersey, but is not resident here.

Current Status: The Red-spotted Purple is widespread and sometimes fairly common, occurring throughout the state. The White Admiral or Banded Purple race occurs in the Catskills and as close as Bear Mountain (Rockland County, NY) and perhaps occasionally in northwestern New Jersey (Opler and Krizek 1984). It is recorded from Passaic County (Opler's Atlas); there are recent reports from the Delaware Water Gap and highlands of Morris County (Wander).

Historical Status: No apparent change for the Red-spotted Purple. From Smith's account it is likely that the White Admiral or the white-banded form 'albofasciata' has declined, although Beutenmüller (1893) did not mention the White Admiral at all. Leck (pers. comm.) reported several records from Princeton in the 1970s, and there are specimens from Cape May and Cumberland; these are intergrades rather than true White Admirals (Schweitzer, pers. comm.).

Smith (1890–1910): Red-spotted Purple "common throughout." The White Admiral is listed only as local, and apparently scarce, in northern hills, with records south to Schooley Mountain.

Comstock (1940): "Throughout." Only the Red-spotted Purple occurs in New Jersey, and "white admirals" are actually the form 'albofasciata.'

Delaware Valley (1966): "Fairly common." Widespread but rare in Pine Barrens.

Staten Island (1973): "Infrequent, local." Has declined since 1910. The form 'albofasciata' was collected on Staten Island (8/22/16; Hall 1916).

New York City Area (1993): "Reasonably common in woods, thickets, overgrown fields and gardens."

Cape May (1993): "Common."

Habitat: This is primarily a woodland species occurring in open areas in and around deciduous forest. Often visits gardens.

Phenology: Two broods in North and three in South. North, April 30–mid-September (extreme date Oct. 11). South, late May and June, mid-July–early August, and mid-August–September.

Caterpillar Foodplants: Mainly Wild Black Cherry (*Prunus serotina*) and other cherries and various poplars (*Populus* spp.) and Oaks (*Quercus* spp.). Smith (1910) lists willows and huckleberries as well, but the latter is doubtful. The race *arthemis* uses birches (*Betula* spp.) and aspen (*Populus* spp.). Scott (1986) lists thirty-four tree species in six families as hosts of the species throughout its range.

Overwintering Stage: Early-stage larva.

Comment: The banded pattern is reported to be disruptive while the non-banded pattern mimics the Pipevine Swallowtail (Platt and Brower 1968) (photo 2 on page 49). Platt et al. (1971) showed that Blue Jays *Cyanocitta cristata* trained to avoid the unpalatable Monarch, rejected Viceroys, but readily ate Red-spotted Purples; those trained to reject Pipevine Swallowtails, rejected Red-spotted Purples, but readily ate Viceroys or White Admirals. Scott (1986) recognized four subspecies. The Red-spotted Purple *astyanax* and a southwestern race *arizonensis* co-occur with the Swallowtail and are mimics; *arthemis* and *rubro-fasciata* occur across Canada and northern United States, north of the range of the Swallowtail, and are white-banded. In New Jersey the identification of the two subspecies is confused by the presence of intergrades ('albofasciata'), which can have a complete white band. This is due to introgression of White Admiral genes from former or occasional interbreeding. This is a distinct phenomenon from hybridization, for white bands of varying intensity can show up at various points in the Purple range (south to western Virginia, Clark & Clark 1951), even among offspring of Purples that never encountered a White Admiral. The form 'proserpina' has only a trace of the white band across the wings.

The distribution of these forms in northern New Jersey deserves careful study. The main line of demarcation between the white-banded and the purple forms is shown across Ulster and Sullivan Counties, NY, passing just northwest of New Jersey (Shapiro 1974a) or through extreme northwestern New Jersey (Opler and Krizek 1984). It continues from Maine to western Maryland. In some areas one finds both pure forms as well as intergrades. We have seen apparently pure White Admiral types as close as northern Rockland County. There are records of the form 'albofasciata' from various parts of New Jersey (Comstock 1940), including the Delaware Valley (Shapiro 1966). The white banding of the White Admiral is controlled by a single pair of autosomal genes with incomplete dominance (Platt and Brower 1968), and produces a disruptive pattern.

The Red-spotted Purple is frequently seen flying through woodland canopy and coming to rest on leaves as much as 10 m above the ground. Adults often nectar at *Buddleia*, but in general use fermenting fruit, tree sap, dung, and rotting carcasses.

In central New York, males showed territorial behavior along flyways used by females, but the location of individual territories changed from day to day (Lederhouse 1993). Males congregate on peaks in hilly country (Pavulaan).

Viceroy, *Limenitis archippus* (Cramer, 1776)

Range: Maritime Provinces to eastern Washington and California, south to Florida and Mexico in Tropical to Transition Zone habitats; central Maine to southern Florida. The nominate subspecies *archippus* occurs throughout New Jersey.

Current Status: Widespread, usually uncommon, but sometimes common. Over much of its range this species is certainly less common than the Milkweed butterflies (Monarch and Queen) that it mimics.

Historical Status: No dramatic change, but listed as "common" in early reports and as "uncommon" or "fairly common" in current publications. It has apparently declined somewhat in the past 25 years.

    Smith (1890–1910): "More or less common throughout."
    Comstock (1940): "Throughout."
    Delaware Valley (1966): "Locally common." Occasionally numerous.
    Staten Island (1973): "Frequent, but local."
    New York City Area (1993): "Fairly common in wet meadows," "commonest inland."
    Cape May (1993): "Common."

Habitat: A variety of open habitats including pastures, old fields, marshes, and forest edge, often on the edge of old orchards.

Phenology: Three broods May–October.

Caterpillar Foodplants: A variety of willows including Black Willow (*Salix nigra*), also *S. sericea* and various poplars (*Populus* spp.). Has been reared on Weeping Willow (*S. babylonica*; Platt et al. 1971).

Overwintering Stage: Small larva.

Comment: The apparent mimicry of Monarchs by Viceroys is one of the best-studied examples. The northern Viceroys (*L. a. archippus*) found in our area have the same pattern and are the same shade of orange as the Monarch (*Danaus plexippus*, while in Florida the race *floridensis* is a darker chestnut mimicking the distasteful Queen (*D. gilippus*), a close relative of the Monarch. Jane Brower (1958a,b) showed that both cases represent Batesian mimicry. This continues to be a fruitful area of study since recent research suggests that Monarchs are not always unpalatable (depending on the alkaloid concentrations in their local host plants), while Viceroys sometimes are unpalatable (in which case it represents Müllerian rather than Batesian mimicry; Ritland and Brower 1991). (See photo 1 on page 48).

There is increasing interest (Platt and Maudsley 1994) in the apparently regular hybridization of Viceroys with Red-spotted Purple, White Admiral (Shapiro and Biggs 1968), Weidermeyer's Admiral (*L. weidermeyeri*; Simpson and Pettus 1976), and Lorquin's Admiral (*L. lorquini*; Perkins and Gage 1970).

In early summer adults often use aphid honeydew, tree sap, or carrion, but in late summer they regularly nectar and feed on overripe fruit such as apples. Males are highly territorial (Pavulaan).

Subfamily *Apaturinae*, Emperors

The two emperors are variously treated as members of the Apaturinae (Scott 1986) or are lumped with the Leafwings in a larger subfamily, Charaxinae (Opler and Krizek 1984). Earlier authors treated these groups as family-level taxa. The Apaturinae contains about fifty species, mainly in tropical regions; it is not consistently distinguished from the Nymphalinae except for a characteristic wing shape (Scott 1986). All five North American species feed on Hackberries (*Celtis* spp.). Friedlander (1986) prepared a major review of the biology and biogeography of the Emperors, based on his studies in Texas.

Hackberry Emperor [Hackberry Butterfly], *Asterocampa celtis* (Boisduval and LeConte, 1834) Plate 3a

Range: Southern New England to Minnesota, south to Arizona, northern Mexico, and Florida; southern New York to southern Florida; the subspecies *celtis* occurs throughout New Jersey.

Current Status: Localized to areas with its host species, Hackberries (*Celtis* spp.). Usually not numerous, but occasionally common, as at Higbee Beach. Usually seen singly, but occasionally fairly common in central New Jersey with up to four per day at the Rutgers Busch Campus (Piscataway; C. Leck). Maximum 4JC total 13 (1995, Cape May).

Historical Status: This species has clearly increased in the past 50 years since it is now widespread and at least uncommon. Neither this species nor the next are listed as regularly occurring in New Jersey by Smith (1890–1910), perhaps because early collectors did not frequent Hackberry groves. Indeed, Shapiro and Shapiro (1973) mention that even in 1970 this species, though common on Staten Island, did not occur near Philadelphia.

Smith (1890–1910): Not listed.

Comstock (1940): "Locally" north of Fall Line. No records from southern New Jersey. {Now known to be fairly common in Cape May area.}

Delaware Valley (1966): "Uncommon and local."

Staten Island (1973): "Locally abundant at Tottenville and occasional elsewhere." Not recorded by Davis (1910) {further evidence that it has increased this century}.

New York City Area (1993): "Confined to bottomland hackberry thickets" {by implication local and usually uncommon}.

Cape May (1993): "Uncommon to common."

Habitat: Open or woodland habitats where its host occurs.

Phenology: Two broods June–September.

Caterpillar Foodplants: Various species of Hackberry trees (*Celtis* spp.), mainly *C. occidentalis*.

Overwintering Stage: Usually as larva; occasionally as adults.

Comment: This is one of three obligate Hackberry feeders in New Jersey. It often perches head downward on posts, tree trunks, or walls. It is a pugnacious species, readily flying out to circle one's head before returning to its perch. It occasionally lands on a human to drink sweat. This species shows increased activity in the late afternoon and evening. In Ohio it has been reported to become abundant, defoliate its host trees causing them to die, and then subsequently become rare (Langlois and Langlois 1964).

Tawny Emperor, *Asterocampa clyton* (Boisduvel and LeConte, 1833)

Range: Southern New England to the Great Plains, south to Florida and northern Mexico. In East from western Connecticut to central Florida; throughout New Jersey. The subspecies *clyton* occurs in New Jersey.

Current Status: A hackberry specialist; apparently quite local and usually rare to uncommon, although sometimes abundant at Cape May and in Northwest with up to 30/day in Sussex County, and regular at Greenwood Sanctuary; 23+ at Cape May (8/21/93; Tudor). Not yet found at the Rutgers Busch Campus, where Hackberry Emperor is fairly common.

Historical Status: Although still highly local, this is one of the species that has increased dramatically in the past 20 years. It is now fairly common at Tottenville, Staten Island, where it was not recorded by Shapiro and Shapiro (1973), and it is sometimes common at Cape May. It has also increased elsewhere in southern New York.

Smith (1890–1900): No records from New Jersey.

Smith (1910): Listed only from Maplewood based on larvae on *Celtis*.

Comstock (1940): "Locally," north of Fall Line. More common than Hackberry Emperor.

Delaware Valley (1966): "Quite local . . . usually uncommon . . . widespread." Only Mercer County listed, suggesting it is rare or absent in Burlington, Gloucester, Camden, and Atlantic Counties.

Staten Island (1973): Not listed.

New York City Area (1993): More local and rare than Hackberry Butterfly.

Cape May (1993): "Uncommon."

Habitat: Open areas to woodland edges where Hackberries occur.

Phenology: Two broods late May–June and mid-August–early September.

Caterpillar Foodplants: Hackberry (*Celtis occidentalis*) and other species of *Celtis*.

Overwintering Stage: Small larva.

Comments: This is one of three Hackberry specialists. Adults rarely nectar, but more often feed on tree sap, carrion, decaying fruit, dung, or aphid honeydew. Friedlander (1985) found that about two-thirds of egg masses in Texas are parasitized by tiny wasps; eggs are laid in pyramid-shaped clusters which help protect interior eggs from parasitism.

Subfamily *Satyrinae*, Satyrs and Wood Nymphs

The Satyrids are treated either as a family (Satyridae) or by most recent authors as a subfamily (Satyrinae) of the Nymphalidae. This group contains about 2000 species worldwide, with forty-three in North America. Nine have been recorded in New Jersey, including the recent invader, Common Ringlet. Two of the species have disappeared from the state (Carolina and Mitchell's Satyrs). In our region all species are generally brown with a variety of eyespots or ocelli arranged in rows across both wings. The forelegs are greatly reduced in size and have a sensory rather than locomotary function. Most species are grass feeders (Scott 1986) and have palatible, cryptic larvae.

[Southern Pearly-Eye, *Enodia portlandia* (Fabricius, 1781)]

Range: Southeastern United States from Virginia to northern Florida and westward to Oklahoma and Texas. The race *portlandia* would occur in New Jersey. Opler's Atlas records it from Cape May County.

Current Status: Hypothetical and/or accidental. No evidence that it was ever resident.

Historical Status: Only distinguished from next species by Gatrelle (1971). Comstock (1940) mentions a Pearly-Eye from Wildwood which may refer to this species.

Habitat: Damp wooded habitats of the Lower Austral Zone.

Phenology: Long flight period April–November.

Caterpillar Foodplant: Giant Cane (*Arundinaria gigantea*) and Switch Cane (*A. tecta*) (Opler and Krizek 1984), neither of which occurs in New Jersey.

Comment: All three species of Pearly-Eyes were reported together near Fayetteville, AR (Heitzman and dos Passos 1974).

Northern Pearly-Eye, *Enodia anthedon* (Clark, 1936)

Formerly treated in the genus *Lethe*, and only recently split from *portlandia*.

Range: Maritime Provinces to Manitoba through the Appalachian Mountains to northern Georgia, central Mississippi and the southern Great Plains. Opler and Krizek (1984) map shows it throughout New Jersey except extreme East, but it is probably absent from the Coastal Plain and southern New Jersey.

Current Status: Generally rare to uncommon, occasionally fairly common, particularly in swampy woods in northern New Jersey (e.g., Great Swamp, Hibernia). Maximum count, seventeen (Springdale 1995, 4JC). Rare or absent from most of the state. Does not occur in the southern Coastal Plain.

Historical Status: Was collected in most northern counties (Opler 1983), but has declined, possibly due to insecticide spraying. Documented records are from Sussex, Passaic, Bergen, Morris, Essex, Hudson, Union, and Somerset Counties (Opler's Atlas).

Conservation Status: Natural Heritage ranking is S3–4. Its known populations should be monitored regularly to detect significant trends.

Smith (1890–1910): "Local throughout, not common."

Comstock (1940): "Locally throughout," includes record from Five Mile Beach (Wildwood). Otherwise all other records are in northwestern New Jersey. {The Wildwood record could refer to the Southern Pearly-Eye.}

Delaware Valley (1966): "Very rare . . . damp dark woods." No New Jersey records in area covered.

Staten Island (1973): "Apparently rare. Two records in serpentine highlands."

New York City Area (1993): "Fairly common but never abundant," "absent from coastal plain."

Cape May (1993): "Historical" This listing was no doubt based on a misidentification of Appalachian Brown (P. Sutton).

Habitat: This is one of our most forest-loving species, seen mainly along trails and dirt roads in deciduous and mixed deciduous-coniferous woodlands, often around wet depressions or bogs. Often rests on tree trunks.

Phenology: One brood June–August. Farther south there are two broods, and a partial second brood should be sought in September.

Caterpillar Foodplants: Grasses. Opler and Krizek (1984) list Plume Grass (*Erianthus*) in Maryland and Bearded Short-husk grass (*Brachyelytrum erectum*) in New York.

Overwintering Stage: Larva.

Comments: The Northern Pearly-Eye was described as a subspecies of the Pearly Eye (*E. portlandia*) by Clark with the type locality in Sullivan County, NY. Gatrelle (1971) recognized that two distinct sibling species were involved. Heitzman and dos Passos (1974) verified this, based on its darker, grayer coloration, differences in eyespot patterns and antennal knobs, and subtle differences in the male genital structures, in an area where the two were sympatric. These two species occur sympatrically in the southern United States (Tennessee, Arkansas, Alabama) without interbreeding, and occupy somewhat different habitats.

Populations fluctuate dramatically from year to year (Shapiro and Shapiro 1973); some colonies persist, others disappear. Shapiro (1966) commented that the upland "race" *anthedon* is found in the Delaware Valley, while the southern Coastal Plain form *portlandia* occurred in Cape May, Cumberland, and Atlantic Counties, but that "neither subspecies is found in most of New Jersey." However, these old Coastal Plain records may have been in error since the Southern Pearly-Eye, which otherwise occurs north to Maryland (Opler and Krizek 1984; Scott 1986), is not known to have occurred in New Jersey.

This woodland butterfly frequently perches on the ground or head-down on tree trunks. The latter behavior separates them from the next two species, which seldom do so. This species has a tendency to be active in the late afternoon and evening.

Adults seldom use nectar, preferring sap, rotting fruit, dung, and especially carrion.

Where to Find It: The boardwalk in the Great Swamp, and mature woodlands in Sussex County.

[**Creole Pearly-Eye,** *Enodia creola* (Skinner 1897)]

Range: Southeastern United States from southeastern Virginia to Georgia and west to Oklahoma and Texas. Its range almost completely overlaps the Southern Pearly-Eye.

Status: No New Jersey records; recorded once in southern Delaware (Sussex County; Opler's Atlas). It is not likely that such a sedentary species would wander to New Jersey; but if it has wandered to Delaware, it is not a major leap to Cape May.

Eyed Brown [Northern Eyed Brown], *Satyrodes eurydice* (Johansson, 1763)

Usually referred to as the Northern Eyed Brown. The English Names Committee of NABA (1995), in its effort to reduce reliance on English trinomials, recommends referring to this as the Eyed Brown and the next species as the Appalachian Brown.

Range: A northerly distribution from the Maritime Provinces across to the northern prairie provinces of Canada and the Rocky Mountains, south to extreme northern Delaware and North Dakota. In East from northern Maine to Pennsylvania; northern and central New Jersey. The subspecies *eurydice* occurs in New Jersey.

Current Status: Documented at least from Sussex and Morris Counties. To distinguish from the next species, see Glassberg (1993b), but caution required. Sometimes common, e.g., at Vernon, where up to fifteen seen per day (Wander).

Historical Status: The two species of Eyed Browns were only recognized by Cardé et al. (1970) and were therefore not distinguished by Comstock (1940) or Shapiro (1966); hence the details of their distribution in New Jersey are uncertain. They are often difficult to identify, and this is the less numerous of the two species. There are historic records of Eyed Browns from Ocean, Atlantic, and Burlington Counties which are questionable.

Conservation Status: It is possible that this species was formerly more common before the draining of wetlands and before widespread pesticide use. It has declined dramatically in Ohio (Iftner et al. 1992) due to habitat loss. The Natural Heritage ranking is S1–3, indicating the lack of adequate information, due in part to the difficulty in distinguishing this species.

Smith (1890–1910): {Not distinguished from next species.}

Comstock (1940): {See next species.}

Delaware Valley (1966): {See next species.}

Staten Island (1973): "Very local but frequent."

New York City Area (1993): "Rare . . . widely scattered local colonies." Westchester and Long Island.

Cape May (1993): "Historically present but may no longer occur." {May be an error referring to the next species.}

Habitat: Not usually in woods. This species prefers extensive open sedge marshes and bogs while the next species tends to be in more wooded habitats (Shapiro and Cardé 1970). In two New York studies (Cardé et al. 1970; Angevine and Brussard 1979) and one Ohio study (Shuey 1985), the authors reported that no Eyed Browns were taken in woods and few or no Appalachian Browns were taken in wet meadows. However, in New Jersey, habitat may be less reliable for identification; the two species may occur together along the same dirt road through wet woodlands in the Great Swamp. This requires further study.

Phenology: One brood June–early August (June 17 to July 25; Cech 1993). This is a much more restricted flight period than the next species.

Caterpillar Foodplants: Various sedges (*Carex* spp.).

Overwintering Stage: Late-stage larva or possibly pupa.

Comments: The type locality of this species is the Morris Arboretum in Philadelphia, where the species no longer occurs. For details on distinguishing these two species, see Glassberg (1993b). The Eyed Brown and Appalachian Brown differ in subtle and inconsistent wing markings, in genitalia structure, and in the markings on the larvae. The Eyed Brown is the more sedentary of the two. Based on genetic studies, Angevine and Brussard (1979) confirmed the earlier conclusions (Cardé et al. 1970) that the Eyed Brown and Appalachian Brown are different species.

Appalachian Brown [Appalachian Eyed Brown], *Satyrodes appalachia* (Chermok 1947)

Range: Central New England and Minnesota south to northern Georgia and Mississippi; disjunct population in northern Florida; throughout New Jersey. The subspecies *appalachia* occurs in New Jersey.

Current Status: This species is probably widespread, though usually not numerous, except in the Northwest where it is often common (Wander). Common in Great Swamp (MG). Has been found around wet woods at Lakehurst (MG), Pigeon Swamp (Williams), and Trenton Marsh (Leck); locally common in South.

Historical Status: It was uncommon at the turn of the century, but may have been more common in midcentury than today.

Smith (1890–1910): Throughout (Hopatcong to Cape May) but uncommon.

Comstock (1940): Recorded "throughout." Records are from Newton to Five Mile Beach.

Delaware Valley (1966): "Locally common, in moist meadows and fresh-water marsh." Recorded from Atlantic, Burlington, Camden, Mercer, and Gloucester Counties.

Staten Island (1973): "Local but frequent."

New York City Area (1993): "Uncommon to locally fairly common in wet, sedgy bottomland woods." "Regular at Springdale, NJ."

Cape May (1993): "Locally common."

Habitat: Originally described as a species of wet woodlands and forest swamps and edges. Frequently seen along trails and road cuts through wet woodlands. Fairly common in bogs in southern New Jersey.

Phenology: One brood mid-June–mid-August, mainly in July. In North, June 8–Sept. 5. A partial second brood occurs in Delmarva (Pavulaan) and could occur in southern New Jersey.

Caterpillar Foodplants: Sedges, including *Carex lacustris* and probably Tussock Sedge (*C. stricta*).

Overwintering Stage: Nearly grown larva and possibly pupa.

Comment: Adults do not nectar but feed on tree sap. Glassberg (1993b) cautions that identification of the two Browns is tricky, but provides details for distinguishing them.

Carolina Satyr, *Hermeuptychia sosybius* (Fabricius, 1793)

Often treated as a subspecies of the very widespread Hermes Satyr, *H. hermes* of the Neotropics.

Range: Southern Maryland (first collected in 1960) and southern Missouri to the Gulf Coast, including all of Florida and Texas. Opler and Krizek (1984) show its range as disjunct, including the Coastal Plain of New Jersey. Not listed for Delmarva (Woodbury 1994). The commonest satyr in much of the southeastern United States.

Current Status: Status uncertain; Either formerly a rare and local resident in southern New Jersey which is now EXTIRPATED, or only a historic stray which may have occasionally bred.

Historical Status: There are very few records, including those from Burlington, Salem, Gloucester, and Cape May Counties; historical information is inadequate but it has declined. No twentieth-century records (Schweitzer). It may have colonized New Jersey briefly concurrent with a population explosion in the southern states (Pavulaan), but there is no evidence that it was ever an established part of our fauna (Schweitzer).

Smith (1890–1910): "Occasional in South," Mount Holly.

Comstock (1940): On Supplemental List of nonregular species, based on specimens from Mount Holly, Burlington County.

Delaware Valley (1966): "Straggler in southern New Jersey." Rare in Cape May "where it may breed." Recorded from Salem and Gloucester Counties.

Staten Island (1973): Not listed.

New York City Area (1993): Not listed.

Cape May (1993): "Historically present but may no longer occur." {No evidence that it was ever resident.}

Habitat: Usually a species of pine woodlands (Opler and Krizek 1984). Reported, perhaps erroneously, to occupy shaded bogs in New Jersey, which is not its usual habitat in the southern states. In Maryland, found in semi-open floodplain woodlands (Simmons and Andersen 1971).

Phenology: One brood July–early August.

Caterpillar Foodplants: Grasses, including Centipede grass (*Eremochloa ophiuroides*) in Virginia, elsewhere on Bermuda Grass (*Cynodon dactylon*), and on *Poa* in the laboratory.

Overwintering Stage: Does not overwinter.

Comment: This species closely resembles the Little Wood Satyr. Authorities are divided on whether to consider the Carolina Satyr a distinct species (*H. sosybius*; Pyle 1981; Iftner et al. 1992; Opler 1992; NABA 1995), or a subspecies *sosybius* of the wide-ranging Hermes Satyr (*H. hermes*; Opler and Krizek 1984; Glassberg 1993b), or part of Hermes Satyr not even subspecifically different (Scott 1986). The Hermes Satyr has been extensively studied in Costa Rica (Emmel 1968) and the Carolina Satyr has been studied in Florida (Kilduff 1972).

Georgia Satyr, *Neonympha areolatus* (J.E. Smith, 1797) Plate 4b

Range: Virginia south to Florida and eastern Texas with a disjunct population in central and southern New Jersey. Not listed for Delmarva (Woodbury 1994). The subspecies *septentrionalis*, described by Davis in 1924, occurs in New Jersey, but is probably a separate species, the Lakehurst Satyr, *Neonympha septentrionalis*.

Current Status: Sometimes common in abandoned cranberry bogs and up to twenty-five have been found at Lakehurst in late June. May be widely distributed in Pine Barrens bogs, but highly local and not found in all bogs. This habitat is declining due to succession and development. There has been no current assessment of the generality of its distribution. It has occurred in Ocean (Lakehurst), Burlington, Camden, and Atlantic Counties, and rarely in Cape May County (Opler's Atlas). No recent record for in Cape May or Cumberland counties (Dowdell).

Historical Status: For at least the past century this has been a highly local but occasionally common species.

Conservation Status: It should be considered at least a species of special concern, and it is vulnerable due to its narrow habitat requirements. Suitable bogs should be surveyed to determine the number of New Jersey colonies, and if small, it should be listed as THREATENED due to loss of habitat. Its habitat is severely threatened by development and by natural succession, and requires aggressive management. The Natural Heritage ranking is S3.

Smith (1890–1910): Localities on Coastal Plain from Toms River to Seven Mile Beach, occasionally common; also recorded from Morristown by Edwards prior to 1890.

Comstock (1940): "Pine barrens and coastal district." {Reasonable records are from Lakehurst and Browns Mills south to Richland (northern Atlantic County), with puzzling records from coastal localities at Deal and Atlantic City which were, even then, inappropriate habitats for this highly local species.}

Delaware Valley (1966): "Locally distributed . . . sometimes not uncommon."

Staten Island (1973): Not listed.

New York City Area (1993): "Never recorded from the New York City area."

Cape May (1993): "Locally uncommon."

Habitat: In New Jersey this species inhabits mainly bogs, but also wet savannah. In the southern U.S. it occupies wet meadows.

Phenology: Usually one brood late June–mid-July at Lakehurst, but two broods reported (June and August) at Fort Dix (Schweitzer). The geographic pattern and ecologic correlates of this variation remain to be investigated.

Caterpillar Foodplants: Not known. Shapiro (1966) suggested grasses, "perhaps favoring *Panicum*," but Opler and Krizek (1984) suggest that sedges are used. Pavulaan (in litt.) reports raising it on Yellow Nut Sedge (*Carex esculenta*) in captivity and suggests *septentrionalis* does not use grass.

Overwintering Stage: Larva.

Comment: It is likely that the New Jersey form will be considered a distinct species when more detailed studies are undertaken. The form *septentrionalis* is reported to occur south to the Carolinas, where there is limited intergradation with the nominate subspecies *areolatus*, and probably to western Florida. The southern populations of true Georgia Satyr are bivoltine. The males of *areolatus* and *septentrionalis* differ in their genital structure (Schweitzer, in litt.).

Mitchell's Satyr, *Neonympha mitchellii* (French, 1889)

Range: Disjunct distribution. The subspecies *mitchellii* was known from only about thirty locations in seventeen counties from southern Michigan, northern Indiana, northeastern Ohio, and extreme northwestern New Jersey (Schweitzer 1989; Wilsmann and Schweitzer 1991). The subspecies *francisi* is known from North Carolina.

Current Status: EXTIRPATED from the state in the mid-1980s. Recorded from several "bogs" (actually calcareous fens) with only one recent colony known, and no records from there since July 15, 1985 (Cech 1993).

Historical Status: Was formerly rare and localized with records from Sussex, Warren, and Morris Counties. Its last known location was near Johnsonberg/ Long Bridge, Warren County. Darrow (in litt.) reported seeing 3–4 on each visit in the 1970s. The history of this species in New Jersey was remarkably brief. Although first collected in 1890 (the year after it was described by French, 1889), it was not known to be resident until 1966 (Rutkowski 1966) and was gone 20 years later. Last reported in Ohio in 1950, and believed extirpated there as well (Iftner et al. 1992).

Conservation Status: This federally ENDANGERED species was listed in June 1991 (USFWS 1991), after both the Ohio and New Jersey populations had been extirpated. The species suffers from loss of habitat, and probably spraying, but the New Jersey population is believed eliminated by overcollecting. The last New Jersey record was in 1985. This is the only butterfly currently on the New Jersey ENDANGERED list. Its Natural Heritage ranking is SH (historical records only) and G2 (globally endangered). Several factors contribute to the disappearance of its colonies. Habitat changes include urbanization and agriculture as well as natural succession to upland forest. The New Jersey fens are sufficiently wet that fire should not pose a problem. "Collecting has clearly caused the demise of two populations in New Jersey" (Wilsmann and Schweitzer 1991).

Smith (1890): Not listed; not described until 1889.

Smith (1900–1910): Only from Dover, NJ, and two localities in Michigan.

Comstock (1940): On supplemental list only based on a specimen from Dover, Morris County (7/10/1890).

Delaware Valley (1966): "Recorded probably erroneously from northern New Jersey" {it turned out not to be erroneous; Rutkowski 1966}.

Staten Island (1973): Not listed.

New York City Area (1993): "Extirpated."

Cape May (1993): Not listed.

Habitat: This species is apparently confined to fens, which are wetlands, mainly of sedges, on calcareous soils over alkaline springs. It has erroneously been attributed to bogs, which are mainly acidic *Sphagnum* communities. The association of sedges, Shrubby Cinquefoil (*Potentilla fruticosa*), Poison Sumac (*Rhus vernix*), and Tamarack (*Larix laricina*) mark its preferred habitat.

Phenology: One brood early–mid-July, very brief flight period. Males precede females.

Caterpillar Foodplants: Presumably sedges. Michigan females were induced to lay on *Carex stricta*, but larvae refused to eat it; larvae were successfully raised on *Carex alopecoides*, and also ate bulrush (*Scirpus atrovirens*) (McAlpine et al. 1960).

Overwintering Stage: Fourth instar larva (McAlpine et al. 1960).

Comment: This species was under pressure from collecting coupled with habitat loss. As it became more rare, the collecting pressure increased, and Darrow (in litt.) observed several collectors visiting the last known colony repeatedly and capturing all adults they encountered. Its disappearance from New Jersey is attributed to collecting (USFWS 1991).

The original petition to list Mitchell's Satyr as ENDANGERED was made in 1974 (when the Ohio population was probably already extirpated), and it took 17 years (and extinction in New Jersey) before the species was federally listed (USFWS 1991). Surprisingly, the original listing did not include the St. Francis Satyr *N. m. francisci*, discovered at Fort Bragg, NC, in 1983 (Parshall and Kral 1989), which was also severely reduced before being placed on the ENDANGERED list separately in February 1995 (USFWS 1995a). Only one metapopulation survives there (USFWS 1995b). The subspecies *mitchelli* survives in only nine counties in Michigan and Indiana (Wilsmann and Schweitzer 1991).

McAlpine et al. (1960) published the most detailed account of the biology of this species, providing limited information on their use of sedges and on their maturation. It has a limited ability to recolonize fens by moving along narrow watercourses, and populations tended to occur at more than one point in a watershed (Wilsmann and Schweitzer 1991).

The original New Jersey specimen collected by C. W. Johnson (7/10/1890) has long been attributed to Dover, but there are no suitable habitats nearby, and

Wilsmann and Schweitzer (1991) suggest that this locality label is inaccurate, and the specimen may have been taken miles away. Engelhardt (1936) suggested the specimen may have been taken near Lake Hopatcong.

Little Wood Satyr, *Megisto cymela* (Cramer, 1777)

Systematic status requires study. It represents most likely two species.

Range: Central Maine to central Florida west through the Great Plains; the nominate subspecies *cymela* occurs throughout New Jersey.

Current Status: Widespread, often abundant in open woodland, forest edge, and brushy meadows.

Historical Status: No apparent change.

Smith (1890–1910): "Common throughout."

Comstock (1940): "Throughout."

Delaware Valley (1966): "Common and general . . . throughout including pine barrens."

Staten Island (1973): "Common and widespread."

New York City Area (1993): "Widespread and very common."

Cape May (1993): "Common."

Habitat: Open areas in and around deciduous woodland.

Phenology: Considered univoltine over most of its range (Opler and Krizek 1984), but in New Jersey two "broods" mid-May–June, and late June–August. Extreme dates in north May 7–Aug. 9 (Cech 1993).

Caterpillar Foodplants: Orchard Grass (*Dactylis glomerata*) documented in New York and Centipede Grass (*Eremochloa ophiuroides*) in North Carolina (Opler and Krizek 1984). Larvae raised on *Poa pratensis* (Oliver 1982).

Overwintering Stage: Larva.

Comment: Often flies in partial shade through forest understory, with a characteristic bounding flight close to the ground. Rarely visit flowers; sometimes feeds on tree sap, aphid honeydew, and rotting fruit.

It is likely that there are two species, identical in appearance, but differing slightly in phenology (see Glassberg 1993b). A spring form disappears in the North by late June, while the summer form flies late June to August. On average the earlier form is slightly smaller and darker. It tolerates more open country, while the later form prefers deeper woodlands with a grassy understory. Any locality may have one or both species (Pavulaan 1990). It is remarkable that such a wide-ranging and abundant species should have such a narrow host range.

Common Ringlet, *Coenonympha tullia* (Mueller, 1764)

Usually listed as Inornate Ringlet, *C. inornata*.

Range: Holarctic. In North America from Maritime Provinces to Alaska, south along the Rocky Mountains and to southern California; in the East from Newfoundland to northwestern New Jersey. Also Europe. The subspecies *inornata* described by Edwards in 1861 is invading New Jersey. The map in Opler and Krizek (1984) shows it reaching only northern New York, and Opler's Atlas shows its range to Albany County (updated to 1985). The species is now common in the lower Hudson Valley. It extended its range southward to Westchester County, NY, in the early 1990s (Cech 1993) and first invaded New Jersey in 1994.

Current Status: Recently (1994) invaded New Jersey, and is already widely established as a resident in Sussex County (1995; Wander). Reported as widespread in Orange County, NY (1994; Yrizarry). Will likely spread farther south quickly. (see photo 14).

Photo 14. Common Ringlet has been extending south-ward through New England and finally invaded New Jersey in 1994. It is now fairly common in northwestern New Jersey and it is likely to expand its range to cover most of western New Jersey before the end of the century. (Photographed by Joanna Burger at Stokes State Forest)

New York City Area (1993): "A northerly species, gradually but steadily expanding its range southward into our region" since 1988.

Historical Status: Not applicable.

Habitat: A species of open grasslands, occurs commonly over mowed lawns along highways which serve as corridors for its range expansion.

Phenology: Two broods late May–late June and August.

Caterpillar Foodplants: In the western states feeds on grasses, and *inornata* is presumed to feed on grasses. Not yet studied in New Jersey.

Overwintering Stage: Larva.

Comment: This species has a characteristic flight, bouncing low over grassy fields, revealing a flash of rufous in its wing which is unique in our region. The eastern race *inornata*, formerly listed as a distinct species *C. inornata* (Opler and Krizek 1984), is now considered a race of the widespread *tullia* complex, which includes the Large Heath (*C. tullia*) of Europe. The systematics in eastern North America also require further study since Brown (1961) suggested that in some areas the August brood is not produced by the June brood, suggesting that two species may be involved.

Common Wood-Nymph, *Cercyonis pegala* (Fabricius, 1775)

Range: Southern Maritime Provinces to British Columbia and south to central Florida, central Texas and central California. Occurs throughout New Jersey. The subspecific status in New Jersey is unclear. The dark northern subspecies *nephele* or dark intermediates occur in northwestern New Jersey, with records from Sussex and Warren Counties (Opler's Atlas). The coastal population is sometimes separated as a subspecies *maritima* based on poorly defined forewing patch (Shapiro 1966), except in southern New Jersey where they blend with *pegala* (Pavulaan).

Current Status: Widespread in or near woods; often abundant.

Historical Status: No apparent change. Iftner et al. (1992) suggest that it has increased in parts of Ohio.

Smith (1890–1910): "Common throughout." Variety 'maritima' common in southern and central New Jersey and variety 'nephele' common in Northwest (Smith 1910).

Comstock (1940): "Throughout." "Form *nephele* occurs in northwestern part of state."

Delaware Valley (1966): "Very common to abundant."

Staten Island (1973): "Frequent and widespread."

New York City Area (1993): "Common and widespread."

Cape May (1993): "Common to abundant."

Habitat: Open areas in and around deciduous woodland, also brushy fields and pastures. Often flushed from tall grasses near trees.

Phenology: One prolonged brood late June–early September, occasionally to late September. Females tend to persist longer than males.

Caterpillar Foodplants: Various grasses including Purple Top (*Tridens flavus*).

Overwintering Stage: First-stage larva.

Comment: Nectars more frequently than most other satyrids, but often feeds on decaying fruit. Although the characteristic mark of this species is the rectangular yellow patch on the forewing, this is obscure or lacking in many individuals in northern New Jersey.

A century ago, Smith (1884) recognized the extreme variability of this species in southern New Jersey, and many of the variants that differ in size, in presence or absence of the yellow wing patch, and in the eyespot pattern have been considered full species in the past. Emmel (1969) provided evidence that this is one highly variable species that ranges across North America. From central New York northward there is a dark form *nephele* which lacks the yellow patches. Individuals with no apparent yellow wing patches are seen as far south as Morris County. It is not clear whether these are intergrading subspecies or morphs since both forms can occur in the same population area, but as Smith (1884) predicted, intergradations occur in intermediate areas (Iftner et al. 1992). Any morph may be represented in a population outside its normal range (Pavulaan). This may represent migration, mutation, or perhaps some other genetic process.

Wood Nymphs are often used as a palatable control in studies of mimicry and predation. Bowers and Wiernasz (1979) found that 7–10% of individuals show wing damage, evidence of attempted predation by birds. Yet one does not see birds attempting to capture them despite their conspicuous weak flight.

Subfamily *Danainae,* Milkweed Butterflies

This large tropical group is often treated as a separate family. In their monumental monograph, Ackery and Vane-Wright (1989) recognized 157 species, of which three occur in the eastern United States. Only the Monarch regularly ranges north of Florida. Caterpillars generally store cardiac glycosides, rendering themselves and their adults noxious to predators. The recognition of unpalatability in this family dates back to Swynnerton's (1915) study of African birds fed various Milkweed Butterfly species. These butterflies are classically mimicked by other palatable species. The naturalist Henry Bates published the first description of mimicry based on Amazonian forms of Milkweed and Heliconian butterflies (Bates 1862).

Monarch, *Danaus plexippus* (Linnaeus, 1758) Plate 8b

Range: A nearly cosmopolitan species or species complex occurring in North and South America, Africa, Europe (Spain), and Asia with populations established on Hawaii, New Zealand, Australia, and elsewhere. Throughout North America from central Canada to southern Florida and Mexico and the Caribbean.

Occurs throughout New Jersey. The nominate subspecies *plexippus* occurs in North America.

Current Status: Varies from year to year, but common to abundant, and often the most conspicuous butterfly, particularly in coastal habitats. Frequently seen migrating high in the air in September–November. Forms large communal roosts numbering from dozens to thousands (millions in Mexico), and some roosts are subject to commercial exploitation for scientific supply houses. Numbers fluctuate dramatically from year to year (e.g., low in 1990, abundant in 1991, low again in 1992, abundant in 1994).

Historical Status: The number of Monarchs fluctuates greatly from year to year, partially obscuring long-term trends. Longtime experience along the shoreline in autumn suggests that the species has declined somewhat in the past 40 years, but there are no quantitative data to support this.

Conservation Status: It is hard to think of a butterfly as abundant as the Monarch as requiring conservation attention. Yet only about a dozen wintering sites are known in Central Mexico (Brower 1995). This habitat is severely jeopardized by logging, and it is likely that only ecotourism to see the wintering hordes will provide a countervailing economic infusion to the remote montane region (Brower and Malcolm 1991). Malcolm and Zalucki (1993) edited an entire volume on the ecology and conservation of the Monarch.

Smith (1890–1910): "Common throughout."

Comstock (1940): "Throughout."

Delaware Valley (1966): Occurs throughout; varies in abundance annually.

Staten Island (1973): "Abundant everywhere."

New York City Area (1993): "A conspicuous migrant and colonist."

Cape May (1993): "Abundant" and migratory.

Habitat: Ubiquitous, occurring from coastal dunes to open areas in and around forests. Often visits gardens. Migrates conspicuously along the coast (including over the ocean) and through urban areas as well.

Phenology: First arrival in mid-May; first brood in late June, with 2–3 later broods throughout the summer. Southward migration first noted in late August, peaks in September, but continues through October, with smaller numbers still moving south in early November.

Caterpillar Foodplants: Various species of milkweeds (*Asclepias* spp.), most often on Common Milkweed (*A. syriaca*) and Swamp Milkweed (*A. incarnata*), less common on Butterfly Weed (*A. tuberosa*). Twelve species of milkweeds occur in New Jersey (Anderson 1983), and these other species should be checked for larvae. The larvae sequester heart-poison chemicals from the plants, and these persist in adult tissues as well. Female Monarchs prefer to lay their eggs on milkweeds that offer intermediate concentrations of these chemicals (Hook and Zalucki 1991). The larvae are brightly banded in green, yellow, and black and are therefore conspicuous. This is considered a case of warning or aposematic coloration, since predators that encounter them should have learned that such items are unpalatable or toxic.

Overwintering Stage: Migratory adult.

Comment: Probably no North American species has received more study than the Monarch. The close resemblance between the Monarch and Viceroy is the classic example of Batesian mimicry among North American butterflies. Each spring Monarchs migrate northward with a series of broods, and each fall they migrate southward. We have seen them migrating more than 30 miles offshore in October.

The Monarchs of the eastern half of North America converge on fall migration and funnel down to a relatively few wintering areas in the mountains of central Mexico. The fall movement of Monarchs southward along the New Jersey coast, particularly at Cape May, is a well-known event which characterizes the season as much as the famous bird migration (Walton and Brower 1996). In view of habitat destruction on the wintering grounds, this migration is now being called an "endangered phenomenon" (Brower and Malcolm 1991). Like the migrating hawks, the Monarchs take advantage of warm thermal air currents to speed them on their way while conserving energy.

The seasonal average number of Monarchs observed migrating past Cape May Point State Park ranged from 10 per hour in 1992 to 142 per hour in 1991, with peaks of 618 in one 8-minute period and counts regularly exceeding 1000 per day. The peak is usually the third week in September, with a secondary peak in early October (Walton and Brower 1996). None of these numbers compare, however, with estimates of millions reported late in the nineteenth century (Walton 1993). The bulk of New Jersey's migrating Monarchs continue down the Atlantic and then westward along the Gulf Coast to their Mexican wintering grounds (Urquhart and Urquhart 1976, Brower 1977). Some may cross the Gulf of Mexico or may cross from southern Florida, through Cuba, to the Yucatan Peninsula, perhaps to winter in the Guatemalan or eastern Mexican highlands. This latter pathway remains hypothetical (Brower 1995).

The wintering congregations contain many millions of Monarchs, and some of the sites are preserved as local tourist attractions, hence are at least temporarily stable. Others are being jeopardized by logging for firewood. For a well-illustrated article on these roosts, see Lincoln Brower's article in *Natural History* (Brower 1977). The behavior and thermal biology of the Monarchs in these high-altitude forests where they spend several months has been studied by Urquhart's group (Urquhart 1987) and Brower et al. (1977).

By January, Monarchs are beginning to move northward, reaching the southern United States. There they breed and produce a new generation, which itself moves northward before breeding. After several generations, the Monarchs have repopulated their summer range, where insects in very different habitats are subject to different selective pressure and may actually undergo incipient genetic differentiation. Soon, however, the Monarchs from all over migrate southward, where there is complete mixing on the wintering grounds. The current evidence suggests that there is no subsequent site fidelity. Thus the offspring of a Monarch hatched in New Jersey and breeding in Mexico may move to Texas and produce young that colonize the central United States. Genetic analyses showed that by late summer there are some genetic differences among Monarchs in central versus eastern United States, but these are swamped each winter when the butterflies come together and mate with individuals from other areas (Eanes and Koehn 1978).

The maximum local count is an estimated 50,000 at Great Kills, Staten Island (10/7/70; Glassberg 1993b). Leck estimated 3000 in a roost at Kendall Park (8/31/91). At least one reason for some periodic population crashes is infestation of the larvae with a polyhedrosis virus (Urquhart 1987).

A national tagging program begun in 1938 documents the migration and wintering grounds of Monarchs. Although some of the high-altitude fir forests where the Monarch winters are designated as preserves, logging continues and the habitat is becoming degraded. Tall trees provide crucial shelter from winter storms, such that even selective logging jeopardizes Monarch survival (Calvert et al. 1984, Alonso-Mejia et al. 1992). Heavy snow in Mexico in December 1995 killed large numbers of wintering Monarchs. The impact of this mortality on future numbers should be studied.

Hesperiidae, Skippers

The Skippers, family Hesperiidae, have often been omitted from books on butter-flies, yet they make up over 40% of our butterfly fauna. Their markings are subtle and many species pose challenging identification problems. Scott (1986) esti-mated that there are 3650 species worldwide, with 263 in North America. In our region there are two subfamilies.

Subfamily *Pyrginae*, Spread-winged Skippers

The Pyrginae have been called the Pyrgines (Opler and Krizek 1984), or the 'Herb, Shrub and Tree' skippers (Scott 1986). Neither of these names is very meaningful. These Skippers have the habit of perching with their wings opened flat most of the time, hence are referred to here as Spread-winged Skippers, the name also used in the NABA Checklist (NABA 1995). The names of the Cloudy-wings, Duskywings, and Sootywings are sometimes listed as two words, but we follow NABA's (1995) convention here. Many of the species rely extensively on members of the Fabaceae (Leguminosae), but the hosts of the Duskywings are very variable.

Silver-spotted Skipper, *Epargyreus clarus* (Cramer, 1775)

Range: Across southern Canada and south to central Florida, northern Mex-ico, the southwestern states and southern California. The subspecies *clarus* oc-curs throughout New Jersey.

Current Status: Widespread and sometimes abundant. A familiar visitor to gardens.

Historical Status: Apparently has remained a widespread and abundant species.

Smith (1890): "Common throughout."

Smith (1900–1910): "Throughout the state, not rarely."

Comstock (1940): "Throughout."

Delaware Valley (1966): "Permanent resident, often abundant."

Staten Island (1973): "Common and general."

New York City Area (1993): Common and widespread.

Cape May (1993): "Common."

Habitats: Very diverse, including gardens, brushy fields, open woods and cuts, and even coastal scrub.

Phenology: Three broods April–October. Extreme dates in North Apr. 28–Oct. 10 (Cech 1993). Common throughout the summer.

Caterpillar Foodplants: Main host in our area is apparently Black Locust (*Ro-binia pseudoacacia*); elsewhere feeds on other legumes such as *Wisteria*, Tick Tre-foils (*Desmodium* spp.), Kudzu (*Pueraria lobata*), and Hog Peanut (*Amphicarpa bracteata*).

Overwintering Stage: Pupa.

Comment: This species uses a great variety of nectar sources depending on availability, with a preference in central New Jersey for *Buddleia* and Everlasting Pea (*Lathyrus latifolia*). Males typically perch on branches, tall grass, or other vegetation from which they make rapid sorties to chase other insects or even to "attack" human observers. Their flight is extremely rapid and erratic, and they frequently engage in aerial chases at heights of 10–15 m.

Long-tailed Skipper, *Urbanus proteus* (Linnaeus, 1758)

Range: A widespread Neotropical species which is a permanent resident from North Carolina to Florida and south through the Caribbean and Mexico to Argentina; occasionally irruptive to central and southern New Jersey and to Long Island and Massachusetts. The subspecies reaching New Jersey is *proteus*.

Current Status: A rare southern vagrant to southern New Jersey, Staten Island, and New York City, not found in most years prior to 1990, but annually since (Dowdell), only partly because of increased number of observers. The greatest influx known occurred in 1994, with about fifteen reports from Cape May and Cumberland counties in September. The 1995 influx was even greater with 3–5 seen every day at Cape May (Dowdell). Two Sandy Hook Records (10/20–23/95).

In New York it was not recorded between 1947 and 1990, when it turned up on eastern Long Island (Shapiro 1974a; Glassberg 1993b).

Historical Status: Always very rare or absent until recent records. Beutenmüller (1893) knew of only one New York City record. Opler's Atlas shows records for Cape May, Cumberland, Salem, and Camden counties as well as Long Island, NY.

Smith (1890): Collected by Aaron at Cape May; also on "Newark" list.

Smith (1900): "Occasional," but apparently no new records.

Smith (1910): Additional record from Five Mile Beach.

Comstock (1940): On supplemental list based on specimens from Five Mile Beach and Cape May.

Delaware Valley (1966): "Infrequent and irregular migrant . . . Coastal Plain . . . somewhat more frequent in New Jersey," with scattered records from Salem, Cumberland, Gloucester, and Camden counties. Not in the Pine Barrens.

Staten Island (1973): Not listed. {Observed in 1990; Peter W. Post.}

New York City Area (1993): "An accidental stray up the coast." Recent records include Staten Island (9/2–4/90), Manhattan (10/14–17/89), and Jamaica Bay, NY (1993). Otherwise not recorded in New York City since 1880.

Cape May (1993): "Stray."

Habitat: Woodland edges, road shoulders, brushy fields, and parks and gardens in the southeastern United States.

Phenology: In New Jersey, late June–October, mainly after mid-August.

Caterpillar Foodplants: Leguminous vines, including Tick Trefoil (*Desmodium*) and *Wisteria*. On Wild Bean (*Phaseolus polystachios*; Smith 1900) and garden beans (Pavulaan).

Comment: Reported injurious to beans in the southern United States (Comstock 1940).

Where to See It: Not reliable anywhere in New Jersey. Most records are in Cape May region in September.

Golden-banded Skipper, *Autochton cellus* (Boisduval and LeConte, 1837)

Range: From Delaware (rarely) to Florida and west to southern Mexico and Arizona. Opler and Krizek (1984) show it occurring in central New Jersey.

Current Status: No recent records.

Historical Status: Probably only an accidental visitor, but possibly a rare resident, now EXTIRPATED. Only one record reported by Comstock (1940) and only two additional ones by Shapiro (1966). Shown in Salem, Gloucester, and Essex counties (Opler's Atlas), corresponding to "a few old records from west central New Jersey, early–mid June" (Glassberg 1993b). Probably never resident in New Jersey. It has declined greatly over the northeastern part of its range and is now extirpated around Washington, D.C. (Pavulaan, in litt.).

Conservation Status: National Heritage ranking G4/SH. There is no evidence that this species was part of New Jersey's fauna any time in the present century.

Smith (1890): "Taken rarely by Newark collectors."

Smith (1900–1910): No additional records.

Comstock (1940): On supplemental list based on Smith's (1890) report from "Newark."

Delaware Valley (1966): "One of the rarest butterflies of the East." "Very rare and sporadic in New Jersey." Records are Salem County (Harrisonville, 6/9/59) and Gloucester County (Wilson Lake, 6/8/62).

New York City Area (1993): Not listed. {Shapiro 1974a mentions an old Brooklyn report by Forbes.}

Cape May (1993): No record, but listed as a "species to look for."

Habitat: A species of wooded ravines in the Upper and Lower Austral Life Zones (Opler and Krizek 1984).

Phenology: Early–mid June, "possibly later" (Shapiro 1966).

Caterpillar Foodplant: Only Hog Peanut *(Amphicarpa bracteata*; Opler and Krizek 1984). The report (Smith 1900) of "Convolvulaceae" as a host is presumably in error.

Comment: This species is generally rare and highly localized throughout its range in eastern United States (Burns 1984). It could possibly be overlooked because of its superficial similarity to the ubiquitous Silver-spotted Skipper or the Hoary Edge. Its nearest population is in the mountains of Virginia.

Hoary Edge, *Achalarus lyciades* (Geyer, 1832)

Range: East of Great Plains, from central New England to southeastern Minnesota, south to northern Florida and eastern Texas; throughout New Jersey.

Current Status: Widespread and usually uncommon, but occasionally fairly common in early summer. Up to twelve per day at Lakehurst in late June.

Historical Status: Recorded as common and abundant by Smith and Comstock, and uncommon by Beutenmüller (1893); usually uncommon today, hence may have decreased.

Smith (1890): "Quite generally distributed, but rare."

Smith (1900–1910): All sections of the state; locally common.

Comstock (1940): "Throughout. . . . Sometimes locally abundant."

Delaware Valley (1966): "Locally quite common."

Staten Island (1973): "Locally common."

New York City Area (1993): "Locally common . . . commonest near Tick-trefoils."

Cape May (1993): Common mid-May–mid-July.

Habitat: It occurs along woodland edges and cuts.

Phenology: One brood May–mid-July. In northern New Jersey, May 27–late July, with extreme date Aug. 20 (Cech 1993). Recorded mid-May in southern New Jersey.

Caterpillar Foodplants: Various Fabaceae including Tick Trefoils (*Desmodium paniculatum* and other *Desmodium* spp.). Also reported on Bush Clover (*Lespedeza*) and Blue False Indigo (*Baptisia australis*).

Comment: Late individuals are either immigrants from south or a partial second brood (Cech 1993). This is an uncommon but widespread butterfly that favors Common Milkweeds (*Asclepias syriaca*) as a nectar source but uses various other species. The large population in Van Cortland Park (Bronx, NY) nectars on Spreading Dogbane (*Apocynum androsaemifolium*; Tudor).

Cloudywings, Genus *Thorybes*

Seven species occur in North America, three in New Jersey. The common names are inappropriate. The Northern Cloudywing (*T. pylades*) does range farther north, but also farther south, than the Southern Cloudywing (*T. bathyllus*). The

Confused Cloudywing (*T. confusis*) does not act confused at all, and is so-named because it is confusing to identify. This is one species which Glassberg (1993b) says should be identified only by experts. Scott (1986) uses the name Eastern Cloudywing for *bathyllus*, and this species is indeed confined to the eastern U.S., while *pylades* ranges across the continent. However, the former is "eastern" only to a westerner, so the name is no help. Scott (1986) calls *confusis* the Dark Cloudy Wing, but it is not appreciably darker than the others.

Southern Cloudywing, *Thorybes bathyllus* (J. E. Smith, 1797)

Range: Southern Maine and central New York to southeastern Colorado and northeastern New Mexico, and south to central Florida and Texas; throughout New Jersey.

Current Status: Widespread and usually uncommon; seldom numerous but not rare. Maximum 4JC ten (1992, Cape May).

Historical Status: Probably no change in status. May be fairly common locally, but usually only 1–3 seen in a day.

Smith (1890–1910): "Common throughout."

Comstock (1940): "Throughout." Localities from Newton to Dennisville.

Delaware Valley (1966): "Resident in the Coastal Plain, but sporadic north of the Fall Line."

Staten Island (1973): Recorded by Davis but "no modern records." "There is no obvious reason for the absence."

New York City Area (1993): "Locally and thinly distributed."

Cape May (1993): "Common." {Shapiro (1966) reported it "very common in Cape May County."}

Habitat: Dry meadows and clearings, sandy barrens, edges of oak woodlands and cuts. Frequently occurs with the next species.

Phenology: One brood in northwestern New Jersey early June–mid-July; two broods in southern New Jersey early May (occasionally late April)–early July, with second brood, mid-August to early September.

Caterpillar Foodplants: Tick Trefoils (*Desmodium* spp., including *D. rotundifolium*), Bush Clover (*Lespedeza capitata*), and various other legumes.

Overwintering Stage: Full-grown larva.

Comment: The three Cloudywings are difficult to distinguish in the field (see Glassberg 1993b). This species has the hourglass mark on its forewing. Males are often seen perched on a grass stalk or twig, rarely nectaring.

Northern Cloudywing, *Thorybes pylades* (Scudder, 1870)

Range: Across southern Canada to British Columbia and south to southern Florida, Texas, and northern Mexico; throughout New Jersey.

Current Status: Widespread and occasionally fairly uncommon. Seldom more than three per day in most locations. Recorded on 4JC, only in southern counties, with maximum of fifteen (1991, Cumberland).

Historical Status: No evidence of any change in status, but would not be considered abundant anywhere today.

Smith (1890–1910): "Quite generally distributed," not common.

Comstock (1940): "Throughout."

Delaware Valley (1966): "Sometimes very abundant."

Staten Island (1973): Only found once in 1971, apparently rare.

New York City Area (1993): "Widespread but seldom abundant."

Cape May (1993): "Uncommon."

Habitat: Dry meadows and clearings, sandy barrens, edges of oak woodlands and cuts. Frequently occurs with the former species.

Phenology: One brood mid-May–mid-July in North and to early July in South.

Caterpillar Foodplants: Fabaceae, mainly Bush Clover (*Lespedeza*) and Tick Trefoils (*Desmodium*), but also on Alfalfa (*Medicago sativa*), White Clover (*Trifolium repens*), and other legumes.

Overwintering Stage: Full-grown larva.

Comments: The two commoner species of Cloudywings are distinguished by the hourglass mark on the forewing of the Southern and by its pale whitish or grayish face. The Northern Cloudwing has a dark face. The two species are likely to occur together, and males have the similar pugnacious habit of flying out from a dead stalk to investigate passing objects (Iftner et al. 1992).

Confused Cloudywing, *Thorybes confusis* (Bell, 1922)

Range: New Jersey and southeastern Pennsylvania (marginally) and Maryland west to Nebraska, south to central Florida and Texas. Opler and Krizek (1984) show it as an immigrant to central–western New Jersey.

Current Status: Uncertain. This species is very difficult to identify, hence its apparent rarity may reflect that it is overlooked. There is only one New Jersey specimen documented (Fort Dix, Burlington County, by Ray Stanford, 1972). Putative specimens from Cape May and Cumberland Counties proved to be Southern Cloudywings on genital examination (Schweitzer, in litt.). The species is more common to south and west of New Jersey.

Historical Status: Not recognized from New Jersey until very recently.

Smith (1890–1910): Not described at the time.

Comstock (1940): Not listed.

Delaware Valley (1966): Rare. No records reported from New Jersey.

Staten Island (1973): Not listed.

New York City Area (1993): Not listed.

Cape May (1993): Its occurrence not yet confirmed.

Habitat: Scrubby woodlands and glades and forest edges.

Phenology: Two broods late May–early July, and August.

Caterpillar Foodplants: Not documented but presumably legumes. "Possibly" *Lespedeza* (Shapiro 1966).

Comment: This is one of the very few local butterflies which Glassberg (1993b) considers virtually impossible for most people to identify visually. He comments "identification . . . should be left to experts." "Most individuals cannot be identified to species." Schweitzer (in litt.) notes that examination of male genitalia is definitive, but that females may not be distinguishable; he cautions that Northern and Confused cannot be separated by spot pattern and Southern and Confused would be impossible in some cases.

The Confused Cloudywing was first recognized and named in 1922. Due to its similarity to the more common Cloudywings, it has possibly been overlooked even by collectors (Iftner et al. 1992). However, There is no evidence that it is or was resident in New Jersey.

Hayhurst's Scallopwing [Southern Sooty Wing] *Staphylus hayhursti* (W. H. Edwards) 1870

Also called Scalloped Sooty Wing (Scott 1986).

Range: Eastern United States from southern New Jersey and Maryland to Nebraska and south to central Florida and central Texas.

Current Status: Local, but sometimes fairly common in disturbed habitats. Colonies in Cape May, Cumberland and Salem Counties. It is extending its range (Schweitzer).

Historical Status: It is difficult to tell whether the population in southern New

Jersey is of recent origin or was overlooked by earlier collectors. Recently seen in Ocean County (Dowdell).

Smith (1890–1910): Not listed.

Comstock (1940): Not listed.

Delaware Valley (1966): Not in area. Closest record is Maryland "I know of no New Jersey record."

Staten Island (1973): Not listed.

New York City Area (1993): Not listed.

Cape May (1993): "Uncommon" and local; {can be found at Higbee Beach}.

Habitat: A species of woodland edge habitat with a tendency for favoring shady locations (Iftner et al. 1992).

Phenology: Apparently 2–3 broods with peaks in late May, July, and a smaller brood in August–September.

Caterpillar Foodplants: Lambsquarters (*Chenopodium album*). Also reported to use an amaranth host (Scott 1986).

Comment: Although southern in its distribution, this is the northernmost member of a genus that deserves recognition for the distinctive scalloped margin to the hind wing; hence the NABA Committee dropped "Southern" since it is inappropriate, and uses a more descriptive common name for the genus: "Scallopwing." Heitzman (1963) published a brief life history account of this species in Missouri. Hayhurst's Scallopwing was originally thought to be confined to salt and tidal marshes in Maryland, but Simmons and Anderson (1970) reported that it invaded the Piedmont, moving along river valleys. It prefers shaded woodlands.

Where to See It: This species is regular at Higbee Beach, and can be found along the interface between fields and woods or along roads through the woodland. Also seen at Cape May Point State Park and the Beanery (Dowdell 1993).

The Duskywings, Genus *Erynnis*

There are at least fifteen species of Duskywings in North America (Scott 1986) of which nine have occurred in New Jersey. They represent some of the most challenging identification problems and some are virtually identical except for their host preferences. Their appearance varies with gender and wear, and sometimes with season (Burns 1964). Many cannot be identified definitely in the field, and even museum specimens have been misidentified (Schweitzer, pers. comm.; Iftner et al. 1992).

Males of one species are often more similar to males of another species than they are to conspecific females. Males have an upward fold on the costal (front) edge of the forewing as well as elevated hairlike scales (most prominent on Persius Duskywing), while females lack the fold and have flattened scales (Burns 1994a). Additional guidance on identification is provided by Glassberg (1994a,b), while Burns (1964) provided a technical revision of the genus.

For identification purposes, there are three groups: (1) the nearly unspotted Dreamy and Sleepy Duskywings are very similar; (2) the large, conspicuously spotted Juvenal's and Horace's Duskywings are also similar to each other; (3) the remaining species all have a row of four small spots on the subapical region of the dorsal forewing. Of these, only the Wild Indigo is widespread and is the only one that is definitely resident in New Jersey today. The Mottled Duskywing is the most distinct of this group, while the Zarucco Duskywing is challenging to identify. The Columbine and Persius Duskywings are virtually indistinguishable from the Wild Indigo in the absence of their host plants. Writing of the Persius Duskywing, Holland (1898) remarked: "The student may be pardoned if, in attempting to classify the species of this genus, and the present species in particular, he should grow weary." Beginning with Fabricius, who named Juvenal's

Duskywing in 1793, many of the Duskywings are named after Roman poets (Zirlin 1993).

Dreamy Duskywing, *Erynnis icelus* (Scudder and Burgess, 1870)

Range: Across southern Canada to northern Georgia and Arizona; northern and central New Jersey.

Current Status: Inadequately known. Probably widespread; usually uncommon, but may be locally fairly common (Wanders). Absent from Pine Barrens (Schweitzer) and extreme southern New Jersey (Schweitzer; Dowdell).

Historical Status: Smith did not give a clear picture of its status, but showed it as local, while Shapiro considered it common. It may have declined since it is now usually not common. On the Coastal Plain, documented only from Burlington County (Opler's Atlas). Recently seen in Ocean County (Dowdell).

Smith (1890): Delaware Water Gap and "Newark."

Smith (1900–1910): Also Fort Lee, Plainfield, Jersey City, and Staten Island.

Comstock (1940): North of Fall Line. {No localities on Coastal Plain.}

Delaware Valley (1966): "Usually common to . . . locally abundant."

Staten Island (1973): "Frequent."

New York City Area (1993): "Fairly common locally in open woods."

Cape May (1993): Not listed.

Habitat: Widespread; edges and cuts in woodlands. Often rests on dirt roads.

Phenology: One brood mid-May (rarely late April)–late June. Collected in July in Jersey City (Smith 1900).

Caterpillar Foodplants: Primarily poplars and willows (Burns 1964); also on Black Locust (*Robinia pseudoacacia*; Schweitzer). Iftner et al. (1992) suggest that oaks may be host in Ohio. Smith (1900) mentioned Witch Hazel (*Hamamelis virginiana*) which has not subsequently been reported.

Overwintering Stage: Full-grown larva.

Comment: Slightly smaller than the next species and often distinguished by darker bases of the wing and a white costal spot on the forewing (Glassberg 1993b). The antennal club is pointed in this species, but blunt in the next (Iftner et al. 1992). This is a species of deciduous woodlands frequently found on road and trailsides, glades, and cuts, whereas the next species is found mainly in the Pine Barrens. Both species are often found basking on the ground or on fallen leaves or twigs.

Sleepy Duskywing, *Erynnis brizo* (Boisduval and LeConte, 1834)

Range: Disjunct distribution from extreme southern Maine to California and south to central Florida and northern Mexico; map in Opler and Krizek (1984) shows it throughout New Jersey.

Current Status: Uncommon to common in Pine Barrens and other well-drained sites in central and southern New Jersey; rare to uncommon elsewhere where Scrub Oak occurs. Uncommon in Cape May County, occurring south to Great Cedar Swamp.

Historical Status: It has declined in northern New Jersey and we know of no reliable localities there. It is still fairly common in the Pine Barrens.

Smith (1890): Newark, Gloucester, and Westville (Camden).

Smith (1900): From Greenwood Lake to Staten Island and in south near Camden.

Smith (1910): "More or less common throughout."

Comstock (1940): "Throughout." Localities listed are from Warren to Bergen Counties (but not Sussex) south to Ocean County.

Delaware Valley (1966): "Resident not usually very common."

Staten Island (1973): Recorded by Davis but not observed in 1970–71.

New York City Area (1993): "Locally common in Scrub Oak and pine-oak barrens."

Cape May (1993): "Uncommon."

Habitats: Pine Barrens and in oak and mixed pine-oak woodlands along trails, cuts, and in open glades.

Phenology: One brood early April–mid-May. Shapiro (1966) reports second brood June–July.

Caterpillar Foodplants: The Scrub Oak (*Quercus ilicifolia*), but in the southern United States it uses other oaks (Scott 1986). In Florida it occurs where this oak is absent (Opler and Krizek 1984). Oviposits on Black Oak (*Q. velutina*) in Ohio (Iftner et al. 1992). Also reported on American Chestnut (*Castanea dentata*).

Overwintering Stage: Full-grown larva.

Comments: Often fairly common in the Pine Barrens in early May, although usually greatly outnumbered by Juvenal's Duskywing. Frequently basks on the ground—often directly on dirt roads.

Where to Find It: Along dirt roads in the Pine Barrens in early April, look for this smaller, unspotted species among the abundant Juvenal's Duskywings. Known locations include Assunpink WMA, Warren Grove, and the Pine Barrens along Route 72.

Juvenal's Duskywing, *Erynnis juvenalis* (Fabricius, 1793)

Range: Nova Scotia and southern Maine west to the Rocky Mountains from Manitoba and south to New Mexico. In east to southern Florida, and Mexico; throughout New Jersey.

Current Status: Widespread and fairly common in early spring, and often superabundant in Pine Barrens, where several hundred can be seen in a day (JB, MG). Occurs throughout New Jersey. 1993 was a poor year with low counts in the Pine Barrens (Tudor, MG, JB).

Historical Status: No apparent change. Always considered common to abundant.

Smith (1890–1910): "More or less common throughout."

Comstock (1940): "Throughout."

Delaware Valley (1966): "Abundant and general."

Staten Island (1973): "Abundant."

New York City Area (1993): "Common and widespread."

Cape May (1993): "Common to abundant."

Habitat: Widespread in open habitats, particularly cuts and edges of oak and pine-oak woodlands.

Phenology: One brood mid-April–mid-June. Shapiro (1966) reports some individuals in mid-July as a partial second brood, and both Smith (1910) and Comstock (1940) mention two broods (May-July), perhaps due to confusion with the next species. Iftner et al. (1992) report a single specimen in late July, but this is probably rare. The species is considered univoltine over most of its range (Scott 1986).

Caterpillar Foodplants: Various oaks (*Quercus* spp.).

Overwintering Stage: Full-grown larva.

Comment: Difficult to distinguish from the next species, but Juvenal's almost always shows two subapical spots on the ventral hindwing (Glassberg 1994a); Horace's usually has one. These two species are relatively large for the genus, and the four subapical spots on the forewing tend to be larger than on other species. Both have a conspicuous white spot in the cell of the forewing, which the Wild Indigo lacks. This is the commonest early spring Duskywing. On Pine Barrens' roads in early May one often disturbs hundreds of Juvenal's and smaller numbers of Sleepy Duskywings. Although it is almost entirely univoltine, the belief that only Horace's flies after that period would preclude recognition of any late-flying Juvenal's or a partial second brood.

Where to Find It: Probably anywhere in the Pine Barrens in early May.

Horace's Duskywing, *Erynnis horatius* (Scudder and Burgess, 1870)

Range: Disjunct. Massachusetts and southern New York to Minnesota and south to central Florida and Texas (also in southwestern U.S.); throughout New Jersey.

Current Status: Uncommon throughout. Sometimes fairly common at Lakehurst and in Somerset, NJ, but not encountered at all in some years (MG). In Somerset it has been less common since 1993 than previously, and this is reflected on the Raritan Canal 4JC.

Historical Status: Since this species is difficult to distinguish from Juvenal's and sometimes from Wild Indigo Duskywings, its apparent rarity at the turn of the century may be an artifact. It was not reported at all by Beutenmüller (1893). But it has certainly increased on the Coastal Plain, particularly Cape May County. Shapiro (1966) reports it very common in Morris County and fairly common in the Pine Barrens.

Smith (1890–1900): New Jersey shown on the range map of Scudder, but no documentation found.

Smith (1910): Specimens listed from Orange Mountains, Woodbury, Jamesburg, and Atco. No mention of status.

Comstock (1940): "Throughout," with localities from Pompton and Orange Mountains to Jamesburg. {No southern localities listed.}

Delaware Valley (1966): Not as common as *juvenalis*.

Staten Island (1973): "Frequent."

New York City Area (1993): "Far less common than Juvenal's. Most frequently reported from the Coastal Plain."

Cape May (1993): "Common."

Habitat: Fields, open woodlands, glades, and cuts. Sometimes enters bogs in dry years. In Rhode Island usually in oak woods, infrequently at edge (Pavulaan).

Phenology: Two broods late April–early June and early July–August and occasionally September. Cech (1993) identifies three peaks (mid-June, mid-July, late August).

Caterpillar Foodplants: Various oaks (Burns 1964), especially Blackjack Oak (*Quercus marilandica*) and Scrub Oak (*Q. ilicifolia*) in Pine Barrens and Chinquapin (*Q. muhlenbergii*) in Morris County (Shapiro 1966).

Comment: Very similar to former and probably overlooked in early spring when outnumbered by *juvenalis*. Conversely in midsummer it is identified mainly by season rather than specific pattern.

Mottled Duskywing, *Erynnis martialis* (Scudder, 1869)

Range: A complex disjunct distribution from western Massachusetts and northern New York to Minnesota, south to central Georgia and Texas, with populations in the Black Hills and Colorado (Opler and Krizek 1984); formerly northern and central New Jersey.

Current Status: Uncertain. It has definitely declined and is ENDANGERED and possibly EXTIRPATED from New Jersey. It occurs on serpentine barrens of southeastern Pennsylvania and in Albany Pine Bush. Does not occur in New Jersey Pine Barrens, nor does its food plant (Schweitzer).

Historical Status: "Has declined greatly in Northeast" (Glassberg 1993b). Has probably declined in northern Ohio in the past 25 years (Iftner et al. 1992). It has always been rare and local in New Jersey, but now it must be very rare. Schweitzer (pers. comm.) attributes its decline to the heavy Gypsy Moth spraying, and there are very few subsequent records from New Jersey. Opler's Atlas reports records from Sussex, Essex, Middlesex, Mercer, Burlington, Camden, and Gloucester Counties.

Conservation Status: The Natural Heritage ranking is G4/SH. There are no recent records for this species. Surveys should look for this species in places where its host occurs.

Smith (1890): An Aaron specimen from unspecified location in New Jersey. The form 'ausonius' attributed to New Jersey is undocumented.

Smith (1900): *Martialis* from Sparta and Normannock. The form 'ausonius' was previously reported in error from Woodbury.

Smith (1910): Additional localities include Staten Island, Westmont, Paterson, Eagle Rock, Laurel Springs, Woodbury.

Comstock (1940): North of Fall Line. {However, one site is Woodbury, which is in the south.} Additional locations include Newton, Great Notch, and Jamesburg.

Delaware Valley (1966): "Rather rare . . . resident," recorded from Gloucester, Mercer, and Burlington Counties. {These records are unlikely to reflect residence since the foodplant does not occur there.}

Staten Island (1973): At least two specimens recorded by Davis, and one taken 7/16/71. Its host plant is rare.

New York City Area (1993): "Formerly bred on Staten Island, seen as late as 1971."

Cape May (1993): Not listed.

Habitat: Cuts in hilly woodlands and brushy fields on acidic soil. In New York pine barrens and Pennsylvania serpentine found in low brushy glades amid woodlands.

Phenology: Two broods late April–mid-May and early July–early August.

Caterpillar Foodplants: New Jersey Tea (*Ceanothus americanus*); the host plant is local but not rare.

Comments: The host plant is not uncommon in some parts of New Jersey (e.g., Springdale, Hibernia), and this Duskywing should be looked for wherever the plant occurs.

Where to Find It: There is no reliable location at this time in New Jersey, but it can be found in May in serpentine barrens at Nottingham County Park, southwest of Philadelphia and in the Albany Pine Bush Reserve, albeit in small numbers.

Zarucco Duskywing, *Erynnis zarucco* (Lucas, 1857)

Range: A species of the southeastern United States. On the Coastal Plain from North Carolina through Florida to Texas and the Caribbean, irruptive fairly regularly to Maryland and rare strays or possibly accidental in New Jersey.

Current Status: Status of recent records unknown. Shapiro's (1966) account suggests it may have been less rare in New Jersey 30 years ago. No recent record.

Historical Status: If this species was "occasionally common" on the Coastal Plain in the 1960s, it has certainly declined dramatically. Only records are Shapiro's from Camden, Cape May, and Salem Counties.

Smith (1890–1910): New Jersey shown on the range map in Scudder, but no documented records. {At this time the Wild Indigo Duskywing had not been described.}

Comstock (1940): Not listed.

Delaware Valley (1966): "Ranging barely into our area . . . not uncommon some seasons." "Doubtful resident north of . . . Cape May." "Scarce to occasionally common, Coastal Plain only." Records from Salem and Camden Counties.

Staten Island (1973): Not listed.

New York City Area (1993): Not listed.

Cape May (1993): "Stray."

Habitat: Scrubby fields and forest edges on the Coastal Plain.

Phenology: Recorded in August. Two broods in southern United States.

Caterpillar Foodplants: Legumes including Hairy Bush Clover (*Lespedeza hirta*) and Black Locust (*Robinia pseudoacacia*). Probably also other legumes.

Comment: This species is very similar to the Wild Indigo Duskywing (Glassberg 1993b, 1994a). There is no apparent reason that this species should be less common today than a generation ago.

Columbine Duskywing, *Erynnis lucilius* (Scudder and Burgess, 1870)

Range: Disjunct distribution from central New England and southern Quebec to Minnesota and south to Appalachians of Virginia. Map in Opler and Krizek (1984) shows it throughout New Jersey except the Southeast, though it was documented only from Sussex, Burlington, Camden, and Gloucester Counties (Opler's Atlas), with additional records from Passaic and Essex Counties. Also reported from Mercer and Hunterdon (Shapiro 1966). Recorded in most central and eastern New York counties including Orange by Shapiro (1974a), who did not have specimens from Rockland County, where it has recently been found.

Current Status: Unknown. Very difficult to identify. No recent records. As name indicates, should be found around Columbines. It is rare and probably local. Recently found at Hook Mountain, Rockland County, NY (Tudor), where seen ovipositing on Columbine (Lawrenson).

Historical Status: Uncertain. Beutenmüller's account (1893) suggests he knew of only two records in the New York City vicinity (one in Orange Mountains, NJ). No recent documented New Jersey records, hence appears to have declined compared with Shapiro's (1966) report. However, its host is common in northern New Jersey, and there has been a great increase in plantings of horticultural Columbines. Burns (1964) wrote: "I can definitely say that *lucilius* occurs in . . . most if not all, of New Jersey, Pennsylvania."

Conservation Status: Natural Heritage ranking is G4/SU, indicating the need for careful surveys in wooded areas where Columbine occurs.

Smith (1890): New Jersey included on Scudder's range map, but no documented record.

Smith (1900): Greenwood Lake and Orange Mountains in May and June.

Smith (1910): Also at Paterson.

Comstock (1940): North of Fall Line.

Delaware Valley (1966): "Common . . . in rich 'Alleghenian' woodland." Records from Camden (Haddonfield), Gloucester (Browns Mills, Whitesbog), Burlington (Mount Holly, Medford, Indian Mills), Mercer (Washington Crossing), Hunterdon (Raven Rock). {Browns Mills is actually in Burlington County.}

Staten Island (1973): Not listed.

New York City Area (1993): "Historically absent from Coastal Plain. Recent possible records from Hook Mountain, Rockland County, and the palisades." More common in upstate New York. {Absent from Long Island; Shapiro 1974a.}

Cape May (1993): Not listed.

Habitat: A woodland or edge species, fond of hilly slopes and forested ravines; identified mainly by its association with Wild Columbine (but see comment section). Also found in gardens around Columbines.

Phenology: Two or three broods late April–May, July–August, and September. Recent Rockland County, NY, records have been in mid-May.

Caterpillar Foodplants: Burns (1964) reported it only on Wild Columbines (*Aquilegia canadensis*). But it oviposits on horticultural varieties of *A. vulgaris* as well. Old reports of *Chenopodium*, willow, and poplar (Smith 1910) have not been validated and are apparently in error.

Overwintering Stage: Full-grown larva.

Comment: Glassberg (1993b) says that this slightly smaller species "cannot be distinguished on the basis of appearance from Wild Indigo Duskywing." This species should be found in rich woodlands where Wild Columbines grow, and it is identified by its association with Columbines. We have seen a Duskywing in a greenhouse in Schenectady County, NY, exploring horticultural Columbines, which may prove to be a predictable habitat. However, Pavulaan (pers. comm.) provides a cautionary note. Females laying on his garden Columbines in Maryland, and young raised on the Columbine, were identified by H. A. Freeman as Wild Indigo Duskywings. This complex clearly requires further study. In New York State, Shapiro (1974a) considered it widespread, except for Long Island, and locally common.

Wild Indigo Duskywing, *Erynnis baptisiae* (Forbes, 1936)

Range: Central New England and Minnesota, south to northern Florida and central Texas; throughout New Jersey.

Current Status: Widespread from Northwest to Cape May; usually in vicinity of Crown Vetch, therefore along many roadways. Often abundant in central New Jersey (JB, MG), but not as common in Northwest (Wanders). Highest 4JC total 249 (1989, Raritan Canal).

Historical Status: This species was first described in 1936, in time for Comstock (1940) to include it in his list. With the widespread planting of Crown Vetch to stabilize highway shoulders, the Wild Indigo Duskywing has certainly increased. It was rare in central New Jersey before the 1970s (Leck). Shapiro (1979) reports that in areas where Crown Vetch was abundant in southeastern Pennsylvania, this species had become the commonest butterfly.

Smith (1890–1910): Not mentioned {species was described in 1936}.

Comstock (1940): "Possibly throughout," localities range from Northwest to Fort Lee from late May to August.

Delaware Valley (1966): "Resident," no comment on abundance.

Staten Island (1973): "Infrequent sporadic."

New York City Area (1993): "Fairly common."

Cape May (1993): "Uncommon."

Habitat: Open fields, gardens, and road shoulders, particularly where Crown Vetch has been planted.

Phenology: Probably three broods mid-May–mid-June, July–August, and September. Sighting in Hackensack Meadows (10/23/93) may represent a partial fourth brood (Tudor, Cech). In central New Jersey the early summer brood is most numerous.

Caterpillar Foodplants: Historically its main host has been Wild Indigo (*Baptisia tinctoria*), other species of *Baptisia*, and Lupines (*Lupinus*). Shapiro (1979) was the first to demonstrate that this species could utilize Crown Vetch (*Coronilla varia*), but this is certainly its main host in New Jersey. Larvae can be raised on Columbine (Burns 1964), and females occasionally lay on Columbines (Pavulaan).

Overwintering Stage: Full-grown larva.

Comment: Because this species is so common, the Columbine and Persius Duskywings, and to a lesser extent Mottled and Zarucco Duskywings, which less closely resemble it, could be easily overlooked. Simmons and Andersen (1970) reported that they could easily find the larvae of this species on Wild Indigo (*Baptisia*), but seldom saw adults; however, they also remarked that Zarucco Duskywing adults were frequently seen but were hard to catch. Given the similarity between the two (Glassberg 1994b), it seems likely that the elusive adults were the missing Wild Indigo Duskywings. Although adults spend relatively little time nectaring, they are opportunistic, using a wide variety of flowers, including *Buddleia*, but infrequently Crown Vetch. This is a territorial species. Males sit on the tips of grass and fly out to attack intruders; however, at high density of the host plant the butterflies cease being territorial (Shapiro 1979).

Persius Duskywing, *Erynnis persius* (Scudder, 1863)
Range: Very disjunct distribution from northern New England and New York across North America, south to Virginia; Opler and Krizek's (1984) map shows it throughout New Jersey, except in extreme South, but there are very few confirmed and no recent records. The subspecies in New Jersey would be *persius*.
Current Status: Almost certainly EXTIRPATED if it was ever resident. No recent records known to us since 1950.
Historical Status: Impossible to determine since identity of some or most old records in doubt. Any interpretation must take into account the fact that the very similar Wild Indigo Duskywing was not described as a separate species until 1936 (Forbes 1936). For example, Beutenmüller's (1893) account of this species as "not rare" lists habitats entirely inappropriate for this boreal species. If it was indeed widespread, as Comstock (1940) suggested, it has declined dramatically. Schweitzer (1987) reports specimens from Franklinville, Gloucester County, in the Peabody Museum at Yale University, but it was always rare in southern New Jersey. Records from Sussex, Passaic, Middlesex, Ocean, Camden, and Gloucester Counties shown in Opler's Atlas. The Passaic specimen was identified by Burns (1964).
Conservation Status: Since many old records are suspect, one can only guess that this species has had a drastic decline from Massachusetts to New Jersey. It is possible that this is another of the boreal species that has retreated northward. Iftner et al. (1992) consider it endangered in Ohio. The Natural Heritage ranking is G4/SH. Vigilance is required to detect this species among the much more numerous Wild Indigos. Attention should focus on its leguminous hosts, and small duskywings associating with Lupines could be captured for expert determination.
Comstock (1940): "Possibly throughout." Specimens recorded from Old Bridge, Jamesburg, Runyon, Lakewood, and Greenwood Lake from late April to late May. {It is probable that some or all of these were misidentified Wild Indigo Duskywings.}
Delaware Valley (1966): "Rare . . . rich woods." Records from Gloucester and Camden Counties.
Staten Island (1973): "Davis . . . record of *E. persius*, . . . almost certainly refers to" *E. baptisiae* (Shapiro and Shapiro 1973).
New York City Area (1993): "Never common in New York State (few records, all in May). No definite recent sightings, but populations could be easily overlooked."
Cape May (1993): Not listed.
Habitat: "Open areas within boreal forests . . . sandy areas . . . or open fields and boggy places" (Opler and Krizek 1984). In New England and New York, this rare species appears to be "least rare in sandy pine barrens" (Schweitzer 1987).

Phenology: One brood May, possibly into early June.

Caterpillar Foodplants: Controversial. Comstock (1940) lists willows and poplars and Opler and Krizek (1984) consider these the chief host in the East, but also mention that Wild Lupine (*Lupinus perennis*) is used. Schweitzer (1987) provides evidence that this species uses primarily *Baptisia tinctoria* and *Lupinus perennis* in the Northeast, and indicates that *Baptisia* was probably its host in New Jersey. Iftner et al. (1992) report oviposition on lupine in Ohio. Scott (1986) mentions the use of willows and poplars in eastern North America, but this is probably erroneous. Various leguminous plants are used in western North America (Burns 1964, Scott 1986).

Overwintering Stage: Full-grown larva.

Comment: This species is very similar to the Wild Indigo (Shapiro 1974a), and it is probable both that old records are misidentified, and that it if it occurred it would be easily overlooked. It is very difficult to identify, requiring microscopic examination and experience for positive confirmation (Schweitzer). In New York it is considered "rare and poorly understood" with records shown scattered in northeastern, central, and southeastern counties including Westchester and Rockland (Shapiro 1974a). In Maryland the first documented specimen was collected in 1955 (Simmons and Andersen 1978c). The main distinguishing marks are the short whitish hairs on the forewing of the male, from which it receives an alternative name, Hairy Duskywing (Scott 1986).

Holland (1898) lamented that the color plate in his book "does not show these delicate but constant marks of difference as well as might be desired." This was surely both an understatement and a handicap for the generation of lepidopterists who relied on Holland's illustrations for identification. Perhaps misleading plates contributed to misidentifications in the past.

Appalachian Grizzled Skipper, *Pyrgus wyandot* (Edwards, 1863)

We follow compelling arguments of Shapiro (1974a) and Schweitzer (1989) that this be treated as a distinct species. The NABA Checklist (1995) and many other sources treat it as a race of the Grizzled Skipper (*P. centaurae*), which is primarily a Eurasian species, but has a race *P. centaurae freija* extending from Alaska to eastern Canada.

Range: Disjunct distribution from southern New York to Kentucky, and in Michigan. Formerly in New York with records from Erie, Tompkins, Tioga, and Rockland Counties (Shapiro 1974a). Formerly in extreme north of New Jersey with records in Passaic, Bergen, Morris, and Essex Counties and adjacent Rockland County, NY (Opler's Atlas).

Current Status: Formerly occurred in northern New Jersey. No recent records. Has declined in the Northeast. It has probably been EXTIRPATED, but if it survives it must be rare and local and should be considered ENDANGERED.

Historical Status: Beutenmüller (1893) reported this as exceedingly rare within 50 miles of New York City, but mentioned that it had occurred on eastern Long Island, which seems highly unlikely. The early records in Smith and Comstock are mainly from Little Falls, Great Notch, and Paterson, which are all within 5 miles of one another. The Rutgers University Collection has specimens from Pompton (5/4/37) and Normanock (4/25/38). It formerly occurred on trap rock glades in the Orange and Watchung Mountains and a few other sites, but was apparently eliminated by pesticide use since the former habitats are mostly intact (Schweitzer 1989). Additional localities include Montclair and Pompton (Glassberg 1993b).

Conservation Status: Should be listed as ENDANGERED and probably EXTIR-

PATED. It had already declined by 1940 (Comstock), but its disappearance from New Jersey was probably accelerated by pesticide use, since there are no records after the period of heavy mosquito spraying in the 1950s (Schweitzer 1987). It is declining throughout the northeastern United States, even today after pesticide use has declined. It is avidly sought by collectors. It is ranked G2/SH, indicating that it is a candidate for the federal ENDANGERED list.

Smith (1890): Recorded from adjacent states "and almost certain to occur here."

Smith (1900): Little Falls.

Smith (1910): Westmont, Paterson, Little Falls (late April through May).

Comstock (1940): "Crystalline Highlands . . . Formerly numerous at Paterson and Great Notch."

Delaware Valley (1966): Not in our area, but found in Lancaster County, PA, in April. "It also occurs in the mountains of northern New Jersey."

Staten Island (1973): Not listed.

New York City Area (1993): "Historically rare . . . the Grizzled Skipper seems to have disappeared entirely from this region."

Cape May (1993): Not listed.

Habitat: This is a species of dry barrens. In Pennsylvania it is found mainly in powerline cuts through shale ridge forests (Schweitzer 1989), in Ohio mainly in openings in mature oak forest, and in central New York on acid heath barrens.

Phenology: One brood late April–early May.

Caterpillar Foodplants: Dwarf Cinquefoil (*Potentilla canadensis*; Schweitzer 1987); in Michigan on Wild Strawberry (*Fragaria virginiana*).

Comment: Often treated as a race of the Grizzled Skipper (*P. centaurae*), but Shapiro (1974a) argued that *wyandot* was specifically distinct based on genitalia, and Schweitzer (1989) pointed out that habitat, food plants, and larval characteristics supported its distinctness.

Common Checkered-Skipper, *Pyrgus communis* (Grote, 1872)

Range: A widespread Neotropical species resident from southern Virginia to the Pacific Coast and thence southward to Argentina. It irrupts regularly north to Long Island and less frequently to southern New England and southern Canada; recorded in most of New Jersey.

Current Status: Recorded annually in varying numbers. Occurs mainly in southern New Jersey in late summer and sometimes common, with up to ten seen in a day, but rare in 1994 (Dowdell) and more common in 1995. June and July records in northern New Jersey in recent years may represent immigrants from a second brood just south of New Jersey, but their occurrence in the same locality suggests that it may sometimes overwinter in New Jersey. Three recent records from Warren County (Wander). In 1995 they were scarce near Cape May but unusually common northward, with a regional high count of 150 in a field in southern Orange County, NY (1995; Yrizarry).

Historical Status: Confusing. The reports below mention "common" and "abundant," words that would not usually describe its status in New Jersey today. However, Beutenmüller's (1893) account for the New York City vicinity considered it "very rare." Nor does it occur throughout since it is now rare in the Northwest and was not documented there by Opler's Atlas (1983, 1995). It is likely, therefore, that in some areas it is less common now than formerly, a situation suggested also for Ohio (Iftner et al. 1992), perhaps due to a decline in agricultural land. However, in other areas it has increased.

Smith (1890): "Quite common throughout the State."

Smith (1900): "Throughout the State and seasonally common; very abundant near New Brunswick" (August 1898).

Smith (1910): "Throughout" "seasonally common."

Comstock (1940): "Piedmont Region and southward . . . sometimes locally abundant."

Delaware Valley (1966): "Usually common, occasionally . . . abundant." Throughout, but mainly in Coastal Plain, where breeders are "reinforced by immigration from the south."

Staten Island (1973): Davis (1893) knew of only one record, but Davis (1910) listed records from August to October. "No modern records . . . an irregular immigrant."

New York City Area (1993): "Irregular southern immigrant." Does not overwinter.

Cape May (1993): "Common" as an immigrant.

Habitat: Open, fairly barren grasslands with bare ground.

Phenology: A southern immigrant arriving by July (sometimes in May), with largest numbers in September. Three broods May–November.

Caterpillar Foodplants: Common Mallow (*Malva neglecta*) and Hollyhock (*Althaea officinalis*) and occasionally other species of Malvaceae; also Flower-of-an-Hour (*Hibiscus trionum*) and Prickly Mallow (*Sida spinosa*) (Comstock 1940). In Orange County, NY, apparently used Velvetleaf (*Abutilon theophrasi*; Yrizarry).

Overwintering Stage: Larva.

Comment: In New Jersey it occurs mainly on the Coastal Plain, yet in New York it has been recorded in almost all central and western counties (Shapiro 1974a). On five successive Raritan Canal 4JC, it has been recorded on the edge of the same alfalfa field within a 50 m radius, while it is rare elsewhere (see Photo 15). This suggests a permanent colony rather than random immigration and colonization. Shapiro (1974) reported that this species does not overwinter in southeastern New York but does in western New York, and suggested that there may be biological differences between the two populations. Thus the latter may be represented in central New Jersey, for the species does not overwinter regularly in Cape May or even in Maryland (Pavulaan). This species is often seen on bare ground or mowed trails. Nectaring noted mainly on Alfalfa (*Medicago sativa*) and Red Clover (*Trifolium pratense*).

Common Sootywing, *Pholisora catullus* (Fabricius, 1793)

Range: Occurs across southern Canada from Quebec to British Columbia; in East from southern Maine to northern Florida and Texas, but may not overwinter north of southern New York; throughout New Jersey.

Current Status: Occurs in open, disturbed habitats throughout the state and fairly common; occasionally abundant.

Historical Status: Unclear. Opler's Atlas does not list records from Monmouth to Atlantic Counties nor from the northeastern counties. This suggests that the species was much less common during the period of great collecting activity prior to 1940.

Smith (1890–1910): "Common throughout."

Comstock (1940): "Throughout, generally common."

Delaware Valley (1966): "Abundant resident."

Staten Island (1973): "Very common."

New York City Area (1993): "Locally common along the coast."

Cape May (1993): "Common."

Photo 15. Checkered Skipper on Rabbits Ear Clover. The colony at Cook College along Route 1 has persisted for several years. (Photographed by Joanna Burger)

Habitat: This species benefits from urbanization and agriculture; occurring in weedy fields and vacant lots and early successional stages, including bare ground, pastures, roadsides, and lawn edges, even in urban parks.

Phenology: Three broods early May–September. In North mid-May–mid-September; in South early May–September, with peaks in early June, mid-July, and late August (Glassberg 1993b).

Caterpillar Foodplants: Usually on Lamb's Quarters (*Chenopodium album*), but also on Amaranths (*Amaranthus* spp.) and Ragweed (*Ambrosia*). Reports that it uses mints (*Marrubium, Monarda*, and *Mentha*) are considered erroneous (Scott 1986) since in the laboratory larvae reject these plants.

Overwintering Stage: Full-grown larva.

Comment: This is such a widespread and often common species that it is puzzling that its occurrence is localized. It is absent from many fields and parks where its host plants are abundant. Shapiro (1974a) also commented that its distribution in New York was "spotty." We have fewer than ten records in our yard over 10 years, despite the fact that it can be abundant nearby.

Subfamily *Hesperiinae*, Grass or Folded-Wing Skippers

The remainder of the species to be discussed are the Grass, Folded-Wing or Branded Skippers. All but one species (Brazilian Skipper) rely on grasses or sedges as larval hosts, and most have the habit of sometimes sitting with their hind wings folded flat and their forewings elevated at a 45–60° angle. The Common Roadside and Pepper and Salt Skippers hold the forewings nearly perpendicular (Glassberg 1993b). The brand refers to the black stigma of the male, which is a dark, scent-producing patch on the dorsal forewing.

These skippers are various combinations of yellow to dark brown with various spots and lines and patches. Some have fine white "frosting" on the underwings. Glassberg (1993b) calls these the "little brown jobs" of the butterfly world. The entry for *Overwintering Stage* has been omitted for virtually all of the Grass Skippers because of lack of documented information for New Jersey.

Scott (1986) estimates that there are 2150 species of Grass Skippers worldwide, with 137 species and 47 genera in North America; 39 species in 21 genera have been recorded from New Jersey.

Arctic Skipper, *Carterocephalus palaemon* (Pallas, 1771) Plate 2a

Range: A Holarctic species of boreal regions of Eurasia and North America. From Nova Scotia to Alaska south to extreme northwestern New Jersey and northern California. The subspecific name *mandan* has been applied to the North American form.

Current Status: Recently discovered in High Point State Park. Probably occurs elsewhere in extreme northwestern New Jersey, which is at the southern limit of its range. It can be quite common during its brief flight period; maximum fifteen per day (Wander).

Historical Status: No New Jersey records shown in Opler's Atlas, but Opler and Krizek (1984) include northwestern New Jersey in its range. Little known in New Jersey until discovered by Halliwell in late 1980s.

Conservation Status: This species is marginal in New Jersey. Surveys should be done to determine the extent of its range in the state. The Natural Heritage ranking is S1.

Smith (1890–1910): Not listed.

Comstock (1940): Not listed.

Delaware Valley (1966): Not in area.

Staten Island (1973): Not listed.

New York City Area (1993): "A northerly species which barely reaches the edge of our region . . . in far northwest Sussex County."

Cape May (1993): Not listed.

Habitat: Open cuts through Canadian Zone forest. Found nectaring on road shoulders.

Phenology: Probably one brood late May–late June.

Caterpillar Foodplants: In Europe found on brome grasses (*Bromus*) and in California on Purple Reed Grass (*Calamagrostis purpurascens*), but its host(s) in the East not known (Shapiro 1974a). Larvae will eat a variety of grasses in captivity (Scott 1986).

Comments: Shapiro (1966) predicted that this species of Canadian and Hudsonian Zone forests would "probably be found widespread in the Poconos and in northern New Jersey." The only southeastern New York record that Shapiro (1974a) reported was in western Ulster County; he remarks that the name 'Arctic' is inappropriate for this Canadian Zone species.

Where to Find It: At High Point State Park nectaring on Wild Geraniums (*Geranium*) on road shoulders in late May and early June.

Swarthy Skipper, *Nastra lherminier* (Latreille, 1824)

Range: Rhode Island to Missouri thence to southern Florida and Texas; shown throughout New Jersey as an immigrant in Opler and Krizek (1984). In New York recorded only from Long Island and Westchester (Shapiro 1974a).

Current Status: Widespread and sometimes fairly common, particularly in late summer. Usually fewer than ten individuals per day, but rarely over 100 can be found. New Jersey is near the northern limit of its range, and it is quite rare in the Northwest (Wander), and uncommon in the Great Swamp. Fairly common in northern Rockland County, NY (Glassberg).

Historical Status: This species apparently increased greatly in the early half of this century. It was not listed at all by Beutenmüller (1893).

Smith (1890): Not listed.

Smith (1900–1910): "Local," from Orange Mountains, Staten Island, and Sandy Hook to Camden and Anglesea.

Comstock (1940): "Coastal Plain and a little above the Fall Line," including Ramsey and Green Village {Great Swamp}.

Delaware Valley (1966): "Common . . . general . . . including the pine barrens."

Staten Island (1973): "Frequent to locally abundant." {Davis (1910) had only one record.}

New York City Area (1993): A common resident, mainly near coast and in Hudson Valley.

Cape May (1993): "Common."

Habitat: Variable, often found in dry fields and cuts, where its host is found.

Phenology: Two broods late May–early October, mainly mid to late June and again early August–mid-September in North and mid-June–early July and early August–mid-September in South.

Caterpillar Foodplants: Little Bluestem (Andropogon scoparius). No other host has been recorded (Opler and Krizek 1984).

Comment: This dark-brown skipper has an indistinctly veined appearance which separates it from the Tawny-edge Skipper. The Dun Skipper can also appear unmarked below, but is blacker. Other skippers may lose their underwing markings when worn, and could be confused with this species. Swarthy Skippers tend to stay close to the ground, infrequently nectaring at tall flowers such as milkweeds.

Clouded Skipper, *Lerema accius* (J. E. Smith, 1797)

Range: Southeastern Virginia to southern Florida and westward through southern Great Plains to eastern Texas; also Mexico to northern South America; irruptive occasionally to central and southern New Jersey and rarely to Long Island. Not recorded in New York away from Long Island (Shapiro 1974a).

Current Status: Erratic. Essentially unknown until 1990. Present in Cape May in some years in good numbers; absent in other years. Has been regular since 1990. A major invasion occurred in 1991 when the species became abundant at Cape May with up to fifty in a day (Dowdell); scarce in 1994. Since it has also been recorded in Staten Island and Long Island, it should be looked for throughout the Coastal Plain.

Historical Status: Uncertain. Very rarely recorded prior to 1990.

Smith (1890–1910): Reported from Salem by Aaron in June and July. No additional records after 1890.

Comstock (1940): On supplemental list based on specimens from Salem and Atlantic City.

Delaware Valley (1966): "Uncommon immigrant . . . scattered records from" Salem, Gloucester, Camden, and Atlantic Counties, usually singly.

Staten Island (1973): "Infrequent to rare immigrant." "Breeds in New Jersey some years."

New York City Area (1993): "Southern accidental. Invaded . . . in fair numbers in the fall of 1991 (five records 9/16 to 10/3), when it was "exceptionally common" in southern New Jersey.

Cape May (1993): "Stray." First Cape May record in 1991 (Dowdell); several in 1991 and 1993-95 (P. Sutton).

Habitat: At Cape May found in various open habitats, including gardens and weedy fields. Shows some preference for patches of Everlasting Pea (Lathyrus; Dowdell).

Phenology: In New Jersey, one flight August–September or rarely to mid-October.

Caterpillar Foodplants: Grasses—*Paspalum*, *Erianthus*, particularly Woolly Beard Grass (*E. alopecuroides*), and *Echinochloa*.

Comment: This species is most likely to be mistaken for a female Zabulon Skipper. It also resembles a Dusted Skipper, but that species flies only in spring, long before Clouded Skippers reach New Jersey.

Where to Find It: Check flower gardens and patches of Everlasting Pea at Cape May Point, including the State Park in September. Its numbers vary from year to year.

Least Skipper, *Ancyloxypha numitor* (Fabricius, 1793)

Range: From Atlantic Coast across the Great Plains; Nova Scotia to southern Saskatchewan, south to Florida and Texas. Throughout New Jersey.

Current Status: Widespread and often common, particularly in wet meadows and marsh edges; sometimes abundant.

Historical Status: No evidence of change.

Smith (1890–1910): "Common throughout."

Comstock (1940): "Throughout."

Delaware Valley (1966): "Generally abundant . . . throughout."

Staten Island (1973): "Common and widespread."

New York City Area (1993): "Common to abundant."

Cape May (1993): "Common."

Habitat: Marshes and wet grassy fields and meadows; fens and grassy cuts in forest. Also margins of lakes, particularly around Pickerel Weed (*Pontederia cordata*).

Phenology: Three broods late May (or more often early June) to October.

Caterpillar Foodplants: Cutgrass (*Leersia oryzoides*), *Poa*, *Zizianopsis*, and cultivated rice are natural hosts (Opler and Krizek 1984).

Overwintering Stage: Larva.

Comment: This diminutive species has a characteristic weak flight through the grass, often remaining within 50 cm of the ground and infrequently rising above 1 m. It is distinguished from the European Skipper by its uniformly brighter orange underwings, black upper wings, and its more slender body.

European Skipper, *Thymelicus lineola* (Ochsenheimer, 1808)

Range: Originally a Eurasian species introduced to North America, where it now occurs from southern Maine to Wisconsin and south to Virginia and Missouri. Opler and Krizek (1984) show it for all of New Jersey except extreme south, where it now occurs.

Current Status: Widespread and often abundant in northern New Jersey (MG, Wanders), less common in central New Jersey as far south as Ocean County; uncommon to rare in southern New Jersey (Dowdell).

Historical Status: First North American record was at London, Ontario, in 1910 (Opler and Krizek 1984). It reached the United States near Detroit in 1927 (Rawson 1931). Since then it has spread over the northeastern U.S., but its main colonization of New Jersey has been in the past 40 years. Joseph Muller (1958) collected the first New Jersey specimens at Lebanon, Hunterdon County (6/26/58). Leck did not find it at Kendall Park before 1980.

Smith (1890–1910): Not listed.

Comstock (1940): Not listed.

Delaware Valley (1966): "An introduced species that will probably turn up in our area." Already present in Hunterdon County.

Staten Island (1973): "Common to locally abundant."

New York City Area (1993): "Widespread and often remarkably abundant."

Cape May (1993): "Uncommon."

Habitat: A characteristic species of wet or dry fields and pastures.

Phenology: One brood early June–late July; extreme dates in North: May 27–July 27 (Cech 1993).

Caterpillar Foodplants: Timothy (*Phleum pratense*).

Comment: Sometimes reaching great abundance, with many hundreds of individuals. We estimated over 500 in one field near Newton (7/5/92), and 1350 were estimated at Meyer Sanctuary in Westchester County (6/29/89; *Mulberry Wing*).

Fiery Skipper, *Hylephila phyleus* (Drury, 1773)

Range: Massachusetts to California and south to southern Florida, the West Indies, and Central and South America; the subspecies *phyleus* occurs as an immigrant throughout New Jersey.

Current Status: A regular immigrant from the South recorded almost every year, particularly around Cape May. Occasionally common in South (up to twenty-four in one day at Cape May; Dowdell). Rarer in north, and generally absent in Highlands and Northwest. We have had three sightings in Somerset in 10 years, but it is regular at the Rutgers Display Gardens (New Brunswick) in September. 1991 was a peak year for Fiery Skipper populations and it was even fairly common in southeastern New York.

Historical Status: This species was apparently rarer at the turn of the century than today. Beutenmüller (1893) listed only three specimens. But it was perhaps more common in midcentury than at present, based on Shapiro (1966). Opler's Atlas shows records for Sussex, Bergen, Hudson, Mercer, Ocean, Burlington, Cumberland, and Cape May Counties.

Smith (1890): Specimens from Atlantic City and Clifton.

Smith (1900): Additional location: Bayonnne.

Smith (1910): "Not common." Additional locations: Hopatcong, Five Mile Beach.

Comstock (1940): "Throughout." Localities range from Englewood and Hopatcong to Dennisville.

Delaware Valley (1966): "Common and widespread . . . many seasons . . . restricted to the Coastal Plain."

Staten Island (1973): "Frequent after early August." "Not recorded by Davis."

New York City Area (1993): "A rare immigrant along the Coastal Plain and extremely rare colonist."

Cape May (1993): "Common" as a migrant.

Habitat: Usually found in disturbed habitats such as lawn edges, gardens, brushy meadows, vacant fields with weeds.

Phenology: Arrives in late summer, usually not before September in the North, but rarely as early as June in the South. Extreme early date in New York City area is June 29, but typical arrival is in early September.

Caterpillar Foodplants: Grasses, favoring Crabgrass (*Digitaria*).

Comment: The reproductive behavior of this species was investigated in detail by I. Shapiro (1975). The species is readily recognized in the folded position by the orange rays that extend across the black margin of the dorsal hind wings. With wings closed, it has distinct dark spots that are smaller and more numerous than on the Whirlabout, a much rarer species.

Where to Find It: Cape May Point parks and gardens and Higbee Beach in September.

Leonard's Skipper [Leonardus Skipper], *Hesperia leonardus* Harris 1862

Range: Nova Scotia to Minnesota, south to northern South Carolina and Arkansas. The subspecies *leonardus* occurs throughout New Jersey.

Current Status: Uncommon and local. The only skipper that first emerges in late summer and fall, with no spring or early summer brood. There is a large colony in Cumberland County (up to 75 seen in a day), but no active colony is known in Cape May County (Dowdell). Rare and local in central and northern New Jersey, with few colonies known. A colony in Somerset (MG, JB) and one at Delaware Water Gap (Wanders).

Historical Status: This striking skipper appears to be dependent on extensive meadows with tall grass, and it has disappeared from most parts of the state. It was formerly recorded in most counties. However, it was always probably local and never common. Beutenmüller (1893) considered it rare.

Conservation Status: This vulnerable species has a Natural Heritage ranking of S2–3. It should be considered for listing as a THREATENED species. Few colonies are known and these should be monitored. It is not faring well in some other parts of its range. It is disappearing in southern New York (Tudor), and a western race *montana* of Colorado is THREATENED as well (Wooley et al. 1991).

Smith (1890): "Rare" in East; on "Newark" list.

Smith (1900–1910): "Quite generally distributed, but not common," localities range from Newark and Staten Island to Camden.

Comstock (1940): "Throughout" Aug. 23–Sept. 17. Locations: Fort Lee to Dennisville.

Delaware Valley (1966): "Local breeding resident. . . . More common in New Jersey," with records from Camden, Gloucester, Salem, Atlantic, and Burlington.

Staten Island (1973): Two old specimens (1887–88) and one modern specimen (Tottenville, 9/22/71); "should be fairly widespread."

New York City Area (1993): "Much reduced and locally threatened; . . . only a few outposts."

Cape May (1993): "Uncommon." {Based on historic records.}

Habitat: It occurs in marshy meadows as well as in old fields with tall grasses and is vulnerable to habitat destruction by mowing and, of course, by development. Said to use the same habitat used earlier in the spring by Dusted Skippers (Opler and Krizek 1984). Associated with *Andropogon* grasses and often nectars on Ironweed (*Veronia novaboracensis*) (Wander).

Phenology: Single brood first week of August–mid-September.

Caterpillar Foodplants: Various grasses including Switch Grass (*Panicum virgatum*) and *Eragrostis alba* (Shapiro 1966), Poverty Oatgrass (*Danthonia spicata*), Bent (*Agrostis* spp.), various *Andropogon* spp.

Overwintering Stage: Early larva.

Comment: This is the only univoltine skipper in New Jersey that flies in the late summer and fall. The conspicuous white, v-shaped, postmedian spot band on the underwing surface is distinctive. It is declining, probably due to development or mowing of its habitat. Its habitat preferences and requirements should be carefully studied at localities where colonies thrive. It should be looked for nectaring on Ironweed (*Vernonia* spp.; Wander) and spotted Knapweed and Joe-Pye-Weed in southern New Jersey (Dowdell and C. Sutton). Scott and Stanford (1981) provided morphological, behavioral, and ecological evidence that Leonard's Skipper is conspecific with the Pawnee Skipper. Best studied in Iowa where the nominate subspecies *leonardus* and *pawnee* intergrade (Spomer et al. 1993).

Cobweb Skipper, *Hesperia metea* (Scudder, 1864)

Range: A highly disjunct distribution from extreme southern Maine and southern Vermont to Wisconsin to central Georgia, Mississippi, and eastern Texas. The subspecies *metea* occurs throughout New Jersey {but highly local and rare away from Coastal Plain}.

Current Status: Widespread in early spring, and occasionally common; mainly Coastal Plain and Pine Barrens, where it prefers sparsely vegetated areas and sandy roads, occurs south to Rio Grande in Cape May County where up to six seen in a day (Dowdell) and in Ocean County (5+ at Warren Grove, 5/8/93; Tudor). Scarce north of Fall Line (Wander).

Historical Status: No apparent change in southern New Jersey, but Beutenmüller (1893) reported no records at all from within 50 miles of New York City, hence it is apparently more common now than a century ago.

Smith (1890): Schooley Mountain.

Smith (1900–1910): Localities from Morris County and Staten Island to Camden. {Apparently widespread but local.}

Comstock (1940): "Throughout." Localities: Hopatcong to Clementon.

Delaware Valley (1966): "Locally very common," general in the Pine Barrens.

Staten Island (1973): "Common or locally abundant."

New York City Area (1993): "Locally fairly common but thinly distributed in sandy habitats."

Cape May (1993): "Common."

Habitat: Occurs in barren habitats such as oak-pine scrub and rocky barrens, grassy swales, and along dirt roads and powerline cuts, but mainly on sandy soil (Shapiro 1965). Reported associated with Sand Myrtle (*Leiophyllum buxifolium*) by Smith (1900), but this was undoubtedly a habitat indicator rather than a host plant.

Phenology: One brood, mainly May. Extreme dates in North May 6–June 9 (Cech 1993); in South, late April to mid-May.

Caterpillar Foodplants: Little Bluestem (*Andropogon scoparius*) and other species of *Andropogon*.

Overwintering Stage: Full-grown larva.

Comment: Often found perched on bare ground. This is the first Grass Skipper to appear in spring. The half-developed larvae bury deeply into the base of a Bluegrass clump, where they estivate. They hibernate in the center of the grass plant in a sealed silk chamber. In spring the larvae emerge and pupate immediately (Heitzman and Heitzman 1969).

Where to Find It: On dirt roads or bare dirt areas in Pine Barrens in early May. The Bearberry Flats at Warren Grove (see under Hoary Elfin) is a good location.

Dotted Skipper, *Hesperia attalus* (Edwards, 1871) Plate 4a

Range: Disjunct distribution. Main range is from central New Jersey to central Florida and along the Gulf Coast and also to Texas; but mostly very sparse records shown in Opler's Atlas. Recorded in central and southern New Jersey. The subspecies in New Jersey is *slossonae* described by Skinner in 1890.

Current Status: Several locations known from Monmouth County south through the Pine Barrens to Cumberland County (Manumuskin). Highly local, but may be fairly common when found (Dowdell).

Historical Status: Apparently always rare and local. Opler's Atlas shows records for Ocean, Burlington, Camden, and Atlantic Counties. Davis (1909) recorded taking "several" at Lakehurst (7/3–4/1909). Its status may not have changed, but observers are more educated on where and how to look for it.

Conservation Status: Natural Heritage ranking is S2–3. The species has generally been considered rare. Surveys are required to determine how widespread it might be and what protective measures are required to maintain colonies.

Smith (1890): Hypothetical in New Jersey. Reported for New Jersey by Edwards, but "not taken by either the Philadelphia or Newark collectors."

Smith (1900): Specimens from Clementon and DaCosta.

Smith (1910): Local in South. Additional localities: Lakehurst and Manumuskin.

Comstock (1940): "Pine Barrens, Swamps." Lakehurst, Lakewood, DaCosta, and Clementon.

Delaware Valley (1966): "Uncommon to rare . . . mainly in the Coastal Plain."

Staten Island (1973): Only New York State record, 7/16/71.

New York City Area (1993): Only area record was on Staten Island in 1971.

Cape May (1993): Listed as a "species to look for."

Habitat: Now aware of its presence, researchers have found it at various localities in the Pine Barrens; it occurs in wet areas (Davis 1909) and dry fields.

Phenology: One brood early June–August with peak in mid–late July.

Caterpillar Foodplants: "Presumably a grass" (Shapiro 1966); uses Little Bluestem (*Andropogon scoparius*) and perhaps African Lovegrass (*Eragrostis*) in New Jersey (Schweitzer); in Florida uses Wire Grass (*Aristida* spp.) which occurs along abandoned railroad right-of-ways where the skipper also occurs (Schweitzer 1987).

Comment: This species has been considered "one of the country's rarest butterflies" (Simmons and Andersen 1978a). Although highly local, it may occur over most of the Pine Barrens. It must be distinguished with care from the similar Crossline Skipper (see Glassberg 1993b).

Where to Find It: The Lakehurst area in mid-July seems to be consistent. The butterfly is not in the bog, but has been seen in weedy fields as well as on wide trails around the bogs.

Indian Skipper, *Hesperia sassacus* (Harris, 1862)

Range: Northern Maine to Minnesota, south to western Virginia and northern Indiana; the subspecies *sassacus* occurs in northern and western New Jersey.

Current Status: An uncommon or occasionally common and probably fairly widespread spring species in the North. However, rare or absent in southern New Jersey and not resident on the Outer Coastal Plain (Schweitzer). Only one Somerset record in 10 years (MG).

Historical Status: This species was rarely collected at the turn of the century, with only six localities known by 1910, nor was it common around New York City (Beutenmüller 1893). It has apparently increased since that time. Shapiro (1966) lists records from Mercer to Salem Counties, suggesting it may have been more widespread on the Coastal Plain in the recent past than it is today, since it is currently rare there.

Smith (1890): "Newark," Caldwell, Trenton.

Smith (1900): Additional localities: Hopatcong, Staten Island, Plainfield.

Smith (1910): Additional localities: Westmont, Newfoundland, Orange Mountains.

Comstock (1940): North of Fall Line.

Delaware Valley (1966): "Quite local" in northern part of region, with records from Salem, Gloucester, Camden, Burlington, Mercer, and Hunterdon Counties.

Staten Island (1973): Recorded by Davis in May–June, but not found in 1971.

New York City Area (1993): "Uncommon to locally fairly common."

Cape May (1993): Never recorded, but listed as a "species to look for."

Habitat: A species of scrubby fields and short grasslands and dry hillsides, mainly in North.

Phenology: One brood May–June.

Caterpillar Foodplants: Grasses, *Panicum*, perhaps *Poa annua* (Shapiro 1966). In Ohio, oviposited on Red Fescue (*Festuca rubra*) and associated with *Andropogon* (Iftner et al. 1992).

Comments: Can be confused with Long Dash and Peck's Skippers. This species has received little study.

Peck's Skipper, *Polites peckius* (Cramer, 1775)

Often listed as *Polites coras* and sometimes called Yellow-patch Skipper.

Range: Maritime Provinces to British Columbia, south through Appalachians to northern Georgia and Texas and northern California. Opler and Krizek (1984) map shows northern and central New Jersey; however, it occurs south to Cape May.

Current Status: Widespread and sometimes very abundant in most of state, but highly local and uncommon in Cumberland County and quite rare in Cape May County (Dowdell); elsewhere often the commonest of the skippers and fortunately very easy to identify.

Historical Status: No evidence of change.

Smith (1890–1910): "Common throughout." "Perhaps the most common species throughout the State" (Smith 1900).

Comstock (1940): "Throughout," "usually common."

Delaware Valley (1966): "Most common skipper northward, less common in south." Occurs throughout.

Staten Island (1973): "Common and widespread."

New York City Area (1993): "Fairly common to abundant."

Cape May (1993): "Uncommon."

Habitat: Very diverse. This is often the most abundant skipper in overgrown fields and gardens, also on cuts and forest edges.

Phenology: Three broods May–October. In central New Jersey, least common in early July, most numerous in August. In North, extreme dates May 14–October 15. The timing of the Fourth of July Counts lies between the first and second broods, so it has been recorded on only 23% of the New Jersey counts with a maximum of only 36 (1991, Raritan Canal).

Caterpillar Foodplants: Grasses; "generalized in its tastes" (Shapiro 1966). In New York, used Rice Cut-grass (*Leersia oryzoides*; Shapiro 1974a); also probably Kentucky Bluegrass (*Poa pratensis*; Scott 1986).

Overwintering Stage: Full-grown larva and pupa.

Comment: Frequently seen by the hundreds, for example in fields of Black Knapweed (*Centaurea nigra*) and Alfalfa (*Medicago sativa*). Uses a great variety of nectar sources.

Tawny-edged Skipper, *Polites themistocles* (Lattrielle, 1824)

Range: Nova Scotia to southern British Columbia and south to central Florida, central Texas, and northern California; throughout New Jersey.

Current Status: Widespread and sometimes common, though much less common in southern Coastal Plain. Local in Delaware Valley. Uncommon to rare in Pine Barrens but common on its periphery (Schweitzer); fairly common in Cumberland County but rare at Cape May (Dowdell). In Northwest, widespread, but uncommon to fairly common, and usually less numerous than Crossline Skipper (Wander).

Historical Status: No clear evidence of change.

Smith (1890–1910): "Common throughout."

Comstock (1940): "Throughout."

Delaware Valley (1966): "Very common . . . throughout, but rare . . . in the pine barrens."

Staten Island (1973): "Infrequent and sporadic," mostly solitary. Davis did not distinguish this from the next species.

New York City Area (1993): "Locally common to abundant."

Cape May (1993): "Uncommon."

Habitats: Very diverse. Open grassy areas including wet meadows, dry pastures, cuts, and gardens.

Phenology: Two broods May–November. Extreme dates in North May 16 to November 4, with peaks in late May and August (Cech 1993). In South early June–mid-July and late July–late September.

Caterpillar Foodplants: Mainly the smaller species of Panic grasses (Panicum spp.).

Overwintering Stage: Pupa.

Comment: It is similar to the larger Crossline Skipper but usually lacks the pale postmedian spot band on the ventral hind wing. It is reported to occupy moister habitats than the Crossline, but in central New Jersey the two are often found together, occasionally on the same flowers.

Opler's Atlas does not document records from Camden, Gloucester, Salem, or Atlantic Counties, but this is an omission since Shapiro (1966), the main source for that area, lists it as "common throughout" without specifically identifying those counties.

Crossline Skipper, *Polites origenes* (Fabricius, 1793)

Range: Southern Maine to the Rocky Mountains of Wyoming and south to central Florida, central Texas, and northern New Mexico; throughout New Jersey.

Current Status: Widespread and sometimes common throughout. Common on Coastal Plain (Schweitzer). Sometimes common at scattered localities in Sussex County, with up to fifteen per day (Wanders).

Historical Status: Unclear, probably stable. This species was considered uncommon at the turn of the century. Shapiro considered it abundant both in the Delaware Valley and on Staten Island, and it is possible that it has declined in the past 25 years, since it is hardly abundant anywhere at this time.

Smith (1890–1900): Generally distributed, not common.

Smith (1910): "Local and uncommon," seven localities listed from Newark to Gloucester.

Comstock (1940): "Throughout."

Delaware Valley (1966): "Often locally abundant."

Staten Island (1973): "Frequent . . . locally very abundant."

New York City Area (1993): "Locally fairly common."

Cape May (1993): "Common."

Habitat: Variable fields, meadows, cuts, and gardens. Prefers drier habitats than Tawny-edged Skipper.

Phenology: One or two broods. Usually considered univoltine in New Jersey, occurring late June–late July in Pine Barrens, but in north occurs early June–mid-August, with an extremely late date of Sept. 10 (Cech 1993). A partial second brood occurs in some areas in some years. September individuals may be southern immigrants.

Caterpillar Foodplants: Purple Top grass (*Tridens flavus*). Also on Little Bluestem (*Andropogon scoparius*) in Michigan (Scott 1986).

Comments: This species seems to us confusable with pale individuals of the Northern Broken Dash.

Long Dash, *Polites mystic* (W. H. Edwards, 1863)

Range: Maritime Provinces to British Columbia and south to western central New Jersey (with records south to Burlington County), West Virginia, the northern Great Plains, and Colorado and Washington. The subspecies *mystic* occurs in New Jersey.

Current Status: Generally uncommon, but locally common in northwestern New Jersey. Status in central New Jersey unknown. Probably absent from southern New Jersey and most of Coastal Plain.

Historical Status: No apparent change; it has always been listed as local, but the term "common" was not applied by any author since neither Philadelphia region nor Staten Island is within its regular range. However, Beutenmüller (1893) considered it rare around New York City. Reported as common in northern New York, rare on Staten Island, and local on Long Island and New York City area (Shapiro 1974a). On Coastal Plain, documented from Ocean and Burlington Counties (Opler's Atlas).

Conservation Status: This local species has a Natural Heritage ranking of S3?, indicating the need for additional information on its distribution and habitats. There is no evidence that it has declined.

Smith (1890): Schooley Mountain, "Newark," Trenton.

Smith (1900): Additional localities: Orange Mountain, Staten Island.

Smith (1910): "Throughout northern part of the State," with localities from Morris County to Trenton.

Comstock (1940): North of Fall Line.

Delaware Valley (1966): "Resident . . . local . . . northward only," with records from Burlington, Mercer, and Hunterdon Counties.

Staten Island (1973): "Scarce and local." Recorded in June by Davis (1910).

New York City Area (1993): "Fairly common well upland in wet meadows."

Cape May (1993): Not listed.

Habitat: Wet meadows, marshes, fens, and cuts through moist habitats.

Phenology: Mainly one brood mid-May–mid-July. Smith (1900) reports broods in May–June and August–September, but the second brood is questionable or irregular. Extreme dates in North May 23–mid-July, with a record on September 9.

Caterpillar Foodplants: Grasses. In Pennsylvania reported on bluegrass (*Poa* sp.; Shapiro 1966).

Overwintering Stage: Larva.

Comment: It is superficially similar to the Indian Skipper.

Where to Find It: High Point State Park in late May; look where road crosses grassy stream beds and in wet meadows. The Blue Flag Iris appears to be an indicator of its habitat.

Whirlabout, *Polites vibex* (Hubner, 1832)

Range: Atlantic Coastal Plain and Piedmont from North Carolina to southern Florida and Texas; rarely irruptive to southern New Jersey. Strays north to Connecticut. Only New York sites are Staten Island and Brooklyn (Shapiro 1974a). Not listed from Delmarva (Woodbury 1994), but one specimen from St. Mary's County, Maryland (Simmons and Andersen 1978c).

Current Status: Vagrant. Very rare in northeastern United States, even as far as Maryland; few documented records.

Historical Status: Very rare between 1890 and 1940, but apparently more common in 1960s and 1970s, prompting Shapiro (1974a) to remark, "Apparently a fairly frequent immigrant, perhaps overlooked by many collectors because it resembles common species." Specimen from Middlesex and Cape May (Iftner and Wright 1996).

Smith (1890): Not listed.

Smith (1900–1910): Camden, three specimens collected by Carney prior to 1900.

Comstock (1940): On supplemental list based on three specimens from Camden.

Delaware Valley (1966): "Uncommon immigrant in the Coastal Plain." Frequent in some years and rare in others. Records from Salem, Atlantic, and Camden Counties.

Staten Island (1973): "A frequent immigrant . . . in 1971," these were first reports for New York City area.

New York City Area (1993): "No known sightings from New York or New Jersey in recent decades."

Cape May (1993): No record, but listed as a "species to look for."

Habitat: Open woodlands to Pine Barrens and beaches, often on sandy soil.

Phenology: Three broods in the South, but only recorded in New Jersey late August–mid-October.

Caterpillar Foodplants: Grasses, including Bermuda Grass (*Cynodon dacty lon*), Slender Paspalum (*Paspalum setaceum*), and, in the southern U.S., St Augustine grass (*Stenotaphrum secundatum*).

Comment: Superficially similar to several other more common skippers, including Fiery, Zabulon, and Sachem. Females are difficult to identify, but males have a unique stigma pattern and it is unlikely that they would be overlooked by careful observers.

[**Southern Broken-Dash**, *Wallengrenia otho* (J. E. Smith, 1797)]

Usually listed as Broken Dash. No New Jersey records. This southern species ranges from southeastern Virginia to Texas, and is rarely irruptive to northern Maryland. The two Broken Dashes were not distinguished as separate species until about 1950. The Southern Broken Dash could occur in the lower Delaware Valley.

Historical Status: Confusing, since Smith (1890–1910) refers to *egeremet* as more common, implying that *otho* may have been collected in New Jersey as well. However, there are no documented records (Opler's Atlas). It has been collected in Sussex County, Delaware. Burns (1985) discusses the relationships and distribution of the two species.

Northern Broken-Dash, *Wallengrenia egeremet* (Scudder, 1864)

Range: Central Maine, southern Quebec, and northern Minnesota to central Florida, northern Texas, and Nebraska; throughout New Jersey.

Current Status: Widespread and often abundant. Fairly common in Sussex County (Wanders). Common but somewhat local in southern New Jersey (Schweitzer).

Historical Status: No apparent change, although Beutenmüller (1893) considered it scarce near New York City.

Smith (1890–1910): "Throughout"; "locally common."

Comstock (1940): "Throughout."

Delaware Valley (1966): "Occasionally abundantly . . . throughout."

Staten Island (1973): "Current and widespread."

New York City Area (1993): "Fairly common to common."

Cape May (1993): "Common."

Habitat: Any open areas from pastures to wet meadows, often near woodlands or in forest cuts; frequently visits gardens.

Phenology: One prolonged brood early June–mid-September. Peak occurrence mid-June–early August. Fresh individuals can be seen at any time probably indicating asynchronous emergence, but may also have a partial second brood.

Caterpillar Foodplants: A variety of larger species of Panic grasses *Panicum*, including *P. clandestinum* and *P. dichotomum* (Shapiro 1974a); in New Jersey, usually near Switchgrass (*P. virgatum*; Schweitzer).

Comment: Listed simply as "Broken Dash" in much of the literature, and Shapiro (1966) says "probably specifically distinct from *W. otho*." Burns (1985) published the definitive account of the relationships between these two species. Abundance varies from year to year. The Northern Broken Dash was surprisingly uncommon in central New Jersey in 1994. This species resembles not only the Dun Skipper and Little Glassywing but the Tawny-edge and Crossline Skippers, and depending on their freshness or wear, care should be taken to arrive at a correct identification. Observers are cautioned that not all individuals and not even all photographs are identifiable.

Little Glassywing, *Pompeius verna* (W. H. Edwards, 1862)

Range: Southern Vermont to eastern Nebraska to northern Florida and eastern Texas; throughout New Jersey.

Current Status: Widespread throughout; usually not common but sometimes locally and briefly abundant. Uncommon in South, with few recent Cape May County records (Dowdell). Apparently rare on Coastal Plain and in southern New Jersey, even where Purple Top grass is common (Schweitzer), but common on eastern Long Island.

Historical Status: From Smith's reports we infer that it was rare and local, mainly away from the Coastal Plain, but that it may have been increasing between 1890 and 1910. It is therefore more common today than a century ago.

Smith (1890): "Recorded by Mr. Aaron, without definite locality." {This could have meant it was hypothetical, rare, or too common for Aaron to mention localities.}

Smith (1900): Fort Lee, Lake Hopatcong, Orange Mountains, and Staten Island. {No southern localities.}

Smith (1890): Additional localities: Westmont, Elizabeth, Five Mile Beach.

Comstock (1940): "Throughout."

Delaware Valley (1966): "Common and widespread"; "rare in pine barrens."

Staten Island (1973): "Frequent and widespread."

New York City Area (1993): "Common to very common . . . most frequent inland."

Cape May (1993): "Uncommon."

Habitat: Very diverse, including old fields, woodland edges, pastures, cuts, and gardens.

Phenology: One brood June–August, emerging late June in North and early June in South. Extreme dates in north June 5–August 5. Its peak of abundance is the last week of June–early July.

Caterpillar Foodplants: Only known on Purple Top (*Tridens flavus*). Probably on other grasses as well (Schweitzer).

Comments: A small dark skipper. Females with wings closed resemble a female Dun Skipper, but when wings are folded the large whitish, squarish spot on dorsal forewing is diagnostic.

Sachem, *Atalopedes campestris* (Boisduval, 1852)

Range: Permanent resident from Virginia to California and south to Florida and Brazil. Immigrant to Long Island (and rarely Massachusetts) and most of New Jersey (except extreme Northwest). The subspecies *huron* described by Edwards in 1863 occurs in New Jersey.

Current Status: Immigrant, may be resident in South in some years. Occurs annually in southern New Jersey and in most years north to New Brunswick; is sometimes abundant near Cape May. In most years uncommon in central and northeastern New Jersey, but up to twenty a day seen at Rutgers Display Gardens, East Brunswick. Very rare in Northwest; absent in most years (Wander). In South, populations were high in 1994 and 1995 and superabundant in 1996.

Historical Status: Early in the century it was more widely collected than species such as Northern Broken-Dash. It was "very rare" within 50 miles of New York City a century ago (Beutenmüller 1893) and unaccountably rare on Staten Island in early 1970s, suggesting that it may be on the increase in the past two decades.

Smith (1890): From Mount Holly (Aaron) and "Newark."

Smith (1900): Additional localities: Hopatcong, Camden (common in August–September), Cape May (common in September).

Smith (1910): "Locally common."

Comstock (1940): South of Fall Line from New Brunswick to Cape May.

Delaware Valley (1966): "Regular immigrant . . . most records from the Coastal Plain."

Staten Island (1973): "A rare stray." No old records, one 1971 record.

New York City Area (1993): "Rare and irregular near New York." Not seen in most years. Recorded in 1991 and 1992, but not for many preceding years.

Cape May (1993): "Common" as a migrant.

Habitat: Dry grassy fields, barren weed fields, and gardens.

Phenology: One or multiple broods late July–late October, with peak in September.

Caterpillar Foodplants: Crabgrass (*Digitaria* spp.), Goose Grass (*Eleusine indica*), Bermuda Grass (*Cynodon dactylon*).

Comment: Often very common on Coastal Plain in late summer. At Philadelphia, 431 recorded 7/15/91 (Bryn Mawr 4JC); at Cape May Point, more than 1000 recorded 9/96.

Arogos Skipper [Beardgrass Skipper], *Atrytone arogos* (Boisduval and LeConte, 1834)

Range: Disjunct distribution formerly from Long Island to central Florida; also ranges in the northern Great Plains and on the Gulf Coast; occurs in northern and central New Jersey. Only New York site is Staten Island (Shapiro 1974a).

Current Status: No New Jersey records between 1974 and 1994; then "rediscovered" on Fort Dix in 1995 (Schweitzer). Reported from Morris County in 1995. A species of the bluegrass prairies and serpentine barrens.

Historical Status: Formerly in Pine Barrens, Coastal Plain, and Staten Island. Recorded from Sussex, Ocean, Burlington, Camden, and Gloucester Counties (Opler's Atlas), but the Sussex County record is questionable (Schweitzer 1989). "Several" collected at Lakehurst July 3–4, 1909 (Davis 1909). Not known in New Jersey prior to 1900, and apparently not collected between 1910 and 1940. Observed at Batsto in 1974 (Schweitzer 1989).

Conservation Status: Believed EXTIRPATED, but now should be considered ENDANGERED, and populations should be monitored. Its Natural Heritage ranking is G4/S1. Existing population(s) should be monitored annually. Many populations have disappeared and the species requires survey work throughout its range.

Smith (1890–1900): Not listed.

Smith (1910): Specimens from Brookville, Lakehurst, Browns Mills (July–August).

Comstock (1940): "Pine Barrens. Swamps."

Delaware Valley (1966): "Rare and sporadic . . . but apparently breeding," with records from Salem County (Salem), and Gloucester (Pitman, Williamstown), Camden (Atco), and Burlington (Chatsworth, Mount Misery) Counties.

Staten Island (1973): "Known only from the serpentine barrens . . . Sea View, there quite common." "The northern-most record of this little known insect."

New York City Area (1993): The Staten Island colony is now EXTIRPATED.

Cape May (1993): Not recorded, but listed as a "species to look for."

Habitat: This species is characteristic of undisturbed prairies. Davis (1909) reports it in wet fields near the Lakehurst bogs.

Phenology: One brood late June–early August, with stragglers into September. Shapiro (1966) gives dates from early July–early August.

Caterpillar Foodplants: Big Bluestem (*Andropogon gerardi*); Little Bluestem (*A. scoparius*) recorded on Staten Island. Will accept *A. glomeratus* (Shapiro 1974a).

Comment: It is now very rare on the Atlantic Coast north of Florida, where it has "always been apparently rare" and local, with few specimens from areas where it formerly occurred, despite the fact that its host species is widespread and very abundant. Considering that there were no records prior to 1900 and apparently none between 1910 and 1940 or between 1974 and 1995, we wonder whether this species, here near the extreme of its range, was ever truly resident in New Jersey.

Delaware Skipper, *Anatrytone logan* (W. H. Edwards, 1863)

Usually listed in the genus *Atrytone*, but separated by Burns (1994b), and sometimes listed as *A. delaware*.[1]

Range: Southern Maine and central Vermont to southern Alberta, south to southern Florida, Texas, and New Mexico; throughout New Jersey. The subspecies *logan* occurs in New Jersey.

Current Status: Widespread and occasionally common.

Historical Status: It is remarkable that this species was obviously rare and highly local at the turn of the century, for such a conspicuous and striking skipper would not have been overlooked by collectors. Like Smith, Beutenmüller (1893) labeled it "exceedingly rare" around New York City. It obviously increased greatly between 1910 and 1940, and perhaps benefited from habitat change. Shapiro (1974a) suspected that it was extending its range northward in New York.

Smith (1890): Only from Maurice River area (Aaron).

Smith (1900–1910): "Rare near New York," specimens from Westville as well as Maurice River. {Apparently rare and local.}

Comstock (1940): "Throughout."

Delaware Valley (1966): "Common . . . throughout."

Staten Island (1973): "Not recorded by Davis . . . frequent" near Tottenville. "Locally common on Staten Island" (Shapiro 1974a).

New York City Area (1993): "Common to very common."

Cape May (1993): "Common."

1. Edwards described *Hesperia logan* on p. 18 of the *Proceedings of the Entomological Society of Philadelphia* in 1863, and *Hesperia delaware* on p. 19. Thus *logan* has page priority, if it indeed refers to the insect we now call the Delaware Skipper. The type of the *logan* specimen is believed to be from Lansing, MI, while the type of *delaware* is from Philadelphia (Miller and Brown 1981:41).

Habitat: Very variable including dry meadows and pastures, road cuts, and marshes, bogs, and fens.

Phenology: One brood June–September, in North mainly in July. In southern salt marshes, two broods mid-June and August (Glassberg 1993b).

Caterpillar Foodplants: Grasses *Andropogon*, *Erianthus*, and Switchgrass (*Panicum virgatum*). Association with sedges suggests possible use as hosts (Iftner et al. 1992).

Comment: This widespread species is distinguished from the very similar but highly local Rare and Arogos Skippers by the black veining on the upper hind wing (hence its alternative name, Black-veined skipper; Scott 1986). On the female this takes the form of an oval that reminds us vaguely of a snowshoe. At Ward Pound Ridge, NY, we saw 205 in one day, mostly nectaring on Common Milkweed (7/8/89; MG, Tudor). The maximum 4JC total is 27 (1994, Springdale).

Rare Skipper, *Problema bulenta* (Boisduval and LeConte, 1834) Plate 6a

Range: Disjunct distribution from New Jersey to southern Georgia; no New Jersey records in Opler and Krizek (1984), but now known to occur on Atlantic coast and Delaware Bay coasts of New Jersey in several estuaries.

Current Status: Has been found recently at several sites in southern New Jersey, where it can appear locally common in July. It is known from both Delaware Bay and the Atlantic coast from Burlington, Atlantic, Cape May, Cumberland, and Salem Counties (Cromartie and Schweitzer 1993).

Historical Distribution: This tidal marsh species was only discovered in New Jersey in 1989.

Conservation Status: This habitat-restricted species with a disjunct distribution is given a Natural Heritage ranking of G2–3/S2. Selected, accessible populations should be monitored.

Smith (1890–1910): Not listed.

Comstock (1940): Not listed.

Delaware Valley (1966): Not listed.

Staten Island (1973): Not listed.

New York City Area (1993): Not listed.

Cape May (1993): "Locally common."

Habitat: Estuaries, and edges of salt marsh.

Phenology: One brood, late June–early August, mainly July.

Caterpillar Foodplants: Careful study confirms that Tall Cordgrass (*Spartina cynosuroides*) is the host in New Jersey (Cromartie and Schweitzer 1993). Scott (1986) mentions it associating with *Zizianopsis miliacea*.

Comment: The history and biology of this fascinating species are discussed by Cromartie and Schweitzer (1993). The species was discovered simultaneously in Atlantic and Cape May Counties in 1989. Previously it was known from only five estuaries in five states (Opler and Krizek 1984). It uses a variety of nectar sources, including mallows, milkweed, Buttonbush (*Cephalanthus occidentalis*), and Morning Glories (*Ipomea* sp.). Although it appears sometimes common at its favored flowers, surveys in stands of the host plant suggest that it is possibly a scarce species, albeit widespread in the southern coastal part of the state. The authors suggest that this species has been overlooked in the past due, in part, to its similarity to the Delaware Skipper, although others suggest that it may recently have invaded the state (Opler 1992).

Mulberry Wing, *Poanes massasoit* (Scudder, 1864)

Range: Disjunct distribution from Massachusetts and central New York to Maryland; isolated populations occur in south-central New York and from

Michigan to Minnesota. The subspecies *massasoit* is found in northern and central New Jersey.

Current Status: Localized to tussock sedge marshes, but sometimes common. In Northwest, uncommon to fairly common (Wander). In central New Jersey, recorded at Plainsboro (7/28/71) and Helmetta (7/21/82; Leck). Regular and fairly common near Lakehurst. Generally absent in the core of the Pine Barrens, and absent from many seemingly suitable sites in the South (Schweitzer), but up to 100 seen in a day (Dowdell).

Historical Status: No apparent changes. At the turn of the century this species was apparently very local, but occurred in both northern and southern New Jersey. It occurs mainly in wet meadows, a habitat that is dwindling.

Smith (1890): "Not common," records from Gloucester, Westville, and "Newark."

Smith (1900): Additional records from Staten Island, Jamesburg, Camden.

Smith (1910): Additional records from Westmont, Paterson, Elizabeth.

Comstock (1940): "Locally, throughout . . . at times common."

Delaware Valley (1966): "Very local, but often common."

Staten Island (1973): "Local . . . frequent." Restricted to bogs with tussock sedge. Plentiful near Bull's Head in 1891 (Davis 1893).

New York City Area (1993): "Generally scarce to uncommon; scattered populations."

Cape May (1993): "Locally common."

Habitat: A species of freshwater marshes, wet meadows, and bogs and fens.

Phenology: One brood in North, early July–mid-August. Late June–late July at Lakehurst.

Caterpillar Foodplants: Tussock Sedge (*Carex stricta*).

Comment: The large yellow patch on the ventral hind wing has variously been considered a large bird footprint, an airplane, and a Celtic cross (Tudor). However, there is a variety "suffusa" which lacks this mark and is uniformly colored on the ventral surface. Often found together with Black Dash.

Hobomok Skipper, *Poanes hobomok* (Harris, 1862)

Also listed as Northern Golden Skipper.

Range: Eastern North America to Rocky Mountains. Nova Scotia to Saskatchewan and south to central New Jersey, northern Georgia, and New Mexico. The subspecies *hobomok* occurs in New Jersey.

Current Status: Widespread in northern New Jersey; occasionally common or abundant. Rare or absent from Pine Barrens and Coastal Plain.

Historical Status: No apparent changes.

Smith (1890): Listed as a form under *zabulon* but considered the more common of the two.

Smith (1900): "Generally distributed"; apparently not uncommon, including on Staten Island.

Smith (1910): "Probably local throughout the State" {but all localities listed are in the North}.

Comstock (1940): North of Fall Line.

Delaware Valley (1966): "Very common in the northern part of our area . . . not in pine barrens."

Staten Island (1973): "Probably frequent."

New York City Area (1993): "Very common and widespread."

Cape May (1993): Not recorded, but listed as a "species to look for."

Habitat: Characteristically at edges, glades, and cuts in deciduous woodlands.

Phenology: One brood mid-May–mid-July, although scarce in July.

Photo 16. Ho-bomok Skipper feeding on a bird dropping. This species particularly seems to favor bird droppings, though other butterflies feed this way as well. (Photographed at Somerset by Joanna Burger)

Caterpillar Foodplants: Panic grasses (*Panicum*) and bluegrasses (*Poa*). In New York associated with broad-leaved species of *Panicum* (Shapiro 1974a).

Overwintering Stage: Can be egg, larva, or pupa.

Comment: The females are dimorphic; 25% are the dark brown *pocahontas* form. This species is similar to Zabulon Skipper and the dark females are especially similar to female Zabulon, from which they may be distinguished by a series of sharply delineated spots on the dorsal forewing in Zabulon that are blurred in Hobomok females. Female Hobomok do not have a white costal margin to the ventral hind wing.

Males act territorial perching on twigs or leaves about 1–2 m above the ground and flying out to investigate passersby, including humans. They frequently return to the same perch, which facilitates careful identification. Frequently seen feeding at bird droppings (photo 16).

Zabulon Skipper, *Poanes zabulon* (Boisduval and LeConte, 1834)

Also listed as Southern Golden Skipper.

Range: Eastern United States to Great Plains; also in Rocky Mountains. Massachusetts to central Iowa and south to central Florida and Texas; throughout New Jersey. In New York, was known only from Long Island and southern Westchester and Rockland Counties (Shapiro 1974a), but now common in Orange County, northern Westchester, and probably further up the Hudson Valley (Glassberg).

Current Status: Widespread and often very common even to Cape May, but rare in recent years in Sussex County (Wander).

Historical Status: No apparent changes.

Smith (1890): "Not rare throughout the State" {in reference to both *zabulon* and *hobomok*}.

Smith (1900–1910): "Generally distributed, but seems to be local and not common," with localities from Paterson and Staten Island to Camden and Cape May.

Comstock (1940): "Locally, throughout."

Delaware Valley (1966): "Resident." Occurs throughout but "not common in pine barrens."

Staten Island (1973): "Frequent and widespread."

New York City Area (1993): "Common and widespread."

Cape May (1993): "Common."

Habitat: An adaptable species found in parks and gardens as well as woodland edges and cuts.

Phenology: Two broods mid-May–early October. The first peaks in June, the second in August; the latter is more numerous. In Sussex County, the first brood is often rare or absent (Wander).

Caterpillar Foodplants: Purple Top *Tridens flavus*, *Eragrostis* and perhaps other, narrow-bladed grasses.

Overwintering Stage: Undetermined.

Comments: A highly sexually dimorphic species. All males are brown with large golden area on ventral wing surface. All females are dark chocolate brown (similar to the Pocahontas form of Hobomok), with pale markings and a frosted margin to the ventral wings. They are usually seen with wings closed. It is similar to Hobomok, and the two may be found together in central New Jersey in late May and June.

Aaron's Skipper, *Poanes aaroni* (Skinner, 1890)

Also listed as Saffron Skipper.

Range: Disjunct distribution along Atlantic Coast from southern New Jersey to North Carolina, in South Carolina, and in Florida; occurs on both coasts of southern New Jersey. Unconfirmed record from Brooklyn, NY (Shapiro 1974a).

Current Status: Originally described from New Jersey. Regular in salt marshes and adjacent fields on both coasts; occasionally abundant with hundreds seen in a day (Dowdell). Northern limit of range is uncertain. We do not find it on the Barnegat Bay salt marsh islands.

Historical Status: Data are inadequate to assess change, but no evidence that it has declined.

Conservation Status: This locally common species has a Natural Heritage ranking of G4/S1. Its known populations should be monitored. New Jersey has very extensive salt marsh habitat which is secure at present, but the skipper does not occur throughout the habitat.

Smith (1890): Not listed {the initial description was in 1890}.

Smith (1900): "Common," Cape May and Anglesea.

Smith (1910): "Common on the salt marshes from Tuckerton south to Cape May . . . recorded by all collectors."

Comstock (1940): "Coastal District. Salt Marshes."

Delaware Valley (1966): Not in our area, but occurs in coastal salt marshes of New Jersey, where locally common.

Staten Island (1973): Not listed.

New York City Area (1993): No records in area.

Cape May (1993): "Common."

Habitat: Primarily a salt marsh species that wanders out of marshes to adjacent dry fields, sometimes several miles inland, for nectar.

Phenology: Two broods June and August–September, rarely to early October.
Caterpillar Foodplants: Uncertain, possibly *Distichlis spicata*.
Overwintering Stage: Undetermined.

Comment: Cape May is the type locality for this species. New Jersey is probably the center of its abundance, and recently Cumberland County had the national high 4JC total (269 in 1993). A late record was one at Delmont (10/2/93; Tudor).

Broad-winged Skipper, *Poanes viator* (W. H. Edwards, 1865)

Range: Disjunct distribution from Massachusetts to northern Florida and along central Gulf Coast to Texas; also in Great Lakes region to the eastern Great Plains (Shapiro 1970b). The Coastal Plain subspecies *zizaniae* (described by Shapiro 1970a) is found throughout New Jersey.

Current Status: Local where there are Phragmites, but then often abundant. Mainly occurs on Coastal Plain, but since Phragmites are widely distributed inland, it may show up almost anywhere. Uncommon in the Piedmont. We have five Somerset records in 10 years. Rare in Sussex County, with recent records at Vernon (Wander) and Springdale (Tudor).

Historical Status: This species was clearly uncommon in northern New Jersey a century ago. Beutenmüller (1893) listed specimens from Newark, Snake Hill (Essex), and Brooklyn. Between 1890 and 1910 several new localities were added. As the aggressive Phragmites has extended its range, this species has probably increased, and it is now locally abundant along the coast. Not listed from any northwestern counties in Opler's Atlas, though now known from Sussex and Somerset Counties.

Smith (1890): Cape May, "Newark."

Smith (1900): Various localities listed from Hopatcong to Cape May.

Smith (1910): "Not uncommon at the edge of salt meadow."

Comstock (1940): "Locally, throughout . . . marshy land. Occasionally numerous in salt meadows."

Delaware Valley (1966): "Very local . . . marshes along the Delaware, but there often abundant." Recorded from Trenton Marsh (Mercer County) and in marshes from Camden southward.

Staten Island (1973): "The most abundant skipper," but local. Davis knew only one locality.

New York City Area (1993): "Abundant . . . less common inland."

Cape May (1993): "Common to abundant."

Habitat: A species of coastal habitats near *Phragmites*. Occasionally seen in gardens on Coastal Plain.

Phenology: One brood mid-June–late September, with peak abundance in early–mid-July.

Caterpillar Foodplants: Mainly on *Phragmites communis* but also on Wild Rice (*Zizania aquatica*). The subspecies *viator* is reported to use sedges (*Carex*) in Ohio (Shuey 1985; Iftner et al. 1992).

Comment: The Atlantic coast population was designated as a distinct subspecies *zizaniae* by Shapiro (1970a), with Tinicum, Philadelphia, as the type locality. The center of abundance is in southern New Jersey, and Cumberland County or Cape May often has the national high 4JC total (maximum 455 in Cape May in 1991). This is the largest of the tawny-colored skippers; when wings are folded, it reveals bold cream-colored spots on the dorsal forewing. It has a typical bobbing flight through the grass, and then frequently perches on a reed stem with its body vertical. Frequently nectars at Purple Loosestrife.

Dion Skipper, *Euphyes dion* (W. H. Edwards, 1879)

Has been referred to as Sedge Skipper.

Range: Eastern United States; disjunct distribution from Connecticut to northern Florida; also in Great Lakes region, and along the Gulf Coast; sparsely distributed over much of New Jersey, but status poorly known for most areas.

Current Status: Local in wet habitats and usually uncommon to rare. Locally common in Cape May County, with up to twenty seen in a day (Dowdell); 3–6 per day at Lakehurst. Recent records are mainly from Sussex (Springdale), Morris (Great Swamp), Ocean (Lakehurst), and Cape May Counties.

Historical Status: Always a local species. Usually seen singly. Given the large number of observers looking for butterflies, it has apparently neither increased nor decreased since 1940. However, it was apparently more rare a century ago (it was recognized as a species in 1879). It was not listed by Smith (1890) nor by Beutenmüller (1893). Recorded from most northern counties and from Burlington, Cape May, and Cumberland (Opler's Atlas) Counties.

Smith (1890): Not listed.

Smith (1900): First New Jersey record at Anglesea (July 7).

Smith (1910): Additional localities at Brookville, Lakehurst, and Browns Mills.

Comstock (1940): "Pine Barrens, Appalachian Valley." Localities include Stockholm and Great Meadows in the North and Jamesburg, Lakehurst, and Browns Mills on the Coastal Plain.

Delaware Valley (1966): "Very sporadically, in New Jersey . . . marshes . . . most numerous in Ocean and Monmouth Counties."

Staten Island (1973): Rare; collected only once in 1970–71.

New York City Area (1993): "Rare and very local resident."

Cape May (1993): "Locally common."

Habitat: Wet grasslands and meadows, marshes, bogs or fens; cuts and ditches with tall vegetation. Can be found in very small marshy areas in otherwise dry habitat.

Phenology: One brood early July–mid-August (only to mid-July in North; Cech 1993). In South, normally July 20 to Aug. 10 (Schweitzer). A Sept. 15 record from Browns Mills (Smith 1910) is aberrant.

Caterpillar Foodplants: Various sedges (*Carex* spp.) and rushes (*Scirpus* spp.). Reported on Lake-bank Sedge (*C. lacustris*) in New York (Shapiro 1974a).

Overwintering Stage: Undetermined.

Comment: There appear to be two disjunct populations, a northern one and a Pine Barrens one. Glassberg (1993b) points out both habitat and behavioral differences which suggests these could represent sibling species.

Black Dash, *Euphyes conspicua* (Edwards, 1863)

Range: Northeastern United States. Disjunct from Massachusetts to Virginia along coast and Appalachians, and southern Great Lakes region from Ohio to central Minnesota. The subspecies *conspicua* occurs throughout New Jersey except the northern coast.

Current Status: Local and usually uncommon to rare; may be locally common in wet sedgy areas in northwestern New Jersey (near Springdale, Sussex County, and Great Swamp, Morris County). Rare and local in the Coastal Plain (Schweitzer); one colony known in Cape May County (Dowdell).

Historical Status: This is a conspicuous species where it occurs, and there is no evidence of increase or decrease since the turn of the century. It has always been rare on the Coastal Plain, but has essentially disappeared from Staten Island.

Smith (1890): Recorded only from Westville by Aaron.

Smith (1900): Several localities from Hopatcong to Camden {apparently local}.

Smith (1910): Few additional localities.

Comstock (1940): "Throughout." Most locations listed are north of Fall Line.

Delaware Valley (1966): "Rare and local in Pennsylvania, more common in New Jersey."

Staten Island (1973): "Formerly widespread on the island," according to Davis (1910), but only collected once in 1970–71.

New York City Area (1993): "Local and usually uncommon . . . almost always inland."

Cape May (1993): "Locally uncommon."

Habitat: Usually in marshy or sedgy meadows or fens.

Phenology: One brood mid-June–mid-August (mainly in July).

Caterpillar Foodplants: Sedges (*Carex* spp.); in New Jersey only on Tussock Sedge (*C. stricta*).

Comment: This species is superficially similar to, but more numerous than, Dion Skipper. Often found with Mulberry Wing.

Two-spotted Skipper, *Euphyes bimacula* (Grote and Robinson, 1867)

Range: A northern species ranging from Maine to northeastern Colorado and south to central New Jersey and in the mountains to western Virginia. The subspecies *bimacula* occurs in northern, central, and southern New Jersey, but very locally.

Current Status: A very local, bog-dwelling species, that is usually uncommon. Occurs locally in Pine Barrens north of Mullica River (Schweitzer). Regular but uncommon at Lakehurst. First Cape May County record in 1993 (Dowdell). Reported from Mashipacong Bog (Wander), where it has been historically collected, and at Hutcheson Forest (6/26/86; Leck).

Historical Status: Rare and apparently local at the turn of the century; possibly more common 50 years ago, but rare and local today. The population exploded in the northeastern United States in 1968, but it has since declined. Surprisingly, Shapiro (1974a) considered it local, and "usually frequent to common" in eastern New York, including Long Island, but it is rare in southeastern New York today. It has apparently declined recently in Ohio (Iftner et al. 1992). Its disappearance from much of northern New Jersey is apparently part of a regional decline (Schweitzer).

Conservation Status: Should be considered THREATENED due to its limited and declining habitat. There are few known populations, and a survey of suitable bogs will probably reveal some additional colonies. Natural Heritage ranking is G4/S3.

Smith (1890): "A specimen labeled 'N.J.' is in Mr. Aaron's collection; source unknown."

Smith (1900): No additional information. "New Jersey is well within the range of this species."

Smith (1910): Additional localities at Oak Ridge (June 26–July 3) and Lakehurst (June 27).

Comstock (1940): "Pine Barrens, Appalachian Valley. Swampy spots," recorded from Mashipacong, Greenwood Lakes, Ogdensburg, Stockholm, and Oak Ridge in the North and only from Lakehurst on the Coastal Plain.

Delaware Valley (1966): "Very local" with records from Camden, Gloucester, Burlington, and Mercer Counties.

Staten Island (1973): Taken once in a bog 7/12/71, "no old records."

New York City Area (1993): "Reported very rarely from northwestern New

Jersey. Regional influx in summer of 1968. Nearest active colony is in central New Jersey."

Cape May (1993): "Uncommon."

Habitat: Apparently narrow requirements for bogs, fens, or sedge meadows.

Phenology: One brood mid-June–mid-July.

Caterpillar Foodplants: Various Sedges. Hairy-fruited Sedge (*Carex trichocarpa*) is used in New York (Shapiro 1974a). In Ohio, always associated with Tussock Sedge (*C. stricta*; Iftner et al. 1992). Hosts in New Jersey need documentation.

Comment: This Skipper is rare over much of its range. Simmons and Andersen (1970) encountered one or two individuals in five Maryland counties, but reported that they were unsuccessful in finding colonies, nor have we seen more than two individuals at a time at Lakehurst. When we observed it at Lakehurst, it had a tendency to sit conspicuously perched on a plant stalk for minutes at a time and then to disappear into the sedges, particularly during cloudy moments, only to reappear after 15–30 min.

Dun Skipper, *Euphyes vestris* (Harris, 1862)

Listed as *Euphyes ruricola* in various sources; *ruricola* has priority by two pages, but there is doubt as to what species that name applies.

Range: Nova Scotia to Manitoba, south to southern Florida and eastern Texas. The subspecies *metacomet* occurs throughout New Jersey.

Current Status: Widespread, often abundant in early summer, but uncommon in late summer.

Historical Status: Either no change or an increase in the present century. Was not listed for most southern counties (Opler's Atlas).

Smith (1890): Few records. Caldwell, "Newark," and "taken by Mr. Aaron."

Smith (1900): "Quite generally distributed" localities from Hopatcong to Camden.

Smith (1910): "Throughout the State from June to August, records ranging from Hopatcong to Cape May."

Comstock (1940): "Throughout."

Delaware Valley (1966): "Common . . . general, rare in pine barrens."

Staten Island (1973): "Infrequent."

New York City Area (1993): "Common inland."

Cape May (1993): "Uncommon."

Habitat: Very variable, including densely vegetated, brushy moist meadows, dry fields, forest edges, and cuts. Tolerant of disturbed habitats and often visits gardens.

Phenology: In South, two broods mid-May–early July, late August–late September. One or two in North May 29–Sept. 30.

Caterpillar Foodplants: Sedges (*Carex* spp.) are probably the only host.

Comment: Frequently seen nectaring in stands of Common Milkweed (*Asclepias syriaca*). Similar species include Northern Broken-Dash and Little Glassywing.

Dusted Skipper, *Atrytonopsis hianna* (Scudder, 1868)

Range: Southern Vermont to the Dakotas and eastern Wyoming, south to northern Florida and Mississippi Valley. Disjunct populations occur in Michigan, northern and southern Great Plains. Occurs in northeastern, north-central, and central New Jersey. The subspecies *hianna* occurs in New Jersey.

Current Status: Early spring, local; not common; current status unknown. Fairly common and widespread in Northwest (Wander). One Lakehurst record

(6/25; Tudor). Recently found in Cape May County, where fairly common (up to ten per day at Dennisville), but highly local (Dowdell).

Historical Status: Unless we assume that early collectors shunned the barren habitats where this and the Cobweb Skipper occur in the spring, it appears that this uncommon, local species has probably increased in the present century. Beutenmüller (1893) reported only one New York area record, an unlabeled specimen of S. L. Elliot, and mentioned a record from eastern Long Island. Shown from Sussex, Warren, Union, Mercer, Ocean, Burlington, Camden, Gloucester, and Cumberland Counties (Opler's Atlas).

Smith (1890): Not listed.

Smith (1900): Recorded from New York, but not yet from New Jersey, although it is within its range.

Smith (1910): Specimens from Iona and Browns Mills.

Comstock (1940): "Pine Barrens" from Lakewood, Browns Mills, and Iona.

Delaware Valley (1966): Uncommon and local. General in the Pine Barrens.

Staten Island (1973): "Seen on serpentine-limonite barrens . . . probably frequent."

New York City Area (1993): "Local and usually uncommon."

Cape May (1993): Listed as a "species to look for."

Habitat: Occupies oak-pine scrub and sandy barren areas, where it is seen in open glades, sandy roads, cuts, along edges, and on dry hillsides.

Phenology: One brood late May–early June (very short flight period).

Caterpillar Foodplants: Beardgrasses, Little Bluestem (*Andropogon scoparius*); also Big Bluestem (*A. gerardi*).

Comment: Often found in same area as Cobweb Skipper, emerging as the latter is declining, but it is much rarer and more local (Shapiro 1966).

Pepper and Salt Skipper, *Ambylscirtes hegon* (Scudder, 1864)

Often listed as *samoset*.

Range: Nova Scotia to Manitoba, south in Appalachians to northern Georgia and Texas; occurs in extreme northwestern New Jersey.

Current Status: No recent New Jersey records until 1993. Not uncommon, but highly local, in late spring in Stokes State Forest–High Point State Park, with up to twelve per day (Wander). Found also at Hibernia, Morris County (1995; Barber and Elia).

Historical Status: It has probably always been a highly local and uncommon species. It may have been overlooked in the past, and apparently ranged more widely. It was recorded as far south as the Great Swamp (Comstock 1940). It may have suffered from pesticide spraying; its disappearance in western Maryland coincided with Gypsy Moth spraying (Pavulaan, in litt.).

Conservation Status: This species is marginal in New Jersey, where its local population is vulnerable. Surveys may reveal that its range is more extensive in the forested areas of the Northwest. Its Natural Heritage ranking is G5/S2–3.

Smith (1890–1910): New Jersey is within its range, but no specimens yet taken.

Comstock (1940): Very brief entry. Ogdensburg and Green Village {Great Swamp}.

Delaware Valley (1966): Not listed.

Staten Island (1973): Not listed.

New York City Area (1993): "Recently located in Sussex County, NJ."

Cape May (1993): Not listed.

Habitat: Openings and cuts in coniferous or mixed woodlands; often at edges of bogs and along roads where Blue Iris (*Iris versicolor*) and Wild Geranium

(*Geranium maculatum*) are found. Absent from the Coastal Plain throughout its range (Shapiro 1974a).

Phenology: One brood mid-May–early July. Partially double brooded in central New York (Shapiro 1974a).

Caterpillar Foodplants: Kentucky Blue Grass (*Poa pratensis*; Klots 1966), species of *Sorghastrum* spp. and on *Uniola latifolia*.

Comments: To be looked for in wooded areas of northwestern New Jersey. The life history of this species is poorly known. Klots (1966) provided the first modern description of the larval stage.

Common Roadside-Skipper, *Amblyscirtes vialis* (W. H. Edwards, 1862)

Sometimes referred to as Roadside Skipper.

Range: Disjunct distribution from Nova Scotia to British Columbia, south to central South Carolina, Texas, and central California; shown throughout New Jersey except extreme south (Opler and Krizek 1984), but this is misleading, because it is rare and local. Occurs throughout New York, including Orange County, but not Rockland County or Staten Island (Shapiro 1974a).

Current Status: Rare and apparently local; current status unknown. Recent specimens from Hamilton Twp, Atlantic County (Dowdell), and Downe Twp, Cumberland County (May 1989; Schweitzer). Two 1994 records: Lakehurst (May 7; Cech, photographed), and Newton (in June; Wanders). A species of serpentine barrens, but apparently formerly also in the Pine Barrens, where now rare and sporadic.

Historical Status: Apparently slightly more common in past, although Smith's (1890) statement of "locally common throughout" is contradicted by his subsequent reports, and Comstock (1940) does not indicate status. Many years passed without any records. Was recorded near Batsto in 1970s (Schweitzer). Rutgers Collection has eight specimens, including three from Lakewood (5/22/1907).

Conservation Status: Current status is really unknown. There are very few sightings, and these are from scattered locations. Its Natural Heritage ranking is G5/S3–4. Vigilance is required to detect this species, and monitoring of its known sites may reveal resident colonies.

Smith (1890): "Locally common throughout the State. Not on the Newark list."

Smith (1900): "Local, early in the season"; localities given are Clementon and Westville.

Smith (1910): Additional localities at Newfoundland and Lakehurst.

Comstock (1940): "Throughout. Moist roadsides." Additional localities at Ogdensburg, Jamesburg, Lakewood.

Delaware Valley (1966): "Uncommon . . . local," recorded from Camden, Mercer, Burlington, and Gloucester Counties.

Staten Island (1973): Not listed.

New York City Area (1993): "Declining . . . exceedingly rare in this area."

Cape May (1993): Not recorded, but listed as a "species to look for."

Habitat: Varied habitats, including glades, edges, and cuts in Pine Barrens or deciduous forests. Also occurs on serpentine barrens.

Phenology: One brood mid-May–early June.

Caterpillar Foodplants: Grasses—*Poa, Avena, Agrostis, Cynodon*, and *Uniola*.

Comments: It is now very rare, considering the number of field observers combing New Jersey. Likely to be seen on the ground on a dirt road or along a forest trail.

Where to Find It: At present no reliable sites in New Jersey, but should be looked for on dirt roads near Lakehurst and Lakewood. Has recently been found both in Sussex and Ocean Counties as single individuals. This species is fairly common in May in the serpentine barrens (Nottingham County Park) in southeastern Pennsylvania.

Eufala Skipper, *Lerodea eufala* (W. H. Edwards, 1869)

Range: Resident from coastal South Carolina to Florida and across southern United States to central California. Also in Cuba and throughout Central and South America. Experiences late summer population expansion occasionally to the Great Lakes and North Carolina. Rare in Maryland (first record in 1973; Simmons and Andersen 1978a). Now rarely reaches New Jersey, although it may have been overlooked in past.

Current Status: Vagrant. First state record (specimen) Sept. 18, 1991 (Dowdell), and another photographed (9/19/91; Tudor, Cech, Lawrenson) at Cape May Point. Recorded at Cape May Point in 1993 (MG).

Smith (1890–1910): Not listed.

Comstock (1940): Not listed.

Delaware Valley (1966): Not listed.

Staten Island (1973): Not listed.

New York City Area (1993): Not listed.

Cape May (1993): A straggler in September.

Habitat: Disturbed areas, grassy cuts, and edges of southern woodlands. Further south occurs in salt marshes and behind coastal dunes (Pavulaan).

Phenology: Year round in Florida, but two broods in Georgia (Opler and Krizek 1984), spring, and late summer. Vagrants arrive in New Jersey by late summer.

Larval Host: Sorghum (*Sorghum* spp.) and Sugar Cane (*Saccharum officinalis*).

Comment: A very few recent records. This species must be distinguished from Tawny-edged Skipper. Distinguishing marks are apparent in folded position, but the ventral surface (closed position) is more challenging.

Twin-spot Skipper, *Oligoria maculata* (Edwards, 1865)

Range: North Carolina to southern Florida, west to Texas; isolated records shown near Philadelphia and Camden (Opler and Krizek 1984). First Maryland record was in 1979 (Simmons and Andersen 1978c). Record from Albany area of New York is hypothetical (Shapiro 1974a); recorded from Massachusetts (Shapiro 1966).

Current Status: Accidental. Two Camden specimens were mentioned by Smith (1910) and Comstock (1940) but not by Shapiro (1966). Otherwise we know of no New Jersey records.

Historical Status: Only recorded once. In addition to the Camden and Delaware specimens noted below, Opler's Atlas shows only two Maryland records and a hypothetical Connecticut record, north of its range in coastal North Carolina.

Smith (1890–1900): Not listed.

Smith (1910): Two specimens at Camden, July 15.

Comstock (1940): On supplemental list based on two specimens from Camden {both apparently taken the same day}.

Delaware Valley (1966): One specimen from Marcus Hook, DE. No mention of the above Camden specimens.

Staten Island (1973): Not mentioned.

New York City Area (1993): Not listed.

Cape May (1993): Not listed.

Habitat: This is a species of flat pine woodlands and coastal swamps of the Southeast.

Phenology: In southeastern U.S. has spring (April–May) and summer (July–August) broods.

Caterpillar Foodplants: Grasses.

Comments: The occurrence of this species in New Jersey requires verification. It is common as far north as South Carolina. Unfortunately, Scott (1986) called this the Three-spot Skipper, a name most other authors apply to a tropical species, *Cymaenes tripunctus*, which reaches southern Florida.

Brazilian Skipper [Canna Skipper], *Calpodes ethlius* (Stoll, 1782)

Range: A tropical species ranging from southern Florida and southern Texas through the West Indies and Central America to Argentina. Map in Opler and Krizek (1984) shows it irruptive to northeastern, central, and southern New Jersey. In New York, recorded only from Long Island (1911, 1912) and Albany (1893; Shapiro 1974a). First Maryland record in 1956 (Simmons and Andersen 1978c).

Current Status: Uncertain whether it always arrives as a natural vagrant or has been human assisted. Few recent records. Recent specimen from Cape May Point, Oct. 4, 1991 (Dowdell), and photographed at Goshen (10/15/92, Suttons).

Historical Status: Apparently always a vagrant, but may have reached our area more frequently in past, perhaps associated with inadequately controlled fruit shipments from the tropics. Shapiro (1966) mentioned at least three specimen records from Salem and Camden Counties, and reported sight records from Cape May. Opler's Atlas shows records for Salem, Gloucester, and Burlington Counties. Apparently bred on Long Island in 1911, where it was reported as a pest on *Canna* (Engelhardt 1912). A northward invasion in the 1930s reached at least Virginia.

Smith (1890–1910): Not listed.

Comstock (1940): No New Jersey records, "but taken at several places on Long Island in 1911."

Delaware Valley (1966): "Quite rare, mainly in the Coastal Plain, but very sporadic," with single specimens from Salem County (Salem), Camden County (Camden, Mount Ephraim), and observations at Cape May.

Staten Island (1973): Not mentioned.

New York City Area (1993): "A South Florida resident which occasionally makes its way northward." In early 1900s, briefly established on Long Island.

Cape May (1993): A "stray."

Habitat: The natural habitat of this species is not clear. In the West Indies and Florida it is mainly a "garden" species, occurring where ornamental cannas are grown (Brown and Heineman 1972; Opler and Krizek 1984; Smith et al. 1994).

Phenology: Recorded August–September.

Caterpillar Foodplants: *Canna*.

Comment: Reported to be destructive to Canna (Comstock 1940). The Miami Parks Authority stopped growing cannas because of their vulnerability to this insect (Smith et al. 1994). This butterfly is reported to be crepuscular.

Salt Marsh Skipper, *Panoquina panoquin* (Scudder, 1864)

Range: Long Island, NY, to southern Florida and Louisiana, including eastern and southwestern New Jersey (coastal areas).

Current Status: Widespread but usually uncommon (though sometimes abundant) in salt marshes and nearby beaches and fields on both coasts. Populations may be reduced by mosquito control programs in the salt marshes.

Historical Status: It has been considered a common salt marsh species by all authors, hence no apparent change in status. Despite the extensive salt marshes of New York City, Long Island, and northern New Jersey, it was not recorded by Beutenmüller (1893).

Smith (1890): Atlantic City; not on "Newark" list. {Probably few collectors visited this habitat.}

Smith (1900): "Very common in the salt meadows . . . Atlantic City . . . to Cape May Pt."

Smith (1910): "Common on the salt marshes from Tuckerton, south to Cape May . . . taken by all collectors."

Comstock (1940): "Coastal District. Salt Marshes . . . common in salt meadows."

Delaware Valley (1966): "Occasionally common" in salt and brackish marshes of Delaware Bay.

Staten Island (1973): "Infrequent."

New York City Area (1993): "Occurs in salt marsh . . . rarely occurs far from coast."

Cape May (1993): "Common."

Habitat: Salt marshes. It appears to show a preference for mixed marsh vegetation rather than for islands with predominantly Salt Marsh Cordgrass (*Spartina alterniflora*), and this is consistent with its presumed hosts. Its ecology remains to be studied.

Phenology: On Staten Island, two broods, early July and August–September. Elsewhere, June–September. Shapiro (1966) lists mid-July, late June, and possibly May.

Caterpillar Foodplants: Probably Spike-grass (*Distichlis spicata*). Reported on *Scirpus* (Shapiro 1966).

Comment: This and other salt marsh butterflies were probably greatly reduced in some areas by the ditching of salt marshes as well as annual spraying for control of the Salt Marsh Mosquito (*Aedes sollicitans*), and have probably benefited from Integrated Pest Management (IPM) programs, which rely less on pesticides. New Jersey often has the national 4JC high, with 691 recorded on the Galloway Township 1992 count. This species frequently seeks flowers in areas adjacent to the salt marsh, including Pickerel Weed (*Pontaderia*) in ponds and milkweeds (*Asclepias* spp.) in fields.

Ocola Skipper [Long-winged Skipper], *Panoquina ocola* (W. H. Edwards, 1863)

Range: A tropical species ranging from South Carolina, Florida, and Texas to Argentina. Frequent immigrant northward to Virginia, occasionally New Jersey, and rarely southern New England.

Current Status: Rare visitor from South. Very few late summer records in 1993 and 1994, but widespread in 1995, with the biggest influx yet recorded. Mainly confined to Coastal Plain but records from Morristown area (Glassberg) and Orange County, NY (1995; Yrizarry). In 1995 it reached Brooklyn, Central Park, and even Massachusetts. Not usually found north of Philadelphia, but should be watched for in late summer.

Historical Status: Difficult to determine. It was obviously rare before 1890, with two "invasions" in 1896 and 1899, and then became rare again, with only a few records before 1940. Records from Bowne (8/21/37 and 9/12/37) suggest an invasion in 1937. However, Shapiro (1966) considered it a frequent visitor to both Philadelphia and southern New Jersey. It then was apparently very rare again until 1993–94.

Smith (1890): "Salem, rare—Aaron."

Photo 17. Ocola Skipper is a rare late summer visitor from the southern United States. A vagrant until recently, it became increasingly common in the early 1990s, with an invasion in 1995. Note the long forewings that extend well beyond the hindwing, giving this a characteristic shape. (Photographed on our *Buddleia*, September 1995, by Michael Gochfeld).

Smith (1900): Reported from Camden, Sept. 1899, as "common, never before seen (Carney)," and also from Staten Island (Davis).

Smith (1910): No additional records.

Comstock (1940): No status given. Localities include Lakehurst, Atlantic City, Salem, and Camden, and a Delaware Valley location, Bowne (Hunterdon).

Delaware Valley (1966): "Regular immigrant . . . sometimes common . . . south of the Fall Line." "Common in Tinicum Reserve most seasons." "General from Camden and south edge of pine barrens southward," but more numerous to west of Delaware Bay.

Staten Island (1973): Recorded in 1896 by Davis, and in 1970 and 1971, but "no evidence of breeding locally."

New York City Area (1993): Staten Island, fall records in 1896, 1970, and 1971, September 1980, and in 1990; central New Jersey in 1991. {Beutenmüller (1893) reported a single, unlabeled Elliot specimen from New York City area.}

Cape May (1993): "Stray" first county record 10/2/93 (P. Sutton).

Habitat: In southern states, often in wet open areas, but also on flowering hedges and gardens. In New Jersey most often recorded from gardens.

Phenology: Late August–October, occasionally to early November.

Caterpillar Foodplants: Various marsh grasses.

Comments: Adults particularly attracted to white Orpine (*Sedum*) flowers at Cape May. This skipper is readily recognized by its very long forewings, which are unmarked below. This species was presumably named after Ocala, Florida, hence its English name should probably be Ocala Skipper. See photo 17.

Gazetteer of Butterfly Locations in New Jersey

The locations indicated on these maps represent those mentioned in the historical publications as well as in the recent literature. Those marked with an asterisk were apparently favorite collecting sites reported by Smith and by Comstock. There are many other suitable butterfly sites not specifically identified in this book that are not shown on these maps.

Due to scale, some sites could not be identified uniquely. The same letter pair may be used more than once in different counties, and locations that straddle county lines may be indicated for both counties.

If you do not know the county for a location, check in the index where county is given in parentheses for each locality mentioned in the text.

Several publications are particularly useful for locating butterfly sites.

Boyle, William J., Jr. 1986. *A Guide to Bird Finding in New Jersey*. Rutgers University Press, New Brunswick.
Cape May Bird Observatory/New Jersey Audubon Society. 1995. "Birding and Butterflying Map to Cape May County." Cape May Point, N.J.
Department of Environmental Protection. No date. *Guide to Wildlife Management Areas*. Trenton, N.J. Lists 50 Wildlife Management Areas (WMAs).
Department of Transportation. 1991. *New Jersey Place Names*. Trenton, N.J.
Glassberg, Jeffrey. 1993. *Butterflies Through Binoculars*. New York: Oxford University Press.

Codes

NWR = National Wildlife Refuge
SF = State Forest
WMA = NJ Wildlife Management Area
* A traditional collecting site reported often by Smith or Comstock

Sussex

AN	Andover	MA	Mashipacong Lake and Bog
BR	Brighton	NO	Normanock
BS	Bear Swamp WMA	*NT	Newton
FF	Franklin Furnace	*OG	Ogdensburg
HM	Hamburg Mountain	SD	Springdale
*HO	Hopatcong	SF	Stokes State Forest
HP	High Point State Park	SM	Sunrise Mountain
LH	Lake Hopatcong	SP	Sparta
*LL	Lake Lackawanna	ST	Stockholm

Figure 12. Appendix A: Gazetteer locations for northern New Jersey.

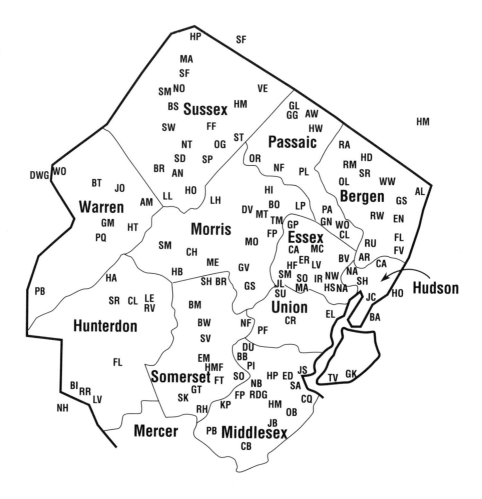

Passaic

AW	Awosting	HW	Hewitt
CL	Clifton	NF	Newfoundland
* GG	Greenwood Lake and Glens	OR	Oak Ridge
* GL	Greenwood Lakes	* PA	Paterson
GN	Great Notch	PL	Pompton Lakes and Pompton

Bergen

AR	Arlington and North Arlington	PP	Palisade Park
EN	Englewood (including Palisades)	RA	Ramapo
FL	Fort Lee	RM	Ramsey
FV	Fairview	RU	Rutherford
GS	Greenbrook Sanctuary	SR	Saddle River and Upper Saddle River
HD	Hillsdale		
OL	Oakland	* WW	Westwood

Warren

AM	Allamuchy SF	HA	Hackettstown
BT	Blairstown	JO	Johnsonberg
DWG	Delaware Water Gap	WO	Worthington SF
GM	Great Meadows		

Morris

CH	Chester	LP	Lincoln Park
*DV	Dover	MO	Morristown (includes
	Frelinghuysen Arboretum		Frelinghuysen Arboretum)
	(Morristown) (see MO)	MT	Mount Tabor
GS	Great Swamp NWR	*SM	Schooley Mountain
GV	Green Village	TM	Troy Meadows
*HI	Hibernia		

Essex

BV	Belleville	LV	Livingston
*CA	Caldwell	MA	Maplewood
ER	Eagle Rock	MD	Montclair
GP	Great Piece Meadows	ML	Millburn
HA	Harrison	NW	Newark
HF	Hemlock Falls	NA	Newark Airport
HS	Hillside	*SM	Orange Mountains
IR	Irvington		= South Mountain Reserve

Hudson

BA	Bayonnne	*JC	Jersey City
CA	Carlstadt	SH	Snake Hill
HO	Hoboken (includes Liberty State Park)		

Hunterdon

BI	Bull's Island	LV	Lambertville
CL	Clinton	RR	Raven Rock
FL	Flemington	RV	Round Valley Reservoir
HA	Hampton	SR	Spruce Run Reservoir
LB	Lebanon		

Somerset

BM	Bedminster	NP	North Plainfield
BR	Basking Ridge	RH	Rocky Hill
BW	Bridgewater	SH	Scherman-Hoffman Sanctuary
EM	East Millstone		and Bernardsville
FR	Franklin Park	SK	Skillman
FT	Franklin Township	SO	Somerset
GT	Griggstown	SV	Somerville
HMF	Hutcheson Forest		
KP	Kendall Park		
	(center of Raritan Canal Count)		

Union

CR	Cranford	PL	Plainfield
*EL	Elizabeth	SU	Summit

Middlesex

HM	Helmetta	PB	Plainsboro
IS	Iselin	PI	Piscataway, including
JA	Jamesburg		Rutgers Busch Campus
KP	Kendall Park	RDG	Rutgers Display Gardens
NB	New Brunswick		at Cook College
OB	Old Bridge	SA	South Amboy

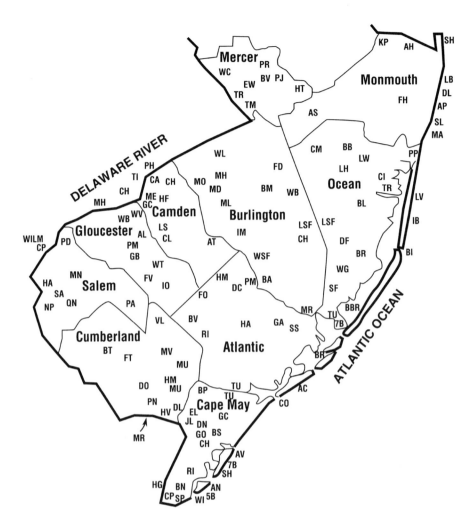

Figure 13. Appendix A: Gazetteer locations for southern New Jersey.

Mercer

BV	Bakersville	TM	Trenton Marsh
EW	Ewingville	TR	Trenton
PJ	Princeton Junction	WC	Washington Crossing
PR	Princeton		

Monmouth

AH	Atlantic Highlands	LB	Long Branch
AP	Asbury Park	MA	Manasquan
AS	Assunpink WMA	SH	Sandy Hook (Gateway National
DL	Deal		Recreation Area)
FH	Freehold	SL	Spring Lake
KP	Keyport		

Ocean

7B	Seven Bridges Road	BR	5 mi west of Barnegat–Brookville
BB	Butterfly Bogs WMA	CI	Cattus Island Park
BBA	Barnegat Bay (extensive	CM	Collier's Mills
	salt marshes)	DF	Dwarf forest, Pine Barrens
BI	Barnegat Inlet		(Route 72)
BL	Bamber Lake	IB	Island Beach

*LH	Lakehurst	SF	Stafford Forge
LSF	Lebanon State Forest	TR	Toms River
LV	Lavallette	TU	Tuckerton
LW	Lakewood	WG	Warren Grove
PP	Point Pleasant		

Burlington

BA	Batsto	*ML	Medford Lakes
*BM	Browns Mills	MM	Mount Misery
*CH	Chatsworth	MO	Moorestown
FD	Fort Dix	MR	Mullica River
IM	Indian Mills	WSF	Wharton SF
LSF	Lebanon State Forest	WB	White's Bog
MD	Medford	WL	Willingboro
MH	Mount Holly		

Atlantic

*AC	Atlantic City	HA	Hamilton Twp
BR	Brigantine NWR	HM	Hammonton
BV	Buena Vista	PM	Pleasant Mills
CO	Great Egg Inlet and Mullica River	RI	Richland
DC	DaCosta	SS	Stockton State College
FO	Folsom	TU	Tuckahoe WMA
GA	Galloway		

Camden

AT	Atco	GC	Gloucester City
*CA	Camden	HF	Haddonfield
CH	Cherry Hill	LS	Laurel Springs
*CL	Clementon	ME	Mount Ephraim

Gloucester

AL	Almonessen	PM	Pitman
FV	Franklinville	WB	Woodbury
GB	Glassboro	WT	Williamstown
IO	Iona	WV	Westville

Salem

CP	Carney's Point	PA	Palatine
HA	Harrisonville	PD	Pedricktown
MN	Mannington Marsh	QU	Quinton
NP	Salem Nuclear Plant	SA	Salem

Cumberland

BT	Bridgeton	MR	Maurice River area
DL	Delmont	MU	Manumuskin
DO	Downe	MV	Millville
FT	Fairton	PN	Port Norris
HV	Heislerville WMA	VL	Vineland

Cape May

5B	Five Mile Beach	BS	Beaver Swamp
7B	Seven Mile Beach	CH	Cape May Court House
AN	Anglesea	CP	Cape May Point
AV	Avalon	DN	Dennisville
BN	Beanery (Cape May)	EL	Eldora
BP	Belleplain SF	GC	Great Cedar Swamp

Cape May (*continued*)

GO	Goshen	SP	Cape May Point State Park and Hawk Watch
HG	Higbee Beach (Cape May)		
JL	Jakes Landing	TU	Tuckahoe WMA
RI	Rio Grande	WI	Wildwood
SH	Stone Harbor		

Outside New Jersey

Staten Island

FW	Fort Wadsworth	*TV	Tottenville
GK	Great Kills		

Brooklyn / Queens

CA	Canarsie (Brooklyn)	FT	Fort Tilden (Queens)
FL	Flushing (Queens)	JB	Jamaica Bay

Manhattan

CP	Central Park	RP	Riverside Park

Long Island

RH	Riverhead (Suffolk)

Orange County

SF	Sterling Forest	SH	Stanhope

Rockland County

BM	Bear Mountain	HM	Hook Mountain

Pennsylvania

CH	Chester	NH	New Hope (Bucks County)
MH	Marcus Hook	PH	Philadelphia
MO	Monroe (suburb NE of Philadelphia), Cheltenham Twp	PO	Poconos
		TI	Tinicum

APPENDIX B

Glossary of Terms

The definitions given in this glossary are only for technical terms used in this book. There are many technical terms applied to the anatomy, biochemistry, and physiology of butterflies which are not defined here. See glossary in Opler and Krizek (1984) and Scott (1986) for additional terms. In addition to the terms defined below, there are definitions in the sections on "Status and Distribution" and "Butterfly Conservation."

aberration: a butterfly specimen showing a distinct color, shape, or pattern that differs noticeably from the normal pattern for the population. It is more extreme than normal variation. Some aberrations are genetically determined, and others are caused by conditions during development. Some recur from time to time and others are unique. Many were given "scientific" names by early collectors.

abundance: the number of individuals present at any one time.

alkaloids: a general term for many of the plant chemicals that protect some plants against some herbivores. Caterpillars of some species can tolerate these chemicals and store them in their bodies. The chemicals may have distasteful or toxic properties that render the caterpillars and the resulting adults unpalatable or noxious (see *palatability spectrum*).

allochronic: two genders, morphs, or species which fly at different times with little or no overlap between their flight periods.

allopatric (allopatry): two forms, subspecies, species, etc., whose ranges do not overlap. When two forms are allopatric, it is impossible to determine whether they interbreed freely in nature, hence whether or not they are conspecific.

aposematic: warning coloration of distasteful, unpalatable or toxic organisms. Bright colors and conspicuous patterns reinforce a predator's learning that this species should not be eaten.

authority: the name of the author(s) who described and named the species or subspecies; often listed after the scientific name.

Batesian mimicry: the close resemblance of a palatable species to an unpalatable one, thereby protecting it from predation.

biennialism: requiring two years to complete the life cycle. May result in adults flying only in alternate years.

biodiversity: the variety and number of different life forms (normally given as the number of species in an area).

biological species concept: the belief that species can be defined by their reproductive interactions where they are in contact. Two populations that interbreed freely and produce offspring with high viability and fecundity are considered the same species. If the two populations are unable to mate for anatomical, behavioral, or biochemical reasons, or if their offspring are at a disadvantage, they are said to be reproductively isolated and therefore are considered separate species.

bivoltine: a phenology pattern characterized by two periods of adult emergence during a season.

brood: a single generation of a butterfly during which the adults have a more or less synchronous emergence.

canalization: the opposite of plasticity; the fixation of development in a particular character so that it is not vulnerable to changing environmental conditions. Thus polyphenism occurs in characters that are not canalized.

chrysalis: the pupal stage of a butterfly.

cladistics: a formalized study of systematics, which requires that relationshpis be defined by shared characteristics that are derived rather than primitive. Cladists avoid making a priori judgments about the importance of any particular character.

classification: the product of taxonomy; the organization of organisms according to some method or plan, usually reflecting their known or presumed evolutionary relationships. It is an orderly arrangement of organisms, either on the basis of their overall similarity (*phenetic* classification using *numerical taxonomy*) or on the basis of their presumed relationships (based on *phylogenetic systematics* or *cladistics* or on *evolutionary systematics*).

cline: a gradual change in size, color, or some physiologic function, as one goes from north to south, from east to west, or up or down a mountain.

colony: a term loosely applied to a local population of butterflies that persists at one location for a number of years.

congeneric: two species that are assigned to the same genus.

conspecific: used to refer to two forms, races, or subspecies that are believed to belong to the same species, usually based on their ability to interbreed where they come in contact.

crypsis: camouflage.

cryptic species: a less desirable synonym for "sibling species."

cuts: a linear open habitat through woodland such as a powerline cut, railroad line (active or abandoned), a firebreak, or dirt road.

description: the process of identifying and naming a species or subspecies new to science. It must meet certain requirements in order to achieve recognition.

diapause: a delay in the normal developmental cycle of a butterfly, usually in response to changing day length or other climatic events. Diapause can occur at any life stage.

dichromism: the presence of two or more distinct color forms.

dimorphism: a situation where the members of a species, subspecies, or population have two distinctive forms which may differ in size, color, pattern, or some other characteristic. Where males and females differ in size or appearance, this is termed sexual dimorphism.

disjunct: referring to distributions where there are one or more gaps in a range, leaving populations that are not in contact with other populations of the species.

distractive pattern: a pattern that can suddenly be revealed when a butterfly takes flight and shows a conspicuous color patch or wing bar that may confuse or frighten a predator.

diversity: can refer to species (the presence of a large number of species in an area), plant hosts, habitats, etc.

ecdysis: the shedding of skin by a caterpillar.

eclosion: the emergence of the adult butterfly from the chrysalis.

ecotypes: two forms which differ ecologically, such as the upland and marsh populations of Baltimore Checkerspot.

emigration: a long-distance movement of individuals out of an area in one direction. The same individuals do not return again.

endangered: a rare and local species or population that is likely to disappear in the foreseeable future without some intervention.

evolutionary systematics: the study of the relationships among organisms which distinguishes among or weights different characteristics or adaptations, rather than assuming that all characters have equivalent weight or meaning.

extinct: a species that no longer survives anywhere. In North America, only one full species, the Xerces Blue, is known to merit this dubious distinction, although others such as the Uncomphagre Fritillary and perhaps Mitchell's Satyr may be approaching that condition.

extirpated: a species which has become extinct in a geographic region (such as a state) but still survives in other places.

Fall Line: a line running from northeast to southwest, roughly from Perth Amboy to Trenton, separating the Coastal Plain from the Piedmont.

flight period: the time of year during which the adult butterfly can be found.

fragmentation: referring to habitat where once continuous stands of fields or forest have been broken up by any discontinuity, usually caused by agriculture or urban development, leaving small islands of original vegetation which may be too small to support viable populations of certain butterfly species.

genitalia: the structures of the male and female butterfly used for mating and insemination. Often the structure of these organs holds clues to the relationships or differences among highly similar related species. The distinctive genitalic structure of closely related species may serve to prevent their interbreeding.

genotype: the genetic makeup of an individual.

geographic isolation: a geographic or spatial barrier that separates two populations for a long period of time, allowing them to accumulate mutational differences that may lead to their being considered two separate species.

hibernation: the period of dormancy during the winter which corresponds to a diapause in the life cycle. Metabolic processes slow nearly to a halt and biochemical changes take place to protect tissues from the effects of freezing.

Holarctic: The faunal region comprising the North Temperate and Arctic regions of both North America and Eurasia.

ICZN: abbreviation applied to the International Code on Zoological Nomenclature and to the International Commission on Zoological Nomenclature (see below).

imago: the adult butterfly.

immigration: the periodic movement into the state of butterflies from another region; for example, the annual immigration of southern species to southern New Jersey.

industrial melanism: the evolution of dark coloration of moths and butterflies living in industrial areas. The darker individuals are better camouflaged in the sooty environs, and therefore experience lower mortality and higher reproductive output.

instar: as the developing larva grows, it periodically sheds its skin, passing through five stages or instars before pupating.

intergradation (see also *secondary contact*): where two subspecies of a single species are in contact, interbreeding can occur, resulting in intermediate individuals.

International Code on Zoological Nomenclature: the document that states the principles and laws regarding the scientific names of animals. Often abbreviated ICZN.

International Commission on Zoological Nomenclature: the body responsible for the standardization of the scientific names of animals and for implementing and revising the

International Code. The abbreviation ICZN sometimes applies to the Code and sometimes to the Commission.

introgression: a genetic term. Where two populations come in contact and interbreed, genes from one population eventually become part of the other population.

irruptive: species that periodically invades from an adjacent or distant area; they occur in New Jersey only intermittently. Most of these species invade NJ from the south or west.

lek: refers to a polygynous mating system in which groups of males display to each other on small clumped territories, and wait for females to approach and select one of them. In birds, the common display arena is referred to as "the lek."

lumper: a taxonomist who calls attention to the similarities among different taxa (species, genera, families) by combining them under one name. This is usually accomplished in the course of a revision.

mark-release-recapture (MRR) techniques: butterflies are captured at one time period, marked, and then recaptured or resighted at a second time period (usually 1–7 days later). This allows an estimate of the initial population size.

melanism (see also *industrial melanism*). Butterflies with excessively dark pigmentation.

mesic: refers to habitats that are neither wetlands nor arid, but have a moderate degree of moisture.

metapopulation: applied to a group of populations that have a slight exchange of individuals. This is becoming an increasingly important concept in conservation biology. If one of the populations becomes extinct, its area may be repopulated or colonized by individuals from another population of the same metapopulation.

migration: a long-range movement from one location to another, and often back again. To distinguish this from "emigration," it is customary to consider migration a two-directional phenomenon.

mimetic: a pattern that is similar to or "mimics" the pattern of another butterfly, presumably to confer protection.

monophagy: a species that feeds on a single host plant.

monophyletic: two taxa that share a common ancestor.

morphs: multiple forms of the same species, as, for example, the white female morph of the Clouded and Orange Sulphurs or the black female morph of the Tiger Swallowtail.

Müllerian mimicry: the presence of conspicuous or warning colors that are shared by several species of noxious or unpalatable insects, each enhancing the ability of predators to recognize what *not* to eat.

myrmecophily: associating with ants. The larvae of many Lycaenids are regularly attended by ants, which provide food or protection against predatory wasps.

nomenclature: the technical process of applying unique names to organisms. It is conducted according to a series of formal rules that are overseen by the International Committee on Zoological Nomenclature.

numerical taxonomy: the classification of organisms based solely on their qualitative and measurable similarities. This has been applied extensively to insects where there are large numbers of highly similar species.

obligate: the larvae can only feed and develop on one kind of host.

old field: This is a successional stage when a cleared field, whether an abandoned farm field or pasture, or a burned area, begins to grow up in tall grasses, brambles, and bushes. On sandy soil, Red Cedar is a common early successional tree.

palatability spectrum: variation in palatability from completely edible to completely inedible. Individuals within a single population of Monarch, for example, may vary in the amount of toxic alkaloids in their tissues.

panmictic (panmixis): all members of a population have a possibility of coming in contact and breeding with all other members of that population.

phenetics: the study of relationships among organisms based on the presence or absence of characters (these may be morphological, behavioral, physiological, biochemical, or ecological), as in numerical taxonomy.

phenology: the timing of appearance and disappearance of organisms during a single year.

phenotype: the body form and appearance of an organism, shaped by an interaction between its genotype and its environment.

pheromones: specific chemicals used for communication between individuals, usually in the process of attracting mates and recognizing species. Lepidoptera have highly evolved olfaction and can detect pheromones at long distances.

photoperiod: the alternating pattern of daylight and darkness, and the change in the number of daylight hours during the season. Many aspects of plant growth, flowering and fruiting, and of butterfly life cycles are influenced by change in photoperiod.

phylogenetic systematics: see *cladistics.*

Piedmont: the zone between the highlands and the Coastal Plain; a foothill region.

Pine Barrens: an area of poor, usually sandy soil, where pine trees (*Pinus*) form a stable successional stage, and which is not usually suitable for a mature hardwood forest. However, many areas of the barrens include a mixture of pine and various oak trees, thereby forming a pine-oak or oak-pine barrens. In New Jersey, they occupy most of southern New Jersey except the immediate coastal regions.

plasticity: the opposite of canalized; a character that can vary depending on environmental conditions during development.

polymorphism: a species or population where there may be two or more distinct forms, usually of one sex. Thus the female Eastern Tiger Swallowtail is polymorphic, as are females of the Sulphurs. The term is not used when the variation is continuous.

polyphagous: organisms that consume more than one food species.

polyphenism: the presence of two or more distinct forms, usually due to environmental factors, such as seasonal polyphenism, where a species has a different appearance in spring, summer, and fall.

priority: in reference to nomenclature, the first valid name that was applied to a species or other taxon is the one that must be used for it, even though other scientists subsequently gave it other names.

protandry: males emerge several days or weeks before females.

race: another term for subspecies, but may apply to forms that appear different due to ecologic factors (hosts or habitats), not only geography.

relict: a species or population that was formerly more widespread but has become restricted to a small area, usually by habitat loss.

revisions: the technical process of studying a taxon (species, genus, family, etc.), redefining the relationships, and often changing the nomenclature to conform to the author's understanding.

scoli (scolus): conical projections on caterpillars bearing branching spines or hairs that are often sharp.

seasonal polyphenism: the presence of distinctly different forms at different times of the year.

secondary contact: when two populations that have been geographically isolated come in contact. They may or may not interbreed, depending on how much they have differentiated during the period of isolation (see *biological species concept*). If they interbreed freely, they would be considered a single species. If not, they are considered to have evolved into distinct species. In some cases many generations are required to ascertain whether hybrids are at a disadvantage. This is necessary in order to ascertain whether they will or can interbreed freely.

serpentine barrens vegetation: a depauperate flora comprising of species that can tolerate the high nickel/chromium/magnesium content of serpentine soil.

sex-limited inheritance: inheritance modified by the genetically determined sex, such that a particular pattern or phenotype occurs only in one sex, usually the female.

sibling species: two species that are so similar that they were long thought to be a single species, until new research or techniques revelaed that they were separate. The various azures that have masquereded as "Spring Azure" would be considered sibling or cryptic species.

sloppydoptera: A term coined by Henry Skinner to describe damaged specimens that appear to have been captured with a baseball bat or temporarily loaned to a new baby (Mallis 1971:323).

speciation: the process by which two isolated populations accumulate genetic differences over time, such that they gradually become more and more different until they can no longer interbreed successfully.

species: This is the basic biologic and taxonomic unit, and theoretically all individuals of one species can interbreed freely with all other individuals of that species. Forms that do not freely interbreed or whose hybrids are either not fertile or have reduced survival or fecundity are usually considered different species.

spermatophore: the packet containing sperm and nutrients which the male transfers to the female during mating.

splitter: a taxonomist who emphasizes the differences among closely related taxa by assigning them to different groups and giving them different names. This is usually accomplished in the course of a "revision."

stigma: a patch or "brand" of specialized scales, usually appearing black, on the dorsal forewing of male Grass Skippers.

subspecies: A named category below the species level. Populations that are recognizably distinct, usually on morphological characters (but occasionally on ecologic or other characters), yet can freely interbreed with members of another subspecies where they are in contact.

sympatry (sympatric): two populations that co-occur in the same place.

synonyms (synonymy) (in reference to scientific nomenclature): when a name is used for a species that has previously been named; one must retain the name that has priority, and the subsequent name(s) are considered synonyms, and are relegated to synonymy.

systematics: the study of the evolutionary relationships among organisms. Classification is the organization of organisms according to some method or plan.

taxa (taxon): can refer to any taxonomic collection of organisms at any level; thus a subspecies is a taxon, as is a species, genus, family, etc.

taxonomy: the study of how organisms are related and how they should be classified and named.

teneral: the period after eclosion when adult butterflies do not fly.

territoriality: a behavior involving the defense of an area or a feeding station or a mate.

thorax: the middle portion of an insect's body, to which the wings and legs are attached.

threatened: a species what has declined and become so localized that it is likely to become endangered if there is no protection or other change in status.

type specimen: when a taxon is newly described, one specimen is identified as the type, to which the name is uniquely linked. Many North American butterflies do not have an extant type specimen, and for some, the type is a painting.

univoltine: a phenologic pattern with a single emergence or flight period in a year.

vagility: the tendency of members of a population or species to disperse widely (opposite of sedentary).

variety: a nontaxonomic term used in reference to a recognizable morph or aberration of a butterfly. A century ago, varieties were given scientific names, and today these are indicated in 'single quotes.' They were much prized by collectors.

vulnerable: a species that is not threatened or endangered, but is likely to become so without protection or habitat management.

APPENDIX C

Chronological List of Publications (1758–1940)

Linnaeus, C. 1758. *Systemae Naturae*. 10th ed.

Clerck, C. 1759–64. *Icones*. Stockholm.

Fabricus, J. C. 1775–98. Several publications.

Cramer, P. 1775–1800. *Papillons éxotiques*.

Hubner, J. End of 18th c. *Sammlung exotischer Schmetterlinge*.

Smith, J. E. 1797. *The Natural History of the Rarer Lepidopterous Insects of Georgia*.

Boisduval, J. A., and J. E. LeConte. 1833. *Histoire générale et monographie des lépidoptères et des chenilles de l'Amérique septentrionale*. Paris. 228 pp. 78 color plates.

Harris, T. W. 1841. *A Report on the Insects of Massachusetts Which Are Injurious to Vegetation*.

Morris, J. G. 1860. *Catalogue of the Described Lepidoptera of North America*.

Morris, J. G. 1862. *Synopsis of the Described Lepidoptera of North America*. Smithsonian Institution, Washington, D.C.

Edwards, W. H. 1868–97. *The Butterflies of North America*. 3 vols.

Strecker, H. 1872–79. *Lepidoptera—Rhopaloceres and Heteroceres—Indigenous and Exotic*. Illustrated with 15 color plates.

Scudder, H. 1872. A Systematic Revision of some of the American Butterflies. *Ann. Rep. Peabody Acad. Sci.* 4:24–83.

Strecker, H. 1878. *Butterflies and Moths of North America: A Complete Synonymical Catalogue*. Reading, Penn.

Edwards, W. H. 1884. Revised Catalog of the Diurnal Lepidoptera of America North of Mexico. *Trans. Amer. Entom. Soc.* 11:62–337.

French, G. H. 1886. *The Butterflies of the Eastern United States*. 402 pp., 93 figs.

Scudder, S. H. 1886. *The Butterflies of New England*.

Maynard, C. J. 1886. *The Butterflies of New England*. 72 pp., 8 color plates.

Scudder, S. H. 1889. *The Butterflies of the Eastern United States and Canada with Special Reference to New England*. 3 vols. Cambridge, Mass. 1958 pp.

Smith, J. B. 1890. *Catalogue of Insects Found in New Jersey*. Geological Survey, Trenton.

Maynard, C. J. 1891. *A Manual of North American Butterflies*. Boston.

Scudder, S. H. 1893. *The Life of the Butterfly*. Henry Holt and Co., New York.

Beutenmüller, W. 1893. Descriptive catalogue of the butterflies found within fifty miles of New York City, together with a brief account of their life histories and habits. *Bull. Amer. Mus. Nat. Hist.* 5:241–311.

Scudder, S. H. 1893. *A Brief Guide to the Commoner Butterflies of the Northern United States and Canada*. Henry Holt and Co., New York.

Skinner, H. 1898. *Synonymic Catalogue of the North American Rhopalocera*. Academy of Natural Science, Philadephia. 100 pp.

Holland, W. J. 1898. *The Butterfly Book*. 1st ed. Doubleday, Page, New York.

Godman, F. D., and O. Salvin. 1879–1901. *Biologia Centrali-Americana: Rhopalocera*.

Privately printed, London. Vol. I (1879–86, 487 pp.); Vol. II (1887–1901, 782 pp.); Vol. III (1879–1901, 112 plates).

Smith, J. B. 1900. *Insects of New Jersey*. 1899. MacCrellish and Quigley, Trenton.

Dickerson, M. C. 1901. *Moths and Butterflies*. Ginn and Co., Boston. 200 photographs.

Fiske, W. F. 1901. An annotated catalogue of the butterflies of New Hampshire. *New Hamp. College Agric. Exper Station Tech. Bull.* 1:3–80.

Dyar, H. G. 1902. A list of the North American Lepidoptera and key to the literature of this order of insects. *U.S. Natl. Mus. Bull.* 53:1–723 (first 62 pp. are butterflies).

Beutenmüller, W. 1902. The butterflies of the vicinity of New York City. *Amer. Mus. Nat. Hist. J. Suppl.* 2(5):1–52.

Comstock, J. H., and A. B. Comstock. 1904. *How to Know the Butterflies: a Manual of the Butterflies of the Eastern United States*. D. Appleton, New York. 311 pp. and 45 color plates.

Wright, W. G. 1905. *The Butterflies of the West Coast*. 257 pp., 32 color plates; illustrates 483 species or varieties.

Smith, J. B. 1910. *Insects of New Jersey*. Annual Report of the State Museum 1909. MacCrellish and Quigley, Trenton.

Robertson-Miller, E. 1912. *Butterfly and Moth Book: Personal Studies and Observations of the More Familiar Species*. Charles Scribner's Sons, New York.

Barnes, W., and J. McDunnough. 1917. *Check-list of the Lepidoptera of Boreal America*. Decatur, Ill.

Holland, W. J. 1931. *The Butterfly Book*. 2d ed. Doubleday, New York.

McDunnough, J. H. 1938–39. *Check Lists of the Lepidoptera of Canada and the United States of America (1938–1939)*.

Comstock, W. P. 1940. Butterflies of New Jersey. *J. New York Ent. Soc.* 48:42–84.

Resources: Books, Clubs, Binoculars

Books on Butterflies

There are hundreds of books on butterflies, and many new ones are published each year. Publishers take advantage of the intrinsic beauty of these insects to issue a wide variety of books, many of which are of the "100 pretty butterflies of the world" variety and are of little use to anyone except perhaps to arouse the latent interest of a curious child. There are, however, many fine books that vary greatly in scope and price, and most butterfly watchers and students will soon accumulate a substantial and costly library. It is difficult to attempt to provide a complete listing of relevant books, but we provide a list we think is valuable for appreciating and understanding New Jersey's butterflies. Some books deal with the butterflies themselves and others with their habitats. (See also chapter 9 on butterfly gardens.)

Some butterfly watchers will want to immerse themselves deeply in the behavior, ecology, and life history of butterflies, while others will be content to get to know them more superficially.

More detailed reviews are provided by Brian Cassie (1993) and in subsequent "Roundup" columns in *American Butterflies* reviewing books on butterflies.

How to Identify Butterflies

The following three books are listed in their order of priority for identifying New Jersey's butterflies. Most serious butterfly watchers will want to have all three because they have different strengths.

Glassberg, J. 1993. *Butterflies through Binoculars*. Oxford University Press, New York. 160 pages, 323 color photographs. $19.95 (paperback). This is the essential identification guide for all species that are likely to occur in the state. The excellent photographs have been well chosen and well placed to highlight differences between similar species. There is brief mention of habitats and hosts. The five-year phenology graphs are a unique and valuable feature for northern New Jersey, as is the butterfly-finding section for New Jersey and adjacent states.

Opler, P. A. 1992. *A Field Guide to the Eastern Butterflies*. Houghton-Mifflin Co., Boston. $16.95 (paper). Illustrated by V. Malikul. This is a much revised second edition of volume 4 of the Peterson Field Guide Series, first published by the late A. B. Klots in 1951. It provides photographs of many species and plates showing all eastern species in the typical "flattened" pose.

The 1951 edition by Klots is worth getting for the historical information it includes.

See also the Opler and Krizek book in the next section.

Pyle, R. M. 1981. *The Audubon Society Field Guide to North American Butterflies*. Alfred Knopf, New York. 925 pp., 759 color photographs. $18.50 (flexible). This book covers all of North America and provides photographs of all widespread and common species. Some species have two or more photos illustrating both sexes, and dorsal as well as ventral surfaces. The descriptive text is brief but covers similar species, the butterfly life cycle, a summary of phenology, and habitat and range. The author is somewhat of a generic splitter, and some of the common names he uses have not been widely adopted. Nonetheless, even for New Jerseyans who can use the Glassberg and Opler books, this book is a valuable asset because it provides additional photographic views.

Wright, Amy Bartlett. 1993. *Peterson First Guide to Caterpillars of North America*. Houghton Mifflin, Boston. $4.95. Not all butterfly watchers care about caterpillars, but for those who do this is a unique volume. The fifty-five color plates illustrate the larvae of most common butterflies.

Learning about Butterflies

The field guides listed above devote minimal space to the behavior, ecology, and life history of butterflies. The following books provide more details on the various aspects of a butterfly's life; the first is a book for children.

Cech, R. 1993. *A Distributional Checklist of the Butterflies and Skippers of the New York City Area (50-Mile Radius) and Long Island*. New York City Butterfly Club.

Craighton, LuAnn. 1991. *Discover Butterflies! An Activity Book for Families, Students and Teachers*. Callaway Gardens, Pine Mountain, GA. $7.95. This is a well-written and engaging introduction to the lives of butterflies, including their anatomy and classification, metamorphosis, behavior, conservation, and how to watch butterflies. There is a chapter on the Monarch and its migrations as well as educational activities for families.

Douglas, M. M. 1986. *The Lives of Butterflies*. University of Michigan Press, Ann Arbor, MI. $45 (hard cover). Both a scientist and a teacher, Douglas has succeeded in covering many aspects of butterfly biology, providing extensive examples from experimental studies. It covers anatomy, development, physiology, ecology, community and population biology, as well as behavior and evolution. It is both an excellent introduction and a detailed review of these topics.

NABA. 1995. *Checklist and English Names of North American Butterflies*. North American Butterfly Association, 4 Delaware Road, Morristown, NJ.

The result of long deliberation, this book lists all butterflies that have occurred in North America, with up-to-date scientific names and their proposed standardized English names. Names are provided for species that have been recently lumped or split. Detailed explanations are given for new English names.

Miller, J. Y. 1992. *The Common Names of North American Butterflies*. Smithsonian Institution Press, Washington, D.C. $15. This is a list of the common names that have been used in books about butterflies. It will be of interest only to people who have many old butterfly books from different regions in North America and want to be sure to what species a name refers. Many of the names preferred by Miller are the same as those adopted by NABA.

Opler, P. A., and G. O. Krizek. *Butterflies East of the Great Plains*. Johns Hopkins University Press, Baltimore. 1984. 402 pp., 324 color photographs. $49.50. This is a wonderful book that illustrates virtually all butterflies likely to be encountered in New Jersey, with high-quality photographs. It is very helpful for identification but is not primarily an identification guide. Each species account includes some basic life cycle, habitat, and biological information. The range maps are generally good, although for some rare species one would gain a mistaken impression that they are widespread in New Jersey. The introductory material is very valuable.

Pyle, R. M. 1986. *Handbook for Butterfly Watchers*. Houghton Mifflin, Boston. $11.95 (paper). This is another general introduction to the biology of butterflies, but provides an emphasis on how to watch and study them. Chapters cover the study of life histories and behavior, gardening, butterfly rearing, photography, and conservation.

Ruffin, Jane. 1993. *Where Are the Butterfly Gardens?* Lepidopterists' Society, 1013 Great Springs Road, Rosemont, PA 19010. 42 pp. $5.75. Butterfly gardens have become a significant tourist attraction in the past decade. This book lists many of the gardens to be found in the United States and Canada.

Scott, J. A. 1986. *The Butterflies of North America: A Natural History and Field Guide*. Stanford University Press, Stanford, CA. 637 pp., 64 color plates. $25.00 (paperback).

Despite its subtitle, this is not a field guide. It covers the entire continent, and has much valuable information in its introductory sections and species accounts. It is worth having in one's library despite several drawbacks. The color plates cover most species as they would appear in a collection rather than in life, and the cross-referencing between the text, the figure legends, and the figures is awkward. The range maps are small, and therefore the details are not always reliable (particularly in the East). However, there are good illustrations of eggs, larvae, and pupae.

Wright, D. and P. Sutton. 1993. "Checklist of Butterflies of Cape May County, N.J." Cape May Bird Observatory/New Jersey Audubon Society. Clearly shows seasonality and modern-day states.

More Technical Information about Butterflies

There are many books and scientific journals that cover butterflies. For those who want to pursue more technical information, several books and publications are recommended:

Vane-Wright, R. I., and P. R. Ackery. 1984. *The Biology of Butterflies.* Symposium of the Royal Entomological Society of London, no. 11. Academic Press, London. Reprinted 1989 by Princeton University Press. Contains thirty-three chapters on systematics, population ecology, food, habitats, predation, genetics and evolution, mating, migration, and conservation.

Gilbert, L. E., and M. C. Singer. 1975. Butterfly ecology. *Annual Review of Ecology and Systematics* 6:365–97. Although twenty years old, this paper provides an excellent introduction to butterfly ecology.

Nijhout, H. F. 1991. *The Development and Evolution of the Butterfly Wing.* Smithsonian Institution Press, Washington, D.C. $20. This book explores the marvel of butterfly wing patterns as a basis for understanding how developmental patterns have evolved among closely related species. This is a fairly technical volume but is well-illustrated so that one can follow the general points.

Pollard, E., and T. J. Yates. 1993. *Monitoring Butterflies for Ecology and Conservation.* Chapman and Hall, London. Describes the technical aspects and methods for monitoring butterfly populations, and discusses the distribution, population fluctuations, and the processes of colonization and extinction for British butterflies.

Pullin, A. S., ed. 1995. *Ecology and Conservation of Butterflies.* Chapman Hall, London. Contains twenty-two chapters on the ecology and conservation of European butterflies, including a chapter specifically on the Arctic Skipper in Scotland.

Journals that emphasize butterflies include *American Butterflies, Holarctic Lepidoptera, Tropical Lepidoptera, Journal of Lepidopterists' Society, Journal of Research on Lepidoptera, Evolution.*

Learning about New Jersey

Anderson, K. 1983. A Checklist of the Plants of New Jersey. Rancocas Nature Center, Mount Holly. A 51-page list of the plants found in New Jersey. Listed by family, with scientific and common names only; no distributional or habitat information.

Boyle, William J., Jr. 1986. *A Guide to Bird Finding in New Jersey.* Rutgers University Press, New Brunswick. Provides detailed instructions and maps and brief habitat descriptions to more than seventy-five bird-finding locations in New Jersey. More than half of these are good for butterflies as well. This is a valuable resource for anyone interested in New Jersey butterflies.

Collins, Beryl Robichaud, and Karl H. Anderson. 1994. *Plant Communities of New Jersey.* Rutgers University Press, New Brunswick. This is a useful book for a butterfly watcher's library. It provides valuable details and insights into the distribution of habitats and landscapes in New Jersey and will facilitate finding new and interesting places to seek butterflies.

Dann, Kevin, and Gordon Miller. 1992. *30 Walks in New Jersey.* Rutgers University Press, New Brunswick. Covers natural history and other items of interest along thirty public access trails scattered over most of the state with the exception of the lower Delaware Bay region.

Held, Patricia C. 1988. *A Field Guide to New Jersey Nature Centers.* Rutgers University Press, New Brunswick. Brief descriptions, instructions, and maps to twenty-nine nature centers throughout the state.

McPhee, John. 1967. *The Pine Barrens*. Noonday Press, New York. Nothing on butterflies, but this is an engaging and informative account of the culture, history of human activities, and changes in the Pine Barrens landscape.

Radko, T. R. 1982. *Discovering New Jersey*. Rutgers University Press, New Brunswick. This is a guide to all sorts of tourist activities, including parks, nature centers, and natural areas. It is more for the general interest tourist visiting New Jersey than for the serious naturalist.

Department of Environmental Protection. No date. *Guide to Wildlife Management Areas*. Trenton. Available for a fee from the N.J. Department of Environmental Protection, 401 East State Street, Trenton, NJ 08625. It describes the fifty Wildlife Management Areas, with maps of each and general habitat descriptions.

Department of Transportation. 1991. *New Jersey Place Names*. Trenton. Available free from the N.J. Department of Transportation, CN600, Trenton, NJ 08625. A pamphlet with the names of many New Jersey localities, their counties, and townships. This includes many places not on typical road maps or county atlases.

In addition, Rutgers University Press publishes a large number of books on the state's geography, culture, history, etc., in its New Jerseyana series.

Telephone Hotlines

Birdwatchers have long communicated unusual sightings over a series of "Rare Bird Alerts" or "Hotlines." This hasn't permeated butterfly watching yet, but New Jersey Audubon Society's Cape May Bird Observatory regularly includes butterfly watching information on its Birding Hotline (phone 609-884-2626).

Butterfly Clubs and Activities in New Jersey

Clubs and societies focused on the study of insects in general and butterflies in particular were formed in the latter part of the nineteenth century. Photographs of the early meetings of these societies show a number of men in suits and ties, in a living room or meeting room, puffing on pipes and no doubt discussing the best location for collecting butterflies or the fine points of variation and taxonomy.

The North American Butterfly Association (NABA) was formed in 1992. NABA is designed to meet the recreational, educational, and social needs of a new breed of butterfly watchers or butterfliers—those who attract, watch, and photograph but do not collect their quarry (Glassberg 1993c). NABA has taken this responsibility very seriously. Through a Standing Committee on English Names it has offered a standardized list of names for North American Butterflies (NABA 1995). Most of these are names already in widespread use, but a few are new variants that may themselves be controversial. Nonetheless, it offers a common language for butterfly watchers, and most of these names will be adopted in books and data bases in the future.

NABA publishes a quarterly journal, *American Butterflies*, as well as a newsletter, *The Anglewing*. It has also undertaken the coordination and publication of the Fourth of July Counts, and under its encouragement the number of counts and participants has greatly increased. Its first national meeting, held at Stockton State College, New Jersey, in May 1994, attracted over one hundred enthusiasts, both amateur and professional from all over the United States as well as other continents. For membership in NABA, write to the Treasurer, 909 Birch St., Baraboo, WI 53913.

NABA is rapidly forming local chapters and is participating in the development of butterfly atlases.

Formed in 1994, the Northern New Jersey Butterfly Club is one of the first local NABA chapters. Its meetings, usually held the first Tuesday of the month, are at the Frelinghuysen Arboretum, Morristown, New Jersey. It plays an active role in encouraging public interest in watching and preserving butterflies and their habitat, and is taking a lead role in developing a *New Jersey Butterfly Atlas*. For additional information, contact the Secretary, Jane Scott, 4 Delaware Road, Morristown, NJ 07960.

The New York City Butterfly Club was organized in 1985 and has focused its attention on finding and watching butterflies within 50 miles of New York City, which includes most of northern New Jersey. It initiated a periodical, *The Mulberry Wing*, which is now published in conjunction with local NABA chapters. For membership information, contact

Don Riepe, Gateway National Recreation Area, Building 69, Floyd Bennett Field, Brooklyn, NY 11234.

New Jersey Audubon Society's Cape May Bird Observatory offers weekly butterfly walks each spring and fall, as well as special workshops on butterfly watching and creating a butterfly and hummingbird garden, special tours of private butterfly gardens and operates the Monarch Monitoring Project, which wing-tagged 5,000 plus Monarchs in the fall of 1996. The Cape May Bird Observatory's "Birding and Butterflying Map to Cape May County" is revised regularly with butterfly watching sites and public gardens (most recent update was 1995). A log of butterfly and dragonfly sighting sheets are maintained at CMBO.

The Xerces Society, an international invertebrate conservation organization headquartered at 10 Southwest Ash Street, Portland OR 97204, publishes an attractive quarterly journal, *Atala*, as well as a newsletter, *Wings*.

The Lepidopterist Society was formed in 1947 and began publishing *Lepidopterist News*, which became the *Journal of the Lepidopterists' Society*. It is an international society of amateurs and professionals who also report, in their quarterly newsletter *News of the Lepidopterists' Society*, the occurrence of butterflies in different areas of North America. For membership, write to the Lepidopterists' Society, 257 Common Street, Boston, MA 02026.

Binoculars for Butterflies

With the aid of close-focusing binoculars, the butterfly watcher can get adequate to excellent views of any butterfly. The key to success is to purchase a quality binocular that focuses as close as 6 feet; some do even better. The closeness of focus depends not only on the optical properties of the binoculars but on a person's vision. Glassberg (1994d) provides a comparison-shopping guide to binoculars, taking into account close focusing, brightness, clarity, field of few, size and weight, and ability to use with glasses. This article is worth reading, particularly for anyone who plans to spend more than the $100 required to buy the popular Minolta 7 × 21 binocular, available in many camera stores. One drawback we find is that the Minolta is not durable, and we have had several pairs simply lose their ability to focus closely. We also use a Leitz compact 8 × 22 glass which has proven more durable, but costs about $200. The better-quality glasses are more likely to serve a dual purpose for bird watching as well. New and improved close + focusing binoculars are being developed and are reviewed periodically in the pages of *American Butterflies*.

APPENDIX E

Where to Find Butterflies in New Jersey

The following entries have been selected with two purposes in mind: (1) to provide a selection of the diverse habitats in New Jersey, and (2) to provide directions for some of the more localized butterflies. These supplement the "Where to Find" section in the Species Accounts.

We have not provided directions involving widespread, common species that might be found anywhere in New Jersey, nor to THREATENED or VULNERABLE species that might be jeopardized by disturbance or collecting. The best way to find these is to participate on one of the organized field trips of a local butterfly club.

The following areas can hardly be considered an exhaustive representation of New Jersey's butterfly-finding potential. Indeed, few of the areas have been exhaustively surveyed. The development of a statewide atlas program will certainly augment our understanding of the butterfly fauna of these and other locations.

We are a long way from having a comprehensive picture of butterfly distribution in New Jersey. Many of the sites in Boyle's book, not included here, deserve surveys for butterflies, and many other sites that may not be unusual for bird watching may contain special butterfly species. The suggestions below must be regarded as preliminary.

The layout of this section corresponds to Boyle's *A Guide to Bird Finding in New Jersey*. No attempt is made to duplicate the specific instructions therein, except to highlight special areas for butterfly watching.

In the descriptions below, WMA refers to a New Jersey Wildlife Management Area, managed by the Department of Environmental Protection for hunting and fishing; NWR refers to a National Wildlife Refuge, managed by the U.S. Fish and Wildlife Service. Areas marked with * are not specifically listed in Boyle's book.

Northwest Region

High Point State Park and Stokes State Forest. About 28,000 acres of mainly deciduous forest in the Kittatinny Mountains, at elevations up to 1803 feet in the northwest corner of Sussex County. Specialties include Arctic Skipper and Pepper and Salt Skipper, as well as the possibility of Gray Comma and other northern specialties. Edwards' Hairstreaks and Long Dash are common, but local.

The hawk-watching lookouts on Raccoon Ridge and Sunset Mountain should be productive for hilltopping and migrating butterflies. The upland population of the Falcate Orangetip occurs here, and the Columbine Duskywing should be sought around Columbines.

The two parks abut each other, but High Point is usually the more productive.

Wayawanda State Park. Straddling the Sussex/Passaic County Line, this park merits exploration. It is close to Upper Greenwood Lake, which was one of the favored collecting areas a century ago. Little is known of its butterfly fauna.

Worthington State Forest and Delaware Water Gap. This is another area to explore for the northern species that should be entering New Jersey's northwestern forests.

* Springdale. The specialty here is the Northern Metalmark, which occurs on the ridge under the powerline, north of Sticklepond Road (not to be confused with Stickles Pond in Passaic County). South of the road, the powerline traverses an area with Scrub Oak, where Edwards' Hairstreaks are sometimes found. Appalachian Browns are common, and the marsh at the bottom of the powerline near the road has had Mulberry Wing, Black Dash, and Dion Skippers, but is now overgrown. The powerline crosses other ridges where the Metalmarks occur.

Scherman-Hoffman Sanctuaries. In Bernardsville, the New Jersey Audubon Society runs this sanctuary along the Passaic River, which includes a variety of fields and forests. The Harvester occurs here and should be sought among the beech groves, where it feeds on the Woolly Aphid infestations.

Northeast Region

Palisades Park. Exit from the Interstate Parkway or Route 9W onto Palisades Avenue. Go east toward the river. The road winds steeply down the face of the Palisades and ends in a parking lot. Walk about 50–100 yards up the road and find a foot trail on the left. The dominant plant on the slope is Pipevine, and adults and larvae of the Pipevine Swallowtail can be numerous. Late morning is best, while the east-facing slope is still in sunshine.

Greenbrook Sanctuary. A private 165-acre reserve on the Palisades, one mile north of Tenafly. The specialty here is the Pipevine Swallowtail. Permission is required to enter. It is reached from Route 9W. Contact the Palisades Nature Association, P.O. Box 155, Alpine, NJ 07620.

South Mountain Reservation (southwest of Newark). This is another historic butterfly area from a century ago, visited by the "Newark" collectors. There is no recent information on its butterfly fauna.

Troy Meadows. The powerline at the southeast corner of Troy Meadows provides excellent access. Park along Beverwyck Road just north of Perrine Road and walk east. Black Dash and Dion Skippers are found here. Troy Meadows is a historic site for the Bronze Copper, though none have been found there recently. The boardwalk along the powerline in the northeastern part of the Meadows is another access point. The third point worth exploring is Troy Meadows Road, which penetrates the northwestern part of the meadows through tall swamp forest and ends at a gun club and lake. This is a good area for satyrids and anglewings.

Great Swamp NWR. The wet swamp forests and wet meadows of this 7000-acre refuge provide excellent habitats, and there is a rich butterfly fauna. Both Eyed and Appalachian Browns occur here. At some times, the Northern Pearly Eye is common along the boardwalk. Mulberry Wings frequent the wet meadows.

Schooleys Mountain Park. This park with open fields and mixed forests is located in western Morris County, southeast of Hackettstown, and is of mainly historic interest. A century ago, many northern species, now rare in New Jersey, were found here, including the Bronze Copper (in wet meadows), Harris' Checkerspot, and Milbert's Tortoiseshell.

Central Region

*Rutgers University Display Garden. Located on the Cook College campus just east of Route 1, the gardens are accessible from Ryder's Lane. Make the first left turn from Ryder's Lane and follow the signs for Holly House. The display gardens are located to the left of Holly House and feature a large garden of annuals plus a special butterfly garden.

In addition to many common species, this is the best spot in central New Jersey for southern immigrants, including Sachem and Fiery Skipper.

Bull's Island and Vicinity. This well-known birding location has not been recently surveyed for butterflies. The island is mainly wooded and represents the best of the Delaware Valley's riparian habitat. Open areas in the vicinity should be explored for butterflies that might range into New Jersey from Pennsylvania.

Washington Crossing State Park. This is a traditional butterfly location. However, when last visited it was highly manicured, and much of it was unsuitable for butterflies.

Trenton Marsh (John A. Roebling Memorial Park). The ecology of this marsh has been extensively studied by Mary and Charlie Leck. The Baltimore Checkerspot breeds here, and a colony of Checkered Whites has occurred here as well. Located off Route 206 southeast of Trenton, this is an extensive (ca. 300 acre) remnant of freshwater marsh and ponds of the lower Delaware Valley. Like so many habitats, it has been significantly altered by highway construction.

Assunpink WMA. Occupies about 5400 acres of open fields managed for game birds and forests. This is an important area for butterflies, particularly in early spring. The two specialties are Frosted Elfin and Falcate Orange Tip. The latter is widespread along forest edges in early spring, but the latter form is highly local.

Take Imlaystown Road north and bear left onto a dirt road just before entering the parking lot at the edge of the lake. This road winds past field and forest for about a mile before it peters out. This is a good spot for Orangetips. When you can drive no further, continue walking along the trail until you reach the end of the field and bear left along the far side of the field until the trail intersects a dirt road. Follow this to the right for about 100 yards. There is a stand of Wild Indigo on the right of this track. This is the location for the Frosted Elfin. The barren patches of dirt along the trail are good for Cobweb Skipper.

Colliers Mills WMA. Located in northern Ocean County, it is one of the largest of the WMAs (12,000 acres). It is at the edge of the Pine Barrens and combines typical oak-pine habitat with dikes and hardwood swamps. There are several White Cedar swamps that can be checked for Hessel's Hairstreak.

Whitesbog. A mosaic of active and abandoned cranberry bogs interlaced with pine forest. It lies within Lebanon State Forest.

Lakehurst. An important historic insect-collecting area. Several sites are worth checking: (1) Park at the point where Union Avenue crosses the railroad tracks at what was once the RR station. The fields to the west of the tracks are good for Dotted Skipper. Coral Hairstreaks are sometimes abundant here on Butterfly Weed. Walk south following the right-hand fork of the RR tracks; watch for Mulberry Wings. After crossing an old wooden "bridge," watch for a trail leading left over a plank into Klots' Bog (unmarked). Walk around and through the bog looking for Bog Copper, Georgia Satyr, and Two-spotted and Dion Skipper. This habitat is threatened by the overgrowth of Red Maples. (2) Use a Hagstrom Ocean County map. Find the junction of Ridgeway Blvd. and the Legler Cutoff. At the southeast angle of this junction there is an old field with mixed vegetation. Look for stands of Milkweed and Butterfly Weed. This is very good for Olive and Hickory Hairstreaks, Cloudywings, and Hoary Edge. (3) Proceed north on Whitesville Road; about 1.5 miles north of the Legler Cutoff you will find extensive fields with large Milkweed stands west of the road. Excellent for all Hairstreaks, including Southern/Northern and White M in early July.

Warren Grove. A village on Route 539 in southwestern Ocean County. At the south end of the village, turn west on Sims Place, then right on Beaver Dam Road and pass through a White Cedar swamp, where Hessel's Hairstreak occurs. After about a mile, you reach a junction with a large, open field and a tall radio tower. The open flats are covered by Bearberry, and Hoary Elfin can be abundant here. Brown Elfin is less common. Sleepy Duskywings and Cobweb Skippers occur here as well.

North Coast Region

Sandy Hook (Monmouth County, Gateway National Recreation Area). This barrier beach extends 7 miles into Raritan Bay, forming a migration corridor for birds and butterflies moving to and from Breezy Point, Brooklyn. It has extensive stands of pines, Red Cedars, and American Holly. Its specialty is Henry's Elfin, which can be found on the ground under and in the canopy of the holly trees in late April and early May.

One can begin at the visitors' center and follow trails or stop at parking lot F and walk back along the road to the main north-south trail. We found the Elfin commonly here as well as near parking lot G. Other specialties are Olive Hairstreak among the Red Cedars and Falcate Orange Tip in late April.

Island Beach State Park. This area should be surveyed for butterflies, particularly in spring and late summer, when it should be a migration corridor. The salt marshes behind the barrier beach are generally not very extensive. It has holly forests that should be checked in spring for Henry's Elfin.

Southwest Region

Wharton State Forest and the Pine Barrens. There are many subtle variations in the Pine Barrens vegetation. White Cedar Swamps may have Hessel's Hairstreak and abandoned cranberry bogs should have Bog Copper, Georgia Satyr, and Two-spotted Skipper. Recent fieldwork shows that the Dotted Skipper, once considered exceedingly rare, is quite widespread in open fields in this area. In early spring, Orangetips, elfins, and duskywings are sometimes abundant. In July, however, many areas of the Barrens are virtually devoid of butterfly activity.

Pine Barrens

Tuckerton Marshes: there is ready access from Seven Bridges Road to salt marsh. This area can be checked for Salt Marsh Skipper, and seems to be the northern limit for Aaron's Skipper as well.

Brigantine [Forsyth] National Wildlife Refuge. The Forsyth NWR contains about 36,000 acres, much of it water and salt marsh. The main area of interest is the Brigantine Division, still known to many as Brigantine NWR. En route to Brigantine, take Exit 49 from the southbound Garden State Parkway. Shortly after leaving the parkway, the road runs along salt marsh that can be accessed easily. Check the Salt Marsh Fleabane for Aaron's and Salt Marsh Skippers. The dikes of the refuge itself often have large numbers of Black Swallowtails and Buckeyes.

Tuckahoe WMA is a 12,500-acre site in northern Cape May and Atlantic County. The main attraction here is wet forest and holly forests, but there are also lakes, salt marshes, and pine forest. The dirt road through the wet forests are often productive, and this is a good spot for Henry's Elfin.

Cumberland County Salt Marshes. Between Port Norris and Dividing Creek, several roads go south and west through expanses of salt marsh, where Aaron's Skipper may be found. Some of these areas have Rare Skipper as well.

Heislerville WMA. Check the salt marsh areas for Aaron's, Salt Marsh, and Rare Skipper.

Belleplain State Forest. Follow dirt roads through the forest, and check the woodland edges and powerline cuts for Brown and Frosted Elfins, hairstreaks, cloudywings, duskywing, and Cobweb Skipper. Henry's Elfin is a regular along Pine Swamp Road. Olive Hairstreak occurs in old fields. Check edges of White Cedar swamps for Hessel's Hairstreak. The Pine Barrens reaches its southern limit in the northern part of the county, and the Southern/Northern Hairstreak occurs here regularly. Bog Copper can be found in cranberry bogs and Hessel's Hairstreak in White Cedar swamps.

Jakes Landing Road. This road leads south from Route 47 through a rich part of the Belleplain State Forest (see above), where Falcate Orangetips occur on road shoulders, and then out through the salt marshes of the Dennis Creek WMA, where Aaron's and Salt Marsh Skippers nectar on Salt Marsh Fleabane.

Beaver Swamp WMA. 2700 acres of forest and swamps accessible mainly via Route 585 south of South Dennis.

Cape May Peninsula

This area is also known as Cape Island, which refers to the area south of the Cape May Canal. Several areas are described in detail below. The geography of Cape May is confusing. One has the illusion that Cape May Point ought to be south of Cape May, but in reality it is west (and slightly northwest, at that). The Cape May area has long been famous for its bird migration, and it is equally important for butterfly migration as well. Many butterflies rare elsewhere in New Jersey are found here regularly. Some probably occur elsewhere in southern New Jersey, but the concentration of fieldwork at Cape May, as well as its protected habitats and butterfly gardens, make it special.

Regular summer immigrants are Little Yellow, Cloudless Sulphur, Variegated Fritillary, Checkered Skipper, Fiery Skipper, and Sachem. Rarer visitors, but seen with increasing frequency in recent years, are Long-tailed Skipper, Clouded Skipper, and Ocola Skipper. Still rarer vagrants have included Gulf Fritillary and Eufala Skipper. In a good year, Cloudless Sulphurs should be seen almost everywhere. In New Jersey, Hayhurst's Scallopwing is found mainly in the Cape May area.

Cape May. The town of Cape May has planted a butterfly garden in the Water Conservation park on Madison Avenue. Although surrounded by residential areas, it attracts a variety of migrants as well as many American and Painted Ladies and Buckeyes.

Cape May Point. Reached from Sunset Boulevard leading south from Cape May. The road dead-ends at a parking lot overlooking the hulk of a partially sunken cement ship. The barren fields to the right of the parking lot are worth checking for Variegated Fritillary.

To enter the town of Cape May Point, go back to Sunset Boulevard about 1/2 mile to Cape Avenue. Follow Cape Avenue to the circle and check the gardens in the circle. The Cape May Bird Observatory "Backyard Habitat for Birds and Butterflies" booklet and program were the inspiration. Wander the streets of Cape May Point and beach front. Many yards have butterfly flowers, such as Orpine and Butterflybush. Check these for Little Yellow, Ocola, and Long-tailed Skipper. The Cape May Bird Observatory on East Lake Drive (phone 609-884-2736) has planted a butterfly garden.

Cape May Point State Park. Affords access to a different scrub habitat. From the Hawk Watch Platform, several trails penetrate into the mosaic of marshes, ponds, and wooded islands. Butterfly migration is often conspicuous with Cloudless Sulphurs, many species of nymphalids, and Monarchs. The Monarch migration and subsequent roosts are often spectacular in September and October. It is a good location for Clouded Skipper. The Scallopwing occurs here, and on rare occasions the Gulf Fritillary has been sighted.

Cape May Migratory Bird Refuge (owned by The Nature Conservancy). When driving east from Cape May Point on Sunset Boulevard, one finds the parking lot on the right just before reaching Bayshore Road. This large open expanse of brackish and fresh coastal marsh is traversed by a loop trail. Mostly one sees common species such as Black Swallowtails, Common Buckeye, and Monarchs, but the patches of flowering plants attract various species of skippers as well, so this site is worth checking on any visit to Cape May.

Hidden Valley, part of **Higbee Beach Wildlife Management Area.** Proceed east toward Cape May and turn onto Bayshore Road (Route 607). Continue on Bayshore Road until it intersects with New England Road. Turn left onto New England Road. Go 0.3 miles and turn into small clamshell parking lot. The first field was planted as a wild flower meadow in 1995 and is excellent for butterflies

Higbee Beach Wildlife Management Area. Continue on New England Road; the road ends at Higbee Beach WMA, a mosaic of open fields and woodlands just behind the sandy beach. Between the fields and the beach is the only surviving remnant of natural Delaware Bay dune vegetation. The weedy fields are managed to keep them from becoming overgrown, but their floral composition varies from year to year. This is the best location for Hayhurst's Scallopwing; White M Hairstreaks can often be found in late summer. Other specialties include Falcate Orangetip, Red-banded Hairstreak, and Henry's Elfin. There is a Hackberry grove next to the parking lot, and Hackberry and Tawny Emperors and American Snout are found here with some regularity.

The New Jersey Nongame and Endangered Species Program planted a butterfly garden next to the parking lot. From the parking lot, walk left (south) along the edges of the fields, until you reach a pond, and return to the road by a different route. This is a good place for Variegated Fritillary and Fiery Skipper. Then follow a dirt road north from the parking lot, for a few hundred yards to the Cape May canal. This is good for the Henry's Elfin, anglewings, and the Scallopwing. The hackberry specialists are best found right near the parking lot.

Checklist: Regularly Occurring New Jersey Butterflies

Name(s) _____ Date _____

Location/habitat 1: _____ Time _____

Location/habitat 2: _____ Time _____

Location/habitat 3: _____ Time _____

Weather AM: Cloud Cover _____% Temp _____F _____

   % of Time sunshining _____

Weather PM: Cloud Cover _____% Temp _____F _____

   % of Time sunshining _____

USE REVERSE SIDE FOR NOTES ON UNUSUAL OCCURRENCE AND BEHAVIOR

Pipevine Swallowtail				Banded Hairstreak			
Black Swallowtail				Hickory Hairstreak			
E. Tiger Swallowtail				Striped Hairstreak			
Spicebush Swallowtail				South/Northern Hairstreak			
Checkered White				Brown Elfin			
Cabbage White				Hoary Elfin			
Falcate Orangetip				Frosted Elfin			
Clouded Sulphur				Henry's Elfin			
Orange Sulphur				Eastern Pine Elfin			
Cloudless Sulphur				Juniper [Olive] Hairstreak			
Little Yellow				Hessel's Hairstreak			
Harvester				White M Hairstreak			
American Copper				Gray Hairstreak			
Bronze Copper				Red-banded Hairstreak			
Bog Copper				Eastern Tailed Blue			
Coral Hairstreak				Spring Azure			
Acadian Hairstreak				'lucia'			
Edwards Hairstreak				'marginata'			

'violacea'				Northern Cloudywing		
Summer Azure				Hayhurst's Scallopwing		
Appalachian Azure				Unident. Duskywing		
Northern Metalmark				Dreamy Duskywing		
American Snout				Sleepy Duskywing		
Variegated Fritillary				Juvenal's Duskywing		
Aphrodite				Horace's Duskywing		
Silver-bordered Fritillary				Wild Indigo Duskywing		
Meadow Fritillary				Com. Checkered Skipper		
Silvery Checkerspot				Common Sooty Wing		
Harris' Checkerspot				Swarthy Skipper		
Pearl Crescent				Least Skipper		
Baltimore Checkerspot				European Skipper		
Unident. Anglewing				Fiery Skipper		
Question Mark				Leonard's Skipper		
Eastern Comma				Cobweb Skipper		
Compton Tortoiseshell				Dotted Skipper		
Mourning Cloak				Indian Skipper		
Unidentified Lady				Peck's Skipper		
American Lady				Tawny-edged Skipper		
Painted Lady				Crossline Skipper		
Red Admiral				Long Dash		
Common Buckeye				Northern Broken Dash		
Red-spotted Purple				Little Glassy Wing		
Viceroy				Sachem		
Hackberry Emperor				Delaware Skipper		
Tawny Emperor				Mulberry Wing		
Northern Pearly Eye				Hobomok Skipper		
Eyed Brown				Zabulon Skipper		
Appalachian Brown				Aaron's Skipper		
Georgia Satyr				Broad-winged Skipper		
Little Wood Satyr				Dion Skipper		
Common Ringlet				Black Dash		
Common Wood Nymph				Dun Skipper		
Monarch				Dusted Skipper		
Silver-spotted Skipper				Pepper & Salt Skipper		
Hoary Edge				Com. Roadside Skipper		
Southern Cloudywing				Salt Marsh Skipper		

APPENDIX G

Forms for Recording Data on Butterflies

This section has four forms that can be duplicated for recording data on different kinds of butterfly observations.

1. Form for reporting the seasonal occurrence of butterflies. The purpose is to document the dates of occurrence and the dates of peak occurrence.
    a. Use one form for each locality.
    b. List each species in checklist order (see Appendix G).
    c. Include an actual count or indication of relative abundance.
    d. It is useful to indicate the date that a species is last regularly seen, as well as noting any unusual late stragglers.
2. Sample form for recording predation events.
3. Sample form for recording observations on butterfly mating activities.
4. Sample form for recording nectar choices by butterflies.

NOTE: On the same page, be sure to define any abbreviations you use. Include the year as well as the month and day.

Annual Occurrence Report for Local Butterflies

Observer _____ Year _____

Place: NJ _____ County _____ Township/Town _____

Location _____

Indicate date by month/day (e.g., May 7th = 5/7)

Species	First Brood Peak				Second Brood				Last regular date	Very last date
	First seen	Peak date	Count	Last seen	First seen	Peak date	Count	Last seen		

Predation on Butterflies

Observer: MG, JB   Location: NJ: Somerset Co, Franklin Twp
                                 54 Hollywood Ave., Somerset, backyard

Date: June 30, 1994   Encounter Time: 13:35   Event #: 94-11

Victim: Cabbage White female
Predator: Crab spider
Substrate: Purple loosestrife flower head   Height: 34"
First Condition: Butterfly freshly caught, struggling intermittently
1 hr: lifeless butterfly hanging down
2 hr: no change
4 hr: no change
6 hr: intact butterfly on grass under flower, spider present

Additional Notes:
8 A.M. (7/1/94): butterfly gone, spider still present
4 P.M. (7/1/94): spider still present
9 A.M. (7/2/94): spider found 15 cm away on adjacent flower head
8 A.M. (7/3/94): spider could not be located

Observations of Mating Butterflies

Location _____ Observer _____

Species	Date	Time first noted	Time last noted	Substrate (flower, leaf, etc.)	Tolerance distance*	Which sex carries	Other**

*How close an approach the butterflies tolerate before flying.
**Include other notes on courtship and events following mating.

Observations of Nectaring

Location _____ Observer _____

Butterfly species	Flower species	Color	Date	Time	Duration*	Other

*Distinguish brief explorations that result in no nectaring from actual nectaring bouts. Butterflies explore many flowers and other colored objects that they don't or can't actually nectar from.

Definitions of personal abbreviations used:

References

Abbott, C. H. 1951. A quantitative study of the migration of the Painted Lady Butterfly, *Vanessa cardui* Linnaeus. *Ecology* 32:155–171.

Abbot, C. H. 1962. A migration problem—*Vanessa cardui* (Nymphalidae), the Painted Lady Butterfly. *J. Lepid. Soc.* 16:229–233.

Ackery, P. R. 1984. Systematic and faunistic studies on butterflies. In *The Biology of Butterflies*, edited by R. I. Vane-Wright and P. R. Ackery, pp. 9–21. Academic Press, London. Reprinted 1989 by Princeton University Press.

Ackery, P. R., and R. I. Vane-Wright. 1984. *Milkweed Butterflies: Their Cladistics and Biology.* Cornell University Press, Ithaca, N.Y.

Alcock, J. 1983. Territoriality by hilltopping males of the Great Purple Hairstreak, *Atlides halesus* (Lepidoptera, Lycaenidae): Convergent evolution with a pompilid wasp. *Behav. Ecol. Sociobiol.* 13:57–62.

Alonso-Mejia, A., A. Arellano-Guillermo, and L. P. Brower. 1992. Influence of temperature, surface body moisture and height above ground on survival of Monarch butterflies overwintering in Mexico. *Biotropica* 24:415–419.

Anderson, K. 1983. *A Check List of the Plants of New Jersey—1983.* Rancocas Nature Center, Mount Holly, N.J.

Angevine, M. W., and P. F. Brussard. 1979. Population structure and gene frequency analysis of sibling species of *Lethe. J. Lepid. Soc.* 33:29–36.

Anon. 1874. Introductory: Cambridge Entomological Club. *Psyche* 1(1):1.

Aridjis, H., and L. P. Brower. 1996. Twilight of the Monarch. *New York Times*, January 26, 1996.

Arms, K., P. Feeney, and R. C. Lederhouse. 1974. Sodium: Stimulus for puddling behavior by Tiger Swallowtail butterflies, *Papilio glaucus. Science* 185:372–374.

Austin, E. J., and G. T. Austin. 1956. What's in your backyard? *Lepidopterists' News* 10:55.

Bates, H. W. 1862. Contributions to an insect fauna of the Amazon Valley. *Trans. Linn. Soc. London* 23:495–566.

Bauer, D. L. 1961. Midge-flies biting butterflies. *J. Lepid. Soc.* 15:91–92.

Beers, F. W. 1874. *County Atlas of Warren, New Jersey.* F. W. Beers and Co., Trenton.

Benson, W. W., K. S. Brown, and L. E. Gilbert. 1976. Coevolution of plants and herbivores: Passionflower butterflies. *Evolution* 29:659–680.

Berger, T. A. 1986. Habitat use and reproductive ecology of the Eastern Tiger Swallowtail, *Papilio glaucus* L. Ph.D. diss., Rutgers University, Newark, N.J.

Beutenmüller, W. 1893. Descriptive catalogue of the butterflies found within fifty miles of New York City, together with a brief account of their life histories and habits. *Bull. Amer. Mus. Nat. Hist.* 5:241–311.

Beutenmüller, W. 1902. The butterflies of the vicinity of New York City. *Amer. Mus. Nat. History J.* (Supp.) 2(5):1–52.

Biel, E. 1958. The Climate of New Jersey. In *The Economy of New Jersey*, pp. 53–98. Rutgers University Press, New Brunswick.

Bitzer, R. J., and K. C. Shaw. 1979. Territorial behavior of the Red Admiral, *Vanessa atalanta* (L.) (Lepidoptera: Nymphalidae). *J. Res. Lepid.* 18:36–49.

Boisduval, J. A., and J. E. LeConte. 1833. *Histoire générale et monographie des lépidoptères et des chenilles de l'Amérique septentrionale*. Paris.

Bowers, M. D. 1980. Impalatability as a defense strategy of *Euphydryas phaeton* Drury (Lepidoptera: Nymphalidae). *Evolution* 34:586–600.

Bowers, M. D. 1983. Mimicry in North American checkerspot butterflies: *Euphydryas phaeton* and *Chlosyne harrisii* (Nymphalidae). *Ecol. Entomol.* 8:1–8.

Bowers, M. D., and D. C. Wiernasz. 1979. Avian predation on the palatable butterfly *Cercyonis pegala* (Satyridae). *Ecol. Entomol.* 4:201–209.

Boydon, T. C. 1976. Butterfly palatability and mimicry: Experiments with Ameiva lizards. *Evol.* 30:73–81.

Boyle, W. J., Jr. 1986. *A Guide to Bird Finding in New Jersey*. Rutgers University Press, New Brunswick.

Braun, E. L. 1950. *Deciduous Forests of Eastern North America*. Hafner, New York.

Brooks, R. R. 1987. *Serpentine and Its Vegetation*. Dioscorides Press, Portland, Oregon.

Brower, A. E. 1960. Maine butterfly seasons—good or bad? *J. Lepid. Soc.* 14:78–80.

Brower, J. V. Z. 1958a. Experimental studies of mimicry in some North American butterflies. Part 1. The Monarch, *Danaus plexippus*, and Viceroy, *Limenitis archippus archippus*. Evolution 12:32–47.

Brower, J. V. Z. 1958b. Experimental studies of mimicry in some North American butterflies. Part 3. *Danaus gilippus berenice* and *Limenitis archippus floridensis*. *Evolution* 12:273–285.

Brower, L. P. 1958. Larval foodplants in the *Papilio glaucus* group. *Lepidopterists' News* 12:103–114.

Brower, L. P. 1969. Ecological chemistry. *Scient. Amer.* 220:22–29.

Brower, L. P. 1977. Monarch migration. *Natural History* 86(6):41–53.

Brower, L. P. 1984. Chemical defence in butterflies. In *The Biology of Butterflies*, edited by R. I. Vane-Wright and P. R. Ackery, pp. 109–134. Academic Press, London. Reprinted 1989 by Princeton University Press.

Brower, L. P. 1995. Understanding and misunderstanding the migration of the Monarch Butterfly (Nymphalidae) in North America: 1857–1995. *J. Lepid. Soc.* 49:304–385.

Brower, L. P., and J. V. Z. Brower. 1962. The relative abundance of model and mimic butterflies in natural populations of the *Battus philenor* mimicry complex. *Ecology* 43:154–158.

Brower, L. P., and J. V. Z. Brower. 1964. Birds, butterflies and plant poisons: A study in ecological chemistry. *Zoologica* 48:65–84.

Brower, L. P., J. V. Z. Brower, and C. T. Collins. 1963. Experimental studies of mimicry. 7. Relative palatability and Mullerian mimicry among neotropical butterflies of the subfamily Heliconiinae. *Zoologica* 48:65–84.

Brower, L. P., and W. H. Calvert. 1985. Foraging dynamics of bird predation on overwintering Monarch butterflies in Mexico. *Evolution* 39:852–868.

Brower, L. P., W. H. Calvert, L. E. Hedrick, and J. Christian. 1977. Biological observations on an overwintering colony of Monarch Butterflies (*Danaus plexippus* Danaidae) in Mexico. *J. Lepid. Soc.* 31:232–241.

Brower, L. P., and S. C. Glazier. 1975. Localization of heart poisons in the Monarch butterfly. *Science* 188:19–25.

Brower, L. B., B. E. Horner, M. A. Arty, C. M. Moffitt, and B. Villa-R. 1985. Mice (*Peromyscus maniculatus, P. spicilegus* and *Microtus mexicanus*) as predators on overwintering Monarch Butterflies (*Danaus plexippus*) in Mexico. *Biotropica* 17:89–99.

Brower, L. P., W. N. Ryerrson, L. L. Coppinger, and S. C. Glazier. 1968. Ecological chemistry and the palatability system. *Science* 161:1349–1351.

Brown, F. M. 1961. *Coenonympha tullia* on islands in the St. Lawrence River. *Can. Entomol.* 93:107–117.

Brown, F. M., and B. Heineman. 1972. *Jamaica and Its Butterflies.* E. W. Classey Ltd. London.

Brown, K. S., Jr. 1984. Adult-obtained pyrrdizdine alkaloids defend ithomiine butterflies against spider predators. *Nature* 309:707–709.

Brown, J. W. 1990. Urban biology of *Leptotes marina* (Reakirt) (Lycaenidae). *J. Lepid. Soc.* 44:200–201.

Bull, J. 1964. *Birds of the New York Area.* Harper and Row, New York.

Burger, J. 1996. *A Naturalist along the Jersey Shore.* Rutgers University Press, New Brunswick.

Burger, J., and J. Shisler. 1978. The effects of ditching a salt marsh on colony and nest site selection by Herring Gulls (*Larus argentatus*). *Amer. Midland Nat.* 100:54–63.

Burns, J. M. 1964. Evolution in skipper butterflies of the genus *Erynnis. Univ. Calif. Publ. Entomol.* 37:1–216.

Burns, J. M. 1966. Preferential mating versus mimicry: Disruptive selection and sex-limited dimorphism in *Papilio glaucus. Science* 153:551–553.

Burns, J. M. 1984. Evolutionary differentiation: Differentiating gold-banded skippers—*Autochton cellus* and more (Lepidoptera: Hesperiidae: Pyrginae). *Smithsonian Contrib. Zoology.* 405:1–38.

Burns, J. M. 1985. *Wallengrenia otho* and *W. egeremet* in eastern North America (Lepidoptera: Hesperiidae: Hesperiinae). *Smithsonian Contrib. Zool.* 423:1–39.

Burns, J. M. 1992. Genitalic recasting of *Poanes* and *Paratrytone* (Hesperidae). *J. Lepid. Soc.* 46:1–23.

Burns, J. M. 1994a. The sex of duskywings. *Amer. Butterflies* 2(3):19.

Burns, J. M. 1994b. Genitalia at the generic level: *Atrytone* restricted, *Anatrytone* resurrected, new genus *Quasimellana*—and Yes! we have no *Mellanas* (Hesperiidae). *J. Lepid. Soc.* 48:273–337.

Calvert, W. H., L. E. Hedrick, and L. P. Brower. 1979. Mortality of the Monarch Butterfly [*Danaus plexippus* L.]: Avian predators at five overwintering sites in Mexico. *Science* 204:847–851.

Calvert, W. H., W. Suchowski, and L. P. Brower. 1984. Monarch butterfly conservation: Interactions of cold weather, forest thinning and storms on the survival of overwintering Monarch butterflies (*Danaus plexippus* L.) in Mexico. *Atala* 9:2–6, 24–28.

Cape May. 1993. *Checklist of Butterflies of Cape May County.* Edited by David M. Wright and Pat Sutton. Cape May Bird Observatory, Cape May, N.J.

Cardé, R. T., A. M. Shapiro, and H. K. Clench. 1970. Sibling species in the *eurydice* group of *Lethe* (Lepidoptera: Satyridae). *Psyche* 77:70–103.

Carpenter, G. D. H. 1933. Attacks of birds on butterflies. *Trans. Entomol. Soc. London* 81:21–26.

Carpenter, G. D. H. 1937. Further evidence that birds do attack and eat butterflies. *Proc. Zool. Soc. London (A)* 107:223–247.

Carpenter, G. D. H. 1941. The relative frequency of beak marks on butterflies of different edibility to birds. *Proc. Zool. Soc. London (A)* 111:223–231.

Carson, R. 1962. *Silent Spring.* Houghton Mifflin, Boston.

Cassie, B. 1993. Round-up review of butterfly books. Part I. *Amer. Butterflies* 1(2):17–21.

Cech, R., ed. 1993. *A Distributional Checklist of the Butterflies and Skippers of the New York City Area (50 mile radius) and Long Island.* New York City Butterfly Club, New York.

Cech, R. 1995. Checkered White. *Anglewing* 2(1):6.

Chew, F. S. 1977. Coevolution of pierid butterflies and their cruciferous hostplants. II. The distribution of eggs on potential hostplants. *Evolution* 31:568–579.

Chew, F. S. 1979. Community ecology and *Pieris*-crucifer coevolution. *J. New York Entom. Soc.* 87:128–134.

Chew, F. S. 1981. Coexistence and local extinction in two pierid butterflies. *Amer. Nat.* 118:655–672.

Chew, F. S. 1995. From weeds to crops: Changing habitats of pierid butterflies (Lepidoptera: Pieridae). *J. Lepid. Soc.* 49:285–303.

Clark, A. H., and L. F. Clark. 1951. The butterflies of Virginia. *Smithsonian Misc. Collections* 116:1–239.

Clarke, C. A., and P. M. Sheppard. 1959. The genetics of some mimetic forms of *Papilio dardanus* and *Papilio glaucus*. *J. Genetics* 56:236–260.

Clarke, C. A., and P. M. Sheppard. 1962. The genetics of the mimetic butterfly, *Papilio glaucus*. *Ecology* 43:158-161.

Clarke, C. A., P. M. Sheppard, and U. Mittwoch. 1976. Heterochromatin polymorphism and colour pattern in the Tiger Swallowtail butterfly, *Papilio glaucus* L. *Nature* 263:585–586.

Clench, H. K. 1961. *Panthiades m-album* (Lycaenidae): Remarks on its early stages and on its occurrence in Pennsylvania. *J. Lepid. Soc.* 15:226–232.

Clench, H. K. 1967. Temporal dissociation and population regulation in certain Hesperiinae butterflies. *Ecology* 48:1000–1006.

Clench, H. K. 1979. How to make regional lists of butterflies: Some thoughts. *J. Lepid Soc.* 33:216–231.

Codella, S. G., Jr. 1986. Intersexual comparison of mimetic protection in the Black Swallowtail butterfly (*Papilio polyxenes asterius* Stoll). M.S. diss., Rutgers University, Newark, N.J.

Collenette, C. L. 1935. Notes concerning attacks by British birds on butterflies. *Proc. Zool. Soc. London* 1935:200–217.

Collins, B. R., and K. H. Anderson. 1994. *Plant Communities of New Jersey*. Rutgers University Press, New Brunswick.

Comstock, J. H., and A. B. Comstock. 1904. *How to Know the Butterflies*. D. Appleton, New York.

Comstock, W. P. 1940. Butterflies of New Jersey. *J. N.Y. Entomol. Soc.* 48:47–84.

Cottrell, C. B. 1984. Aphytophary in butterflies: Its relationship to myrmecophily. *Zool. J. Linnean Soc.* 79:1–57.

Courant, A. V., and F. S. Chew. 1995. Latent polyphenism and direct development in *Pieris virginiensis* (Pieridae). *J. Lepid. Soc.* 49:84–87.

Courant, A. V., A. E. Holbrook, E. D. van der Reijden, and F. S. Chew. 1994. Native pierine butterfly adapting to naturalized crucifer? *J. Lepid. Soc.* 48:168–170.

Covell, C. V., Jr., L. D. Gibson, R. A. Henderson, and M. L. McInnis. 1979. Six new state butterfly records from Kentucky. *J. Lepid. Soc.* 33:189–191.

Cromartie, W. J., and D. F. Schweitzer. 1993. Biology of the Rare Skipper, *Problema bulenta* (Hesperiidae), in southern New Jersey. *J. Lepid. Soc.* 47:125–133.

Cruickshank, A. D. 1942. *Birds around New York City*. American Museum of Natural History Handbook No. 13, New York.

Davis, W. T. 1893. Catalogue of the butterflies of Staten Island, New York. *J. New York Entomol. Soc.* 1:43–48.

Davis, W. T. 1909. The camp at Lakehurst. *J. New York Entomol. Soc.* 17:95–98.

Davis, W. T. 1910. List of the Macrolepidoptera of Staten Island, New York. *Proc. Staten Island Assoc. Arts and Sci.* 3:1–30. [Dated 1909.]

Davis, W. T. 1911. *Vanessa milberti* in New York City and vicinity in 1910. *J. New York Entomol. Soc.* 19:198.

Davis, W. T. 1912. A migration of Red Admiral butterflies. *J. New York Entomol. Soc.* 20:293–294.

Department of Environmental Protection. No date. *Guide to Wildlife Management Areas*. Trenton, New Jersey.

Department of Environmental Protection. 1992. *Special Animals of New Jersey*, Trenton, New Jersey.

Department of Labor. 1991. *Census of Population and Housing*. Trenton, New Jersey.

Department of Transportation. 1991. *New Jersey Place Names*. Trenton, New Jersey.

Dethier, V. G. 1941. Chemical factors determining the choice of foodplants by *Papilio* larvae. *Amer. Nat.* 75:61–73.

Dickerson, M. C. 1901. *Moths and Butterflies*. Ginn-Athenaeum Press, Boston.

DiGiovanni, D. M., and C. T. Scott. 1990. *Forest Statistics of New Jersey—1987*. U.S. Dept. of Agriculture, Northeastern Experiment Station Resource Bull. #112. Radnor, PA.

Dirig, R., and J. F. Cryan. 1991. The status of Silvery Blue subspecies (*Glaucopsyche lygdamus lygdamus* and *G.l. couperi*: Lycaenidae) in New York. *J. Lepid. Soc.* 45: 272–290.

dos Passos, C. F. 1936. Life history of *Calephelis borealis* (Lepidoptera). *Canadian Entomol.* 68:167–170.

dos Passos, C. F. 1948. The eye colors of some *Colias* collected in New Jersey. *Proc. Entomol. Soc. Wash.* 50:35–38.

dos Passos, C. F. 1956a. William Phillips Comstock, 1880–1956. *J. New York Entom. Soc.* 64:1–5.

dos Passos, C. F. 1956b. A bibliography of general catalogues and check lists of Nearctic Rhopalocera. *Lepid. News* 10:29–34.

dos Passos, C. F. 1965. A synonymic list of the Nearctic Rhopalocera. *Mem. Lepid. Soc.* 1:1–145.

dos Passos, C. F. 1966. *Pieris narina oleracera* (Harris) in New Jersey (Lepidoptera: Pieridae). *J. New York Entomol. Soc.* 74:222–223.

dos Passos, C. F., and A. B. Klots. 1969. The systematics of *Anthocharis midea* Hubner (Lepidoptera: Pieridae). *Entomol. Amer.* 45:1–34.

Dorwort, J. M. 1992. *Cape May County.* Rutgers University Press, New Brunswick, N.J.

Douglas, M. M. 1986. *The Lives of Butterflies.* University of Michigan Press, Ann Arbor.

Douwes, P. 1976. An area census method for estimating butterfly population numbers. *J. Res. Lepid.* 15:146–152.

Eanes, W. F., and R. K. Koehn. 1979. An analysis of genetic structure in the Monarch Butterfly *Danaus plexippus. Evolution* 32:784–797.

Edinger, G. 1995. Native *Eupatoriums* for the butterfly garden. *Amer. Butterflies* 3(4): 24–29.

Edmunds, M. 1974. Significance of beak marks on butterfly wings. *Oikos* 25:117–118.

Edwards, W. H. 1878a. Life history of *Danais Archippus. Psyche* 2:169–178.

Edwards, W. H. 1883. On the polymorphism of *Lycaena pseudoargiolus.* Bois. *Papilio* 3:85–97.

Ehrlich, P. R. 1957a. The higher systematics of the butterflies. *Lepid. News* 11:103–106.

Ehrlich, P. R. 1957b. Systematists and subspecies. *Lepid. News* 11:155–157.

Ehrlich, P. R. 1958. The comparative morphology, phylogeny and higher classification of the butterflies (Lepidoptera: Papilionoidea). *Univ. Kansas Sci. Bull.* 39:305–370.

Ehrlich, P. R. 1961. Has the biological species concept outlived its usefulness? *System. Zool.* 10:167–176.

Ehrlich, P. R. 1964. Some axioms of taxonomy. *System. Zool.* 13:109–123.

Ehrlich, P. R., and A. H. Ehrlich. 1961. *How to Know the Butterflies.* Wm. C. Brown Co., Dubuque, Iowa.

Ehrlich, P. R., and A. H. Ehrlich. 1967. The phenetic relationships of the butterflies. I. Adult taxonomy and the non-specificity hypothesis. *System. Zool.* 16:301–317.

Ehrlich, P. A., and A. H. Ehrlich. 1982. Lizard predation on tropical butterflies. *J. Lepid. Soc.* 36:148–152.

Ehrlich, P. R., and D. D. Murphy. 1981a. Butterfly nomenclature: A critique. *J. Res. Lepid.* 20:1–11.

Ehrlich, P. R., and D. D. Murphy. 1982. Butterflies and biospecies. *J. Res. Lepid.* 21: 219–225.

Ehrlich, P. R., and P. H. Raven. 1964. Butterflies and plants: A study in coevolution. *Evolution* 18:586–608.

Emmel, T. C. 1968. The population biology of the Neotropical satyrid butterfly *Euptychia hermes.* I. *J. Res. Lepid.* 7:153–165 (published 1970).

Emmel, T. C. 1969. Taxonomy, distribution and biology of the genus *Cercyonis* (Satyridae). I. Characteristics of the genus. *J. Lepid. Soc.* 23:165–176.

Emmel, T. C. 1972. Dispersal in a cosmopolitan butterfly species (*Pieris rapae*) having open population structure. *J. Res. Lepid.* 11:95–98.

Emmel, T. C., M. C. Minno, and A. Drummond. 1992. *Florissant Butterflies: A Guide to the Fossil and Present-Day Species of Central Colorado.* Stanford University Press, Stanford, Calif.

Engelhardt, G. P. 1912. *Calpodes ethlius* on Long Island. *J. New York Entomol. Soc.* 20:70.

Engelhardt, G. 1913. *Iphiclides ajax* Linnaeus on Long Island and *Catopsilia philea* Linnaeus in New York City. *J. New York Entomol. Soc.* 21:161–162.

Engelhardt, G. P. 1936. *Cissia mitchellii* in New Jersey. *Bull. Brooklyn Entom. Soc.* 31:110.

Erwin, T. L. 1983. Beetles and other insects of tropical forest canopies at Manaus, Brazil, sampled by insecticidal fogging. In *Tropical Rain Forest: Ecology and Management*, edited by S. L. Sutton, T. C. Whitmore, and A. C. Chadwick, pp. 59–75. Blackwell, Edinburgh, U.K.

Evans, W. H. 1955. A catalogue of the American Hesperiidae indicating the classification and nomenclature adopted in the British Museum (Natural History). Part IV. Hesperiinae and Megathyminae. British Museum, London.

Evans, W. H. 1958. A breeding experiment with pupal coloration of *Eurema nicippe* (Pieridae). *Lepidopterists' News* 12:95.

Fales, J. H. 1976. More records of butterflies as prey for ambush bugs (Heteroptera). *J. Lepid. Soc.* 30:147–149.

Fales, J. H., and D. T. Jennings. 1977. Butterflies as prey for crab spiders (Thomisidae). *J. Lepid. Soc.* 31:280–282.

Fee, F. D. 1979. Notes on the biology *Battus philenor* (Paplionidae) in Centre County, Pennsylvania. *J. Lepid. Soc.* 33:267–268.

Ferris, C. D. 1989. *Supplement to: A Catalogue/Checklist of the Butterflies of America North of Mexico*. Lepitoperists' Society Memoir No. 3.

Fiedler, K. 1994. Lycaenid butterflies and plants: Is myrmecophily associated with amplified host plant diversity? *Ecol. Entomol.* 19:79–82.

Field, W. D., J. H. Masters, and C. F. dos Passos. 1974. A Bibliography of the catalogs, lists, faunal and other papers on the butterflies of North America north of Mexico arranged by state and province (Lepidoptera: Rhopalocera). *Smithsonian Contrib. Zoology.* 157:1–104.

Fink, L. S., and L. P. Brower. 1981. Birds can overcome the cardenolide defence of Monarch Butterflies in Mexico. *Nature* 291:67–70.

Forbes, W. T. M. 1936. The *persius* group of *Thanaos*. *Psyche* 43:104–133.

Ford, E. B. 1964. *Ecological Genetics*. Methuen and Co., London.

French, G. H. 1886. *The Butterflies of the Eastern United States*. J. B. Lippincott Co., Philadealphia.

Friedlander, T. P. 1985. Egg mass design relative to surface-parasitizing parasitoids, with notes on *Asterocampa clyton* (Lepidoptera, Nymphalidae). *J. Res. Lepid.* 24:250–257.

Friedlander, T. 1986. Taxonomy, phylogeny and biogeography of *Asterocampa* Rober 1916 (Lepidoptera, Nymphalidae, Apaturinae). *J. Res. Lepid.* 25:215–337.

Gall, L. F. 1985. Measuring the size of lepidopteran populations. *J. Res. Lepid.* 24:97–116.

Garrahan, W. D., Jr. 1994. Early capture of *Phoebis sennae* in Rhode Island indicating historically significant early migration in 1992. *Lepid. Soc. News* 1994:64–65.

Garraway, E., and A. J. A. Bailey. 1992. Parasitoid-induced mortality in the eggs of the endangered Giant Swallowtail Butterfly *Papilio homerus*. *J. Lepid. Soc.* 46:233–234.

Gatrelle, R. R. 1971. Notes on the confusion between *Lethe creola* and *Lethe portlandia* (Satyridae) *J. Lepid. Soc.* 25:145–146.

Gilbert, L. E., and M. C. Singer. 1975. Butterfly ecology. *Ann. Rev. Ecol. Syst.* 6:365–397.

Glassberg, J. 1989. Searching for Bronze Coppers in the New York area. *Mulberry Wing* 5(1):3.

Glassberg, J. 1992. *Aglais urticae* (Nymphalidae): A nascent population in North America. *J. Lepid. Soc.* 46:302–304.

Glassberg, J. 1993a. The butterflying revolution. *Amer. Butterflies* 1(4):2.

Glassberg, J. 1993b. *Butterflies through Binoculars*. Oxford University Press, New York.

Glassberg, J. 1993c. The birth of butterflying. *Amer. Butterflies* 1(1):2.

Glassberg, J. 1993d. Binoculars for butterflying. *Amer. Butterflies* 1(2):22.

Glassberg, J. 1993e. Marine Blues flood North America. *Amer. Butterflies* 1(4):12.

Glassberg, J. 1994a. Identification of Eastern duskywings. Part I. *Amer. Butterflies* 2(1): 10–17.

Glassberg, J. 1994b. Identification of Eastern duskywings. Part II. *Amer. Butterflies* 2(3): 14–18.

Glassberg, J. 1994c. Editorial: A Rosa by any other nomen. *Amer. Butterflies* 2(2):2.

Gochfeld, M. 1990. The Checkered White (*Pontia protodice*): From abundance to rarity. *Friends of the Endangered and Nongame Species Program (NJDEP) Newsletter* 1(1): 2–3.

Gochfeld, M. 1993. Common vs. scientific names. *News Lepid. Soc.* 1993(3):86.

Gochfeld, M. 1994. New location for Checkered White: Newark Airport. *Mulberry Wing* 9(3):5.

Griscom, L. 1923. *Birds of the New York City Region.* American Museum of Natural History, New York.

Grossmueller, D. W., and R. C. Lederhouse. 1987. The role of nectar source distribution in habitat use and oviposition by the Tiger Swallowtail butterfly. *J. Lepid. Soc.* 41: 159–165.

Guppy, R. 1959. Host plants of *Strymon melinus atrofasciata. J. Lepid. Soc.* 13:170.

Hagen, R. H., R. C. Lederhouse, J. L. Bossart, and J. M. Scriber. 1991. *Papilio canadensis* and *P. glaucus* (Paplionidae) are distinct species. *J. Lepid. Soc.* 45:245–258.

Hall, G. C. 1916. *Limenitis ursula var. albofasciata. J. New York Entomol. Soc.* 24:93.

Hamilton, J. 1885. Entomology at Brigantine Beach in September. *Canadian Entomol.* 17:200–206.

Hammond, P. C., and D. V. McCorkle. 1983. The decline and extinction of *Speyeria* populations resulting from human environmental disturbances (Nymphalidae: Argynninae) *J. Res. Lepid.* 22:217–224.

Hazel, W. N., and D. A. West. 1979. Environmental control of pupal colour in swallowtail butterflies (Lepidoptera: Papilioninae): *Battus philenor* (L.) and *Papilio polyxenes* Fabr. *Ecol. Entomol.* 4:393–400.

Heitzman, J. R. 1963. The complete life history of *Staphylus hayhurstii. J. Res. Lepid.* 2:170–172.

Heitzman, J. R., and C. F. dos Passos. 1974. *Lethe portlandia* (Fabricus) and *L. anthedon* (Clark), sibling species, with descriptions of new subspecies of the former (Lepidoptera: Satyridae). *Trans. Amer. Entomol. Soc.* 100:52–99.

Heitzman, J. R., and R. L. Heitzman. 1969. *Hesperia metea* life history studies (Hesperiidae). *J. Res. Lepid.* 8:187–193.

Heston, A. M. 1924. *South Jersey: A History, 1664–1924.* Lewis Historical Publishing Co., New York.

Hoffmann, R. 1978. Environmental uncertainty and evolution of physiological adaptation in *Colias* butterflies. *Amer. Nat.* 112:99–1015.

Holland, W. J. 1898. *The Butterfly Book.* Doubleday and McClure, New York (rev. 1931).

Holland, W. J. 1931. *The Butterfly Book.* Revised edition. Doubleday, Doran, Garden City, N.Y.

Hook, T. V., and M. P. Zalucki. 1991. Oviposition by *Danaus plexippus* (Nymphalidae: Danainae) on *Asclepias viridis* in northern Florida. *J. Lepid. Soc.* 45:215–221.

Hovanitz, W. 1962. The distribution of the species of the genus *Pieris* in North America. *J. Res. Lepid.* 1:73–84.

Hovanitz, W. 1963. The relation of *Pieris virginiensis* Edw. to *Pieris napi* L: Species formation in *Pieris? J. Res. Lepid.* 1:124–234.

Hovanitz, W., and V. C. S. Chang. 1962a. The effect of various food plants on survival and growth rate of *Pieris. J. Res. Lepid.* 1:21–42.

Hovanitz, W., and V. C. S. Chang. 1962b. Three factors affecting larval choice of food plant. *J. Res. Lepid.* 1:51–62.

Hovanitz, W., and V. C. S. Chang. 1963. Change of food plant preference by larvae of *Pieris rapae* controlled by strain selection and the inheritance of this trait. *J. Res. Lepid.* 1:163–168.

Howard, L. O., F. M. Webster, and A. D. Hopkins. 1912. Dr. John Bernard Smith. *Proc. Entom. Soc. Wash.* 14:111–117.

Howe, W. H. 1958. What's in your backyard? *Lepidopterists' News* 12:130.

Howe, W. H., ed. 1975. *The Butterflies of North America*. Doubleday, New York.

Iftner, D. C., J. A. Shuey, and J. V. Calhoun. 1992. Butterflies and Skippers of Ohio. *Bull. Ohio Biological Survey* 9:1–210.

Iftner, D. C. and D. M. Wright. 1986. *Atlas of New Jersey Butterflies*. Self-published by the authors. Sparta, N.J.

Jeffords, M. R., J. R. Sternberg, and G. P. Waldbauer. 1979. Batesian mimicry: Field demonstration of the survival value of Pipevine Swallowtail and Monarch color patterns. *Evolution* 33:275–286.

Johnson, K., and P. M. Borgo. 1976. Patterned perching behavior in two *Callophrys* (*Mitoura*) (Lycaenidae). *J. Lepid. Soc.* 30:169–183.

Kettlewell, H. B. D. 1955. Selection experiments on industrial melanism in the Lepidoptera. *Heredity* 9:323–342.

Kilduff, T. S. 1972. A population study of *Euptychia hermes* in northern Florida. *J. Res. Lepid.* 11:219–228.

Kirby, W. F. 1837. Polyommatus in *Fauna Borealis Americana (Richardson)* 4:2.99.

Kirby, W. F. 1872. On the geographical distribution of the diurnal Lepidoptera as compared with that of the birds. *J. Linn. Soc. London Zool.* 11:431–439.

Klots, A. B. 1951. *A Field Guide to the Butterflies of North America East of the Great Plains*. Houghton Mifflin Co., Boston.

Klots, A. B. 1966. The larva of *Amblyscirtes samoset* (Scudder) (Lepidoptera: Hesperiidae). *J. New York Entomol. Soc.* 74:185–188.

Kohler, S. 1977. Revision of North American *Boloria selene* (Nymphalidae) with description of a new subspecies. *J. Lep. Soc.* 31:243–268.

Langlois, T. H., and M. H. Langlois. 1964. Notes on the life-history of the Hackberry Butterfly, *Asterocampa celtis* (Bdvl & Lec.) on South Bass Island, Lake Erie. *Ohio J. Sci.* 64:1–11.

Leck, C. F. 1973. Butterflies of Hutcheson Memorial Forest, and their ecological organization. *William L. Hutcheson Mem. For. Bull.* 3(1):1–2.

Leck, C. 1984. *The Status and Distribution of New Jersey's Birds*. Rutgers University Press, New Brunswick, N.J.

Lederhouse, R. C. 1982. Territorial defense and lek behavior of the Black Swallowtail butterfly, *Papilio polyxenes*. *Behav. Ecol. Sociobiol.* 10:109–118.

Lederhouse, R. C. 1983. Population structure, residency and weather-related mortality in the Black Swallowtail butterfly, *Papilio polyxenes*. *Oecologia* 59:307–311.

Lederhouse, R. C. 1993. Territoriality along flyways as mate locating behavior in male *Limenitis arthemis* (Nymphalidae). *J. Lepid. Soc.* 47:22–31.

Lederhouse, R. C., and J. M. Scriber. 1987. Ecological significance of a postmating decline in egg viability in the Tiger Swallowtail. *J. Lepid. Soc.* 41:83–93.

Levin, M. P. 1973. Preferential mating and the maintenance of the sex-limited dimorphism in *Papilio glaucus*—evidence from laboratory matings. *Evolution* 27:257–264.

Lorkovic, Z., and C. Herman. 1961. The solution of a long outstanding problem in the genetics of dimorphism in *Colias*. *J. Lepid. Soc.* 15:43–55.

McAlpine, W. S. 1971. A revision of the butterfly genus *Calephelis* (Riodinidae). *J. Res. Lepid.* 10:2–125.

McAlpine, W. S., S. P. Hubbell, and T. E. Pliske. 1960. The distribution, habits, and life history of *Euptychia mitchellii* (Satyridae). *J. Lepid. Soc.* 14:209–225.

McDunnough, J. 1938–39. Check Lists of the Lepidoptera of Canada and the United States of America. Part 1. Macrolepidoptera. *Mem. South. Calif. Acad. Sci.* 1:1–272.

McIsaac, H. P. 1991. The capture and release of a Monarch Butterfly (Nymphalidae: Danainae) by a Barn Swallow. *J. Lepid. Soc.* 45:62–63.

McPhee, J. 1967. *The Pine Barrens*. Noonday Press, New York.

Malcolm, S. B., and M. P. Zalucki, eds. 1993. *Biology and conservation of the Monarch Butterfly*. Los Angeles County Museum of Natural History, Los Angeles.

Mallis, A. 1971. *American Entomologists*. Rutgers University Press, New Brunswick.

Marshall, L. D. 1985. Protein and lipid composition of *Colias philodice* and *C. eurytheme* spermatophores and their changes over time (Pieridae). *J. Res. Lepid.* 24:21–30.

Masters, J. H. 1979. A documentation of biennialism in *Boloria polaris* (Nymphalidae). *J. Lepid. Soc.* 33:167–169.

Maynard, C. J. 1886. *The Butterflies of New England*. N.p.

Mayr, E. 1954. Notes on nomenclature and classification. *System. Zool.* 3:86–89.

Mayr, E. 1963. *Animal species and evolution*. Harvard University Press, Cambridge, Mass.

Mayr, E. 1969. *Principles of Systematic Zoology*. McGraw-Hill, New York.

Miller, J. S. 1987. Phylogenetic studies in the Papilioninae (Lepidoptera: Papilionidae). *Bull. Amer. Mus. Nat. Hist.* 186:365–512.

Miller, J. Y. 1992. *The Common Names of North American Butterflies*. Smithsonian Institution Press, Washington, D.C.

Miller, L. D., and F. M. Brown. 1981. *A Catalogue/Checklist of the Butterflies of America North of Mexico*. Lepidopterists' Society Memoir #2.

Morris, J. G. 1862. Synopsis of the Described Lepidoptera of North America. Part I. Diurnal and crepuscular Lepidoptera. Smithsonian Institution, Washington, D.C. *Smithsonian Misc. Collections* 1:1–420.

Muller, J. 1958. *Thymelicus lineola*, a European Skipper (Hesperiidae), new for New Jersey. *Lepidopterists' News* 12:174.

Muller, J. 1972. Is air pollution responsible for melanism in Lepidoptera and for scarcity of all orders of insects in New Jersey? *J. Res. Lepid.* 10:189–190.

Muller, J. 1976. Aberrant species of New Jersey Lepidoptera. *J. Res. Lepid.* 15:144–145.

Murphy, D. D., and P. R. Ehrlich. 1983. Opinion: Crows, bobs, tits, elfs and pixies: The phony "common name" phenomenon. *J. Res. Lepid.* 22:154–158.

Murphy, D. D., and P. R. Ehrlich. 1984. On butterfly taxonomy. *J. Res. Lepid.* 23:19–34.

NABA. 1993. English names for North American butterflies. *Amer. Butterflies* 1(1):21–29.

NABA. 1995. *Checklist and English Names of North American Butterflies*. North American Butterfly Association, Morristown, N.J.

New, T. R., ed. 1993. *Conservation Biology of the Lycaenidae (Butterflies)*. International Union for the Conservation of Nature, Occasional Paper No. 8, Gland, Switzerland.

Nielsen, V., and J. Monge-Najera. 1991. A comparison of four methods to evaluate butterfly abundance, using a tropical community. *J. Lepid. Soc.* 45:241–243.

Nijhout, H. F. 1980. Ontogeny of the color patterns on the wings of *Precis coenia* (Lepidoptera: Nymphalidae). *Develop. Biol.* 80:275–288.

Nijhout, H. F. 1991. *The Development and Evolution of Butterfly Wing Patterns*. Smithsonian Institution Press, Washington, D.C.

Odendaal, F. J., M. D. Rausher, B. Benrey and J. Nunez-Farfan. 1987. Predation by Anolis lizards on *Battus philenor* raises questions about butterfly mimicry systems. *J. Lepid. Soc.* 41:141–144.

Oliver, C. G. 1970. The environmental regulation of seasonal dimorphism in *Pieris napi oleracea* (Pieridae) *J. Lepid. Soc.* 24:77–81.

Oliver, C. G. 1972. Genetic and phenotypic differentiation and geographic distance in four species of Lepidoptera. *Evolution* 26:221–241.

Oliver, C. G. 1976. Photoperiodic regulation of seasonal polyphenism in *Phyciodes tharos* (Nymphalidae). *J. Lepid. Soc.* 30:260–263.

Oliver, C. G. 1979a. Experimental hybridization between *Phyciodes tharos* and *P. batesii* (Nymphalidae). *J. Lepid. Soc.* 33:6–20.

Oliver, C. G. 1979b. Genetic differentiation and hybrid viability within and between some Lepidoptera species. *Amer. Nat.* 114:681–694.

Oliver, C. G. 1980. Phenotypic differentiation and hybrid breakdown within *Phyciodes* 'tharos' (Lepidoptera: Nymphalidae) in the northeastern United States. *Ann. Entomol. Soc. Amer.* 73:715–721.

Oliver, C. G. 1982. Distinctiveness of *Megisto c. cymela* and *M. c. viola* (Satyridae). *J. Lepid. Soc.* 36:153.

Olson, L. 1962. Song sparrows feeding on Lepidoptera. *J. Lepid. Soc.* 16:136.

Opler, P. A. 1983. *County Atlas of Eastern United States Butterflies (1840–1982)*. U.S. Fish and Wildlife Service, Washington, D.C. (see Opler 1995 for revised title).

Opler, P. A. 1992. *Field Guide to Eastern butterflies*. 2d ed. Houghton Mifflin, Boston.

Opler, P. A. 1995. Lepidoptera of North America. 2. Distribution of the Butterflies (Papilionoidea and Hersperioidea) of the Eastern United States. C. P. Gillette Museum of Insect Biodiversity, Colorado State University, Fort Collins (revision of Opler's 1983 County Atlas updated through 1987).

Opler, P. A., and G. O. Krizek. 1984. *Butterflies East of the Great Plains.* Johns Hopkins University Press, Baltimore.

Osborn, H. 1912. John Bernard Smith. *J. Econ. Entomol.* 5:234–236.

Owen, D. F. 1971. *Tropical Butterflies.* Clarendon Press, Oxford.

Parshall, D. K., and T. W. Kral. 1989. A new subspecies of *Neonympha mitchellii* (French) (Satyridae) from North Carolina. *J. Lepid. Soc.* 42:114–119.

Pavulaan, H. 1990. The skippers (Hesperioidea) of Rhode Island with recent records of the true butterflies (Papilionidae). *Atala* 16:6–13.

Pavulaan, H., and D. M. Wright 1994. Out of the Azure and into the Lab: The Current State of *Celastrina* Research. *The Mulberry Wing* 10(1):406.

Perkins, E. M., and E. V. Gage. 1970. On the occurrence of *Limenitis archippus* x *L. lorquini* hybrids (Nymphalidae). *J. Res. Lepid.* 9:223–226.

Platt, A. P., and L. P. Brower. 1968. Mimetic versus disruptive coloration in intergrading populations of *Limenitis arthemis* and *astyanax* butterflies. *Evolution* 22:699–718.

Platt, A., R. Coppinger, and L. Brower. 1971. Demonstration of the selective advantage of mimetic *Limenitis* butterflies presented to caged avian predators. *Evolution* 25:692–701.

Platt, A. P., and J. R. Maudsley. 1994. Continued interspecific hybridization between *Limenitis (Basilarchia) arthemis astyanax* and *L. (B.) archippus* in the southeastern U.S. (Nymphalidae). *J. Lepid. Soc.* 48:190–198.

Pollard, E., and T. J. Yates. 1993. *Monitoring Butterflies for Ecology and Conservation.* Chapman and Hall, London.

Porter, A. H. 1994. Implications of introduced Garlic Mustard (*Alliaria petiolata*) in the habitat of *Pieris virginiensis* (Pieridae). *J. Lepid. Soc.* 48:171–172.

Porter, B. A. 1952. *Resistance to Insecticides. Yearbook of Agriculture.* U.S. Government Printing Office, Washington, D.C.

Powell, J. A. 1989. Presidential address, 1988: Lepidopterists—collectors *and* biologists? *J. Lepid. Soc.* 43:157–166.

Pratt, G. F., D. M. Wright, and H. Pavulaan 1994. The various taxa and hosts of the North American *Celastrina* (Lepidoptera: Lycaenidae). *Proc. Entomol. Soc. Wash.* 96(3):566-578.

Proctor, N. S. 1976. Mass hibernation site for *Nymphalis vau-album* (Nymphalidae). *J. Lepid. Soc.* 30:126.

Pullin, A. S., ed. 1995. *Ecology and Conservation of Butterflies.* Chapman and Hall, London.

Pyle, R. M. 1867. Conservation and the lepidopterist. *Bull. Assoc. Minn. Entomol.* 2:1–5.

Pyle, R. M. 1981. *The Audubon Society Field Guide to North American Butterflies.* Alfred A. Knopf, New York.

Pyle, R. M. 1984a. *Handbook for Butterfly Watchers.* Houghton Mifflin, Boston.

Pyle, R. M. 1984b. Rebuttal to Murphy and Ehrlich on common names of butterflies. *J. Res. Lepid.* 23:89–93.

Pyle, R. M. 1995. A history of Lepidoptera conservation, with special reference to its Remingtonian debt. *J. Lepid. Soc.* 49:397–411.

Rausher, M. D. 1979. Egg recognition: Its advantage to a butterfly. *Animal Behav.* 27:1034–1040.

Rawson, G. W. 1931. The addition of a new skipper, *Adopaea lineola* (Ochs.), to the list of U.S. Lepidoptera. *J. New York Entomol. Soc.* 39:503–506.

Rawson, G. W. 1945. Interesting problems connected with the Checkered White Butterfly *Pieris protodice* Boisduval and LeConte. *Bull. Brooklyn Entom. Soc.* 40:49–54.

Rawson, G. W., and J. B. Ziegler. 1950. A new species of *Mitroura* Scudder from the pine barrens of New Jersey (Lepidoptera, Lycaenidae). *J. New York Ent. Soc.* 58:69–82.

Rawson, G. W., J. B. Ziegler, and S. A. Hessel. 1951. The immature stages of *Mitroura hesseli* Rawson and Ziegler (Lepidoptera, Lycaenidae). *Bull. Brooklyn Entomol. Soc.* 46:123–134.

Remington, C. L. 1954. The genetics of *Colias* (Lepidoptera). *Adv. Genet.* 6:403–450.

Remington, C. L., and R. W. Pease, Jr. 1955. Studies in foodplant specificity. I. The suitability of Swamp White Cedar for *Mitoura gryneus* (Lycaenidae). *Lepid. News* 9:4–6.

Riepe, D., J. Ingraham, and G. Tudor. 1992. *Butterflies of the Jamaica Bay Wildlife Refuge.* Gateway National Recreation Area, New York.

Ritland, D. B. 1986. The effect of temperature on expression of the dark phenotype in female *Papilio glaucus* (Papilionidae). *J. Res. Lepid.* 25:179–187.

Ritland, D. B., and L. P. Brower. 1991. The Viceroy butterfly is not a Batesian mimic. *Nature* 350:497–498.

Robbins, R. K. 1982. How many butterfly species? *News Lepid. Soc.* 1982(3):40–41.

Robbins, R. K. 1987. Logic and phylogeny: A critique of Scott's phylogenies to the butterflies and Macrolepidoptera. *J. Lepid. Soc.* 41:214–216.

Robbins, R. K. 1993. False heads: The real tale. *Amer. Butterflies* 1(4):19–22.

Robbins, R. K. 1994. Naming hairstreaks. *Amer. Butterflies* 2(3):28–32.

Robertson-Miller, E. 1912. *The Butterfly and Moth Book.* Charles Scribner, New York.

Rothschild, M. 1961. Defensive odours and Müllerian mimicry among insects. *Trans. Royal Soc. Entom. London* 113:101–121.

Rothschild, M. 1972. Some observations on the relationship between plants, toxic insects and birds. In J. B. Harborne, ed., *Phytochemical ecology*, pp. 1–12. Academic Press, London.

Rothschild, M. 1991. *Butterfly Cooing Like a Dove.* Doubleday, London.

Rothschild, M., and C. Farrell. 1983. *The Butterfly Garden.* Michael Joseph, Ltd., London.

Ruffin, J. 1993a. Round-up review of butterfly gardening books. *Amer. Butterflies* 1(4): 27–29.

Ruffin, J. 1993b. *Where Are the Butterfly Gardens?* Lepidopterists' Society, Manhattan Beach, Calif.

Russell, E. W. B. 1981a. Vegetation of northern New Jersey before European settlement. *Amer. Midland Nat.* 105:1–12.

Russell, E. W. B. 1981b. Indian-set fires in the forests of the northeastern United States. *Ecology* 64:78–88.

Rutkowski, F. 1966. Rediscovery of *Euptychia mitchellii* (Satyridae) in New Jersey. *J. Lepid. Soc.* 20:43–44.

Rutowski, R. L. 1984. Sexual selection and the evolution of butterfly mating behavior. *J. Res. Lepid.* 23:125–142.

Rutowski, R. L. 1994. Questions about butterfly behavior: The case of the Empress Leilia. *Amer. Butterflies* 2(2):20–23.

Sakai, W. H. 1994. Avian predation on the Monarch Butterfly, *Danaus plexippus* (Nymphalidae: Danainae), at a California wintering site. *J. Lepid. Soc.* 48:148–156.

Sargent, T. D. 1995. On the relative acceptabilities of local butterflies and moths to local birds. *J. Lepid. Soc.* 49:148–162.

Saunders, A. A. 1932. Butterflies of the Alleghany State Park. *N.Y. State Mus. Handbook* 13:1–270.

Schweitzer, D. F. 1987. Identification and prioritization of New Jersey's rare Lepidoptera: 1981–1987. Proceedings of N.J. Rare and Endangered Plants and Animal Conference, Ramapo State College, October 1987.

Schweitzer, D. F. 1989. A review of category 2 insecta in USFWS Regions 3,4,5. Unpublished report for USFWS, Newton Corners Regional Office.

Scott, J. A. 1968. Hilltopping as a mating mechanism to aid the survival of low-density species. *J. Res. Lepid.* 7:191–204.

Scott, J. A. 1973. Lifespan of butterflies. *J. Res. Lepid.* 12:225–230.

Scott, J. A. 1975. Variability of courtship of the Buckeye butterfly, *Precis coenia* (Nymphalidae). *J. Res. Lepid.* 14:142–147.

Scott, J. A. 1984. The phylogeny of butterflies (Papilionoidea and Hesperioidea). *J. Res. Lepid.* 23:241–281.

Scott, J. A. 1986. *The Butterflies of North America.* Stanford University Press, Stanford, Calif.

Scott, J. A. 1988a. *Speyeria atlantis* in Colorado: Rearing studies concerning the relation between silvered and unsilvered forms. *J. Lepid. Soc.* 42:1–13.

Scott, J. A. 1988b. Biology of *Polyggonia progne nigrozephyrus* and related taxa (Nymphalidae). *J. Lepid. Soc.* 42:46–45.

Scott, J. A. 1994. Biology and systematics of *Phyciodes* (*Phyciodes*) *Papilio* (n.s.) 7: 1–120.

Scott, J. A., and R. E. Stanford. 1981. Geographic variation and ecology of *Hesperia leonardus* (Hesperiidae). *J. Res. Lepid.* 20:18–35.

Scott, F., and Wright. 1972. Small Tortoiseshell imported to Nova Scotia. *J. Lepid. Soc.* 26:116.

Scriber, J. M., R. V. Dowell, R. C. Lederhouse, and R. H. Hagen. 1990. Female color and sex ratio in hybrids between *Papilio glaucus glaucus* and *P. eurymedon, P. rutulus,* and *P. multicaudatus* (Papilionidae). *J. Lepid. Soc.* 44:229–244.

Scriber, J. M., and M. H. Evans. 1986. An exceptional case of paternal transmission of the dark form female trait in the Tiger Swallowtail butterfly, *Papilio glaucus* (Lepidoptera: Papilioninidae). *J. Res. Lepid.* 25:110–120.

Scriber, J. M., R. C. Lederhouse, and L. Contardo. 1975. Spicebush, *Lindera benzoin,* a little known foodplant of *Papilio glaucus* (Papilionidae). *J. Lepid. Soc.* 29:10–14.

Scudder, S. H. 1875. Fossil butterflies. *Mem. Amer. Assoc. Adv. Sci.* 1:1–98.

Scudder, S. H. 1877. The introduction and spread of *Pieris rapae* in North America, 1860–1885. *Mem. Boston Soc. Nat. Hist.* 4:53–69.

Scudder, S. H. 1889. *The Butterflies of the United States and Canada with Special Reference to New England.* 3 vols. Cambridge, Mass.

Scudder, S. H. 1893a. *The Life of the Butterfly.* Henry Holt, New York.

Scudder, S. H. 1893b. *A Brief Guide to the Commoner Butterflies of the Northern United States and Canada.* Henry Holt, New York.

Shapiro, A. M. 1962a. Notes on *Satyrium acadica* and other unusual hairstreak records (Lycaenidae) in southeastern Pennsylvania. *J. Lepid. Soc.* 16:199.

Shapiro, A. M. 1962b. *Colias* activity in November and December in Pennsylvania. *J. Lepid. Soc.* 16:129–130.

Shapiro, A. M. 1965. Ecological and behavioral notes on *Hesperia metea* and *Atrytonopsis hianna* (Hesperiidae). *J. Lepid. Soc.* 19:215–221.

Shapiro, A. M. 1966. *Butterflies of the Delaware Valley.* American Entomological Society, Philadelphia.

Shapiro, A. M. 1967. The origin of autumnal "false broods" of common Pierid butterflies. *J. Res. Lepid.* 6:181–183.

Shapiro, A. M. 1970a. Notes on the biology of *Poanes viator* (Hesperiidae) with the description of a new subspecies. *J. Res. Lepid.* 9:109–123.

Shapiro, A. M. 1970b. Postglacial biogeography and the distribution of *Poanes viator* and other marsh butterflies. *J. Res. Lepid.* 9:125–155.

Shapiro, A. M. 1971. Occurrence of a latent polyphenism in *Pieris virginiensis* (Lepidoptera: Pieridae) *Entomol. News* 82:13–16.

Shapiro, A. M. 1974a. Butterflies and skippers of New York State. *Search* 4:1–60.

Shapiro, A. M. 1974b. Beak-mark frequency as an index of seasonal predation intensity on common butterflies. *Amer. Nat.* 108:229–232.

Shapiro, A. M. 1978. Weather and the lability of breeding populations of the Checkered White butterfly, *Pieris protodice. J. Res. Lepid.* 17:1–23.

Shapiro, A. M. 1979. *Erynnis baptisiae* (Hesperidae) on Crown Vetch (Leguminosae). *J. Lepid. Soc.* 33:258.

Shapiro, A. M. 1982. Taxonomic uncertainty, the biological species concept, and the Nearctic butterflies: A reappraisal after twenty years. *J. Res. Lepid.* 212–218.

Shapiro, A. M. 1993. Long-range dispersal and faunal responsiveness to climatic change: A note on the importance of extralimital records. *J. Lepid. Soc.* 47:242–244.

Shapiro, A. M., and J. D. Biggs. 1968. A hybrid *Limenitis* from New York. *J. Res. Lepid.* 7:149–152.

Shapiro, A. M., and R. T. Cardé. 1970. Habitat selection and competition among sibling species of Satyrid butterflies. *Evolution* 24:48–54.

Shapiro, A. M., and H. Geiger. 1986. Electrophoretic confirmation of the species status of *Pontia protodice* and *P. occidentalis* (Pieridae). *J. Res. Lepid.* 25:39–47.

Shapiro, A. M., and A. R. Shapiro. 1973. The ecological associations of the butterflies of Staten Island (Richmond County, New York). *J. Res. Lepid.* 12:65–126.

Shapiro, I. 1975. Courtship and mating behavior of the Fiery Skipper, *Hylephila phylaeus* (Hesperiidae). *J. Res. Lepid.* 14:125–141.

Sheppard, P. M. 1975. *Natural Selection and Heredity.* 4th ed. Hutchinson, London.

Shields, O. 1967. Hilltopping. *J. Red. Lepid.* 6:69–178.

Shields, O. 1976. Fossil butterflies and the evolution of Lepidoptera. *J. Res. Lepid.* 15:132–143.

Shields, O. 1989. World numbers of butterflies. *J. Lepid. Soc.* 43:178–183.

Shields, O., J. F. Emmel, and D. E. Breedlove. 1969. Butterfly larval foodplant records and a procedure for reporting foodplants. *J. Res. Lepid.* 8:21–36.

Shuey, J. A. 1985. Habitat associations of wetland butterflies near the glacial maxima in Ohio, Indiana and Michigan. *J. Res. Lepid.* 24:176–186.

Shuey, J. A. 1986. Comments on Clench's temporal sequencing of Hesperiid communities. *J. Res. Lepid.* 25:202–206.

Shuey, J. A., E. H. Metzler, D. C. Iftner, J. V. Calhoun, J. W. Peacock, R. A. Watkins, J. D. Hooper, and W. F. Babcock. 1987. Status and habitats of potentially endangered Lepidoptera in Ohio. *J. Lepid. Soc.* 41:1–12.

Silberglied, R. E., and O. R. Taylor. 1973. Ultraviolet differences between the Sulphur butterflies, *Colias eurytheme* and *C. philodice*, and a possible isolating mechanism. *Nature* 241:406–408.

Silberglied, R. E., and O. R. Taylor. 1978. Ultraviolet reflection and its behavioral role in the courtship of the Sulfur butterflies *Colias eurytheme* and *C. philodice. Behav. Ecol. Sociobiol.* 3:203–243.

Simmons, R. S., and W. A. Andersen. 1962. Notes on five new butterfly records for the state of Maryland. *J. Lepid. Soc.* 15:99–101.

Simmons, R. S., and W. A. Andersen. 1970. Eighteen new or scarce butterflies for the state of Maryland. *J. Res. Lepid.* 9:175–184.

Simmons, R. S., and W. A. Andersen. 1978a. Notes on Maryland Lepidoptera No. 7: Eight new butterfly records for the state of Maryland. *J. Res. Lepid.* 17:253–255.

Simmons, R. S., and W. A. Andersen. 1978b. Notes on Maryland Lepidoptera No. 8: *Erora laeta* (Edw.). *J. Res. Lepid.* 17:255–257.

Simmons, R. S., and W. A. Andersen. 1978c. Notes on Maryland Lepidoptera No. 9: Seven new butterfly records for the state of Maryland. *J. Res. Lepid.* 17:257–259.

Simpson, R. G., and D. Pettus. 1976. Records of *Limenitis* hybrids from Colorado. *J. Res. Lepid.* 15:163–168.

Singer, M. C., and P. Wedlake. 1981. Capture does affect probability of recapture in a butterfly species. *Ecol. Entomol.* 6:215–216.

Skinner, H., and E. M. Aaron. 1889. Butterflies of Philadelphia, Pa. *Canadian Entomologist* 21:126–131, 145–149.

Skinner, H. 1896. Impressions received from a study of our North American Rhopalocera. *J. New York Entomol. Soc.* 4:107–118.

Slansky, F., Jr. 1972. Latitudinal gradients in species diversity of the New World butterflies. *J. Res. Lepid.* 11:201–217.

Slosson, A. T. 1893. Common versus proper. *J. New York Entomol. Soc.* 1:1–5.

Smith, D. S., L. D. Miller, and J. Y. Miller. 1994. *The Butterflies of the West Indies and South Florida.* Oxford University Press, New York.

Smith, J. B. 1884a. Synopsis of the N.A. species of *Satyrus* West. with notes on the species collected by the N. Transcontinental Survey. *Bull. Brooklyn Entomol. Soc.* 6:125–135.

Smith, J. B. 1884b. An introduction to a classification of the N.A. Lepidoptera. *Bull. Brooklyn Entomol. Soc.* 7:70–74, 81–83, 141–149.

Smith, J. B. 1890. *Catalogue of Insects Found in New Jersey.* Report of the Geological Survey, Trenton.

Smith, J. B. 1900. *Insects of New Jersey.* Supplement to the Twenty-seventh Annual Report of the State Board of Agriculture, 1899. MacCrellish and Quigley, Trenton.

Smith, J. B. 1910. *Report on the Insects of New Jersey.* Annual Report of the New Jersey State Museum 1909. MacCrellish and Quigley, Trenton.

Smith, J. E. 1797. *The Natural History of the Rarer Lepidopterous Insects of Georgia*. With plates by John Abbot.

Sokal, R. R., and T. J. Crovello. 1970. The biological species concept: A critical evaluation. *Amer. Nat.* 104:127–153.

Sokal, R. R., and P. H. A. Sneath. 1963. *Principles of Numerical Taxonomy*. W. Freeman, San Francisco.

Spomer, S. M., L. G. Higley, T. T. Orwing, G. L. Selby, and L. J. Young. 1993. Clinal variation in *Hesperia leonardus* (Hesperiidae) in the Loess Hills of the Missouri River Valley. *J. Lepid. Soc.* 47:291–302.

Stamp, N. E. 1981. Effect of group size on parasitism in a natural population of the Baltimore Checkerspot *Euphydryas phaeton*. *Oecologia* 49:201–206.

Stamp, N. E. 1982. Behavioral interactions of parasitoids and Baltimore checkerspot caterpillars (*Euphydryas phaeton*). *Environ. Entom.* 11:100–104.

Stamp, N. E. 1984. Interactions of parasitoids and checkerspot caterpillars *Euphydryas* spp. (Nymphalidae). *J. Res. Lepid.* 23:2–18.

Stamp, N. E., and T. M. Casey, eds. 1993. *Caterpillars—Ecological and Evolutionary Constraints on Foraging*. Chapman and Hall, New York.

Stanford, R. E. 1994. Presidential address 1993: On the comparative distributions of Lepidoptera and lepidopterists. *J. Lepid. Soc.* 48:1–7.

Stein, S. 1995. The Little Bluestem meadow: Plant your field of dreams and the butterflies will come. *Amer. Butterflies* 3(2):24–28.

Stone, W. 1909. *The Birds of New Jersey*. Annual Report, New Jersey State Museum—1908, Trenton.

Stone, W. 1910. *The Plants of Southern New Jersey with Especial Reference to the Flora of the Pine Barrens and the Geographic Distribution of the Species*. Annual Report, New Jersey State Museum—1909, Trenton.

Straatman, R. 1962. Notes on certain Lepidoptera ovipositing on plants which are toxic to their larvae. *J. Lepid. Soc.* 16:99–103.

Swengel, A. B. 1990. Monitoring butterfly populations using the Fourth of July butterfly count. *Amer. Midland Natur.* 124:395–406.

Swengel, A. 1993a. 4th of July butterfly count column. *Amer. Butterflies* 1(1):30.

Swengel, A. 1993b. 4th of July butterfly count column: History of the count program. *Amer. Butterflies* 1(4):38.

Swengel, A. 1993c. Regal Fritillary: Prairie royalty. *Amer. Butterflies* 1(1):4–9.

Swengel, A. B. 1994a. 4th of July butterfly count column: News from the 1993 counts. *Amer. Butterflies* 2(1):38.

Swengel, A. B. 1994b. 4th of July butterfly count column: Monarch monitor. *Amer. Butterflies* 2(2):38.

Swengel, A. B. 1995. Population fluctuations of the Monarch (*Danaus plexippus*) in the 4th of July Butterfly count, 1977–1994. *Amer. Midland Nat.* 134:205–214.

Swynnerton, C. F. M. 1915. Birds in relation to their prey. Experiments on wood-hoopoes, small hornbills, and a babbler. *J. South African Ornith. Union.* 1915:22–108.

Tasker, R. R. 1975. A second extant colony of *Pieris virginiensis* in Ontario (Pieridae). *J. Lepid. Soc.* 29:23.

Taylor, O. R. 1972. Random vs. non-random mating in the sulfur butterflies, *Colias eurytheme* and *C. philodice*. *Evolution* 26:344–356.

Tedrow, J. C. F. 1963. *Soils of New Jersey*. Robert E. Krieger, Malabar, Fla.

Tilden, J. W. 1962. General characteristics of the movements of *Vanessa cardui* L. *J. Res. Lepid.* 1:43–49.

Treat, A. 1975. *Mites of Moths and Butterflies*. Cornell University Press, Ithaca, N.Y.

Turner, J. D. 1990. Vertical stratification of hilltopping behavior in swallowtail butterflies (Papilionidae). *J. Lepid. Soc.* 44:174–179.

Turner, J. R. G. 1977. Butterfly mimicry: The genetical evolution of an adaptation. *Evol. Biology* 10:163–206.

Tutt, J. W. 1908. Form *neglecta-major*. *Natural History of the Lepidoptera* (London) 9:407.

Tyler, H., K. S. Brown, Jr., and K. Wilson. 1994. *Swallowtail Butterflies of the Americas*. Scientific Publications, Gainesville, Fla.

U.S. Department of Commerce. 1993. Climatologic Data, New Jersey. 1992. *Natl. Oceanic and Atmospheric Admin. Annual Summary* 95:13–30.

Urquhart, F. A. 1976. Found at last: The Monarch's winter home. *National Geographic* 150:160–173.

Urquhart, F. A. 1987. *The Monarch Butterfly: International Traveler*. Nelson-Hall, Chicago.

Urquhart, F. A., and N. R. Urquhart. 1976. The overwintering site of the eastern population of the Monarch Butterfly (*Danaus p. plexippus*: Danaidae) in southern Mexico. *J. Lepid. Soc.* 30:153–158.

USFWS. 1991. Endangered and threatened wildlife and plants: Proposal to list the Mitchell's Satyr as endangered. U.S. Fish and Wildlife Service. *Federal Register* 56(176): 46273–46277.

USFWS. 1995a. Endangered and threatened wildlife and plants: Saint Francis' Satyr determined to be endangered. U.S. Fish and Wildlife Service. *Federal Register* 60(17): 5264–5267.

USFWS. 1995b. Technical/agency draft recovery plan for St. Francis Satyr (*Neonympha mitcellii* ssp. *franciscii*). U.S. Fish and Wildlife Service, Southeast Region, Atlanta.

van Sommern, V. G. L., and T. H. E. Jackson. 1959. On protective resemblance amongst African Lepidoptera. *J. Lepid. Soc.* 13:121–150.

Vane-Wright, R. I., and P. R. Ackery. 1984. *The Biology of Butterflies*. Symposium of the Royal Entomological Society of London, No. 11, Academic Press, London. (Reprinted by Princeton University Press, Princeton, N.J., 1989).

Vasconcellos-Neto, J., and T. M. Lewinsohn. 1984. Discrimination and release of unpalatable butterflies by *Nephila clavipes*, a neotropical orb-weaving spider. *Ecol. Entomol.* 9:337–344.

Vawter, A. T., and P. F. Brussard. 1975. Genetic stability of populations of *Phyciodes tharos* (Nymphalidae: Melitaeniae). *J. Lepid. Soc.* 29:15–23.

Vawter, A. T., and P. F. Brussard. 1983. Allozyme variation in a colonizing species: The Cabbage Butterfly *Pieris rapae* (Pieridae). *J. Res. Lepid.* 22:204–216.

Vawter, A. T., and J. Wright. 1986. Genetic differentiation between subspecies of *Euphydryas phaeton* (Nymphalidae: Nymphalinae). *J. Res. Lepid.* 25:25–29.

Vermeule, C. C. 1899. Report on forests. *Annual Rep. New Jersey State Geologist*. Trenton, N.J.

Wagner, D. 1995. Rearing Regals for reintroduction: Playing the odds but still losing ground. *Amer. Butterflies* 3(2):19–23.

Waldbauer, G. P. 1988. Aposematism and Batesian mimicry. *Evol. Biology* 22:227–260.

Walter, S. 1993. Marine Blue: A first East Coast record. *Mulberry Wing* 9(3):7–8.

Walton, R. 1993. Tracking North American Monarchs. Part I. The East. *Amer. Butterflies* 1(3):11–16.

Walton, R. K., and L. P. Brower. 1996. Monitoring the fall migration of the Monarch Butterfly *Danaus plexippus* L. (Nymphalidae, Danainae) in eastern North America: 1991–1994. *J. Lepid. Soc.* 50:1–20.

Watt, W. B. 1973. Adaptive significance of pigment polymorphisms in *Colias* butterflies. III. Progress in the study of the "alba" variant. *Evolution* 27:537–548.

Watt, W. B. 1995. Descent with modification: Evolutionary study of *Colias* in the tradition of Charles Remington. *J. Lepid. Soc.* 49:272–284.

Webster, R. P., and M. C. Nielsen. 1984. Myrmecophily in the Edwards' Hairstreak butterfly *Satyrium edwardsii* (Lycaenidae). *J. Lepid. Soc.* 38:124–133.

Weed, C. M. 1917. *Butterflies Worth Knowing*. Doubleday Page, Garden City, N.Y.

West, D. A., and W. N. Hazel. 1979. Natural pupation sites of swallowtail butterflies (Lepidoptera: Papilioninae): *Papilio polyxenes* Fabr., *P. glaucus* L. and *Battus philenor* (L). *Ecol. Entomol.* 4:387–392.

West, D. A., W. M. Snellings, and T. A. Herber. 1972. Pupal color dimorphism and its environmental control in *Papilio polyxenes asterius* Stoll (Lepidoptera:Papilionidae). *J. New York Entomol. Soc.* 80:205–211.

White, R. R. 1986. The trouble with butterflies. *J. Res. Lepid.* 25:207–212.

Widmer, K. 1964. *The Geology and Geography of New Jersey*. D. Van Nostrand Co. Princeton, N.J.

Wilkinson, R. S. 1988a. Cyril Franklin dos Passos (1887–1986). *J. Lepid. Soc.* 42: 155–163.

Wilkinson, R. S. 1988b. Annotated bibliography of the entomological publications of Cyril F. dos Passos (1887–1986). *J. Lepid. Soc.* 42:168–183.

Williams, C. B. 1958. *Insect Migration.* Macmillan, New York.

Williams, R. C. 1941. Butterflies which may be found within 50 miles of Philadelphia. *Entomol. News* 52:217–218.

Wilsmann, L. A., and D. F. Schweitzer. 1991. A rangewide status survey of Mitchell's satyr *Neonympha mitchellii mitchellii* (Lepidoptera: Nymphalidae). Unpublished report for USFWS, Twin Cities Regional Office.

Wilson, E. O. 1988. *Biodiversity.* National Academy Press, Washington, D.C.

Wilson, E. O., and W. L. Brown, Jr. 1953. The subspecies concept. *System. Zool.* 2: 97–111.

Wolfe, P. E. 1977. *The Geology and Landscape of New Jersey.* Crane Russak, New York.

Woodbury, E. N. 1994. *Butterflies of Delmarva.* Tidewater, Centreville, Md.

Wooley, R. L., L. C. Keenan, M. N. Nelson, and R. E. Stanford. 1991. Oviposition behavior and nectar sources of the Pawnee Montane Skipper, *Hesperia leonardus montana* (Hesperiidae). *J. Lepid. Soc.* 45:239–240.

World Almanac and Book of Facts. 1993. World Almanac/Scripps Howard, New York.

Worth, C. B. 1972. *Of Mosquitoes, Moths and Mice.* W. W. Norton. New York.

Wright, A. B. 1993. *Peterson First Guide to Catepillars of North America.* Houghton Mifflin, Boston.

Wright, D. 1985. *Butterflies of Cape May County.* Cape May Geographic Society 39th Annual Bulletin, pp.1-5.

Wright, D. 1989. *Checklist of Butterflies of Cape May County.* New Jersey Audubon Society, Cape May Bird Observatory.

Wright, D. 1995. the American Azures: Our blue heaven. *Amer. Butterflies* 3(1):20–28.

Wright, D., and P. Sutton. 1993. *Checklist of Butterflies of Cape May County.* 2d ed. Cape May Bird Observatory.

Wright, D. M. 1983. Life history and morphology of the immature stages of the Bog Copper butterfly *Lycaena epixanthe* (Bsd & Le C.). *J. Res. Lepid.* 22:47–100.

Xerces Society. 1990. *Butterfly Gardening.* Sierra Club Books, San Francisco.

Ziegler, J. B. 1953. Notes on the life history of *Incisalia augustinus* and a new host plant record. *J. Lepid. Soc.* 7:33–35.

Ziegler, J. B. 1960. Preliminary contribution to a redefinition of the genera of North American Hairstreaks (Lycaenidae) north of Mexico. *J. Lepid. Soc.* 14:19–23.

Zirlin, H. 1993. Taxonomists just wanna have fun: Oh those poetic duskywings. *Amer. Butterflies* 1(3):21–23.

Zirlin, H. 1994a. Taxonomists just wanna have fun: Swallowtails of the Trojan War. *Amer. Butterflies* 2(1):25–27.

Zirlin, H. 1994b. Taxonomists just wanna have fun: Fauns, satyrs and nymphs still inhabit our woodlands. *Amer. Butterflies* 2(3):25–27.

Subject and Locality Index

Place names followed by a two-letter abbreviation in parentheses are locatable in the Gazeteer (Appendix A). Whether or not they are shown on the maps, place names are also followed by the county (in parentheses). Pages in boldface refer to the species accounts for butterflies in the main text and for plants in the gardening chapter.

146, 153, 157, 171, 174, 180–181, 204, 224, 236, 238, 241, 244, 249, 252, 255
conspecifics, 20, 268
Cook, Captain, 76
Coppers (Lycaeninae), 12, 13, 114, **144–147**
county records, 113–114
Cramer, Peter, 76
cranberry bogs, 83, 146, 182, 207
Cranford (CR) (Union), 262–263
Cretaceous period, 10
Cromartie, William J., 81
crop pests, 122, 133, 216
Cruickshank, A. D., xviii
crypsis, 51, 52, 89, 197, 268
Culver's Pond (Sussex), 194
Cumberland County: 4JC, 90, 162, 185, 196, 250; salt marshes, 284

DaCosta (DC) (Atlantic), 264–265
daily rhythm, xv, 38, 151, 161, 205
Danainae (Milkweed butterflies), **212–214**
Darrow, Harry, 81, 115
Davis, William Thompson, 79, 194
DDT, 33. *See also* insecticides
Deal (DL) (Monmouth), 208, 263–264
deforestation, 66–67, 73, 86
Delaware Bay, 71, 162
Delaware–Raritan Canal, 182
Delaware Valley, 69, 70, 72, 141, 239, 250, 259
Delaware Water Gap (DWG) (Warren), 70, 134, 159, 221, 262, 281
Delmarva, 119, 131, 146, 148, 151, 171, 176, 178, 198, 206, 207
Delmont (DL) (Cumberland), 162, 250, 264–265
Dennisville (DN) (Cape May), 182, 235, 236, 254, 264–265
diapause, 40, 126, 166, 181, 189, 268
Dickerson, Mary, 77, 128
dimorphism, 136, 248, 249; larvae, 157; sexual, 125, 248, 249, 268
Dismal Swamp (VA), 126, 148
dispersal, 15, 16
distraction, 197, 268

distribution, xviii, 30, 31, 57, 87; cosmopolitan, 196, 212; disjunct, 112, 150, 155, 156, 172–174, 186, 187, 208, 221, 224, 228, 237, 246, 249, 251, 253, 268; holarctic, 133, 145, 192, 196, 211, 228, 234
ditching, 72
diurnal cycle, 205. *See also* daily rhythm
diversity, 7, 108, 164
dos Passos, Cyril, 79–80, 129–130
Douwes Method (censusing), 92–93
Dover (DV) (Morris), 149, 209, 262
Dowdell, Jim, 81, 115
Downe (DO) (Cumberland), 255, 264–265
dragonflies, 49–50
Dutko, Rick, 81
Dwarf Forest, (pine barrens) (DF) (Ocean), 264
Dyar, Harrison Gray, 78

Eagle Rock (ER) (Essex), 224, 262–263
East Brunswick, 235
East Millstone (EM) (Somerset), 262–263
eclosion, 40
ecological chemistry, 53
ecological races and variation, 29, 157, 188–189
ecology, 16, 57, 82–86
ecotourism, 213
ecotypes, 157, 188–189, 268
edge habitat, 82
Edwards, William H., 76–77, 166, 168–169
egg laying, 6, 52, 120. *See also* host discrimination
egg masses, 188
eggs, 41, 53; predation on, 52
Ehrlich, Paul and Ann, 9, 15, 17, 18, 22, 26, 29, 77
Eldora (EL) (Cape May), 264–265
electrophoresis, 186
Elfins (Theclinae), **147–164**
Elia, Vince, 81
Elizabeth (EL) (Union), 142, 146, 152, 177, 243, 247, 262–263
Elks Neck State Park (MD), 121
emergence, 41
Emmel, Tom, 207
Emperors (Apaturinae), 14, 114, **201–203**

Endangered and Nongame Species Program, 5, 39
endemism, 107
Englewood (EN) (Bergen), 235, 262
environmental variability, 167
Eriosomatidae (Woolly Aphid), 144
escapes, 177. *See also* butterfly releasing; species, introduced
estuaries, 246
evolution, 10, 15, 18, 27, 51, 57. *See also* speciation
Ewingville (EW) (Mercer), 263–264
experiments, 212; hybridization, 186
extinctions, 8, 38, 85, 109, 180, 269. *See also* extirpations
extirpations, 8, 108–111, 123, 148, 160, 173, 180, 183, 187, 190, 193, 207, 208, 216, 223, 227, 228, 244, 245, 269
eye spots, 52–53. *See also* Satyrinae

Fabricius, Johann Christian, 76
Fairton (FT) (Cumberland), 180, 264–265
Fairview (FV) (Bergen), 126, 262
Fall Line, 65, 67, 128, 146, 157–158, 178–179, 183, 184, 194, 202, 221, 224, 233, 237, 238, 244, 247, 252, 269
farming, 65
fens, 72, 73, 83, 107, 149, 208, 209, 241, 251, 252
fire, 7, 65, 73, 86, 209; suppression, 187
Five Mile Beach (5B) (Cape May), 6, 120, 151, 152, 159, 216, 235, 243, 264–265
Flemington (FL) (Hunterdon), 262–263
flight period, 41; allochronic, 41, 267. *See also* phenology
Flushing (FL) (Queens, NY), 265
Folded-Wing Skippers (Hesperiinae), 13, 15, **231–259**
Folsom (Gloucester), 154
Ford, E.B., 3
forelegs, 12–14, 143, 203
forest cover, 66–67

host switching, 188, 226
Hubner, Jacob, 76
Hudson Valley (NY), 171, 248
Hudsonian Life Zone, 7
human-assisted occurrence, 32, 34, 176, 177, 195, 257
human population, xvi, **66–67**, 214
human settlement, 65
Hutcheson Memorial Forest (HMF) (Somerset), 7, 144, 177, 262–263
hybridization, 17, 20, 130, 135, 137–138, 186, 201

Iftner, David, 9, 81, 224
immigrant, seasonal, 139, 141, 142, 175, 177, 192, 197, 198, 215, 228, 230, 233, 235, 244, 256, 258
Indian Mills (IM) (Burlington), 224, 264
industrial sites, 129
industrialization, 94, 173
insect classification, 9
insecticides, xvi, xvii, 7, 33, 85, 98, 171, 204, 205, 209, 224, 228, 254, 257
Integrated Pest Management, 258
interbreeding, 17, 130, 160. *See also* hybridization
intergradation, 212
International Code of Zoological Nomenclature (ICZN), 21, 269
introgression, 200, 270
invasion, 8, 30, 45, 73–74, 137, 210, 257, 258
Iona (IO) (Gloucester), 254, 264–265
Irvington (IR) (Essex), 262–263
Iselin (IS) (Middlesex), 119, 262–263
Island Beach State Park (IB) (Ocean), 264, 283
isolation, 17

Jakes Landing (JL) (Cape May), 264–265, 284
Jamaica Bay (JB) (Brooklyn, NY), 91, 128, 129, 216, 265
Jamesburg (JA) (Middlesex), xix, 147, 148, 150, 152, 180, 182, 223, 224, 247, 262–263
Jersey City (JC) (Hudson), 121, 221, 262–263
Johnsonberg (JO) (Warren), 262

Kendall Park (KP) (Middlesex), 113, 128, 159, 182, 262–263
Kennedy Airport (NY), 146
Keyport (KP) (Monmouth), 263–264
King method (censusing), 92–93
Kirby, W. F., 11, 166
Kite Swallowtails, 121
Kittatinny Mountains, 70, 82
Klots, Alexander, xiii, 80, 129, 132
Klots' Bog (Lakehurst, Ocean), xiii, 147, 283
Kudzma, Linas, 81, 115

Lake Hopatcong (LH) (Sussex), 6, 70, 128, 148, 161, 184, 206, 210, 235, 261–262. *See also* Hopatcong
Lake Lackawanna (LL) (Sussex), 261–262
Lakehurst (LH) (Ocean), xix, 86, 87, 121, 128, 135, 144, 145, 147, 152, 153, 156, 161, 162, 193, 206–208, 217, 223, 237, 245, 247, 252–255, 259, 264, 283; 4JC, 90, 153
Lakewood (LW) (Ocean), xix, 156, 254, 255, 264
Lambertville (LV) (Hunterdon), 262–263
landscape, 7
larvae, 42, 46, 53; bird-dropping mimics, 119, 126; coloniality, 189; development and growth of, 133, 138; hosts for, 98, 103–104, 118; predation on, 51, 52
Laurel Springs (LS) (Camden), 224, 264–265
Lavallette (LV) (Ocean), 264
Lawrenson, John, 115
leaf litter, 163
Lebanon (LB) (Hunterdon), 262–263
Lebanon State Forest (LS) (Ocean–Burlington), 264
Leck, Mary and Charles, xvii, 30, 81, 115, 283
LeConte, J. E., 77
Lederhouse, Robert, 80, 122
lek, 123, 270
LeMarchant, Michelle, 115
Lepidoptera, general, 4, 10
Lepidopterists' Society, 113
Libytheinae (Snouts), **175–176**
life cycles, 40, 41, 53, 56, 94, 95, 138

life histories, 56. *See also* life cycles
Limenitidinae (Admirals, Viceroy), **199–201**
limestone ridges, 83, 174
Lincoln Park (LP) (Morris), 262
Linnaeus, C., 22, 75–76
Livingston (LV) (Essex), 262–263
lizards, 46, 49, 55, 120
logging, 214
Long Island (NY), 126, 137–139, 142, 149, 156, 163
longevity, 193, 194
lumping of taxa, 20, 154, 159, 270
Lycaenidae (Harvesters, Blues, Coppers, Hair-streaks), 11, 13, 107
Lycaeninae (Coppers), **144–147**

McAlpine, Wilbur, 173
McDunnough, James Halliday, 77
McPhee, John, 66
Manahawkin (Ocean), 147
Manasquan (MA) (Monmouth), 139, 142, 163, 263–264
Mannington Marsh (MN) (Salem), 264–265
Manumuskin (MU) (Cumberland), 237, 264–265
Maplewood (MA) (Essex), 203, 262–263
Marcus Hook (MH) (Pennsylvania), 256, 264, 266
mark-release-recapture techniques, 88–89, 270
Mashipacong Lake and Bog (MA) (Sussex), 147, 180, 252, 261–262
mate attraction, 125, 197
mating, 40, 41, 55–56, 125, 198
Maurice River area (MR) (Cumberland), 245, 264–265
Maynard, C. J., 77
Mayr, Ernst, 15–20
Medford (MD) (Burlington), 224, 264
Medford Lakes (ML) (Burlington), 154, 264
melanism, 28, 125, 135, 270; industrial, 28, 269
Metalmarks (Riodinidae), 13, 114, **173–174**
metapopulation, 16, 209, 270
mice, 46
midges, 50

Taxonomic Index to Butterflies, Other Animals, and Plants

Pages in boldface refer to the species accounts for butterflies in the main text and for plants in the gardening chapter.

Abutilon theophrasi, 230
Acanthaceae, 199
Acer rubrum, 86
Aceraceae, 86, 124
Achalarus lyciades, 24, 36, 45, **217**
Actinomeris alternifolia, 171, 184
Adelgid, Woolly, 73
Admiral, 14; Lorquin's, 201; Red, 23, 25, 36, 44, 52–53, 92, 98, 99, 103, **197**; Weidermeyer's, 201; White, 23, 53, **199–200**
Aedes sollicitans, 258
African Lovegrass, 238
Aglias, 24, 43, **194–195**. *See also Nymphalis*
Agraulis vanillae, 23, 25, 32, 43, **176–177**
Agrostis spp., 236, 255
'alba.' *See Colias*; Sulphur
Alder, 144
Alfalfa, 43, 97, 98, 103, 136–139, 165, 219, 230, 239
Allaria petiolata, 45, 131, 133
Allium, 99, **103**
Alnus spp., 144
Althaea spp., 45, 196, 230
Amaranth, 220, 231
Amaranthus spp., 220, 231
Amblyscirtes: hegon, 25, 44, 83, 111, **254–255**; *vialis*, 24, 33, 37, 44, 85, 111, **255–256**
Ambrosia, 231
Ambush Bugs, 50
Ameiva lizards, 49, 55

American Lady (also American Painted Lady), 3, 23, 33, 36, 39, 92, 98, 103, **195–196**
americana (subsp. of *Lycaena phlaeus*), xviii, 23, 24, 32, 35, 43, 92, **145**
Amorpha fruticosa, 139
Amphicarpa bracteata, 43, 215, 217
Anacardiaceae, 43, 163, 170, 209
Anaphalis spp., 196
Anartia jatrophae, 23, 25, 199
Anatrytone logan, 25, 33, 37, 44, **245–246**
Ancyloxphya numitor, 23, 37, 44, **234**
Andropogon spp., 98, 99, 100, 103, 106, 188, 236, 237, 239, 245, 246; *gerardi*, 44, 245, 254; *glomeratus*, 245; *scoparius*, 44, 99, 100, 103, 106, 118, 233, 237, 238, 240, 254
Anethum, 98, 122
Anglewings, 98, 103, **189–194**
annickae, 24, 76, 79, 84, 110, **134–135**. *See also Anthocharis midea*
Annonaceae, 43, 121
Anole, 120
Anolis carolinensis, 120
Antennaria spp., 196
Anthocharis midea, 24, 76, 79, 84, 110, **134–135**
Antirrhinum, 198

ants, 51, 143, 151
Apaturinae, 12–14, 97, **201–203**
Aphid honeydew, 190, 200
Aphids, Woolly, 45
Apiaceae, 13, 98, 122, 170
Apocynaceae, 97, 102, 104, 217
Apocynum: androsaemifolium, 217; *cannabinum*, 97, 102, 104
Appias drusilla, **127**
Aquifoliaceae, 43, 73, 84, 96, 153, 157–158, 168, 170
Aquilegia: canadensis, 43, 226; *vulgaris*, 45, 226
Arabis spp., 46, 130, 135
Aralia hispida, 169
Araliaceae, 169
Arctium spp., 196
Arctostaphylus uva-ursi, 43, 84, 96, 155–157
Aristida spp., 238
Aristolochia, 13, 43, 44, 53, 119–120; *durior*, 82, 98, 120
Aristolochiaceae, 13, 43–45, 53, 82, 98, 119–120
Aronia melanocarpa, 153
Arrowwood, 188
Artemesia spp., 196
Artogeia. See Pieris
Arundinaria: gigantea, 203; *tecta*, 203
Asarum canadense, 43, 45, 120
Ascia monuste, 134
Asclepiadaceae (milkweeds). *See Asclepias*

Watercress, 130, 132, 133
Whirlabout, 24, 44, 235, **241–242**
White (White butterflies), 12, 13, 56, 114, **127–135**; Cabbage, xv, 23, 28, 29, 32, 33, 35, 38, 40, 42, 44, 46, 50, 74, 92, 127, 128, 131, **132–134**, 135, 137; Checkered, 24, 33, 43, 76, 110, 111, **127–129**; Florida, **127**; Great Southern, 134; Mustard, 23, 24, 25, 28, 30, 111, **129–131**, 132; West Virginia, xvi, 25, 30, 33, 43, 76, 85, 110, 111, 130, **131–132**
Wild Ginger, 43, 45, 120

Wild Indigo, 44, 57, 73, 96, 156–157, 226–227
Wild Rice, 44, 250
Willow, 45, 98, 191, 193, 194, 221, 226; Beaked, 150; Black, 43, 150, 194, 201; Silky, 43, 149, 201; Weeping, 201
Wingstem, 171, 184
Winter Cress, 130
Winterberry, 144
Wisteria, 45, 215, 216
Witch Hazel, 221
Wood Sorrel, 99
Wood-nymph, 47, 211; Common, 23, 28, 36, 44, **211–212**
Woolly Beard Grass, 234

Xanthoxylum americanum, 43, 123–124. *See also Zanthoxylum*

Yellow, Little, 24, 32, 91, 110, 127, **141–142**. *See also* Sulphur

Zanthoxylum: americanum, 43, 123–124; *clavaherculis*, 43, 124
Zerene, 23, **138–139**. *See also Colias cesonia*
Zizania aquatica, 44, 250
Zizianopsis miliaceae, 234, 246

About the Authors

Michael Gochfeld is Professor of Environmental and Community Medicine at the Robert Wood Johnson Medical School of the University of Medicine and Dentistry of New Jersey. Trained in both environmental medicine and ecology, he has been very interested in the quality of New Jersey's environment and its impact on human health and biodiversity. He has written many scientific papers on human health and on the effects of chemicals on behavioral development, and has edited several books, most recently a textbook, *Environmental Medicine*. He now serves as president of the North Jersey Butterfly Club, a chapter of the North American Butterfly Association.

Joanna Burger is Professor of Ecology and Evolution at Rutgers University, where she teaches courses in animal behavior and ecological risk assessment. She has published many scientific papers and several books on a wide variety of animals (birds, reptiles, mammals, fish) and on various environmental problems (mercury pollution, lead exposure, oil spills). She has served on several committees of the National Academy of Science including its Board of Environmental Studies and Toxicology. She is author of *A Naturalist Along the Jersey Shore* (Rutgers University Press).

For ten years the authors have chronicled the populations of butterflies in many parts of New Jersey, particularly around their home in Somerset, in order to prepare this volume. Recognizing that butterfly populations are dynamic in New Jersey, they have documented the changing patterns of butterfly abundance, both in the past decade and with reference to works published over the past century. Their task does not end with the publication of this book, and their field work will continue unabated, leading them to all corners of this small but fascinating state.